Freeland

by Tim Pompey

Published by Tim Pompey

ISBN-13: 978-1470183615
ISBN-10: 1470183617

Cover Illustration:
"Freeland"
by Julinya Vidigal De Vince
and Victor Vidigal de Avila
Used by Permission

Back Cover Photo:
Jacqueline Woods

Cover Design:
Nancy DeLucrezia

1.

Truth is what we create, like clay in the hand
or the turn of a sentence.

2.

That which comes in darkness can be observed.
That which comes in light can be disguised.

3.

What we know, what we think we know,
flows swift as a running brook.

PROLOGUE

May 18, 1871

As the sun's dying embers glowed on the horizon, the evening shadows began to press across the wagon.

"How far you wanna go today?" Ruth said.

Jeremiah crossed his arms with the reins held loosely in his calloused fingers and turned his lanky body toward her. His sweat stained floppy hat and long beard gave him the appearance of a downtrodden wizard.

"Don't know," he replied. "Gettin kind of late. Think this might be a good place to camp?"

Ruth shrugged. "Good as any I spose. Stop here, I'll see what's in the wagon."

Spring in eastern Oregon and the Rolf family, with all their belongings stuffed in a creaky Conestoga wagon, had come to rest in a clearing down slope from a mountain ridge. Jeremiah, his wife Ruth, their 4-year-old daughter Esther.

From their home in Jones Cove, Tennessee, it had been a long trip westbound to the Oregon trail. Jeremiah wasn't sure where they would end up, but guessed he would know it when they got there. For the moment, out of habit from his pensive nature, he simply sat and gazed up at the spiral tops of a nearby pine grove.

Little Esther broke into his thoughts and pointed. "Look, Daddy, is that a squirrel?"

Jeremiah followed her finger and smiled. "Sure is. Probably happy to be out of the cold and busy workin." Then he returned to his daydreaming.

Ruth, tall with waist length brown hair and a strong square face, let herself down, walked to the back, and grabbed some small food items, a pot, and a couple of old benches. "I'll start a fire," she said. "Maybe take that rifle a yours and see what might be around. Could use a little meat to go with these fixins."

Jeremiah peered down at her and nodded. "I'll do that."

After wintering in Fort Boise, the Rolfs were once again on the move along the Oregon Trail—the family just one small part of a great wheeled herd eager to head west.

After purchasing their wagon in St. Louis, they had threaded their way across the great plains and through the mountains for the better part of a year. And now here they were in Oregon, alone in the wilderness. Jeremiah wondered if they would ever settle down, if this trail might actually end somewhere.

As an expert marksman, he went about his business and returned in an hour with a rabbit and a couple of squirrels to add to the family dinner. They all gathered around the fire and sat quietly as Ruth prepared the meal. She threw some stew meat in a pot and glanced over at him. "How far you think we went today?"

Jeremiah rested his large frame on one of the small benches she had pulled from the back. He ran his hands several times through his beard. "Hard to tell out here, no towns and all. Ten, fifteen mile I reckon."

Ruth let the stew simmer over the campfire. She watched her husband's face, his eyes focused on the flames licking the pot. Then she asked the real question on her mind. "How long till we get somewhere?"

Jeremiah shifted slightly but kept his eyes on the fire. "Oh, Lord, honey, I got no idea, you know. We go west till we find a town, I spose."

"And then?"

Jeremiah straightened and looked at his wife. "Then we stop and decide what we wanna do."

She grew quiet.

Jeremiah could feel her silence, the same as the land. Looking east, he could make out the shadows of the Oregon and Idaho foothills. Craggy. Rugged. The territory painted with patches of evergreen, plateaus, and high desert.

He had never seen a place with so much wildlife. Deer, bear, wild sheep and goats, large eagles. For a hunting man like himself, this was paradise. Yet the land itself, this ruthless wilderness, left him feeling vulnerable and unprotected. He knew she felt similar, even without saying so. For his sake and that of the children, she chose to remain silent.

"Pretty out here, don't you think?" He hoped a little cheerfulness might calm her fears.

Ruth looked around and nodded. "Pretty, yes—and lonely."

"That it is, but damned if it don't seem like a little piece of paradise too. Maybe find a town out here, a house for the kids."

She stopped stirring for a moment. "That would be good."

Jeremiah could read her face and feel the ache in her soul. She was thinking of their home in Tennessee—her family and friends, the horse she owned, the small cabin they used to have, and how they remained pilgrims after all these months, headed to God knows where. He knew she wondered. About this trip. About him.

As she disappeared into the back of the wagon, a solemn ache crept into his soul. He would be glad when they gathered some company again, maybe joined a group of fellow travelers, rode through a town or two as reassurance that there was civilization out here. He wanted desperately to pack up and get moving again.

It was now well after dark. Esther had been fed and put to sleep under the wagon. Ruth spread an extra blanket and crawled next to her by the front wheel. Jeremiah hovered by the campfire with his solitary thoughts. The longer he sat, the more afraid he became. Of what, he was unsure, but he sensed that something or someone was watching.

He kept his rifle near as he recalled tales he'd heard of Indian raids, women raped, children kidnaped. Tales of the dangerous west. He hadn't noticed signs of any Indians, but those damn stories kept popping into his head.

Just as he was ready to doze off, he heard a sound. Grabbing his rifle, he spun around. Then, out of sheer surprise, he dropped it and gaped at what he saw.

About ten feet in front of him, a man, black as a starless night—shirtless, shoeless, maybe seven feet tall, lean and muscular. The only clothes he wore were an old pair of buckskin pants like an Indian might wear. But he was no Indian.

The man's coal skin blended with the night. His eyes were fierce, steady, and focused on Jeremiah. "Good evening, my brother," he rumbled in some type of strange accented English.

Jeremiah didn't move.

The man continued. "You are surprised to see me, no?"

Jeremiah worked up the nerve to speak. "Yeah, I guess you could say that."

"I do not blame you. I am a stranger to this land. Perhaps no one knows I am here, except you of course."

"That so?"

"Yes, it seems we're alone." The stranger smiled.

Jeremiah took a moment to size him up. "Where you from?"

"Ah, such a far distance. From as far away as Africa."

"Africa?" Jeremiah was immediately suspicious. "Now what would a nigga boy from Africa be doin out here?"

The stranger moved closer. His full body appeared in the firelight. He looked graceful, at ease with his surroundings, as if it was normal for a man like him to be wandering in Oregon this time of night.

Jeremiah knew the war was over, knew that many slaves had been freed, but he didn't think they'd traveled this far west. And this one in particular—tall, dignified, speaking a melodic kind of English. It made no sense.

The stranger bent down, picked up some dried grass, and twirled it with his elegant fingers. "I think this place will be my new home. It is pleasant here, with good water and land, far removed from the wars of men."

Jeremiah scratched his chin. "Seems to be in the middle of nowhere, if you ask me, a far piece to be settlin."

The stranger looked off toward the dark plains. "Sometimes nowhere is the best place to be."

There was a stir by the wagon. Ruth woke and rolled over. "Honey?" she said in a sleepy voice. Then she saw the stranger and froze.

"It's okay," Jeremiah said, though truthfully he had his doubts. "This man's travelin, just like us."

They all stared at each other as the dwindling fire crackled and spit.

Jeremiah broke the silence. "You got a name?"

"Ah, yes, indeed," the stranger said. "I am Sarihaba Kinyaga, but you may call me simply . . . Sari."

"Sari, huh? Never heard a that name. I'm Jeremiah, this be my wife Ruth. My daughter over there, she's Esther. We're on our way out west."

"A family?" Sari said. "Looking for someplace to settle, I imagine?"

Jeremiah hesitated and wondered if he should say more. "You could say that."

"Someplace that would be good for a family. A town or a village, perhaps?"

"A town of some sort, yeah."

"Perhaps a new town?"

Jeremiah shifted uncomfortably. "I don't really care, as long as it's safe, maybe with a school for my child."

Sari nodded. "Ah, yes, the child."

By now, Ruth was fully awake. She slid protectively in front of Esther. "What about you?" she asked. "Where you goin?"

"Oh, me," Sari said. "I have traveled a great distance to be right here. This, I think, is where I shall settle."

"Here?"

"Yes, the perfect spot. I have picked out some land for a village not far from here. I am amazed by all the animals, and the birds are quite beautiful. They represent for me beauty and . . . freedom."

Jeremiah leaned forward. Despite his misgivings, he was now curious. "You gonna live out here all by yourself?"

Sari shook his head. "Oh no. Eventually others will come to be with me."

"You got family?"

"No, they are long dead. But there are many like yourself coming down this road, and I can be quite persuasive."

"You think they'll come out here just cause you ask em? White folk, no less?"

"Yes, indeed. As I have said, it would be a good place for a village where families could settle. You, for instance, and your family. This place would be ideal."

Jeremiah didn't like the turn this conversation was taking. Tales of raiding Indians came back to mind. Settlers killed or forced into slavery. Children sold off to other tribes. And what if they were captured by this large man? He found these thoughts distressing and reached down to touch his rifle. It was ready when needed. His hand on the hilt reassured him. "No offense to you, Mr.— "

"Sari."

"Sari, but I don't think so. I'm afraid we're on our way somewhere else."

Sari maintained his smile, a broad persuasive grin. "There are always choices to make, choices you might not imagine at first. It would not be so hard to choose this place, no? Not hard at all."

Jeremiah's eyes flashed. "Well, if there's a choice to be made, I think we've already done it. As I said, we're moving west."

Sari stood up and put his full height on display. "But this is a good place, no?" The tone in his voice became soothing, more hypnotic.

Ruth began to slide under the wagon. "Jeremiah," she whimpered.

Jeremiah reached down to grab his rifle and came up empty. To his surprise, the weapon had disappeared. He looked down by his feet and discovered it had slid to the far edge of the campsite. He stood up and stumbled back toward the wagon. "You . . . you oughta go now. We're not interested in what you have to offer. Go on now. Be on your way."

Sari grinned and kept quiet. Then his eyes widened and his arms flew in the air.

Jeremiah and Ruth felt something pop in their head, a painful pressure that seemed to mushroom and spread.

Ruth screamed and wailed. "Oh, Lord, help us!" Then she began to writhe like a dog in the dirt. "Jeremiah, make it stop!"

Jeremiah rushed over to comfort his wife, but he had similar pain and struggled to focus. It was like something was alive in his brain. "Jesus Christ, who are you?" he shouted.

Ruth grew quiet and still. Jeremiah thought maybe she had died.

His daughter began to wake up. "Daddy?" she whimpered.

Jeremiah glanced over at her. He reached out a hand to come to her aid, but darkness clouded his thoughts. Then, he blacked out.

I

June 25, 1977

The building was old, but quaint—red brick, antique windows. Even though Stan Blankenship was late for his first day of work, he seemed in no hurry. He wanted to drink in the sight of The Idaho Statesman, one of the last original newspapers from the old west. Standing like a lawman with hands on hips, he eyed the building. This was his kind of vibe. Atmospheric, rawboned, immune to modernity, a shade above flea bitten.

People often said the same about him. Tall, wiry, with dark hair rolling loose down his back and questionable taste in clothes, that impression wouldn't be far from the truth. Stan was a writer. He didn't give a shit for properness. As long as he wore a shirt and pants, the rest would take care of itself.

He gave the big arcing sign one last look and stepped through the colonial front door. A receptionist—petite, blond, maybe Stan's age—glanced up and gave him a good once over. She was buried behind a large counter. From the doorway, Stan could just make out her head and neck. *Nice head, nice neck*, he thought.

"Can I help you?" she said.

Stan gave her his best easygoing smile. "Yeah, actually, I'm here to work."

She smiled back. "Are you now?"

"Yes, ma'am. First day. Need to see Hank Aleano."

Her lips puckered to a glossy O, then returned to smiling. "Oh, lucky you."

Stan leaned on her office counter and caught sight of the rest of her. "Yup, lucky me, I guess."

The receptionist fed him a flirtatious eye. "And who might you be?"

"Stan. Stan Blankenship, new reporter for the Idaho Statesman."

"Well, Mr. New Reporter, let me see if Hank will summon you to his throne room." She reached out a prim finger and dialed an extension. "Hank, your new guy is here. Should I let him in?"

Stan heard a loud cackle coming from her phone, something between the growl of a lion and the whine of a witch. The receptionist held the receiver back from her ear. "Okay," she said. "I'll let him know. You too, Hank." Another pause. "No, Hank, remember, I already have a boyfriend." The receptionist hung up and smiled at Stan. "He'll be out in a minute."

Stan straightened up and fixed his tie. "What's your name?"

She delicately placed a finger on her cheek. "Jessica. Jessica Rawley, but most folks around here just call me Jess."

"Well, Jess, it's nice to meet you. Thanks for summoning his highness."

"No problem."

At that moment, Hank banged through a set of doors leading into the back office. "Hank Aleano," he said with a meaty hand outstretched.

Stan shook it. "Stan. Stan Blankenship."

With his shaved scalp and hard eyes, Hank looked more like a union boss than a news manager. He had a round body and a head like a bulldog. He was a Boise news veteran and the steely-eyed desk editor at the Idaho Statesman. When he spoke, his sentences sounded chewed up and spit out. "News guy, huh?"

"Yes sir, mostly community newspapers on the east coast, but I did do a two-year stint with The Pittsburgh Gazette."

"Oh, Pittsburgh. Big time. Very impressive."

Hank stopped and gave Stan a dubious stare. There was heavy silence in the room. Jessica tilted back in her chair and observed with interest.

"Ever have a regular job?" he growled.

Stan fumbled for something intelligent to say. "Like—"

"Washing dishes, mowing lawns, that sort of thing."

Pressure began to build in Stan's chest. He wondered if he might be fired before he even started. "I used to work the counter at McDonald's."

"McDonald's?" Hank squinted. "You're a burger guy?"

Stan fidgeted with his fingers. "Among other things."

Hank grinned and started to laugh. It was a rumble of sorts, like thunder burdened with a serious smoker's cough. "From hamburgers to news, I like that." He clapped his big paws together. "Well, let's get to it Mr. Macky D news guy. Let's see if you can write as well as you cook."

He spun, hit the door again, and was down the hall before Stan could take his first step.

Hank sang something familiar—an old McDonald's theme song. It was loud and off key.

Jessica smoothed herself and folded her hands on her desk. "Better get to work Mr. Macky D news guy. Hank doesn't like it when his reporters don't keep up."

"Oh, right," Stan said. "Well, see you around."

"Definitely," she said with another flirtatious grin.

August 13, 1977

They worked the downtown Boise beat together. Stan and fellow reporter, Amy Nigel. She taught him the ropes about local sports, politics, business. He tried to keep up and learn fast.

Amy was tall, auburn haired, with hazel eyes, a perfectly round face, and a sure-footed gait when she strode across the room. The cowboy boots she wore gave her a country girl feel, but her news savvy was as sharp as a chef's knife.

A local girl and graduate of Boise State, she had served a summer journalism internship at the paper in the early '70s and managed to impress Hank. He hired her right out of college.

Hank was infamous for pelting his reporters with various bits of blue humor and salt-of-the-earth wisdom. Some found it annoying, but Amy enjoyed it. She was one of the few who could take Hank's humor and give as good as she got. That and the fact she was pretty helped him stay off her ass, more or less. Plus she was a damn good reporter.

Amy and Stan had hit it off from day one, which explained why they were hanging out together on this late Saturday night at the Mustang Bar near the Boise State campus. They both liked their hangouts dark, greasy, loud. Tonight the bar featured Jimmy Ray and the Herders playing country rock.

Seated in a booth in the back, they drank beers and chatted.

"So," Amy yelled over the music, "how you like it here so far?"

"Like what?" Stan said.

"The job, the beat—working with me."

Stan leaned forward to make himself heard. "Happy as a clam," he said. "Nice town, good job, great teacher, what's not to like?"

Amy eyed him and smiled. "Are you kissing my ass?" She turned her Budweiser bottle three quarters up and took a long swig.

Stan rubbed his chin thoughtfully. "Not yet. Someday maybe, when you're my editor, but tonight's a no bullshit night." He noted her suspicious eyes. "Like I said, everything so far is peachy."

Amy wrapped her long fingers around the bottle neck. "Speaking of bullshit, how's things with Hank?"

Stan laid his elbows on the table. "Hank gives everybody shit. I don't take it personally."

She paused a moment and looked around the bar. "How'd you get out to this cowpoke town anyway, if you don't mind my asking?"

Stan lifted his legs and stretched them lengthwise across the booth. He leaned his lanky figure against the wall and put his hands behind his head.

"I like to travel," he said. "Didn't want to settle down too fast. When I finished UCLA in '71, I decided to get out and see the country."

Amy looked puzzled. "Six years is a long time to travel."

Stan cocked his head. "I worked at different newspapers, none of them too long, except for the Pittsburgh Gazette. I actually liked it there."

Amy took another long drink. "Pittsburgh, huh? I wouldn't mind going to Pittsburgh or Philadelphia or anywhere else for that matter, long as it's far from here."

"Lived here a long time?"

"Born and bred, branded and roped, corralled, stuck, whatever you want to call it."

Now it was Stan's turn to look puzzled. "You're young. You're talented. What's stopping you?"

Amy set her bottle on the table and began to pick at the label. "Oh, you know, it's home here—family, stuff like that. They like to keep me close."

"No husband, boyfriend?"

She grimaced. "Husband once. Divorced. Gun shy. Not anxious to go down that road again."

As the music picked up, Stan closed his eyes and drifted off for a minute. They were playing Neil Young's "Cowgirl in the Sand." His wandering thoughts were pulled back by Amy's voice.

"You going somewhere without me?" She had leaned over the table to stare at him.

Stan glanced up and noticed her steady eyes, as if they saw everything and gave nothing away. Her delicate hands were flat on the table.

"What? Oh, sorry," he said. "I just like Neil, that's all. Sometimes I get lost when I hear his music."

"Well, that makes me feel better."

Stan moved his feet to the floor and gazed back. Their faces were no more than a foot apart. "It's too damn noisy in here. How about we go for a drive?"

"What'd you have in mind?" She smiled coyly.

"I've heard there's some nice views out on Warm Springs Road by Lucky Peak. I haven't been out there much. You know the area?"

She settled back in her booth. "Ah yes, I know it well. The local lover's lane around here." Once again she eyed Stan with a joker's smile. "I also know, if you're truly interested in sightseeing, you can see more in the daylight."

Stan couldn't tell if she was serious or joking, whether he had said something wrong or she was just cracking wise. He went with the latter. "I can see just fine in the dark, thank you. That's why I come to this bar. I have radar vision."

Amy chuckled. "That's a great pick up line. I'll have to remember that one."

Stan eased out of the booth. "Well?"

Amy moved one leg out to the aisle. "Well, okay, but I'm not riding out to lover's lane without taking my own car." She grinned, held up her keys, and shook them.

"No problem. You have a nicer car than me, anyway."

"I do, my reward for taking Hank's shit."

As Amy rose, she brushed her fingers across Stan's cheek. "You be nice to me now, lest I tell Hank you've been a bad boy. He gets a little protective sometimes."

"I promise you're safe. Hank has nothing to worry about."

No doubt, though, walking out of the bar, Stan could feel the heat rising from her jeans.

Amy parked near a beach area about 20 yards from the lake. She pulled two beat up lawn chairs from her trunk and plunked them down in the sand on the edge of the water. They sat and looked over the watery landscape drenched by a full moon. There was a white plume trail on the water like a bridge stretching shore to shore.

As they sat and watched the ripples, Stan blurted out, "This is why I came."

Amy loosened her pony tail and fluffed out her hair. "Why's that?"

Stan slouched, dug his heels into the sand, and looked up at the moon. "Sounds corny, but I do like the great outdoors."

"You're kidding. You don't strike me as much of a camper."

"Looks are deceiving."

"Where you from?"

"San Diego, originally, but I spent four years at U.C.L.A. God awful. Couldn't wait to get out. Smog, traffic. Guess I'm more of an open road kind of guy."

"So, I've been here all my life and can't wait to leave, and you can't wait to leave home, you've been everywhere, and you end up here? Isn't life funny?"

Stan nodded. "It is indeed."

Amy kicked off her boots. "I must seem like a country hick to you."

"Don't forget, we just hung out at Mustang's. There's nothing wrong with a little country."

"Wish I could bleach mine out."

Stan eased out of his chair and sat cross-legged on the sand. He motioned her to follow.

She sat next to him with her knees pulled to her chest. "You're a funny man, Stan Blankenship."

They both sat silently for several minutes transfixed by the horizon.

"So," Amy said, "what's next for you?"

"Next?" said Stan.

"Yeah, your next big step in life."

He dug his hands into the beach. "No idea. I'm just getting used to Boise."

"Oh come on now, you've traveled around for six years, you have to have something in mind."

Stan put his hand under his chin. "Seriously?"

"Yeah, seriously. Remember. You called this a no bullshit night."

He held his breathe for a moment. "I think . . . that I'd like to own my own small town newspaper, print up all the little town stuff—ladies socials, PTA events, town hall meetings, things like that."

Amy paused. "See, that wasn't so hard."

"I don't think too much about it, but you asked, so I dug deep."

"Not much of a planner, huh?"

"It's not one of my strong points. I'm pretty spur of the moment sometimes."

"You plan to get married?"

Stan gave her a long look. "Now that—I have no idea. When it comes to women, I'm good for a few fucks, but they usually figure me out pretty quick. I think most of them aren't into my lifestyle."

"What lifestyle is that?"

"Work, travel, work, travel. I'm really a nomad."

"Who wants to settle down and own a paper."

"Well, maybe someday, in my 40s."

She turned and stared out at the lake. Something in her mood shifted.

Stan pulled his hands from the sand and brushed them off. "Did I say something wrong?"

Amy shook her head. "There's nothing wrong, you're just—different from most guys, and I mean that as a compliment."

"I know, my folks always worry about me."

"As they should," she said, "or they wouldn't be your folks." Suddenly, Amy stirred and stood up. "Well, in the meantime—"

"What?"

"We're young, we're a little drunk and crazy, and there's a full moon, in case you hadn't noticed."

"Yeah?"

"There's a beach, it's warm tonight, and the water is waiting."

Stan looked up at her.

Amy began to strip down.

"You're kidding," he said.

"What, in all your adventures, you never skinny dipped with a naked woman?"

He shook his head and grinned. "In my lifetime, never."

"Well, let me introduce you to what we do when we're hot here in Boise." She was now bare except for her panties. In the moonlight, her breasts reflected the milky smoothness of the moon. "So get up and start shedding." She kicked sand in his direction and ran down to the water.

Stan could hear her splash in and wade out.

"Don't tell me you didn't think of this when you brought me here," she shouted. Her voice echoed off the surrounding trees.

Stan stood up and started to undress. "Nope, didn't plan it, but I'm not complaining either."

"Then shut up and get moving. I'm going to teach you to swim Boise style."

Stan stood naked on the shoreline. He put his toes in the water and marveled at how warm it was, just the right temp for a midnight swim. As he gazed once more across the lake, it occurred to him that this was a very rare moment.

And then he heard it. His name, faint like a whisper. An image of a shrouded face passed through his thoughts and disappeared.

Though the night was windless, a breeze enveloped him like the texture of a fine sheet. The air formed a gentle vortex, swirled faintly like a funnel, then vanished.

For a moment, Stan lost track of where he was. He was brought back by Amy's voice. "Are you coming in or what?"

He felt a little dizzy. His heart palpitated. He looked out at Amy. He looked up at the moon. He looked back at Amy.

Something had happened, something only he could detect. Strange as it seemed, a mysterious other had blown through his mind, invaded it, and peeked inside.

Standing on the shoreline, he saw nothing unusual, except for the lovely woman in the water and his bare body. A word crossed his mind. *Magic.* Something about tonight was different from any other night he remembered. *Magic* he thought again, though he couldn't figure out why this word stood out. It just seemed—appropriate.

He shook off the breeze and splashed into the lake.

September 21, 1977

Stan couldn't sleep. Even this late in the season as fall began to infiltrate Boise, the weather was unseasonably warm. His apartment had no air conditioning and despite all his open windows, the atmosphere inside was stagnant.

He sat on his bed and looked out over the squared-off complex. Like the air in his room, nothing moved. An eerie quiet had settled in, as if the half-moon and the night anticipated something. Even the pool was perfectly still.

Amy slept soundly next to him. In what seemed like a budding romance, she had been spending more nights at his place, an inkling that they might be moving toward something beyond just sex.

Stan threw on a pair of gym shorts and walked through his apartment, a nondescript two bedroom one bath rental located a couple miles from the Statesman. It was cheap and temporary until he could afford something better. He lived on the second floor with a front entrance overlooking the pool.

Grabbing his keys, he opened the door and stepped out onto the concrete walkway bordered by a black iron railing. Turning left, he eased along the corridor and down the stairway to the patio.

He unlocked the pool gate and slid into one of the aluminum lounge chairs that dotted the deck. Stretched out, looking straight up, he eyed the stars and the face of the half-moon that jumped in and out of low-hanging clouds.

Ever since that night on the lake, Stan had found it hard to sleep. Strange dreams followed by a mysterious presence that invaded his thoughts. Often he would be startled awake.

Stan had no reason to be this troubled. Things seemed to be going well for him. The job was good. He liked Amy. His life was coming together nicely. So what did he have to be stressed about? And why did he constantly feel like he was being watched?

Stan stared at the rippling reflections from the pool water, the pool lights, the edge of the glassy tide that lapped the side. For a moment, he forgot his problems and let himself be mesmerized.

Water, he thought. *Was it something about being near water, or maybe it was the moonlight?* It made no sense, but whatever he felt inside his head was palpable. His brain was aware that a presence had prowled through his body.

"Can't sleep, huh?" said a voice near the railing. It was Jeff Brewster, the complex manager, looking over the pool fence as he smoked a cigarette.

He was a pale-faced man, skinny, with crooked teeth and a reputation for being nosy. Jeff's hair had thinned considerably, which only further accented his chinless face. A lit cigarette was jammed between his knuckles.

Stan pushed up and dropped his feet on the pool deck. "Shit, Jeff, you scared the hell out of me."

"Sorry, I'm a light sleeper. Heard a noise outside, thought I'd investigate. We've had some break-ins recently. Really would like to catch the bastards."

Stan settled back in his chair.

Jeff took a drag and motioned with his cigarette hand. "What're you doin up so late?"

"You're right, can't sleep." Stan shook his head. "Too damn hot tonight."

"Yeah, can't blame you for wanting to get a little air."

They both settled into a long silence. Jeff smoking, Stan staring into space.

Jeff pointed up. "See anything interesting?"

Stan lowered his eyes. "Just stars and moon. If any aliens are up there, they're not talking tonight."

"Yeah. Wonder if they're hot, too. Wonder if they have bad nights like tonight."

"Good question," Stan said hesitantly.

Jeff finished his cigarette and threw his butt in a nearby trash can. "Well, if you see any punks out trying to steal my car, don't hesitate to wake me up." He pointed at a nearby window. "I'm definitely within earshot."

"Okay, Jeff, will do."

Jeff walked away and disappeared through his apartment door. Stan could hear through his open window the faint squeak of bedsprings, the rustling of covers. A woman's voice whispered, "Who the hell is out there?"

"No one," he heard Jeff murmur and then all was quiet.

Stan sat for another half-hour and lost himself in the skyline. It was so quiet, he could hear his heart beat. He folded his hands in his lap and closed his eyes.

That's when he felt it again—the presence. Faintly, but it was there. Stan could almost visualize it in his head. "What the hell do you want?" he said in a low voice.

But no answer came. Instead, the presence roamed around and searched his mind. Stan wanted to protest, but his tongue seemed pinned to the roof of his mouth. His body had suddenly become a library, his life an open book.

He was being drawn somewhere, forced to travel without moving, beckoned to visit some place unseen. He realized that the invisible trip was against his will, but, in this case, his will didn't matter; for that matter, his will barely existed in the presence of the presence.

Stan was being called into a court of law to wait for a jury's verdict. What would the presence decide? Would he be imprisoned or freed? Would he be found guilty or not? All he knew was that his life, his mind, his soul lay in the balance and he could do nothing to defend himself.

As the presence entered the court and filled the room with energy, Stan could feel a body not made of flesh, far beyond human form, emerge inside him. It was ethereal but real, floating like the clouds he had been staring at, floating lazily and without any sense of urgency. Stan's verdict would come when it came. There was no rush.

A foggy pair of eyes followed him, eyes that penetrated Stan's head and invoked panic. Stan believed that looking into those eyes would finish him. He wanted to fight but his body had been pinned by the presence.

This was always the worst part of his nightmares—fighting to wake up, deathly afraid, trapped inside a sleeping limbo. He opened his mouth to scream.

A faint voice entered the room. Someone speaking from a distance, then moving closer until he heard someone shout in his ear. "Stan. Wake. Up."

He started and jumped from his chair.

It was Amy, standing in her pajamas, looking terrified. "Stan," she shouted again.

He stood still and tried to regain his bearings. As he looked at the sky, he noticed faint traces of daylight, an emerging blue dawn. "Shit," he muttered.

Amy stood straight and folded her arms. "What the hell are you doing out here? Why are you yelling in your sleep?"

Stan felt each part of his body begin to come back. The pieces that had been wrenched loose were now being plugged back in. "Couldn't sleep," he said.

Amy watched him carefully. "Well, you sure looked asleep to me."

Stan glanced around and noticed the lounge chair, its frame still locked in a wide V shape. "Yeah, guess I did."

"Jesus," she whispered. "You scared me, scared the whole complex. I saw a couple neighbors peak through their windows."

Stan was speechless. He shook his head and shrugged.

Amy's face transformed from fear to tenderness. "Come on, baby, come back inside. We can talk if you want, but you need to come back." She reached out a hand.

Stan held it lightly and let her lead him up the stairs and back to his apartment. Then he sat down in a kitchen chair and gazed numbly at the table.

Amy walked over to his coffee machine and began to brew a pot. She glanced at him with an anxious look. "Bad nightmare, huh?"

Stan didn't answer. He had no explanation or defense and he was completely exhausted.

As Amy stood by the stove, she searched his face for a response. Nothing.

After several minutes, she gently pulled the pot from the machine and poured two cups of coffee. The kitchen clock read 6:10. Time to get ready for work. She took both cups, set them on the table, and sat opposite him. "Was it like a nightmare?" she asked.

"Well," Stan said, "that's the thing."

"What?"

"I—I can't remember a thing."

She paused and sipped from her cup. "Really?"

"All I know is that I laid down in that chair and the next thing I know, you're screaming at me."

Amy took another sip and waited.

Finally, Stan raised his cup and took a long drink. He glanced over at the kitchen clock and began to stir. "Time to go to work," he said, as if whatever had bothered him had conveniently passed on.

He stood up, patted Amy on the shoulder, and went directly to the bathroom.

Except for an occasional swallow of coffee, Amy sat still for ten minutes and listened to Stan move around in the bathroom. Then she drained her cup, shook her head, and stood up.

He was right. It was time to get ready for work.

October 8, 1977

Hank hollered from his office. "Ship, got a minute?"

Stan jumped out of his creaky chair and strolled down the corridor into Hank's paper-strewn kingdom and leaned his wiry frame against the doorway. "Hey Hank. What's up?"

"Got a job for you. A solo job. No Amy required."

"That right?" Stan's interest picked up a notch. "Doing what?"

"Oh, you're gonna like this. Ever hang out with hillbillies?"

Stan sensed that Hank was about to launch into some of his typical dark humor. He rubbed his chin and smiled. "Hillbillies?"

"Thaaaat's right."

Stan paused. "Well, Hank, correct me if I'm wrong, but isn't this Idaho?"

"Yeah? What's your point?"

"Aren't hillbillies usually from the South?"

"Well now, let's define the word itself according to Aleano's exhaustive dictionary. Do hillbillies live in the mountains?"

"Yeah."

"Do they live off the land, marry their cousins, that sort of thing?"

"Well—"

"Do they fire first, ask questions later?"

"Maybe, sometimes, you know, if you watch too much TV and believe that sort of shit."

Hank tilted forward. "Well, I hate TV, but I do believe that sort of shit, thank you very much. You see, out here in Idaho, not far from this fine civilized city, we got people that live up in them thar mountains. They may not be as sophisticated as our good folk from the South, but still, in every sense of the word, they're the same.

Same situation, different state. So, if our hill folk here in Idaho fit my definition, then tell me, what's the difference?"

Stan crossed his arms. He had to admit. Hank had a point. "Okay, hillbillies, Idaho style. So?"

"Got word there's some type of skirmish between sheriff's deputies and hillbillies, er, pardon me, some of our fine Idaho patriots, out near the state line. Somewhere close to—what the hell is the name of that place?—O yeah, Payette. Sounds like your cup of tea, and I think it's time you left Amy's nest and spread your wings. So, you game?"

Stan was game. Getting out of the office and roaming around, especially if it involved exploring the unusual, was right up his alley. "Yessir. Payette. Hillbillies. I'm ready."

"That's the spirit." Hank leaned back in his chair with his drool-soaked cigar perched between his lips.

"What's the angle?" said Stan.

"Angle? Now young Ship, just exactly what kind of a reporter are you? Am I your mama? Do I have to spell it out for you?"

Stan shrugged his shoulders.

Hank shrugged back. "Find someone out there who looks dangerous. Look for gun totting crazies holed up in a cabin somewhere. Seek out death and destruction. Dead children, bleeding bodies, dying cops, you know, real human interest." He took his cigar and held it between two fingers. "Got it?"

Stan fought the urge to argue. After all, It was his first solo byline. He'd write it and hope that Hank would cut him some slack. "Got it."

Hank's chair groaned as he put his meaty arms on his desk. "Now isn't this just swell? Mr. College Kid from California, my new protégée, learning the ropes. This'll be good for you, open your eyes to some of our dee-lightful local culture. Yeah, yeah, it's true, you know. We got culture out here. It ain't just for folks like you from Hollywood."

"Culture?" Stan said. "As in hillbilly culture?"

Hank put his cigar between his teeth and bit down. "Yeah, you little west coast snob. Those are survivalists out there. Years of inbreeding and some real good recipes for rabbit. Stewed, fried, baked. I hear they got a way of roasting the ears, kind of like Chinese won tons. Care to hear more?"

"Nope, think I got it, Hank. I'll be happy to cover the story, minus the won tons."

"Well now, don't be too snooty. You have my permission to stop and sample the merchandise."

Stan smiled. "Thanks. I just might do that."

Hank relit his cigar and blew smoke rings toward the ceiling. "Well, that's being real open-minded."

Stan waited for Hank to give him any other bits of information, but he had returned to writing notes on a pad. Hank, as he was prone to do, had quickly moved on.

"So," Stan said. "Got any maps? I could use some help finding the place."

"Talk to my secretary, Sheila," he growled. "She'll *draw* you something." Hank began to scribble again, ignoring the fact that Stan remained in the doorway.

"Okay," Stan said. "I'm on my way."

Hank kept scribbling.

Stan stuffed his maps and reporter gear into a well-worn black leather bag. On his way out, he passed Amy working the phone in her cubicle.

She saw him, finished her call, and hung up. "Going out?"

"Yeah, Hank is generously sending me out to do a story on hillbillies."

"Hillbillies? Is this a little Hank humor here?"

"Yeah, probably, but it's also a solo assignment, my first real byline. So, what can I say? He made me an offer I couldn't refuse."

"What's the story?"

Stan leaned on her cubicle wall. "Guess some sheriff's deputies are having trouble with folks up in the mountains, a little place called Payette."

Amy grimaced. "Ah, yes. Payette. Lovely place."

"Know about it?"

"Yup. I was wrong about Hank. He's not sending you out as a joke. He's trying to get you killed."

Stan paused. "That right?"

"Payette is a hot spot for a little compound called Liberty or Die. Ultraconservative with lots of guns and a nasty attitude."

"Sounds interesting."

"Be careful up there, Stan. Just do your job and get the hell out. They wouldn't mind putting a bullet or two in some nosy reporter like you."

Stan gently touched her shoulder. "If Hank wants a story, I'll give him a story. Don't worry. I can take care of myself."

Amy swung her chair around and faced him. "Do that and we'll have some fun tonight, okay?"

Stan's face lit up. "Sounds great. Pick you up at your place?"

Amy stood up and glanced around. Except for a few secretaries in the back, the office was empty. She stepped forward and gave him a peck on the cheek. "For good luck," she said.

"I feel better already."

It was overcast, a long drive, made even longer by the fact that he was headed in the wrong direction. Hard to tell why at this point, but he knew when he crossed the bridge over the Snake River into Oregon, this was not the way to Payette.

Still, the further he drove into Oregon, the more he was enchanted with these beautiful valley views. His freewheeling nature kicked in and he kept driving until he reached Ontario. Then he continued northwest along Interstate 84.

The foothills. The rugged terrain. The wild feel of this land. All of this was new territory to him. Though the days of the Oregon Trail were long past, driving up this highway made him feel like a pioneer in search of a home. His hands, attached to the steering wheel, had tapped into a pulsating current of curiosity.

A half-hour past Ontario, Stan took a turnoff. A little sign pointing right that read "Exit 345 Vale." Once off the Interstate, he traveled west, then south on a small thread of highway that shot straight through miles of canyon terrain and dry grassland. Only spare signs of human habitation. It was as if he had jumped back in time three-hundred years or so when the only settlers here were Indians.

"Well, here we are on our great adventure," he said, not quite sure what he was thinking or why he was talking to himself. He was not even sure if he was talking to someone specific. Call it an urge. He knew where he was supposed to be and this definitely was not his assignment. Still, he kept going.

Chugging along in his old green Volkswagen, a beat up clunker he had bought off a used lot on the outskirts of Boise, he grew excited.

Rolling down a window, he stuck his long arm out to channel the spirit of the land into his thoughts. As the cool October breeze rushed past his face, he began to wonder if hillbillies might live here on the plateau. Was there such a thing as a desert hillbilly?

On a whim he began to sing the refrain to Lynard Skynard's *Sweet Home Alabama.* Not because he had ever been to Alabama. Only that Alabama and hillbillies seemed synonymous; though, now that he thought about it, he realized there were very few mountains in Alabama. Hard to have hillbillies without mountains. He concluded that in Alabama and eastern Oregon, there were no such things as hillbillies.

This road seemed symbolic of his life. He had set out to find a different path from his father and brother. Journalism instead of engineering. Travel instead of the usual San Diego surf and sun.

That search led him out to the east coast where he picked up various news jobs. As the '70s dissolved into the disco era, he worked hard to survive as a holdover hippie carrying on what was becoming a fast-fading tradition.

The morning sun lit up the eastern mountain ranges along the Oregon and Idaho border. Stan marveled at the shades of color that coalesced into a series of crooked ridge lines. He admired the contrast of the beige prairies. He counted himself lucky to see this, lucky to experience the solitude of this two-lane road at this exact time of day.

It struck him, why he had moved to this part of the country. Taking a vacation to Idaho, driving through Boise, he had simply fallen in love with the area and never left. He had discovered the last remaining frontier in America. Here it was, in the rural Northwest. His move was cemented when he found a job as a reporter with the Statesman.

Stan let all these thoughts roll through his head like cool water. He found that his surroundings and his life had, for better or worse, become a smooth river. Except for his damn nightmares.

The wind from his open window circulated through his long brown hair. It flew around and revealed more than usual of his Irish skin and angular face. Every so often, he would wipe a bit of dirt from his eyes. A deer of some sort casually ate grass on the side of the road—red spotted, no horns. Probably a doe.

A phrase popped into his head. An invisible voice whispering. "Round and round and round we go," he chanted. "And where we land—"

He slowed down and stared at the deer. It raised its head and stared back.

"Wonder what he's thinking?" Stan murmured. He couldn't help but notice a poetic cadence as he repeated the words *round and round and round* several times in different meters. Then his thoughts drifted off like fog down a river.

Stan wound his way through Vale, then southwest on Highway 20 until he came to a small turnoff that read *Sand Hollow Creek Road*. Traveling south, he kept going straight for 10 miles, maybe more.

Suddenly, from the corner of his eye, he saw a large handmade sign with a rather odd name: *Freeland*. To the right of the name, a hand sketched arrow that pointed west.

"Freeland?" he said. "What kind of a name is that for a town?"

Of course, he had no intention of following the sign. After all, he was headed somewhere else on a mission. To find the remote town of Payette (eventually), get the skinny from the local sheriff's deputies (maybe, maybe not), worm his way into an interview with an actual hillbilly under siege (slim chance), and sample some rare mountain delicacies (odds of that—even slimmer).

Why should he care about an old beat-up sign with a strange sounding name? Yes, he noted, the town's title was a little unusual, but so what? As far as he was concerned, it was only a blip on the radar in his daily plan.

So why did he slow down? Why did he pull off to the side of the road, check his mirrors, and circle back? Why did he park next to the sign and examine it like some type of sacred monolith? Old, beat up, certainly not worth spending fifteen minutes tracing the hand-drawn curves in each letter with his fingers.

How could he possibly understand at his young age that driving blithely down a highway, life, so unpredictable and capricious, could throw an unwary driver a sudden curve. He hadn't learned to anticipate these types of road hazards, silent and airy, that dart from nowhere, hit a man in the forehead, and heave him somewhere else. An interview. A deer. An unexpected summons from a distant spirit. A turn in the road. A road sign that read *Freeland*.

Most discoveries of genius happen like this. Engineering. Art. Death. They don't come when invited. Whether from inspiration or an aneurism, they generally fly from nowhere, strike a windshield or a fender, or a forehead, and wreak their own brand of havoc.

Stan's curve came in the form of a flash behind his eyes, a jolt like a surge of electricity. It buzzed and stung like a pin prick, then quickly passed. His mind, however, was snatched like a ball in flight. Payette instantly became a passing thought. Thoughts of Freeland, that old sign, the arrow pointing west, took over like a zealous mother steering her child toward law school.

Stan returned to his car, put the key in the ignition, and gently pressed the gas. His hands swung the vehicle right at the sign. As he did so, he was acutely aware. Someone else was driving.

Suddenly, Stan knew there were two brains in his head working simultaneously. One rational, standing outside his body, watching and wondering what he had just done. The other, mysterious, overpowering, pushing him toward a far-flung destination.

As of this moment, the mysterious part was in control. Without understanding why, he had instantly forsaken his news assignment and followed a black narrow asphalt road in the direction of what he hoped would be Freeland.

"Freeland," he said with some defiance. "Not Payette. Screw Payette. No sir, I'm going to Freeland."

He couldn't help but feel that some concealed reporter was hiding just around the corner waiting to stick a microphone in his window and ask, "Mr. Blankenship, you've just turned off on a tiny road to nowhere. Where the hell are you going?"

To which Stan answered out loud, "I'm going to Freeland." Not Disneyland. Not Hawaii. Not even Payette or Boise. As he drove down the road, a tune he had never heard before began to play in his head. He sang in response, "I'm a goin to Freeland, Freeland, Freeland, oh yes I am. Where oh where is Freeland?"

His mind was disjointed, yet unafraid. Whatever had urged him to travel this way also kept him calm. The question of *why* remained as distant as a bystander in the high gallery of an auditorium. For the moment, as *why* looked down and observed, the mysterious *other* led him deep into nowhere. Well, not exactly nowhere. He was going to Freeland.

Stan continued for several miles along the isolated road. Road in name only. More like a trail barely big enough for an automobile, but paved and smooth, as if the State of Oregon had made access to Freeland a priority.

The surrounding country seemed to swallow him. He saw nothing resembling a town and wondered if he had made some kind of mistake. Miles and miles of grass and canyons against a winding string of asphalt, but no Freeland. Not even a house or a barn. The further he drove, the more he assumed he had somehow missed a turnoff.

"Jesus, what am I doing out here?" he groaned as he logged more mileage on his journey toward foolishness. A wild goose chase into the middle of nowhere, wandering when he should be working. Then again, he knew he was not here by accident.

Suddenly, tucked away in some bushes like an old shoe under a bed, a battered city limit sign that announced: *Freeland.*

"Ah," Stan exclaimed. "Pay dirt."

Rounding a curve, he saw a most remarkable sight. A quaint town with a few small shops, a café, an old-fashioned school, and many houses. So neat and picturesque, it could have come straight out of a Norman Rockwell painting.

He spotted a butcher shop, a flower shop, a small auto garage and gas station. As he drove around, neat bungalows were laid out on tree-lined streets. In appearance, it looked like a small town that had been pulled straight from its New England roots and dropped square in the middle of this remote stretch of Oregon.

"My God," he said as he circled around. "What the hell is this place doing out here?"

As he completed his circle, he noticed another odd sight. In stark contrast to the rest of the town's well-scrubbed feel, there was a grungy old building with a beat-up banner that read *Matty's Grocery*.

The clapboard sides were cracked and the roof was in desperate need of repair. Stan wondered if it was still in business. He decided to pull in and look around, buy a snack, snoop. It was open. *Lucky me*, he thought as he walked inside.

Expecting the typical food mart, he was fascinated by what he found. An old hand-operated cash register sat on a long counter made out of plywood. Yes, there were food items crammed in shelves, but also pistols and rifles lined along the wall and general merchandise that might have been from the Civil War. Not to mention knick knacks and dinnerware from the turn of the century and cans full of bolts and nails shoved in a corner. It seemed more like an antique shop than a grocery store.

At first glance, the place looked deserted. Then he heard a shuffle and cough from somewhere deep in the store. "Hello?" he called out.

A woman's cranky voice replied, "Yeah?" Stan heard her march toward him. She turned a corner with hands on hips. "Yeah?" she repeated.

Stan was surprised by what he saw. An old woman, no more than five feet tall, maybe ninety pounds soaking wet, with white hair that looked like it hadn't been combed in a decade. She wore a faded red cotton shirt, old blue jeans several sizes too large, and laced up work boots you might see on a lumberjack. But despite her appearance, her expression was sharp. She might have been old. Her eyes said otherwise.

Stan tried his best to sound friendly. "I just arrived here, thought I might look around for snack food, candy bars, that sort of thing."

The woman looked annoyed. "That right?"

He paused, looked her over, and tried again. "You sell groceries here, right? The sign outside? Matty's Grocery?"

"Well now, aren't you observant," she sneered.

"I'm just looking for junk food, sodas, snacks, that kind of stuff."

The woman's eyes narrowed. "I don't carry any junk in this store, if that's what you're implying. The store may look junky, maybe could use a coat of paint, but I can assure you, I only carry top quality items."

"Okay, sorry," Stan said. "That's not what I meant. All I'm looking for is a snack."

The old lady squinted. "Where you from?"

"Boise."

She raised an eyebrow. "They don't have snacks in Boise?"

"Yeah, but at the moment, I'm here, wherever this is—"

"Freeland."

"Right, Freeland."

The woman raised a hand to her chin like an attorney questioning a witness. "So, if I'm understanding this right, you got in your car in Boise, drove all the way into Oregon, took a wrong turn off the highway, and landed in this dipshit little town." Her voice now rose like a preacher concluding her sermon, "And to top it off, you wandered into my broken down grocery store so you could maybe, just maybe, buy a candy bar?"

Stan thought about it and saw the humor in her observation. He broke out in laughter. Then, to his surprise, so did she.

"Well?" he said.

"You're one strange, gas wasting son of a bitch," she replied as she moved behind the counter. "But, as to your question about snack food, the answer is—" her face grew serious, "no."

"No?"

"Don't carry that stuff. People here don't ask for it. I do have beer, liquor, milk. And some fresh pepperoni sausage I got from Larry's Butcher. Good stuff, you know. Any of that interest you?"

"What kind of grocery store is this?"

"My store. Been here for nearly fifty years so I must be doing something right."

"Fifty years?"

"That's right. Name's Matty Rolf, owner, collector, whatever you want to call me, and you're in my store acting mighty rude, if you ask me."

"Gee, lady. I'm sorry, really. I just came in to get a snack, that's all."

"Well, as sorry as you seem, you're not helping your case."

Stan threw up his hands. "All right. All right. No problem. I'm leaving."

Matty stuck out her chin and pointed at the door. "The quicker, the better. Head back and don't stop till you hit the main drag, Sand Hollow Creek I think is the name. Have a safe trip and don't let the door hit you in the ass."

Stan stormed out. Batting the rickety screen door and hearing it slam gave him a moment of satisfaction.

As Stan headed toward his car, he was startled by the sight in front of him. A lanky black man, at least seven feet tall, perched on his hood. He had fierce looking eyes and wore some type of vest over a brown cotton shirt. Even with his shirt on, Stan could see that the man's arms were chiseled like a bronze sculpture.

"Uh . . . hello," said Stan.

"Welcome to Freeland, my brother," the man said in accented English, perhaps Jamaican or African. His smooth bass voice was sonorous and calming.

Stan stopped and crossed his arms. "Excuse me?"

"You are a guest in my town, are you not?" The man extended his hands toward Stan.

Stan glanced back and forth between the grocery store and his car and noticed that Matty had perched herself behind the screen door. He heard her mumble, "Ah, hell's bells."

"Well," Stan said, "I just stopped in for a snack." Staring back at her, he continued in a slightly louder voice. "But since this store doesn't carry snacks, I'm on my way out."

"Then that makes you my guest," the man said.

"Well, I guess, if you say so. But . . . why is this your town?"

"I've been here a very long time, brother, longer than anyone else who lives here. That makes me the village elder, and as such, I always take the opportunity to welcome visitors."

"Well, gee now, that's swell of you—brother," Stan said, "but it just so happens I'm leaving, so thanks, but no thanks."

"It is almost noon. I suspect you have driven some distance. You must have a meal, as my guest of honor."

"Guest? What's with this guest bit? I don't get it."

The man's face broke into a huge smile. "What don't you get? I am inviting you to a meal at my café. See?" He pointed to a building about fifty yards across the town square. "That is my business. I serve meals, drinks, and do it all with great care and friendliness. And today, at no cost to you, you are my guest."

Stan put his hands on his hips. "You own that place?"

"Yes, exactly. Officially, it's called the Kinsho."

"The what?"

"That is my language. It means the village circle, but since most folks here don't speak my language, they just call it the Circle."

"You're kidding. Who calls their restaurant the Kinsho, the Circle, whatever?"

Taking a half-bow and extending his arms, the man replied, "I do."

Stan thought about the man's invite. His offer seemed gracious and for a starving reporter living on a shoestring budget, the chance for free food was always welcome. "Well, okay then, I'll come over. Hell, that's actually pretty nice of you."

"I am a generous man. You will learn that soon enough."

The man turned his long, elegant frame and strode across the square to his café. As Stan turned again to look at Matty, she stared at him, shook her head, and disappeared into the store.

Inside the Circle, some folks had gathered for lunch. The café had the feel of a long rustic cabin. Near the front door was a bar counter with three stools. Across from the bar were two well-worn naugahyde booths parallel to a wide bay window overlooking the town square. Beyond the booths sat five square wooden tables, each with two chairs.

The down home atmosphere was reinforced by floor to ceiling wood paneling stained in a brown walnut color. The smell of coffee permeated the room. It was a place built to suit folks who liked their coffee black and their gossip fresh off the grill.

As Stan walked in, the room went silent. He sat in a booth near the front door. The tall black man came over to greet him.

"Welcome again. We have not yet been formally introduced. My name is Sarihaba Kinyaga, Sari for short. I come from an ancient African country, now called Kenya, but I have traveled around the world, only to rest my head in this small village. Freeland, I have called it. On behalf of all of us, I would like to welcome you to our little home." Sari motioned to the waitress to take Stan's order. "If I can be of assistance, you let me know. I usually sit over there behind the bar."

Sari bowed, walked behind the counter, and settled in a corner. He wiped a glass with a clean dish towel and began to chat with folks. As he sat and talked, the mood lightened and people returned to their conversations.

The waitress approached. "Welcome to the Circle, sir. My name's Amanda and I'll be serving you today. Can I start you off with some drinks or maybe an appetizer?"

As she stood poised with a pen and pad, he immediately noticed how pretty she was. Dark hair, dark eyes, a slim body poured into jeans and a cotton T-shirt.

"Well . . . Amanda," he said in his best friendly tone, "My order's pretty simple. I guess I'll just have the usual hamburger and French fries. And maybe a beer. You got any Budweiser?"

"Yes, we do." She sounded very professional. No wasted words.

"That's it, then. Thanks."

"You're welcome," she said and hurried away.

Stan watched her work and admired her efficiency. Also her legs, thighs, breasts, and face. He thought he might give her a decent tip just on looks alone.

When she returned with his order, he munched on his hamburger and fries and took in the Circle's quaint atmosphere. Maybe there was a story here with some type of offbeat human interest angle. If he could manage to sneak back and finish reporting on Payette, he might ask Hank to let him return and scope out the place. Hank would find this small hole in the wall amusing, especially if Stan could get an interview with this Sari character.

As he prepared to leave, Stan looked around for Sari, but the man had disappeared. He motioned to Amanda. "Say, that Sari guy. Where'd he go?"

"Out there," she said.

He followed her finger and noticed through the bay window that once again Sari was standing by his car. "Thanks," he said and exited out the front door.

As Stan approached his car, Sari spoke. "You are happy with your meal?"

Stan nodded. "Yeah, it was all right."

He didn't want to appear ungrateful, but he wished the man would leave him alone. He tried to conceal his annoyance, but beyond all his smiles and courtesy, Sari really pushed his buttons. Something about him just didn't add up. Something about all of this didn't add up. Stan was ready to get the hell out of Dodge.

Sari persisted. "You are happy with your visit?"

Stan decided to humor him. "Well, it started out a bit rough, but, all in all, I'd say yes."

"This town. Would it not be a good place for a young man like you to settle in, perhaps raise a family?"

Stan paused and stared at Sari. "I don't know. I honestly hadn't given it much thought. I suppose if I had a good reason to be here, like a job or someone nice to marry, then maybe."

"All that can be arranged."

Stan's irritation leaked out. "I'm sorry, what?"

"There is work here, women here, a house for you to settle in."

"Well, now, that's a nice arrangement if I lived in some place like, say, India, but I have a job and I don't need help finding a wife. Thanks anyway, but I'd just as soon go home."

"But, my brother, that is where you are."

"Excuse me?"

"You have arrived—home."

Without warning, Stan felt a surge in his head, the same as when he noticed the Freeland sign, only stronger, more painful. It vibrated inside his skull like the rumble of train wheels.

He raised his hands to his forehead. "Ow, stop, what is this?" The shock buzzed his brain and made him shake violently. His limbs went weak. Within seconds, everything grew dark.

When Stan woke, he looked around and saw that he was in a room, perhaps an old bedroom. He lay sprawled in a bed on top of a thick mattress. Sari sat peacefully off to the side. Stan glanced at him and immediately jumped up.

"Be calm, my brother," Sari said.

"Be calm my ass," Stan answered. "What's this all about?"

"It's about you, coming to Freeland. You were my guest. Now you are one of our residents. On behalf of the town and myself, I would like to welcome you."

"What the hell are you talking about?" Stan's face went flush. His fingers curled into a fist.

"You will learn as you go, no doubt. My sense tells me you will be a very valuable asset around here."

"I don't plan on staying, if that's what you're getting at. I told you. I live in Boise. I'm not interested in moving. So, move your sorry ass. You want me to call the cops?"

Sari looked amused. "You can call, of course, provided you can find a telephone, but I can assure you, they will not come."

"Why?"

"There are very few of them out here, and those that work out here are quite afraid of this place."

"Yeah?"

"And besides, I am the master of this village. That is my role here. To be your leader, and the leader of those who depend on me. If you need help, you simply come to me and ask."

"I didn't ask for your help. I don't know you from Adam, and given your little performance here, I wouldn't trust you anyway, even if I *did* need help. Come on. What's this all about anyway?"

Sari leaned his tall frame toward Stan. "It's quite simple, really. I have requested that you stay."

"You're kidding."

"As the leader of this community, I have made you a generous offer. I think it would be most impolite to refuse."

Stan sprang off the mattress. "I don't give a goddamn what you think, polite or impolite. Who made you emperor?"

"By your coming here, it is implied, and because of my generosity, your citizenship has been approved."

"Well, I didn't ask to come here and I certainly didn't vote for you."

"You will understand soon enough, my brother." Sari stood up. In such a small room, he filled most of the empty space. "You have traveled a far distance to be with us. Rest assured, there is no going back." He glanced around the room. "I hope you will find this house comfortable, a good place to live and raise a family. I will assist you, if you like, to start your own newspaper. That is, after all, what you want. To write your own stories?"

"How did you—" Stan stopped. His mind went blank.

"I know much about you already and soon, you will tell me more. For now, I must return to work. You are free to move about anywhere in town. This place, this village, is now your home."

"Really? What's to keep me from leaving?"

"You are part of my flock. I can assure you. The power of my spirit will keep you here. Perhaps unwillingly at first, but, as you grow accustomed to our town, my hope is that you will be happy."

Stan moved back and braced himself against a wall. "Who are you?"

Sari grinned, a broad grin that stretched across his face. Not evil, not dangerous. A grin closely attached to his eyes that revealed his good nature. "Some would call me a shaman. I like to think of myself as a molder of souls, and as such, your soul is now under my care."

"Whether or not I want to be molded?"

Sari gestured with his elegant arms. "We must all serve someone. By fortunate circumstance, you have come to me. Yours is the start of a long life of service, not just to me, to the whole town. We are a village. These people are now your family."

Stan eyed Sari for a moment, then made a desperate attempt to bolt. Within seconds, he found himself thrown back on the bed by an invisible hand. He struggled to rise, but whatever held him was unyielding. "Let me up, goddamn you."

"Soon enough, my brother," said Sari.

"Why am I pinned here?"

"To help you see that I have great powers. All for your benefit, I might add."

Stan tried again to sit up, but his arms and legs were paralyzed. He began to panic. "What kind of parlor trick is this?"

"I assure you, no trick at all. I told you. I am the village leader and I am asking you to stay."

For a moment, they watched each other—Sari with his confident smile, Stan reeling from his imprisonment.

Stan was amazed at Sari's magnetic attraction. How else to explain the force that held him down? His eyes, his words, all aimed in Stan's direction. His approach, mysterious, yet effective.

Then he recalled the lake, the nightmares, the invisible presence in his head. As he watched Sari, he realized where all that had come from. "You?" he said.

Sari nodded. "Ah, you finally recognize me."

"How the hell—"

"It is a long story, brother, one which I will happily share with you at some future date."

"You mean you brought me here?"

"Yes, by powers I learned long ago. Many who are here have come through my beckoning. We all have a purpose here."

"Purpose? A purpose for being kidnaped?"

"A purpose for finding their better being."

The room went quiet. For Stan, it began to sink in. "Seriously," he pleaded. "You mean I'm stuck here? Forever?"

"I prefer to think of it as recruited, as in your national army," Sari said. "Remember, all the things you want—home, job, wife, a newspaper—I promise to give." Sari paused, smiled, and walked out of the bedroom.

The power that held Stan released him. He jumped up and tried to tackle Sari, but some powerful force held him back. The harder he pushed forward, the more weight fell on his shoulders. Heavy, like large sacks of concrete. It pressed down and forced him to fall back on the bed. Sari paid no attention to Stan's struggles and stepped out the front door of the house. Stan staggered onto the porch.

Sari stopped at the gate and looked back. "I will give you much assistance. You will lack for nothing to get started."

As Stan watched him walk away, he took a few cautious steps forward and sat on the porch step. He looked over his surroundings. A small house, a road bordered by a hardy bit of forest, and the slopes of the rugged foothills. How was it possible he could end up fixed to this house, this small town? What would his family think? What would Amy think?

Yet, his intuition told him that Sari spoke the truth. He could sense his presence firmly planted in his head and in this town. Strange how he had become lost and found at the same time. Some large invisible wind had picked him up and dropped him on this street. The wind was frightening, but its purpose and his purpose was clear. Stan assumed the rest would unfold soon enough. For now, taken off guard, a prisoner in this haven, he had officially moved to Freeland.

March 13, 1820

Sari was tall and strong, an able-bodied man who had no trouble finding work as a crewman sailing west through the island colonies. It had been a long journey. Nearly three months in rough weather in a boat he had boarded in Cape Coast, Africa.

Still, he endured the storms and long days of sailing with great patience. When the going was particularly tough, he always used his unique powers of concentration to focus on his goal. America. A gleaming adventure. A bright new world of possibilities.

He had heard stories in Abidjan about a land lush and green, a paradise spread so far, a man could travel for months without seeing another soul. There was talk of clear rivers, unending forests, and magic animals.

Sometimes when he listened to the old men in the marketplace, he wondered if all this was really possible. He knew how the elders loved to make up stories. But where did these stories come from? Was there a kernel of truth underneath that kept them alive?

To satisfy his curiosity, Sari spent hours sorting through their tales. He determined that even if half of what they said was true, it would be worth a journey.

He had often thought about this on the deck of the trade boat Elizabeth late at night. He swore that sometimes, even in the middle of the ocean, he could smell the new world approaching.

It was early evening as they pulled into Charleston Harbor. He felt excitement, the anticipation of touching American soil. They would dock for the evening and unload early in the morning.

Their plan, not his. Sari had no intention of staying. This was his moment to discover for himself what was true or just idle gossip. As soon as the boat cast anchor and the Captain retired to his quarters, Sari slipped off the ship and disappeared.

A few blocks from the Elizabeth, a sailor was coming home from a drinking binge at one of the local pubs. His head spun and he had just stepped into an alley to puke up his rum soaked dinner. Rounding a corner, he nearly collided with the tallest darkie he had ever seen.

"Hey, mate, what the hell?" he said a little too loudly. "What you doin out at this hour—" The sailor suddenly froze.

Sari's eyes widened as he raised his hands, palms upward. "Destales farkuna," he said in a deep, quiet voice.

The sailor was lifted like a piece of paper in the wind and slammed into the side of a wall. Sari lowered his hands and the sailor floated to the ground. He bent over and brushed his hands across the man's face. "Sleep . . . well," he said, his first official words in America.

Raising up, he looked both ways down the street, then checked the stars. West was where he wanted to go. He would work his way across the land, learning as he went. The sense of mystery enticed him. This was America. So much to see and experience.

Looking back one last time at the sailor, he hurried down the street. It might take him several hours to reach the outskirts. This seemed like a large city, but eventually he knew there would be open land. He was an expert tracker. These skills would come in handy.

Moving, hiding, scouring the terrain, he took long strides down the street, creeping along as carefully as a lion hunting his prey.

November 1, 1977

It was late afternoon, a touch of early winter in the air. Stan sat in his living room and stared out at the trees along the hillsides. He tried to wrap his mind around his predicament; how he had become pinned inside this town by a power that, up until a few days ago, he would never have believed.

But this was no hallucination. Freeland was real. Sari was a powerful ruler. Stan was a prisoner. The town itself existed by Sari's imperial will. All who lived here were beholden to him. And yet no one except him seemed to mind.

Looking out his front window, Stan tried to muster enough energy to push against the bars of a mysterious cage with a secret door, but no amount of mind power could open it. It was hidden, locked, and sealed.

This was fate at its worst. Stuck in Freeland, friendless, powerless. He could not imagine continuing to live this way.

Stan started when he heard a knock at the door. Rising from his couch, he peered out the window and saw Matty at the front door.

"Yeah?" he said. He wondered if she also had powers, if by association with Sari she could read his mind.

"Open up," she said.

Stan waited for a moment, then stepped to the door and pulled it ajar. "Yeah?"

Matty looked at him crossly. "Well, you gonna let an old lady freeze out here?"

Stan eyed her small frame, her wrinkled face, her defiant expression. He pushed the door open.

"Thank you," she said and made her way to the small kitchen. In her arms was a sack full of groceries. "Brought you some stuff to survive on."

Stan stood by the kitchen entrance and watched her unpack the bag.

"Well," she said, "you gonna stand there or help?"

He walked over and pulled out bread, milk, some type of meat he didn't recognize, a few household items.

Matty began loading groceries into his cabinets. "Haven't seen you around the store much."

Stan stopped and folded his arms. "You're right. I guess I haven't gotten around to meeting my neighbors."

"Sounds like you're moping to me."

Stan leaned against a counter and folded his arms. "Yeah, that would be one way of looking at it."

When Matty finished, she pulled out a chair and sat with her legs crossed. Dressed in oversized jeans, a scarf, a wool hat, and her typical lumberjack shirt, she looked absorbed in the fabric. Clasping her fingers across her waist, she said, "You got to decide."

Stan stared down at the woman. His eyes widened. "Decide what?"

"Whether or not to make due."

He gave her a dubious look. "Is this your way of cheering me up?"

"It's the best I have to offer and it's more than you'll get from anyone else in this shitty little town, including grandmaster Sari."

Stan walked to the opposite side of the table and sat down. "And the alternative?"

Matty raised her hands. "Come on, you're a smart boy. There ain't no alternative. You seen what we're up against. Hell, I been here all my life. It's all I've ever known. Trust me, I wish I could've had what you had. But it don't do no good to complain. It is what it is. So. You make due."

Stan tapped his fingers on the table. "Swell. I feel better already."

"You should." Matty's voice faltered. "At least you have something worth remembering."

Stan noticed the lines on Matty's face. He supposed they might be lines of anguish from being captive all her life. But there was something else as well. The firm way she held her mouth, the determination in her eyes. "You mean you don't believe in Sari?"

Matty leaned forward and folded her hands on the table. "I believe in what it takes to survive. Beyond that, my thoughts are off limits and what I say here won't ever be repeated. Not by me anyway."

Stan grimaced. "Damn, you're one tough broad."

"Tougher than you know."

He paused and watched a smile spread across her face. "Okay," he said. "Survival, step one."

"Survival, step one. First, trust no one . . . but me." She waited for her words to sink in. "Step two. Don't go blabbing your sorrows around town. You need an ear, come to me. Otherwise, keep your gripes to yourself."

Stan waited, then propped his chin on his half-closed fist. "All right, then. Anything else?"

Matty laid a pile of wafer thin coins on the table, each one roughly the size of a quarter. They all looked similar. Black with grey and white marbling throughout. "This is what we use for money around here." She pushed them like casino chips across the table. "We call them—no surprise here—Saris."

Stan fingered the coins and rubbed one between his thumb and forefinger. "They feel like stone."

"Probably, though where he gets his supply and how he makes these all look alike is way beyond my small level of comprehension."

"So, this is official Sari money, huh?" He held one of the coins up to the light.

"Yeah. Among other things around here, Sari is the town's official banker and doler-outer. He makes sure everyone gets a weekly allotment, based on what he thinks you earn in loyalty. The more you kiss his ass, the more you get. Needless to say, you use these around town when you need to buy stuff . . . like groceries."

Stan placed the coin on the table and rubbed around its edges. "And how much ass have you kissed over the years?"

"You seen my store?"

"Yeah."

"That should give you a clue. Then again, he needs my store and I know how to run the place better than anyone else in town. As I said, I do what I need to survive. So, we've come to terms. I keep my mouth shut and he leaves me alone."

Stan sat quietly.

Matty continued. "He gave you this to get you started. The more or less part is up to you."

"All right, then. My allowance for the week. Where do I go for my next allotment?"

"You're looking at her."

"Ah, so the banker has his own personal teller."

"You got a problem with that?"

Stan watched Matty carefully. She was well-practiced at the amount of information she gave out. He guessed that he was dealing with a shrewd politician. "No, none at all."

"So, now you know."

"Know what?"

"Come by the store. Don't be such a stranger. And, since it's my store, I give discounts to whoever I want. Be nice to me and I could make your life a lot easier." Another smile broke across her face.

Stan put his elbows on the table and blew into his cupped hands. "Okay, Ms. Matty. You have my promise. I will be extra nice to you."

"Good," she said and eased to her feet. "Gotta go. Much as I love to chat, the store needs tending." She walked to the front door, adjusted her clothing, and stepped out on the porch.

"Thanks, Matty," said Stan.

"Don't mention it." She paused on the steps. "Life here has its good moments. You just gotta work hard to find em."

"I'll remember that."

She walked through the gate and headed toward town.

Stan watched with admiration as the old woman hobbled up the road. Somehow listening to her gave him inspiration. Life in Freeland. *Make lemons out of lemonade* his father would say. Stan closed the door, went to the refrigerator and decided what to make for supper.

April 12, 1978

It was one of those beautiful spring mornings. Some signs of green in the desert shrubbery. A mockingbird crooning. Daylight lengthening. Stan welcomed some much needed warmth on his face as he hiked from his house to the grocery.

People were starting to be out and about, taking walks, talking in the Circle about warmer weather. Johnny Nelson, for instance.

Johnny had befriended Stan when he first arrived here almost six months ago. He had taken him under his wing and done his best to make him feel a part of the community.

An elderly, gregarious man, he was always about town greeting neighbors and hiking along Paradise Road. Today, he caught up with Stan as he walked to work.

"Morning, there, Stan," he said cheerfully.

Johnny was spry for his age. Stan had to increase his pace to keep up. "Morning, Johnny. I see you're out and about early."

Johnny spoke between breaths. "Up with the birds. Guess that's the price of being old. Don't sleep as much. Weather turns warm, I like to get a fresh start. Does me good to walk."

"I'd say it's done you a world of good. I can barely keep up."

"What, you? With an old guy like me?" Johnny looked over his shoulder and laughed.

"I think, Johnny," Stan said between breaths, "you could walk most of us under the table."

"Well, I do get around. Pretty good athlete when I was young. Guess I still got a little get up and go."

As they reached a small path cutting off to the side of the road, Johnny veered right. "Well, I like to make a trip or two up in the hills round about this time of year. Mother Nature can't be beat in the spring."

"See you, Johnny," Stan called out as he stopped for a minute to catch his breath. He watched with admiration as Johnny skimmed up a hillside.

After a long winter in Freeland, Stan was beginning to get on with his life. Did he enjoy being trapped here? No, but he was trying to take Matty's advice and make the best of it. Soon, his paper, The Freeland Reporter, would get off the ground. Equipment in place. Legwork done. Launch imminent.

Matty had agreed to let him set up shop in a small storage room in the back of her store. The room was doorless, windowless, and stuffy. For Stan, it seemed more like a tool shed, but it had electricity and just enough space to cram in office supplies and a small printer. The end result. Next week, a new rag would appear in print.

"Morning, Matty," Stan called out as he walked in the front door of the grocery store.

"Morning yourself," she replied tersely.

"Nice weather we're having."

"Thank God for small favors. Same town, same life. Always the same, snow or sun."

"Well, I happen to like the sunshine."

"Well then, yippy skippy for you. Wouldn't want to spoil your fun."

Stan knew Matty could be crusty. He'd learned that from day one. Today, in particular, she seemed to have her axe sharpened and ready. Still, he knew there was a soft spot under all that armor. Every so often he could coax some warmth out of her. "Well, there's no starting my day on the right foot unless you smile. How about it. Hmm?"

She eyed him and perked up at the game to be played. Matty loved to banter and Stan had thrown down a gauntlet. She cracked a thin smile. "And which foot would that be?"

"Whichever one gets you to smile."

"Well now, how about if I take *my* foot and kick you in the ass? That would be pretty fun. Could cheer me right up." Her smile broadened.

Stan broke into laughter. "You know, lady, you've got some mean streak in you."

She leaned on the counter. "Yeah, not very grandmotherly, am I? But I got one thing going for me."

"What's that?"

"You need my storage space."

Stan watched her face slowly break into another grin. "All right then," he said. "Have a great day."

She stepped back and did a mock curtsy. "Thank you. From here on out, it's all downhill."

He conceded game, set, and match to Matty.

Stan ran through his mockups, deciding which items to put in the first edition. An ad for Roy's Firewood Service. An article on the upcoming ladies' luncheon. Someone's plea to help them find their lost dog. Not exactly earthshaking or worthy of the Pulitzer Prize.

When he worked at the Statesman, he and Amy had covered some interesting news. Human interest stories, breaking news, even a few gigs covering the Mayor's office. Here, it was all small stuff.

On the other hand, it was nice being his own boss. He was the owner, editor, printer, chief cook, and bottle washer. And living in Freeland offered some opportunities to investigate things well beyond the normal. After all, he lived in one of the strangest towns on earth.

Case in point—Sari. Who was he? What kind of powers did he wield to keep people pinned here as prisoners?

Stan had lived in Freeland for several months and still struggled to understand answer that question.

But did he dare write about it? And if he did, what would happen to him? He was still learning the rules. What was inbounds, out of bounds, what might save him or get him in hot water.

Always, when he talked to Sari, he sensed danger. A man with that kind of power was unpredictable. And those damn eyes. Looking in them reminded him of looking in a very dark pool. The water on top might be smooth, but underneath—

He shook his head as if Sari's name was automatically hypnotic. Regaining his focus, he laid out the various stories on his desk and realized their order made absolutely no difference to anyone. It was all small news. Besides, the paper only ran eight pages. Stan grabbed the article on the ladies' luncheon and decided to post it on the front page. *Good politics*, he thought.

That evening, he left the office about five or so. It was a comfortable, cool evening. After he rousted some dinner, he ate out on the porch of his little house, a one room bungalow parallel to Paradise Road, the main drag through town. The paint had faded to a weathered grey and the roof was in desperate need of repair.

As he finished his dinner, Stan heard footsteps on the pavement and looked up. It was Larry Levin, owner of Larry's Butcher Shop on the south end of the town square.

Larry was a stocky man with massive arms, dark crew cut hair, and a pumpkin-size head. Tonight he wore old overalls, steel-toed boots, and a Navy pea jacket. He was not tall, but his build suggested he could handle heavy loads and his hands were the size of dinner plates.

But what Stan noticed most about Larry was his eyes, brooding and fierce. When he looked at someone, he always stared a hole through them.

As Larry strolled by, he stopped at Stan's teetering picket fence. "Evening there, Mr. Blankenship."

"Evening—Larry, is it?" Stan replied.

"That's right."

"Well, just call me Stan, please."

"All right. Stan."

Stan laid down his dinner. "What can I do for you, Larry?"

"Out for a walk tonight." Larry looked up and down the road. "Summer's coming."

Stan watched him nervously shuffle his hands in and out of his coat pockets. "Yeah, you're right," he said. "Warm weather's just around the corner."

"You the newspaper guy, I hear."

"That's right. Due to launch in a week."

"Never thought Freeland was big enough to have its own paper." He sniffed and wiped his nose on his jacket sleeve. "Then again, you never know what Sari's up to. Guess you arrived here unexpected like the rest of us. So, who knows what's coming tomorrow?" Larry smiled and revealed a mouthful of square teeth.

Stan remained quiet.

Cramming his hands back in his pockets, Larry continued. "You hunt?"

Stan draped his hands between his legs and paused. "No, never," he said.

Larry tilted his head. "Where you from?"

"San Diego originally, but I came here from Boise."

"Oh, California, huh? Lots of crazies down there. Probably not many hunters, though."

Stan stood up and braced himself against his porch post. "I worked for a paper in Boise, even traveled a bit around the country. I can tell you, there's a whole lot of crazies everywhere." He stopped short of mentioning Freeland.

Larry shifted uncomfortably from one foot to the other. "Yeah, guess so." He glanced around, then zeroed in on Stan. "Around here, we hunt—a lot."

"Really," Stan said. "For what?"

"Deer, mostly, sometimes ducks, whatever critters fly or live near water—and some things that don't." He gave this line a pregnant pause. "If we can eat it, we hunt it." Again, that big oafish smile. "I carry lots of it in my store. You ever need fresh game, I can get it."

"Well thanks, Larry," said Stan as he puzzled over the *some things that don't* part.

Larry cleared his throat. "Let's see. Where was I? Oh yeah, hunting." He took his hands out of his pockets, rubbed them together, and returned to his line of questioning. "You interested in learning?" He assumed a wide stance and stared at Stan with those radar eyes.

Stan was unsure if this was an invitation or a challenge. "Honestly, Larry, I wouldn't be much good to you."

"Well, you can always start. I got an extra rifle. Teach you to shoot, skin, make your own dinner."

The more Larry talked, the more Stan was repulsed. It wasn't that Stan was afraid of guns. He *was*, however, afraid of Larry. "Thanks, Larry, but I'll pass on this. Think I'll rely on you to keep me stocked."

Larry looked disappointed. "Oh, well then, just thought I'd ask. Never hurts to try. I've been a good teacher to a lot of folks around here. We got a nice little group of us that hang together."

"I'm sure."

He pulled his coat tighter and turned his back to the fence. Stan thought he might be deciding which way to walk. Then he turned and gave Stan one more hard look. "Just a word of caution, though."

"What's that, Larry?"

"We tend to go out a lot, sometimes at odd hours. Gotta go where the game is, you know."

"Yeah?"

"Everyone knows around here."

"What's that?"

"Don't wander these hills at night."

Stan grew chilled. He rubbed his arms to ward off the fear. "Dangerous, huh?"

"Can be if you don't know where you're going. Hunter thinks you're a deer, could be painful." Larry grinned.

Stan was curious about whether or not this might be one of Larry's odd jokes. Or maybe a warning. He also wondered what other things these guys tracked besides deer. "Thanks. I'll keep that in mind." He lifted his hands to his mouth, cupped them together, and blew into his palms. "Getting kind of cool, Larry. Think I'll go in now."

"Okay," Larry said and waved. "Be seeing you around. Won't be long. Bag em, skin em." He turned, gave another glance up and down the road, then crossed over and disappeared.

Stan peered into the hillsides. Sari, Larry. Now this damn invitation. Picking up his dinner, he hurried back into the house, painfully aware that, as Larry had ironically pointed out, he was surrounded by crazies.

April 19, 1978

The night before, Stan had worked late and fussed over every detail to get his small publication out the door. He fretted over the logo, did some last minute editing, carefully measured the ink, and made sure the newsprint fed straight. Despite the paper's diminutive size, he treated it like his first major novel.

When he finished printing and bundling, it was nearly one in the morning. He dumped his tired body in his creaky wooden office chair, stretched his feet on his desk, and took a long, satisfied look at the pile of small town news in front of him.

"Not bad," he said, "for a little paper that nobody gives a shit about. Ladies and gentlemen of Freeland, I present to you—the Freeland Reporter."

He stood up and danced around the room, did a mock cheer, and raised his hands in a victory salute. Then he stopped and eased back in his chair with his fingers locked behind his head. The question popped in his head: *One down, how many more?*

The thought hit him like a slap to the face. He was proud of his paper, but he knew why it existed. As therapy. Occupational therapy. Otherwise, like a felon behind bars, he was still a prisoner.

Pushing back the thought, he took one last look around before leaving the store. He walked home and tried not to let the darkness overwhelm his sense of accomplishment.

He woke early and was back in the office by eight.

"Aren't you the early bird this morning?" Matty said as he entered the store.

"It's ready, Matty, my dear," he responded. "I am the father of a brand new baby paper."

Matty looked skeptical. "Bit dramatic, now, aren't we?"

"Yes, ma'am, I am. But today, I don't care. The paper has arrived. Would you like to be my first customer?"

"Is it gonna cost me anything?"

"No. That's the beauty of this little plan. Thanks to the generosity of our beloved Sari, it's all free."

"Well, then, lay it on me."

Stan hurried into his office and emerged with a single bundle of papers. Pulling one off the top, he handed it to Matty. "You, my dear, are at the front of the line. First copy, first edition. Would you like me to sign it?"

Matty browsed through the pages and gave several *huhs* before looking at Stan. "Not bad. Could use a gossip column."

Stan pretended to write on a pad and paper. "Okay, Matty's opening suggestion. Gossip column. Who's my mole?"

"You're looking at her. I know everything that goes on in this little pinhole town."

Stan gestured toward her with both hands. "Lady, you're hired."

"I expect you'll put my name in here, right under yours. Maybe a nice title like Community Gossip Editor, some such nonsense."

"You got it."

She grinned and pointed toward the door. "Better get out there, Stan, and start pounding the pavement. Paper business is pretty competitive around here." She walked to the middle aisle, shook her head, and disappeared.

The printing was just the first step. It also fell on Stan to be his own delivery man. He had often thought about this as he laid the groundwork for his paper's launch. Every so often, he took small opportunities to get the word out—making house calls, asking permission to deliver, that sort of thing. There was no harm in doing a bit of good marketing.

Still, it was an anxious moment when he picked up his pile and began delivering to various houses and small businesses. As Stan passed out each paper, he sent positive thoughts to make sure it was well received.

By ten o'clock, he was finished and back in his office, thinking about next week. It had all gone by in such a blur. *Now what*, he wondered?

He sat at his desk without turning on his lamp. Only the daylight from the store illuminated his office. Stan often did this to calm himself and think. To his surprise, Sari stepped in the doorway and blocked what little light he had. Sari, whose presence in his office seemed as immense as a tall building.

"Good morning, my brother," he said gently.

"Morning, Sari," Stan said. "Care for some light?" He reached over and turned on his lamp.

Sari located the one folding chair Stan kept for visitors and sat down. His legs were so long, he was forced to sit sideways to avoid banging his knees on Stan's desk. Yet, even as he settled in, Sari never took his eyes off Stan.

"It is a good morning for you, no?" he said with his usual soothing rumble.

"You mean the paper?" Stan shifted in his seat and picked up a pen. He laid his hand on his desk and pretended to take notes. In fact, he just needed an excuse to doodle and avoid Sari's intense eyes. "Well, now that you mention it, I guess it is."

Sari sat quietly for a moment. "The paper is a good thing, no?"

"It keeps me busy, that's for sure."

"The word is a powerful tool. I myself take great pride in its use."

Stan scratched out a series of intersecting lines. "I can imagine."

"Now, you are officially a part of Freeland."

"Really?"

"You've found your path, I think."

This assumption annoyed Stan. Like he really had a choice in the matter. "I think it's more accurate to say the path found me."

"Yes," Sari said as he folded his hands around his knees. "Sometimes these two things must find each other, like a man's soul finds his body."

Stan was not a mystical person. Sari's tone sounded like a philosophy lecture with Stan as the neophyte. Stan didn't consider himself a neophyte and had no desire to be tutored on metaphysics. "Can I help you with something, Sari?"

"I am checking on your well being," he said. "After all these months, I am hopeful—"

"That I'm ready to live here? Ready to be your little tool for the rest of my life?"

The atmosphere in the room shifted like the temperature of the wind from a fast-moving weather system. Sari's energy could be felt by all around him. Stan had learned this over the course of his few conversations with the man and knew what the change in temperature meant. He braced himself.

"I am hopeful you will come to feel at home here. It is, after all, your village."

Several deep breaths later, Stan calmed himself and regained his composure. "I have no choice in the matter, Sari, but, given what I'm doing now, I'd say this helps."

"Then we are moving in the right direction."

Stan choked down a retort. He realized his predicament and thought better of pushing back too hard. After all, Sari *was* the shaman in charge. Better to live with some small measure of purpose than die. The paper was his baby. It would keep him busy and out of trouble. Maybe.

Sari's tone softened. "In time, perhaps you will be happy."

"Perhaps."

Sari rose from his chair and towered over him for a few moments. Stan stared up and examined him like a large dark totem pole. Sari's mind and body, mysterious and full of indecipherable hieroglyphics. Stan would have to work harder at understanding the symbols.

"We will speak again, soon," he promised.

Stan remained silent.

Sari turned and walked through the door. The light disappeared and reappeared so suddenly, Stan questioned whether or not he had just witnessed an eclipse. He sat at his desk and stared at the empty folding chair.

Matty came to the door. "Visit from the big kahuna, huh?"

"Yeah," said Stan.

"He's a real mystery, ain't he?"

"Very true."

"Man gives me the heebie jeebies."

Stan took his eyes off the chair and glanced at Matty. "Why's that?"

"Sometimes he knows what you're thinking before you can say it. Never seen anything like it. I try to keep out of his way."

Stan stood up, turned off his lamp, and stretched his arms toward the ceiling. "I'm afraid he's got his eye on me."

"He's got his eye on everyone. You can't spit around here without him knowing it."

"Well, I guess that's good to know."

Matty turned and leaned against the doorframe. "One thing I'm glad about."

"What's that?"

"When I die, he ain't gonna follow me. Hell, heaven, wherever I go, least *he* won't be there."

Stan noticed how her eyes flared. "Well, that's some consolation, isn't it."

"Damn straight. Fact of the matter is, I can't wait."

Stan crossed his arms and watched Matty. He noted how there was something rebellious and determined in her expression.

"Don't look at me like that," she said. "You and I both know what death really means around here."

"What's that?"

"Freedom."

She blinked for emphasis, pushed off the doorway, and went back to work.

December 7, 1978

The holidays always arrived early in Freeland. Not Thanksgiving, Christmas, or New Year's. Hunting season. Stan had learned this from numerous chats with locals at the Circle. As a result, this year he printed reminders in the Reporter about the official start dates for hunting season.

Even so, he knew it didn't matter. Freeland was different from the rest of the state. Hunters securing licenses, checking guns, scouting out the best areas to find game. No one here seemed to live by those rules anyway.

In Freeland, the talk centered around outsiders who came into this area to hunt. In the local vernacular, they were referred to as DAWGs (damn assholes with guns). Numerous conversations in the Circle could be overheard about these so-called intruders and how they always showed up uninvited.

Stan picked up on this, even printed a story or two about what he'd overheard, which was why on this cold December morning, he tromped into the Circle to see if he could catch any more gossip.

As usual, sitting on his favorite bar stool, his prime source of information—Walt Renier. And next to him, his best friend, Larry Levin. The two of them appeared to be having some important discussion, probably about their favorite subject. Hunting.

Walt, the town's local tow truck driver, was a heavy set man with a round jowly face and a large bald spot on the top of his head. What remained of his grey-brown hair hadn't been combed in years.

In every sense, from his coveralls to his greasy hands, Walt looked like a redneck, but Stan knew that he was much more complicated than he looked on the outside.

True, he loved a good beer and a crude joke, but get him started on topics like modern philosophy or international politics and he could amaze everyone with what he knew. In short, Walt had a tow truck body and a renaissance mind.

"Morning, Walt," Stan called out. "What's keeping you busy these days?"

"Well, hey there, Stan. Enjoyed your paper the other day. Good story on Daisy's canning techniques. Might try it myself for Christmas."

"Thanks."

"Morning, there, Stan," Larry said. "Can you smell it in the air?"

"What's that, Larry?"

Larry took a deep breath and exhaled. "Smells like—" he put his finger to his nose, "hunting season."

Stan shivered. "If you say so. You guys do that all year around out here. Not sure why now is so special. Besides, you know I'm not a hunter. Any meat I get is from your store."

"Well, around here, if you go to my store, most likely we're the ones that put it there."

"Okay, then. I'm in good hands."

Larry raised his coffee cup in salute. "You betcha."

Stan sat down in his favorite booth near the front door and settled in for breakfast. Amanda came up, took his order, and hurried off. After she left, he turned to Walt. "So, what's the latest news?"

"Don't miss a beat, do you, Mr. Reporter?"

"I try to stay on my toes. Hard to keep ahead of you, though."

"That's cause you drive a Volkswagen and I drive a truck." Walt and Larry had a good chuckle over that remark.

"True enough." Stan put a notepad on his table and reached in his jacket to pull out his pen.

Walt seemed pleased to be interviewed. "You want gossip, huh?"

Stan nodded. "Got any?"

"Well, I hauled another vehicle last night over to Vale. Damn, this was a nice truck. Looked like a new Chevy '78 4x4 1500, pretty silver color, jacked up, nice big tires, runners. Probably had, I'm guessing, a 350 engine in it. Sheriff's deputy called me last night to come get the damned thing off the highway."

Stan stopped writing and rubbed his chin. "Just left it, huh?"

"Abandoned like a baby on a door step."

"How come, you think?"

"Insurance, divorce settlement, hell if I know."

"No clue, huh?"

Walt leaned back on his stool, arm propped on the bar counter, with a big grin on his face. "You accusing me of something, Stan?"

"Just seems strange, that's all."

"Hell, Stan, haven't you noticed? You're in Freeland. Strange is the norm around here."

Again, Walt and Larry laughed.

"Good one, Walt," Larry chuckled.

Stan nodded and smiled. "Isn't that the truth." He paused as he scratched out some notes. "What's that, like the third one this week?"

"Yeah," Walt said, "and it's not like the Sheriff seems to care that much. Probably hopes no one calls so they can auction them off, pocket a few bucks between them."

Sari chimed in. "I think he doesn't want to know. He's too spooked to spend much time in this place anyway, especially this time of year. Word is out, you know."

Stan looked puzzled. "About what?"

Sari motioned with his fingers. "Around here, a very scary place." He grinned wide and put his finger to his mouth. "Shhh. No police, no army, nobody wants to know." Sari waited, then whispered, "Where are the drivers?"

It was not true, what Sari said—this bit about not wanting to know, at least for one person in the room. Stan was curious. Also petrified about what Sari and his cohorts knew and protected as their jolly little secret.

"Well, keep me posted," Stan said to Walt. "I'll file it under my missing truck section."

Walt laughed. "Detail person, ain't you Stan?"

"Fills my paper."

"That tidbit get me a free ad?"

"Maybe." Stan's eyes wandered to the bay window. An approaching snow storm gave the horizon an ominous appearance.

"Put me down then. Be sure it's in the front."

"You got it. Thanks, Walt."

As Stan took a break from his afternoon work, he decided to bundle up and go for a walk. Just west of his house, he stopped for a moment to look up and down Paradise Road.

It was overcast, foggy, about three-thirty in the afternoon. As Stan gazed west, the road bent and disappeared into the hills. With the asphalt blanketed by drizzle and fog, it looked like a little thread that simply dropped off the face of the earth.

He wondered if that's what happened to the missing owners of the trucks. They took a wrong turn, headed toward Freeland, and poof, fell off the face of the earth. He wondered if they really ended up here by accident.

As he gazed down the road, he thought about an opening line for a story: *Hunters arrive each year, drive through Freeland in their fancy trucks, and each year some trucks never go home. The question is, why?*

His paper may be small, but he believed this story had potential. Too bad no one outside of Freeland would ever read it.

Stan decided to walk down Paradise Road and see if he could spot any hunters. Maybe he could do some interviews and gather clues to this mystery. He hiked another quarter mile to a quiet clearing and sat down on a rounded boulder by the road.

In the December half-light, with wind and mist blowing around his face, the atmosphere was ominous. Perhaps an approaching storm. Perhaps a premonition. It made him shiver and hope for someone to pass by just to distract him from his dire thoughts.

As if on cue, an old Ford pickup appeared, something from the late '50s. Stan could tell they were hunters. Gun racks in the cab. Orange vests in the rear bed. Some type of setup for hauling game. As they drove by, the passengers in the cab spotted him and waved.

Stan waited until they dipped over the horizon, then stood up and followed.

He walked west another quarter mile, his breath steaming, his hands stiff from the cold. The hunters had parked off to the side in a small clearing. Since the guns and camouflage were missing, he assumed they were already out hunting.

Turning in a complete circle, Stan tried to calculate which way they'd gone. Truthfully, he had no clue. "Oh well," he said. "One direction's as good as the other."

Making a random choice, he headed south. There was no apparent trail. He realized how easy it would be to get lost out here, especially with dusk approaching. Still, he pushed on.

He traversed up toward the foothills in complete silence. The only audible sounds—the dry grass and dirt under his feet and the wind. Loneliness crept through his neck and shoulders. And something else. Fear. He could smell it in the air. His own. Someone else's.

Suddenly, Stan heard a voice in the distance. A long, clear human scream, the kind someone utters when they're afraid of dying. It was followed by the noise of crashing brush and snapping twigs. Then, silence. "Oh, Jesus," he whispered.

He fought off panic and kept listening. Nothing more. He took a guess as to where the voice had come from and started walking in a slightly different direction.

It was not long before the land cleared at the crest of a hill and revealed a small lake in the shape of an oval. Ten yards or so in front of him was a hunting blind about five feet high, six feet wide, set between two large pine trees. Perhaps the hunters had come looking for ducks on the water or deer on the shoreline.

The blind was deserted, but a small ice chest, an orange vest, and a couple rifles still remained. It appeared whoever had been here left in a hurry.

Stan stood between the two trees and looked out, imagining what he might see if he was a hunter. His eyes circled the water and browsed along the hilltops. He picked up a rifle, extended his arms, and pretended to aim. As he squinted through the scope, he prepared to fire on some imaginary varmint.

Through the cross-hairs, Stan thought he spotted movement. Briefly. A twitch in the landscape.

He was surprised when, somewhere close by, a gunshot cracked the air. Then a second. More shouts. Another scream. Stan dropped the rifle and ducked behind the blind. "Shit, shit," he kept muttering. The oppressive presence of death pressed against him. His pulse quickened and in the stillness, he could hear his own heart beat.

Another noise. What was that? Hard to make out from such a distance. A snarl? A growl? For several minutes, he remained hidden behind the blind. The noise repeated, approached closer, stopped.

Another few minutes passed. Hearing nothing, he stood up and looked around. Still no movements that he could make out in the growing darkness. Sound was tricky on this open plateau. It was possible that the gunshot, the scream, could be miles away.

Stan heard something or someone crash through some brush straight toward him. He collapsed behind the blind again and waited.

It approached from his left, near the shoreline—the distinct patter of running feet. Not boots like a man. Lighter, faster, like the gait of a deer or a dog.

As Stan waited, a pack of dogs broke out and rushed past the blind. Passing within a foot or so, he heard their barks and huffed breathing as they traveled at breakneck speed. Dogs in hot pursuit of their prey. Within seconds, they disappeared back into the brush.

Stan hid until he was sure the pack had passed. Cautiously, he stood and turned toward the pond. What he saw startled him so badly he jumped backwards, tripped over a rock, and fell flat on his back. As he hit the ground, he yelled, "Holy shit!"

There, standing with a strange look on his face—Walt. Heavy black coat, rugged winter boots, a bright orange stocking cap on his head.

"Well, hey there, Stan," he said. "Can't imagine what you'd be doing out here in the middle of nowhere. You lost?"

"Walt?" Stan gathered himself and stood up.

Walt strode toward him. "Looks like you could use some help getting back. Pretty far from home for a news guy."

"I followed some hunters out here, wondered what they might be doing. Looks like they were here. Now they're not." Stan stopped and watched Walt's expression. "Know anything about that?"

Walt looked blankly at Stan. "Not a thing. I've been out here a couple hours. Haven't seen any hunters."

Liar, Stan thought. "You're hunting, huh?"

"That's right. As you well know, I do that occasionally, especially this time of year."

"Where's your rifle?"

"Don't need one. There's lots of ways to hunt without having to shoot."

"Like?"

"Traps, bow and arrow, knife—"

That's when Stan noticed the hilt on Walt's right hip. He shivered from the images that popped into his head. Walt, dogs, hunters, blade to flesh. It was all he could do to keep from turning tail and running down the hillside.

Walt remained calm, his body relaxed.

Stan pointed toward the brush. "You have dogs, I see."

"That's right," said Walt as he looked out over the lake. "It's a tried and true method you know. My daddy's from Tennessee. Used to love to go with him when he brought out the blue ticks. Could smell a coon from miles off. Smartest dogs I ever knew."

"There's a blind here. Yours maybe?"

Walt crossed his arms. "Nope, no idea who that belongs to. Probably some DAWG left it. Looks like he's gone now. Not a good idea to leave your stuff out in the open like this. Nice couple of rifles. Never know who might steal it."

"I heard screams somewhere around here. You hear them?"

"Lots of noises out here that sound funny. I once heard a bobcat cry that sounded like a fire siren. Strangest thing I ever heard."

There was something peculiar about Walt's response, his presence out here, the nature of his hunt. By now, it was almost dark. As Walt's face faded, Stan became even more afraid.

"Getting pretty dark, Stan," Walt noted. "Maybe you should start for home. Gets cold out here at night. Wouldn't be good for you to get lost, dressed like you are."

Stan watched Walt carefully. His darkened face, the tone of his voice, seemed threatening. "You're right," he said. "Guess I should be heading home."

Walt reached into his jacket. "Need a flashlight? Maybe I should walk you back."

The thought of Walt following him in the dark was not pleasant. "That's okay. It's not that far. The extra light would be nice, though."

Walt handed over the flashlight and pointed north. "Just keep walking in that direction. You can't miss the road."

"Thanks, Walt. Much appreciated."

Walt turned and hiked in the direction Stan last heard the dogs run. "See you tomorrow," he called out.

Standing for a moment, Stan puzzled over Walt and the hunters. His guess. More would go missing. Walt would get another call from the Sheriff and have another abandoned truck story to talk about in the Circle.

Judging by this encounter, Stan had a good idea what happened to these hunters. They walked in here and vanished without a trace, leaving families and curious reporters like him to ask where they went.

Except, in his case, Stan suspected the answers. Walt and his crew. What they loved to hunt were the DAWGS. What they did with them was anyone's guess.

As Stan walked back down the hill, the awful pictures of bushwhacked hunters left him jumpy and paranoid. The wind sounded like the voices of lost spirits, maybe the ghosts of those who died here. Shadows darted across his flashlight beam.

He shivered and repeatedly patted himself to stay warm. It wasn't just the cold that bothered him. For Stan, the wintry landscape had become a symbol of death.

When he reached the road, he realized what he had to deal with. Not only the oddities of life in Freeland, but also murder, the knowledge of murder, and the guilt about keeping it secret. For his own survival. There were dangerous powers at play here and men who prowled the canyons hunting other men. They were the real beasts of Freeland.

Stan let his beam roam up and down the road. He watched it bounce around in some trees, a solitary white pole against an avalanche of black branches. As he walked back home, he finally came to understand. The warnings were true. Don't wander around these hills at night.

In the morning, as Stan walked into the Circle for breakfast, Walt sat on his favorite stool drinking coffee.

Sari, from his usual perch, greeted Stan. "Hey, my brother, I heard you got lost yesterday. You hear spooky noises, maybe see a ghost or two?"

Walt joined in. "Ever find your hunters?"

Stan took his normal seat. "Morning guys. News travels fast I see."

"Little town, big ears," Sari joked.

"See you made it home all right," said Walt.

Stan reached over and fiddled with a coffee cup. "Yeah, thanks, Walt. Flashlight really helped."

"Got another call for an abandoned truck. A real clunker. Sheriff'll probably be lucky to get fifty bucks out of it."

"No surprise there, huh, Walt?"

Walt's hands froze in midair. He put down his coffee cup and rotated his chair. Face to face with Stan, his eyes narrowed and his jaw grew taut. "Something you're accusing me of, Stan?"

"Hmm, not without evidence. That's the way it works in this country."

"Damn straight," said Walt.

"Doesn't mean I don't know what's going on."

Walt and Sari grew quiet and eyed Stan, sizing up his last statement. Walt grinned, turned around, and slapped a coin on the counter. "Thanks, Sari. Gotta get to work. Busy time of year, you know."

Sari rose from his chair. "Always in Freeland this time of year, especially for you."

Walt hung by the door. "You take care, Stan."

Stan remained still, his eyes locked on Walt. "I'll do that."

"And don't go wandering these hills at night." He strolled out, jumped in his tow truck, and drove off.

As he rolled out of sight, Stan grabbed his pen and started scratching on a napkin:

Hunters drive through Freeland each year—in trucks—beat up and fancy—and every year—a few—well, more than a few—never go home. The question—for me—is—why?

October 7, 1641

It was a warm night in Sari's coastal village of Dishaba. The ocean was calm and thousands of bright stars gleamed in the sky.

Sari was very excited. Sitting on the beach, he anticipated "Prava" night, when the whole town gathered in the central square to watch the shaman Benlama demonstrate his powers. All the residents chatted about whether the master would show them any new tricks tonight or accurately predict someone's fortune.

Though a family man and a respected leader in his village, Sari loved to watch Benlama and yearned to become a shaman. He often watched him closely to see if he could discern the difference between trickery and genuine magic.

"Benlama," he would sometimes call out. "Teach me some of this."

The master would always stop and smile. "If this is what you want, you must leave your family and dedicate yourself. This, above all else, requires great focus."

"But who will feed my family, my wife and children?" Sari asked.

Benlama would always shake his head. "Then you, my friend, are not ready."

Sari would go home and ponder about what he meant. How hard was it to learn magic? And what did Benlama mean when he said that Sari was not ready? He was greatly puzzled and hoped in the future to ask more questions, perhaps in private when the two of them could talk at length.

Tonight in particular, as Sari sat in the audience, Benlama was spectacular. The village cheered his performance as he made one of their elders float in the air.

Late that night, after most were asleep, Sari slipped out of his hut and over to the lodging of the great shaman. Light reflected through the cracks of his tent. *Good*, he thought. *Benlama is still awake.* He stepped inside and saw the shaman sitting motionless by his fire.

"Good evening, great master," Sari said quietly so as not to disturb him. "I see you are still perfecting your craft."

Benlama looked up and greeted Sari with a mischievous grin. "Ah, the man who wants to know all my tricks. You are willing to watch but not learn. When will you understand? Magic requires that you free yourself."

Sari huddled with Benlama near the fire. He noticed how the shaman's face glowed in the half-light. Though Benlama must have been very old (the local elders often talked about how long he had been coming), he marveled at how the man never seemed to age.

Rocking slowly and rhythmically, Sari's eyes locked on the fire. "I would truly like to learn," he said as he folded his arms around his knees. "I've watched you for years. I have a feeling that something draws me to this."

"Perhaps the wind," said Benlama. "The wind goes where it goes and sings to whomever it pleases. It leaves when it chooses and draws whomever it wants."

They sat silently together for several minutes.

"What would you give to become like me?" said Benlama.

Sari took some time to consider this. It was the moment he had hoped for—an invitation. He weighed his options carefully. "I think several of my best cattle. That seems more than fair to me."

Benlama laughed. "Foolish man. The wind does not need cattle."

They sat quietly for several more minutes.

Sari spoke again. "Perhaps one of my daughters? She would give you many children."

This time Benlama simply grunted. "The wind does not need daughters or children."

Sari thought about what he had left to offer. "I have several gold coins. Perhaps the wind could use these?"

Benlama shook his head. "The wind does not need gold."

Sari was perplexed. He had run out of things to trade. "Then—what?"

With a quick snap of his arm, Benlama slammed a thin knife into Sari's chest.

It happened so fast, Sari had no time to protest. He remained upright as the blood dripped down his torso. Like a feather floating to the water, his head slumped and his eyes closed.

Benlama slid over and laid Sari gently on his back. "This, my friend, is what the wind desires. Now, exactly like the wind, you will be free."

When Sari woke, he was lying on his back in a small dark tent. There were no sounds around him. No village noises, women chatting, children playing. Just the constant moan of the wind and the smothering intensity of insufferable heat. He remained still, his eyes moving around the tent. Through small cracks, he could see the bright sunshine and dry landscape.

He raised up on his elbows and tried to remember what happened. A flash of Benlama's hand, a blade to his heart. Death. Yet, here he was, breathing, seeing, hearing. Carefully, he pushed himself to his knees and peered out the tent door. As far as he could see. Desert. And Benlama on top of a sandy knoll scanning the horizon.

When Sari emerged from the tent, he stretched out his full frame and shielded his eyes from the sun.

Benlama's eyes found him. "Ah, my student," he proclaimed, "you have risen at last."

In the light, Sari could see the scar from his knife wound. Fully healed. Just a thin pink line on his chest. "Where are we?"

"Far from home, in a place where I will teach you what you have always wanted to know. Is this not what you asked for?"

"And my family?"

"They released you to me. A dead father is no good to them. But do not worry. I paid them well. They will not go hungry. Your wife and children are well cared for."

Sari brushed the scar on his chest. "I was—dead."

Benlama stood up and walked briskly down the slope. He passed Sari and waited by the tent door. "Indeed you were."

"How is this so?"

"That also I will teach you. For now, it's enough to know that you are still quite alive. In fact, you will live longer than anyone in your village. Blood breeds life, and now you are, let's say, stronger than human."

"But—how?"

"That is why we are here, my friend, but for now you must rest and get better. In due time, you will understand."

Sari was dumbfounded by all of this. His mind reeled and his legs gave way. He collapsed in front of the tent and sat cross-legged.

There was no returning from death and he was certain he had died. Yet, his mind perceived, his body reacted. In flesh and spirit, he was alive.

"It is time to eat," said Benlama. "Come inside. I will make you something." He slipped through the tent door into the stifling darkness and readied some containers.

As Sari followed him inside, he recognized a familiar odor and noticed Benlama in a corner chanting something foreign.

"Here," Benlama offered. "Taste this."

In the dark, Sari could not see what he offered. His fingers squeezed around a small cup. He raised it and drank something liquid, thick, metallic tasting. Given his experience on the battlefields, given the smell, he knew what this was. Blood.

"Now for the first lesson," Benlama said. "Remember this. Blood is life and man's blood will give us life—forever."

Sari sat down in the darkness. Once dead, now alive, he realized how Benlama had lasted all these years. The master shaman had discovered the secret to eternal life.

Sari eagerly took another sip. Already, as he the blood slid down his throat, he looked forward to the next lesson. He was excited to learn, excited to be alive.

January 18, 1979

It was late evening. Bitter cold, temperature near zero. No wind, clear skies. As winter kicked into high gear, an icy gloom descended on Freeland like an enormous blanket.

Stan sat alone in his office sorting through story ideas. His only light—a small desk lamp and a glowing floor heater. The reflections on the wall, changing from black to orange and back. Now he knew what cave dwellers went through on long cold nights with nothing more than campfires for light.

Perhaps this depressing atmosphere explained why, as he jotted notes and arranged scraps of paper, the screams of panicked hunters kept haunting him. Winter had descended. Hunting season was over. Still, he knew some poor soul's remains lay out there, frozen, perhaps buried in an unmarked grave.

What he struggled with was why. In such a peaceful town with an abundance of good things, what led men to prey on other men? Was there something more sinister behind this? And what did Sari know or condone?

He picked up his napkin with the notes he had scribbled last month at the Circle. Did he dare write a story? Stan's fingers ran over the lines, his eyes focused on the phrase: *Every year—a few—well, more than a few—never go home.*

It was a good story, but risky and very personal. Still, his journalist instincts buzzed. Taking out a pen and notepad, he wrote furiously. Lots of questions. How, in this town of secrets, could he investigate and come up with answers?

That night, after he went to sleep, he dreamed of being chased by wild animals. Not just animals. Strange half-human animal beings with sharp teeth and bloody faces. They were calling his name and taunting him. Even worse, there was no hiding from their hunt. They knew exactly where to find him.

"Morning, Sari," Stan said as he walked into the Circle for his usual breakfast.

"Good morning, my brother," Sari replied. "This cold, I think, could break off your limbs, couldn't it?"

Stan sat down and laid his pen and pad on the table. "Must be hard for you, being from Africa. They don't usually get this kind of cold."

"No, quite true. My family would think this weather is some type of punishment from the gods."

Stan gave his order to Amanda. Amanda Beston. Tall, slim, her dark hair pinned back under a ball cap stitched with some unknown logo on it. Her face had that slim almond shape you see with girls on the covers of fashion magazines. And those piercing dark eyes. Very pretty. Seeing her reminded him of Amy. There was an ache in his chest. He missed her companionship, her beautiful body.

Today Amanda wore tight fitting blue jeans, bright white tennis shoes, and a light blue long sleeve polyester shirt. Something perhaps you might wear skiing. The shirt fit snugly over her body, enhancing her figure and the round shape of her breasts.

Stan always tried to pry some conversation out of her, but every morning, she had the same routine. He kept trying to break the ice. She always gave him the same measured response. "Morning, Amanda," he said hopefully.

"Morning, Stan," she said.

"Cold weather we're having."

Amanda's expression did not change. "It usually is in January. Anything different for you this morning?"

"Nope, the usual. Scrambled eggs, toast, bacon, coffee. You've got me pegged."

"All right, be back in a few." She scribbled on her pad and hurried over to the kitchen.

Oh well, he thought. Spreading out some papers on the table, he glanced over at Sari. "You ever miss it?"

"Miss what?" Sari said as he sat on his stool and surveyed the café.

"Africa, Kenya, the hot climate."

"Hmm, sometimes, but never enough to return. This country is much too interesting."

"Really?"

Sari picked up something in Stan's question. Stan could see it in the man's eyes. He looked away, afraid of what those eyes might uncover. His thoughts. His story.

Still, Sari read his face perfectly. "Perhaps you are interested in why."

"Perhaps," said Stan.

"In America, where so much abounds, there is such a strange fascination with freedom, so much so that men are willing to kill for it. And usually, this quest for freedom, it ends up killing them."

Stan was surprised by Sari's observation. He didn't realize the man was such an astute observer of American culture. "And?" Stan encouraged.

"Sometimes, freedom can be healthy, sometimes destructive. In my tribe, there was a certain order to things which could not be questioned. Here everything is questioned. Much is gained, much gets lost."

"And that's interesting to you?"

"I have formed an entire village around it. In case you have not noticed, freedom and order have much to do here."

Stan paused and chewed on Sari's last statement. He had the feeling this personal nugget was revealed, not out of kindness, but as a lesson. "Good to know," he said and pretended to work on his notes. In fact, he was doodling and thinking. More Sari. More mystery. Typical. "Seen Walt around lately?"

Sari picked up a glass and examined it. "Every morning, like clockwork."

He gave Stan one last glance and walked back into the kitchen. Did he know why Stan had questioned him? Did he suspect what Stan was really after?

Stan's breakfast arrived. As Amanda placed his plate on the table, they shared a warm glance, a momentary thaw in the frigid ice between them.

"Thanks, Amanda," he said.

"You're welcome," she replied. "Anytime."

As she walked away to serve another customer, Stan's hope was revived. *Winter can't last forever*, he thought.

He spent the next several days watching Walt on the sly, noting his movements, who he hung out with, where he went at night.

So far, he had not detected anything suspicious. He had become familiar with his whereabouts, could even predict his schedule. But when it came to understanding anything more about his involvement with dead hunters, his scorecard read zero.

Tonight he sat in his Volkswagen with an old pair of binoculars he had found in Matty's store. As he watched Walt having dinner in the Circle, he was freezing his ass off and questioning his worth as an investigative reporter. How much longer would he have to wait? Maybe next fall, when the hunters returned. In the meantime—

"Ah, cripes, it's cold," he kept repeating.

Every so often, he would turn on the engine in his Volkswagen to get a small amount of defrost. What he ended up with was a large pair of binoculars peering through a hole about the size of a coffee plate.

He picked up Walt rising from the counter, paying his bill, walking through the front door. As Walt approached his tow truck, he stopped for a minute, peered in Stan's direction, and waved. *That's odd*, Stan thought just seconds before his door jerked open.

Binoculars and all, Stan was hauled out of his car and thrown to the ground. Some type of covering was thrown over his head and he was heaved up into the back of someone's truck bed.

"Goddamn it, let go of me," he yelled, more out of shock than actual hope. No one listened. He was covered halfway down his torso and secured like a gunny sack. His arms were pinned and someone took a few seconds to bind his ankles.

The truck screeched and took off in a hurry. Stan was jolted by bumps and potholes in the road. His head bounced around on the hard metal surface like a basketball.

In a few minutes, the truck stopped. More sets of hands pulled him out and carried him up some steps into a building. Stan was laid out on a floor and let loose. He rubbed his arms and took a few seconds to scope out his location.

An old house. A living room. Square-shaped, plainly decorated, with furniture that might have dated from the 1950s. There were no pictures on the walls.

Stan noticed how he sat in the middle of a threadbare throw rug with a worn picture of a large lion in the center. Stan sat directly on top of its gaping toothy mouth. Around the lion's body were a variety of dirt and grease stains. The room and the lion made him queasy.

A group of men stood around him. He knew them all. Larry Levin, Rick Dumont, George Romero, and Walt. What was surprising was the last person he recognized standing in the background. Sari.

"Good evening, my brother," he said in his usual calm voice.

"Sari?" said Stan.

"You have been out and about, I see."

Stan kept quiet and waited.

Sari squatted down beside him. "You are curious, I believe?"

"More than a little," Stan said. "You didn't need to snatch me, you know. Maybe just a simple invite."

"Ah, perhaps, but caution and stealth are the signs of a good hunter, and that is perhaps a much more effective message, no?"

Stan sat upright on his butt and massaged his ankles. "Is that what this is all about?"

Sari looked at the circle of men. They backed off and sat down on some old folding chairs.

Sari motioned to Stan. "You have questions, I believe?"

"Questions?" said Stan.

"About me, the hunters, Walt?"

Stan realized his pursuit had been discovered. No sense continuing to pretend. He took a deep breath. "They disappear," he said. "Someone's obviously killing them. You, Walt, your crew here, maybe. I don't understand. Why?"

Sari remained perfectly still, his eyes searching Stan.

Stan could not return his gaze. He looked around at the circle of men. They all had weird grins on their faces. Dangerous grins, if Stan had to guess.

"I am very old," Sari said. "But looking at me, you would not guess that."

"No, you're right," said Stan. "No idea—no idea how you do it."

"I have learned a saying over these last few centuries taught to me by a very wise man. Blood is life and man's blood will give us life—forever."

Stan ran this saying repeatedly through his mind several times. Finally, it clicked. His eyes widened. "You're—a vampire?"

Sari let loose a low laugh. The circle of men joined in. Stan failed to grasp the joke.

"Vampires are myths," said Sari. "They are the dark things dreamed up from men's imaginations, beings you find in books." He pointed a finger at his chest. "I, however, am a real man."

Stan rubbed his hands through his hair. "I don't understand."

"Think carefully, my brother. If you follow the trail of an animal long enough, perhaps you might surprise him."

Sari's cat and mouse game made Stan angry. "I don't know why you've got to be so damn mysterious about this. Why not just tell me what the hell you're talking about?"

Sari sat on the floor cross-legged. "For a man skilled with words, you are most impatient. Where magic lives, sometimes the obvious is missed. Because you do not understand these powers, I am perhaps telling you more than you can grasp." He gave Stan a coy look and glanced around at his posse. "Then again, perhaps not."

Stan mumbled the saying, this time thinking of how it might be taken literally. As he whispered it one more time, its meaning began to seep in. "You drink blood," he said, "because it somehow gives you life?"

"Well done. That is my secret," Sari said, "and I have learned my lessons well. The skill with which I practice this should tell you. I had a great teacher."

"And these guys, they're your goons?"

"Oh, hey now," Walt protested.

Sari silenced him with a raised hand. "They are accomplished hunters, men of great skill."

"Blood suckers too, no doubt?"

"Learning their craft, with my assistance, of course. They are not there yet, but they are my students—"

"These guys? You're giving these stone-cold killers a chance at eternal life?"

"They have sought out my secrets and proved themselves worthy in my service."

"No doubt, but any way you paint it, they're still killers."

"Yes, but not without purpose. During the fall, the hunters we capture help build up my supply."

This revelation hit Stan like a bullet to the gut. True enough, Sari was not a vampire. He was something much worse. A man who enticed and murdered the innocent while posing as a benevolent leader. Not to mention his inner circle of butchering cronies.

Stan's stomach groaned. He jumped up and bolted out the door, doubled over a porch railing, and vomited. As he finished heaving, Sari appeared by his side.

"Bloody hell," Stan croaked. "You plan to knock me off too? Is that why you brought me out here?"

Sari remained quiet.

Stan was all the more unnerved. "Shit, go ahead then, get it over with. I think I'd prefer that to living with what I know."

"Now is not the time," said Sari. "Your purpose is laid out. You have much work to do. You are quite safe as long as you fulfill that purpose."

"I'd rather die than be your toady, live with these snakes in this dipshit little hole you call a village."

"I can assure you from my own experience, being alive is better than being dead. For now, that will not change."

"What do you want from me, you sick bastard?"

"To be a part of this village, to live happy, to learn about life in its fullness, life beyond just . . . living, and perhaps one day, to join me as a student."

Stan was astonished. "Goddamn, happiness? Really? Didn't I just wish I was dead?"

"Over time, I think that will change. You will see. Life in Freeland is good."

"And if I don't change?"

"There are always options. That is what is most profound about Freeland. As things change, the mystery of our lives gives us new direction."

"Direction?"

"Yes, life is about adapting. As a man who has survived much, I know this to be true. I could teach you, if you would trust me to guide you."

Stan took two steps to his left and sat on a porch step. He was exhausted and overwhelmed by this terrible knowledge. He hung his head between his knees.

Sari continued. "Of course, you will not write about this in your paper or mention anything about the missing hunters. But you are free to explore our purpose for being here. I would be very happy to sit down and talk with you. Perhaps there is even a story or two in it."

Stan looked up and stared across the dark snowy landscape. Raising his hands to his head, he muttered, "And what if I do write about these so-called missing hunters?"

"I'm sure you're aware by now. There are many other interesting things to write about. If you want, tomorrow at the Circle, I might offer a few suggestions."

Stan caught a whiff of his own vomit. It was foul and sour smelling.

Sari walked by him and out to the street. He looked back at Stan. Those eyes—dark, powerful, eternal. "I will see you for breakfast. Walt will be glad to give you assistance." He turned and marched away.

Walt came out on the porch. "Need a ride?"

"From you?" Stan huffed. "No thanks." He twisted around and gave Walt an angry glare.

"Awful cold tonight to be wandering around."

"If I'm lucky, maybe I'll freeze to death."

"Suit yourself," he said. Throwing Stan's coat on the porch, he walked out to the truck. After the others followed and piled in, Walt peeled off, wheels crunching snow, smoke spitting out the tailpipe.

Stan stood and looked up at the crystal stars. They seemed far removed from his little spot on this planet. He questioned whether God or anyone else outside of Freeland cared about his terrible predicament.

February 8, 1979

Stan sat at his desk and read the flyer about the community Valentine's Day Party. It was bordered by red hearts and little pictures of cupid. He was placing it as an ad in the paper.

It was painful to read. He missed Amy. He missed sex. He thought about a couple of old girlfriends in San Diego. Then he thought again about Amy. He crumpled up the paper in frustration and tossed it like a baseball toward the wall. It bounced off and rolled on the floor.

Whatever Amy had meant to him in the past, Stan realized he had to move on. But how? There weren't many single women available in Freeland and he had no desire to hook up with anyone married. Not in this nosy little town. Particularly when so many men owned weapons.

As he laid out the print type for the party, Stan found himself wishing he could invite someone. One name kept crossing his mind—Amanda Beston.

At the Circle, he had inched his way into her life through their daily breakfast routine. Amanda, however, remained very shy. As a waitress, she was efficient and pleasant with his order. Beyond that, she hardly said boo. Stan could tell from watching her work that she didn't care much for gab. In fact, he wasn't sure if she cared at all for men.

He mulled over his options. Could he ask her to the dance? What if he asked and she turned him down? How embarrassing would that be? And even if she did decide to go, would she be willing to have a good time?

Then he remembered her occasional smile, the one she sometimes gave him as she finished his order. *What are the odds*? he thought.

He was determined to go to the dance and he didn't want to go alone. Without a doubt, Amanda was pretty, sizzling pretty, worth the risk pretty. As he finished laying out the paper, he decided to consult with his good friend Matty for some helpful advice.

He headed for his favorite chat point by the counter. "Say, Matty," he called out. "Mind if I ask you a question?"

Matty lumbered around the corner of the aisle and waved her hand. "I don't mind if you don't mind the answer. Most folks who ask advice don't really want to hear what I've got to say. So, if you don't want to know something, don't waste my time asking. How's that for a roundabout answer?"

Stan watched her pass by him and ease up next to the cash register. "Okay then," he said. "Well, if you'll give me an honest answer, I promise to listen."

"Shoot."

"What can you tell me about Amanda?"

Matty gave him a sly grin. "You want her biography or her bust size?"

"Give me the bio first."

"Came here about two years ago, not long before you arrived. Don't really know much about her, except she rents a room over on Liberty Street from Dotty Bustamente. Quiet girl. Hardly says a thing when she comes in the store. Far as I know, I've never seen her with a guy, fact, with anyone at all. She keeps pretty much to herself. Now go ahead, ask your real question."

"What question is that?"

"The one about the guy who wants to ask the girl to the Valentine's Day dance."

Stan looked sheepish. "Okay, my dear. Think she'll go to the party with me?"

"Can't tell you one way or the other. Guess you're stuck with the old-fashioned method."

"What's that?"

"Ask her, you big blockhead. Don't know why men think you need a crystal ball to talk to a woman."

"Because," Stan said deliberately, "I haven't been able to get much out of her. She hardly says hi when she takes my order, and—"

"And?" Matty put a finger to her cheek.

"Frankly, I have no idea if she'll say yes."

Matty pointed that same finger. "She won't if you don't ask her, that's for sure."

"Okay," Stan said. He shrugged his shoulders. "I'll ask."

"Okay. There you go." She lurched off the counter and began walking toward the aisle. "That's all the free therapy you get today. Now, I gotta get back to work."

"Well," Stan said, "since you now know how desperate I am, if she says no, would *you* go to the party with me?"

Matty pulled up and put her hands on her hips. "No thanks, dear. Been there, done that. I like my peace of mind and men are nothing but trouble."

"Well, I love you too, sweetheart."

She waved her hand and threw Stan a playful glance. "I know you do. Wouldn't let you stay here otherwise. Just remember, you're on a short leash."

"Thanks, Matty. I promise to behave myself."

"34C by the way."

"What's that?"

"Her bust size. She bought a bra from the store a couple weeks back. I got an eye for things like that."

Stan's eyes widened. "I didn't even know you sold bras."

"Well, I do, over in the far corner, away from prying eyes. Got a pretty nice selection, if you ask me."

"Really?"

"Really." Matty gave Stan a triumphant grin and walked away.

She was already near the end of the aisle when he called out, "Well, thanks, Matty."

"You're welcome," she said from the other side. "Next time I charge you, and I have to warn you, my asking price is steep."

Stan pushed off the counter. "One way or the other, you always get your pound of flesh out of me."

"Yes, I do," she said, "and don't you forget it."

Matty was right. The only way to know if Amanda would go was to ask. But how and when?

Stan knew she usually left the Circle about four or so. He sometimes stood at the store's front door in the late afternoon and watched her walk home. Gauging the time of day and his work schedule, he moved various projects around so he could take a break when she got off work. Maybe he could catch her as she slipped out the back door.

It was a cold, blustery day. Temperatures hovering in the teens, a stiff wind blowing down from Canada. The kind of day that made going outside a severe chore.

Stan drove in his car to the Circle's back entrance and waited for Amanda to emerge. His ears burned and he kept smacking his gloves together in a vain attempt to stay warm. Finally, she came out. Tonight, with her slim frame braced against the cold wind, she looked fragile. Stan jumped out of the car.

"Hey, Amanda," he called out. She stopped and watched him approach. "Cold day, isn't it. You want a ride?"

Amanda hesitated and pulled her coat tight over her shoulders. "It's not that far."

Stan could tell by the look on her face he was already in trouble. Maybe he should have asked her while she was indoors.

"Well, I was thinking—" He hesitated for a moment, trying to push the words out of his mouth. "You have any plans for the Valentine's Day party?"

She looked surprised and puzzled. "No, not really. No one's—" Her eyes grew curious.

Like a diver on a high ledge, he took the plunge. "Well, I just thought maybe you'd like to go. With me that is."

She hesitated and peered down Paradise Road. "I'd have to find a dress," she said.

Stan rubbed his hands together and waited.

She appeared to be lost in thought.

He scuffed a shoe in the snow. "Yeah, that's true."

"It's next week, right?"

"Next Wednesday."

The wind kicked up in their faces. Both of them winced against the frigid sting.

"Okay, but just to the dance, all right? Don't expect anything else."

Stan was taken back. "I'm sorry?"

"Well, you know sometimes guys—" Suddenly, she blushed and turned away.

"Yeah?" Stan said. "Sometimes guys—"

This time, Amanda was on the hot seat. She turned sideways and grabbed her collar. "Sometimes guys—well, you know."

"It's just a dance," said Stan, deliberately keeping his voice even. "Honestly, I promise to be a gentleman. It's just, I'd like to go with someone. To the party. I guess what I'm saying is, I'd like to go with you. "

Amanda's eyes were searching, inquisitive. "I'm sorry," she said. "I know I'm being very rude." She paused. "Okay, yes, I'll go to the party. Thanks for asking." For the first time, she smiled. It was a vulnerable smile, a small crack in her armor.

Stan was relieved. The tension in his arms and legs suddenly released. "Great, then. Pick you up Wednesday, about seven or so."

"Okay, I'm over on Liberty Street. I rent a room from Dotty, but you probably already know that, you being a newspaper guy."

"No," he lied. "First I've heard of it. Liberty Street. Dotty. Got it."

"Thanks." She turned to walk down the road.

"Say, I'm serious," he called out. "It's damn cold out here. Can I give you a ride?"

She hesitated. "Sure, that would be nice."

As they rode toward Dotty's, Stan realized it was the first time they'd been alone together. It was both pleasant and unnerving.

When they arrived, he opened her door and waved as she hurried up the steps. "Have a nice night," he said.

"You too," she replied and disappeared into the house.

Well, he thought, *step one complete. Now what?*

For the next several mornings, Stan hoped that his invitation might help thaw her out. No such luck. Same efficiency. Same tone of voice. As usual, she scribbled his order and rushed it to the cook. Nothing to indicate she was interested in him or happy to be going to the party.

Her toughness struck him as strange, but whatever the cause, he didn't want to push her too hard. Maybe she would be embarrassed if people in the restaurant knew about her personal life.

Still, Stan knew that in Freeland, privacy was nonexistent. Sooner or later the news would get out, a fact verified by Matty the day before the party.

"Heard you had a date," she told him during one of his breaks.

Stan stopped and folded his arms. "Heard from who?"

"It's Free-land," Matty said in a musical voice. "You know, lots of little birdies chirping."

"Really. It's too cold for birds this time of year. You must be psychic."

"Well, if I am, you should be careful. Most men have dirty minds."

Stan grimaced.

Matty leaned against the front counter. "There's a tradition at our party. We like to play mix and match, pick the best couple."

"Who does?"

"All the old hens on this farm, that's who."

"And you're telling me this because—"

"You and Amanda, you're on our list of potentials."

Stan waved his hands in protest. "Oh hell, what are you, a yenta?"

"Call me whatever," she said with a grin. "I'm also a prophet."

Stan shook his head. "A what?"

"You know, like in the Bible." She tapped her finger on the counter. "You're on our list. Don't be surprised."

"Please, do not do anything to spook this girl. It's all I could do to get her to the party. If you scare her off—"

"Oh, don't worry," Matty laughed. "Everything will take its normal course, just with a little prophetic help, that's all. You'll barely know I'm around."

"I have no idea what you're talking about."

"And you don't need to. Just go and have a good time. That's all you need to know."

"Well, thank you, I think."

"You're welcome. We don't choose just anyone you know. Only the cream of the crop."

Stan wagged a finger. "You're starting to scare me."

"No need to be afraid. Take what help you can and enjoy yourself."

Stan returned to his office and mulled over the type of help he was being offered.

The following night, Stan, in a new black suit he had bought with Sari coinage from one of the local clothing stores, picked up Amanda at her front door. Since he'd only seen her dressed as a waitress, he was surprised at how stylish she looked. A V-neck silk dress in a dark shade of blue that flowed around her ankles. She had her black hair stylishly parted in the middle so that the ends wrapped delicately around her cheeks. Her outfit was complimented by a pair of bright silver heels with delicate straps around the back. It was a profound transformation.

"Wow," Stan exclaimed. "You look . . . really nice."

"Thank you," she said and smiled. It was a shy smile, but Stan could tell she was pleased. For the first time, he noticed how her eyes brightened and the corners of her mouth gently curled up. In this outfit, with that smile, he thought she was stunning.

They arrived at the Danny Akern Recreation Center and walked into the decorated hall. "Geesh," he said, "All this for Valentine's Day?"

Amanda followed his eyes across the room. "Your first party, huh?"

"Yeah, why?"

"Well, they take their romance pretty serious here."

"Really? How so?"

"I can't explain it in twenty-five words or less. You'll have to watch it unfold."

Stan stood near the refreshment table taking it all in. There were pretty red hearts on the ceiling, streamers that crisscrossed wall to wall, lots of sparkling decorations, even a stage and some ambient lighting to provide atmosphere.

"Nice," he said.

Amanda stopped and looked squarely at Stan. "You really don't know, do you?"

Stan stopped in mid-step. His face began to burn. "Know what?"

"What Valentine's Day means in Freeland."

"Other than candy, flowers, occasional hanky panky?"

"Oh my God, here I thought you were serious."

"About what?"

"About asking me to the party."

Stan looked puzzled. "Well, I asked you to the party. Isn't that serious enough?"

Amanda put her hands on her hips. "Apparently not, if you haven't figured out what's going on."

Stan stepped back and shrugged his shoulders. "Okay, I'm confused. So. What's going on?"

"This is their annual pairing off."

"Their what?"

"Singling out couples as potential mates."

"You don't mean—"

"You never knew, huh?"

"Not a clue."

"Okay, well, that's a load off, now that I know." She kept her steady eyes focused on him. "I thought you were asking—"

"You mean like marriage?"

"Well, the start of that process, anyway. It's a pretty old tradition here. There are a lot of rituals built into this, but it all starts here."

Stan tapped his fists together and rubbed his right shoe on the parquet floor. He had to admit, given what Matty said, it all made sense. "Hell, I was just hoping to get some punch, hang out with you, maybe dance a little."

Amanda searched his face for clues.

He wished a hole would open in the floor. He wished he had never—well, maybe not.

"Okay," she said flatly. "Now that you know, you want to stay or not?"

There it was, his options clearly laid out. An escape route back to singleness or a chance to be paired off and get married—maybe.

Stan took a deep breath and imagined what she must be feeling. Maybe dread, maybe anticipation. Still, she'd gone to a lot of trouble to look this nice. It seemed a shame to turn around and walk out. "Well, if we stay, do we have to get married?"

"They don't force you to do anything. It just creates a channel, so to speak, sort of like water running through a canal."

Stan rubbed the floor again with a shoe tip and hung his head.

She crossed her arms and eyed him suspiciously.

"All right," he said. "Let's be clear. I'm here to enjoy myself, and you, of course. Let's put a hold on the canal thing for a bit and just relax. How about it?"

Amanda held out for a moment. "Fine, but I have to warn you, it could get a little crazy."

"Ground rules established. Crazy, fine. Marriage, out."

Once again, her dark eyes scanned his face. "Okay, but go easy on the punch." She took his arm and led him over to a row of folding chairs.

As they sat, he noticed a large punch bowl in the center of the room. He wondered if that was the punch she had warned him about. From where he sat, it looked pretty harmless. He pointed at the bowl. "Is that the punch?"

Amanda's head turned. "Yup, that's it."

"Well? Is it safe?"

"I said go easy, not avoid it."

Stan gestured toward the bowl. "Would you like some?"

Amanda paused. "Sure, thanks."

After Stan filled two cups and returned, they sat for a moment and watched the party start.

A small folk band arrived. They laid a hand-lettered sign on the stage that read *Donnell's Irish Hearts Band*. There were three of them, a fiddler, a bone drummer, and a guitarist.

Stan pointed toward the stage. "Wow, a band, huh?"

"Yeah," she said. "Believe it or not, they all live here and play on special occasions. We just call them Donnell's for short."

Stan watched them set up. "Pretty impressive," he said.

"It always is," she responded.

As Donnell's began to play, people gathered on the large central floor and danced. The happy atmosphere and music put Stan in a good frame of mind. After a few minutes, he worked up his nerve. "Want to dance?"

"Sure, let's," she said.

For the first time, Amanda seemed to relax. She was a good dancer. After a couple of rounds, they started to get in synch.

As they circled the floor, Stan noticed some people watching them. A few whispered and pointed. He remembered Matty's prophetic utterance. Maybe she was hiding in a corner somewhere saying *I told you so* to her close friends. But so what? At this point, he was having a good time.

After an hour or so, the evening's emcee, Diana Newt, owner of Pin A Rose Flower Shop, took the stage and announced the next few dances for party goers. Amanda looked at Stan. "You really want to stay for this?"

"Sure, why not?" he said. "No one's forced me to do anything—yet."

Amanda looked back and forth at Stan and the stage. "Your choice."

Stan and Amanda worked their way through a couple of dances, men switching partners, women switching partners, everyone dancing to an Irish reel.

Ignoring Amanda's warning, he drank a few more glasses of punch and started to warm up inside. It didn't taste alcoholic. More like a spicy kind of kool aid. Quite tasty.

Each time he drained his little plastic cup, his mind and body became a little more lively, as if the punch was some type of elixir. After a half-dozen cups, he could feel his joints loosen and his mojo find its groove. He was ready to party.

He spotted Matty making conversation with her good friend, Johnny Nelson. She and Johnny often chatted together at the store. Johnny always took those crusty moods of hers in stride and served as the straight man for her dark sense of humor. Tonight it looked like they were enjoying a dance or two.

Stan walked over to them with a wide grin on his face. His tie had loosened and his hips swayed. "Well, Ms. Prophet," he said. "What does your ESP tell you tonight?"

"Same as before," she said. Matty looked over at Johnny, then back at Stan with a mischievous grin. "Having a good time, I imagine?"

"Not bad, not bad at all. She seems to be warming up to me."

"Judging by how you look, I think you're the one that's doing the warming."

Johnny enjoyed her joke.

"Maybe," Stan said. "Hell, it's Valentine's Day. Why not?"

"My point exactly."

"So, the tea leaves say—"

"I don't need to tell you that. I said it happens naturally. All we do is give it a little nudge or two."

"Nudge away, then," he joked.

"Already have." She turned to Johnny. He took her arm. "Help yourself to some more punch," she said.

Stan waved at Matty and trotted back to find Amanda. She had finished the dance and was standing next to her chair. "You're a really good dancer," he said.

Amanda placed her head gently on his shoulder. "Thanks, I took lessons when I was a kid, even did a bit of clogging in high school. It all comes back, like riding a bicycle."

"Great," said Stan. "I'll have to work hard to keep up with you."

"I'm a good teacher. Very patient."

A group of women gathered center stage for some type of announcement. Diana, Matty, and Dotty.

Amanda and Stan breezed over and stood in the middle of the crowd.

"Well," Diana said to the crowd. "Are we all excited?"

The crowd responded with cheers and hand claps.

"Okay, now, as you all know, Valentine's Day is pretty special around here. We like to think of this as the start of a whole new life for some lucky someone and tonight could be your lucky night. So, let's get started." More cheers arose. "Now, those among us who think of ourselves as divinators, we like to look into our crystal ball and believe that we're giving just a little help to young people and their futures. Kevin, would you and the boys please bring out the table and chairs?"

Kevin Roust, a local auto mechanic, quickly responded. He and his crew brought out a six-foot portable table, a nice tablecloth, and three folding chairs.

The three women strode around to the back of the table, sat down, and folded their hands primly on top. Some square cards lay on top of the table.

"Okay," said Diana. "We've consulted among ourselves and here are our picks for the year. Each chosen couple gets to spend a lovely night courtesy of Dahlia Rutan at her home in the hills of Freeland. This comes complete with a spacious room overlooking our beautiful town, a queen size bed, and a gourmet dinner courtesy of Dahlia herself, plus free access to all her accommodations. You also get a nice jar of Nadine's aromatic bubble bath. Dahlia will give you a gift certificate to use whenever you like. The bubble bath you can take home, use it tonight if you want." She giggled and pretended to be embarrassed.

Stan glanced over at Amanda.

She looked dubious. "I tried to warn you."

Reaching for a card, Diana announced, "Dan Reynolds, Wanda Watson."

A small cheer went up. Dan Reynolds, with a sheepish grin, marched up to take the gift certificate and the bubble bath. He looked out over the room and tried to hide the bubble bath behind his back.

"Congratulations," Diana said.

Stan glanced again at Amanda. She read the panic in his eyes. "Remember, no obligation," she said.

"Ricky Dwarte and Belinda Singe," Diana said as she pulled another card off the table. Ricky ran on stage, flush with his moment in the limelight. "Yahoo," he hollered. The crowd laughed at his enthusiasm.

As Ricky walked down the stage steps, Stan asked Amanda, "How many couples are we talking about here?"

"Usually three," she said.

Diana paused, then reached for the next card. "And we're especially pleased to announce this next couple. Stan Blankenship and Amanda Beston." A loud round of cheers went up followed by hearty clapping.

Stan was stunned. Someone pushed him from behind. He dragged himself toward the stage. Standing in front of Diana, his face flushed and he could feel heat down his back.

"Congratulations, Stan . . . and Amanda," Diana said as she clapped.

He stood doe-eyed for a moment before trudging down the steps with the envelope and one very noticeable jar of bubble bath. All eyes in the room followed him as he searched for Amanda.

Diana made one last announcement. "And now, for our best couple's dance, selected for what we believe is the most promising pairing. Stan and Amanda, would you please come to the center of the floor."

More cheering and clapping. Someone shoved him toward the middle of the dance floor.

As he and Amanda joined together, some rousing music kicked in. The crowd swarmed around them. Everyone in the room (except Stan) knew their dance steps. Amanda took Stan by the arms and, in contrast to the music's fast pace, she danced with him in a slow circle. He relaxed and followed her lead.

Then something strange kicked off in Stan's head. The room's atmosphere was energized by a powerful force. A set of invisible hands drove Stan closer to Amanda, more in tune with her steps. Amanda's face and body took on a glow and her dress became drenched in phosphorescent light.

The dancers moved in, physically lifted them up, and held them horizontal above the crowd. Everyone picked up the pace as the music became faster and louder. Stan and Amanda, held by dozens of hands, spun around the room.

Stan heard a wind roar in his ears. He was moved to raise his hands toward the ceiling in praise to whatever force created this dynamic moment. His soul left his body and moved around in search of Amanda.

The music continued to increase in speed and volume. Stan's head reeled from the tremendous G force. Within moments, he became unconscious.

Stan and Amanda were together in a small bedroom. They undressed and stood completely naked, circling around each other like tango dancers. As they stopped and embraced, Amanda's body grew bright and her mouth radiated intense heat.

When she pulled him close, her thighs and breasts became snow white. In contrast, her hair turned the color of blood. She wrapped her arms around him and they kissed. Pain like a heart attack shot through his chest. She pushed him on the bed and crawled between his legs. She was uttering something, but her words were unintelligible. As they joined together, the thrust of her pelvis was sharp like sandpaper and her pitch black eyes seemed sharp as arrows.

Whether in agony or ecstasy, she let out a primal scream. Her hands grew claws and cut into his chest. Trapped beneath her, Stan experienced both pleasure and pain. Responding to her body movement, he also screamed. Blood began to run down his torso. As their thrusts increased, the room exploded and their bodies dissolved into dazzling white light.

It was morning. Still in his suit, Stan woke up and found himself lying on his back in a small bed in an unfamiliar bedroom, a single window visible through a sheer curtain. When Stan realized he wasn't home or anywhere else he recognized, he panicked and bolted up.

Amanda sat in a corner chair. Not speaking, just looking. She was dressed in a terrycloth housecoat, hair pinned up, hands folded in her lap

"What the hell?" he exclaimed.

She leaned forward in her chair. Her elbows slid to her knees. "They got you good, didn't they?"

"Who did? Where am I?"

"My room, obviously."

His eyes darted around, then glanced down at the bed. He looked up at Amanda. "Why? How?"

"Well, after the dance, you were kind of out of your mind. You certainly couldn't drive. I was afraid you might hurt yourself, and I don't know where you live, so, against my better judgment, I found your car keys and drove you here."

"What time is it?"

"Noon."

Stan's head throbbed. He lay back and fixated on the ceiling. "Great God Almighty—"

"Well, you can't say I didn't warn you. Mostly the punch I imagine. I'm not sure what they use, but it sneaks up on you. Probably some ancient African concoction they cooked up centuries ago. I'm always careful when I drink it. I'd say you were up a dozen or so when we started the last dance. That and all the spinning kind of put you in orbit."

"Ohhhhhhhhh—"

"You'll be okay. Bet you had some weird dreams though. That's one of the side effects."

"We didn't—"

"Oh no, not in your state of mind. I doubt you knew where your zipper was, let alone your belt or the buttons on your shirt. You can check everything if you don't believe me. You're all tucked in."

Stan put his hands on his forehead. "Oh, my God," he groaned. "I'm really sorry. This town just gets stranger by the minute."

"Trust me. You're just beginning to scratch the surface."

"Yeah, but this is the worst. Definitely not how I pictured our first date."

"It's okay. Maybe this works out in my favor. You give me any crap at the Circle, I can hold this over your head."

Stan detected a trace of a smile on her face.

Amanda sat back, crossed her legs, and put her hands behind her head. "The trouble is not you, Stan. It's Freeland."

She grew quiet and glanced at one of her bedroom walls. Her brow furrowed in concentration. "I know it sounds strange, coming from me. We've barely said boo to each other since you came, which makes this hard to talk about—Sari being who he is, always poking around. Truth is, you and I, we're marooned in weirdness. It's kind of the nature of this town. The closer you look, the stranger it gets. I can't really paint you a picture. It's just something you've got to learn for yourself."

Stan rolled over, sat on the edge of the bed, and hoped his head would clear. When he regained his sense of balance, he stood up and hurried toward the door. "Hope this won't cause you any trouble with Dotty."

"Long as I'm quiet, she doesn't care. As you can see, she's part of the committee that chose us. I would guess she's happy to know you're up here."

"Thanks for your help. I'm sure the birds will be chirping about this."

"That's kind of the point. The party feeds their frenzy. Now that we've officially been chosen, they're free to gossip."

He stood by the door and grinned sheepishly. "How about another chance, maybe away from prying eyes, not quite so intense?"

*

Amanda's dark eyes were busy reading his thoughts. She tugged on her belt and smoothed her robe. "Sure."

"Maybe I can cook you dinner at my house?"

She looked surprised. "You actually cook?"

"Well, okay, not so much. Maybe snacks and drinks, or a picnic."

"Give this thing a chance to cool down, then we'll talk."

"Right. Well—thanks."

He closed the door and eased himself down the stairs, hoping to avoid meeting Dotty.

As he walked briskly down the front sidewalk, he turned to look up. Amanda was watching him through her window. For an instant, Stan swore there was a flash in her eyes, a small bright light of some sort, like the sun's reflection in a mirror. Then, she closed the curtain.

As Stan drove home, he thought about the dream. It struck him as odd—what he remembered about him and Amanda. In his dream, when he woke, the same bedroom.

The dream, the bedroom. He questioned whether or not there was some truth to his vision. Was the wild Amanda and the quiet Amanda one and the same? If that was the case and the powers that ran this town were right about their pairing, he knew they were in for a one hell of a courtship.

II

June 28, 1979

The headline in this week's issue read: *4ᵗʰ of July, How Families Celebrate*. Corny, yes, but for Stan, this was Freeland and a headline like this made for good reading.

He grabbed the mockup, held it up to the light, and enjoyed a sense of satisfaction. Stan Blankenship, editor and publisher. Not many thirty-year-old men could make that claim. Then again, not many lived as journalists and prisoners in such a strange town.

Stan rose from his desk and walked over to his office doorway. He called out to Matty as she stocked items on a shelf. "So, Matty, what're you doing for the Fourth?"

"What I always do," she growled. "Eat some fried chicken, wave a sparkler or two, go to bed. Yippee."

"Some folks are getting together to shoot off fireworks in the town square. You going?"

"Oh, probably. Not much else to do around here. You?"

"Same, I suppose. Yippee."

"Right, now you're in the spirit."

"Seems like there should be a parade or something."

Matty paused. "A parade? In Freeland? Now there's an idea that could burn up five minutes or so. Circle round the Circle, wave some flags, then what?"

"I don't know. Just seems like we should celebrate."

"Gee, Mr. Paperman, are you going soft? Where's that hard edge, that truth at any cost kind of attitude? I'm sure there's a scandal or two somewhere around here you could dig into. I might even point you in the right direction if you're actually interested."

"Maybe, but this issue's family oriented. It's the Fourth of July. I'm looking for some small town schmaltz, some old fashioned bang and boom."

"Well, I'm all banged and boomed out. At my age, all the fizzle's gone out of the wick. I'll settle for a sparkler, thank you."

"I'll be sure you get one in each hand."

Mattie waved at Stan. "There you go. Like you said. Yippee."

In the afternoon, Stan decided to take a break. With the weather hot and the days long, he had the urge to throw some hamburgers on the grill and have a cookout. He caught Amanda at the Circle and invited her over. After dinner, he'd come back and finish the paper. Browsing through the store, he yelled, "Okay, Matty, I'm cooking tonight. Time to do a little shopping."

"Shop away," she said. "I'm always here to take your money."

Stan did just that. Buns and beer plus some barbeque sauce and charcoal briquettes. Later, fresh chopped meat (Stan didn't ask what kind) from Larry's Butcher Shop. It cooked up as a nice dinner for the two of them. The hamburgers were good, the company even better.

Around eight-thirty, Stan headed back with a couple more hours of work to finish. This was his favorite part. Watching the ink roll on the paper, witnessing each copy as it jumped off the press. Great stuff if you're a writer *and* publisher.

Matty was just closing up when he came in. "You've got a visitor," she said.

"Really?" Stan was not expecting anyone to drop by at this hour. "Someone important?"

"How should I know? Why don't you go and see?"

"All right then, I'll just do that."

"Fine. I'm leaving. Let yourself out when you're finished. And don't forget to lock up."

"Sure, Matty, have a good night."

"Will do," she said as she walked out the front door.

His interest piqued, Stan entered his office. Someone sat in his one and only folding chair with the main mockup of the Reporter spread in front of their face.

Stan stood by the doorway and checked out the visitor. "Can I help you?"

"I don't know," said a familiar voice. "I think I'm actually here to help you." The visitor lowered the paper and grinned. It was his older brother, Dave.

His stout frame, short cropped hair, tailored business suit, and wire rimmed glasses were in stark contrast to Stan's slim build, straight flowing locks, and casual attire. One thing they shared in common. The same dark eyes.

"Dave?" Stan leaned back against the doorway.

Dave seemed amused. "Dave? Is that all you can say to your long lost brother?"

"How'd you find me?"

"Not easily, I can tell you. Your trail of bread crumbs dried up in Boise. I had to put on my detective's hat and do a hell of a lot of driving around. I think I got lucky when I noticed that old Freeland sign back on the road a few miles. I said, 'That sounds like somewhere my brother would go.' And sure enough, here you are."

"Yeah, we're a bit off the beaten path."

"Congratulations, by the way."

"For—?"

"Your rag here. The Freeland Reporter, as you cleverly call it."

"Thanks." He pushed off the doorway, headed for his desk, and plopped down in his chair. "Oh my God," he mumbled. "I can't believe you actually found me."

Dave folded his hands together and laid them across his crisp white shirt. "Nice spot you picked for yourself. Having so much fun, you forget your family?"

"Well, it sort of picked me." Stan wedged an elbow on his desk and planted his chin deep in his palm. "But here again, that's a long story."

"I asked some guys over at that diner next door. They pointed out where you might be. Guess it's my lucky day."

"You went to the Circle?"

"Is that what you call it? Yeah, strange place. Who's that big black guy behind the bar? He could play for the Lakers."

"That's Sarihaba. Sarihaba Kinyaga."

"Who?"

"Sari for short. He owns the place."

"He play basketball?"

"No."

"Whole place was weird." Dave laced his fingers behind his head. "They stared at me like I was from another planet. Couple guys looked like they could eat me for lunch."

"They might," Stan mumbled.

"What's that?"

"I said you're probably right. This place can be a little strange to outsiders."

Dave gazed around the office. "Bit of a shoe box you're in here. How the hell'd you end up in this hole?"

"By accident, mostly." Stan buried his face in his hands. "Ohhhh, shit."

Dave watched him intently. "You don't seem happy to see me. Everything okay?"

Stan shook his head. "Not really. Your being here is a big problem."

Dave angrily flipped the mockup to Stan. "Well here you go then. Looks like you have work to do. Don't let me stop you. Thanks for the visit." He stood up and headed for the door.

"That's not what I meant." Stan leaned forward and put his hands flat on his desk. "What're you doing here, Dave?"

Dave blinked at his brother. "Looking for you, dumbass. I've been at this for months now. Lots of time and money and detective work. You dropped off the face of the earth. Mom and Dad are upset. I'm upset. Here I am after all this time and you ask me what I'm doing here. What the fuck?"

"It's hard to explain."

"Start from the beginning."

"I can't. I don't have time. You don't have time. We need to get you out of here, fast."

"Why?"

"Dave, listen to me. There's no time to explain."

"Hey, Stan. It's your brother here. I always thought we were close. Close as brothers, close as family. I came a long way to find you. I don't deserve this."

Stan stared at his brother. "Neither do I, for that matter, but here I am."

"You're not making sense." Dave folded his arms. "You in trouble here?"

"Not legally, no, but in other ways, yeah."

"Someone giving you shit, harassing you, that sort of thing?"

"Uh, not exactly."

"Then why don't you leave?"

"I can't."

Dave stopped asking questions. In fact, he stopped moving, except for his eyes. Watching, blinking, searching his brother's face.

Stan knew he was struggling. After all, Dave was his big brother and he wasn't offering him much help. He could read it all in his brother's face.

"You need help?" said Dave.

Stan exhaled and sat quietly for a moment. "I do, but you can't . . . help."

"Why not?"

Stan grew frustrated. His voice leaked irritation. "Dave, did I not tell you this was beyond explanation? Even if I could tell you about my dilemma, you wouldn't believe me, and even if you did believe me, there's nothing you can do about it."

The lamp on Stan's desk silhouetted Dave's frame. In the darkness, it seemed to grow larger.

Stan shook his head. "Trust me, Dave. You need to get in your car and get out of here, now."

"What do I tell Mom and Dad?"

"Don't tell them anything. You know nothing about where I am. We never had this conversation."

Dave threw open his arms. "You want me to lie to them? You want them to grieve as if their son is dead, when I know he's alive? Sorry, bro. No can do. If I walk out of here, I tell them everything."

Stan aimed a finger at Dave. "You can't."

"I will, trust me."

"Dave, you're in big danger right now and if you tell them and they get involved, you put them in danger, too."

"Why, Stan? Just give me a clue, will you?"

"It's Freeland. This is a very strange place. Those folks in the restaurant, if they know you're here and they find you, it's bad news."

"Because—"

"Because nothing. This town is a wormhole in the universe. These people aren't your normal small town folk."

"What, some kind of religious cult, commune?"

"No, trapped. We're all trapped here."

"Hostage, prisoner?"

"Hostage, no. Prisoner, yes."

"So, you're trapped here, living in a small town, everything looks normal but—"

"I can't leave, and if you don't get out of here—"

"I'll be trapped."

"Right."

Dave curled a finger to his chin. "Jesus, this is fucking strange, you know?"

Stan rose from his chair, moved over to Dave, and put a hand on his shoulder. "It is and so is this town. I'm trying to warn you. Get the hell out while you can."

For the first time, Dave looked frightened. "Christ, Stan, this is some scary shit you're telling me."

"Worse than you can imagine. Come on, I'm going to check outside. If it's clear, don't ask questions. Just get in your car and go."

"You're serious?"

"Absolutely. Go. Now."

Dave grabbed a pen and some paper off Stan's desk. "I'm not leaving here without giving you my contact info." He scribbled it down and handed it to Stan. "Hide this somewhere. You may want to send a message or something. At least let me know how you are."

Stan crammed the paper in his shirt pocket. "Okay. Thanks. Now, hurry, get your ass out of my office before Sari finds us."

"Sari? The guy in the restaurant? What's he got to do with this?"

"Never mind, just go."

Dave slipped through Stan's office door. Stan jumped in front of him and ran to the front entrance.

The lights were still on at the Circle. Stan could see movement through the bay window, but he had no idea who was there. More important, he couldn't see Sari.

One thing he *was* sure of. Sari would find them. He always knew
when strangers came to town. For all Stan knew, he could have
beckoned Dave. Maybe he had some sinister family plan in mind.

Checking left and right, he noted that the coast was clear and
signaled Dave to move forward. "Come on, Dave. All clear. Where's
your car?"

"Right over there, that red Datsun."

"Got your keys handy?"

"Sure, right here."

"Ready—"

Dave peered out the door and prepared to run to his car.

From the darkness, a familiar voice spoke. "You are sending our
guest away, no? And without even so much as an introduction?" It
was Sari, about 10 feet to the right of them, his black skin invisible in
the night. He walked over and stood between Dave and the Datsun
with his arms crossed. "How impolite."

For a moment, they all stared at each other. The only sounds
around them were the usual night noises and an occasional burst of
wind.

Sari spoke up. "He has come a great distance to visit you, this
man. Why send him away?"

Stan stood in front of his brother. "My brother came by accident,
but he's chosen to go back home. His stay is only temporary. You
should honor his wish."

Sari wagged a long index finger. "No, no, my brother, you have it
all backwards. I should do what *I* think is best, and in Freeland, there
are no accidents. You of all people should know this."

Dave grew agitated. "What the fuck, man? This is America. What's
to keep me from knocking you on your ass?"

Sari extended his arms as an invitation. "Nothing, my brother.
Come try, if you can. You are right. America is a land of freedom and

choice. That is why we celebrate the Fourth of July, no? So, in the spirit of the holiday, come knock me on my ass."

"Dave, shut the fuck up," Stan hissed. "Trust me. Don't move a muscle."

"Your brother is a smart man," Sari said. "He is a writer, a very good writer. He knows this town well. You should listen when he speaks."

Dave refused to back down. "Stop spouting bullshit to me. If you don't get out of my way, I promise, you'll be flat on your back."

Sari chuckled a slow, rumbling laugh. "Oh, I never speak bullshit my brother. No, no, no." He wagged his finger. "What I speak, plain and simple, comes to pass."

Once more Stan pleaded, "Dave, back up, shut up, please."

Dave bowed his arms. He glanced at Stan with furious eyes. "No, I won't shut up. I don't know why you're backing off this dickhead, but maybe you need someone to help lead the way. Maybe a big brother is just what the doctor ordered." He darted around Stan and took two steps toward Sari.

Sari in one easy motion moved his hand across his chest. Dave catapulted through the air and landed fifteen feet from where he first stood. He lay motionless on his back in the dirt.

For a moment, Stan thought he'd been killed. As he rushed over to check, Dave groaned.

"Find your freedom yet, brother?" Sari mocked. "Perhaps it is buried somewhere underneath you. Feel free to dig around."

Stan kneeled by Dave and raised his head. "C'mon, Dave. C'mon bro. Speak to me."

At last, Dave came around, focused his eyes, and recognized his brother. His glasses were bent and dirt-smudged. His body was covered in dust. "What the hell?"

"Stay here, Dave. I told you. Don't move."

"Yes, Dave, stay with us, please," said Sari.

Dave heeded Stan's advice and remained quiet. He stretched out his arms, bent one leg at the knee, and remained still.

Stan stood over his brother and glared at the shaman. "What do you want, Sari?"

Sari looked amused. "Are you making me an offer?"

"I'm trying to save my brother's life. So, yes, if that's the way you want to play it, what do you want?"

Sari became quiet for a moment, his eyes locked on Stan. "What I always want. What you gave me. What he gives me. Another fascinating soul to come to Freeland. Fresh souls are the lifeblood of my village."

"What can I give you in exchange? What will it take to let my brother go?"

The question intrigued Sari. He raised his hand to his chin and stroked it. "We are bargaining here, no?"

"If that's what it takes, then yes."

"You are offering a service to me?" His eyes intensified.

"We're all servants here, Sari. Everything we have, everything we do, you own us. We have no choice. You know that."

"It is one thing to be living under my dominion. But service to me, that is something very different. Much more demanding. It calls for sacrifice, devotion, perhaps someone's blood. You wish to make that offer?"

Stan moved forward a few steps. "I want to free my brother. You hold the cards here. Tell me what it takes."

Sari extended his hands. "A brother is a valuable commodity, no? Your flesh and blood, very valuable indeed."

Stan waited for his offer. Once Sari intuited the depth of his desperation, he had no doubt the price would be steep.

Sari lowered his hands. "You must bring me two new souls, young, vibrant, smart. They must add to the life of our town and they must be bound to me here in Freeland. For this, I will let your brother go."

The impact of his offer hit Stan hard. Two more souls imprisoned. Two people he must look in the eyes as he worked and lived in Freeland. Two people who would blame him for their plight.

He glanced at Dave lying helpless in the dirt. He glanced at Sari. His wide smile revealed that he knew Stan's position. Like a grand master at chess, he had him in check. Stan forced out the word. "Agreed."

"Let it be so," Sari said like a priest. He moved to the side a few steps and spoke to Dave. "Get up, my brother. My good servant has saved you, for now. Rise, get in your car, and go."

Dave, still woozy, struggled up and eyed both Sari and Stan. He limped over and hugged his brother.

When he let loose, he stepped back and gave Sari a hard stare. "I will come back for you, Stan. I promise. And when I do, I'll come prepared."

Sari nodded. "Ah, yes, brother Dave, you will return to knock me on my ass, as you say. A good brother you are. I insist when you come back, by all means, come prepared to do battle. I welcome the challenge."

Dave removed and cleaned his classes. He put them back on his face and took time to straighten his clothes. "I don't know how you managed this, or what you've done to my brother," he said. His eyes narrowed as he pointed a finger at Sari. "But I can promise you. We'll meet again."

Sari chuckled. "I look forward to it. I will someday receive two new souls from this agreement. And in the end, you will be my third. Of this, I am sure."

"Don't bet on it. You can't be the only fish in this pond."

"No sir, I am not, but I am a big fish, no?" Sari shot his arms in the air and began to laugh loudly. His eyes grew fierce. They were the eyes of a warrior.

Dave put his hand on his brother's shoulder. "Count on it, bro. Someday. I'll be back."

Then he staggered past Sari, stepped in his Datsun, and drove off.

Stan found his resistance reassuring. A seed of revolution had been planted in his heart.

Sari walked over and stood next to him. For a moment, they both watched Dave's taillights disappear.

"We have not seen the last of him, no?" said Sari.

Stan let out a long sigh. "Probably not."

"Your brother will come for you?"

"Yeah, I have to admit. When he says something, he'll do it. He's pretty stubborn that way."

"He will come with a plan, and that is good, the sign of a brave man. He will be a welcome addition to Freeland."

Stan glanced at Sari and scuffed his foot in the dirt. "I hope not, for his sake."

Sari turned and gave Stan a cunning smile. "Be certain, my brother, it will all work out, as life always does in the long run. Perhaps in time you will come to see the wisdom of it all."

Stan reached down and dusted himself off. "Perhaps."

"And perhaps in time both you and your brother will come to enjoy life in our village."

Stan looked up at Sari, the hovering oracle whose optimism and confidence was so immutable. He tried to muster something cutting to say, to probe for some crack in Sari's solid wall of faith, but under that watchful gaze, his will to fight dissipated.

He turned back in the direction from where the car had disappeared. Dave gone. Taillights gone. Hope and freedom gone. He kept silent.

Sari turned toward the Circle. "I have to close down. I will see you tomorrow for breakfast, as always." He hurried to the restaurant. At the Circle's front door, he waved and disappeared.

Stan was left alone with his thoughts—mostly this one unpleasant thought. Finding it in his heart to doom two new souls to Freeland.

July 8, 1863

Sari had returned east after all these years.

He had done his traveling, seen marvelous sights, met interesting people.

Always exceptional with words and language, he had picked up enough English over the years to talk with Americans and learn a great deal about this wide-open land.

It was strange to him, the obsession this country had with independence. Contrast that with the need for violence and the willingness to kill over land and gold.

Sari spent hours thinking about these matters. He constantly observed and learned more as he traveled on foot through middle and western America. This country never ceased to fascinate him.

Along the way, some had died to keep him going. He was selective, choosing those whom he discerned would be least missed. Drunks, thieves, a few prostitutes. Still, at certain points, he had to choose. A settler's family in Kansas. An Indian village in Nebraska. Some fur trappers in Montana. It often came down to availability, whoever happened to be in the wrong place at the wrong time.

For a man his height, Sari was quite efficient and barely noticed. Some of this was stealth. Some of it had to do with his skin color. Some was through the power of the mind. Some of it was outright magic.

Tonight he had turned west again, slipping through enemy lines across northern Alabama, spending considerable time avoiding troops, weaponry, and landowners on the lookout for runaway slaves.

As usual, he traveled late and moved rapidly along small roads and byways. In the dark, he could make better time.

As Sari walked a deserted dirt road, he gave serious thought to settling down and creating a village to nourish his soul, somewhere far from this war. He set a goal for himself—to find that perfect spot and pick out residents who would help him form his own community.

The bloody bodies he had crossed on battlefields in Mississippi and Tennessee had pushed him toward this conclusion. If people on their own were helpless to fend off this violence, perhaps he could use his great knowledge to create the right setting. Perhaps people needed some higher guidance to create harmony, a certain order that would help them live better.

He would build a town, handpick his residents, and install himself as Chief. This was what he was planning when he came upon a group of white men on horses.

A fat man with a whip spotted Sari. He had drooping jowls and a body that looked like an oversized watermelon. His short legs, squeezed into tight boots and tucked in stirrups, were pointed outward at an awkward angle. Three other men rode behind him single file, all younger, perhaps his sons or a posse.

When the fat man stopped, they all trotted up and formed a wall across the road. Sari halted about ten yards in front of them.

"Where you goin?" the fat man growled in a deep, threatening voice.

"West," said Sari. "Far, far west."

The fat man eased his hambone fingers around his saddle horn. "You got some place you sposed to be?"

"Not yet," said Sari. "Soon, perhaps, I will turn toward the mountains."

The fat man snorted, "Shiiit. That right?" He laughed loudly and the others joined in. The fat man tilted forward in his saddle. "And just where exactly you from?"

"From many places actually," Sari said calmly. "I am what you call a traveler."

The fat man looked astonished. He eyed Sari coldly. "Traveler, huh? You don't sound like no traveler to me. Maybe traveled here in a boat, maybe run away. That the kind of travelin you talkin about?"

"Not in the least," said Sari.

The fat man glanced at his cohorts and grinned. He turned back to Sari. "Hell nigga, you got any idea what's goin on around here?"

"Yes," Sari said. "I know quite a bit. I have witnessed war and bloodshed here and elsewhere, perhaps more than you."

The fat man adjusted himself on his horse and pulled at his groin. "What's that sposed to mean?"

Sari smiled. "I am aware of the war. I myself have been a warrior. But I have no quarrel with you or those you are fighting. This is not my battle. I am doing my best to avoid it."

The fat man's voice grew irritated. "Don't talk to me like I'm a fool, nigga. You best be straight with me er I got a rope here just for you. You a runaway? Belong to somebody else?"

Sari was aware of widespread slavery in this area. He had seen it firsthand. He sensed in the man's thoughts that they were about to capture him for that purpose. Straightening like a tall tree, he crossed his arms in defiance. "No, my friend. I am Sarihaba Kinyaga, a son of Africa, and I am quite free. Neither my body or my soul have ever been captured."

The fat man shifted once more in his saddle and hocked a wad of tobacco on the road. "Well, now, who's to say you're free or slave cept those a us that make the rules around here? You're in Alabama, boy. Free states er a might long ways from here. I'd say, if you believe what you say, you're pretty stupid, not to mention," The fat man tightened his fist around his whip, looked left and right at the men beside him, and grinned, "—lost."

The group joined in a hearty laugh.

Sari remained planted in the road. "If you think I am a slave, you are welcome to come capture me."

The fat man edged his horse forward a step. "Well now, I may not be the best educated man aroun here, but I can still count, and right now there's more a us then there are a you. A rope, a gun, we got both. What you got?"

Sari's eyes flared. "You are right, my brother. You have weapons enough to kill me many times. But you have overlooked one thing."

"Really?" the fat man sneered. "And what might that be?"

Sari threw his hands above his head. "I, my brother, am magic." Then he thrust them forward.

The horse flew out from underneath the fat man's butt, sailed in the air about ten feet to the left, and landed on its side in a corn field. The fat man hurtled straight down and collapsed on his back. He lay unconscious, spread out on the road like an oversize sack of flour.

"Goddamn," one of the other men exclaimed. He reached for a rifle, but before he could grab it, the gun sailed high in the air. When the weapon fell, it cracked him on the head. He did a slow droop and teetered off his horse, one foot stuck in the stirrup. The horse whirled and bolted, dragging the man like a rope behind him. They both disappeared in the dark.

The two men who remained yanked on their reins and made a sharp u-turn. Whipping their horses, they were out of sight in less than a minute.

Sari walked over to the fat man. He bent down and carefully examined him, picking tokens off his body that might prove useful in his travels. Some money. A pipe and tobacco. The bullwhip.

He spread his legs and straddled the fat man's torso, standing tall and proud like a victorious boxer. He dangled the whip and let it crawl like a lazy snake across the fat man's bulging face. "You will not use this on anyone else," he declared.

For a moment, Sari stood motionless with hands on hips and stared down the road. "Today," he declared, "I will let you live." Then stepping over the fat man, he walked away.

After some distance, his thoughts returned to his new village. Given what he had just witnessed, he was sure, with some persuasion and magic, he could bring a group of people together who would appreciate a more peaceful way of living.

"Freeland," he muttered to the darkness. "That will be what I call it." He walked several steps and nodded. "That is a very good name."

July 26, 1979

The threat of rain, so typical this time of year. Lots of thunder, angry clouds, rough winds. As usual, it created a show of force and gave folks something to talk about.

One brainstorm of Stan's—to add a 7-day forecast as a regular weekly column for the Reporter. It was good local information and added a nice graphic touch to the front page. It also allowed him to add "weatherman" as a feather in his editorial cap.

Today, the forecast called for possible tornadoes. A big front mixed with cool air from Canada blew east. There was talk in the grocery, talk at the Circle. Weather here meant more than just sunshine and rain.

Matty had talked with Stan about some rumors she had heard regarding these storms—that some sort of town council used the power from these storms to post calls for new residents. She described it as Sari's ability to combine the storm's energy with his own powers and pass his call via his body to his followers. The more followers who gathered, the stronger the convergence and the clearer the message.

It was hard to tell in this place who believed in or supported this type of recruitment. Power was power. Stan assumed that those who spent the most time with Sari had the most to gain.

Today, he had no doubt as he headed to work that with so much thunder and lightning in the forecast, Sari and his tribe would be gathering.

"Morning, Matty," he said as he walked into the grocery store. "Feels like rain."

"Lots of it," she replied. "I don't know what it is, but these storms always get me excited."

"How come?"

Matty gestured dramatically. "I like to watch all those things going on in the sky—big clouds, lightning. Kind of gets me going, like seeing a fireworks show."

"You're a storm fan, huh?"

"Yeah. Give me a cup of coffee, some popcorn, let me sit down in my chair on the porch. Zowie. Great stuff."

"You're not afraid of the lightning?"

"Me? Naw. I get zapped, so what? I'm ready to leave anyway. Nothing here to keep me tied down. What've I got to be afraid of? I'm an old lady stuck in Freeland running a shitcan grocery store. I've done my time. See ya later, I say."

Stan stopped at the counter and watched her work. She was thumbing through some paperwork. "How long've you lived here Matty?"

She stopped sifting. The question hit a nerve. "Too long," she said. She glanced at Stan, then at the front entrance, then back at Stan. "Say, I've got work to do, Stan. You got a paper to run. We best get busy, you and I." Matty picked up a pencil and started writing on a notepad.

In her few brief comments, Stan believed she had given him the essence of her life. Stuck here unwillingly, eager to make her final exit, reluctant to say too much. He kept quiet, kept watching her write.

"Your mother teach you it's impolite to stare?" she said.

"Sorry, Matty, but your beauty is dazzling. I can't take my eyes off of you."

She put down her pencil and folded her hands. "Your bullshit is touching. Fifty years ago I might've cornered you behind the counter and had my way. Today, I'm giving you a pass. Keep at it though and you might regret being so loose with all that flattery. I still got a little gas in the tank."

"Okay, I've been warned."

"Save your hoochikoochie for Amanda."

Stan pointed at her. "Now you're meddling."

"It's what I do best."

"See you later, Matty."

"You started it."

"You're right."

"I'm always right."

Stan nodded and bowed in deference.

"Chivalrous little bastard," she growled. "Come over here and finish what you started."

Stan escaped to his doorway. "Maybe later."

"You big tease."

Her story, the story of most folks who lived here, piqued Stan's curiosity. They were stories of people who worked at jobs or ran their own small businesses in Freeland. People who appeared as normal as any other citizen in this country, yet remained concealed from the outside world. People like Matty who were permanently stranded in Freeland. Stan thought about how he might pry into their lives without being noticed. A reporter's challenge.

For the moment, though, he focused on the weather. Not for what it brought, but whom. Having lived here for almost a year and a half, he had no doubt the power boiling under the surface was strong enough to draw in the curious and unsuspecting.

His contract with Sari was in the back of his mind. Typical of human nature, he sought to fulfill his end of the bargain and avoid the cost.

For the first time in his life, he yearned for a priest; someone he could trust, confide in. With no one readily available, he called Amanda and invited her for dinner. That night, at his house, she brought over fixings and fried some chicken.

Amanda, as it turned out, worked at the Circle for a reason. She was a hell of a good cook. On occasion, when Freddy Mantel, the normal short order cook, was out, Amanda filled in as his sub.

Tonight she was Stan's chef and the scent of fried grease in his little house was delightful. When dinner was ready, they sat on folding chairs on his porch and enjoyed the warm summer evening.

"Damn girl, this is good," Stan said as he tore meat from a breast and munched on some fresh sweet corn.

Some late blue sky broke through the steel grey cumulus clouds. Amanda appeared relaxed and peaceful. She dissected a wing, ate a small piece, and peered over the rail.

Stan thought the storm was not the only thing around him receding. And for his part, he was thinking more and more about things that had never occurred to him in the past. Scary things like love, commitment, settling down. No woman had ever inspired him to dig this deep.

Not that he believed he and Amanda had reached that point. Marriage, kids, those kind of things. It's just that lately he caught himself thinking about it, particularly when she was with him on nights like tonight, sitting peacefully on his porch eating chicken. Simple, basic, beautiful.

He nodded at her. "Long way from Valentine's Day, huh?"

Amanda chewed on some chicken and paused thoughtfully. "Yeah. It is."

Stan hesitated. "You mind if I ask you something?"

Amanda put down her chicken. "About politics, religion, or me?"

"You in particular."

Her fingers stopped peeling. "Well, there's really not much to tell."

"Hmm, I actually think there's a lot, if you'll open the door a bit." He dropped a bone on his plate and wiped his mouth. "Look, I'm sorry. I'd just like to get to know you, that's all. We have these little dates but I never find out who you are. You're always the same mystery coming in and going out the door."

Amanda laid her plate on the porch. "I'm not sure what to tell you, Stan."

"Well, how'd you come to Freeland? Let's start there."

"Hmm, now that's very personal."

"Okay," he said, scratching his cheek. "Where'd you grow up? Is that easier?"

"Yeah, much. I grew up near Cleveland. Shaker Heights, actually. Pretty normal childhood. Dad worked for Skyco Plastics. My mom was your everyday housewife. I have two older brothers."

"There you go," he said. "That wasn't so hard, was it?"

She smiled and pointed. "Your turn. How about you?"

"I grew up in San Diego. Chula Vista to be precise. I have an older brother, Dave. He and my dad work for an engineering outfit called Rohr and my mom is a librarian. I finished at UCLA back in '71. Majored in journalism, minored in creative writing."

"I like to read, myself."

"Really? What?"

Amanda reached down and played with her chicken wing. "You're going to laugh."

"Why?"

"Because—"

"Because why?"

"I like romance novels."

Stan kept a straight face, then broke into a big grin.

Amanda reached over and punched his arm.

"Okay," he said. "I held it as long as I could. You're right. That's funny."

"What's funny about it?"

"Serious, quiet Amanda with a chick book."

"Don't be an ass." She looked at Stan slyly and grinned. "What about you? What do you read?"

"Hmm. I can promise. Not romance. Mostly mysteries—and biographies. Lincoln is my favorite."

"Well, now," she said, drawing out the words. "Biographies about Lincoln, huh? That sounds really . . . boring."

Stan laughed. "Yeah, I guess that's what most people think. Call it the geek in me. That and comic books. I was a big Spiderman fan." He began to hum the Spiderman theme from the old TV cartoon show. Amanda snickered.

Stan changed the subject. "You go to college?"

"No, finished high school in '72, became a traveling flower girl, in hippie speak. You know, wanted to experience life, live off the land, that sort of thing. Took me to some pretty strange places along the east coast. None stranger than here, though."

"Where'd you learn to cook?"

"One of the advantages of having a stay-at-home mom. We spent a lot of time in the kitchen feeding my family. Having a girl was a big help to her. None of the men in my family ever lifted a finger. She and I became a good team." Amanda began to tear up.

Stan shifted uncomfortably. "Hey, you okay?"

She took a moment to regain her composure. "Yeah, I miss my mom. That's all. She was a good mother."

"Mine too, and my dad. Get's pretty rough sometimes being stuck here."

"Tell me about it."

Stan put down his plate and snuck his arm around her shoulder. She took his hand and squeezed. They remained quiet for several minutes.

Amanda broke the silence. "All right. I'll tell you something else." She peered across the road, as if doing so might bolster her courage. "I didn't come here by accident."

"Well, I assume that somehow or other Sari brought us all here. He's got some strange ability to bring in whoever he needs to run this place."

"No, you're not listening. I came here—deliberately. I knew what I was doing and chose to do it."

Stan dropped his arm. He glanced over to see if she might be joking. She was not. "You chose to come and be enslaved here?"

"I chose to come. I didn't see it as enslavement, at least not at the time."

"Why not?"

Amanda waited and took a deep breath. "Because I'm a witch."

"A what?" Stan watched her eyes, her mouth.

"A witch, genuine, from a coven in Ohio. My specialty is love spells. That's why Sari wanted me. If I could cast love spells on people, he thought they might be less inclined to want to leave. Having people attached to each other would make them form bonds in the village."

"And in exchange, he offered—"

"The chance to practice my art. You know, when you make a spell work, create genuine magic, well, it can give you quite a buzz."

"But the long-term, to be trapped here—"

"I was young, I wasn't thinking long-term. It was the attraction of using my powers. You don't think about consequences when Sari makes his case. He's really quite persuasive."

Stan kept staring at her.

"Well," she said testily, "you wanted to know."

"I did. It's just not what I expected."

"What did you expect?"

"Waitress, stuck in Freeland, falls in love, decides to tell me. Something to that effect."

"All true."

"I didn't count on the witch part."

"Most people don't. I keep it under raps."

"So, you and I?"

"Yes?"

"How does that fit in?"

"I'm not sure yet. It's still a work in progress."

"Goddamn, Amanda, you're just confusing the hell out of me. A little insight would be nice."

"You have to be patient, Stan. I'm in a tough spot here. I owe allegiance to Sari, but I also like you. I may be a witch, but I'm also a woman. I can't help how I feel but Sari is watching us closely. He doesn't quite trust you, not after the incident with your brother."

"You know about that?"

"Yes."

"You discussed this with Sari?"

"Yeah, I guess you might call me part of his inner circle."

"Inner circle?" Stan froze, then shook his head. "Ohhhh, no, no, no, now I get it. You, me, Sari. I'll be damned. Tell me you're not a spy?"

"I do his bidding."

"What's that supposed to mean?"

"What he asks, I carry out," she said flatly.

"Including keeping an eye on me?"

"If he asks me, yes."

Stan paused. A troublesome question crossed his mind. "You know about the hunters?"

"I know what they do, yes. Most anyone who's lived here long enough finds out sooner or later. Do I participate in the murders? No. The ones who do that are his personal caretakers. Creepy people. Dangerous people. Thank God I don't have much to do with them."

Stan's hands shook. He could feel his temper build. He raised his voice a notch. "Can you see why I'm having a hard time here?"

Amanda crossed her legs. One foot began to bounce nervously in the air. "I can. Yes."

"While we've been going out, you've been spying. Double dipping I would say."

Amanda began to tear up. The color in her face drained. As Stan watched her body language, her face grew blank and her shoulders drooped. The warmth she had exuded dried up.

Stan knew he had crossed a line. He clasped his fingers together and exhaled, allowing for a moment to pass between them.

"Look, Amanda. I'm sorry. I'm surprised and hurt, but that's no reason to take it out on you."

Stan hoped for some signs of a thaw. None were forthcoming. "Amanda?"

Her eyes flashed angrily. "We're all trapped here, Stan. Whether I'm double dipping or not, every one of us serves the same master, you as well as me. It's all shades of the same color."

"Okay."

"Just be aware that you do what Sari wants as well, when he wants it. We're all in this together, you know."

"Right."

"He's got you under his radar."

Stan leaned back in his chair. "Well, where does that leave us?"

"It leaves you with a choice."

"What's that?"

"Trust me. Don't trust me. You can't have it both ways."

Stan reached over and touched her cheek with his fingers. "Tell me you care and I'll believe you."

Amanda held his gaze. "I do care. Even in a place as whacked out as Freeland, that counts for something."

Stan thought about Amanda's words. It began to sink in, how they both were in a dangerous position. Love existing as a competing loyalty to Sari.

"I could kill you," she said. "He could ask me to do that. Just because I can do love spells doesn't mean there aren't other things in my arsenal."

"Knowing Sari, I'm guessing that's something you're familiar with?"

"Very."

"Jesus, you're scaring me."

"You should be scared. This is really very serious."

"How am I supposed to respond to that?"

"That's up to you, Stan. Hard as it is to hear, knowledge is information, information is power."

Night descended on the house. Crickets, dogs barking, an occasional gust of wind. The blue sky disappeared. In the remaining half-light, the clouds reformed and their rain soaked curtains descended.

"I have to go," said Amanda.

Stan started to protest, saw her face, and held back. "Thanks for dinner," he said as she stood on the porch steps.

"Anytime."

"Apologies accepted? I hope?"

"None needed. I understand."

Stan wanted desperately to touch her, but he was hesitant. The distance between them still stretched wide. And lodged between their fragile connection—Sari.

Their eyes met. He leaned forward in his chair and made his declaration. "I trust you."

Some color returned to her cheeks. A small smile. She reached out and hooked his finger. "That's good to know. Somewhere down the line, it'll be put to the test."

"Still friends?"

"More than friends, Stan. You know that. I wouldn't say these things otherwise."

"Does that make us official?"

"We were unofficially official in February. You just didn't know it. I had to be sure you could be trusted."

"Good to know."

She turned to walk down the steps. "Gotta go. We'll talk some more."

"Count on it."

Amanda stepped off the porch and hurried down Paradise Road.

Stan remained on the porch and watched the boiling clouds overhead. More than a typical thunderstorm, something powerful brewed in this little town. He wondered if it had anything to do with them.

An hour passed. As Stan observed the storm, he had the sudden urge to take a walk. Even with the bad weather, he needed to get out and think. He grabbed a light jacket and hat, walked past his gate, and hiked west on Paradise Road.

For a half mile or so, Amanda's words filtered through his head. He remembered the Valentine's Day party, the vivid dream, waking up in her bedroom.

He thought about the chicken dinner they had eaten tonight and her confession. Perhaps this was all part of one of her love spells, but why? What did it mean for them to be matched up? Nothing in this town happened by accident. What purpose would Sari have for pairing up a witch and a reporter? It didn't make sense. Yet here they were, serving Sari, caring for each other. The idea seemed quite combustible.

A car approached—an old Ford Pinto—driving east. The bright headlights caught Stan's attention. As the car pulled alongside, he noticed there were two young adults inside. A man and woman. Maybe college age.

The man rolled down the window and stopped the car. "Hey there. We're lost. You know how we can find our way out of this goddamned maze?"

Stan hesitated. His promise to Sari flashed through his head. He tried to ignore it. "Yeah, just stay straight on this road for a few more miles, don't stop until you hit the highway, then head north to Vale. You can't miss it."

"Damn, that's good news. I've been driving up and down this road for hours looking for a way out."

"No problem," Stan said and started to move away.

The man stuck his head out the window. "You know anywhere around here we can eat?"

There it was. The promise. The obligation. The temptation.

Stan stopped in mid-step. Yes, he knew the answer. He also knew how to keep them out of trouble. He could save their lives and maintain their freedom. But opportunity and need were strong intoxicants. A simple choice could fulfill his contract and leave him with unsullied hands, at least in the short-term.

Stan turned and faced the car. There they sat. Lost, young, and confused. It must have seemed strange to them. The pause, the empty air as Stan's mouth opened without speaking.

"You live around here?" the man asked.

Stan resigned himself to the inevitable. "Yeah, I do."

"Well? Can you help us?"

Pushing guilt aside, he crossed that thin grey line. "Sure, right up the road, a bar and café. It's called the Circle."

The man earnestly scanned his face. "You think it's still open?"

"Should be. Usually closes at nine."

"Good place to eat?"

"Not bad. Basic food. Hamburgers, chicken, fries."

"All right." The man glanced at the woman, then back at Stan. "Well, thanks for the help."

"You're welcome."

The man rolled up his window and sped away, anxious to eat, eager to get back home.

As they drove out of sight, Stan knew they would never make it.

He also knew that even though he made his suggestion seem subtle, off the cuff, he was as guilty as if he had personally led them to Sari. He had delivered their souls as promised. Contract completed. Life could move on. He felt relief. He felt wretched.

As darkness descended, the night sky looked ominous. A few drops of rain splattered on the pavement. The words of Amanda came to mind. *We serve the same master, you as well as me. It's all shades of the same color.* Whether intentional or not, he had served Sari well.

December 27, 1979

Christmas was over, and with it, all the ads and announcements that made running a paper this time of year so interesting. Not only did Christmas news fill up space, it gave Stan a solid sense of purpose in the community.

Now, with New Year's approaching, the well was a bit dry. So he resorted to what every newspaper did this time of year. Print a year in review. In this case, Freeland news for 1979. Things to look back on, moments to remember, the usual sentimental shtick. This was what he was thinking of this morning as he walked into the grocery store and headed to his office.

"Well," Matty announced to him as he passed. "Another year."

"Gone bye bye," he said.

"You doing anything for New Year's?"

He leaned on the counter with both elbows. "Guess I'll hit up the town's New Year's Eve party, at least until midnight. Beyond that, no idea."

"Time sure flies. Older you get, the faster it slides."

Stan halted and looked at his old friend. "Oh, now don't you get morose on me, Matty. I count on you to be the little miss ornery sunshine in my life."

She gave him a melancholy glance. "Even the best entertainers get blue occasionally."

Stan brushed his fingers along the counter top. "Don't like New Year's, huh?"

"Don't like being old. New Year's reminds me of too much water under the bridge."

"O now, what's floating loose in that lovely head of yours?"

"Don't be nosy." Her face turned stubborn.

"It's my job. You should know that by now."

"Well, if you must know, I always think of my late husband Frank. Don't know why. He wasn't good for much anyway, cept maybe pushing a broom around, but he was company and he was nice to me, so I guess it balanced out."

"Frank, huh? How long has he been gone?"

"Died about ten years ago. Heart attack. They said he never knew what hit him, which I spose is a blessing, if you gotta go. Quick and painless."

"You miss him, huh?"

"Not so much till this time of year. Maybe it's just time passing and remembering who you knew. Beyond that, I can't explain it."

"Well, what can I do to cheer you up?"

Matty pointed a bony finger at him. "Marry that girl you've been dicking around with for months. Stop frittering time away. Guess I should know. Love ain't forever."

"So now who's being nosy?"

"You stick it in my affairs, I return the favor." She crossed her arms in an I-told-you-so stance.

"Thanks for sharing."

"You're welcome."

At that moment, one of the town's newest souls, the driver of the Pinto that Stan had so helpfully guided into their town last summer, shuffled through the front door.

Brent Plymouth, originally from Boise, formerly a student at Boise State, with ambitions to be an architect. Now, along with his girlfriend, Rita Towson, a servant of Freeland.

Brent was a tall, awkward looking fellow. He wore black-rimmed glasses that sat crooked on his nose and his clothes always seemed to be the wrong size. His curly brown hair looked like a perm gone awry. When he walked, he reminded Stan of Jughead from the Archie comics.

Brent noticed Matty and hesitantly approached the counter. "Scuse me, ma'am."

Matty cast a curious eye. "Would you by chance be talking to me?"

"Yes, ma'am."

"There's that ma'am again. I'm afraid you have me confused with someone else. My real name is Matty. No ma'am in any form or fashion attached to it."

Brent had yet to understand Matty's sharp wit. A serious fellow with an engineer's personality, he reminded Stan of his father. Good fellow, warm heart, lousy sense of humor.

"Sorry, uh, Matty." He looked confused and lowered his head like a school kid who had just been scolded by his teacher.

"That's better," said Matty. "So, whatta you want?"

Brent shuffled his feet for a moment. "Uh . . . do you by any chance . . . carry any feminine hygiene products?"

Matty stopped, opened her mouth, and stared at Brent. Then she took a deep breath and smiled. "Oh, Lord. She send you on a mission, huh?"

Stan could tell. Matty's was about to have some fun.

"Poor guy. You tell her if she wants women's stuff to come get it herself. Some things shouldn't be left to men."

Brent was tongue-tied and thoroughly embarrassed. He looked around the store, perhaps searching for the feminine hygiene aisle, perhaps hoping for a quick escape.

Matty zeroed in like a dog to a rabbit. "What type she want, she tell you?"

Brent remained speechless.

"Oh, never mind," She pointed. "Over there, against this wall, next to the bras. Take your time but choose wisely. If she's on the rag, you know, your life could be in danger."

All this Matty managed to handle with a straight face. Stan knew better. She was enjoying herself.

Matty circled around the counter and headed toward the back wall. She stood quietly and waited while Brent shuffled over. She pointed again. "Right here. Don't worry when you buy them. I'll put them in a brown bag. They'll look just like groceries. No one will ever know the difference."

Stan watched this unfold from his vantage point at the counter. He was doing his best to hold back his laughter and save Brent any further angst.

As Brent took time to analyze each brand, Matty returned to the counter and shook her head. "That boy needs a leash," she growled.

It was Stan's cue to get back to work.

At his desk, Stan sorted through all the special occasions, town gatherings, and announcements for 1979. Everyone's life was important when it came to the paper. He didn't want to leave out an event and tick someone off. It was a sensitive matter.

Sifting through his pile, he noticed Brent standing in the doorway. He and Stan hadn't said much in the five months since Brent and Rita moved here.

"Morning, Brent. Something I can do for you?"

Brent stepped into his office holding his anonymous brown bag. "I'm not sure, but I thought I'd ask."

"Okay, shoot."

"I was wondering, you being involved in the paper business, if you could get a message to my parents. I know they're really worried about where I'm at."

Stan took in a sharp breath. "Ooo, that's a tough one."

"Well, you're the only one I know around here that might have some connections to the real world, outside of Sari and maybe a few of his friends. And I don't get a good feeling about them, so I thought I'd ask you."

"Worried, huh?"

"Terribly."

Stan's guilt kicked in. He knew exactly what Brent was going through. "You're new around here, Brent. I know it takes a while to get adjusted and find some working purpose. But contacting people from the outside, well, that's just not a good idea."

"I don't want them to come. I just want them to stop worrying."

"If they know you're here, they'll come and that will only make things worse. Trust me." Thoughts of Dave ran through his head.

Brent sat in Stan's lone office chair. He put down his bag and stared at the floor. "This is the shits."

"It is," said Stan.

Brent let out a deep breath. "You could have helped me, you know."

The accusation stung but Stan remained calm. "You're right. You're absolutely right."

They both sat and listened to Matty work in the next room.

Stan realized he had let loose one obligation only to pick up another. The contract he fulfilled had left him with another pressing load. "You're asking me to do something very risky, you know."

"I'm sorry," Brent said. "I just don't know what else to do. Rita was beside herself this Christmas. Neither of us like being here. It's too small, too weird. This Sari guy gives me the creeps. I'm kind of desperate."

"You can't tell your family you're here. That's out of the question."

"Well, what do you suggest?"

"I don't know, yet, but give me a chance to think about it. In the meantime, buck up and keep quiet." Stan clasped his hands together on his desk and let his warning sink in. "Do not talk about this to anyone else. Understand?"

Brent's eyes pleaded like a lost dog aching to go home. "Right. I get it." Those eyes—searching Stan's face, searching for some sign of hope. "I'll keep quiet, for now, if you promise to help."

Stan admired his pluck. They had more in common than he first thought. "I promise to think about it and get back to you. That's all I can say at this point."

"Okay." Brent sighed and laid a scrap of paper on Stan's desk. "In case you decide, here's their address and phone number in Boise."

"Right," Stan said as he picked up the paper and gave it the once over. "As I said, I'll think about it. In the meantime, keep busy, stay quiet."

Brent stood up. He gave Stan one last sorrowful glance, picked up his bag, and trudged out of the store.

Stan read the address on the piece of paper and tucked it safely away in a manila folder underneath a stack of papers in his bottom desk drawer. As he returned to his pile of recollections for 1979, there's one announcement he had deliberately overlooked. New arrivals in Freeland.

At the Circle during lunch, Stan caught Amanda as she waited on tables. "Doing anything tonight?"

"Same as usual, go home, eat, relax, sleep. What's up?"

"Can you come over to my house after dinner?"

She eyed him. "Okay—"

"I've got something I need to chat about."

"What?"

"Can't talk here, but tonight?"

>

"What time?"

"Eightish?"

"All right. Sure." She gave him another puzzled look. "Well. Gotta go. Later."

He watched her scurry to another table and glanced over at Sari to see if he was watching. Sari seemed occupied with another customer. He had skirted his attention—for now. That was good. Stan finished his lunch and hurried out the door.

On his porch that night, Stan sat bundled up as he perused the clear night sky. When Amanda approached, he met her at the gate and gave her a strong hug. For a moment, she nestled her head on his shoulder, then wrapped her arms around his neck and gave him a kiss.

"That's a very nice Christmas present," he said.

She brushed his cheek. "We'll celebrate Christmas all year long, if you like."

"Come on, let's get you out of the cold."

They hurried inside the house. Stan took her coat and put it in the bedroom.

Wearing a blue knit sweater, hair pulled back in a pony tail, Stan thought Amanda looked enchanting. Her dark eyes said she was happy to see him. He put his arm around her shoulders and pulled her close. "I could eat you for dinner, you know, if I hadn't already had dinner."

Amanda gave his shoulder a gentle nudge with her cheek. "You're sweet."

They nestled on his couch and basked for a moment in the comfort of the house.

"You had something to talk about?" she said.

"I do. Hate to spoil the mood, but I need an ear."

"I assume that's why I'm here."

Stan gave her a gentle hug. "I had a chat with Brent today."

"Oh, I know that's not going well," she sighed.

"How much does Sari know?"

"Let's just say he knows enough." She turned away from Stan, her face troubled. "Nothing gets past him."

"Damn, I was afraid of that."

"He complain to you?"

"More than that, he wants me to get a message to his parents." She looked across the living room and chewed on a thumb. "More bad news."

"He's very lonely and unhappy here. He misses his family terribly."

"Don't we all."

"I don't know what to do. Me being his messenger would just puts us both in the dog house."

"And you want to know how to help Brent and presumably Rita as well?"

"Yeah, if possible. I don't know how to tell him no. You should see the look on his face. He's desperate."

"I know. Poor guy."

"So?"

"I'm thinking—"

"Think out loud."

"Don't be a pest. Shut up and be still for a minute."

As they pressed together, Stan focused on the small wall clock and watched the needle tick rhythmically around the face.

Five minutes passed before she tapped on his shoulder. "Leave it to me."

Stan waited for an explanation. Nothing came. "And?"

Amanda pressed her palm against his chest and shook her head. "Don't ask. The less you know, the better."

"Hey," he said with mock indignation. "Where's the trust here?"

"I'd rather do this myself. In this case, it's your turn to trust me." She pressed her head on his shoulder. "Now, let's not discuss this anymore. We have more pleasant things to talk about."

"Like—"

"Like what we're doing for New Year's."

"You mean go to the party?"

"Afterwards, I mean."

"You have a plan?"

"No, but you do."

"What?"

She gently dragged a finger across his chest. "I seem to remember a gift certificate laying around, still unused if I recall."

"Ohhhh. Right, you're right. Been a while but I know it's here somewhere."

Her eyes turned amorous. "Get on the stick tomorrow, make a reservation for two."

Stan loved those eyes, especially now as they revealed her want. As she smiled at him, he imagined her as a fine china doll that he cradled in his hands. He rubbed his fingers lightly along her cheek. "Really?"

"Yeah. A night at Dahlia's would be lovely."

"And after that?"

"I'll leave that to your imagination."

Stan touched her cheek. She grabbed his hand and kissed it. He leaned down and kissed her. Indeed, his imagination was working overtime.

Another week passed. Stan, absorbed by work and life with Amanda, forgot about Brent and Rita. That is, until Brent walked in the store one morning. Stan could tell who he was by the sound of his voice and the lumbering clop of his feet on the wood floor.

The thought of his dilemma came rushing back. He heard him shop, have a chat with Matty, shuffle up and down the aisles. Something about him was different. His tone, his cheerfulness. Stan perked up and eavesdropped.

Brent surprised Stan at his office door. "Hi," he said.

"Hi, Brent," Stan replied.

"Hey, I'm sorry about putting you in a tough spot."

"What?"

"You know, asking you to send a letter and stuff."

"No problem, man."

"I don't know, I was thinking about it and really, it's not so bad here. Kind of nice actually. Small town, nice people. Rita and I met the Darseys a couple days ago. Looks like we may become pretty good friends."

"Really?" The Darseys were an older couple, square as a box. Not the kind of friends Stan imagined for Brent and Rita.

"Yeah, and Rita's found a job at Pin a Rose Flower Shop. Something she really enjoys."

Stan feigned enthusiasm. "That's good news."

"Anyway, I just wanted to stop by and let you know how much I enjoy your paper."

"Hey, that's nice of you, Brent. Thanks."

Brent's eyes landed on Stan's old print machine. "I always wanted to work on a paper. I thought maybe you might need some help. And you don't have to pay me. I'm looking for things to do around here. You ever want an assistant?"

"Well, now that you mention it, there are times when I could use a hand. I tell you what. Why don't you come around next Monday and we'll talk."

Brent's face lit up. "Great. See you then." He hurried down the store aisle and out the door.

Stan left his office and stood next to Matty by the screen door. They both spied on Brent as he did his funny little camel walk across the town square.

Stan spoke up. "He seem different to you?"

"Like how?" she said.

"Like he's actually glad to be here in Freeland kind of different?"

Matty rubbed her fingers lightly on the beat-up screen. "Yep, I'd say you're right."

Stan raised his hands and shrugged his shoulders.

Matty shrugged back. "Not the first strange thing you've seen around here, is it?"

"No, you're right."

She returned to her perch behind the counter. "At least he's not hanging out in the women's section anymore."

Stan sat at his desk with his hands flat on the table. *What did Amanda do*, he wondered?

One of the odd things about having a witch for a girlfriend. He never knew what she might do—to others, to him.

Reaching in his bottom drawer, he sifted through his papers and pulled the address of Brent's parents out of the manila folder. It dropped in his lap.

Somehow Stan could not slough off his role in their son's disappearance. Brent may have changed his attitude, but they wouldn't. He thought of his own parents, how they must worry about him every day.

Stan put a sheet of white paper in his old IBM Selectric and typed:

Dear Mom and Dad:

I'm sorry I've been out of touch for so long. I just wanted to let you know I'm all right and miss you very much. I can't tell you the whole story, but I've decided to do some traveling. You know, get out and see the country. I promise someday to go back to school, but, for now, this is something I really want to do.

I'll send you an occasional card and letter. I know you're worried. Don't be. Really. I'm okay. Will be in touch soon.

Love,

Brent

He folded the letter and inserted it in an envelope. Then he addressed it to Brent's parents and put it in his coat pocket. He knew that even if he succeeded in pulling this off, the letter would be small comfort to them. Still, at least they would know their son was alive.

He jumped from his chair and hurried down the aisle of the grocery store. "Going out for a while, Matty," he called out.

She lifted her eyes from a stack of invoices and watched him head toward the door. "I'll stand guard," she said in her usual deadpan voice and immediately went back to work.

Stan drove on Sand Hollow Creek Road south toward Lake Owyhee State Park and pulled his car in front of a combination gas station, post office, and food mart. The station served as the hub of a very small community called Forestview. The store bordered a tall sign on the highway that read *Forestview Texaco.*

He had heard about this little hole-in-the-wall from Walt, who often told him that he gassed up his truck here when he went out on tows. Walt had mentioned there was a small post office inside.

The room was warm, suffocating. He pulled off his heavy jacket and folded it over his left arm. He clutched the letter to Brent's parents in his right hand.

Stan knew he had to move quickly. He browsed through the store and bought some stamps. Frequently checking the front door, he placed a single stamp on the envelope's top right corner.

He spotted the box for outgoing mail. As he reached for the slot, he was overcome by panic. Did Sari know what Stan was about to do? Like a boy making his first full confession, Stan's heart raced and his mouth felt dry. The shaman. The penitent. What penance would be required for this sinful act?

Stan threw off his doubts and lifted his hand toward the mail box. As an act of defiance, he used extra force to push the letter through the slot. *There you go, Sari*, he thought. *Here's a fine fuck you.*

On his way back to Freeland, Stan considered doing the same for his folks. He wondered if they still missed him. Maybe the grief had passed and his memory had become distant. By this time, perhaps he had become just a picture on a wall. Something to glance at in passing. It hadn't been that long, had it?

As he approached the turnoff for Freeland, the frigid January wind buffeted his Volkswagen. The bright afternoon sunshine gave him no comfort. His hands, his feet, even the steering wheel were ice cold.

Looking at all the surrounding snow piles made him feel worse. The earth and his soul, buried under a crush of white suffocation. Watching the cars pass up and down this road, he felt solitary and lonely.

He remembered seeing the old Freeland sign for the first time. How hard would it be, right now, to make a different choice? Go straight, or make a u-turn. At this instant, he could return home or escape. It was all right here in front of him, one asphalt road branching into thousands of miles to somewhere else.

Stan pulled off the highway and parked on the shoulder. Getting out of his car, he leaned on his door, brushed some slush off his shoes, and checked traffic up and down the road. It was empty and stretched straight as a giant black ruler. North. South. He became acutely aware of direction. Which way to Freeland, which way home.

He thought of Amanda, how she had become a tiny blooming flower among all this frigid winter, a tender respite.

And then, something more disturbing penetrated his thoughts. Sari. Floating through his head like a plane searching for a place to land. His image pushed out everything else, any thoughts of escape, love, or freedom.

Stan recognized the pull, urgent, overpowering. The turnoff. The sign. That damned Freeland sign.

It was the same pull Sari had placed deep in his thoughts back in Boise. It was what drove him to Freeland. It was what Sari had implanted in his head—an aching, involuntary reflex to stay bound to this town.

He knew the old sorcerer must be searching for him, inquiring about why he stood by himself on this lonesome road.

He also understood what Sari had done to him. His thoughts always pointing like a compass toward Freeland. Wherever he went, whatever he chose to do, that's where they would always land. The further from Freeland he ventured, the stronger the pull.

Based on the powerful throbbing in his head, Stan calculated how far he could travel before his body exploded. Vale, maybe. Ontario or Payette. Boise? Out of the question.

It was painful to face, the truth as it stared at him in the form of a sign. Freeland. Tacky, weathered. Permanent. On this cold January day, he was forced to own up to his icy reality; what had happened to him, how he had become locked into this life. Corralled, tied up and tethered like string to a kite.

With reluctance and more than a little agony, he slid back in his car, turned left at the sign, and drove back to his office.

January 15, 1980

Stan had just curled up on his couch in the living room. The weather outside was terrible. Heavy snow, frigid winds. He ached to have Amanda here, but she was busy tonight with some meetings in preparation for this year's Valentine's Day party. It was up to him to entertain himself.

He had just started to leaf through some old magazines Matty had given him when he heard footsteps on his porch. Several sets of footsteps. Then a knock.

"Hells bells," he said. "Who could be out on a night like tonight?"

Stan opened the door and found Sari and two of the men who helped kidnap him. Walt and Rick.

"Damn," Stan muttered as he looked incredulously at the trio covered by parkas and snow. "You guys out for a little stroll?"

Sari, who enveloped the doorway, rubbed his large black gloves together. "In a manner of speaking, yes."

"Well, come on in. No hot chocolate tonight, guys, sorry."

The group tromped through the doorway and quickly filled up his living room. Walt and Rick grabbed two kitchen chairs and dragged them over. Jackets, hats, and gloves were strewn across the floor. Sari sat cross-legged opposite the couch.

Stan waited quietly.

"You are well, I presume?"said Sari.

Stan paused, his mind racing. An unplanned meeting tonight in the middle of a snow storm. What could this mean? "As well as can be expected."

Another long silence.

"Come on, fellas, what's up?" Stan demanded. "You didn't drop by for a friendly chat. That's not your style."

Sari folded his fingers together and rested his hands under his chin. "We are here to offer you an invitation."

Stan tried to look Sari in the eyes, but his gaze was just too powerful. Instead, he glanced at the kitchen. "Invitation?" he said. "Invitation for what?"

"For life," Sari said.

"Life?"

"Yes. Life."

"I don't catch your drift."

Walt and Rick sat with stony faces. Walt, in particular, seemed irritated. "I think he's avoiding your point."

"Right, Walt," Stan said. "I don't get the point because all you've done is throw out a riddle, which I don't mind answering if you give me more clues."

"Then here is one," Sari interjected. "What would it take to live forever?"

Stan thought for a moment, then looked at them in horror. "You guys aren't asking me—"

"Ah," Walt said. "Mr. Smarty Pants finally gets it."

Stan clenched and unclenched his fists. "I get the riddle. I just don't get why you're asking me. After your little kidnaping caper last year, I expected to be persona non grata with you guys."

"Well," Walt said, "if it were up to me—"

Sari raised his hand. Walt went mum.

"You have made great progress," Sari said. "And of course, we're aware of the news about you and Amanda. If life as you know it were to include her, would that not be a pleasant thought?"

Stan scratched his head and forced himself to look at Sari. "Are you baiting me, Sari?"

Sari rested his hands lightly in his lap. "You use a negative, I use a positive. I think I could argue my point as well as you. Life with her, is that not a great offer?"

"At what cost?"

"Simply to choose life as we have come to know it."

"I don't get it. Honestly. Why now?"

Sari rested his hands in his lap. "Why not?"

"Why anything with you, Sari? I never understand what you're doing or why, and believe me I'd like to understand this. I don't like to jump over cliffs on blind faith."

Walt and Rick shifted uneasily in their chairs. Sari laid his palms flat on the floor. "The knowing comes with the living, my brother. First comes life, then knowledge. That is the normal order of things."

Stan could feel his pulse racing. They were squeezed together so tight in the living room, he wondered if they could hear his heartbeat. "I think, if I'm understanding the gist of this conversation, you're asking me to join in your hunts, help with your little blood feasts. In exchange, you'll teach me your bloody magic tricks. Is that the point here? And to sweeten the pot, you're offering to do the same thing for Amanda. Am I on target here, Sari?"

"Yes," he said, rubbing his chin. "You have managed to grasp a complex idea and make it sound very easy. I like how you think. And together, with your insight and Amanda's gifts, our village would be remarkably strengthened. I like the sound of this. I think it would be a wise choice."

"What's the other option?"

For the first time since he and Stan had met, Sari appeared confused. "Other option?"

"Yeah. If I don't choose bloody eternal life, what's the other option. Death?"

There was a sudden downturn in the room's temperature. Despite all Stan had done to warm up the house, the cold suddenly permeated the room. Stan could see his breath misting. He braced himself and shivered.

"You really are a smart ass, ain't you?" Walt said.

"You can lead a horse to water—" said Rick.

Stan gave him a dirty look. "If I were a horse, Rick, I might get your point."

"The offer is a good one," Sari said. "There is no other option that I am implying. There is no negative to my positive. We are simply inviting you to become a trusted leader in our community."

Stan pressed his back against the couch and laced his hands over his head. His fingers were numb and his scalp chaffed from the cold. He was unsure whether Sari actually meant this last statement. The temperature in the room said otherwise.

"I say no thanks," he said. "If I really have a choice, then I opt out."

The cold in the room deepened. Stan absorbed the added chill of three sets of eyes.

"Nevertheless," Sari said calmly, "though you have chosen now, you may choose differently in a matter of time. The offer remains."

"Really," Walt complained. "I think he's made his point pretty clear."

"For now, yes" Sari said. "But the best virtue I have learned by living a long life is patience. Many days roll by. When you see enough of them, you realize how much everything changes—" He took a deep breath and let the word melodically roll off his tongue. "Eventually."

Stan bristled. "God, I hope you're wrong, Sari, at least on my account."

"We shall see, my brother. I have seen many changes in you already. The paper, two new souls, a blossoming love. I am not without hope."

Stan knew Sari was right. Whether he liked it or not, he was doing what it took to survive and prosper. He knew that Freeland had wrapped its roots around him. He questioned just how far he would go to keep the peace. What else would Sari ask him to do?

Sari and his group rose. Jackets and gloves were put back on. Walt and Rick left ahead of him. Sari paused on the porch as Stan waited by the door.

"Perhaps you will choose to make more trips down the road?" he said.

Stan averted his gaze and pushed against the door. He knew exactly what Sari meant. He had no illusion that Sari missed anything in this village, leastwise someone leaving.

Stan's voice faltered. "If it means consoling someone's parents, then yes. Whatever family you've assembled here doesn't mean we don't miss the people we really love."

Sari nodded. "Soon, perhaps, this will be your family as well."

Stan didn't answer. He wasn't going to give Sari any more satisfaction.

"Good night, my brother. Share a greeting with your beloved." He reached Stan's gate and turned east on Paradise Road.

Stan could hear him swish and crunch through the falling snow. He could not help but notice how Sari appeared eerily like a long dark shadow among snowflakes.

His hands began to shake and his knees grew weak. He shut the door, walked into his living room, and collapsed on the floor. For now, he had escaped damage. But for how much longer? If not from Sari, from Walt and his cronies?

Thinking about this gave him a headache. He remained motionless on the floor, waited for his heart to slow, and fell into a troubled sleep.

October 30, 1980

Halloween. A strange time in Freeland. More than just the usual American celebration—trick or treat, harmless parties, scary costumes. In Freeland, magic was real and the paranormal was routine.

No surprise then that so many folks in town looked forward to Halloween because they believed this night encouraged the collision of the living with things otherworldly.

Stan wrote some stories about this in the paper, including interviews with some residents who had encountered the paranormal as well as some who used the evening to dabble in spiritual arts.

He also included a few tales of the macabre. Even in Freeland, everyone enjoyed a spooky story.

"So Matty," Stan said the day before Halloween. "What's your plan for tomorrow night?"

"None," she shot back. "I'm going home, lock my doors, turn out the lights, and hope no one eggs my house like last year. I hate it. Seems this time of year brings out the worst in folks."

"Well, is there any doubt that Freeland is haunted?" He curled his fingers like claws and imitated Boris Karloff. "Hau-nted, hau-nted. Zi dead live here. Go back, go back!"

Matty stared him down. "Very funny. I should make you stand guard outside my house."

"What, and spoil all the fun?"

"Fun, pish. Just another excuse to try and snag more souls." Realizing what she said, Matty lowered her voice and looked around to make sure no customers had overheard. "But that's just between you and me, right?"

"My lips are sealed."

"Ah, hell. Me and my big mouth." She shooed Stan off with two sets of fingers. "Go on, do some work, would you? Write something, run some copies. Just ignore what I just said."

"I'm on my way."

She shook her head and disappeared down an aisle.

As for Amanda and Stan, they decided to stay home and practice their own magic, one of the fringe benefits of being in love with a witch.

Stan had learned that, while Amanda could be tight-lipped and serious, she did have a sense of humor. If he encouraged her, she could keep him entertained for hours with various tricks and spells.

When he came home from work on Halloween night, she met him at the door. "I have somewhere I'd like to take you."

"Really?" he said. "Do we walk or ride a broom?"

She grinned and scolded him. "Don't be an ass or I'll turn you into a lizard."

"Oooh, a lizard." He made his best reptilian face. "Please, Ms. Witch. Don't turn me into a lizard." Tongue flick. Hissing sound. "I promise to be a good boy."

Amanda put her hands on her hips. "Do you want to go with me or not?"

"Okay, if you promise to leave me alone. No funny stuff."

"I promise, if you promise to stop being a smart ass."

Stan gave her a military salute. "Promise."

"Keep your coat on. We're going for a stroll."

"Can I put my stuff down?"

"Yes, yes. Please. Just hurry."

Stan laid his stack of papers on the kitchen table. As Amanda waited by the door, he grabbed her from behind and pulled her close. "Sorry for being such a smart ass." He kissed her on the cheek. "Now, where are we headed?"

She spun in his arms and smiled. "You'll see. Let's go."

Amanda took Stan's hand and led him past the town center, through a series of small residential streets—Bluebird, Oak, Red View—until they reached the west edge of town.

They turned south down a narrow paved street with a weathered sign that read Black Oak Lane. The street was empty. No houses or other signs of human habitation. The pavement ran like an index finger into the hills.

"Jesus," he said. "I've lived here all this time. Never been in this part of town."

Amanda tugged on his hand. "Keep walking."

As they reached the end of the street, Stan noticed a small dirt walkway that lead to a tiny cabin. It looked old but well maintained—brush removed, a small clearing around the perimeter.

Amanda led him down the path and halted at the door. "Well, what do you think?"

"Of what?" he said.

"This." She pointed at the cabin.

Stan took in the rough-hewn structure. "Cozy, rustic, small. So. What is this place?"

She smiled slyly. "My office."

"Your what?"

"My office. You have your office, I have mine. This is it."

Stan walked around the building and rubbed his fingers against the prickly boards. It was quaint, like a little one room cottage a couple might rent for a weekend.

"Wow. Your headquarters. Impressive."

"Don't be sarcastic."

"I'm not. Really. It's beautiful. Do I get to go inside?"

Amanda turned the knob and pushed open the door. "Enter my domain."

Pulling some matches from her coat, she lit candles around the room. As gold illumination flared against the walls, Stan noticed a pretty curtain across the one primitive window and an assortment of items organized on shelves. There were no chairs. They sat spread-eagle, facing each other on the plank floors.

"So," Stan said. "What does a witch do in her headquarters? And by the way, when did you move in here?"

"Sari let me have this not long after I came. It's my think tank, so to speak, where I come to cast spells, or sometimes just relax. Like a getaway. You know, a place to escape from the big city."

Stan chuckled. "Ah, very funny."

"No one knows about this except Sari, and now . . . you."

"Well, thanks for letting me in on your little secret."

"You're welcome."

They sat and watched the candles throw off yellow light and black shadows. Stan noted how much thought she had put into this place. Some shelves. A few books. Various amulets. Small knick knacks. Everything within arm's reach.

"Impressive," he said. "So—"

"So?" she echoed.

"How does a nice girl from Cleveland end up here? I have to admit, it's kind of strange to think you could come from such an ordinary family and become a, well—"

"Witch?"

Stan exhaled. "Yeah."

Amanda brushed her fingers across the floor. "It's a long story."

"It's a long night. We've got lots of time."

She sighed. "The usual kids stuff. You know, fascination with Ouija boards, ghost stories, that sort of thing."

"Yeah, I did the same thing when I was a kid but I didn't grow up to be a witch."

"I read books, got interested in the real thing. I met someone in high school whose parents were involved in spells, conjuring, contacting the dead. We got to be friends and they took me under their wing. When I graduated, I found a coven not far from Cleveland. Guess you could say I had a knack for it. You went to college, so did I, except everything I did was very hands on." She swept a finger over the flame of a nearby candle. "Turns out I'm good at what I do."

"Yeah," he said as he pulled her finger from the fire and held it lightly. "I've seen you in action." He lowered her hand into his lap. Their eyes locked. "And Sari?"

"He found me."

"Really?"

"Well, I guess it's better to say he called me."

"Why am I not surprised?"

"One night—this was maybe four years ago—I had this very strange vision. I actually saw him in a dream, felt the need to seek him out. I moved from Ohio to Oregon, bounced around a bit, and eventually discovered Freeland. That was the start."

"Amazing."

"And now," she said, pulling his fingers into her hands, "here we are."

"You and me—"

"Cozy."

A moment passed as they enjoyed the candles. Stan moved closer, stretched out his legs, and put his head in her lap. "This is nice. Thanks for the invite."

"You're welcome. Now, it's our little getaway."

A thump startled them. Stan raised his head. Something tapped outside on the wall and followed with a long scratching sound, like a nail being dragged across the wood. It moved from the far side of the cabin to the front door. There was a knock and a breathy voice whispered, "Amanda."

They both sat up and stared at each other.

"Expecting visitors?" he said.

She shook her head. "Just you."

"Well, obviously, we've got company."

"Obviously."

Stan turned and faced the entry. "Care to answer the door, or should I?"

"How brave are you?"

"Depends on who's there."

"Well, in that case, we'll both go."

They stood up and eased forward. Stan reached for the knob and pulled cautiously, expecting something or someone to kick the door in his face. Nothing. They stepped outside and waited for their eyes to adjust to the dark.

"Hello?" Stan called out.

"Something's here," Amanda whispered.

"What? I don't see anything."

"It may not be visible. Doesn't matter. I know it's here."

Stan was unsure if she was joking or serious. It was Halloween after all. "Tell me what we're dealing with here."

"I'm not sure. Yet." She stood still and peered down the street.

Another sound floated past them, like a coat or a skirt rustling.

"Hello?" he called again.

A voice rose nearby. Not loud. More gentle and melodic. It began to sing a song eerie and sweet like the tone of a flute.

Amanda and Stan edged forward, looking north up the paved finger. With the help of light from the stars and a rising half-moon, they finally saw something. A woman clothed in black—her body small, thin. She stood with her back to them.

The woman turned to face them. She had dark hair cascading down her flowing garments, intense eyes, and a kind face.

As she moved toward them, her steps were slow and graceful. She lifted her arms with the easy flow of a ballerina. "My music," she said in a lilting voice. "A song for you."

Stan stepped protectively in front of Amanda. "And you are?"

"Breena," she replied. She looked at Amanda and smiled. "Of course, I know you."

Amanda slipped around Stan and bowed. "Deestus procurus."

"Deestus procurus, my sister."

Stan looked back and forth between the two women. He crossed his arms and pointed a finger at each. "You two know each other?"

"Yes," said Amanda, "though not formally. More by reputation. Fellow witches from different regions."

"You mean like the Wizard of Oz, Witch of the North, Witch of the East, that kind of thing?"

"Roughly, yes."

"Well now, what are the odds, the two of you standing here on the same street?"

Amanda waited. "Deliberate, I would guess."

He turned to Breena. She nodded.

A thought popped into his head. "Oh, hell, this isn't a showdown is it? Like, Halloween night, battle of the witches, that sort of thing?"

"It's nothing you have to worry about," Amanda said gently.

"Well, I don't know. For all I know, you guys—"

She interrupted. "Just be patient and wait. You'll see."

Breena paused, then began to sing another tune. This one higher, more melodic, with the haunting quality of a wolf's cry.

Stan had to admit, it was quite beautiful. Not like any singing he had ever heard. By the time she finished, he was mesmerized.

Then, to his surprise, Amanda replied with her own song, equally sonorous and captivating. Different in sound from Breena. Deeper and with an Irish lilt. As she finished, Stan realized something in his soul had been drawn in and massaged.

Breena extended a hand toward Amanda. "Come away with me, my sister."

"Ah, my sister," said Amanda, "I cannot."

Breena glanced at Stan, then her. "You are bound?"

Amanda wrapped her arm around Stan. "Yes, on two counts."

"Ah," she said. "Such a pity."

As Stan watched Breena and Amanda, he sensed his connection to this conversation. There were more than words passing between them and somehow, as he followed their eyes, he was part of the discussion.

"I fear it will not go well for you," said Breena.

"Perhaps not," said Amanda, "but we all choose our own destinies. Mine rests here."

Breena gazed up at the sky, as if she was ready to fly among the stars. "Then I will sing for both of you."

Amanda released Stan and bowed. "And I for you."

As Breena started up the street, she stopped and studied Stan. "And you? Will you also sing for her? Even when she is gone?"

He glanced at Amanda. She squeezed his hand as encouragement. "Yes," he said firmly. "I will sing many songs."

Breena's eyes were inquisitive. She touched her cheek. "Then it's true, you really have been captured."

Stan thought for a moment. "Yes, I suppose that's true."

"You both will endure much sorrow," she said as she wheeled around and drifted into the hills.

Stan and Amanda stood for several minutes and watched where she had vanished.

Overcome with curiosity, Stan turned to Amanda. "What the hell was that all about?"

"A mother witch," said Amanda, "beckoning me to come join her."

"Is that a good thing?"

"It's a great honor. Maybe once in a lifetime."

"You turned her down."

"Yes—I did." She swiveled, her gaze locked on Stan.

He thought he saw it again, that flash in her eyes, the way she looked when he first saw her standing by her bedroom window. "Why?" he said.

"Do I have to spell it out for you, Stan? My heart's here, and my soul. Sari would not take this lightly, though, in the end, he would have to defer."

Stan gently pulled her toward him. "And?"

"And what?"

"You said you were bound by two counts."

"I did, didn't I." She nuzzled her chin on his shoulder.

"Well, I'll be—"

"Don't let it go to your head."

He squeezed Amanda a little tighter. "The only thing in my head right now is you. Not even Sari can compete with that."

Amanda wrapped her arms around his neck.

"What did she mean?" he said.

She pulled back and caught his eye. "About what?"

"About me singing when you're gone? And both of us enduring great sorrow?"

"I don't know," she said and glanced away.

"Amanda?"

"I don't, really." She laid back on his shoulder. "Whatever she saw, we'll just have to wait it out."

Stan put his hands on her cheeks and raised her head. He wanted to see her eyes. He wanted her to see his eyes. "Well, you're not going anywhere if I can help it."

She pulled on his neck and kissed him. "Good. Now, that's settled. Let's go back inside. I'm cold."

"Can do," he said as he cradled her in his arms.

A breeze kicked up and rustled through some nearby trees. By now, the moon had risen. The horizon was shimmering in fluorescent light. They took a slow stroll up the path to the cabin, kissed each other at the doorway, and stepped in.

December 4, 1980

It happened every year in Freeland. The celebration of what was known as the Dark Festival. It always coincided with the weekend of the first new moon in December. Stan guessed the party may have descended from some ancient winter tradition passed down for generations. Most likely Sari had confiscated and adapted it as a celebration of the strange powers that ruled Freeland.

With all the party announcements and special ads Stan ran in the paper, the festival was good business. Of course, Dahlia Rutan put in an ad for the big bash at her house and there were smaller notices for séances here and there.

Matty usually placed an ad for special pricing on party goods. Her odd items were especially popular this time of year. Things like old cat skulls and powders made from snake skins that brought good luck if sprinkled over your left shoulder on the first night of the festival's new moon.

She also carried a line of deer eyeballs preserved in small mason jars—their pitiful white orbs pleading with customers from behind liquid and glass. Rumor had it that the eyeballs had special powers to predict a person's future. They were used at local séances in lieu of Tarot cards.

Always one of her best sellers, her source was a well-guarded secret. And, for whatever reason, she was sneaky about putting them on the shelf. One day the shelf would be empty, the next morning, there would be there, haunting Stan as he walked in his office.

For the Dark Festival, the town gathered at the Danny Akern Recreation Center promptly at midnight and celebrated till dawn. Food and drink were provided by the Circle and Sari was the MC.

At the end of all of this, he oversaw a ceremony which he affectionately called "the eye," similar to what outsiders might think of as a crystal ball. It was Sari's attempt to gaze into the future and predict some things that would give local folks a glimpse into their potential future.

Stan worked overtime to publish a special Dark Festival edition of the Reporter. He was careful to add extra copies to his normal print run and leave an additional pile in a rack near the front entrance to the grocery. To his delight, they always went like hot cakes.

In November, Amanda and Stan had moved in together in his old house and become happily domesticated. Not yet married, but definitely a couple.

Tonight Stan sprawled on the living room couch and perused through an old magazine from the 1930s while Amanda cooked in the kitchen. He had no idea what she was preparing, but whatever it was, it smelled good.

Someone knocked on the door. When Stan opened it, Sari breezed in and stretched his long frame across the couch.

"Come on in, make yourself at home," Stan said as he watched Sari ease himself down.

Sari's legs extended halfway across the room and his arms reached the entire length of the back. He was an imposing figure in their small house.

"Thank you, brother," he said as he gazed around the living room, then let out a long sigh, "You are happy here, no?"

Closing the front door, Stan entered the living room and propped himself against a wall. "Where, in Freeland or this living room?"

Sari searched his face. "Ah, I see your wits are sharp tonight. I would love to stay and match words, but it is not you I am seeking."

At that moment, Amanda walked in. "Sari?"

"Yes, my Amanda. It appears you are the featured chef tonight. Some time you must come and cook for me as well, be my special guest."

For a moment, they all looked at each other. Having Sari as a guest was never comfortable. Something always lurked beneath his surface and any words exchanged with him had to be measured carefully.

"Stay tonight if you want," she invited.

Stan gave her a quick glance.

"I think not," Sari said. "I think your man here would rather have you all to himself." He smiled enigmatically. "Am I not right?"

Stan hated Sari's knack for reading his thoughts. Furthermore, he believed that Sari found the relationship between him and Amanda amusing. The idea of a witch and a journalist in love. Perhaps, in Sari's peculiar way, he was poking fun.

Amanda questioned Stan with her eyes.

Stan glanced between Sari and Amanda and shrugged. "So, Sari, what brings you out tonight?"

"Preparing, as I always do this time of year, for the festival. You are coming, no?"

"I'm always there. You know that."

"There, yes, but really there, I wonder."

"I come and watch. I'm not sure what else you expect."

"Perhaps this year will be different. This year, I hope your lovely woman will participate. I have a special spot for her at the end. And Amanda, perhaps you might see this as something of a coming out?"

Amanda had returned to the kitchen to keep an eye on dinner. She poked her head into the living room. "How so, Sari?"

"Some do not know how talented you are. Not even your special man here. I thought perhaps a small demonstration of your gifts might be appropriate."

"You want me to do what?" she called from the stove.

"Give us an idea of who you are and what you can do."

Amanda wiped her hands with a dish towel and returned to the living room. She looked surprised. "You want me to let other people know—I'm a witch?"

"In so many words, yes. But show us with some type of small demonstration. I know you're capable."

Amanda hesitated. "You're sure this is a good idea?"

"I am. It is time for you to rise." He extended his arms until his long fingers spread straight toward the ceiling.

Stan could tell, by the look on her face, she was taken back. Yet, something told him she was also pleased.

"Well," she said, "let me give it some thought."

Sari tapped his large hands on the couch. "You will do well and our audience will be delighted."

He rose and filled the living room with his tall frame. "You should be proud of your woman," he said to Stan. "She is capable of great things."

"I'm always proud of her," said Stan.

Sari walked to the door, waved at both of them, and strode out to Paradise Road. Stan stood in the doorway and watched as he disappeared into the night.

"Come on," said Amanda. "Dinner's ready."

Stan remained in the doorway. His appetite had disappeared. In its place, an uneasy feeling. Their cozy arrangement had been called out. Amanda was being brought forward.

As he returned and sat at the dinner table, he thought about what this meant for both of them. They ate their meal in silence.

When he finished, Stan sat back with his hands in his lap and watched Amanda eat. "Well, I guess now we're all in this together, huh?"

Amanda put down her fork. "I guess so. Pretty big leap."

"Meaning?"

"He's willing to give you the benefit of the doubt, for my sake. He knows how much I care about you."

Stan reached across the table and covered her hand. "Well, isn't that sweet of him?"

"Don't be snippy. You're part of our family now."

Part of the family, he thought. Not something he cared to hear. Whose family? Certainly not in Freeland. His family had been placed out of bounds. He had been exiled to this tiny outpost in the Oregon foothills minus his family. But Amanda. Family. He saw the possibilities.

On Festival night, Amanda and Stan made the rounds to their friends' houses. People circulated around town, bundled in their best winter garb. There were brief meet and greets on the way to each house. Their last stop was at Dahlia's.

As usual, she had decked out her house and provided a brilliant spread. Lots of folks made this their special destination. No one wanted to miss one of Dahlia's parties, not even Sari.

Dahlia was pleased when Sari arrived and made sure she gave him preferential treatment as an honored guest.

When Sari saw Stan and Amanda in the living room, he approached and spoke to her. "You are ready, no?"

Amanda nodded. "I am. I hope you'll be pleased."

"I have no doubt," he said and passed into another wing of Dahlia's large house.

Amanda was excited. Stan rarely saw her this buoyant and happy, this at ease in her element.

Matty came up and put her arms around their backs. "So, come on you two, when are we going to hear about a wedding?"

"Mind your own business," Stan said playfully.

"I'll mind mine if you mind yours," she said. "But then again, you're a news man. My business is your business, right?"

"Good point."

"Well, then, I'm returning the favor."

Amanda pulled Matty close to her side. "You keep reminding us, Matty. I don't mind."

"I will and you're welcome." She let loose of them and merged into the crowd.

Amanda hugged Stan and gave him a light kiss. "She's our good luck charm, you know."

He put his arms around her waist. "Maybe she is, but so are you, to me anyway."

"You're sweet."

"You're beautiful."

"Guess that makes the vote unanimous."

Near midnight, Stan and Amanda left Dahlia's and moved over to the recreation center. From one decorated venue to another, they entered and gawked at the splendid setup. For such an ordinary building in a very small town, Sari had gathered some outstanding arrangements. Ceiling to floor, special lighting, beautiful floral arrangements.

"He's a genius," Stan exclaimed to Amanda. "Where's he get all this stuff?"

"I told you, he's well connected," she said. "He's got resources all over the world. Never underestimate his contacts."

"He can find anything, huh?"

"Or anyone."

Her last statement brought him up short.

Over the next few hours, a variety of entertainments were provided, ranging from the amusing to the spooky. Donnell's played their usual Irish music. In between games and events, Amanda and Stan took in a few of the dances.

Like children at a carnival, everyone delighted in the spectacle. Combined with good food and drink, time passed quickly and dawn arrived. The crowd was tired but thoroughly entertained and wanting for more.

Sari came on stage and stood in front of the audience. "Good morning, my friends. It's time, you know." There were immediate shouts and clapping. This was the event they had anticipated all morning. "That's right, it's time for . . . the eye." Sari laughed, a low chuckle that rumbled through the auditorium. "Ah, the future, the future. What does it hold?"

There were a few shouts from the audience.

"I'd like a bigger house," someone called out.

"How bout a car?" another said.

From a far corner, a voice shouted, "How about . . . more souls?"

The energy in the center crackled. "Ah, yes," Sari said. "Wouldn't we like to welcome more souls to our little village? Some fresh new faces for our gathering?" Some cheers went up and more hand claps. "In the meantime—"

At a table in the middle of the stage, he seated himself and lowered his head near the curved opening of a long half-moon-shaped wooden bowl. The sides were highly polished and ornate with strange markings near the top.

Sari's head nearly touched the bowl's lip. A light emanated from the bowl and illuminated his chocolate face. "Mmm, what's this?" he said. "Someone will receive a new child into their home. A baby boy, healthy and vibrant."

Some ohs rippled around the room.

"And the village will be blessed with a marriage." He caught the eyes of Amanda and Stan. "Now, I wonder who that might be?"

Several heads turned in their direction. Underneath the table, Amanda squeezed Stan's hand.

"Ah, here's something I know you always wish for. Many deer and duck next year. A very good hunting season."

This drew cheers and whistles from some of the men.

"I see that someone has a mother. Yes, she has died and wants to assure her daughter she's fine and happy. The daughter has her mother's picture in a locket. It's stored in a locked cabinet in her house."

At a table ten feet in front of Sari, Dari Matilda dabbed her eyes with a napkin and murmured, "Thanks, Mommy, I love you too."

"And here is a very momentous announcement." There was a sudden change in the room's atmosphere. The lights in the room flickered and something bright hovered just above his head. Members of the audience gasped with delight.

"There will come an angel among us, God's angel, to heal someone very sick. You have lung cancer, but do not worry. I will speak to this angel and you will be made whole."

A few more women wiped tears from their eyes. Others raised their hands and whispered praise.

Sari looked up at the audience. The soft light from the bowl rose and spread like fog across the ceiling. "And now, my brothers and sisters, I would like to introduce you to a family member who has lived and worked here for some time discretely going about the business of helping and preserving Freeland."

As Sari spoke, Amanda stood up and walked toward the front.

"She has gifts that you may not know about, but here in Freeland, the humble are the mighty and those who serve are the ones anointed."

Amanda reached the side stage.

"She is presented to you this morning, at the break of dawn, to demonstrate a taste of her divine calling. She comes to us now with my blessing. Amanda Beston."

Some gasps rose up. Then a unified cheer. Sari exited off the stage. Amanda was left alone front and center.

She closed her eyes for a few moments. Then, lifting her arms, she stretched her fingers toward the audience. There was an audible buzzing noise, like an exposed power line separated from its generator. The white light across the ceiling drifted toward her and was drawn into her fingers. Her arms began to glow.

Amanda reached both hands behind her head and hurled them forward. The light shot from her fingers and spread through the audience. For a brief instant, they were all covered in white and the stage in front of them disappeared. Then, with a thunderous crash, the room was plunged into darkness.

In an instant, the lights returned, but Amanda had disappeared. Everyone searched around the room until someone pointed toward the main entrance and cried, "Look, she's over here."

From one side of the hall to the next, Amanda had traveled across a space of perhaps two-hundred feet in no more than two seconds. She stood by the door and waited for the crowd to find her.

One by one, everyone turned and recognized where she had landed. A smattering of cheers rose up. Then the whole room clapped.

"Jesus Christ," said Stan.

Someone patted him on the back and said, "Quite a gal you got there, Stan."

Sari reentered the stage. "And that, my friends, is why we live in Freeland. We are an amazing village, are we not?"

This drew more cheers and a standing ovation.

"Go forth now and enjoy the day. Remember how blessed we are to be together."

And that was it. Event over. Entertainment complete.

But where was Amanda? Stan turned and scanned the room. No sign of her. As he ran outdoors, dawn was emerging. In an hour or so, the sun would rise over the hilltops. It was bitter cold and Amanda had left her coat in the hall. Stan couldn't imagine where she would go without it.

His next destination—the Circle. But when he arrived, it was locked tight. No evidence of anyone outside or inside. He grew alarmed. His only remaining thought. Home.

Stan sprinted down the road and up the sidewalk. The front door was open. Encouraged, he hurried inside and yelled, "Amanda." No answer. Living room, dining room, kitchen. Still no Amanda. Finally, he found her in the bedroom face down on the mattress.

"Amanda," he yelled. No response. He stood by the bed and gently shook her. "Amanda?"

She uttered a faint groan.

"Holy Christ, what's happened to you?"

Stan eased her over and put a pillow under her head. He lowered his head next to her lips to check for breathing. Shallow but steady. Her skin was hot and dry and her lips badly parched. He ran to the kitchen, grabbed a glass, and filled it with water.

Lifting up her head, he poured a small amount in her mouth. Some of it dribbled down her neck, but she responded to the taste. Grabbing the glass, she gulped it down. He ran back to the kitchen and brought her more. She drained a second glass.

"Honey, what's wrong?" he said.

Amanda whispered something but he couldn't make out the words. In the bathroom, he wet down a towel, brought it back, and wiped her forehead. Then, he undressed her and applied more wet towels.

After an hour or so, she began to regain consciousness. Slowly at first, then a look of recognition as she woke up and saw Stan's face. Stan removed the towels and tucked her under the covers.

"Stan?" she groaned.

"Yes, dear."

"Where am I?"

"Home, baby. You came home after the festival."

"Oh, did I really—"

"Well, this was where I found you anyway. After that little stunt, I'm not sure if you walked or flew. All I know is, you're here. Alive. Safe."

"Guess I overdid it a bit, huh?"

"Goddamn right. Don't ever do that again, please."

Amanda wrapped her fingers around his wrist. "Worked pretty good, huh?"

Stan carefully slid his hand underneath the back of her head. "Too good. Not worth repeating."

She moved her fingers up and down Stan's arm. "Was Sari pleased?"

"I don't give a damn whether he was or not. It's not important at this point."

She looked distressed. Her voice was hoarse, her words labored. "Don't say things like that, Stan. His good will is important."

"Enough to kill you in the process?"

"Well, blame me if you have to. I didn't anticipate the fallout."

"Now there's an understatement."

"Worked, though."

"Let's not talk about that right now. Let's just focus on getting you back to normal."

Stan helped Amanda pull herself up against their headboard. Minute by minute, she was becoming more lucid. He tried to ensure that she was comfortable.

"I'm not normal, you know that," she said as he adjusted her pillow.

"For sure," he said as he pulled an extra blanket up around her chest.

"You've got to accept that these things will happen from time to time."

Stan stretched out beside her on the bed. "Not too often, I hope. I'm more concerned about your safety. Guess that's why you keep me around."

"You're a good man."

"I'm your good man."

Amanda pulled at a bed sheet and secured it around her body.

Stan could tell she was thinking. He recognized that intense look of concentration and how she nibbled at her thumb.

She nodded at him. "He said there'd be a wedding."

Stan leaned against the headboard and slipped his arm around her shoulders. "He did, didn't he?"

She tilted against him. "You think he knows?"

"What?"

"Our future."

"I have no idea."

"He said there'd be a wedding."

Stan gathered her in his arms. "I'm not disputing that."

"So?"

"So what?"

"Us, we, you and I, let's."

"We'll talk about that when you're better."

Amanda closed her eyes and fell asleep. Then her eyes flew open and she looked up at Stan. "Worked pretty good, huh?"

"Stop that. You're scaring me."

When she looked at him that way, he always felt some deep energy inside her, like something caged in a nuclear weapon, hazardous and explosive. Would she love him or kill him? Hold him tight or blow him to bits? He could never be sure.

Propped lightly on his shoulder, Amanda drifted off to sleep. For an hour or so, Stan just laid quietly and listened to her breathe. Her sheet slipped down. Her arms were delicately crossed, fingers open and relaxed.

Stan was amazed at how peaceful and pretty she was in her prim, naked pose—slim snow white body, symmetrical breasts, dark hair cascading on her shoulders. In this position, she might have been a model for Renoir.

Stan brushed his fingers across her breasts like an artist sketching a delicate painting and realized two things. How much he loved her. How frightened he was to be with her.

III

March 19, 1981

With the coming of spring, Stan always liked to run items in the Reporter about seasonal changes. It gave his readers a sense of what's coming. Warm weather, wild flowers blossoming, hints of summer. Even though it was still cold in Oregon, he knew folks would be anxious to get outdoors. As usual, Johnny Nelson was one of the first to be out and about.

This morning, Stan noticed Johnny hiking toward town and decided to accompany him on his way to the office.

"Hey Johnny," Stan called out as he hurried down his porch steps.

Johnny stopped and waited on him to catch up. "H'lo there, Stan. Beautiful day, ain't it?"

"Still kind of cold, but spring's not far off. You must be getting anxious."

"Yes, sir," he said with a grin. "Man goes stir crazy in winter round here. Wouldn't mind moving to Arizona."

It was an inside joke in Freeland. Every winter, folks would discuss among themselves who they might nominate to convince Sari to move their town south. They always joked about the lucky candidate, daring so and so to take up the challenge. So far, no one had volunteered.

Johnny stopped in mid-step. "How bout you? Wanna go?"

Stan laughed. "Still trying to find a patsy, huh?"

Johnny winked and grinned.

"No thanks," said Stan.

"Well, then, here we are, freezing our asses off, waiting for spring." Johnny started walking again.

Stan thought about it. "I guess you're right."

They marched quietly together for fifty yards or so before Johnny broke off and entered a small trail by the side of the road. "Well, this is my stop," he said and gestured to Stan. "Having breakfast?"

"No, gotta get a little work in first. I'll be over later."

"Well then, be seeing you. Keep up the good work." He waved at Stan and disappeared down the thin path.

As Stan walked over to his office, he was already thinking about upcoming stories. Easter was about a month away. He was mapping out in his head various ideas he might bring to the table. As he stepped into the grocery, Matty wrote notes at the counter.

"Hey, Matty," he said. "I saw your boyfriend on the road this morning."

"Clark Gable's dead, honey," she said without glancing up. "Ain't no one else I'd consider at this point in my life."

Stan laughed. "Clark? Screw Clark. I'm talking about Johnny."

"Johnny? Oh Lord, he may be sweet, but I'm not a bee and I don't need any honey. My hive dried up years ago."

"I don't believe you. I see that look in your eyes when he stops by."

"You mean this look?" She crossed her eyes, clenched her lips, and puffed out her cheeks.

"No, but I bet if you did that to him he'd get excited."

"Yeah, that's the problem. Damned if I do and damned if I don't. Men are like fungus, you know. Useful sometimes but hard to get rid of."

"You're a tough nut, Matty, but I bet he might soften you up."

"Not without a hammer to my head."

Stan winced. "Ouch."

"Ouch is right." She returned to her notes.

Johnny did drop by later that afternoon for a chat. Stan stood in his doorway as a tease to Matty. She saw him, waved him off, and returned to their conversation.

Several days went by without another Johnny sighting. Not unusual for this time of year. It was still early for him to be out on a regular basis. A week passed, then two. One day in his office, it hit Stan. Where had Johnny been hanging out?

On his way out to lunch he asked, "Say, Matty, you seen Johnny lately?"

"No, not since the last time you tried to butt into our conversation."

"Kind of strange, don't you think? He's usually around here a couple times a week."

"Yeah, not like him to avoid me. Think I might have hurt his feelings?"

"Maybe one too many brush offs?"

"Hard to know. You men are so sensitive. Gotta coddle your egos. Maybe I shouldn't have told him about my other boyfriend."

"Clark?"

"No, Cary Grant."

Stan's mouth opened and closed. "Wait a minute. What happened to Clark?"

Matty, who had been stocking a shelf, stopped and planted her hands on her hips. "I've got more than one, you know. At my age, I keep a stable."

Stan shook his head. "Jesus, you're a bad girl."

"Well, play loose, play hard, that's my motto." She returned to her work.

Stan watched her lift canned corn onto the shelf. "Okay. Well, let me know if Johnny comes by. I'm a little worried."

"Go check his house if you want. He doesn't wander far from there."

Good idea, Stan thought.

After lunch, he walked over to Johnny's house to see if he was home. If something had happened, maybe he could help.

Stan knocked. No answer. He eased the door open and stepped inside.

"Johnny?" he called. Still no answer. As he poked around, he noticed some dirty dishes in the sink.

He checked Johnny's bedroom. His bed was made up. His closet was open and a hanger poked out from the rest of the clothes. It was in the middle of a row of coats, a sign that Johnny had taken one off the hanger to go outside.

Stan sat down on Johnny's bed. "Johnny, Johnny, where have you gone?"

Leaving the house, Stan returned to the Circle and found Sari at his usual perch behind the bar. There were a couple of customers at the counter.

"Say, Sari," he said, "I'm kind of worried about Johnny Nelson. Have you seen him lately?"

Sari shook his head. "Not for some time, brother."

"When's the last time he ate here?"

"Hmm, now that you mention it, maybe two weeks ago. We had a nice chat about his past hunts. Claims to be quite a deer expert."

"Two weeks? He's been gone two weeks and you haven't noticed?"

Sari's face went blank. "In this town you are free to appear or not appear without my permission."

It was a challenge. Stan knew it. A warning of sorts.

Stan refused to back down. "There's nothing in this town you're not aware of."

The restaurant went quiet. All eyes turned to Stan. Even Amanda pulled up and watched.

Sari remained quiet.

"Two goddamn weeks," Stan muttered and hurried out.

Stan barged through the front door and bulled past Matty. He was headed for his office to cool down and think.

"Stan?" she called out.

He passed by and disappeared through the doorway.

In a few minutes, Matty slipped into his office. "Everything all right?"

Stan banged a pencil on the end of his desk. "Johnny's missing and no one around here seems to notice."

Matty furrowed her brow and looked at the ceiling. "You're right. I was wondering about that myself. Given I usually have my ear to the ground, I know that sounds kind of strange, but it's not unusual this time of year for him to stay inside."

"That's the problem. He's not at home. He doesn't seem to be anywhere around town. He's gone missing."

"Really?"

"You'd think Sari would notice something like this."

Matty waited. Her eyes never left Stan. "You should know by now, no one understands what that man thinks. It shouldn't surprise you."

Stan took a deep breath. "You're right, as usual, my lady."

Matty smiled. "I'm always right. You know that."

Stan stopped bouncing the pencil on the table and locked his hands together. "All right. We know that no one wanders far from here without returning. So, if he's not home, where might he be?"

Matty sat down in Stan's folding chair, crossed her legs and wrapped her hands around her knees. "Other than here, he usually goes around to places like Larry's, maybe Pin a Rose. I know sometimes he takes meals to Delores Magana. She can't see very well to cook anymore. And—he likes to hike out in the boonies. I always try to talk him out of that but you know how men are. He never listens to me."

Stan loosed his hands and stood up. "Well, at least I have somewhere to start."

Matty smiled. "You're a good friend, Stan."

"Johnny's like a father to me."

"Hope you find him. Wouldn't want anything bad to happen. He's my friend too, you know."

"If I find him, I'll let you know."

"Same here."

He marched up to Matty, gave her a pat on the shoulder, and headed out the door.

Stan went to all the places Matty suggested. He also stopped and talked to several folks on the street. The response was all too familiar. No one had seen him lately. It appeared he had dropped off the planet.

He circled back to Johnny's house and sat on a patio chair by the front door. For a half-hour, he rehashed his steps and questioned whether there was any place he had missed. One idea kept troubling him. Maybe he had gone out into the hillsides for an early spring hike.

Stan remembered the coat hanger jutting out from Johnny's closet and thought back on the weather the day he and Johnny last talked. It was unseasonably warm for March. Highs in the 50s. Warm enough for Johnny to walk with a light coat on, take his usual route down Paradise Road, get back in time for breakfast.

He remembered what Johnny had worn—an orange windbreaker, something a hunter might wear, with some type of sports logo on the chest.

From Johnny's porch, Stan set out on a hunch. East on Paradise Road to the spot where Johnny had veered off after they last met. He knew Johnny had been okay that afternoon. But what about that evening? Had he gone back?

It was a bright day. A brisk breeze blew in Stan's face. Looking side to side, he searched for the small trail that Johnny had used that morning. About a quarter-mile down, he spotted it. A little thread breaking south.

It was quiet. Stan's steps echoed as he trampled on brush and hard-packed dirt.

About twenty yards in, the trail veered east. It was a perfect place for a short hike. Just off the beaten path, not far from the road.

Stan examined the trail for any signs of recent activity. There was new growth along the path. Sprigs of green among the wild brush.

He came to a second trail that turned south again. His heart sank as he remembered Larry's warning. If Johnny had become confused and accidentally taken this trail in the evening, he could be in serious trouble.

Taking a moment to catch his breath, Stan's dread began to build. He remembered his own experience with the missing hunters, the sounds of dogs in a pack, the sight of Walt appearing at the blind. He was lucky to escape that night. Maybe Johnny was not so fortunate.

About a fifty yards in, Stan spotted a trace of orange just off the path. Fighting off panic, he approached it. A coat. As he turned it over with his foot, it looked familiar—Johnny's coat. Nylon. Bright orange with red sleeves. Sports logo on the chest. And there was more. The coat covered a pile of Johnny's clothes. Shirt, pants, shoes, T-shirt, underwear, socks.

Turning in a complete circle, Stan looked for some trace of his body. Seeing nothing, he left the coat and clothes and kept inching along the path as he carefully searched for clues. There were signs of movement. Dried brush broken, the ground dragged, fresh dirt in spots.

About ten steps in, Stan saw something adjacent to a pile of brush. Bending down, he took note of its reddish brown color, the color of dried blood. More of it as he continued on and then, on an open patch of ground, a large brown circular pattern. Here the clues ended. The evidence, however, was clear.

From the looks of it, Johnny was gone for good. He wouldn't be back to cheer up the town, flirt with Matty, or take meals to Delores Magana. Someone caught him out at night and exacted the ultimate price.

Stan's dread now turned to anger. "Shit, Johnny," he cried out. "Who the hell would do such a thing to you?"

It was one thing to do this to outsiders, quite another to do it to someone as gentle and easy going as Johnny. Even if he was out too late, Stan had no doubt whoever did this knew him and still chose to carry out their hideous act. He could barely control his rage.

Backtracking on the trail, he picked up all of Johnny's clothes as evidence for the court.

When Stan arrived at the Circle's front door, he pressed Johnny's clothes to his chest and took several deep breaths to calm himself. "For you, my friend," he said as he entered.

Sari spotted him. "Good afternoon, brother."

The entire restaurant went quiet. Amanda stood near the kitchen entrance. When she spotted Stan holding Johnny's clothes, she froze.

Approaching the counter, he laid them piece by piece across the width of the bar. Coat. Shirt. Underwear. Socks. Methodically, as if creating a collage.

Sari followed him as he unfolded each item, curiosity written across his face. "You have brought me some strange gifts, no?"

"Johnny's clothes," Stan said, "found out in the brush, not far from where someone probably cut up his body."

Sari examined Stan's face. His mysterious eyes narrowed. "You are talking trouble here, brother."

"I would hope so, for someone in this town." Stan waited like a trial lawyer. He turned to face the customers. "One of our own, no less."

"You know this because—"

"I found them right where I told you. This is all that's left. Clothes and a big blood spot on the ground. The rest of him's missing. You and I can guess what happened."

Sari folded his hands together. "I do not guess at these things."

"No, that's right. There's nothing around here you don't know. In fact, my guess is, you probably know the exact moment when it happened. You probably know the where and who and why."

"What I know at this moment is that you have claimed these are Johnny's clothes. What happened to him I cannot say—"

"Or won't say here in public. Another one of your victims, Sari? Maybe you ran out of hunters and decided—"

"Be careful with accusations, my brother. They have a way of coming back to bite you."

"Then let them bite me right in the ass, but don't dick around with the truth here. Someone in this town killed Johnny, but you probably already know this. I want to know who and what we should do about it."

Sari circled from behind the bar to the front of the counter and sorted through each piece of clothing. Everything in the restaurant stopped. Amanda writing. Freddy cooking. Casual conversation. No one spoke or left their seat.

Sari stopped sorting and nodded at Stan. "You can show me the scene?"

"I can. About 50 yards west of here off Paradise Road, a small trail up in the hillsides. I found his jacket just off that path. His blood stains were not far from his jacket. Trouble is, his body's missing. I have no idea where it is, but I can guess what happened to it."

"But you have no proof, other than these clothes?"

"What other proof do you need? I'm telling you exactly what I found. I've seen the blood stains. I've brought you the clothes. You think I'm lying? You think there's something wrong with my eyes?"

Sari lifted up Johnny's shirt and examined it front and back. "I do not doubt your observations. Your passion perhaps is flawed. But at this moment your eyes, sharp as they are, see more anger than truth."

"I'm not sure I have a choice." Stan turned again to the patrons in the restaurant. "I don't want Johnny to get buried under the rug. Some asshole's already dragged him off to God knows where. If we're talking about people in this town killing each other, for all I know, I could be next. Who's to stop anyone in this town from killing anyone?"

Sari looked around the restaurant, then back at Stan. "I can assure you. That will not happen. Does that satisfy you?"

"No. Not even close. What *will* satisfy me is finding Johnny's killer."

Sari put down the shirt. His voice was reassuring. "Then that is what we will seek."

"Fine. Show me a little justice. Find the killer. Johnny deserves it. He didn't deserve to die like this. Whoever did this is a goddamn scumbag. And you, of all people—one of your own."

Sari stood and waited.

Drained by anger, there was nothing else for Stan to do except leave the restaurant and go home.

In his living room, Stan observed the fading light of sunset darken his walls. Stretched out on his couch, he lay with an arm across his eyes and his head propped on a cushion. His mind and soul had grown dull and listless from shock. Several empty beer bottles were piled up nearby.

By the time Amanda walked in, the house was completely dark. She flipped on a hall light, then the living room light.

"Goddamn it, turn that off," Stan half-growled, half-slurred.

She turned off all the lights and waited in the hallway. "I'm sorry about Johnny," she said softly.

Stan sat up. His body slouched forward and his hands dropped between his knees. "Thank you, but sorry doesn't bring him back."

Amanda laid a bag of groceries on the floor and stepped into the living room. "You were pretty gallant in there."

"Foolhardy, too. Who knows if I'm next on the local hit list."

"Johnny was a friend. I think Sari understands that."

"What I don't understand is Sari saying nothing. He knows every tit and tat in this town. He had to know about Johnny."

"Sari doesn't let other people into his thoughts. If he knew, which I don't doubt, then what he thought about it was his own secret. But that's Sari."

Stan buried his head in his hands. "Okay, let's suppose that's true. So why did he keep Johnny's death a secret? I always thought among us, doing harm to each other was off limits. Someone's crossed the line here."

"Yes, he's aware of that. More important, everyone in town knows it too. He'll have to do something about it."

"You think I embarrassed him?"

"You did—not a good thing. Down the line, he may extract his pound of flesh. But, in Johnny's case, your words hit home."

Stan fingered an empty beer bottle and absentmindedly rolled it on the floor. "Why Johnny? I don't get it."

Amanda kneeled in front of Stan and gently rubbed his temples. "Why people kill each other is never clear. Maybe Johnny was just in the wrong place at the wrong time. Doesn't justify it, but shit happens. Innocent people die every day."

The point hit home. Stan could think of nothing else to say. Amanda moved the beer bottles away from the couch, slid next to him and folded her arms around his waist.

When she touched him, he could feel something being released, a great sea of pain, a breaking dam of anger. The image of Johnny being tortured and murdered overwhelmed his thoughts.

"He was such a good man," Stan said as he choked up and cried. She waited patiently for him to let loose his grief.

In the morning, Stan walked into the Circle for breakfast. As he sat in his booth, all eyes veered toward him. Perhaps the word was out, the rumor mill flowing. After Amanda took his order, Stan fiddled with a salt shaker and stared out the large bay window.

Sari approached his table and stood motionless, his great, long frame towering over Stan like a skyscraper. His eyes were intense, his words measured. "There will be no more deaths like Johnny's."

Stan rested his hand on his cheek and looked up. "And you know this because—"

"Because, as you know, I am the village elder. I am also a man of my word."

For a moment, they locked eyes. Then Sari spun around and strolled back to his usual place behind the bar.

As he sat, things returned to normal. People went back to their regular conversations. Sari's priestly declaration had returned order to the town.

Amanda brought Stan his breakfast and brushed her hand on his shoulder. Stan ate in silence and went back to his office.

"Here's a story for you," Matty said as Stan passed by. "Why is Larry Levin not in his butcher shop today?"

Stan stopped and gave Matty a curious look. "I don't know. Why?"

Matty plopped both hands on the countertop. "Well now, you're the reporter. Do your own investigation."

"About?"

"I've given you the clues, now go hunt. The fact I didn't notice Johnny missing, you can understand. He kind of came and went as he pleased. But give me some credit for knowing most of what goes on in this pinhole town."

Stan raised his hands. "You know—"

Matty mouthed each word carefully. "That Larry Levin isn't in his butcher shop."

Stan wheeled around and went directly to Larry's Butcher Shop. It was closed. Unusual for this hour of the day. The butcher shop always opened promptly at nine a.m. It was now ten-thirty.

Larry always carried fresh game. Deer, duck, even an occasional pheasant. Rumor had it that he was an expert hunter with an eye for the exotic. Today, however, the store was dark. No sign of any exotic meat on sale. No sign of Larry.

Larry never returned to his shop. In fact, he was never seen again around town.

The next day, Reid Dammers, a man known around town as equal to Larry in his passion for hunting, took over the place. The details of the transfer were a well-guarded secret. The name was changed simply to Reid's Butcher Shop. No muss. No fuss.

Though Stan was curious, this was not something he could explore in the paper. He did mention the change in ownership as part of his community news. Other than that, it was business as usual.

Whatever happened to Larry happened out of sight. Sari had made his views known. Stan chose to respect his privacy. He also accepted that justice for Johnny was served in some opaque fashion. Invisible justice. Sari justice.

On a warm May morning as Stan sat in the Circle eating his usual breakfast, Sari slipped up behind him and stood next to his booth.

"You seem happy," he said.

Stan put down his fork and looked up. "I miss Johnny."

"But time passes, things work out, life goes on."

"Time passes, things work out, Johnny's not coming back."

"And neither is Larry."

He looked steadily at Stan, his eyes speaking as judge and jury.

Stan put his hands on the table. A loosening of grief and anger ran through his body. It appeared that Johnny had been given his day in court. Maybe an obscure court with its own ideas about truth and justice. A court in the background. A court that remained squarely in the hands of Sari. But at least it carried out a silent code of its own and Larry had been punished.

Sari continued to peer like a warden from his tower. "You are satisfied with this?"

"Stan took a large bite of scrambled eggs and chewed thoughtfully. "I'm happy you found Johnny's killer."

"And that you have found justice, as you requested?"

Stan carefully laid down his fork and stared out the bay window. It appeared Sari was measuring his thoughts, and Stan was acutely aware that he was being measured. "Good enough," he said.

Sari returned to the bar and resumed his perch. He understood. Stan understood. The case was closed.

August 13, 1981

The leading story for this week in the Reporter: *Heavy thunderstorms lead to power outages*. On and off, Freeland had been pelted by bad weather, gusts of wind, lightning strikes, and loss of electric power.

Several times in the last few days Matty and Stan had been left in the dark. When this happened, there wasn't much work to be done. They would just sit near the front door of the grocery store and enjoy the show.

As usual this time of year, a couple of poor stragglers had sought out the Circle for shelter and a bite to eat. Stan assumed, by now, they were in the process of being assimilated into life in Freeland.

In the back of his mind, he thought about Dave. He tried to imagine him planning his rescue. What was his plan, and when would he come back?

In spite of all his years in Freeland, Stan's thirst for freedom had not been quenched. Watching the storms pass through, he tried to picture what his family might be doing at this exact moment. Dave and his Dad working at Rohr. His mom volunteering in the library or digging in the garden.

On the surface, Freeland looked placid. Stan's sense, however, was that there was tension among the troops. In spite of Sari's peculiar sense of justice, the disappearance of Johnny and Larry had made everyone aware. Life in Freeland could be fragile, according to Sari's moods. The ripples this sent through the town were still breaking and for many, Stan's confrontation with Sari put him at the center of the storm.

This morning, as they sat on the porch and waited for the power to return, Matty spoke up. "You know, you're going to laugh at me, but I miss Johnny."

"I'm not laughing. I miss him too," said Stan.

"Can't get over how he just disappeared."

"Me either. Damn shame."

"Guess when it's your time, it's your time."

"Don't say that Matty. It wasn't Johnny's time. Someone just decided that for him. It doesn't matter if he was old. He should still be here."

"You're right there. Kind of leaves a hole, doesn't it?"

"A crater."

"It's a damn shame."

They sat together for an hour without speaking. The storm outside reflected their mood. When the power came back on, they returned to work without their usual banter. Neither of them felt much like kidding around.

That night during dinner, Stan laid down his fork and broached the subject with Amanda. "Lots of folks around town really miss Johnny."

Amanda aimed her fork at a mound of salad on her plate. "I do too, no doubt." She took a bite and chewed thoughtfully.

Stan watched as she held her fork loosely, her eyes fixed on her plate. "The subject ever come up at the Circle?"

Amanda stopped. "Not really. I think most folks assume it's a done deal. Nothing left to discuss."

Stan picked his fork up and began lazily twirling a strand of spaghetti. "Kind of strange how we let things slide around here sometimes."

"They're not sliding, Stan. It's more like pieces moved around on a chess board. Things are always shifting in Freeland. You know that. And you know who's doing it."

Stan watched her watch him. "You happy with the way things turned out?"

"Whether I'm happy or not doesn't matter. It's the nature of things around here."

"That's my point. The nature of things is always in the hands of one man."

Amanda took another bite of salad. "That's our tent. We're stuck with it."

For a moment, Stan watched her eyes and tried to read her face, but she was so adept at keeping her thoughts locked away. He could tell, at this moment, she was playing diplomat. "You really believe that's the high and low of it?"

She stopped eating and placed both hands on the table. "You know where power lies in this town, Stan. Only this power is not just political. It's deep, spiritual, and dangerous. It can tell what you think when you think it. You know you're on dangerous ground here. If you want to feed on discontent, you could easily disappear just like Johnny, or Larry. You know that's the truth in this town."

Stan frowned and pointed his fork. "That sounds like a threat."

"Stop it, Stan. It's not me you have to worry about. Words carry around here. Sari can detect them from a great distance. I'm a thin line of protection for you, but, as you know, that could change at a moment's notice."

Stan knew she was right, but it did nothing to ease his mind. Knowing reality and accepting it were two different things. Ever since the death of Johnny, it seemed his brain had kicked harder against his confinement. Still, for Amanda's sake, he surrendered to the inevitable truth. "You're right."

"I am and I say it because I love you. I want us to live long and be happy together. You know that."

"I do."

"Then stop this discussion and for God's sakes don't spread this around town. Please."

Her eyes flashed at him before she resumed her meal. When he saw that look, he understood where she was coming from. She knew better than he the powers at work here. She was helping him navigate troubled waters. He dropped the subject.

Still, something in Freeland was amiss. It was hard to pinpoint. Vague like a hunch, yet hovering. As Stan watched people on the street, the usual meet and greets were missing. The storms continued for the next several days and, instead of generating excitement, the atmosphere hung over everyone's head like a heavy blanket. Even Matty noticed.

"Say," she said to Stan one morning. "What the hell's going on around here? I swear, people are a little grumpy this week. Reuben Moss asked me where the Farmer's Dairy butter was. I told him we're out but the Dairy Mart is right next to it. Just as good. Butter is butter. Comes from the cow, spreads on toast. He gets mad and stomps out of here, you know, like I was trying to trick him. I don't get it."

"Kind of strange for Reuben," said Stan.

"We've been friends forever. Why's he mad over a stick of butter?"

"Maybe it's the weather."

"Weather, smether. Seems like the whole town is in a snit."

Stan rested his elbows on the counter. "Can't tell you, Matty. Just seems odd around here since Johnny disappeared."

"Well, I hope it passes. It's hard enough being stuck in Freeland without someone making your goddamn life miserable. We all have to get along, you know. I miss Johnny, too. You don't see me chewing out someone else for it."

"I hear ya."

No doubt about it. Stan realized the mysterious bad weather had taken its toll.

For the next edition of the Reporter, Stan ran a small article on how to resolve grief. He hoped, if someone was struggling with Johnny's death, it might help them deal with his loss. He also ran a small memorial about Johnny's life. Some type of tribute seemed fitting for a man who had lived so long in Freeland.

Still, Stan noticed odd things. Alice Johnson and Ramona Deerborn arguing in the street. In the Circle, too, the mood was gloomy. Hardly anyone talked out loud.

He passed Dave Neuman near the front door of the grocery and asked about his garden. Dave blew him off, claiming he was too busy to chat. Dave passing on gardening was unheard of in this town, but his face told the truth. He didn't want to talk to him.

Sari appeared in Stan's office doorway late one afternoon. Rather than his usual diplomatic approach, Sari started the conversation with a blunt question. "You are unhappy, no?"

"Unhappy?" said Stan.

"Yes, I am feeling that you are the source of a great unhappiness."

Stan pushed back in his chair and formed a steeple with his fingers. "I don't understand."

Sari waited a moment, then walked in and sat down. His eyes never left Stan—piercing, dark, foreboding. He leaned forward. "I am aware of your unhappiness. Do not try to hide it."

"I think something's not right, obviously, but it's not just me. The whole town seems to be unhappy."

"Yes, but you, my friend, are the source. You must trust my judgment on this. And if something is not right, then we must see what we can do to change it."

"You mean some kind of magic spell, something like that?"

"There are many solutions, but the first part is the telling. From you to me."

"I said there was a problem. You seem to be aware of what people think around here. Seems to me we all could do with a little airing out."

Sari's eyes zeroed in. "Then let us begin here, with you and your unhappiness."

Stan shrugged. "Why me?"

"Ah, my brother, do not avoid my question. Because I know you are unhappy and I choose to talk to you about it. So, here and now, we must discuss ways to bring you back to happiness. That is my role as leader of this town."

"You know, Sari, you can control a lot of things in this town, but not what I think, or feel."

Sari's movements slowed, like a hunter preparing to pounce. His eyes became even more piercing. "There are many things I control that you are not aware of, things more complex than your feelings. But do not underestimate my powers. I know when you are happy, when you are sad, and I know when you are the source of happiness and sadness in this village. When that happens, I am obligated to do something about it."

"Are you telling me you can make people happy all the time?"

"I can control those things that affect people's happiness, yes."

"Well, obviously, something's off, then, if I'm unhappy. Because, the source of my unhappiness is not something you're able or willing to change."

"There are many routes to restore happiness. Some are easy, others more complicated."

Stan placed his hands flat on the desk and stared back at Sari. "Then I'm a big problem for you, aren't I?"

Sari smiled, but not out of friendship. It was a very cunning smile. "No more than others I have overcome. In the end, they are all solvable."

"I can't help how I feel, Sari. If you're trying to force me to feel different, I don't see how that's a solvable problem."

Sari shifted in his chair and braced himself against the wall. "Stan, my brother, you are unaware how truly old I am. This town has been here in some form or fashion for many decades, and I with it. Can you imagine how it has survived all these years?"

"Let me guess. Hmm, the sheer force of your will?"

"And the ability to create harmony. You, Mr. Blankenship, are unharmonious. I am asking you to reconsider your position."

"Do I have a choice?"

"You have many choices, perhaps not all you would like, but within my sphere, I am giving you options. Choose wisely." The last two words were drawn out for emphasis.

Stan understood all too well the scope of this statement. He let out a slow breath. "All right. I promise. I'll think about it."

"That is a good start. Share my words with your lovely mistress. Count on her for guidance."

He stood up, head almost flush to the ceiling, extended his arms and gave a loud clap. In the close confines of the office, it was so jarring that the sound hit Stan in the chest and rolled him back into a small cabinet.

Sari towered over him for a moment, then strode out of the store.

Stan remained in his chair, the noise still ringing in his ears.

When Sari left, Matty came to the doorway and peeked in. "Everything all right?"

"Hardly," Stan said glumly. He rolled his chair back to his desk and stared blankly at the floor.

"Not a good visit, huh?"

"Nope."

She stared at him, shook her head, and returned to the store.

As Stan walked home, he watched people hurry to escape the first drops of an approaching thunderstorm. There was fear on their faces, more fear than you would think over something as natural as rain. He greeted one of his neighbors. She didn't look up, didn't stop to respond. Perhaps they had been warned off. Perhaps they knew that standing too close to him could bring disaster.

He walked into his house, put down his work stack, and sat at the small dinner table in the kitchen.

From being an esteemed member of Freeland, he had become a gadfly. The impact of that thought, combined with Sari's warning, left him shaken.

His one solace. Amanda. If there was consolation to be found, she would offer it. If there was wisdom, she would find it. Stan took a beer out of the refrigerator and sipped on it as he waited for her to come home. When she stepped through the doorway, he hurried to embrace her.

"Well, this is nice," she said.

"You can't imagine how happy I am to see you."

She pulled back and searched his face. "All right. Tough day huh?"

"Very."

"Want to talk about it?"

"No, just go about the house and let me enjoy your company."

"You're sweet, but I know something's wrong, so when you're ready, we'll talk."

"Fine."

She moved about the kitchen to prepare dinner. Stan sat at the table and engaged her in small talk.

That night, as the two of them ate, a huge squall boiled up and whipped the house with wind and rain. Suddenly, the power went out. They moved their dinners to the living room and huddled on the floor with several candles.

This storm was fierce, the worst Stan had experienced since coming to Oregon. Their small house shook and the windows rattled. The wind pounded the door.

"Jesus," he exclaimed. "Where'd this come from?"

"I do wonder," she said.

He noticed her eyes fixed on him. "You wonder what?"

"You asked the question and I responded."

"I know, and you said, 'I do wonder.' What's that supposed to mean?"

Amanda's expression remained steady. "I'm wondering the same thing as you, where the storm came from."

They listened to the rain build intensity. It howled more like a hurricane than a normal thunderstorm.

"This can't be good," he said.

"No," she said and moved closer to him. "And I think you know more than you're telling me."

Stan laid his dinner on the floor and let his hands fall in his lap. "You're implying something, but I'm lost here. What are you getting at?"

"Talk to me, Stan. I don't think you're being truthful here."

"This is odd coming from you. Tell me what you mean, Amanda. You're giving me the creeps."

"These kinds of storms. I've seen them before, but not just from weather."

"Well then, what?"

Her eyes—dark, demanding. She knew something.

"Come on, spit it out," he said.

Amanda gestured. "Do I have to spell it out for you?"

"Well, some hint would be nice."

She paused and looked away. "It's a spiritual convergence."

The statement hit Stan like a brick. "Sari?"

Her expression said it all.

"Oh, you think he's sending me a message?"

"It's one alternative to consider."

"Now why would you think that?"

"I think you should take his words very seriously."

"What words?"

Amanda gripped her hands together and pressed them to her chin. "I know he came to see you this afternoon."

"Oh, Jesus, now suddenly you two are conferring?"

"Does this surprise you?"

"Okay, so now Stan has become a problem and I'm the subject of conversation between mighty Sari and my lover. Anything else I should know?"

The pain on her face spoke volumes.

Stan stood up and gestured. "You can't do this to me, Amanda. You asked me to trust you. This is not trust. This is trading inside information. You've crossed the line here."

Another flash of lightning and a loud thunderclap brought the conversation to a halt. It was followed by a second bolt and an increase in wind speed. Stan ducked as if it had been aimed at his head.

Amanda eased up and reached out her hand. "I'm trying to help you, Stan."

"Help me do what? Be compliant, stay out of Sari's way, keep your status as his protégée?"

Amanda backpedaled from the room and stood with her back to the door. "I can't help you if you won't listen."

"I can't trust you if you keep ratting me out to Sari."

"I came here at his bidding. I'm part of his community."

"Does that make you his snitch?"

"We all belong to Sari, Stan. Why is this so hard to understand? There's no choice in this matter. In Freeland, it's Sari or die. For you to believe otherwise is just madness."

"And what about love?"

Amanda pushed her palms against the door. "Love only exists if Sari chooses it," she said. "If you want love, if you want me, you have to accept that premise. Nothing, absolutely nothing in Freeland exists apart from Sari."

Stan knew she spoke the truth. Their love, their living arrangement, all purely at Sari's discretion. Still, to accept that their whole lives were connected to Sari's power was more than he could stomach. As he arched his back against the living room wall, Amanda read his face.

She gave him another sad look and opened the door.

The storm's blast pinned him to the wall. Any words he tried to yell were caught in his throat. He watched her brace against the wind and step out on the porch.

At that moment, there was another thunderclap, the loudest of the evening. Stan put his hands over his ears. A blinding flash sent electricity through the house and into his body. He screamed and collapsed in a heap on the floor.

When he regained consciousness, Amanda was gone. He stumbled to the door and called to her but the violence of the wind pushed him back and made it impossible to run after her. There was nothing he could do to bring her back.

As he slammed the door, the storm let up. Within minutes, the wind died and the rain stopped.

The ensuing quiet was painful. Blue sky. Beautiful summer evening, but Amanda's voice and presence—gone.

After sitting in the living room for an hour or so, Stan went out on the porch and watched the night descend.

More than just a sunset, the waning light was his life being swallowed by darkness. His thoughts had bitten him in the ass and so had his misplaced trust. It appeared that, step by step, Sari was squeezing him back into the fold.

First, a warning. Then the storm. Now, the removal of Amanda. If Stan didn't come around soon, he feared what else might happen. Even worse, how long before the reality of Sari's will crushed his soul?

August 20, 1981

Stan's misery had become the town's torment as stifling heat buried the town for a week. Tonight in particular there was no sleep or relief in sight for him. Also, no paper, no visits to the Circle, none of his usual routine. His house had become both a prison and an unbearable sauna.

Stan stripped to a light pair of shorts and a netted jersey.

He was compelled to escape and dig out some moment of solace. His only hope—a long walk in the hills. Under the stars, with the deft touch of the wind, he might find comfort. Or he might be killed. Either one was fine with him.

Throwing on a pair of slip-on shoes, he dragged himself out of the house and walked west on Paradise Road. Despite the evening's oppressive heat, the quiet landscape and occasional small breezes made him feel better.

Perhaps there was magic in these hills far greater than Sari or Amanda. Perhaps the night would take pity and let him fly away.

Was there mercy in this Oregon wilderness? His mind began to float away, toward home, toward Dave, toward hope. All this just from the rhythmic sound of his shoes on the pavement and the pendulum motion of his legs and hands.

A half-mile west, he stopped and stood perfectly still. For the last week, his solitude had haunted him. Here, it seemed to buoy him, the sky and land serving as a genuine comfort to his soul.

He planted his feet on the road and let their presence wash over his body. The idea occurred to him. The answer to his yearning for freedom. To become lost, so lost that no one, not even Sari and his unholy hunters, could find him. Sari could occupy his mind, but could he search an entire state? Could he find a needle in a haystack?

Under this spell, Stan swerved left and plunged into a patch of trees. Whatever direction this was, it was better than being buried in his house with all his damned memories. He would push through until the land refused to let him pass, or his heart gave out from exhaustion.

"Hey, O mighty Sari, you sonofabitch," he shouted. "You want a piece of me? Come and get me." He balled a fist in the air and hurried past a few pines trees, striking out at loose branches and thick shrubbery. As he jogged, he shrieked, "To hell with all of you."

Then he tripped on a root, rolled several times over a rough bed of rock and dirt, and came to rest in the middle of a thick grove of shrubs.

Lying flat on his back, the grove seemed to form a small nest around him that framed the heavens. Stan could make out a few constellations and tiny clusters of stars.

His mind roamed freely. How did starlight make it this far? Did our light make it to them? Were there lonely beings on planets directly above him? Maybe some of those beings at this very moment hiked through their own sandy hills. Maybe two pairs of eyes simultaneously searched the heavens for lost love. These thoughts ran through his head like a Buddhist meditation. Before he knew it, he had fallen asleep.

Something woke him. Voices, not too distant. Low murmurings. Occasional laughter. He lay still and tried to regain his sense of direction.

Carefully and with some pain, he rose up and sat cross-legged. There they were again. The voices.

He had a choice to make. From his vantage point, he could remain hidden and safe. But something dared him to move out.

He recalled Larry and Walt's admonition. *Don't wander these hills at night.*

Why, he asked? And if he found out why, what would happen?

Stan broke out of his brush arbor and trekked as quietly as he could toward the noise. It came and went. Sometimes he had to stand still and wait for it to return. But he knew he was making progress. The voices were louder, closer. Not blaring. The ebb and flow of human conversation.

Stan noticed a flicker over the top of a boulder. A campfire. Sneaking closer, he heard the voices echo from the edge of a clearing. As he peeked from behind a large rock, he could make out men around a fire. And directly across from him, no more than 20 feet—Sari.

Stan's heart pounded uncontrollably. Confronted by actual danger, his fantasies about death and dying vanished like fog under a morning sun. His senses became acute. His hearing. His sight. And fear.

He took a deep breath and peeked around the rock. Who else was here? Sari. And Rick Dumont. And Walt.

"Ah, cripes," Stan murmured in what he hoped was a barely audible voice, at least to the bloody crew sitting around the campfire. Then he saw Sari stop and fix his eyes on his hiding place.

"You are lost, my brother?" he said.

The men around the fire also stopped and stared in the same direction.

Stan had been called out. He stood up and walked toward the fire.

"Well, don't you look dandy," Walt said. "Out for a picnic I guess?"

"I'll be goddamned," Rick added.

Stan was chagrined, like a kid who'd just had his pants pulled down in front of his class. He wanted to run, but he sensed that escape was futile. Whatever happened to him would be their choice, not his.

Sari remained quiet.

Stan could see he was thinking, analyzing, like a finely tuned machine.

"Sit down," Walt invited. "Help yourself to some coffee." He reached to his side, pulled out an empty cup, and poured from a pot that had been sitting near the fire. Holding it up, he waited for Stan to respond.

Stan took the cup and sat.

Sari nodded. "What brings you here, my brother, so far from home?"

Stan took a long swallow, laid down the cup, and set his eyes firmly on the fire. "It's been a hell of a week. Too hot tonight. Can't sleep."

"Yes," Sari said like a doctor to a patient. "I can see you've been troubled. No paper, no visits to my café, no Amanda. Perhaps you've been hiding under a bush waiting for us to find you."

"Well," Stan said with resignation, "If that's the case, I'm not hiding now."

"Yes," Sari said, "here you are and here we are. Perhaps the spirits have called us all together."

Walt crossed his well-worn hiking boots and gave Stan a hard look. "I thought I told you to stay out of these hills at night."

Stan turned his head and stared. "Why, Walt? What goes on out here that you need to keep secret?"

Walt grew silent. Sari as well. The four men watched the fire for several minutes, hypnotized by the flames.

Sari cupped his hands together and gently blew into them. Then he rested an elbow on his knee and spoke. "We have offered you an invitation. Perhaps you have given that some thought."

Stan dropped his head and covered it with his hands. "Jesus," he whispered.

"The offer remains."

Lifting his head and resting his chin on his knees, Stan said, "And if I do?"

Sari extended his hand. "Then perhaps whatever is troubling you will go away."

Stan let out a long sigh. "Why are you doing this to me, Sari?"

Sari wedged his chin in the crook of his thumb. "I am a leader of this village, entrusted to guide you wisely. This, my brother, is my guidance to you."

"And what about Amanda?"

"She remains with us, ready to return. And if you choose to be a part of us, she can be persuaded to rejoin you. You must realize by now how she loves you."

Stan paused and mulled over Sari's words. As he watched and waited, he noticed something strange. Sari, Rick and Walt began to change. They were like framed photos whose pictures were transforming. Their faces, lit gold by the fire, grinned like hungry hyenas. Their bodies shimmered like heat waves rising off a desert highway.

Sari himself grew larger, his eyes wider and more intense. "Give yourself to me," he said with a rumbling voice. Then he pulled out a long sharp knife and held it high in the air. "Give yourself up and move from death to life."

Stan froze in terror. In their hands he noticed they each had a coffee cup tilted so he could see inside. The cups were filled to the brim. The liquid—red, bright red, blood red.

"Remember the saying I taught you," Sari said, his voice increasing in volume. "Blood is life and man's blood will give us life—forever."

Then Sari lowered the knife and pointed the tip at Stan. Stan watched it shine in the firelight.

"Then give me blood," Stan said hesitantly. "Give me whatever it is you have. Give me life. Give me back Amanda."

Sari pulled the knife perpendicular to his body. "That, my brother, is a wise choice."

Before Stan could blink, Sari thrust the blade through his chest. It was painless, surgical, straight to the heart. When Sari removed it, the tip carried a small drop of blood. His blood. Then his head grew dizzy and light. His final thought—how nice it would be to fall asleep.

Stan woke up and was startled to find that he was still in his shrubbery fort. The stars were shining. The night was dark. Sari was nowhere to be seen.

"Goddamn it," he mumbled. A dream, as terrifying as any he had ever had in Freeland. And yet not just a dream. Stan wondered if Sari had stepped back into his head and turned his thoughts into a vision. Had Sari invaded his mind and shown him the future?

Suddenly, a wave of nauseating terror struck him. He scrambled out of his hideaway and fled as fast as he could through the brush. He wasn't sure where he was going. He might be lost. No matter. He had to run somewhere, away from this place. Like the town, it seemed that even the ground around him had been overrun and cursed by Sari's presence.

Bursting onto Paradise Road, he tripped on its asphalt edge and sprawled out like a penitent priest. His skin was scraped and bloodied. Pain shot through his arms and legs. For several minutes, he couldn't move. From terror. From exhaustion.

He anticipated who might be following and what was to come. The hunters. The knives. The bloody feast. But no one arrived to cut out his heart. The silence surrounded and stretched over him like a sheet. He turned his head and saw the tiny crumbs of asphalt melded together into a single road that stretched into infinity.

Stan's head began to clear. He pushed up gingerly and hobbled toward his house.

When he reached his gate, another wave of nausea hit him as he realized there was no Amanda to take care of him. He would have to tend his wounds himself and sleep alone.

He winced as he walked up the steps and into the bathroom. Wearily he cleaned himself and stripped down. Even with his best effort, he was still a mess and would remain so for quite some time. What choice did he have? Simply to bleed on his sheets. Bleed by himself, then look at those blood stains on his mattress for months afterward.

Falling diagonally on the bed, he buried his face and lay still. In this position, he groaned desperately for a moment and dozed off.

September 20, 1981

The evening sunlight slid through the living room window and formed a gold bar on the wall about a foot long.

Stan noticed it and covered his eyes, as if he had been jolted by sudden light in a dark cave. His house had in fact become just that. Curtains pulled, he had barely been out for the last month. Just short trips to Matty's grocery, mostly for beer.

His normal paper delivery had been forgotten. No meals at the Circle. Most of his time had been spent right here where he lay, trashed by a drunken stupor. The waning sun revealed him sprawled on the living room floor amidst a growing collection of beer cans and half-eaten meals.

The loss of Amanda had been the loss of his will. As a result, he had been engaged in a last ditch effort to isolate himself from the tentacles of Freeland and perhaps die by alcohol. But not yet. At this moment his scalded eyes made him quite aware that he was still breathing.

"Shit," he mumbled as pulled himself up with his back to the couch. He looked around the room. "Shit." There was ample evidence of how the wheels had fallen off. The light simply ripped the band-aid off his misery.

Stan's brain had become addled and his sense of location, the day of the week, his routine and purpose, had fizzled out like a leaky balloon.

He stood and wobbled like a worn out fence post. Turning toward the kitchen, he stumbled over a plate and beer bottle. Both went clattering off to the side. He was sober now with a splitting headache and no relief in sight.

Turning on the kitchen light, he waited for his eyes to adjust, then went to the sink, poured himself a glass of water and sat at the table. The same table where she used to sit across from him.

He laid his elbows on that table, rubbed his eyes, and gawked at her old chair. That was as much motion as he could muster for the time being. The walk from the living room to the kitchen had exhausted him.

He heard the sound of footsteps on the porch. A knock on the door temporarily piqued his interest. Then, like a puff of wind, his interest disappeared. He sat and listened as someone continued to bang on the door.

"Open up, Stan," a voice demanded. Matty.

Stan refused to budge. Not with his messy life displayed around the house. Not with his pity party on the verge of discovery.

She persisted. "Come on, Stan, I know you're in there." More knocking.

Stan laid his head on the table and waited for the knocking to stop.

He heard the door creak open and remembered. It had no lock. Slow footsteps entered through the doorway. A moment of quiet ensued before Matty murmured, "I see you've been busy in here."

Stan turned and faced the small woman with the gritty smile, only she wasn't smiling.

"Well, ain't this a fine mess," she muttered. "Fired your housekeeper, I see."

"I didn't fire her," he said. "She walked out the door."

Matty picked her way through trash, entered the kitchen, and leaned against a counter. "And you being a man, I spose you wouldn't know your broom from your ass?"

They looked at each other before a small smile broke out on Stan's face. "You have a way with words, my dear."

Matty folded her arms. "Why, yes I do, thank you very much."

"I hereby bequeath my paper to you for safekeeping."

"Maybe you're right. Maybe I should be the editor and you can run the damn store."

Stan propped his head on his hand and tilted forward in his chair. "That would be a nice change of pace. You could learn to typeset and I could order bras."

"You could, but I pity the woman who bought them."

Matty eased her tiny frame in the chair across from Stan. Amanda's chair. "Brokenhearted, are we?"

"Thoroughly," he confessed. "Not to mention way plastered."

Matty crossed her legs and tapped a finger on the table. "Life's a bitch around here sometimes. Whole town feels like it's been hit with cholera or TB. I don't know what you did, but in your highly educated way, you've managed to bring down one hell of a curse, and considering where we are, that ain't easy to do."

Stan straightened and looked squarely at Matty. "All I did was tell the truth about Johnny. If that's the curse you're talking about, I hope the whole town rots and goes to hell."

Matty turned in her chair and wrapped her hands around her knees. "Well then, I guess that's where we're at. Mule's got a right to be stubborn. That's his nature. Sure does make life inconvenient, though, for the rest of us."

"I guess," said Stan.

"Seems though, that a mule ain't a mule unless he's working. He is a mule after all. What else is he gonna do? That's also in his nature."

"Well, then, that's where your little story falls apart."

"I suppose so, though it seemed to be working there for a bit." A small crack of a grin appeared.

Stan couldn't tell if she was sympathetic or simply amused by his sorry state. Knowing Matty, it was probably some of both. "You're enjoying this, I suppose?"

"Hmm, parts of it, yes, but not the way you're thinking."

Stan put his elbows back on the table and laid his chin on top of his hands. "And just what are you thinking?"

"How you kind of put a crimp in Sari's little bubble. He's got a problem and you're it, but he thinks you can be valuable and he certainly sees the advantage of having you and Amanda together, so he's being oh so patient, and yet you continue to be a little piss ant. You're an ornery son of a bitch. He's not used to that."

Stan chewed on Matty's observation. He looked around the kitchen, up at the ceiling, across to the refrigerator. "Ornery, maybe. Stubborn, definitely. Guess that's why Amanda hightailed."

"Well, orneriness has its limits. Hell, look at me. I've been a bitch my whole life and what've I got to show for it? Nothing but a piece of shit grocery store. Still, I think about the alternative and maybe the store doesn't seem so bad."

"Well good for you, Matty, but I'm not seeing the bright side here."

Matty took a moment to rub her palm across the table top. "There is no bright side, Stan. Thought you'd know that by now. There's only survival and some of that comes with a high price tag. You have to choose your level, so to speak and keep kicking—you know, like a mule's supposed to."

Stan exhaled and grimaced. "Is this your way of giving me a pep talk?"

Matty motioned toward him with her wispy hand. "Aren't I the one who always shows up to pull your butt out of the fire?"

He thought for a moment and looked sheepish. "Yeah, I guess."

"And, given my nature and reputation, why the hell would I do that?"

Again he thought. "Honestly, Matty, I haven't a clue. You are a very mysterious woman."

"Well, don't you dare spread this around, but . . . I like your company, I like the fact you're no stool pigeon and frankly, I kind of like reading your paper. It's grown on me, you know, like a moss on a rock."

Stan was taken back. It was a frank confession he had never heard her make to anyone. He realized the risk she was taking, the effort she was making to pull him out of his spiral. He realized that in the town of Freeland, Matty was his only friend. For the first time, he smiled. "Are you flirting with me?"

Matty kept her eye contact level. "Hell no, why would I do that? You're almost a married man."

"Emphasis on the almost part."

"Like any storm, this will blow over, but for now, you could use some help, especially in this house. And not working just makes it easier for Sari to write you off. If you've got any of that mule left, I'd like to see you use it to stick a wrench up his ass. In my own demure way, I'll be there to help you give it a shove. Not that I could be of much help, given my womanly nature, but whatever oomph I could muster—"

Stan smiled again. The idea of two sets of hands shoving anything up Sari's ass was inspiring. "That's an image I could enjoy."

"Me, too, but first we've got to get the funk out of you." She looked around the kitchen and made a face. "And out of this house."

The picture of his empty house hit Stan again. Hard. His voice cracked. "I think she's really gone, Matty. Not sure how I'll survive that."

Matty placed both feet on the floor and slapped her hands in her lap. "She's not gone, gone, Stan. She ain't dead, just on vacation. Can't say where she is at the moment, but she's one of Sari's birds, so I think he's probably got her stashed somewhere for safe keeping."

"Until when?"

Matty shook her head. "Hell if I know, and it doesn't matter. You can't do much about it right now anyway. All that matters is getting you back on your feet. Leave the rest to work itself out."

Stan tapped an index finger on the table. "How long?"

Matty rose and began to unclog a sink full of dirty dishes. Stan could tell she was done talking, except for the question she hurled over her shoulder. "You gonna sit there like a lump of coal or help me? It's your mess here. Start with cleaning up that damned living room."

Stan paused, thought about his other options, and decided there were really only two. Live or die. Dying had its benefits, but he wasn't ready yet to throw in the towel. Not if he knew Amanda might come back. Picking up trash seemed preferable.

"Okay," he said and left the kitchen to clean up the living room.

October 8, 1981

Stan had managed to get the paper back on track. While he had been away, he discovered that many people had paid his office a visit.

Not that he was surprised. Ever since the paper's launch, Stan's desk had become a mailbox where people dropped off notes incognito. Comments about news articles, requests for information, hand scrawled ads and notices. He honestly had no idea how they slipped in and out without being noticed. Matty had a sharp eye but even she admitted folks around here could be downright invisible.

Stan had gone so far as to set up a box on his office wall where these ghosts could leave their messages. It worked pretty well. And if something was left in his chair, Stan knew the writer considered it urgent.

Since he had returned, he noticed that the mail had picked up considerably and the messages were becoming more strange and angry. There was a divide in town and Stan seemed to be the lightning rod. If he were a politician, the sharp swing downward in his poll numbers would be alarming.

Do yourself a favor and keep your mouth shut was one he pulled off the chair this morning. This one was debatable. Either a warning or a word to the wise. Maybe both.

You are a nice guy but sometimes you cause too much trouble. Stay out of other people's business, please. Oh well. As a reporter, Stan expected some of this.

And yet another. *You had a good thing going. Why are you messing it up?* He assumed this was some veiled reference to Amanda's disappearance.

Stan could see where this was going. A boulder rolled downhill was difficult to stop. Now that he had kicked it over the edge, the rock was picking up speed. He tried to think of some way to do damage control. No options came to mind.

The perception was not limited to letters. In the Circle, when he walked in, he sensed a change in conversation. Heads down, whispering. Often, he overheard discussions about Amanda—where she'd gone, what Stan had done to make her leave.

Susie Orton filled in as her sub. When she waited on him, her voice went flat. She took his order quickly and left. When she delivered his food, she slid his order on the table like a hockey puck and left without a word. No refills on coffee. One delivery and done.

This afternoon, Stan stood in his office and laid out each tiny note on his desk. Public opinion, once in his favor, had slid to zero. "Not good," he said.

His story sources had dwindled to almost nothing. Stan was unsure if the paper could survive. Folks in town no longer seemed interested in having him as their voice.

Looking at the pieces of paper on his desk, he decided, after being savaged by his customers, to pack it in for the day. He stacked up the messages and tossed them in the garbage.

"Going out," he said to Matty as he passed her at the counter.

"Oh?" she said.

Stan gave her a quick glance. "Yeah. See you tomorrow."

She looked at him skeptically. "You do that. Don't make me come get you."

"Promise," he said and hurried out the door.

It was a beautiful fall afternoon, very warm and clear. Stan decided to walk home and hang out around the house. If nothing else, he could kill some time reading or go for a hike.

As he traipsed down the road, Walt pulled up in his tow truck. He was dressed in his typical overalls, dirty hat, well-worn work boots. "Hop in," he offered.

"I'm just going home, Walt. It's not that far."

Walt looked at Stan with a smirk and rubbed his chin. "You got something against tow drivers? My truck not clean enough?"

Stan looked at him curiously

"Hop in," Walt repeated.

Stan opened the door and swung in.

Heading west on Paradise Road, they drove past his house. He turned his head and watched it disappear down the road. "I guess you're not taking me home," he said.

Walt gave him a narrow-eyed glance. "You guess right."

They drove for another mile or so, then made a sharp left on a narrow gravel road.

The longer Stan sat in the truck, the more his dread grew. Images of kidnaping, torture, and murder ran through his head. He had flashbacks about Johnny's clothes, blood in the foothills, and his terrible dream. Dogged by fear and curiosity, he asked, "Where we going, Walt?"

Walt didn't answer, just looked at Stan with an odd grin and leaned back, one hand on the wheel, the other arm perched on the open window ledge. He seemed lost in thought. At last, he spoke. "Why were you out in the hills that evening?"

"What evening, Walt?"

"The night I found you. The night you were hunched down behind a blind."

"Oh, well, I hiked in looking for the hunters who left their truck on the side of the road."

"D'you ever find them?"

"No, no one did. You towed their truck to Vale, remember?"

"Oh yeah. You're right. I did."

"And why would you ask me that? I already know you were out there as Sari's little bloodsucker assassin."

Walt gave Stan a nasty glance. "I do what I'm told and I'm good at what I do."

"And in exchange, you get—"

Walt looked back and forth between the road and Stan. "You're a nosy bastard, ain't you?"

"It's what I do for a living."

Walt put both hands on the bottom of his steering wheel and kept driving. Without speaking. Without looking at Stan. The gravel crunched beneath the tires. The truck lurched over ridges and potholes. Walt seemed to take special pleasure in bouncing him around.

When they came to the end of the road, a clearing opened with a small cabin not far from the edge of a lake. There were other cars parked around the perimeter. It appeared that Stan had been invited to a meeting.

"Out we go," said Walt.

Stan stood for a moment and stared at the cabin. "This your place?"

"Well," he said hesitantly, "not mine exactly. Sort of belongs to the town."

"Town council spot, huh?"

"You could say that. We usually come out here for important business."

"Well, then, I'm flattered. Guess I merit special attention."

Walt's face went flat. "Guess so." He turned and headed for the cabin.

Stan took his time approaching the front door. He was not in any hurry to find out why he'd been hauled out here.

Truth be told, Stan had never asked who might be on the town council, just assumed Sari chose whomever he wanted whenever he wanted. As he approached, he counted cars. Three, including Walt's. Was Sari also in there?

Stepping up to the front porch, he stopped. Panic. Dread. His feet locked to the floor. If he walked in, would he walk out? He had to deliberately engage his leg muscles. He took a deep breath, opened the door, and went inside.

It was a primitive cabin. Rough plank porch, flat shingled roof, no obvious signs of electricity. It was about the size of a small bungalow, with a couple of gas lanterns on the floor. A few windows had been framed to let in light. The inside was one rectangular room, with space set aside for a small kitchen and dining room, a fireplace, and open quarters for a couple of cots.

In the center was a group of people sitting on some old wooden chairs. Stan scanned their faces. Walt for one. Doug Rabin, who ran a small produce store on the south end of town. Reid Dammers. Marla Magan, owner of Marla's Hair Salon in the town square. And finally, Dahlia Rutan. Then, as he turned toward the kitchen, he saw Amanda sitting stoically. She had on some type of silken robe, gold and red, and a headband that appeared to be made out of expensive metal. She appeared quite regal among the group of ordinary townsfolk.

"Well, here he is," Walt said. "Let's get on with it. Sit down, Stan. Make yourself at home." He motioned to a chair in the middle of the room.

Dahlia was the first to speak. "Guess you're a little surprised to see us, huh?" She waited, but Stan gave no response. "Well, obviously there's a problem or we wouldn't be here now, would we?"

Her voice reminded him of his third grade teacher. Students must behave. Teacher always knows best. "If you say so," he said.

"I do," she affirmed. "Amanda?"

All eyes in the room turned toward her. Amanda appeared relaxed, her hands resting in her lap. "Afternoon, Stan. Sorry about getting you out here like this."

"Nice to see you, Amanda," he said. "Guess it goes without saying, I'm a little surprised."

"Just so you're not left in the dark here, we're what Sari refers to as his Zulan, his inside circle. You may have heard rumors about us. We don't usually talk about this in public, so maybe you wondered if we really exist."

"You're right, I've only heard rumors."

"We've never discussed this, Stan, but when Sari asked me here, I came as his Dulami. That's an ancient African term, basically meaning second in charge."

Stan gazed around the room. His reporter's curiosity kicked in. What was this place and what exactly did these folks do? He tried to remain focused. "No, I guess you never mentioned that over dinner."

"I didn't want to, and besides, it's not something you needed to know at the time."

"Right. Just one more Amanda surprise."

"After you came, we recognized your great potential, both as a writer and a leader. We were assigned your oversight, to help bring you along and, hopefully, be my Chakar, a term Sari uses to describe the spouse of a great leader."

Stan slumped in his chair and glanced over at the fireplace. All these terms she was throwing at him. African terms. Political terms. "Chakar?"

"Yes." Amanda's lips went tight. Stress tight. Disappointment tight. She looked around the room. "I hoped you would come to love me and be my husband."

Stan turned back to Amanda. His head began to hurt. "You mean, you wanted to recruit me?"

"No," she said patiently, "more like oversee and encourage you, as anyone would do for someone she loves."

"Sari and you together—you picked me?"

Amanda motioned toward the surrounding audience. "Not just Sari and I. As a group, together, with Sari's consent. Yes, we decided this would be a good thing, for you and for me."

Stan lowered his head and rubbed his temples with both hands. "Jesus, sounds like you were shopping for merchandise. Sounds very African or Indian."

"Yes, I guess, you're not far off. Don't forget where Sari comes from. They do that in some of those cultures—match up mates, so to speak. After long discussions, he came to believe that you and I would be a good fit."

He raised his head and gave her a sharp glance. "Holy shit, so my life, our life together, was part of some kind of grand scheme?"

Amanda waited. "When you say it like that, it sounds so crude, but really, it makes so much sense. And all of this was to your benefit, I might add."

"How so?"

"Well, the spouse of a Chakar is greatly respected and often influential in the affairs of a village."

"Really? And I couldn't be respected and influential without being hooked up to a Dulami?"

Amanda's eyes now reminded Stan of Sari. They had that same intense scrutiny—black orbs with a searing lock-down focus.

"We all have our place here," she said. "Sometimes it comes to us and we don't realize what it is. To kick back simply means to invite chaos in the universe. Chaos can't exist in Freeland, at least not for very long. I've tried to explain this to you but for some reason, you won't listen, and therein lies our problem."

Stan dropped his chin into his hands. "Back to me, huh?"

"Yes," she said and let out a deep breath. "I'm afraid so."

Pushing forward in his chair, he spoke laboriously. "I trusted you, just like you asked. Here's the payoff, I guess."

"Your trust was not misplaced. I can protect you, enrich your life."

"Instead—"

"There's still opportunity."

"To—"

"Be restored."

"To you?"

"And Sari."

"For a price, I imagine."

"For submission and acceptance, things easily adjusted. I think it's a small price to pay."

"And without it?"

Amanda traded glances with each group member and each member traded glances with the others. "It's your choice."

Stan gestured toward Amanda with both hands. "And you? I can't help but believe you feel more for me than just seeing me as part of Sari's little world order."

"All things in their place, Stan. I love you, I accept the world around me. Here in Freeland, we exist by order. If you're part of that, you're part of me, if not—"

"That's not love, not human love anyway."

"It is here. You might not see it that way, but that doesn't change the reality. Love doesn't exist in this town apart from Sari."

"And me?"

"You're lucky. You have a choice. As I said, it's for your benefit."

"Otherwise?"

Amanda straightened in her chair and clasped her hands together. Her straight posture and regal face looked like a princess, perhaps a queen. She gave Stan a pitying look. "It's worth repeating. There is no existence here apart from Sari."

"And these folks here?"

"As the inside circle, in the presence of the Dulami, we will decide what to do with you, once you've made your decision."

"A damn kangaroo court, I imagine?"

"It's up to you to decide whether to see my words as positive or negative. I just want you to understand that, in this room, whatever you may call us, we are your best and only hope—for life."

The last statement brought Stan up short. He sat straight, noted the serious looks on each face in the circle and realized. This was life or death. His existence hung in the air by a thin thread. A committee vote.

He had exhibited defiance. There was no way he would walk out of here without complying, not alive anyway. No doubt about it. As he sized up his situation, conforming was a bitter pill, but the other option was much worse. "And us?"

"If you choose to be a part of our town, we will carry on as planned." She stood up, glided elegantly toward Stan, and touched his shoulder. "Amanda and Stan. Stan and Amanda. Our love as ordained by Sari."

Stan shook his head. "Sari gives. Sari takes away. Whatever Sari wants."

"That's our world, Stan. Better to live in it peacefully than perish. Better to love what exists than die trying to escape."

"And me. What does Sari want?"

"Very simple. Your obedience."

Stan adjusted his legs and rubbed his hands together. "That's the problem, Amanda. Trust is never forced. Whatever I give now will be forced. Even our love."

Amanda broke toward the fireplace and looked into the hearth. "As I said, it's your choice."

"You want a robot for a lover?"

"I want a man who understands his place in our world. Once you accept that, the rest comes easy. I can help."

"Some type of spell?"

"Whatever it takes. I'm very resourceful."

Stan's voice raised a notch. "My God, Amanda. Would you listen to yourself? Is there any part of your soul left that sees how warped this is?"

Amanda locked her arms together and pivoted. "What I see is what is, Stan. That's all that matters in Freeland."

As Stan looked around the room, heads nodded. Everyone agreed with her. In this universe, as the tribe solemnly gathered, he was the only one with a toe outside the line.

It was late afternoon. Through one of the primitive cabin windows, Stan could see the lake—quite peaceful, its existence guaranteed by the natural order of things.

It was a world not unlike his own. Locked in, cyclical, prearranged. Trouble may invade the landscape, but things turned awry could be righted. Trees may be uprooted and die. The water level may rise and fall from floods and drought. The lake, however, survives, its life arranged by a power that oversees, decides, sets things as they should be. Not unlike Sari in Freeland.

Stan had a choice. To be a part of Sari's tribe or disappear. Either way, life would go on. If he vanished, no one would notice much other than a sway or two in the trees from a breeze and a slight ripple in the lake. Here in Freeland, without Sari, there was no life. No paper. No Amanda. No Matty. In a flash, his existence would simply be zero.

Stan stood up and stepped toward Amanda. He gingerly picked up her hands. "If I'm understanding this right, you, this group, Sari's Zulan, you're giving me an ultimatum."

"Yes," Amanda said softly. "You understand correctly."

"You would kill me over this?"

"Not me personally, Stan. It's a town decision, supported by Sari. You can look at it that way or see it as a chance to change. Ultimately, it's up to you."

Around the room, he could read their faces. There was consensus. They were determined to see this through, especially Walt. But the final choice was up to Amanda. Whatever she recommended would sway the group. It was a logical progression. Amanda supported Sari. The Zulan supported Amanda and Sari. And Stan? As he saw it, the ball was now in his court.

As everyone sat and waited, Stan could feel the seconds tick off in his head. The room was still, as if noise and air had stopped flowing. The heat from several sets of eyes bore into his skull.

Stan knew that the doorway to life or death—his life, his death—teetered back and forth between open and shut. He looked tenderly at Amanda. "This would make you happy?"

Amanda brushed his cheek with a finger. "If you chose to live happily with me, then yes."

"Even if we're all just slaves here in Sari's sick little world?"

Amanda looked around the room. "You don't need to see it so negatively. You can choose to be part of a bigger picture, part of the village where we can love and live."

Stan walked back to his chair, sat down, and leaned forward like Rodin's Thinker. The more he thought about it, the more bizarre it all seemed. And yet, his instincts for survival, his love for Amanda. He wasn't ready to capitulate. Maybe down the line, if he could plan an escape—

"All right," he conceded. "You've made your point. God help me, I choose life and I choose you. I guess I can't help it."

Amanda looked pleased. She reached out and gave him a gentle hug. "A wise choice."

Stan pulled her close and wrapped his arms around her waist. "You'll come back to me?"

"Yes, we'll be wed and live long and happy."

"Then that's all I ask. You know, whatever you are, whoever you are, I still love you."

"I know."

"I hope you understand that."

"I do."

Stan waited for some type of response from Amanda or the group. For the moment, there was silence. "What else can I do?" he asked.

Amanda returned and stood in front of her chair. The other council members rose. "You've made a good choice," she said. Her voice grew tender. "Now, Stan, all that remains is for you to be happy in our world. Enjoy the beauty and benefits." She pointed at Walt. "Take him home, Walt. I'll be along shortly."

"Will do," Walt said obediently, though he looked quite disappointed.

As Stan headed toward the door, Amanda touched his back. When he turned around, she took his face between her hands and kissed him. "We will be what Sari intends," she murmured, "and that will be good."

Despite all Stan had witnessed in the last few weeks, despite his sufferings and nightmares, at that moment, with her fingers touching him, he believed her, believed what she believed. For better or worse, he was now her obedient companion.

Walt and Stan climbed back in his truck and headed up the gravel road. There was an uncomfortable silence between them, an unspoken mistrust.

As they turned east on Paradise Road, Walt said, "You're a lucky man."

"Guess so," Stan replied.

"Problem is, you're so damned snooty, you don't know how lucky you really are."

Stan noticed how Walt's face was seething. "I can see your point, Walt and I don't blame you for being angry."

"If it had been up to me, I would have killed you."

Stan paused. "Really, Walt? You hate me that much?"

"Cause I don't trust you. I think you're a snake in the grass and eventually you'll show your colors. When you do and the gigs up, I promise to be first in line to make sure you get yours. Until then, I'll just do what I'm told. But I just bet you're gonna fuck up somewhere, so I'll just bide my time—and keep my knife good and sharp." He gave Stan an evil smile.

"Good to know where you stand, Walt." He tried to steady his hands by laying them flat on the seat but his fingers wouldn't stop shaking.

"Just a warning, that's all. Fuck this up and you're a goner. Understand?"

"Got it," he said. No doubt about it, if he'd missed the point earlier, Walt had clarified.

Walt dropped Stan off in front of his house. As he stepped out of the truck, Walt formed a gun with his thumb and fingers and pointed it at Stan. Mouthing a gunshot, he pulled the trigger, hit the gas, and disappeared up the road.

As Stan stood on his doorstep and looked at his small house, he remembered Walt's words. A lucky man. Lucky to be alive. Lucky to have this home. Lucky to love Amanda. Lucky . . . to be in Freeland?

He strode through the front door and sat on the couch. Gazing around the room, he realized just how close to death he had come and puzzled over Walt's words.

If being alive was lucky, then he supposed that he was truly blessed. It was an irony to consider himself lucky in this town.

Trapped, confined, forced to conform. Still breathing, in love with a Dulami who would soon be coming home.

At what point was the line drawn between lucky and unlucky? For Stan, confined to his life in Freeland, that line always seemed to be shifting. Today he had stepped over to the lucky side. Tomorrow?

For an hour or so, he gathered his thoughts and waited for a familiar face to come home.

When she arrived, it was like nothing had changed. The words during the storm, the town's shunning, the loneliness, the conversation at the cabin, all blown over.

"Good to have you home," he said.

"Good to be back," she said as she sat next to him and put her head on his shoulder.

"There's no life in this house without you."

"You're sweet."

For an hour or so, they sat in silence and held tight to each other.

That night, as he watched her undress in their bedroom, the pleasure of her nakedness seemed more thrilling—her beauty, her knowledge, her power beautifully crafted on her face, her breasts, her thighs.

As she crawled into bed and positioned herself on his chest, she ran her fingers through his hair, kissed his face, and created such intense pleasure throughout his body.

When they made love, he felt her body had been sown to him. He knew, whatever else happened, he simply could not live without her. After they finished, she curled next to him and sighed with pleasure.

"We should fight more often," Stan joked.

"No fighting required," she said. "This is how our life is meant to be."

He ran his fingers gently across her breast. "You're like one of those mysterious fortune tellers. I feel like I'm always waiting for you to read my tea leaves."

She laughed. "Fortune tellers? They're fakes. I'm the real deal."

"You're pretty scary sometimes, at least to me, Stan the ordinary news reporter."

"I promise to be gentle."

"I don't need promises. Just having you back is good enough."

Amanda put her arm across his chest and pulled him close. "You're a good man, Stan. Stubborn, but decent. You've no idea what that means to me."

"Teach me, O most holy Dulami, mighty priestess."

She laughed and swatted his shoulder. "Be careful, I might turn you into a toad."

"Just keep me around. I'll croak whenever you want."

Amanda touched her lips to his and murmured, "This is my down payment."

"Good to know."

After Amanda fell asleep, Stan brushed back stray wisps of hair from her face, laid on his side, and took in the peace and luxury of her presence.

He nodded off and began to dream. It was a troubling dream, another vision of Amanda, like he had the night of the Valentine's Day party. The sharp-clawed Amanda who burned to the touch. But when he panicked and woke up, she remained next to him, lovely and restful.

He couldn't decide whom she really was. But it didn't matter. They were together. Whoever she might be, Stan realized how he had sold his soul—to her and to Sari. It was the smart thing to do and, in spite of his misgivings, what he desired to do. Tonight, in the quiet space of their bedroom, he bound himself to her. For love, and because he had no other choice.

June 10, 1982

Flag Day. One of those strange little American celebrations commemorating the history of the stars and stripes. A precursor to the 4th of July that called for a quart size bottle of patriotism. Year to year, Stan never thought much about it until some of the old timers in Freeland would leave notes in his box asking him to remind folks to post their American flags. This year Flag Day was June 14. Stan thought it ironic that residents would stop to celebrate the flag and its reference to freedom when, in fact, they were all prisoners.

At least the notes were a good sign. Receiving these messages meant that he had managed to work his way back into the good graces of the community. They were talking to him again.

His marriage to Amanda last November had helped smooth most of the town's ruffled feathers. Folks viewed it as his sense of commitment to the community. When Stan was single, he was looked at with some suspicion. As a family man, people believed he had put down roots here. No more causing trouble. As far as they were concerned, he was a regular part of town life and the paper was an expression of his consent to live here.

So, as he did every year, Stan worked up something about Flag Day, throwing in a little history and some appropriate words to reinforce American patriotism.

Besides. Summer was coming. The weather had turned warm. Why not celebrate the flag? Enjoy the benefits, as Amanda had reminded him.

When Stan finished with the layout, he decided to head to the Circle for lunch. On his way out, he chatted with Matty. "Happy Flag Day, Matty."

Matty look perplexed. "Whose day?"

"Flag Day. You know, rah rah for the red white and blue, that kind of thing?"

Matty gave him a skeptical sneer. "People still reminding you about that, huh?"

"Every year, without fail."

She clapped her hands. "Well, hurray for them."

"What, you're not putting out a flag this year?"

Matty looked annoyed. "Have I ever put out a flag?"

Stan thought for a moment. "No, you're right. You haven't."

"Well, then, it's a silly question, isn't it?"

"No more than any other I usually ask."

She scoured him with her sharp eyes. "You don't believe in this any more than I do, now, do you?"

"No, but it makes for good press."

"Well, then, by all means, print it. Wave the flag all you want. Attach it to a beanie and put a sparkler on top. You have my full support."

"Thanks. Now I feel better."

"You're welcome. Always glad to help."

"I'm off to lunch. See ya."

"Good for you. Have a hamburger, why don't you? Can't get more American than that."

"You're a wicked woman, Matty."

"But I'm your wicked woman, Stan. Don't forget how much you love me."

"I will never forget. Ever. I promise."

"You owe me big time, you know."

"I do and I promise to repay my debt."

"Well, that may take a while."

"Probably forever, but I don't mind."

Matty waved as he walked out the door.

It was true. He loved her. He loved Amanda. At this moment, he loved his life. In fact, he had capitulated to the fact that everything he loved was right here in Freeland.

At the Circle, Stan sat in his favorite booth and waited for Amanda to come over. As she approached, he gave her a big grin. "Serve me lunch, O mighty one?"

"I'll take your order, if that's what you're asking."

"And you do it so well."

Amanda giggled. "Come on, now. I'm busy. It's rush hour." She gave him her best gum chewing dumb broad imitation. "Whatta want, buddy? I got customers, ya know?"

"Hamburger, with fries, no lettuce. And a Coke. And make it snappy. I got stuff to write."

"You'll get yours when it's good and ready, Mister. Don't gimme no grief."

"Sorry. Can I at least say you're cute?"

"That and a quarter will get you nowhere. Hands off the merchandise." She strutted off and put his order in, then gave him a coy smile as she hurried over to the next customer.

A half-hour later, Stan pushed back his plate and joked with her as she scurried by. "Dinner, my place tonight?"

"Maybe," she said. "Depends on what you're serving."

"Macaroni and cheese sound good?"

"Sounds like something a cheapskate would cook up."

"I'll do my best to make it yummy. I promise you'll be amply rewarded."

She put a finger to her cheek. "Hmm, well, I like the ample part. That means big portions."

"Deal," he said.

Stan tilted back in his booth and caught Sari smiling at him.

Walt, seated at the counter also glanced over. No smile.

As Stan headed out, Sari breezed by and stood next to him. "A good day you are having, no?"

"Guess so," he said.

"A good life, too, I imagine."

"No complaints."

Sari looked over at Amanda as she served coffee behind the counter. "She is good for you, as well."

Stan nodded. "She is very good for me. On that we heartily agree."

"Worth living here, no?"

Stan held the door open and took a deep breath. "You have a point to make, Sari?"

Sari stretched his long arms up to the ceiling, then let them fall loosely. "I will see you later today," he said and returned to his usual perch.

As Stan left the Circle, Sari's words put a damper on his mood. A meeting with Sari was never good news. It meant he wanted something, and whatever it was, Stan knew it would cost him. Still, whatever Sari desired, he would share in his own good time. No sense dwelling on it.

That night after dinner, Amanda read from an old book of magic spells in the living room while Stan sat out on the lawn and enjoyed the warm evening. The sunlight lingered until well past eight o'clock.

Tonight the sky was clear and some stars appeared above his head. Stan sat in his rickety lounge chair and looked straight up. As he picked out constellations, he heard Sari's voice.

"They are a beautiful sight. I wish you could see them where I come from. They are like diamonds." Sari stood by the corner of the house next to the kitchen window.

"Evening, Sari," Stan said. "See you're out and about tonight."

"Look at you, so cozy, with your lovely wife, on a beautiful summer night."

"I was, yes."

"Life is good in Freeland."

Stan raised his eyes back up to the sky. "You're here for a reason, not just to chat, I presume. What can I do for you?"

Sari joined him in star gazing. "I come from a long way off but still, it's the same sky, the same stars here as in Africa." He swept an arm in the air. "We may see different views at different times of the day or night, but it's always the same sky. I take comfort that my old world, very far away, is still in place. So, when I look at the stars, I feel at home, because Africa and I are still connected."

Amanda had slipped out during this conversation and sat on the porch. Sari looked down and spotted her. "Ah, the queen has arrived. Welcome, my dear."

"Evening, Sari," she said.

"You are both with me tonight as testimony to the goodness of life here. It is a pleasure to see you enjoy the evening."

The three of them remained quiet for several minutes. Stan had the sense that Sari enjoyed their company and was in no hurry to proceed. On the other hand, Stan was in no hurry to find out what he wanted.

"You will forgive me for being so sentimental," Sari continued. "Tonight I am reminded of when, as a boy, we gathered around a fire in the evening and told stories. It was a good time."

"You miss your family?" said Stan.

"Sometimes, yes."

"Huh," he said. "You know, sometimes, so do I. When I was growing up, my family would go out on the beach and build a fire. You could do that way back when in San Diego. My brother and I used to see who could outdo each other with ghost stories. Looks like our families have something in common. Funny, how you remember those kinds of things."

Sari's eyes landed on Stan like a hawk scanning the horizon. Words were never wasted on him. Stan knew that he had caught the underlying drift.

"Yes," Sari replied. "Perhaps so."

There was silence. Uncomfortable silence. Sari's mood had subtly shifted. He was his own weather system and those in his presence could feel atmospheric changes, depending on whether or not he was pleased with them. Stan's barometer told him that Sari was carefully considering his last statement.

"You are right, Stan," he said.

"About what?"

"I have come for a reason. I have a request from someone prominent in our town, a request for a Motiko."

"A what?"

"A Motiko, what you might call a sending ceremony."

"Explain, please." Stan gripped the arms of his chair.

"You'll forgive me. I forget you are still learning new things about this place. A Motiko is when someone, usually elderly and sick, requests as a community event that we gather and send them off into the next life."

Stan sat upright and stared at Sari. "You mean kill them—publicly?"

"Yes, so to speak, but with dignity and ceremony. It is really a beautiful event when practiced properly."

"Holy shit. Euthanasia? You do that here?"

"We do, occasionally, and you are invited to be the Sarabwa."

Stan gripped his chair tighter. "Oh boy. I don't like the sound of that."

"Amanda, as the Dulami, is in charge of the ceremony. I have personally assigned her to preside over events like these."

From his chair, Stan slowly pivoted. Her face confirmed Sari's words. He pivoted back. "Okay, you'll forgive me for being a little put off here, but I'm not used to this idea and once again you guys have bushwhacked me."

"I am a patient man," said Sari.

"What, may I ask, is a Sarabwa?" Stan braced himself.

Sari glanced at Stan, then up at the stars. "The one who administers death."

Stan raised his hands in protest. "No way. You can't ask me to do that."

"I surely can, especially if the participant has made the specific request and the Dulami agrees. It would be impolite to refuse."

Desperate for help, Stan stood up and faced Amanda. "Is this true?"

Amanda nodded. "Yes, that's the proper order of things around here."

"Who's asked me to do this?"

Sari took a pregnant pause. "Your good friend, Matty."

"My Matty?" said Stan. "Grocery store Matty?"

"Yes, she is quite elderly and frail and feels she's at an age where she would like to move on."

"Matty, frail? Hell she outworks all of us and she's sharp as a knife. She doesn't strike me as someone eligible for . . . what'd you call this?"

"A Motiko."

"Right, a Mo . . . whatever. Shit, how can you expect me to do this to her? She's the best friend I have here."

"Exactly the reason she's asked for you. In Freeland, this is the ultimate sign of friendship."

"No, it isn't. It's barbaric."

"It's life in Freeland. We are not afraid to deal with these issues. It is part of the great ebb and flow we experience here. New comings, eventual goings. Life in Africa, life in America, life in Freeland. We are all born. We all die. It's only natural."

"Except for you, of course."

Sari paused and smiled. "Indeed, I have lived a much different life."

"You can't ask me to kill someone I care about." He pointed a finger at Sari. "What's wrong with you people?"

"I am not asking. Someone else is asking."

Amanda stood up, walked over to Stan, and put her hands on his shoulders. "I'll talk to him, Sari. I promise, he'll cooperate."

Sari waited, then looked back at the stars. "The words of a wise woman are convincing. I will leave you to it."

As Sari disappeared into the darkness, Amanda waited for Stan to speak.

"I can't believe you'd ask me to do this," he said.

Amanda reached down and took his hand. "Sari made it quite clear. It's not us. It's Matty herself. She's ready. She has no other family. You've become her stand-in. She wants you to do this."

"*I* don't want to do this. People don't do this to family, or friends, or even their enemies, not without damn good reason. What about my choice in the matter?"

"Your choice is secondary. You've been summoned. You can't refuse."

"The hell I can't."

"Listen to me, Stan, and listen carefully. The whole town is watching and probably most of them know by now about Matty's request. Most important, Sari knows. For your own sake and for hers, you can't refuse."

Amanda's words cut Stan. He sat back in his chair. "Of all the things you'd ask me to do—"

"Matty, Stan, Matty. It's her request."

"Okay, Matty. I'll talk to her tomorrow. I'll bet I can talk her out of it."

"Don't do that. The request has been made. There's no going back."

"You mean, once you decide to die, you can't change your mind?"

"I'm saying, once she's decided and the request has been made, it's considered offensive for someone to try and change her mind. It's her decision. Our town is honor-bound to follow through—"

"Jesus Christ, even after all these years, I can't get over how strange this place is—"

"Not to mention, as the Dulami, I'm honor-bound to carry it out. You're my husband. If you refuse, you bring dishonor to our family."

Stan blinked and shook his head. "Really, Amanda. Dishonor? Isn't that just a little over the top?"

"It doesn't matter what I think, whether I approve or disapprove. What matters is what Sari thinks. This is his world, his ways. Matty's learned to live with that and now she's ready to go. For anyone who's spent their life here, this is a very honorable way to leave. Death is a release. Freedom lies beyond the body. Trust me, she's ready. You should be happy for her."

"I might, if it weren't me doing the killing."

"Oh, so you think it would be better if someone else did it? Someone she didn't choose? It's the same result, except you sit on the sidelines and watch. What's the difference? Either way, she dies."

Checkmate. Stan's arguments had been matched and countered.

"Think about it, Stan."

"And how is this accomplished exactly? Guillotine, noose, maybe a stake to the heart?"

Amanda stepped back and gave him an indignant stare. "Stop it. Just stop this right now. This kind of anger gets you in trouble. You know that."

"Well, then, explain, please."

"Sari has developed a drink that works very well. It's quick, painless, and puts her to sleep."

"Permanently."

"Yes, she will go very peacefully. You don't have to worry about her."

"And yet somehow I do."

"Then focus on her freedom. That's something you're obsessed with. Use it to your advantage."

Double checkmate. Stan could see, as usual, she had the upper hand. He felt an urgent need to escape. "I'm going for a walk," he huffed.

"That's not a good idea right now," she said.

"Don't worry. I'm just walking around town."

"All right then, but please, stay out of the foothills."

"I wish you were that concerned about Matty."

Amanda threw up her arms in exasperation. "Then go, Stan. Take a walk. Take a fifty-mile hike for all I care. Just come back when you're ready and for God's sake, please, cooperate." She wheeled around and stomped into the house.

For the next hour, Stan wandered around town, eventually ending up at the grocery store.

Matty was just closing up. She noticed him sitting on the front steps. "Well, if you want to sleep in the store tonight, I recommend the back corner. Less lumpy, not quite as drafty. Need blankets?" She locked the door and sat next to him.

"Sari came by to visit tonight," Stan said.

"Really," Matty said with her head cocked. "And what's the mysterious gentleman have to say for himself?"

"He told me about your request."

She paused and glanced off into the distance. "Oh. That."

"Why didn't you tell me?"

"It's not something I could tell you, until I cleared it with the big kahuna. Official channels, you know. I ain't dying from any disease, healthy as an ox if you want to know the truth. I wasn't even sure he would grant my request. And not a lot of folks know about it anyway, especially the newer ones. I've been through a couple with some of my older friends. It's really quite nice. Not a bad way to go."

"So, you want me to pull the plug on you?"

"Sure, why not? I got no family. You and I have sort of this good friend thing going. Who else would I ask?"

"You want to go that badly?"

Matty folded her hands and fixed her eyes on him. "I've done my time here, Stan. Really, I've lived here all my life. Think about it. Eighty some odd years in this one place. Every day basically the same. Don't you think I've earned a little freedom? Jesus, you know, Sari's got his pound of flesh out of me and he holds all the cards in this town. If you were my age, in my shoes, I bet you'd do the same."

Stan understood her argument—how she had been confined for so long and how anxious she was for this one brief moment. Given what she'd been through, he saw her point.

"Goddamn," he said. His voice choked. "I still can't believe you'd ask me to do this."

Matty looked at him mischievously. "Yeah, it's the shits, ain't it? Pulling the plug on an old lady. Shame on you. You should run like hell, but I got you so pussy whipped, you just can't help yourself."

Stan broke out in hearty laughter. "Oh, that's cold . . . and funny."

"Hope I don't go to hell for this."

"If you do, I bet you'll charm the devil. Serves you right if he sends you back."

"Well then, I've learned something useful for the afterlife. Maybe it won't be so bad after all. So, quit your whining and let's get on with it. Anyway, it's late and I gotta go feed my cat. You need to stay here tonight? I got a cot and a couple blankets around here somewhere."

"No, I'll go home, thank you."

"Good, apologize to your wife for me, would you? I didn't mean to get you in hot water." Matty stood up, gave Stan a weak smile, and hobbled away.

On Monday, June 21, the first night of summer solstice, everyone gathered in the town square at midnight. Sari was decked out in traditional African garb. Amanda wore a lovely blue dress laced with beading and a necklace with smooth polished stones. Stan sat next to Amanda in his best dark suit.

In the middle of the square, a king size bed was covered with beautiful sheets and decorative flowers. The audience surrounded the bed on three different sides. Sari, Amanda, and Stan sat near the foot.

Sari blew loudly on a ram's horn. The noise echoed mournfully across the town square. Matty appeared out of the darkness dressed in her nicest clothes, dolled up with makeup and a new hairdo. She laid on her back with her arms across her chest.

Amanda rose and addressed the audience. "Friends, on occasion we gather to say goodbye to some of our beloved townsfolk. Tonight, at the request of Matty Rolf, who has resided with us for eighty-two years, we come formally to bid her farewell. Matty has served us and been faithful to life in Freeland. This moment has come for her to leave and fly free."

She paused. Several sobs were heard in the audience. "Matty has requested that her good friend and my husband, Stan Blankenship, be tonight's Sarabwa. Let the ceremony commence."

The Donnells played a lovely, sad tune.

Amanda handed Stan a small, silver chalice filled with some type of dark liquid. Holding it with both hands, he approached the bed. His hands and knees shook.

Matty sat on the bedside and waited for his arrival. She was smiling like a school girl.

About three feet in front of her, he stopped. "You're sure this is what you want? I can throw this away and we can run off together."

"That's sweet of you," she said. "You should have made that offer before you got married. I don't mind fooling around but I'm not a home wrecker."

Stan walked the final three steps and halted in front of her.

Sitting on a large bed, she seemed so tiny, like a child waiting for her night time drink of water. She reached out and took the cup.

"You know, I'll miss you terribly," he said.

Matty sighed. She looked distant, as if her thoughts were already dwelling on the next life. "Well, all things must pass and now it's my time. Be happy for me."

"I am, for you. It's me I'm worried about, having to live without you."

"That's kind. Nice to know someone will miss me."

As they gave each other a farewell glance, the strains of Irish music floated over their heads.

"So long, Stan. Try to carry on," she said. "I think you and I both ache for freedom. Well, here it is. For me, anyway. You know, for the first time in years, I actually have something to look forward to."

Stan reached over and touched her shoulder. "Okay, if it means that much, then I'm happy for you."

Matty raised the cup to her lips, drank it, and handed it back to Stan. Then she laid down on the bed and refolded her arms across her chest. In a few moments, she closed her eyes and fell asleep.

Stan grasped her hand and stood quietly as she dozed off. Her eyes closed and her fingers went limp. "See you in the next life, my friend," he said and returned to his seat.

Everyone remained quiet. Even the band stopped playing.

Sari rose and moved over to Matty's bed. "She was a good woman and will be sorely missed. Mahana to her." Then he raised his arms and chanted, "Darawa sitos, hasban ito dichara."

Something pulsated in the air. An electric charge followed by a warm gust of air. The wind hit Stan and Amanda squarely in the face and grew stronger.

Sari repeated his words a little louder. "Darawa sitos, hasban ito dichara!"

A low roar descended from the sky. Some type of faint light swirled around Sari and Matty. Another gust of air. An increase in noise.

Suddenly, the bed exploded and a large ball of flame shot straight up. The whole square was illuminated with shades of yellow and orange.

Sari stood in the middle of the flame with his arms extended in the air, long fingers stretched to the heavens. He shouted a single word that amplified and bounced through the hills. "Chaaalaaawa!"

"Jesus Christ," Stan said as he wrapped his arms around Amanda.

A flash, a second explosion, then blackness. When their eyes adjusted, Sari stood in the same spot, but the bed, Matty, everything else—gone. No trace of fire or smoke, nothing burnt or scorched. Sari lowered his arms and strode back to his chair.

"Christ," Stan muttered.

"We are finished. You are free to go," Sari announced.

Folks rose from their chairs and strolled past the spot where Matty's bed had been. Most shook their heads in amazement.

Sari stood up and moved in front of Stan. "You should know she is in a better place now."

"No doubt, I wish I could go with her."

Sari gave him a long look. "Perhaps you will someday. For now, you have a family, work, a home, things to keep you busy for a long time." He nodded at Stan and headed for the Circle.

Amanda gripped Stan's arm tightly. "Do you believe me now?"

"Believe what?" he said.

"That all things here are ordered for the best."

"I believe you've shown me the order part, though truthfully, I have no idea how this fits that description."

"It's better here than the outside. Things make more sense."

"They always do when someone else lays down the law."

"You doubt what you saw tonight?"

"No, but none of what I saw makes sense anyway."

"One thing leads to the other, you know. Like Jesus' miracles, a testimony to his rightness."

Stan stared at the spot where Matty had disappeared. "I can't argue there. Maybe Sari, Jesus, they're all the same."

Amanda pressed against his shoulder. "You did good."

He placed his arm around her waist. "All I did was carry the cup. Still, for Matty's sake, I'm happy for her. We're still here. She gets to go play."

Amanda pushed back in her chair and threw him a puzzled look. "Really?"

"Really," he said. More quiet passed between them before Stan stood up. "Come on, let's go home. I'm really exhausted."

"I'm glad you're here to say that word," she said softly.

"What?"

"Home."

"Okay, then, I'll repeat it every day, every night in your ear."

"Do it now."

Stan moved his mouth within an inch of Amanda's ear and whispered, "Home."

She stood up, threw her arms around his neck, and kissed him—hard. "And don't you forget it."

"Not a chance," he said.

IV

September 2, 1982

As summer ended, the hills around town buzzed with activity. Crickets, mockingbirds, sounds that Stan called "night noises."

In the dark, with the heat at its peak, Amanda and Stan often slept with the bedroom window open. Sometimes he would lie awake and listen to all these noises and try to pick out which was which.

Using this inspiration, he decided to run a special series in the paper on local nightlife, giving individual profiles about creatures that thrived in the dark corners of Eastern Oregon. Species like the great horned owl, the Columbia spotted frog, and the western small-footed myotis bat.

Often, after Amanda had fallen asleep, Stan would get up, put on some shorts, sit on the porch for an hour or so, and soak in the night. He called this his "thinking cap" hour, where he sorted through things in his head and chewed on ideas for new stories.

On this particular night, Stan sat on the porch with his back against the front door. Off to the far corner of the house, he caught a rustling sound. Not unusual for this time of year. Raccoons or someone's cat. Perhaps a rabbit.

This sound, however, was bigger. Brush disturbed, twigs cracking. It caught his attention. He stood up, tiptoed across the porch, and leaned on the front railing.

There was whispering near the house, human whispering. "Hello?" he called out. The voices stopped.

Five minutes went by. Stan heard them again, further away. Whomever it was, they had moved down the road. Relieved, he went back in the house and fell asleep.

In the morning, during breakfast, Stan asked Amanda, "Did you hear anyone outside our house last night?"

"Hmm, no," she said as she munched on a strip of bacon. "What time?"

Stan jabbed at his scrambled eggs. "I dunno, maybe two or so?"

"Jesus, you're up that late?"

"Sometimes, yes." He stopped to sip his orange juice. "I was on the porch and heard someone outside our house."

"You know for sure it was a someone?"

Stan set his glass on the table. "Yeah, I heard whispers. Definitely human."

Amanda gazed steadily at him. "You're kidding? No, I slept like a baby. Didn't hear a thing."

"Well, whatever it was, it was prowling around our house."

She crunched on a piece of toast and shrugged. "No idea."

After Stan finished breakfast, he decided to investigate around the house. Nothing unusual at first, until he stood under their bedroom window. Lined up straight, a series of small votives with melted candle wax and ashen wicks. Around each votive, a circle of tiny amulets.

"Hey, Amanda," he hollered through the bedroom window.

"Coming," she said.

"Come here and check this out."

She pressed her face against the screen. "What is it?"

"Don't know, but I think you should come see."

He could hear her moving through the house.

"Be right there," she called.

Within a minute, she was carefully examining the scene. Moving from votive to votive, she picked up each amulet and rubbed it with her fingers. Something about the scene had caught her attention.

"Any ideas?" said Stan.

Amanda rubbed one of the amulets. "Yeah."

Stan waited. Amanda remained quiet. "Well," he said, "don't keep me hanging here."

She stopped sorting and looked toward the road. "I'm guessing someone was trying to cast a spell."

"What?"

"It's crude but clear. Whoever did this knows a little about this type of stuff."

Stan eyed the amulet in her hand. "What kind of spell?"

"I'm still trying to figure that out. Can't be good news though."

"Why?"

"Well, these types of votives and charms in combination usually mean a sickness spell of some sort. I guess the best way to describe it is to call it a curse."

"You mean someone has some type of grudge against us?"

"Seems that way."

"How effective is this type of spell?"

"Can be very, but, fortunately for us, they've got everything in the wrong order. That's why I say, it's probably someone dabbling in basic magic. What we would call a novitiate."

"Would this someone know you're a witch?"

"Well, it's common knowledge, now that Sari has pushed me out into the public. So, yeah, if they're from around here, I'm sure they know."

Stan picked up one of the votives and turned it over. "Okay, this is strange. I guess the question is why."

"People are people, Stan. They get their feelings hurt, they want revenge."

"Well, knowing Freeland, that could be a hundred folks."

"Well, more like a small group, but it's obvious they've been busy."

"Can you find out who's behind this?"

"Maybe. I'll take it in and go over it. It's harmless unless you get everything in exactly the right order. Magic is a very precise art, you know. Even more so than science or engineering."

"This is scary stuff. Who else besides you and Sari know about things like this?"

Amanda bent down and rubbed her hands lightly across the ground. "Good question."

They both quietly surveyed the scene.

"Let's not panic," she said. "I'm certain we're dealing with a novice. That's in our favor."

"Easy for you to say," said Stan. "You can protect yourself."

"I can protect you too, don't forget."

"Not while you're sleeping."

"There are things I can do. Trust me. You're safe."

"Okay, if you say so."

"I do. Go to work. Forget about it."

"Right. Forget."

Stan went to work, but he certainly couldn't forget. He'd learned over the years that damage in Freeland can come in many different ways from unexpected sources. Even with Sari in charge, there were factions in the community. Not everything was as smooth as it appeared on the surface. He knew this by the notes left on his desk every week. He knew this from Walt's threats. Now he was keenly aware. Someone in Freeland was angry enough to curse them.

As Stan hurried in, the new owners of Plymouth's Grocery Store, Brent and his former girlfriend, now wife, Rita, were busy at work.

"Morning guys," Stan said. "Everything going okay today?"

Brent glanced up from a box he was unloading. "Just dandy."

"What's new?"

"Nothing much. Just going through Matty's old stock. Some strange stuff in here."

Stan stopped at the counter. "Yeah, she was more a collector than a store owner."

"No kidding."

Just then, Rita called out, "Brent, we need to order more milk, half-gallon jugs I imagine would be best." She popped around a corner. "Hey, morning, Stan. Didn't hear you come in."

"Just walked in, actually."

Rita reminded Stan of what Matty might have been at a much younger age. She stood maybe five foot two, ninety pounds or so, straight shoulder length blond hair, with a round, expressive face and bright blue eyes.

Her reputation had grown among townsfolk for being vibrant, chatty, and a little sharp-tongued. Brent was the yin to her yang, an easy-going guy who took whatever Rita dished out and followed orders. Stan had no doubt, with his smarts and her energy, the store would thrive.

Rita turned to Brent. "You hear me?"

"Yep," he answered "Half-gallon jugs. Got it."

"Good." She waved to Stan. "Well, ta-ta. More to come." She turned quickly and scooted down another aisle.

Brent glanced at Stan and shrugged. "Well, as you can see, busy busy."

Stan waved at him and ducked in his office. His first thought was to search his inbox for anything unusual.

He found a message scrawled on a piece of notebook paper in black ink: *Vadema pox mucenius kadafer*. It made no sense, except in light of what Amanda had told him. "Jesus," he said as he pushed the paper into his pocket.

During lunch at the Circle, Stan caught Amanda and showed her the note.

She unfolded it and murmured the scrawled words. "Vadema . . . pox . . . mucenius . . . kadafer." Handing it back, she looked genuinely concerned. "Where'd you get this?"

"Someone left it in my office. Another curse?"

"A strange one, yes."

"Well, what's it mean?"

"It's witch speak, sort of code language for 'rain down the curse of the evil dead.' It's a spell to punish someone by inviting in the resurrected presence of evil doers."

Stan took back the note and scanned it several times. "You're right, that is strange. I don't have the faintest idea what that means."

"Well, think of people like murderers, psychopaths, that sort, and imagine if someone could bring them back from the dead and invite them into our house. You can guess the ending to that."

"All right, this has got to stop. Can you please talk to Sari?"

"I can, but even he has his limits. I need more clues. You said you found the note this morning?"

"Probably left in my office sometime last night. The only ones with a key to that place are me and the new owners, Brent and Rita. Can't imagine why they'd want to hurt us."

"You can't imagine why people do all sorts of bad things. Most don't give many clues as to their plans. By the time you see it coming, it's too late."

"Great. So now I'm waiting for someone evil to invade my house, but I won't know he's going to kill me until he actually does it."

"Calm down, Stan. I told you this morning, don't panic. Whoever it is will give themselves away. I promise, I'll catch them, and it won't be pretty when I do."

Stan gave Amanda a wide-eyed stare. "Geesh, you're as scary as they are."

"I can be very scary. Just be happy I'm on your side."

"Okay, I'm happy. See you tonight." He kissed her and went back to work.

The story about night creatures began to take shape, except the actual night creatures Stan imagined had nothing to do with animals. Still, he wrote out their descriptions and characteristics and tried to make them fascinating.

As he pounded out the words on his Selectric IBM, the text sounded wooden. These creatures were not dangerous. The ones leaving votives, amulets, and notes. They were the ones that scared him.

After Stan had finished, he sat quietly for a moment. A thought came to mind. "Say, Brent," he called out.

"Yeah?" Brent appeared and pressed his gawky frame against Stan's doorway.

"You see anyone come in here late last night?" Stan pulled his story out of the typewriter.

"You mean in the store or your office?"

"My office."

"The only one I saw, bout eight or so, was Walt. Came in after he did a tow run looking for beer, but I didn't see him go in your office. Went straight in and straight out."

"Walt, huh?"

"Yeah, pretty slow night last night. Not a lot of customers. I definitely remember him coming in."

"Rita see him too?"

"Naw, she'd already gone home."

"Walt. Okay, thanks, Brent. Appreciate it." Stan laid the story on his desk and sat like a mummy in his chair.

Brent lingered for a moment. "Everything okay?"

Stan waved his hand to ward off Brent's curiosity. "Yep, no problem. Thanks."

Brent hesitated, then returned to work.

Walt. No surprise that he might have something to do with this. Stan knew from their last conversation that the man had a vicious side. He also knew that Walt read voraciously and liked to talk about weird stuff.

And then there was the whole saga of Walt, Sari, and the missing hunters. Stan suspected that Walt had his own ambitions. Perhaps he had managed to get his hands on some books about the occult and had stuck his curious nose into black magic.

"Hmm, could be," Amanda said that night as they laid in bed. "He wasn't happy at our last gathering. I think he expected you to be punished."

"Yeah, he said if it was up to him, he would have killed me."

"Really? Well, no doubt, Walt's got a mean streak. He and that bloody crew of his give me the creeps. Trouble is, he's very close to Sari. I'm not sure, if I speak to Sari, it won't end up backfiring."

"Well, what then?"

From her back, Amanda's eyes traced the ceiling. "Let me think about it, okay? In the meantime, I've got some ideas about protecting the house. But you'll have to stay on the porch if you decide to get up at night."

Stan brushed a hand through her hair. "What, will I get struck by lightning?"

"Not lightning, but something pretty potent. Stay close. Don't wander off."

Stan reached over and gave her a kiss. "Yes, dear. I've been warned."

"Just be careful," she said.

"I will stay close," he promised.

"In the house, or on the porch."

"Got it," he said and rolled over. But he couldn't help dwelling on what evil was out there searching for just the right time to strike. It kept him awake.

Several nights passed without any further disturbance. No curses, no human prowlers around the house. Stan thought perhaps this was all some type of prank to scare them. Hopefully, whoever did this had their laughs and moved on.

Toward the end of September, another hot night kicked in. Stan woke up from a bad dream and kicked out of bed. He could see the glowing numbers of their alarm clock—1:13. Laying on his side, he observed it tick off, minute by minute, for half an hour. No more sleep tonight. Only a burgeoning sense of dread.

The faint sound of voices drifted through the window. Stan woke Amanda and they both waited for the voices to recur. They surfaced again about twenty yards or so from their bedroom window. Stan leaped out of bed, but Amanda grabbed his arm. "Keep still," she whispered. "Don't move."

She crouched next to the window and heard the voices come nearer. From about ten yards away, Stan heard a pop followed by a flash and a small explosion.

Someone in the group screamed. Someone else commanded them to get back. Another angry voice shouted, "Sonofabitch motherfuckers."

Stan ran to the window to see if he could identify anybody.

Amanda jumped up and cried out, "Your Dulami commands you to cease and be gone."

Everyone went quiet, except for the person still whimpering from injury.

"Salama destos rajan," a voice shouted. The surrounding perimeter of the house lit up with various flashes and explosions like a high voltage electric fence gone haywire.

"Salama destos nixtos," Amanda shot back. The lights around the perimeter moved outward and flowed like the slow motion of a big river. It crept toward the group in the dark. Stan could hear them fleeing the scene as the energy inched toward them. Someone was clipped by the light and yelled in pain. Others crashed through brush and headed away from the house. Soon, the surrounding hills were quiet.

"Destos siquan," Amanda said. The energy stopped. The light disappeared. All returned to normal.

Stan slipped next to Amanda, whose body was trembling. "What the hell was that?"

Amanda clamped her arms around him and squeezed. "I used energy spells, pulling up forces from the ground for protection. Every night before I go to bed, I put up a perimeter. They tried a counter spell to crash it but obviously, it didn't work. My spell made theirs backfire."

"Are they hurt?"

"Minor burns, nothing life threatening. More like a severe sunburn. Should keep them away. Hopefully they learned their lesson."

"Great. Now we know there's more than one. A whole group of angry folks out to get us."

Amanda did a slow dive into bed and crawled over to her side. "Yeah, that's troubling. More community knowledge to pass around.

Makes them more dangerous. Still, they're no match for me. I'm miles ahead of them."

Stan sat on the mattress, his eyes glued to the window. "Good to know."

She brushed his back soothingly. "Go back to sleep. They won't bother us again, not tonight anyway."

They kissed each other and, in a few minutes, she was sound asleep. Stan laid wide-awake for a couple of hours. She might be confident. He was unnerved.

It was now well into October and summer had faded to fall. No more hot nights. No more sleeping with the windows open.

Stan believed that Amanda had been right about the night attacks. Since they knew the house was protected, odds were they wouldn't come back.

The last week of October, he was working late to finish up his normal press run. Brent worked with him to set the ink and bundle the copies. They chitchatted as they worked, talking above the din of the print machine.

In between counting, Brent straightened and sniffed. "You smell smoke?"

Stan froze. He was right. Something was on fire.

Rita screamed. They both ran into the store and saw flames behind the counter. The store was on fire, big time. In a matter of seconds, the wall exploded and knocked Rita into the counter. She collapsed and sprawled on the floor. Brent and Stan pulled her to safety and carried her out the door.

At a safe distance, they laid her flat on her back and checked for vital signs. She coughed and started to come around. Then, another huge explosion caught their attention. The entire store roared up into a hellish fireball.

People gathered in the town square to witness the fire. In a few minutes, Amanda ran up to check on them.

"Yeah," Stan assured her. "No harm to me, but the store's gone. Paper's gone."

They both sat down in the dirt and watched the flames. Like Stan, Amanda's face reflected shock. "What happened?"

Stan grabbed her hand. "I don't know. One minute we're working, the next thing I know the whole goddamn place is on fire. It's like someone poured gasoline and lit a match."

As they stood mum for several minutes, the store let out another crackling roar and collapsed in a heap. There was nothing left of Plymouth Grocery but charred timbers, hot cinders, and dancing ash.

"Well, it's official now," she sighed. "This is serious."

Stan brushed his hands through his hair. His fingers left streaks of dust that looked ghostly in the fading fire light. "You're telling me. My career has just gone up in smoke."

Amanda turned and touched his cheek. "You're sure you're all right?"

"Positive. No burns, just some smoke inhalation. Rita took the worst of it but it looks like she's coming around."

Amanda offered her hand. "Come on. Nothing to do now. Let's go home."

As they headed toward their house, they spotted Sari outside the Circle. Even he looked downcast.

"I am sorry, my brother, for your loss," he said with a nod. "This is a blow to our community."

Stan broke away from Amanda. "Nice town we've got here, Sari. People harassing us in the middle of the night and burning down buildings. Someone's really gonna get hurt. We could use some help here, you know?"

Sari, inscrutable as always, did not answer. He continued to watch the burning disaster with one foot propped against the door.

As Stan and Amanda walked into the house, he double checked around the exterior with a flashlight to make sure no one was waiting for them.

Even though the yard was empty, he was sure this would not be the last chapter in this story. He went back inside and sat for an hour in the bedroom watching Amanda sleep, listening carefully for the return of the voices.

Stan woke up. The clock on Amanda's bed stand read 4:22. He wasn't sure why he was awake, but something had startled him. He put on a pair of pants and walked out on the porch.

From the surrounding hills, Stan picked up the sound of voices. Cackling, hooting, tones of glee and lunacy in their laugh.

"Walt, is that you?" Stan hollered.

A voice in the darkness mimicked his question in a high-pitched tone. "Walt, is that you?"

Another voice picked up the mockery. "Oh Walt, can you please step forward. Someone's calling for you. Oh Wallllter."

More laughs echoed. Mad laughs that spoke of lunacy and menace. It appeared there were many of them and they had the place surrounded.

Another voice chimed in. "We're sorry, Mr. Blankenship, it appears that Walt has gone home. Or maybe he's just shy." More laughter.

Stan backed into the house and shouted, "Amanda, get up." No response. Bursting into the bedroom, he shook her. "Come on, Amanda, there's a fucking army out here."

Amanda jumped up and sat bedside. "Where?"

"Around the house. Hell, there's probably a dozen of them."

Amanda hurried to throw on some clothes. "Okay, keep calm. I'll deal with them."

They eased out the front door and stood side by side on the porch listening to the mysterious attackers taunt them.

"Oh looky," a voice cackled, "Little Stanley brought his mummy."

"Come out to the hills, little children," someone else invited. "You must see what lives out here in the dark." The voice changed to a hiss. "It's really quite ... scaaary."

Amanda moved forward and raised her right arm. In a quiet voice she chanted, "Presumas illuminata."

A blue-tinted light glowed around the house. Not bright, but effective in revealing anyone who might be hiding.

"Ahhh, the old light trick," a voice said. "Maybe Walter is here after all. Walter, would you mind turning off the lights? They hurt my eyes."

A deeper voice chanted, "Sequan illuminata," and the light disappeared.

"That's much better. Thank you. You see, we like the dark. Don't you? Well, maybe not." A moment of silence ensued, then another snarling voice. "So it's light you want, do you? All right, here you go. Fluores eglan."

From all sides, flares like giant roman candles shot from the sky toward the house. Striking Amanda's perimeter, they burst and sent sparks high in the air. The force of the blasts broke their windows and started fires around their house.

"Derana himos," Amanda shouted. Instantly, a stiff wind blew from the east and snuffed out the flames.

"Hee hee, what a show," someone taunted. "Talk about a blast."

Amanda pulled Stan down and pinned him against the wall. "Stay here, don't move. As long as you're on this porch, you're all right."

Stan pulled on her arm. "What are you going to do?"

Amanda's face was stern. He could see anger in her eyes. Her voice was steady, her words deliberate. "I'm going to fry these bastards."

Stan let her go and pushed back against the wall. "Why? Your perimeter is holding. You don't need to do anything risky."

"I don't know what other spells they have. Better to stay ahead, maybe get them to reveal themselves, or what they've got in their arsenal. Just stay here—please."

Amanda spun around and shouted, "Your spells are children's games. You want to play, let's play. Let's see what you've really got."

"Ohhhhh, we're so frightened," a high voice mocked.

"You should be, you slimy toads."

Laughter tittered from various points around the house. "Oh, did she just call us toads? Now there's a threat. How about this? Terra xteses seco."

The ground shook. Amanda toppled backward on the porch as the floor rattled and a fissure split open beneath the house, causing the foundation to crack and the porch to sag.

Amanda rolled over, grabbed the front railing, and pulled herself up. "Mundo ceradama," she shouted. The fissure rolled shut. The force was so severe, it snapped some nearby trees and rolled small boulders down toward the road.

She raised both hands in the air and yelled, "Terra magnus incrediso." The wind from the east blew again and began to swirl at a high velocity around Amanda's perimeter. The house, however, remained protected in the eye of the storm.

From somewhere nearby, she heard screams and a loud shout. Then a single chant. "Terra minimus denomo."

The wind stopped. The hills fell silent. Amanda waited for their next move. Some may have cleared out, but the one chanting spells was still there.

"I am a Dulami and master witch," she said.

"We don't believe in Dulamis," the chanter sneered, "or your little village mumbo jumbo. Dulami, salami. Master witch, stupid bitch.

Fuck you and Sari and your shithole village." Another round of laughter scattered around the house.

Amanda stood defiantly on the porch with her feet apart. "And yet, here I stand, more than your equal."

"Not yet," the chanter said. "I still stand as well."

"You're not standing. You're hiding like a roach under a log."

"A roach? Why yes, that's exactly what I am, invading your nest. I'm a very nasty roach."

All went quiet for a moment, then the voice spoke. "Destamo . . . regus . . . formica!"

From the ground a tidal wave of insects poured out of the ground and onto the porch. In a matter of seconds, they crawled up Amanda's legs and across the floor to Stan, who jumped up and frantically swatted at them. "Ah, fucking hell," he screamed as he felt hundreds of stinging pinchers lance his skin.

"Little bugs," yelled the chanter, "time for dinner."

Amanda whirled toward Stan and flung her arms outward. "Besandus niveus," she commanded. A river of white light poured from her hands and covered the porch like a low fog bank. It expanded like a ball of gas, rolling up the bodies of both Stan and Amanda and engulfing them in brightness. The porch glowed like a torch for several seconds. Then the light dissolved and with it, any sign of bugs. The insect pestilence had simply disintegrated and disappeared.

Stan was beside himself with fear. He continued to swat frantically at his arms and legs and fight off his own panic as he scrambled to see if any more invaders were around his feet.

Amanda turned toward the remaining chanter. "You bore me, roach," she challenged. "Clearus ramorsa, dertal mali prosto!"

The protective perimeter glowed again, this time white hot around the house. It rolled outward, expanding like a balloon filled with water.

Once again, flares hit the perimeter with great force. Shock waves, explosions, sparks everywhere. The noise grew deafening.

"Tresto sungere," the chanter shouted. The perimeter wavered for a moment.

"Tresto occludo," Amanda shot back. The perimeter continued to expand. "It's coming for you, roach!"

"Delanto mocido un questus," the chanter replied with a tinge of desperation.

"Sorry, roach, won't work," Amanda screamed. "Wrong curse. Go back to spell school. Get a decent teacher."

"I'll send you to hell," the chanter screamed.

"You first, roach. I'll bring down worse than hell on you if you don't slither out of here!"

The perimeter kept expanding. Amanda heard the chanter cry in pain and flee.

"Fuck off, you pitiful pestilence," Amanda spit out. "Run home to your nasty nest. And if you come back, I promise I'll hunt you down and burn you out of your dirty little hole."

The perimeter grew another five feet, covering more acreage around the house. By now all of the voices had disappeared and there was a distinct smell of burning flesh in the air.

One last chant came from a distance. "Darama indices."

A sudden bright ball sped toward the perimeter. When it hit, the entire house and the land surrounding it shook from the force of the blast. Amanda was thrown to the porch and hit her head. She lay motionless and bleeding. Once again, the brush in the immediate vicinity roared with fire, creating a floor of flame that spread rapidly toward Freeland.

Stan leaped up and rolled her over. "Amanda, Amanda, come on baby, wake up!"

Amanda was limp in his arms, but only for a moment. She started and jumped to her feet. "What happened?"

Stan pointed at the brush. "Fire, lots of it, headed toward town."

Amanda limped to the porch steps and saw the flames. "Besandus nemorosus," she chanted. Another heavy downpour of rain deluged the area and put out the fires.

Amanda collapsed on the porch, crawled into Stan's arms, and chanted "Tresto quies." The perimeter disappeared. The chanter and the attackers were gone.

Stan gripped her tightly. "Cripes, who are they, anyway?"

"I don't know," she said wearily, "but I've done some serious damage to them. May take them a while to regroup."

"In the meantime, they've done some serious damage to us."

"Yeah, no doubt."

"Come on," Stan pleaded. "Let's get you inside and clean you up."

He propped her on his shoulder and helped her into the kitchen. After tending to her wounds, he tucked her in bed and she fell asleep.

"You're one tough broad," he said as she rested her head on his shoulder.

In the morning, Stan served her breakfast in bed and gave her orders to stay home for the day. Inspecting around the house, he noted considerable damage to the walls and roof, but no bodies.

As he wandered the perimeter, he picked through the charred remains of shrubs and found remnants of burnt clothing. More than a few attackers this morning would be tending to some pretty nasty burns. He walked over to the Circle to talk to Sari.

When Sari saw him, he said, "Ah, brother, such bad luck. You've had a hard night, I hear."

Stan sat on a stool in front of the counter. "More than that. Whoever this person is, he wants to do some serious hurt."

"And Amanda has returned the favor, I see."

"She's resting now, but the damage to the store and our house—well, you know."

"And Amanda?"

"She's hurt, lucky really to be alive."

"Yes, so I hear."

"You hear a lot. What do you know about this?"

Sari picked up a glass and wiped it with a towel. "I suspect rovers."

"Rovers?"

"Yes, traveling bands of sorcerers. This town has a reputation. Sometimes, bad people find us and cause trouble."

"Why me, why Amanda?"

Sari held the glass up and inspected his handiwork. "You are married to a high sorceress. More know about her than you suspect."

"Rovers, you say?" Stan paused and tapped a finger on the counter. "No one from Freeland involved in this?"

"That is my learned opinion, yes." He returned to wiping the glass.

Stan pulled a salt shaker from its wire cage. "So our house, the store?"

"Do not worry, we have gone through this before and we always rebuild. I will make sure everything gets put back good as new, perhaps even better. You will trust me on this, no?"

"On the rebuilding, yes. On the rover part, I'm not so sure."

"If anyone in Freeland is involved in this, I will find out. Someone would need much knowledge to do something like this."

At that moment, Walt walked in for his usual breakfast and morning chatter. His face was bruised and swollen and he limped noticeably. The hair on his hands looked singed. Still, he sat next to Stan without so much as a side glance.

"Good morning, Walt," said Sari without his usual cheer. "I see Stan is not the only one who had a bad night."

"Damn right. Car I was towing came off the ramp and hit me. Thought I was a goner there for a minute."

Sari stared at him. Stan stared at him. There was an awkward moment of silence.

Stan turned his stool deliberately in a half-circle to face him. "Busy night, huh Walt?"

Walt glanced at Stan without flinching. "No more than usual, just got careless, that's all."

"You look like you got in a fight of some sort. Maybe with a blow torch?"

Walt never even blinked. "Nope, no fight, unless you count the car I towed."

Stan slid an elbow on the counter and stared. "Hear about all the commotion last night?"

"Bits and pieces of it. Sounds like you had a rough night."

"House damaged, store gone. I'd say so. Still, whoever did it took their fair share of damage. Probably walking around today pretty banged up."

"Big battle huh?"

"You didn't hear any noise?"

"Me? Naw. I slept like a baby." He angled his hand like a jet taking off. "Took some pills and went right off, phew!"

"Sari says he thinks it's rovers. Me, I'm not so sure."

"Sari knows a lot about these kinds of things. I'd probably trust him more than you."

Stan slowed his tapping to a single index finger, an adagio as steady as a metronome. "Well there's some evidence around my house says Amanda took a few out."

"That right?" Walt swung around on his bar stool and came eye to eye with Stan. "Well, I guess you showed them, huh?" His bruised face revealed nothing. He swung back around. "Say, Sari. What's a guy gotta do to get some coffee around here?"

Sari slid off his seat, picked up a cup, and poured it full. Walt eased the cup between his large, beat-up hands. "Thanks," he said and took a healthy swig.

"Well, gotta start cleaning up the mess," Stan said. "You're good with your promise to rebuild, right Sari?"

"I am always good with my promises," Sari said, his eyes flush on Walt.

"Right. We're not gonna let these bastards get away with this. If you know of any used printing equipment, maybe I can set it up in my house. Either way, the Reporter's coming back. Give me a couple months. I'll have it out on the street again. That's my promise."

"We shall indeed bring it all back," Sari said as he walked around the back of the counter and vanished into the kitchen.

Walt and Stan sat motionless in their seats like two gunslingers waiting to pull their pistols. Each stared at the wall in front of them, their faces blank, their hands flat on the counter. Neither made the first move. Not yet.

Stan stood up and prepared to leave. "Walt," he said.

"Stan," Walt replied.

Outside the Circle, Stan paused and watched Walt through the big front window. Walt eased his bar stool around and caught Stan's eye. Just as he did in the truck, he raised his fingers, pointed them like a gun, and shot. Stan pointed his in exactly the same gesture and fired back.

January 6, 1983

Freeland was in the middle of a typical January freeze. Wind severe and cutting. Heavy snow.

True to his word, Sari had helped Stan get the house repaired and the Reporter running again by squeezing some old printing equipment into their living room. This meant the paper could return as a voice in the community. It made moving around inside the house a living hell, but for Stan, getting the paper back on its feet was worth it. At least he was working again.

In the meantime, Stan had given much thought to the attack. He knew the instigator but still had no idea who else was involved.

One thing was certain. He believed Walt would regroup and try another assault at some point in the future. Time was on his side and with it, a chance to plan new strategies.

With this in mind, Stan scratched out ideas for the week and worked on an editorial about the meaning of winter; how in the cycle of nature, things often died, were buried, and came back to life.

He tied this to the renewed publication of the paper and hoped, whoever was behind the attacks, would read it and understand his determination to survive.

He also realized that he might antagonize and speed up their plans. No matter. Amanda was right. Stan was very stubborn. Damned if he wanted to back down from the fight.

As he sat on the couch scribbling, Sari knocked at the door. Stan jumped up to let him in.

"Morning, Sari," he said. "Awful cold to be wandering out today. Shouldn't you be running a restaurant?"

"I do not mind the cold, brother," he said. "I come from a very hot country. I appreciate a little wind and snow. The restaurant is fine, by the way. I have a good second in command." He winked and walked inside.

"Yeah, she is good, isn't she? Runs this house pretty well too."

Sari squeezed his tall frame into the living room. There was just enough room between the wall and the printing press for him to stand. "I see you've moved in your new equipment. Ready to get back to work?"

"Anxious as ever. I miss the paper. Hope the community feels the same."

"They do, I'm sure. I'm ready as well. You are an important voice in this town."

"Well, thanks, Sari. Nice of you to say so."

"And the house?"

"Repaired enough to get us through the winter. Come spring, we can finish up the details."

Sari surveyed the room, then focused on Stan. "You are wondering why I am here?"

Stan sat down on the couch and folded his hands in his lap. "I always wonder when you visit. Just the nature of who you are, I guess."

"Ah, yes, I suppose." He cleared his throat. "Well, the truth is, I am worried."

"Sari? Worried? Now I am curious."

"Yes, I can see why you would feel that way. I know you think I am not interested in your dilemma, but nothing could be further from the truth. Yet, I am a patient man. I think watching and waiting is always the best approach. In my village, we had a saying. It is better, when hunting, to let the animal trap himself." Sari stopped and let the words sink in.

Stan shrugged. "Meaning?"

"I have been watching carefully for signs that someone is angry with you."

"And?"

"It is no secret that Walt and you are at war."

"I could have told you that months ago."

"And yet you didn't."

"I don't like to accuse without proof."

Sari nodded. "A good approach."

"He's threatened to kill me."

"He's a man prone to outbursts."

"He's a violent psycho."

Sari nodded again. "As you say, that is a hard thing to prove."

"Because?"

"If he is what you say, he will work secretly and leave very few clues. Walt is quite a brilliant man."

"My point exactly." Stan jabbed his finger into a couch cushion. "I know what he is, I just can't prove it. You know what he is, but you can't prove it either. That leaves a very smart man, a very dangerous man, loose in our town. He's burned down the store, nearly destroyed my house. Sooner or later, he'll come back with something else. I hate to see what's he's dreamed up next."

"Nothing good, I imagine."

"Right. So, what can we do?"

"Approach him carefully, as if you were hunting a lion."

"I don't plan to approach him at all unless he decides to come after me again. Then, if I get the chance, I might do some serious damage."

Sari folded his arms. "And that is my concern."

Stan slumped back. "What's that supposed to mean?"

"You also are prone to violence."

"I'm not the one who's threatened to kill someone."

"You just did, my brother, or did I misread your intention?"

Sari's sharp observation startled Stan. He took a deep breath, held it, then let it seep out. "So?"

"I am very old, older than you might imagine. Centuries ago I discovered two things. How to live long and when to kill. Both of those discoveries take great wisdom and patience and both have helped me build a village in Freeland. Peace is fragile. Hate is easy. I come here seeking peace."

"Why don't you discuss this with Walt?"

"As I said, I will approach the lion carefully."

"And what about me?"

"You, I have more hope for. Prone to violence, yes. A killer, no. I am asking that you learn from me and seek patience."

"I think I've already been pretty patient." Stan edged forward on the couch and planted his feet. "I'm just worried about our safety. He attacked our house, attacked Amanda. She's my wife and your Dulami. You can't ask me to just sit and wait until he decides to try again. And a little help from you would be appreciated."

"I will grant you that help," Sari said and gestured. "But I ask you not to provoke."

"How is that?"

"Be careful what you write. Think about the depth of words. Many good phrases with smooth lines are turbulent underneath. People read more than just words on a page. They also read you. I could teach you many things about that, if you desire."

Stan was perplexed. Had Sari picked up on his thoughts from a distance? Had he read his mind? Did he know what he was scribbling on his pad? He let out another deep breath. "Okay. I understand. I'll keep the themes low key. No provocation."

"And I will seek your safety from the mouth of the lion."

Stan stood up and reached to shake Sari's hand. "Deal."

Sari returned the handshake. "You are a smart man, Stan. A good man to have in town."

As Sari ducked through the door, he turned. "A good woman is a great treasure, no?"

"She's the best."

Sari headed toward the restaurant. As much as Stan feared this man, he also admired his insights. He could see how Sari had managed to survive for so long. He went back to his notepad and crossed out his editorial. For the time being, something else would have to take its place.

January 7, 1983

The temperature hovered just below freezing and the low-lying overcast promised more snow. In an open field, Walt scanned the horizon for signs of animal life. His dogs hovered around his feet, ready to run, anxious to hunt. He was bundled up in a down filled orange overcoat, laced up black boots with deep treads, pillowed gloves, and a fur lined thermal hat. With all this garb, he didn't mind the cold. In fact, he loved it, loved to watch the dogs trek around, whine with excitement, yip when they caught a scent.

Today, for the fun of it, they were stalking rabbits and other small creatures. All practice of course. Hunting season, Walt's type of hunting, was over. Still, he liked to keep the dogs sharp. Come fall, the hunters would be back. Then the real fun would start.

The dogs caught a scent and begged to be let loose. When he unhooked their leashes, they darted through the snow, feverishly barking. Walt pulled up and enjoyed the moment. An open range all to himself. The hills feathered with ice and snow. And except for the dogs, silence.

Where he was, what he did, it was a good life and soon to get better. He learned new things every day. He had been building his power base for years. Bit by bit, he could feel the momentum shift.

He had made some mistakes, especially with that bitch Amanda, but now, as he looked across the field and posed like a king in his domain, he knew he was that much closer to claiming Freeland for himself.

The dogs' howling stopped. Unusual for them. When they found something, they usually yapped loudly. Walt came to full alert.

Reaching down to finger the .22 caliber holstered to his waist, he set out at a quick pace.

It was easy to follow their tracks in the snow. The longer he trailed them, the more he worried. Good dogs took years to train. This particular pack had special chemistry. No wanderers or fighters. He was anxious to make sure they were all right.

About a quarter mile up, the tracks veered right toward the lake. Walt thought that perhaps they had decided to rest and catch a drink. Across the lake was the town council cabin where he was staying for the night. Maybe they thought it was time to go home.

Through a patch of trees he marched until he broke into the open and noticed him standing with the dogs at his feet—Sari.

Walt started at the sight. Sari dressed all in black. Boots, down jacket, gloves, stocking cap. To Walt, he looked like a tall dark pine tree.

"They are beautiful animals," Sari said. "You have trained them well."

"Thanks," said Walt.

Sari motioned toward the hills. "Out hunting, I suppose? Very cold right now. The game I think is laying low."

"I hunt all year. There's lots out here if you know where to look."

"Hmm, yes. With your expert skills, I suppose so. You are a smart hunter. If I knew you were on my trail, I would be very afraid."

Walt clapped his gloves together and stomped snow off his boots. "What brings you out here, Sari? I know you're a hunter, but I've never seen you out in the winter."

"I hunt many times when you're not aware and you cannot see me. Do not underestimate my ability to track down what I want to find."

Walt knew Sari was a man precise with words. He picked up on Sari's meaning. "So, I assume you're hunting me?"

"A wise assumption."

Sari pressed closer to the dogs. They were very docile around him. He bent down and pulled on the collar of Walt's favorite, Cannon. The dog licked Sari's gloves and face. He rubbed Cannon's head and wrapped his long arms around his neck.

Walt was envious. These dogs were his children. Sari's affection was not welcome. "Well, you've found me," he said. "Let's chat if you want."

Sari gave Walt a long look. "I would welcome that."

Walt pointed across the lake. "You want to talk here or over at the cabin?"

"Here is fine. I like this time of year in, what do you call it, the great outdoors?"

"Yeah, me too," Walt said as he shifted his feet and stomped out clumps of snow. "But I know you're not here to talk weather. So, what's on your mind?"

"Many things, all the time. My mind is always occupied, as is yours."

"Meaning what?"

"I sense you are a busy man. Working, hunting, planning."

"Yeah, I try to stay occupied. I'm a single guy. I live alone. Gotta do something to stay active. I've got lots of hobbies, if that's what you mean."

"Exactly. Many hobbies. Some, for you, very exciting. More than hobbies. Passions of the soul I think."

Walt scuffed his boots across the snowy turf. "Say, Sari. You know we've had a lot of interesting discussions in the past. It's no secret I read a lot and run my mouth more than I should. So, what are you getting at? I know you didn't come out here in the middle of goddamn frigid nowhere for loose chitchat. Come on now, let's have it."

"I would prefer that you tell me."

"Tell you what?"

"Your passions."

"You mean the hobbies I'm excited about?"

"The hobby to which you devote the most attention."

"I don't get it."

"Oh, now, Walt, do not disappoint me. The man who studies so many truths, particularly where language, the mastery of language, is important. I've seen you in action, my brother. I know your clarity of mind, your keen insight into the ways of men."

Walt glanced across the lake and pursed his lips. "Well, I think that's a compliment, but it sounds a little strange. Okay, let's put it this way. What passionate hobby of mine are you interested in?"

Sari zeroed in. From their many conversations, Walt knew that look all too well, the moment when Sari sifted through a man's thoughts and made him squirm.

Walt hunted with dogs, Sari with his mind. Walt as the hunter was now the hunted and Sari was hot on his heels.

Sari turned toward the lake. He stretched his arms forward and waved them in circles. The frozen ice stirred and cracked as if a giant boulder had fallen in its center. Gradually at first, then more rapid, until the water rose from edge to center and formed a whirling dervish of twisting moisture and wind. Part tornado, part fog bank, part water spout, the lake lifted like a wall under construction until it reached hundreds of feet into the sky.

Walt gaped at the scene. Then, the giant wall of moisture hurled forward, belted him in the face, and threw him on his back. The sudden fury blew past his ears like a runaway train. He could feel slivers of ice and spray whisk by his face.

Despite the turbulence, Sari and the dogs seemed unaffected. No more than ten yards from where Walt laid, they were safe in a protected pocket.

Walt assumed, in a few moments, he would die. Desperate, he closed his eyes and yelled, "Stop! Stop!"

The water disappeared. The wind stopped. Walt opened his eyes and noted that his face and clothes were dry. Nothing had changed. Lake, dogs, Sari, peaceful scenery.

Walt bulled his way up and slapped the snow off his clothing. "Shit, man, what the hell was that all about?"

Sari turned back to Walt. "Perhaps you will tell me."

"All right, all right. Hell's bells, you don't have to kill me. Goddamn it, I thought we were friends."

"Nothing has changed. As you can see, everything remains the same."

"Good lord, Sari, you can be hard to figure out sometimes."

Sari bent down once again to pet the dogs. "No more than you, my friend. So, between us, shall we clarify?"

"Well, if you're talking about my interest in magic, okay. I'm interested in magic."

"You seek knowledge from the spiritual arts?"

"I've read some about it. Maybe tried a few things." Walt waved his arm. "With all that goes on around here—this little show for instance—who could blame me? This place is crawling with it. I mean, you're teaching me how to live forever, for Christ's sake. So, yes, I've studied a bit. Blame yourself, if we're being honest here. You're the one pointing the way."

Sari gently ruffled the head of another dog. "And with that comes desire, no?"

"Desire?"

"For mastery, and from mastery comes power."

Even with his gloves and coat, Walt could feel a chill settle in his body. Sari hunting. Sari cornering. "I suppose so."

"And power leads to more desire."

Walt shifted again, avoiding Sari's eyes. "Am I on trial here, Sari? Have I done something to offend you?"

Sari murmured something in Cannon's ear and gave the dog an encouraging pat. Cannon danced in a circle and yipped. He smiled and pulled the dog close to his face. "All of us are on trial every day in this universe, my brother. The balance of what we know is measured against our actions. You and I and everyone else are subject to this. No one escapes that balance."

"Great, good to know." Walt dropped his hands in exasperation. "So you've come out here to balance me? Geesh, man. You could have done that at the diner."

"I think not. I think it is not my role to balance you. My role is to guide you. You must balance yourself. Sometimes, though, when the balance is not right and we are thrown off track, then, I must bring truth into focus."

"Wow, sounds like a warning. Thanks for that thought."

Sari pushed himself up and stamped through some snow drifts toward Walt. His high steps seemed like the deliberate beat of a judge's gavel. He stopped directly in front of Walt. "Your thoughts are dark and sad. I, in turn, feel sad for you."

Walt had to crane his head. The wind whistled down his neck into his coat. "Now you sound like a shrink. I like you better when you're hard to understand."

"Yes, I imagine so." Sari let a moment pass. Then he turned back to the dogs. They crowded around him excitedly. He squatted down and petted Cannon one more time. "It is a good life here, no?"

Walt was puzzled and unnerved. His voice quavered. "I—I like it, yeah."

Sari stood up and gave Walt a final glance, then walked away.

Walt could hear his boots crunch in the snow. He sat down and observed like the expert hunter he was, noting how Sari rounded the lake and took the gravel road back to Freeland. In fifteen minutes, he was nothing more than a dark speck.

The dogs returned and circled around him. He grabbed Cannon and gave him a gentle hug. "Whose your real buddy?" he said. Cannon nuzzled up and licked his face. Walt kept chatting with the dog. "Yeah, I know. You're Walt's boy, now, ain't you? Yes, you are. Don't you be giving that old Sari any more love, now. No, sir. You're Walt's boy."

Walt was ready to finish up. He called to his dogs and pointed in the direction of the cabin. "Come on, guys, let's go home." The dogs knew exactly what he meant and raced off.

He had been digesting everything that happened, every word of Sari's conversation. Despite the fact that Sari was on to him, he was more angry than afraid. His guarded life had been punctured, his road to mastery unmasked. It was a challenge to his ultimate goal of lordship, but no matter.

Sari's little stunt may have revealed Walt's vulnerabilities, but maybe that was not such a bad thing. As much a course correction as a threat. Like chess, a good defense was everything. He would keep working at it and search his armor for weakness. Next time, he would not be so easily startled. He'd be ready for anything and everything, even Sari.

He knew the day was coming. His anger was a good thing. He'd make it work for him. Soon, it would be his turn, and, when that time came, he wouldn't hesitate to carry out what Sari only threatened.

When the old shaman was flat on his back, in the grip of death, Walt wouldn't play around with showboat spells or ponderous lectures. He'd make sure the deed was finished.

May 5, 1983

Spring brought the completion of the grocery store and with it, Stan's new home for the Freeland Reporter. Quite modern, all of it. Updated lighting, electronic cash register, even an automatic sliding door. It was bigger than the old store, divided into two parts. The front grocery and a spacious back office for the paper. The store proudly bore the names of the new owner: *Plymouth Grocery*.

In Stan's office, he had more room for printing equipment. Sari had managed to locate a new press that made the job of setup and copy much easier. There were windows to let light in and, to top it off, he had his own entry off the side, complete with his name and title: *Stan Blankenship, Owner and Publisher, The Freeland Reporter*.

Of course, Stan included the story as this week's lead with the headline: *Fire Victims Return to Business*. It reflected the enthusiasm that Brent, Rita, and Stan felt for this fresh start.

Today Brent and Rita showed friends around and made last minute preparations for the grand opening on Saturday. Stan was busy pulling papers off the press, preparing to pass them out to the gathering crowd.

It was a small town grocery and a small town paper. In the big scheme of things, no one outside of Freeland cared. But to the folks here, to Brent and Rita, and to Stan, it had the impact of a major ship launch. Something old and trusted had been destroyed. Something new had taken its place. Stan liked to think of it as the triumph of light over darkness.

He imagined that the ones responsible for the destruction would also follow this with interest. As he ran out news copy, he tried to anticipate what plans they had to wreak more havoc. It was a disturbing thought. He pushed it to the back of his mind and focused on what was important—the here and now, the reopening, the triumphant return.

Thursday evening, Stan worked late. Amanda stopped by to bring him dinner and chat. They sat in the office and gawked at his great setup.

"Nice digs, Stan," she said.

Stan grinned like a kid with a new bicycle. "Not bad for a small town paper, huh?"

"Your own door and everything. Good to know, if I kick you out, you have somewhere to stay. That corner over there looks like it could fit a nice cot."

Stan followed her finger. "You're right. We could christen it, you know."

Amanda made a face. "Hmm, maybe when it gets warmer. Besides, the carpet still smells."

"Yeah, smells great, huh? Smells like—" Stan inhaled deeply, "new."

"I see you've got the press up and running."

"Ready to roll, baby. Paper, ink, typeset. We're in business." Stan twirled circles in his new office chair and raised his hands in triumph.

Amanda laughed heartily. She didn't laugh like this very often. It was a welcome sound. Rising from her chair, she walked over, snuggled in his lap, and nestled her head on his shoulder. "I love it when you're happy."

"I am and hopefully, so are you, to get all that equipment out of the house."

"Oh, God, yeah. With all the extra space, I feel lost in the living room. I can't get used to walking from couch to kitchen without tripping."

Amanda stood up and pranced over to an empty space where she had laid down a white dinner cloth on the floor. She spread out the food brought over from the Circle—hamburger, fries, Coke, ketchup, along with utensils and napkins. She took extra care to lay it all neatly in a circle, fussing over everything like a 4-star chef. "There," she said, "an indoor picnic."

Stan moved over and sat next to her on the floor. "Nice."

As he chowed down, she watched him with amusement. "You're an animal."

"I'm a hungry animal."

She reached out and dabbed him with a napkin. "You have ketchup on your chin."

"Oops, thank you."

After finishing his burger, he searched around the floor. "What's for dessert?"

Amanda eyed him coyly. "Silly. Dessert is for when you get home."

"Really," Stan said. "What'd you make?"

"I didn't *make* anything. You get—," she did her best camera pose, "me."

Stan stopped chewing and grinned. His hungry eyes scanned up and down her body. "Hell yeah. Even better."

Saturday rolled around, warm and sunny. Most of the town gathered at the front of the store. Official words were spoken by Sari and Amanda. Then a ribbon was cut and the first customers hurried inside to purchase groceries. Some milled around to chat for a while.

A buzz was in the air as folks admired the building. The event was a celebration, the start of a new chapter.

As late afternoon set in, most of the well wishers had cleared out. A few customers were still in the store doing business. Stan sat in a folding chair next to the front entrance. The old grocery porch was gone. He'd have to make-do with this new spot.

What would Matty think if she saw this? he asked himself. Probably pooh pooh the ceremony, complain about the newness, show folks some of her highly prized antique guns.

Walt approached and reached out to shake his hand.

Surprised, Stan glanced up from his chair. "Don't do this if you don't mean it."

Walt looked at him without flinching. No words. A thin smile.

Stan hesitated before reaching out to return his grip. They shook and Walt headed toward the Circle. Stan didn't know if he was congratulating him or laying down a gauntlet. He knew somewhere down the line Walt had a plan. For now, he remained shielded, a regular part of the Freeland community.

That evening, Amanda and Stan prepared dinner and ate on the porch. Fried chicken, French fries, corn. The evenings were warming up and they wanted to get a jump on summer. They both threw on T-shirts and shorts and brought out their food. Propping plates on a TV stand between two folding chairs, they chatted about the ceremony and the excitement of getting the store back. Stan mentioned the handshake with Walt.

"Did he say anything?" she asked.

"Not a word," said Stan. "Just stood there with his hand out. I didn't want to be rude. So, I shook it."

"That's strange. I know he's aware Sari knows about him. Maybe he's decided to back off."

"I don't think so. I think he's keeping his true identity under wraps. I couldn't tell from seeing his face whether or not he was sincere. He's a very shrewd man."

"Yes, he is. From watching him at the Circle, everything seems just hunky dory. Same old Walt."

Stan chewed on a wing. "I'm not fooled. He's got something up his sleeve. You watch."

"I will," she promised. "I'll be the advance scout looking for trouble, protecting the wagon train."

He laughed. "You know, I bet you'd look good on a horse."

"So would you. Big hat and stirrups. Gun in the holster. Yee hah."

"Mr. and Mrs. Get-A-Long."

"Yippee ki."

Amanda leaned over and kissed him. Then she leaned back and smiled.

For the first time since he'd come to Freeland, Stan felt happy.

May 12, 1983

Amanda woke up in a state of panic.

She had only recently begun to have night terrors accompanied by a sense of foreboding. The aura of something ominous hung over her head.

Why? she asked herself. On the surface everything was perfect. Stan was behaving. Sari seemed pleased with their progress. Most of all, she had a husband, a home, an important role in the community. She was happy.

This new sense of dread came and went, like an occasional gust of wind. It flew off in the daytime and returned at night, mostly when she woke up and watched Stan sleeping. Mostly when she sat alone at her kitchen late at night.

"Shit," Amanda muttered and gently eased out of bed. She went to the bathroom, then wandered into the kitchen. Turning on the light, she sat down at the table. Her fingers trailed to a small rack filled with napkins. She pulled one out and started folding it like origami.

Amanda thought about the house they had decorated. Her little touches in every room. She had transformed it into her small castle. She never thought she had it in her, but, as it turned out, she was even more domestic than her mother. And she loved it. Home was what she created and this place was her sanctuary.

But something haunted her. The rovers from last fall, the tension with Walt, her own dread. She put up a brave front for Stan, but in truth, her profession, her calling as a witch, scared the hell out of her. She never dreamed the citizens in her dark world could be so dangerous.

Then again, she recognized her own power, her unleashed fury and rage. The night she battled with the rovers, she had become acutely aware whom she was. More than a title figure, she was a witch, a high priestess, a Dulami capable of conjuring spells that frightened even her.

Amanda felt it again. Fear. Oppression. Danger. Very imminent. Something evil unleashed in Freeland. It was coming. For her.

It was the power she had. Something or someone sought it, sought her. She was being summoned because she had power, and that power was connected to a source, and that source had a presence, a name as yet unknown.

She thought about her life, the choices she had made, how fun it once seemed. But sitting in this kitchen, she had no joy. This was a deadly game she had chosen to play.

A game. That's what it all seemed like in the beginning. But a game with a price. Now it was time to pay the piper. The piper was calling. The piper was coming for her.

"Shit," she muttered again as she rose and turned out the kitchen light. She opened the front door, stood by the screen and stared off into the distance.

Stan had another terrible dream. Always something to do with Amanda. They were less frequent now, making it all the more unexpected and terrifying. Despite all their domestic bliss, his dreams were evidence of her dangerous powers. He woke up—startled, disoriented—and glanced at the clock. 2:48. Then he noticed that Amanda was gone, her normal spot on the mattress a wrinkled white space.

It was hot in the house. Stan thought perhaps she might be catching some cool air outside. Getting up, he hit the bathroom and started his search.

He saw the front door cracked open and peeked around the corner. Amanda sat on the porch in one of their lounge chairs in a thin cotton shirt and light pajamas. Stan eased over and put his hands on her shoulders. "Can't sleep?"

She squeezed his hand. "You too, huh?"

"I had another one of your bad dreams. You know, for being such a nice person, you're pretty scary in my nightmares."

"Your brain knows what you won't acknowledge."

Stan grabbed a chair and sat beside her. "What's that?"

"I'm not your typical housewife."

"That's not a bad thing."

"That's not what your brain is telling you."

He reached over and rubbed her knee. "So, my brain has a vivid imagination. So what?"

Amanda grabbed his hand. "You know this can't last, don't you?"

Stan's eyes grew wide. "What can't last?"

Amanda gently stroked his fingers. "Us, this home, this wonderful peaceful life we have."

"What the hell are you rambling about? We're married, Sari's happy. You're the town's Dulami. We've both gone to a lot of trouble to get here. That sounds pretty permanent to me."

Amanda stood up and drifted over to the railing. "I always knew there would come a time. I just didn't expect it to come so soon."

"Expect what?" Stan rose and followed her. As they gazed out toward the road, he put an arm around her waist and pulled her close.

"I'm just letting you know," she said. "There's war in the air and trouble coming. One of these days, we'll be separated. I think that's inevitable. I can't stop it or shield you from it."

"And?" he prodded.

"And then my true nature will kick in and all we've enjoyed here will be shot to hell. Sorry to be such a downer, but I sense what's coming and feel like I need to warn you."

Stan's head hung over the side. "What makes you so sure?"

Amanda avoided his eyes. "It's the times we're in. When the balance of power changes, everything else gets pushed aside. Everything. Friends, family, house, you, me. I didn't know this when I started down this path, you know. I just wanted something exciting in my life." She paused. "I know the worst is coming. It's just the nature of the beast I deal with."

Stan tried to keep his balance but his knees went weak. He backed up and buried himself in his chair. "So, what's Sari's part in this?"

"Sari is as much a part of this as I am. We're all part of the same web."

"Jesus Christ," Stan mumbled. "Here I thought we'd cleared the hurdle. You said if I behaved myself everything would be all right."

"One hurdle, yes, but there's more coming."

Stan covered his eyes and took several deep breaths. "You have any idea when?"

"No, but soon. My intuition tells me that, and my intuition is usually pretty accurate."

"Where will you go?"

Amanda leaned over the railing. Her head drooped. "I don't know if I'll go anywhere. It's what I may become that's the problem. Power changes a person. When all of this shakes down, you may not even recognize me. I may be somebody completely different."

Stan's voice choked. "First Matty, now you. What the hell am I going to do? I can't survive this place without you."

Sighing, Amanda sat down beside Stan. "You'll go on living, I imagine. Life is a process. Give and take, share and let go. I suppose you'll grieve for a while, then move on."

Stan dropped his arms and stared at her. "Goddamn, that's an ice cold way of putting it."

Amanda sunk deeper in her chair. "Would you rather be shocked and surprised?"

"Yeah, probably."

She looked at him tenderly. "I suppose you would. Who wants to know if the future is bad? Better to enjoy the present and let trouble come when it comes."

"Well, is it coming tonight or can we go back to bed?"

"I'm sorry." She rubbed his arm affectionately. " I'm not good at being gentle."

"Sure you are. Just not tonight."

Amanda pulled Stan's hands under her shirt. He eased his hands over her breasts. "Whatever comes doesn't change the present," she said. "I love you, you love me. I guess that's all that matters right now." She pressed against Stan's shoulder and gave him a kiss. "Does this melt the ice a bit?"

Stan brushed his lips across the top of her hair. "Yeah, it helps. Ice gone. Amanda back. I like this person much better."

"Good, maybe that's why you're so good for me. You always seem to melt my ice."

He let his hands roam freely. "I hope so."

Stan and Amanda stood up and hovered near one another. Then he pulled her close. They gently moved together through the house and landed on their bed like birds in flight. He wrapped himself around her as she searched for his lips.

Maybe it was his imagination, but as their bodies joined and their mouths uttered the pleasures of the moment, their lovemaking seemed more intense and passionate.

Stan felt her fingers dig into him; so deep, it surprised and frightened him. He, in turn, rhythmically massaged her thighs and breasts and used his body to make her back rise until they both cried out.

Spent and tired, they stretched out together, her back to his chest, his arm draped across her waist. This time, when he went to sleep, no dreams haunted him.

May 19, 1983

For Walt, the moment had arrived. His studies, his partnerships, his determination to wreak havoc and gain power. In the early morning hours, he sat in the town council's cabin reading by lantern light, preparing to issue the spell.

Nearby, observing Walt from an old chair—his sorcery companion, the man who had tutored and pushed him toward this high moment. Not a word was spoken between them, but the air was filled with their intense thoughts.

Walt had his head buried in a book. "You're sure this will work?"

Bill squeezed his long fingers around his staff and leaned forward. His voice rumbled, but not unpleasantly. His words seemed to flow up from a deep hole inside his belly, swirl and bounce off his esophagus, and dance off his tongue. "Oh, quite sure. I've never been more sure of anything in my life."

Walt seemed less certain. He glanced over and tried to decipher the man's eyes. "And this book, you've used it enough to know what you're doing?"

"My friend, that book has been my companion for ages. If anyone knows how to use that book, it's me." Bill unfolded his fingers elegantly. "And now, of course, you're the beneficiary. Before you know it, you'll be as good as I am. One spell after another. Wham, bam. Freeland won't have a clue. Like shooting fish in a barrel."

"And Sari?"

"Sari goes down in flames. Poof."

"I just want to be sure I do it right the first time. I've had enough of Sari and his bitch fucking up my plans. Goddamn, I'd like to finish them both off for good, so I know I gotta get this right. There can't be any more foul-ups."

"Just say the words and cast the spell," said Bill. "They're as good as gone."

"Okay, so let's go through this one more time."

Bill seemed amused by Walt's meticulous planning. "All right. Let's."

"I say these words first." Walt pointed at a line in the book.

Bill rose, strode across the room, and peeked over Walt's shoulders. "That's right. I see you've written them out in English letters. That's very good. Make sure you get the accents on the right syllables."

"Then, Johnny's blood goes into the fireplace."

"Yes, yes. Over his ashes."

Walt slid further down the page. "Then I come back and finish with this sentence."

Bill nodded. "See, that's all it takes. Easy enough, don't you think?"

Walt ran a finger along the bottom of the page. "What's this last part here?"

"Oh, you know, that's my part. Can't finish without the big mumbo jumbo. Master sorcerer's words. Blah, blah, blah, then—kaboom. Once I finish, all hell breaks loose. The entertainment starts and you'll have a front row seat. And, of course, that leaves you in charge as the new lord of Freeland, or what's left of it anyway. But I have no doubt, once you take over, the town will bounce right back. After all, with my experience and your genius—"

"Good. Okay." Walt looked relieved. "I think I got this. When do we start?"

"Crack of dawn. You should get some rest."

Walt closed the book. "Yeah, some shuteye would be good."

"Yes, you should be fresh for the show, the first act, so to speak."

Walt turned in his chair. "And you?"

"Me? I never sleep. Bad habit if you ask me, but perfectly understandable for you. Go on, I'm not going anywhere." He wiggled his fingers. "Nighty night."

Walt trudged over to a cot and stretched out his bulky frame. In a few minutes, he was snoring.

Bill returned to his chair and sat quietly. "You just enjoy these last few moments," he said.

Walt woke from his nap and rolled over.

Bill sat in the far corner of the room, motionless with his eyes open.

"You ready?" Walt said as his feet hit the floor.

Bill twitched slightly and came back to life. "Oh yes. Ready when you are."

Walt gave him the once-over. "Christ, you looked frozen."

Bill waved his hands. "Oh, I can assure you, I'm quite warm." He rose and stretched his long limbs. "All right then. Let's get this show on the road."

Walt pulled on his boots and lumbered over to his chair. He eased open the book and found the right page. "Whenever you're ready," he said.

Bill gestured politely. "At your discretion."

Walt checked his watch. 6:48. "Do I need to do it any special time of the day?"

Bill stood near the fireplace, leaned on his staff, and grinned. "Any time you like. Long as the sun is coming up, we're good."

"Standing, sitting?"

"Whatever you're comfortable with."

Walt glanced nervously at him, then back at the book. His hands had a slight tremor. "Where you gonna be?"

Squeezing his staff, Bill spoke kindly. "Right by your side, partner."

"Good, good." Walt took a moment to get comfortable. "Ready?"

Bill raised a hand in affirmation.

"All right. Here we go." He put his finger next to the spell, took a deep breath, and read, "Demana negras, tira vida terreras, bestus dararium—"

"Derarium," Bill corrected.

"Ah Christ, I screwed up, didn't I?"

"You did, but no harm. Just start over. Nothing happens till you get it right."

Walt rearranged himself and started over. "Demana negras, tira vida terreras, bestus . . . derarium—"

"That's good," Bill encouraged.

"Veni teos . . . veni sacrifi."

"Step one," said Bill. "Now, move over to the fireplace—"

Walt picked up the small vial of blood on the table. Carefully, he advanced across the room and poured the vial into the fireplace. A crackling noise boiled from the hearth.

"Step two," Bill said. "Now move back—"

Walt backpedaled to his table and carefully sat down. Looking up and down the page, he appeared to lose his place. "Here?"

"That's right," Bill said. "Those last few words."

Walt followed the sentence with his finger and read deliberately. "Desdos demani agnus destructum."

The crackling noise transformed into a buzzing sound filled with a thousand angry voices echoing through the cabin. It grew so loud, Walt covered his ears.

Bill shouted at Walt, "Well done, my Lord. Now you are the master of Freeland."

Walt, however, did not look pleased. His face twisted in pain and his body writhed. "Ow, shit, turn it off, stop!" he screamed.

Bill walked over and yelled in Walt's ear. "How does it feel? That surge of power, it goes right through you, doesn't it?"

Walt's pale face was tortured by pain and panic. He screamed, "Goddamn it, come on man, stop this!"

An invisible force lifted him off the floor and turned his body vertical. Walt floated face up a foot above the table, arms and legs spastic, voice vibrating and screaming, "Aaaaaaaaaaaaa."

Bill leaned over Walt's head and smirked. "Well done, Master Walt. Now if you don't mind, I'll finish the spell."

He reached for the book and held it in his left hand. Raising his right hand toward an imaginary audience, he spoke clearly above the din. "Demana sacrifi, te deos demana, fium gia sanguis."

The room went silent. Walt's body no longer gyrated. His eyes, however, remained open and panicked.

The invisible force lowered him onto the table, his hands and legs stretched out.

Bill pulled a long narrow knife from his overalls and held it over Walt's head. When Walt saw it, his eyes opened even wider.

"And now for the finishing touch," Bill proclaimed. With centuries of expertise, he lifted the knife high and plunged it hard into Walt's heart.

Walt registered a final terrified look. Blood oozed from his chest. Then his face froze—eyes still open, expressionless.

Bill took his hands off the hilt and leaned over his former protégée. He took a moment to rub his finger across Walt's forehead. Then he took the same finger, dipped it in the blood dripping from Walt's chest, and tasted it. "Hmm, " he said. "Outstanding."

A foul smelling breeze rolled through the window, and an even more unusual hissing noise, like the gathering of millions of insects. Stan woke up and checked the clock. 7:34. Amanda was still asleep.

Rolling out of bed, he threw on a pair of old shorts and ran shirtless onto the porch.

Two things immediately struck him. First, the hills had an odd tinge, greenish grey and orange. Second, there was the strong smell of smoke and rotting flesh.

Then, ghostlike and ominous, it appeared. A grey tinted fog, thick and impenetrable. From that fog came the breeze, the smell, the noise.

"Amanda, honey," Stan shouted. "I think you'd better come and check this out." He scurried back to the bedroom.

"Amanda," he yelled again and shook her.

She stirred and woke up. "Hey, morning to you too," she murmured. "What time is it?"

"You better come outside and catch this. It's too weird to describe."

She read Stan's face and grew concerned. "What's wrong?"

"I don't know, but one thing I can tell you. It's not good."

Amanda rolled out of bed and threw on her shirt and pajamas. Stan stood on the porch and paced as she hurried to the door.

"What's that noise?" Amanda said as she stepped out.

Stan pointed to the hills. "I think it's coming from over there."

Catching sight of the fog, she grimaced and looked long and hard at the spreading clouds.

"Any ideas?" he said.

"Yeah. Someone has conjured up black spirits."

Stan glanced at her, then back at the fog. "I assume that's not good."

"No, and, from the looks of it, we have very little time."

"Meaning?"

"Get inside and don't come out. I need to find Sari."

"Wait a minute. Don't ask me to hide here while you do all the dirty work."

"I'm not asking, I'm telling. There's not a damn thing you can do right now and if that fog finds you, you'll be dead in a matter of seconds. You have to trust me, Stan. I'll do what I can to protect you. Just go in, be extremely quiet, and don't come out till I tell you."

Seeing the concern on her face, Stan hurried inside. Whatever this was, it was well beyond his understanding. Better to do as he was told. He found an empty hall closet, shut the door, and waited.

Amanda hurried down the porch and up the road toward the Circle. She found Sari at the front door.

"So, he's gone and done the deed, I see," said Sari. "It will not go well for Freeland today, I'm afraid."

Amanda kept an eye on the fog. "It's not your average spell, to bring this thing up from hell. I can't help but feel Walt has brought in some big time help, more than just rovers."

"Yes, perhaps. The rovers were one thing, but I underestimated his resolve. He surely wants war, perhaps to be lord of Freeland, perhaps to destroy us."

"What do your senses tell you?"

"I am a man with knowledge, but to pit myself against this darkness is not an easy thing. You, perhaps?"

"To deflect, perhaps to shield, but not to hold back, at least not very long."

"Then let us put our heads together and do what we can."

"We can try, but we both know it's temporary. Sooner or later—"

"Yes, I know."

By now, some folks from the Circle had begun to gather in the square. They looked at the fog. They looked at Sari. Nothing like this had ever threatened them. All these years, they had lived with a sense of security about Sari's power and protection. Captives, yes, but never in danger. Now they looked confused and uncertain.

More people came, enough to form a small crowd. One of the town's longtime elders, Bob Deetz, walked over to Sari. "You know about this?"

"I know what it is," said Sari, "and I know who is doing it."

"Well?" Bob demanded.

Sari slipped into the middle of the group and raised his arms to get their attention. "People of Freeland, I suggest you all go to the community center and stay inside until I tell you it is safe to come out. You cannot fight this but you can remain out of sight. Go inside and be very quiet. If you create fear, it will find you. If you remain calm, there is a chance."

"What kind of chance?" someone hollered.

"I cannot tell, but a chance. Go now and remain hidden."

The crowd broke off. In ones and twos at first, then swarming like a thick line of ants toward the center. In a matter of minutes they were all gone. Sari and Amanda stood alone.

"I must find Walt," Sari said. "Do what you can to hold this off." He gave Amanda a lingering look and touched her shoulder. "You will do well." He turned and sprinted west on Paradise Road.

Call it kismet, coincidence, or something in Stan's subconscious. He had been doing some research on theories of good and evil in other cultures, similar threads held in common in different countries. He thought perhaps some of his readers might share his interest.

So, as he sat huddled in the closet, it struck him as ironic. The timing of what he had just published, the fact that so many cultures acknowledged a division between good and evil; that they believed flesh and spirit wove together to form various shades of darkness and light.

He couldn't explain the timing—this collision of truths that came from completely different directions. Someone thinks about a friend and calls them on a hunch, only to find that friend has also been thinking about them. Mental synchronicity.

A writer considers the meaning of ancient good and evil and finds himself surrounded by both. Spiritual synchronicity?

That these events were happening to him now seemed quite bizarre. He should be frightened. Instead, he was mulling on the nature of metaphysics.

The noise remained steady. Not loud, but persistent, like the sound of leaking gas. Stan had no idea what time it was or how long he'd been in this closet. From the sound, he was sure the house was surrounded. The hissing morphed into thousands of whispering voices. He tried to picture where Amanda was and what she was doing to stop this thing.

It was a long wait, a lonely wait, and sitting in a closet with no windows, hard on the nerves. Still, there was nothing he could do. Just more damn waiting, rehashing his article, wondering what or who might have drawn him to that subject. He found it hard to believe it was mere coincidence.

Amanda whispered to herself as the fog crossed the road. She knew timing was everything and, in her case, time was short. If she could find a way to beat back the fog, at least until Sari returned, that would be a small victory.

"Deutius erot pullus," she chanted to the mist. Then she spoke a little louder. "Deutius erot pullus confestim."

As she uttered the spell, the fog stopped creeping forward. The hissing transformed to creaking and groaning mixed with a sound like breaking glass. It ascended straight up, then floated overhead across the whole town, severely cutting down the sunlight.

Amanda had created a safe space over Freeland. How long it would hold, she didn't know. Whoever had created this would counter and adapt. Already she could hear voices communicating, seeking, probing. The fog was alive with the spirits. Amanda tried to think ahead like a chess player and anticipate its next move. "Delinum progda morphus acetum," she said. "Confuto."

The noise increased in protest to her command—cracking, banging, attacking the barrier with tremendous pressure. It sounded like popping bolts and bending metal.

She was afraid and uncertain, not a good frame of mind for such an ugly presence. Her spells were protective, but they also antagonized. She had no doubt that, if her barrier broke, whatever was around and above her would tear everything and everyone apart. Her intuition was tingling. She could taste the presence of evil.

She was a witch. She knew what this meant. For years, she had skirted the moral borders of her sorcery but somewhere close by, her master had come to claim his student. The fact she resisted just made it more evident. Whatever or whoever waited outside was confident. She might delay, but not avoid. The true master of her art had come to claim her soul.

Sari's long legs picked up speed as he skirted along the edge of the fog. He ran with amazing agility and grace, the same form he once had as a youth on the plains of Africa. Even in his village, he was well renowned. At this moment, to the naked eye, he looked like a graceful black antelope galloping along a gravel road.

He knew his window of opportunity was limited, that the fog would soon consume the town if he did not hurry. He also guessed the true origin of the black spirits. A risky guess, but he suspected the source and ran to head it off. From Paradise Road, he turned south on the gravel lane toward the town council cabin.

He had often spied Walt spending time there. Days, sometimes weeks. With his gait, he could reach the cabin in a matter of minutes.

As he ran, he saw the fog move closer to the road. He, in turn, followed its trail.

When he reached the cabin clearing, his hunch was confirmed. From the smokestack, the fog floated north and east.

Fifty yards off, he stopped and assumed a hunter's position. Keeping low, searching for hiding spaces, he moved to within ten yards of the door before a voice surprised him.

"You wouldn't expect that I would just let you walk in uninvited," someone said from just inside. "And besides, there's no need to sneak. This is, after all, your house."

Sari knew he'd been discovered. He stood up and walked the remaining distance to the cabin's front entrance.

Sitting in a battered chair was an old man, elderly, but not bent. He wore a faded flannel shirt and overalls. His laced work boots were tall, brown, worn out. His white hair was dirty, long, tangled. His skin was white, blotched, and wrinkled. Yet his expression was youthful. Sari could sense the presence of a powerful mind. His sharp eyes examined Sari. "I expected you sooner."

Sari bowed. "I came as quickly as I could."

"Hmm, yes, I see you traveled on foot. Perhaps that explains it. Most of these folks prefer a car, but, frankly, their thirst for speed has made them lazy. You on the other hand seem quite strong and able."

"And you are?"

"Who I am is of little concern. What I can do, or not do, is more important to you. For the sake of simplicity, call me Bill."

Sari nodded and bowed again. "All right then—Bill."

"You are welcome to come in, though I must warn you, I have been quite busy and have yet to clean up."

Bill rose, his frame stretching about five foot ten or so, his weight no more than a hundred fifty pounds. Yet he moved easily, showing no signs of his age.

Sari took a deep breath and followed him inside.

That smell, all too familiar. The smell of dead flesh and blood. From his young days as a spear man to villages filled with great plagues to his numerous flights across battlefields during the Civil War, he knew the smell intimately.

Sari halted at the sight of Walt's remains splayed at length in several pieces around the room. Bloodied arms on the floor. Legs on an old cot. Head and torso still on the table. A cavernous hole where his ribs used to be. And on top of a pole, near the old fireplace, his glistening heart.

"I think you know my subject," said Bill.

"All too well," said Sari.

"He was a good student, though not very perceptive about the subtleties of dark magic. I think you might call him . . . overeager."

Sari folded his hands and stared at Walt's chest cavity. "He was a bright man in my town, always learning."

"Yes, unfortunately, his learning is now over. He spent some useful days with me. Alas, he is useful no more. I promise to clean him up and leave this place as I found it. You will not be inconvenienced."

"Death is always inconvenient," said Sari.

Bill rested his hands on his staff. "How very dramatic." He stood by the table and examined Sari, his eyes sizing up every inch of his long, dark body. "You are the town's ancient leader, I presume, and I hear that you yourself are more than a little familiar with bloody carcasses." He smiled at his joke.

"Yes, I am Sarihaba Kinyaga, a shaman from Africa, but you may call me Sari. I have lived in this town for many decades."

"I am not from this place, though I have traveled through here many times. Seen you occasionally. I find you and your town quite . . . amusing."

"I know where you are from and I know what you do. I am only sorry you have done your deeds here, at the request of someone whose knowledge was fueled by hate."

Bill nodded. "Well, haven't you heard? Hate is my specialty. As far as that goes, Walt was the perfect student."

Sari glanced once again at Walt's lifeless chest. He took a deep breath. "You know then why I am here?"

"Oh do tell, please."

"To convince you to move elsewhere."

Bill leered at Sari, a cruel smile born of arrogance and butchery. "Well, if that's the case, then perhaps we can strike a bargain." He grabbed a chair and sat next to Walt's head. Jabbing his elbow into the skull, he propped himself on the table's edge and grinned. "He was a large man, a lot of work."

"He was a resident of my village," said Sari. "Whatever his faults, he belonged to us."

"Take him, then. I'll be happy to gift wrap him for you."

Sari found a chair, pulled it over, and sat in front of Bill. "Let us talk about the fog. It threatens my village."

"It does indeed."

"May we discuss its removal?"

"My, but you are hasty. No small talk? Chitchat?"

"As you know, time is not on my side. Should you draw it back, I would be happy to be more patient."

"Ah, now that is a smart opening move." Bill clapped his hands together. "A worthy gamble. I can see this is going to be an interesting conversation."

"I thank you for your acknowledgment."

"And courteous too. You really have been well groomed."

"I have lived here for many years. I too, like Walt, am a learner."

"Well, whatever, I give you credit. I would be happy to have you on my team." Bill lowered his elbow and leaned forward with both hands in his lap.

Sari now had his full attention. Under the heat of Bill's scrutiny, he knew that each word he uttered would be crucial. "Then we are negotiating?"

"I suppose so," Bill said. "Though I have to warn you, I'm an expert. You may be surprised at what you end up giving me."

"I do not doubt this in the least. Shall we talk terms?"

"Terms?" Bill said with irritation. "Why must people always be concerned with terms? Why not first and foremost consider gain? That is, after all, what's most important. You get something, I get something. That seems easier than setting up terms. Terms. A waste of time, if you ask me."

"Well spoken. I cannot hide my motive from you. You must know that I do indeed consider gain important."

"Yes, quite right. People establish terms as a front. What's really important is what they want, what they really want, and that's what I am devilishly good at finding out." His grin broadened.

"Have you determined that with me, then?"

Bill brushed a curled finger across his lips. "Well now, I am deciding, even as we speak. Every word you say tells me more than you think."

"Well, let us speak then of wants. I will tell you mine, though I admit, you will discern more than I tell. You are a master of words. I hope you will not hold my simplicity against me."

"I am not for or against anything," Bill said as he caressed Walt's forehead with a finger. "I have no boundaries and therefore am free to change as I see fit. As you will learn, I can be quite flexible."

"A strong position."

"Yes, very. I pride myself on holding strong positions, sometimes subtly, sometimes by force, and yet there is also much to be gained from flexibility."

"Then from my position of weakness—of utmost importance, I seek the safety of my village."

"The whole village, or just certain people in that village?"

"I am its protector and leader. I would hope to keep the whole."

"Ah, but we are negotiating. If there is something you gain, there is something you must give." Bill's eyes narrowed. His voice became a taunt. "So, O wise Sari, what are you and your little village willing to surrender?"

The question startled Sari. Direct, even blunt, as if Bill had already determined how to cut him open with a knife.

Sari skirted Bill's challenge. "Is there something you want? It seems that, in the midst of all this, you also have something to ask."

"I do, of course. Otherwise, why would I sit here and talk?"

"Then let us take your point. Perhaps that would be more satisfying to you."

Bill eased out of his chair and circled around the table where Walt lay. "Here is a prime example of someone I used to want. Alas, want can be tricky. Here today, gone tomorrow. Still, I wouldn't go to this much trouble for just anyone. What I really want are those who I believe also want me."

"And there is someone like this you seek?"

"Oh yes," Bill said firmly. "You have someone who has sought me for quite some time."

Sari folded his arms and glanced across the room. It was a stall tactic to hide his reaction. He understood all too well the gist of Bill's statement.

Bill was not fooled. "Oh, please, Sari, great shaman of Freeland, you must know who I refer to, for you yourself recruited her to bring magic into your village."

"Yes, true enough."

"You can do tricks, amusing tricks I might add, but she has the true knowledge."

"She does."

"So," Bill said with a shrug, "if we both agree, then what's the problem?"

"She is my Dulami," Sari said, "a respected leader in my village."

"A Dulami? Well, very impressive. All the more valuable to me."

Sari turned back to Bill. "I cannot force her to come to you."

"No, but you can be damn persuasive when you try. Look at you, talking to me. Most folks I would have slit and barbequed by now, just like your friend here. But you, you know how to talk to a man. So, you must also have some experience with persuasion. She can be of great service to me, at least for a while. She knows the ropes. I don't have to waste time stringing her along. She knows the deal right up front. No muss, no fuss."

Sari paused, then stood up and walked to the doorway. His eyes followed the fog's trail across the hillsides, a trail that could be traced directly to Freeland. As he turned and faced Bill, he laced his fingers behind his back and planted his feet. "And in return?"

"Well, this fog for instance." Bill pointed his finger toward the fireplace. "I, too, can be quite persuasive."

Sari took a moment to consider Bill's offer. "So, to be clear, you will take my Dulami and move somewhere else?"

"Well, those are the general terms. You never know when I might come back and work out a few more details. Depends on who else you recruit to dazzle your little citizens. Then again, maybe you should just stay solo and stick to doing circus tricks. Drink a little blood, call down fire, tell a fortune or two, things that impress your moronic little village."

Bill sauntered over to the pole with Walt's heart and wedged his shoulder against it.

Sari remained silent.

"Well," said Bill, "you're the one in a hurry. Fog is moving. Won't be long, though your Dulami is certainly impressing me with her spells. I know she can keep it up for a while. Still, I'll get her one way or the other. But you. You've got a shot to save your village. Otherwise, I take the whole lot and throw everyone, including you, to my hungry little friends."

Sari bowed. "You are a wise negotiator. I will see what I can do. In return, if you will draw back the fog and give me time—"

Bill grinned triumphantly. "Time seems important to you."

"In this case, yes."

"Well, then—" Bill faced the old fireplace, inhaled deeply, then spun back to Sari and slowly exhaled. "All right. You have your chance. Now, as the saying goes, you're on the clock." He grinned even more broadly. "Be persuasive my friend."

Sari turned and hurried out the door.

Had it been hours since he had locked himself inside this shoe box? As Stan listened to the frightening noises, it certainly seemed like it. The closet where he hid felt like a coffin, his only light a few dim rays seeping under the bottom of the door. Stan stood for a moment and stretched. As he did, the noise stopped.

After listening for so long to the fearful hissing and groaning, the sudden silence hurt his ears. For a moment, he remained still, afraid that if he moved, the noise would return.

Five minutes passed. Nothing but quiet. Stan put his hand on the knob and twisted it just enough to push the door ajar. Another five minutes. No response to his movements. Emboldened, he shoved the door open and stepped out into the hallway. He was surprised to see sunlight stream through the windows.

As Stan crept to the front door, he noticed the fog had pulled back. Still visible across the road, but no longer spreading toward town. Something or someone had brought it to a halt. Maybe Amanda. The sight gave him hope.

Out on the porch, Stan scanned the hills. So far, so good. His thoughts focused on Amanda, the town, the grocery, his office. He decided to take a brisk walk.

As he snuck up Paradise Road, the area was quiet, too quiet. None of the usual sounds from birds, wind, or bugs. No people either. If Stan had been a stranger traveling through, he would swear the place was deserted. All except for the odd fog bank lingering several yards beyond the road.

The silence was even more frightening than being stuffed in a tiny closet. He worried that perhaps he was the last survivor of a devilish apocalypse.

He spotted them standing on the road—Amanda and Sari. At first, it was a welcome sight. Sari, their leader. Amanda, his wife.

Then it appeared that something was amiss. The look on Amanda's face. So tired and sad. She saw Stan moving toward her but failed to respond. No hand wave or greeting. In fact, when she spotted him, she backed away.

What's worse, Sari put his body between him and Amanda to block his view. He briefly caught sight of her again as she hurried across the road.

Stan picked up his pace, but as he did, she ran faster. "Amanda," he hollered, but she failed to stop.

Why, Stan wondered? Then it became apparent. She was headed toward the fog. Sensing danger, Stan tried to catch her but she was far ahead of him and moving faster with each step. "Amanda!" he yelled. No response.

Sari jumped in front of him again, grabbed his arm, and threw him on his back. The look in his eyes was fierce like a warrior.

"What the hell?" Stan protested.

"She goes to save us from hell," Sari said.

He struggled to get up, but Sari's large foot pushed down on his chest. His poised fist hovered near Stan's head.

When Stan stopped struggling, Sari removed his foot and allowed him to roll over on his stomach.

Perhaps, in a final struggle with her emotions, Amanda turned and looked at him. She did not look afraid. Simply grim and sad.

As Stan's arm reached out, she raised a hand and gave him a final wave. Then she vanished into the fog.

As she disappeared, the sound of a great wind blew through Freeland. The fog backed up into the hillsides and disappeared. In a matter of minutes, Amanda and the black spirits were gone.

Stan jumped to his feet and faced Sari. "What's all this?"

Sari set his feet and crossed his arms. "She chose to sacrifice herself for the village."

"And you let her go?"

"I did," Sari said, "though it would be more accurate to say she weighed her options and chose to go."

"Why?"

Sari pointed toward the hills. "The spirits in the fog required it."

"A trade?"

"Yes, a negotiated settlement."

"That's the best you could do?"

"That was all I could do, my brother. I knew it. She knew it. We both agreed that it was a good thing if one life could save a whole village."

"I didn't hear anything about you volunteering."

"They did not ask for me. If they had, I would have gone."

Stan charged, but Sari jumped out of the way, leaving him to snatch at empty space. "You son of a bitch," he screamed as he whirled back to face him. "You gave up my wife for your own sorry skin."

"I did, and for those in my village, and for you. Not because I am afraid to fight. Because fighting would gain nothing except more death."

"Your death, you mean."

With his fingers pointed sharply, Sari extended his hands.

Stan rose in the air and hung suspended, eye-to-eye with the powerful shaman. Those eyes. Staring at him. Wild, fierce, soul-piercing.

"I have powers you cannot imagine," said Sari, "and knowledge you have yet to witness. Still, if I put all of this into a single command, it would not budge the fog an inch. There are some things beyond human nature and common magic that demand fear and respect. Such is the spirit and power of death. If a bargain is to be made with this great power, a leader should pay careful attention. Your anger is justified, but not wise." His voice rose and echoed across the town square. "Your anger would lead us all to perish."

For a moment, their eyes locked. Looking at Sari's face, Stan could feel the pain and truth of his words.

Sari relaxed his hands and lowered Stan to the ground.

He dropped down and stretched out like a dead man face down in the dirt. Only his digging fingers proved he was still alive.

"In time, you will see the logic," said Sari. "It will never make sense, but at least you may come to understand. The worlds around us are fickle, but, in this case, a door was opened. Amanda chose to step through it. You could not stop her, nor could I. Her fate was inevitable."

Stan remained quiet. Then he let out an exhausted sigh and rolled on his back. His body remained still but his eyes found Sari. "Why her?"

"She had useful gifts coveted by the spirits. Long ago she chose this path and sharpened her talents. Her master called. She could not refuse."

Stan's face filled with anguish. "Not even for love?"

"No, death in particular has no room for love. That is a lesson I learned long ago."

Stan raised himself and sat cross-legged. His face smudged with dirt. His hair dusty. "Now what?" he said.

"Now," Sari replied as he bent down on one knee, "we go on living. That is the choice we make to honor her."

Stan ran his fingers through the dirt again. "You've never been in love, have you, Sari?"

"Oh yes, long, long ago, but I gave up love to continue living. Life and death are intertwined and love has little to do with either. As I grew wiser, I chose to live and forego love."

Stan was not surprised by this answer. Knowing Sari as he did, it made perfect sense. "You're a powerful man, Sari, but an empty man. Without love, there's simply no good reason to live."

Sari's voice softened. "Ah, there, brother, I have learned otherwise. I am a living example. Living in and of itself is a good thing."

Stan shook his head. "I feel sorry for you."

Sari was taken back. He stopped and considered Stan's statement. "Sorry? For me? Do not be sorry for me. No, there is much more to life than love. You will see."

He walked away, his long, slow strides indicative of his patience and survival instincts. After a few steps, he spoke over his shoulder. "I must go and tell the folks hiding in the center that they are safe."

Stan realized that this was the essence of Sari. He had honed his life to a razor sharp edge. All that was left in his body and mind was his will to live. The need for love or any other emotion had been pruned by that necessity.

He remained motionless, eyes peering into the distance for a last glimpse of Amanda. There were only trees and hills and the sound of the wind. The birds had returned and the sky was a deep blue with some puffy clouds. No other sign of anything demonic or human.

Gone again, he thought. *What now?*

V

April 5, 1984

It had been almost a year since Stan had done any work with the paper. After Amanda disappeared, the office, the equipment, everything had been mothballed. Each time Stan worked up the courage to walk to his office, he could only get as far as the Reporter's front door before something gripped him—fear, panic, anger. All he could see was a dark fraction of what used to be Amanda and Stan, Stan and Amanda, Stan and The Freeland Reporter.

Working on the paper or any other project was more than he could stomach. His life had veered beyond his normal routine and his personal awareness about what went on in Freeland. His pain had thrown him into an emotional outer darkness.

For weeks, months, he barely functioned beyond sporadic meals and long rambling walks away from Freeland. Ignoring any warnings, he hoped and welcomed the sight of Walt or one of his cronies, someone willing to put him out of his misery.

He saw Sari occasionally at the Circle and around town, but they seldom spoke. Sari had put it out of his mind, as if Amanda had been a gust of wind passing through.

Stan knew that dwelling on the past had no interest to him. Sari had learned long ago to live without grief, to think only of existing in the present. He expected that everyone who lived in Freeland would eventually learn the same. To him, it was just a matter of time and experience.

Not for Stan. He still held onto the emptiness and hoped, for Amanda's sake, that he would never lose this grief. Observing Sari convinced him of the dangers of having eternal life, at least for humans on this earth. Maybe heaven was better, but here on earth, he'd come to believe it was a good thing to die.

More than anything else, Stan came to this one conclusion. He hated Freeland. He hated the idea of repetitiously publishing a paper destined to be nothing more than an insular expression of one tiny spot on this planet. He hated having his paper read by people who were disconnected from anything else going on in the world.

Most of all, he hated Sari and determined that somehow, someway, he would find an escape hatch to free his soul and body. Given Sari's intuition, he had no idea how he might pull this off. It was a reckless ambition. Yet something irrational pushed him to try.

So day after day in his house or out in the hills, he found himself scheming and making no attempt to hide it, believing that if Sari learned of his plans, he would sentence him to death.

Death, sweet death. Compared to his current circumstance, death would be welcome, the ultimate escape. Matty had managed to slip away peacefully. Stan believed his end would be much worse, but if the result was death, it would still be a blessing.

He remembered his brother, Dave. Had he been working on Stan's rescue? Did he need to be reminded? Stan became obsessed with this question. Mainly because Dave's promise was his last great hope.

This morning he worked up the strength to go into his office. He was greeted warmly by the Plymouths but ignored any invite for small talk.

Stan had brought with him the old piece of scratch paper Dave gave him with his address and phone number, the one he had buried in his closet after Dave escaped.

As he sat in his creaky old chair, it lay unfolded in his lap. Stan was torn about asking for help, putting Dave in more danger. Yet, his desperation forced his hand.

Sitting down at his desk, he pulled out a piece of clean white paper and rolled it into his IBM Selectric. Pausing for a moment, he lowered his fingers on the keyboard and wrote the following:

> *Dear Dave:*
>
> *Five years ago you promised to return and help me escape from Freeland. I'm not sure what if any plans you may have considered during this time, but I would like to send you a note reminding you of your promise. Please help me find a way out of here. I want to come home and would welcome any help you could provide. Remember me as your brother. If there's anything you can do, please think of a way to get me out of here.*
>
> *Here's hoping we meet again.*
> *Stan*

Taking the paper out of the typewriter, he read it over, folded it, put it in an envelope, addressed it, and shoved it under his shirt.

Hurrying out of Plymouth Grocery, he noticed the clear sky, the beautiful weather. Just the simple act of getting in his car and driving to Forestview gave him a renewed sense of hope. If Sari was aware of his act of defiance, all the better.

"Morning," a woman said as Stan walked into the Forestview store. She give him a long look and grabbed a Snicker's bar.

Short and stocky with salt and pepper hair that clung to her scalp, the woman watched Stan hurry down the aisle to the tiny post office.

Outside conversation. Something Stan had not had in years. He felt awkward, like a POW reentering society.

The woman walked up behind him. "You new here?"

Stan hesitated and felt the words stick in his throat. "No, I live a bit up the road."

"Really? Vale?"

"No, more out in the hills."

Her face was a query.

Stan wondered if she thought he might be some mountain hermit from the boondocks who occasionally wandered into town. Her face warned him. She was not far from the truth.

The thought must have struck her as humorous. She laughed. "No mailboxes out in your neck of the woods, huh?"

Stan acted nonchalant. "Nope. Pretty remote."

"Everywhere around here's remote."

"That's true."

"Well," she said. "Have a good one." She moved down the aisle, then turned and gave him another long look. Perhaps to memorize his face in case he might be wanted somewhere.

Stan found the outgoing mail slot and stood in front of it, meditating on its shape. That narrow, rectangular opening, a slim passage to rescue. Somehow, the location, circumference, angle, even the empty space between those four sides, took on a whole new meaning.

"You need help?" someone said. The store cashier.

Startled, Stan glanced over at the counter. "No thanks," he said and threw the letter in the hole.

There it goes, he thought. He tried to bolster his hope by imagining that his decision to mail this letter was an act of freedom, the dissent of a man who chose to publish a significant document about the rights of people to decide for themselves how to live their lives.

He realized it was a silly thought. In the big scheme of things, this was just one more piece of paper connecting writer to recipient. It might be important. It might not. In spite of his immense fantasy, life moved on and this letter was just another envelope taking a routine journey.

The cashier hunched over the counter and kept an eye on Stan. "Anything else I can help you with?"

Time to exit, Stan thought. The letter was on its way. What it would accomplish, he had no idea, but it felt good to send a message. Any message.

As he drove back to his house, he calculated how long it would take the letter to get to San Diego, how long it might be before help came.

He sent out a silent message to Dave as reinforcement. *Come on, my brother. Come and help me get out of here.* He concentrated and let his thoughts travel across the continent in search of deliverance.

May 3, 1984

Stan had thrown caution to the wind—perhaps as a dare, perhaps from grief. Returning to his editorial duties at the Reporter in late April, his thoughts week to week reflected this. Hints here and there of ideas he would never have printed had Amanda been here.

Moreover, he'd been taking chances with his own life. Every so often, when he ate at the Circle, Stan would turn and glare at Sari, daring the shaman to confront him. He had also taken to walking the hills at night, tempting fate to reach out, grab his throat, and leave him in a bloody puddle.

So far, none of it had worked. Sari left him alone. No one in Freeland bothered him. Very few people even talked to him. No hunters or black demons devoured him. In fact, today, as Stan sat at his desk in good health, he looked as normal as the average man on the street.

It was a beautiful spring day, the kind Amanda and he often celebrated with dinner on the porch and love in the sheets. The nights were turning warm. Signs of new foliage sprouted all around Freeland. As of now, death had avoided him.

As he sat and planned the layout for this week's paper, he wondered if anything he might publish could provoke a reaction. So far this morning, nothing came to mind. Just the usual run-of-the-mill ads, listings, and small town news. Strange as it sounded, it felt as if he was being protected.

After dinner, Stan grabbed a flashlight and decided to take another one of his night walks. By now, he was familiar with the terrain. He'd learned to recognize various bird and insect calls and to discern what was normal or amiss in his surroundings. The Stan that Walt met by the water all those years ago was very different from the Stan who headed down the road tonight.

Walt. He puzzled over happened to him since the appearance of the black spirits and where he might have gone. Was he responsible for the disaster? Did Sari punish him as he did Larry Levin?

Sari never talked about him and no mention of his disappearance was ever discussed around town. Just like Larry and Amanda, Walt had been swept cleanly off the planet.

As he walked down Paradise Road, he reached the turnoff toward the cabin, a place he hadn't visited since being interrogated by the town council.

He wondered if they continued to meet there. What if he were to interrupt one of their secret meetings? He even fantasized about finding Amanda there. Not missing, just living undercover, waiting for Stan to discover and take her home.

All these thoughts were intriguing. Who knows? He might discover something fabulous or something deadly. Either one was fine with him. He decided to head toward the cabin.

As he hiked down the road, the gravel under his feet crunched. Each step sounded like a kid chewing on a mouthful of cereal. For his own amusement, Stan played around with how fast he walked. Long steps, extended chewing. Shorter steps, faster chewing. He even ran to make the echoes sound like brief bursts of gunfire.

His mind preoccupied, he paid no attention to distance until the cabin came into view. When he spotted it, he refocused and slowed down.

Stan crept up to the front door. To his disappointment, the property was deserted. No cars, no lights, no signs of anyone inside.

There was still enough daylight to illuminate the house and the lake. A person could easily be enchanted by the quiet beauty of this place. On this spring night, it might be the ideal setting to sit on a stoop and enjoy a peaceful evening. And for a moment, that's exactly what he did.

Then he heard it—the snap of a twig, the faint sound of footsteps. It brought him to attention. Someone was coming down the road. Maybe Walt had returned. Maybe Sari had been tracking him. He sat erect on the porch, his eyes focused on the road.

A shadowy figure snuck toward him, his progress slow and erratic. When he neared the cabin, Stan picked up several nice size stones, snuck over to a porch corner and froze. For now, the element of surprise was on his side.

He couldn't make out who it was, a man perhaps, slightly taller than him. Slim build. Definitely not Sari or Walt.

The tracker seemed unsure where he was going, but Stan had no doubt who he was following. Every so often, the man would swivel around to catch his bearings, then resume his search.

When he came within twenty yards of the porch, Stan threw a stone to his right. It thunked on the ground near the lake. The man ducked and peered in that direction. Cautiously, he followed the echo toward the lakeshore. Now the hunter became the hunted. Stan stepped off the porch and trailed him.

Another ten yards and Stan threw a second stone to his right. It landed in a clearing and struck another stone with a metallic ping. The man heard the sound and moved in that direction.

Letting out a loud cry, Stan charged. Within seconds, he hit the prowler like a defensive lineman—head up, arms around the hips—a perfect three-point tackle. The stalker collapsed and landed flat on his stomach. Stan raised a stone to hit him in the skull.

The man pleaded, "No, no, man, don't hurt me, please."

Stan knew the sound of that voice. Brent. He stood up and rolled him over. "Shit, Brent, I could have killed you, you know. Why the hell are you following me?"

Brent flinched and covered his face with his hands. "I-I saw you on the road, wondered where you were going."

"So?"

"You're one of the insiders here, married to Amanda and everything."

"Yeah, so?"

"I wondered if you might know how to get out of this place."

The words caught Stan by surprise. For a moment, Brent's statement petrified him. Stone in hand, Stan hovered over him like an angel of death. "Goddamn it, Brent, you're stupid to come out here like this. You're lucky it's me and not some fucking hunter looking for a body to carve up. In this place, it's been known to happen, you know."

"Yeah," Brent said quietly. "I keep hearing rumors."

"They're not rumors." Stan's adrenaline took its toll on his knees. Feeling faint, he bent over and tried to regain his sense of balance.

Brent cautiously stood up. "Shit, you really scared me, man. I thought you were going to kill me."

"If you had been someone else, I might have. In case you're not aware, this place is dangerous."

Brent's head drooped, a habit he had when Rita scolded him. "No kidding?"

"Yes."

"Then why are you here?"

"Same reason you are, I guess. Looking for answers."

"To what?"

"You just said it. I'm just like you. I want out of this goddamn freak show."

Brent seemed surprised. "Really?"

"Really."

Brent turned to look at the lake. "Any ideas?"

Stan shook his head. "Hell, you think I've got some inside secret?"

"Well, maybe. I came here because of you. I thought maybe you might help me find a way out."

"Well, now you know. I don't know any more than you." Stan's jaw tensed. "And let's get one thing straight, Brent. I didn't drive you here. I didn't get you lost. And I didn't make you stop. You asked me a question on a road, I answered. Stop blaming me. I'm stuck here too, you know."

Brent took two steps back. Once again, he looked alarmed. Then he sat on the ground and buried his head in his hands. "Goddamit," he groaned.

Stan regretted his outburst, more so as he heard Brent's agony echo across the lake. "Hey, Brent, look, I'm sorry. I don't mean to be such an asshole. We both want the same thing. That's a step in the right direction. Maybe we can put our heads together and think. Maybe there's something to discover here."

Brent stopped groaning and rubbed his hands through his hair. "You think there's a chance?"

"I don't know. It's a gamble, but I want out, you want out. Maybe others do as well. Who knows?"

Brent eyed Stan for a moment before standing and extending his hand. "Partners, then?"

Stan shook and patted him on the shoulder. "Teammates, brothers, whatever. You, me, Rita. Maybe there's hope."

Brent mulled over Stan's offer. "You're part of Sari's inner circle. How do I know you won't turn me in?"

Stan shook his head. "First, I'm not in his so-called circle. Far from it. Second, you can't trust anyone in this town. For that matter, I don't know what you'll do either. Maybe you're Sari's little spy."

Brent dropped his head again.

"But from what I can tell, we both want out. That's enough motivation for me. And even if Sari finds out, so what? It's no big secret to him what I think, or you either for that matter."

"Really?"

"Really. I'd be willing to bet he knows we're here right now. That puts us both in hot water."

Brent stood quietly and thought. His eyes wandered back to the lake. "Okay. Good enough. Where do we start?"

Stan pointed. "How about the cabin over there? I know that's where the town council meets. Let's poke around and see what we can find."

Brent turned to face the cabin and hesitated. "Well—"

"Whatever you do, stay sharp and keep quiet. You hear anything, let me know. I don't know what wanders around out here at night, but I don't want to be surprised."

"Okay. Sharp, quiet. Got it."

"Damn place gives me the creeps."

Standing at the cabin's doorway, Stan shivered. Too much darkness dwelt in this building. Still, there was only one way in. Drawing a deep breath, he entered.

There was an odd odor in the room. A cross between mildew and something more foul. "I've got a flashlight," said Stan. "Let's see if we can locate a lantern."

Rotating the beam, Stan surveyed the room. There was a long table in the middle and chairs lined against the walls. "Check over there in the cabinets." He shined his light toward the kitchen.

Brent broke away and opened the pantry doors. "Hey, they're here. Couple of Colemans and some matches."

"That's great. See if they'll light."

Brent took the two lanterns, lined them up on the table, and lit the pilots. A low flame appeared. Same for the second. He adjusted the kerosene and both lamps flared. "One for each of us," he said.

"If you move something," said Stan, "be sure and put it back. We don't want anyone to know we're snooping."

"Got it."

They poked through various closets and cupboards looking for clues. It was such a small place, it didn't take long to search the whole room. Nothing.

"Hell," Stan said. "I can't believe, with everything I know that's gone on here—"

"Nothing I can see out of the ordinary," said Brent.

Stan pulled out a chair, sat down, and rubbed his chin. "I don't believe it. There's got to be something here."

Standing up, he circled around the room and shined a lantern on the floor, the walls, any crack he could locate. He searched for anything like a hidden drawer or a hole in the floor. "I know for a fact, Walt hung out here. He cooked up all kinds of sorcery and I'm willing to bet he did most of it right here." Round and round he marched like a blind man looking for a door.

"I don't see a thing," said Brent. "Looks pretty straightforward to me."

"Nothing is straightforward in this place, trust me."

Brent grabbed a chair and eased down. "Well, I don't know what else to do. You just want to keep looking?"

"I do. I honestly believe there's something here to help us."

Brent circled his lantern around the room. "Well," he said. "How about we search the ceiling?"

Stan halted. "Hell, you're right. Nothing like the obvious to throw you off. When in doubt, look up."

Raising his lantern, Brent illuminated the roof. "There's something up there. Looks like a shelf of some sort."

Following the light to a small nook high above the fireplace, Stan dragged over a chair. He stood on it, reached up, and felt the shape of a book. Small, rectangular, with a hard cover.

Easing it off the shelf, he stepped down, pulled his chair next to the long table, and began to leaf through the pages. The texture of the thick cover and yellowed pages made it appear like it might have come from a medieval monastery.

"I'll be damned," said Stan. "Must be one of Walt's."

Brent stood behind him. "What is it?"

"No idea. It's not even in English. Lots of drawings, strange markings."

Stan examined the front and back covers. No words, nothing to indicate a title or content. He turned to the inside page. Something resembling a title was scrawled by hand, but not in English. He rifled back and forth through the pages and saw little notes written in the corners and on the sides. "There's stuff written here, looks like in pen. In English. Must be Walt's writing."

As Stan leafed through more of the book, it hit him. His hands fell flat on the pages. "Spells."

"Spells?" said Brent.

"Yeah, magic, sorcery. It's a book of spells. Walt must have used some of these to attack my house."

"But they're not in English. How would he know what they're saying?"

"He wouldn't, unless someone helped him translate."

"Who?"

"My guess—a sorcerer. A damn good sorcerer. That would explain how he called up the black spirits."

"But if that's the case, where'd he go?"

"Well, I know the spirits took Amanda. As to what happened to Walt—"

Stan looked up from the book and scanned around the room. The smell. Musty, yes, but also burnt. Foul burnt, like the smell of rotting flesh. Rising from his chair, he took the lantern and cautiously approached the fireplace. Brent followed just behind his shoulder.

Stan held out the lantern. The light confirmed it. Ash. He reached down to sift through the powder and found some small bits of bone. And then, as confirmation, he uncovered a tooth.

"What's that?" Brent said.

Stan held the tooth up to the light. "Walt, I guess, or what's left of him."

Horrified, Brent scrambled out the door. Stan could hear him wretch outside.

Stan threw the tooth back in the fireplace, lowered the lantern, and stepped back. "You crazy son of a bitch," he said and shuddered. "You deal with the devil, this is what happens."

Stan had the sudden urge to flee. The air in this place made his flesh crawl. But first, he needed to cover his tracks. "Brent, come in here and help me put everything back."

"Not me, man," Brent said from outside the door. "I'm not setting another foot in that place. If we were smart, we'd get the hell out of here."

"That's the plan, but we have to put everything back the way we found it. I need your help."

Brent peeked through the doorway.

Stan pointed toward the kitchen. "Put the lanterns back just the way you found them. I'll arrange the chairs."

Brent and Stan combed the cabin to make sure whatever they disturbed was returned to its original place. Chairs, lanterns, everything except—

"What about the book?" said Brent.

Stan brushed his hand over the cover. "I'll take it, keep it tucked away, do some research. I'll check to see if there might be something we can use."

Brent reached out and timidly touched it. "Sure would like to know what's in here."

"Don't be too curious." Stan held the book just out of Brent's reach. "If you need a warning, just look in the fireplace. This is black stuff. Use with caution."

"And you?"

"What about me?"

"You gonna use what's in there?"

"I have no idea what's in there, but if I find something useful, then yes. Pretty obvious, though, I'm going to need some help. Hopefully not from Walt's sorcerer."

"Hopefully."

With everything returned, they backpedaled out of the cabin.

Stan pressed the book to his side. "Go on home, Brent. I'll let you know what I find."

Brent eyed him suspiciously. "You sure?"

"Yeah, we should split up. Less chance of being noticed."

Brent hovered for a moment. "Teammates?"

Stan gripped Brent's shoulder. "Teammates."

Brent look relieved. "All right, man. See you tomorrow."

"As always."

Brent sprinted for the road, anxious to put distance between him and this crematorium.

Stan sat on the doorstep and watched him disappear. He could feel the book in his hands, heavier than when he first pulled it down. The cover seemed to meld with his fingers and fit into the contour of his palm. He questioned whether or not this might be part of its sorcery. Not just spells, but the power to draw in and entice, to consume body and soul.

Remembering Walt in the fireplace, Stan wanted to heave the book and run for his life, but his curiosity was palpable. Holding it tight, he stood up and started the long walk home. Eerie, the sensation he had as he approached Paradise Road. Having the book in his hand made him feel powerful.

May 10, 1984

Another week. Another paper. Stan inserted bits and pieces of his own thoughts about choice, freedom, the importance of the human spirit. What did this have to do with routine life in Freeland? Absolutely nothing.

He didn't care. His struggle for freedom had become an obsession. And, as editor of the paper, he could print whatever he wanted. Call it his defiant expression. Call it freedom of the press. It was ironic, trapped as they all were in this place, that his printed outbursts were tolerated. For how long was anyone's guess.

One person who certainly seemed interested in the subject was Brent. Every so often he would slip by Stan's door and peek in. He said nothing but his eyes spoke clearly. He wanted some sign of hope.

Stan always shook his head "no" and bore the pain of his disappointment. He had to hand it to him. Brent was persistent. The desire for freedom, a fever. Once caught, hard to quell, at least for two people in Freeland. Stan continued to include something about it in each edition of The Reporter.

As for the book, Stan hid it in his house. To be more precise, he buried it under some boxes in his closet. He didn't dare bring it to work and had to settle for leafing through it after hours late at night.

Try as he might, he couldn't make heads or tails of any of it. Walt's notes hinted at some of the spells, but without a translation, Stan had no idea how to interpret them.

His primary language was English, mixed with some Latin and a smidgen of Spanish. None of this helped. Whoever wrote this came from a world completely foreign to him. When he touched the pages, he was sure his fingers caressed a relic from an unknown civilization.

Yet he kept returning to it, a testament to his belief that it had its own mind and would somehow guide him to its meaning. Sometimes he would sit for hours and just run his fingers over each page.

To Stan, if felt like a séance, an attempt to communicate with spirits from the other world. This thought was both encouraging and frightening. What help did these spirits offer? And what price would they demand for a tour through their dark language?

Late one night, deep into one of his book sessions, Stan heard a mysterious noise drift into his bedroom. It was a warm night. His windows were open and he could easily pick up any sound out of the ordinary.

As it rose and fell, the noise sounded like a cross between a whisper and a moan. Not animal, not human, not of this world. He closed the book, returned it to its hiding place, and sat on his bed.

With great dread, he walked to the front of the house and listened by the front door. No doubt, there was something strange in the street. He crept out on the porch. No one. Nothing visible. The noise had stopped.

Suddenly a gale force hit him in the face and knocked him back into his hallway. It swirled through the house like a mad ghost, ripping at loose papers and pushing around furniture. Then, as quickly as it came, it disappeared.

Rising to his feet, Stan returned to the porch.

A man stood outside his gate. A strange looking man in dingy overalls with long dirty white hair, an old face, and piercing eyes. He stood perched against a long staff. Stan knew who'd come to visit him—the father of the black spirits.

"Good evening, sir," the man said. "Wonderful night to be out and about, wouldn't you say?" Seeing the look on Stan's face, he continued, "Well, I suppose my visit is a bit of a surprise. Where are my manners? My name is Bill. Forgive the intrusion but I already know who you are. Stan, I believe?"

Stan stepped to the lip of his porch. "That's right."

The man looked human, and yet not. Something in his eyes suggested cruelty, arrogance, death. Bill gave a long, graceful bow. "Yes, indeed, we have a passing acquaintance, you and I."

Stan's anger boiled. "More than passing I would say. You took my wife."

"Took? As in kidnaped? Oh, now there is a lie if I ever heard one. I believe she came voluntarily, as your shaman should have explained."

"No one comes voluntarily to you without getting some kind of push."

Bill was amused and touched his finger to his chin. "Why, there's a good observation. Persuading and volunteering often go hand in hand. I would agree. One definitely needs the other." He elevated his staff and held it with both hands behind his neck. "And that would explain, of course, why I'm here."

"Really? You want me to volunteer, too? How did I get so lucky?"

"Sometimes," Bill said with a grin, "you just have to be in the right place at the right time."

"Ah, so a visit from the Prince of Darkness is my good fortune. Great! And, of course, you've just come to have a friendly discussion, maybe add a little black persuasion. Pelt me with a demon or two. Threaten my soul. Otherwise, no big deal. Am I clear on this?"

"Why," Bill said, "I think you've summed it up quite nicely."

"Of course."

"So—" He paused and looked intently at Stan.

Stan sat down on a porch step. "So?"

"My goodness, you wouldn't let a guest just stand in the street, now, would you?"

"I think that depends on the guest."

"Yes, well, I can assure you, I'm a very important guest, to you especially."

"No doubt. Because—"

Bill twirled his stick between two fingers and winked. "I bring good news." He waited, but Stan remained seated. "Well then, I'll just make my point here, without hospitality, though I must say, I'm a bit disappointed. If Amanda was here, I'm sure she'd encourage you otherwise."

"Perhaps, but she isn't, thanks to you, so pardon me if I don't throw down a welcome mat."

For a moment, an odd type of light appeared in Bill's eyes.

Stan guessed that behind his facade lay a brilliant, calculating mind always a step ahead of his next victim. He could throw up resistance but Bill was no fool. Even as he talked, Stan felt the surrounding temperature drop a good twenty degrees. He nodded. "So. Speak."

"I'll make you an offer," said Bill.

"Really." Stan folded his arms.

"Not just an offer." Bill threw his arms wide for emphasis. "Let's call it . . . opportunity."

Stan shrugged. "Whatever. Get on with it."

Bill planted the tip of his stick on the street with a loud clack. "You have something that belongs to me."

Stan leaned back and wrapped his fingers around his knee. "Is that right?"

"Yes, a book, a very valuable book."

Stan gave Bill a dismissive wave. "Oh, that thing. About yea big, kind of old and smelly?"

"Why, I think that describes it quite nicely."

"Your book, you say?"

"From my library, yes, though, on rare occasions, I let good friends borrow it."

"Like Walt, I imagine?"

"Exactly."

"Whose now dead in a fireplace."

Bill froze and for a moment, his grin disappeared. Then, just as quickly, it returned. "Well, yes, unfortunately. I'm afraid he failed to pay his overdue fines."

Stan tilted forward and dropped his hands between his knees. "This book. You wrote it?"

"Well, not technically, but I can assure you. I was its source of inspiration."

"No doubt."

Again, Bill bowed and motioned to Stan. "And now it belongs to you."

"I'm guessing it's more accurate to say that I belong to it, but no matter, yes, I have it." Stan waited. "I suppose you want it back."

"Indeed, I'm quite proud of what's in it. It wouldn't do to have just anybody carry it around."

"Someone like me, you mean?"

Bill looked amused. "Someone who doesn't understand its . . . usefulness. *That* would be an immense waste."

"You'd rather someone else have it? Someone more open to your invitation? Someone who would, say, invite you into his house?"

"Precisely."

Stan noted how Bill seemed to be enjoying himself. The pitter-patter of repartee, the thrust and jab of matching wits. All good fodder and terrifying to watch. "Why not just kill me and take it?"

For a moment, Bill's body went rigid. Then he blinked and returned. "It doesn't work that way."

His last statement puzzled Stan. He thought of Walt's ashes in the fireplace and the demonic energy thrown off by Bill's last visit. He thought of Bill's ability to persuade Sari to surrender Amanda. Surely, with his power, it would be no problem to blast Stan off the face of the earth and simply take back the book.

Yet here he was in front of his house making a polite request. What was holding him back? Only one thing that Stan could imagine. "You can't take it, can you? Not by force anyway."

Bill remained quiet.

"Well, I'll be damned. I get it. Really. The book isn't yours unless someone gives it to you. Your possession depends on my consent."

Bill bowed again and extended his right hand. "I'm impressed, Stan. For a novice, you're a shrewd observer of the rules of magic."

"My God, even the devil has his limits now, doesn't he?" Stan let loose and laughed.

Bill returned Stan's laugh with an odd grin. "Well, as you may know, we all exist in a framework of strength and weakness."

"And to think, I assumed you were all powerful."

"It's all relative, this thing with power. One moment yes, the next, no. You as a resident of Freeland should understand. Up one day, down the next. I've learned from experience, good and evil are a very tricky business."

His shrewd observation put a damper on Stan's glee. True, he had the book, but what he chose to do with it could mean life or death. Each step he took could be his last. "So, you want the book, I have the book. Somewhere in this process it must be surrendered—by choice, I imagine. You know this, now I know this. Where does that leave us?"

Bill elegantly twirled his fingers toward Stan. "Where we started. With opportunity."

"Whose? Yours or mine?"

"That remains to be seen."

"Well, in my mind, that's called stalemate."

"Not necessarily. You see, I also have something that belongs to you."

"You mean—"

"What I took, I can also return."

"For a book."

"Not just any book. This one is quite special."

"You'd trade Amanda for the book?"

Bill paused and pursed his lips. "It's a crude term, trade. I like to think of it as a mutual exchange of gifts, a goodwill gesture on both sides of the aisle."

Stan was never very good at playing games like poker and chess. The challenge of calculating and recalculating seemed exhausting to him. In this case, however, he understood how he might have benefitted from their strategies.

At this moment, Bill held a definite advantage. Stan might guess where Bill was headed, but in reality, he had no clue. It was Stan's desperation versus Bill's gamesmanship, and Bill was smarter, much smarter.

Stan tried the only strategy he could think of—stall. "I have to say the offer is tempting, but, unfortunately, you have a bad reputation."

"An unfortunate misunderstanding."

"There's no misunderstanding here. Take Walt for instance. What opportunity did you offer him?"

Bill's expression went flat. "Ah, yes. Poor Walt."

"Yeah. Poor Walt. Poor Stan, too. Poor anybody who thinks you can be trusted."

"Then, following this logic, there must be something in the bargain that guarantees the outcome, right?"

"I don't know how you can guarantee that a liar won't lie or a killer won't kill. And since you're the king of lies and murder, I suppose you just can't help yourself."

"As I said, there are strengths and weaknesses in every framework."

"Really? You mean there's something in your framework that would keep you from lying, backstabbing, chopping me up into little pieces, burning me in the fireplace?"

"Indeed, there are many ways to ensure boundaries."

"But you're not going to tell me yours, right?"

Bill's eyes turned mischievous. "What's the fun in that?"

Stan frowned and crossed his arms. "Well then, here we are again, back to stalemate. No guarantees, no book."

"No book, no Amanda."

"Then what's the point?"

Bill lifted his right hand and waved it dramatically. "Point? Point? Why, it's the game, my man. It's the process. Most of all, it's the possibility of—winning."

Stan laced his fingers on top of his head. "You can't win if you don't play. This isn't playing, this is running around in circles. The problem is, all games have rules and you can't be trusted to play by any of those rules. Someone like you doesn't think that way. So, technically, there's no game here. There's just you blowing hot fucking smoke up my ass."

Bill went quiet. Something in this conversation gave him pause. Instead of his usual catlike thinking, Stan's blunt analysis had pulled him up short. He could tell by the look on his face. One tactic didn't work. The old sorcerer was shifting strategies.

Stan took some satisfaction that at least the nasty old bugger was working for his dinner. He laid his hands in his lap and waited.

"Within the book," Bill said.

"What about it?" Stan demanded.

"As I said, it's a very special book."

"We're starting to repeat ourselves, aren't we?"

"I can share some of its secrets."

"That doesn't get us off this rock. I don't need secrets. I need something—"

"For protection."

"Call it a guarantee."

"Right, then call it what you like. A guarantee."

Now it was Stan's turn to think. "What's in the book that would guarantee you keep your word?"

"Oh, a number of things. You see, the book is actually neutral in its outcome. Powerful, yes, but not prone to anything, dark or light. So, spells can be used for good or evil. It's up to the one who carries it to know the difference."

A profound revelation. In a few short sentences, Bill had given Stan an important clue about the book's purpose. He considered this a major step forward. "So?"

"Think about it. There are spells that could be used for good. For example, protection."

"So? I'm no sorcerer. How does that help me?"

"It doesn't, but I know someone who could."

Stan came up short. "You'd send someone to show me how to protect me from you?"

"Absolutely. Here's my offer. I'll send you . . . Amanda."

Stan was intrigued. "Yeah?"

Bill leaned forward. "Does that get us off this rock?"

Stan had to admit. He was cornered. "It's certainly a step in the right direction."

Bill's face lit up. "Then we're playing again."

The ball was back in Stan's court. "There's one more thing."

"Ah," Bill exclaimed, "the bargaining chip. I knew we'd get to this sooner or later."

"I want out of this town. I don't want to be trapped any more in Freeland. I want my old life back. I want to go home. I want . . . to be free."

Bill aimed his staff at Stan. "Yes, that's a common sentiment among men. Free. Such a loose term. What does it really mean?"

"It means I'm stuck here under Sari's power and I'd like to go home, my real home, and not be stranded here in this pissy little magic dungeon."

Bill smirked. "And?"

"So this is the bargain. Amanda, protection, freedom for everyone in Freeland. That in exchange for the book."

Bill gave Stan's offer some thought. He raised his head toward the sky and rubbed his chin with a finger.

Genuine thought or more teasing? Stan couldn't tell.

Then Bill fixed his wily eyes on him. "My, oh, my. Who would have thought you could wield so much cooperation from—what did you call me? The devil?"

"As you said, it's a very important book. Your words, not mine."

"Indeed."

"Are we agreed?"

"Why, Mr. Blankenship, I believe we've reached a settlement." Bill lifted his stick straight up in the air. "Congratulations."

Despite his evil reputation, Stan had to admire Bill's suave. It was all he could do not to run up, shake his hand, and pat him on the back. The old goat was that persuasive.

A moment passed between them. Stan was sure that Bill had sensed his admiration. His broad grin proved it.

"So," Stan said. "What's next?"

"Next?"

"A contract, agreement, something to sign?"

Bill laughed, a deep rumble that danced up and down the road. "Ah, those old wives' tales about signing in blood, that sort of hogwash? As if paper and pen could hold all of this together. No, my friend, these are words we speak and words that carry forward." His voice turned serious. "I do not take these words lightly and neither should you. There'll be no mistaking when it comes time to move forward. That I can promise." Bill's eyes narrowed and his smile disappeared. "And if I deliver, you must deliver."

A sudden chill in the air made Stan shiver. He rubbed his arms and thought about the return of Amanda. "She'll come soon, I hope."

"Yes, soon. Very soon. Perhaps sooner than you'd like."

"Why's that?"

Bill swung his walking stick like a pendulum. "Ah, humans love to wish for what they haven't got. Then, when that wish comes true, they're left to deal with the fallout. Still, a bargain is a bargain and what happens after that is of no concern to me."

Stan stretched a hand toward Bill. "We are agreed then?"

Bill gave him an amused look and kept swinging. "Indeed we are. You and I are now partners. You've just made a deal with the devil. How does that sound?"

"Frightening."

"But exciting, too, I would imagine. You see? Not so hard to understand, is it? It's the game that makes all this worthwhile. The fact you're playing is good." Bill raised his right hand and pinched his index finger and thumb together. "Now tell me you don't enjoy this just a wee bit?"

Stan paused."Maybe, maybe not. The problem with you is that the game is never over."

"Well, I prefer to say that there's always a next time. Why stop playing when you're having so much fun? I would say that makes me an eternal optimist. Quite the opposite from the dreary opinion most people have of me. You see, Stan, how sunny and benevolent I can be?"

Bill wielded the stick with two hands like a sword and swung it rapidly over his head in a whirling circle. A loud boom and another gust of wind. Stan raised his hands and covered his eyes. When it all died down, Bill was gone.

Back in the house, Stan checked to ensure the book was still where he'd left it. Given his new bargain, it had become precious and endearing, like a comforting treasure. He felt proud that the book was his. Tucking it back into its hiding place, he went to bed and slept fitfully.

In the morning, as Stan sat at his desk, he waited for Brent to pass by his office door. When he slipped in at midmorning, Stan could tell he was not expectant, just doing this out of habit and meager hope. Stan looked him in the eyes and nodded *Yes.*

"Really?" said Brent.

"Really," said Stan.

"You know something?"

"I do."

Brent sat down and clapped his hands. "What?"

"I can't explain right now, but it's good news, for all of us."

Brent nearly danced for joy. He clapped his hands and did an awkward pirouette. "That's great, man. I'm telling you, I can't wait."

He clapped his hands again. "Can I tell Rita?"

"Not yet. Seriously. Not a word to anyone. Big things are happening but you've just got to be cool. Please. Not a peep."

Brent slid his fingers over his lips. "Sealed."

"Good enough. Now go run the store. Pretend nothing's happened."

"I'll run the store, but I won't pretend anything. Rita will just think I'm in a good mood."

"Okay, then do your best to make her believe that."

"Will do." He stood up and hurried back into the store. Stan could hear him yell, "Hey Rita. Want to eat out tonight?"

"Really?" she squealed.

Stan sat at his desk, also pleased. Help was coming. It wouldn't be long now. And to think, he had bargained with the devil. His dad, so confident in his own ability to negotiate anything with anyone, would be proud.

May 17, 1984

Amanda arrived at dusk while Stan sat on the porch and poured over the paper's mockup. She strolled casually down Paradise Road, a woman out for a nice evening walk.

Stan glanced up and immediately dropped his papers.

She waited by the gate wearing jeans, a light-blue cotton top, and a black nylon jacket. Her dark hair was longer but otherwise she looked exactly the same as when she left.

As husband and wife separated for more than a year, Stan expected to be happy about this reunion, but something in her demeanor seemed detached, not quite in this world, not quite aware of whom Stan was. He sensed it as she gazed at the house, then Stan, then back at the house.

He stood up. "Amanda?"

"Stan?" she said.

Cautiously, he walked down the sidewalk, opened the gate, and stopped in front of her. She looked ethereal, though her body was intact and touchable.

"Amanda? Is that really you?" He touched her cheek.

She firmly grasped his wrist. "Of course, Stan."

"You've come back?"

"Yes, it's me."

Stan folded her in his arms. He kept quiet, afraid that saying something might make her vanish, but he was reassured when she gently nestled on his chest. He broke the silence. "Want to come inside?"

"I do," she said. "I want to come inside and help with the book."

Her comment stopped him cold. He glanced down. "You know about the book?"

"Oh yes, I'm well acquainted with it. I'm here to help you, as promised by Bill. It was part of the agreement."

"The agreement was to have you come back, not just help me with the book. You are staying, aren't you?"

She folded her arms around his waist. "Of course, for as long as you need me."

Stan pulled back and looked carefully at her. In appearance, there was no doubt she had returned. In personality, it felt like someone else, or, as Stan thought about it, the lack of someone. Still, he was glad to see her. "Come on in, then. Come back home." He took her hand and led her inside.

Amanda sat primly on the couch and followed him with curious eyes.

Stan carried in a dining room chair and sat in front of her. He dropped his hands on her knees. "What's wrong, Amanda. You don't look well."

Amanda laid her hands in her lap. "I'm fine, Stan."

"You're sure? Because I'd get you help if you needed it. Just tell me."

"Nothing's wrong, Stan. It's you who needs help. We're going to help you be free."

Stan pushed back in his chair. "Who's we?"

"Bill and I. It was part of the agreement."

She was beautiful, physically present, yet somehow empty. He couldn't bear to see her this way, the body of his wife, the presence of a stranger. "You never really answered my question outside."

Amanda glanced around the room. "What question?"

"Are you back for good? I want you to come back and stay with me."

"I'm here. That's all that matters. If you want me to stay, I'll stay."

"Can you tell me what happened?"

"When?"

"Last year, when you left to be with the black spirits."

"I went to save Freeland, Stan. Sari and I thought it best. One person for a village. The town was spared because I went to my master. That's what I am, Stan—a witch. This is who I serve."

Stan grasped her hands. "All right," he said. "Then stay forever. That's my wish."

"I'll stay as long as you want."

As odd as she acted, Stan was happy to see her and tried to make her comfortable. "You want something to eat?"

"No, I'm not hungry."

"Drink?"

"No, not thirsty."

"Well, can I get you anything?"

"How about the book?"

Stan shook his head. "The book can wait. I'm just happy you're home, Amanda. I just want to spend some time with you, that's all."

"Yes, Stan. I'm home. Home is where the book is. I need to look at the book."

"Yes, I understand, but aren't you glad to be here? Can't we just forget about the book until tomorrow?"

"Bill sent me to help. He said you wanted to be free. It's all in the book. The book will set us free."

Stan finally understood the fine print of his agreement with Bill. Amanda had come home, but this was a different woman. This was not his wife Amanda. This Amanda was sent to carry out Bill's agenda.

He rose from his chair and shook his head. "I doubt we'll ever be free of this place. Seems whatever agreement I make always has a catch."

Amanda would not be swayed. "Bring the book and I'll help you."

"No book tonight, dear. It's you and me this evening, just being together. Whatever's happened in the past, whoever you are, I'm glad you're back. I missed you terribly."

"I'm glad to be back. I'm glad to help you be free."

Going to the kitchen, Stan threw together some dinner. A pot of spaghetti, salad, bread. As he prepared the meal, Amanda sat at the dining room table and watched him closely. As he worked, Stan had a feeling that it was not her watching. It was someone else inside that body that kept an eye on him and on the book.

A noise woke him from his troubled sleep. Stan could see the illuminated face of the alarm clock. 3:18. Then he noticed that Amanda was missing.

He twisted in bed and saw a light on in the hallway. Getting up, he heard rustling in the kitchen, the sound of pages turning. At the dining room table, she sat reading the book.

He stood behind her and watched her work. "Amanda?"

Amanda remained focused on a page. "I'm studying."

Stan approached carefully and noticed how her body bent over the book, how her fingers moved swiftly across the page. "You found the book?"

"Oh, yes, I knew where it was." She turned another page and drew her finger across a line of text.

"How'd you know?"

"The book told me, Stan. The book is alive, you know. It can speak."

Stan put a hand on her shoulder and gently squeezed. "You don't need to read that now. Come back to bed."

"I'm studying, Stan. I can help you but I have to read the book first. There's a lot to learn."

"Why tonight? Why not tomorrow?"

"Time is precious. The book wants to help."

"You're not tired?"

"No."

"Then let me stay here with you."

Amanda kept reading. "That's fine. Just don't interrupt. I have so much to cover. The sooner I learn, the sooner I can help."

"Fine." Stan took a step back. "Want some coffee?"

"No thanks."

Amanda leaned forward and studied like a student cramming for a final exam.

Stan had never seen her so intense. At this moment, her sole focus was the book. His presence was barely noticed. "Suit yourself."

Reluctantly, he left the kitchen and buried himself on the couch. His mind raced. Bill was still maneuvering. He realized the real meat of their agreement was in the nuance of the word, the implied interpretation. Stan revisited what he had said to Bill, the exact wording of their final agreement. As he dozed off, he tried to remember what he'd missed.

May 18, 1984

In a remote canyon corner, the morning sun peeked above the crest line. Bill looked up and observed the nimble rays of light washing down the rock wall. He pointed his right index finger and squinted through one eye as he followed a single ray to the canyon floor.

O yes, it appeared innocent enough, but add a few of the right words, a touch of darkness, and it could be as deadly as a bullet and twice as hot. It wouldn't be the first time he played with nature.

He laughed at the thought. Today, he had plans in mind, big plans that he intended to launch from this cozy little cove, and he would do it without a single person noticing. It was a tiny, well-hidden fortress, perfect for a day of delicious mischief.

With Amanda distracting Stan, he was ready to move forward, ready to unleash a flurry of surprises on that pretender Sari and his ignorant village. When that was taken care of, he'd deal with whoever or whatever was left, especially Stan and the book. He'd bring his powers to bear on all of them.

Of course, he could use Amanda in a variety of ways—as an offensive weapon or a bargaining chip. After that, he'd move in for the conquest. He liked his plan. He liked his odds. Most of all, he liked to win.

Bill danced around elegantly in a circle, toeing his boots, twirling in his overalls, waving his hands and fingers. For a man his age, he was extremely nimble and quite knowledgeable about dances he knew from around the world. Europe, Asia, Africa, South America. He knew every step in great detail. He'd seen them all, even helped inspire some of them. Dancing was a symbol of victory and today he would be victorious.

When he finished, he rested on a chair that he had carried with him for a couple of centuries. Taken as a memento during one of the many European wars he had launched to ravage the continent. Carved from oak. Very ornate.

From his royal perch, he stretched out his fingers to start the process. "Carniglias," he said in a soothing voice. "Drustoe hapen des cretado." He thrust his right hand forward and aimed at the ground. A hot beam of light struck the earth and left a charred two-foot wide hole. From the hole spewed dark forces, beings of hell that floated overhead.

The cries they emitted were piercing and horrid to the ear. But not to Bill. These were his children. He lounged in his chair and enjoyed watching his great steaming mass of evil.

He pointed his arm toward Freeland. "Go my friends," he said. "Go and wreak havoc. Do what you do best." The demons sped away. Bill would soon follow, bringing his guns to bear when the town had been overrun.

"So long, little clearing," he said. "We've had fun. Now it's time to go hunting."

He stood up and started his deliberate trek toward town. He was in no hurry. By the time he arrived, the game would be on. He would appear just in time to catch the highlights and step in as the star. He was ready and eager for his grand performance.

The morning sunlight streamed into the living room and woke Stan. He jumped up, as if some emergency bell had gone off in his head.

Hurrying into the kitchen, he saw Amanda sleeping with her head down on the book. Good to know she was human after all. He left her alone and let her rest.

But out the window he saw a disturbing sight. Sari, sitting cross-legged in front of Stan's porch dressed in something that Stan guessed to be traditional African garb. He was bare-chested with his face and arms painted. Perhaps as a chieftain, perhaps as a warrior.

Throwing on some shorts and a shirt, Stan opened the door and stepped out.

Sari saw him and stood up. Dressed as he was, with his long limbs and imposing height, he looked formidable. Arms across his chest, legs planted like tree trunks, he spoke. "At last, you are awake, my brother."

Stan sat down in his rickety porch chair and laid his hands across his chest. "Yeah, it's been a long night." He laced his fingers together. "A very long night."

Sari's eyes drank in Stan and the house. "Yes, I would imagine much activity is taking place here. You have been quite busy."

"And I would imagine, with your gifts of intuition, you've been following the conversation."

"As I would with anyone in the village who may need my help."

"Is that what you believe?"

"My intuition, as you call it, tells me yes."

Stan dug deeper into his chair. "And what help have you come to offer?"

Sari took a step forward. "You are dealing with the unknown here, a great darkness. In your position, you are at a disadvantage against a very formidable foe."

"So, you've camped out on my lawn in some kind of weird garb and face paint to tell me I'm in danger? Is that really news around here?"

"I've come to offer my guidance."

"Really? You know, I just pulled off a deal with the devil. What's your offer?"

"Return Amanda to her master and I will work to see that no harm comes to you."

"Jesus, between you and Mr. Evil in Dungarees, you guys have been passing out a lot of guarantees. Trouble is, I don't believe you or him. I thought as a writer, as a newspaper editor, I understood English. Apparently not. Apparently the two of you can make agreements without really having to abide by them. Oh yes, you'll slit my throat if I don't keep my end of the bargain, but hold your hands to the fire and I always have to read the fine print. It's all just semantics to you guys, isn't it?"

Sari's face remained stoic, but Stan's shot seemed to have hit its mark. He spoke hesitantly. "That is his nature, not mine."

"Well, now, how's this deal sound? He wants his book back and he'd like to kill me. You want Amanda returned but you'd like to keep me locked away. Either way, I get royally screwed."

Sari's eyes narrowed. "The book?"

"That's right," Stan said, "that damn book Walt used to unleash hell on us. Remember that little incident last year? Remember how you sold my wife to the devil?"

Sari paused. "Yes."

"Yeah. Well, that book seemed to have launched it all. I did some exploring and I found it tucked in your secret hideaway. Of course, you probably knew about it. You seem to know everything that goes on around here. Then again, maybe not. Maybe Walt actually managed to pull the wool over your eyes. Not by himself of course. Seems that old Farmer Bill helped him. Yeah, you've met Bill, I think. Tall, skinny guy in overalls. Old, very smart, very dangerous. The man who took my wife as a hostage in exchange for your skin. That Bill, remember? Well, now I have the book and Bill would like it back." Stan took a deep breath and slowly exhaled. "What about it, Sari? Would you like it too? Seems to be a hot item around here."

Sari raised his right arm and covered his head with a massive hand. It glided across his scalp, behind his ear, and came to rest like a pillow on his cheek. "You are in a quandary, my brother."

"Ah. You mean the quandary I've been in ever since coming to this little fucking prison of yours? That quandary? You know, I didn't ask to be here. You sucked me in and now I'm stuck between you and Bill looking for a way out. I would say, yes, that's a quandary as I understand it in my language."

Sari folded his arms. "You are still not happy with my leadership."

"No, Sari. Most people in this country like to choose where they live, like to choose their own leaders. It's called freedom and democracy. You, on the other hand are what we call a dictator. We all cow tow to you without a choice in the matter. It's your way or the highway. So, no, I'm not happy with your leadership. I'd like a chance to go home and be free. I'd like to see my family. I'd like for them to meet my wife. And one day, I'd like to have my own home. Kids, house, picket fence. The whole nine yards. I'd like to live . . . a normal life."

Sari shifted his stance and put his hands behind his back. "As I've learned over the years, my brother, freedom is an illusion. Better to live under wise leadership than suffer the consequences of freedom."

Stan rose from his chair, marched down the sidewalk, and posted himself squarely in front of Sari. "So, here's the lofty benefit of your experience. You'd rather enslave people than allow them to make their own choices?"

"In the long run, my brother, good leadership is not enslavement. In this village, people learn to live and exist without fear. The real enslavement was before they came. In Freeland, they are . . . free . . . to be better."

"Really? Better? Larry vanishes? Johnny is murdered? Walt gets chopped up for playing with black magic? These I suppose are examples of better?"

"They are unfortunate aberrations. The town itself remains intact and at peace."

"Am I the only one around here who thinks this arrangement is crappy? Hmm. I think not."

"You are the only one with whom I'm having this conversation."

"Well, that says nothing about wanting to live here. Seems to say more about them being afraid . . . of you."

Sari flinched and dropped his hands. "Then I assume you are refusing my offer."

"If your idea of help is to set us all free and let us get the hell out of Dodge, I'm listening. Otherwise, no."

Sari, eyes wide and intense, looked down at Stan. Standing straight, he said, "Very well, we shall see the outcome, who indeed is the wiser."

Stan spread his feet defiantly and pointed a finger at Sari's chest. "I guess we shall."

"As you say here in America, the proof is in the pudding."

"I don't need proof, Sari. Just the right to leave with my wife and go home. Seems simple enough."

Sari grew pensive. "Nothing in this life is simple, my brother. That is the point of living. To endure and survive as I have for hundreds of years. It changes the way you see the world, the way you think."

"Isn't it obvious by now? I don't want to be like you, Sari. I don't want to live like you. I don't want to think like you. I don't want to drink blood or be a Chakar or a Dulami or any of the other bullshit titles you've made up. I don't want to live in Freeland. I want to go home. Haven't I made that abundantly clear?"

Sari looked sadly at Stan. "For now, I believe you have." He
pivoted and took his usual long strides up the road.

As Stan watched him go, he realized they had irrevocably
divided. Stan had smashed Sari's ideal of unity. Sari had dashed
Stan's hope for release. No more pretense about their roles in
Freeland. Stan was sure that, from this point on, Sari saw him as his
enemy.

Back inside the house, Stan shook Amanda awake.

Her head jerked up as she grasped the book. "What time is it?"

"I don't know," said Stan. "Maybe seven or so."

She rubbed her eyes and forehead. "Late."

"For what?"

Amanda looked at him, but her eyes and thoughts seemed
focused elsewhere. "This town, you, me. The time is short."

Stan knelt and pulled her to him. "Why?" In truth, he didn't want
to know and dreaded what she might say.

"War, coming. I must help you."

"War?"

"Yes, the reason I came."

"I don't understand."

She raised her head. Her steady eyes locked on him. "That's okay.
I will help you understand."

Shaking his head, Stan's mind and body felt burdened. Then he
began to clatter around in the kitchen. "You want something to eat?"

"No time to eat. I must read the book."

He spun around, snatched the book, and held it behind his back.
"If you don't eat, you can't read. It's that simple."

Amanda seemed unperturbed. "Then I'd like two eggs over easy
and some coffee."

"That's better. A good start. Two eggs and coffee coming up."

She placed her hands on the table and waited.

In his small room behind the Circle, the room that Sari called home, he lit a small bit of sage and let the smoke float past his face and into his lungs. The smell and sight of the incense helped him focus his thoughts on the hours ahead.

It had been years since Sari felt the need to prepare himself. Perhaps, by living in such isolation, he had grown complacent and forgotten just how dangerous and violent life could be.

In his younger years, his tribe had engaged in conflicts with rival tribes. He had learned to expect the unexpected, to adapt on short notice. But that was centuries ago. Since living in this village, Sari had let down his guard.

Still, the memories returned—how he prepared for battle, brought himself to be single minded, readied himself for attack.

He was taught the importance of a good offense, to be the doer rather than the victim, to be strategic and bring surprise into battle. He knew that the strong do not always win, that outmaneuvering a foe could be equal to having great strength.

But in this case, Sari knew the enemy was both strong and smart. He knew it was possible that he might lose everything, even his life. He recalled the teaching of his tribe on what makes a brave warrior and how death with honor was the highlight of one's legacy.

On the other hand, he was also careful to consider escape routes. Sari had not lived all these years without learning valuable lessons about retreating and vanishing. There was no shortage of villages in this world, many other places to set up home. He was not afraid to start over.

He mulled over these thoughts as he closed his eyes in meditation, as the smoke clouded the room, as the growing heat made him sweat. Each minute he spent preparing might be the minute that saved his life, or the life of the village. In this case, he must plan an attack, anticipate the enemy, and have a clear awareness of the fine line between winning and losing.

In the distance, he could hear the noise, faint at first, gradually building. He knew what this was—a horrible dark army stampeding across the hills, eager to overrun all he had built. He knew what battle was approaching and prepared himself for the worst.

As Amanda returned to the book, Stan dressed and decided to take his mockup to the office. The paper was a convenient way to take his mind off his problems. Odd to think that, with what he was dealing with, he could consider publishing another edition. *Why*, he asked himself? *What was the point? Who would be around to read it?*

There were no good answers to these questions. Simply put, the routine was more important than the work. Already, he was behind schedule. Usually the mockup was done by Wednesday night, ready to print first thing Thursday. Stan still had a couple hours of work before he finished.

Brent and Rita were already in the grocery doing stock work in the aisles. Brent greeted Stan eagerly, his eyes asking if this was the day they might see freedom. "Hey, Stan. Going to be a good day today?"

Not wanting to burst his eager bubble, Stan said, "Could be. I'm certainly working on it."

"Good news, I hope."

"What's good news?" Rita said as she came around a corner.

Brent looked at her, then Stan. "Nothing, dear. Just feeling chipper today, that's all."

Rita looked peeved. "Well, you've been feeling awfully chipper the last few days. Anything I should know about?" She walked between them, looked Stan in the eyes, then wheeled on Brent.

"Nope," Brent said. "Guess you're just lucky to have a happy husband."

Rita wasn't buying it. "You two have secrets to share?" She put her hands on her hips and turned toward Stan.

"What's wrong with having a happy husband?" said Stan.

"Cause he's not usually this happy, at least not since he came to Freeland. Kind of makes me wonder."

Stan retreated to his office doorway. "If he's happy, I wouldn't ask too many questions. Just enjoy his company. Better than the alternative."

Rita stomped over with her typical mad hen eyes and stared up at him. She was determined to peel the truth out of someone. "That's a good, safe answer, Stan. Unfortunately, it tells me nothing."

"Best I can offer," he replied and fled to his desk.

Rita stood in his doorway for a moment before calling out to Brent. "All right, happy man, let's see what else needs to be stocked." For the moment, she had been held at bay.

Out of habit, Stan grabbed the notes stuffed in his inbox and began to shuffle through scraps of paper. A few comments about last week's articles. None of them positive.

At the bottom was an envelope with his name handwritten on it. Regular business size, plain white. He threw the stack of notes on his desk and sat down to inspect it. Other than his name centered across the front, nothing unusual about it.

Picking up an opener, he cut through the top and pulled out a letter scrawled in cursive. His eyes widened as he scanned the page:

Dear Stan:

Sorry It has taken so long to correspond with you. Over the years, I've been doing periodic research to try and understand your situation and figure out a way to help. I'm not much on mysticism, so it's taken me a while to catch up. My apologies.

Sorry for not sticking around this time, but, given my previous experience, it wouldn't do to get both you and I stuck here, so I came in undercover. Please be assured I think I've found someone who can help you. Don't be surprised to see me pop up soon, maybe give that Sari bastard a taste of his own medicine.

Thinking of you. Hoping to get you home soon.

Sincerely,

Dave

As Stan finished, his hands started to shake. Dave hadn't forgotten. The thought of him being nearby gave him hope.

Hiding the letter under a stack of papers in his bottom drawer, he sprawled in his chair. This could be it, his last paper. He should make it his controversial best.

Looking over the mockup, Stan decided to take some extra time and spice it up. If it was revolution he wanted, why not make this edition revolutionary? Scrapping a couple of articles he had planned, he put another piece of paper in his Selectric and began to type a letter from the editor. He focused on creating a good opening line:

There is, in all men, the basic desire for freedom.

Stan thought of Thomas Jefferson and the Declaration of Independence. Though he would not compare himself to the master, he felt a strong sense of kinship. And, like Jefferson, there was an urgency to his situation. It seemed appropriate. If Stan was going to declare independence, he wanted to use him as his inspiration.

However noble men's intentions are for guiding other men, there is no guidance that should interfere with, stifle, or kill the desire for freedom.

Stan fixed his eyes on the sentence and read it several times. *Good start*, he thought.

Amanda sat at the kitchen table with her eyes closed and her palms secure on the book. By touch she felt the connection, the spells seamlessly flowing through her hands into her head.

Bill had sent her on a mission. On the one hand, to help Stan. On the other, to help Bill.

She was aware of the conflict in her mission. Something deep in her knew both love and treachery. The man with whom she shared her body and the man who controlled her soul. They were both powerful forces drawing on her devotion.

Whether through hearing or sensing, she sensed the coming chaos, a great roaring tsunami of evil that rushed toward Freeland. She urgently soaked up those spells that would assist in her mission. Spells that worked toward good and evil. Protection and destruction, each present in the book. She straddled these worlds and memorized both.

Ah, she thought. *Here's one that might keep Stan safe. And here's another that might overpower Sari. This one could reign down fire on the village. This one might create an opening for Stan to escape.*

It never occurred to her to take a stand, make a choice one way or the other. The two forces in her life were equal; to be called upon as commanded, depending on whom she believed was most demanding in the moment.

She rocked back and forth in her chair, whispering, preparing. The powerful forces came closer. In her head, gaining volume, the noise, the call for love. Stan and Bill. Bill and Stan. She could protect. She could destroy. There was no differentiation in her loyalties or the outcomes she anticipated. One was as good as the other.

Stan burst into the house and hurried to the kitchen. "Hey, Amanda. I've got a good feeling about this week's paper. Look, I wrote an editorial this morning. Want to hear it?"

Amanda opened her eyes and lifted her hands off the book. "Of course."

Stan read through what he'd just typed. "What do you think?"

She placed her hands in her lap and smiled. "Very elegant."

Lowering his paper, Stan added, "There's something else I found out today."

"What's that?"

"My brother's coming back."

"Brother?"

"Yeah. My brother. Dave."

"Dave?"

"Yeah, you remember, years back, he came to see me, almost got caught by Sari. I had to make a deal with Sari to let him go. He promised he'd come back one day. He's here, well, not in Freeland, but some place close. I got a note from him. I don't know how, but he's bringing help."

"Help?"

"Yep. Help." Stan pulled up a chair and sat face to face with Amanda. "You know, I really believe you and I are going to get out of this place. You and me, Amanda. We're going home."

Amanda seemed puzzled. Her eyes searched his face.

"Home, baby. White house. Quiet life with kids and a yard. Home."

"Home," she repeated. There was a moment of quiet between them. "That would be great, Stan. You and me. Home."

"You betcha. Fuck Sari. Fuck Freeland. Fuck Bill. We're outta here."

Amanda now picked up noise from a different source. She didn't recognize this sound but it disturbed her. Another tsunami from a new location. What would she do against this new wave? Was this another love she had to deal with?

Stan knelt by the table and kissed her. "Won't be long now."

Amanda's eyes remained fixed on him. "No, it's coming soon. You're right. It won't be long."

She picked up the intensity of Stan's heat, let it overwhelm her focus and her body. His arms wrapped around her waist. She followed his lead. This was good. He believed in her. She also believed in him—and Bill—but not this other force, this interfering third party.

Stan gently pulled her from her chair and, as they both inched toward the bedroom, he eagerly undressed her.

As he laid her on the bed and drew her body to him, she knew his physical hunger mirrored his attachment to her soul. In that moment, she was sure he would follow her anywhere.

Amanda stayed in the moment, taking in his pleasure, returning his love. *One is as good as the other* she reasoned. Both loves, both equal. For now, she loved him most.

When they finished, Stan dozed off, spent from work, stress, joy, and lack of sleep. Amanda gently rolled him on his side and rose from the bed. She put on some clothes and returned to the kitchen.

Closing her eyes, she placed her palms back on the book and began to search. For more spells, spells that might help her deal with this other. These spells wouldn't go both ways. These spells were meant to stop and destroy. Whoever this third other was, she did not want him to succeed.

After an hour of intense study, Amanda closed the book and took a deep breath. She knew what was coming and had done her best to be ready. For Bill. For Stan. For love. Braced for battle, Amanda left the house and headed down Paradise Road. Toward town. Toward Sari. The army was coming.

Sari knew it like he knew when the weather changed. The coming of the horde. An approaching storm front. His mind a barometer measuring atmospheric pressure. He walked out of his smoke-filled room, took a deep breath, and drew on his inner power.

From the back of the Circle, he stepped toward the town square. As anticipated, he saw Amanda, but not the Amanda he had brought to Freeland. This was Amanda's body with something or someone else in control of her soul. He watched her approach.

The sound of buzzing demons filled the square with menace. A hot wind whipped through the town carrying a smell like rotting flesh. Amanda stood in front of Sari. Behind her, speeding toward Freeland, a dark army.

Sari shook his head. "I am sad for you, my sister."

Amanda looked puzzled. "Sad because—"

"I feel responsible. I brought you here for a purpose, yet I failed to see your full potential."

"It was always my intention to serve my master."

"Yes, and for that I believe you are well prepared."

"And now my purpose has arrived."

Sari spread his feet apart and lowered his arms to his side. "And what is that purpose?"

Amanda made wide gestures with her hands. "I promised Stan freedom and protection. I promised the town freedom and protection. I promised them freedom and protection . . . from you."

"Yes, I'm sure you did."

"Beyond that, my master will reveal more when the time comes."

Sari reached out his hand. His face grew tender. "It must be difficult to be so divided."

"Not at all," Amanda said. "In fact, I'm perfectly content."

Sari let out a long sigh. "Then you must feel no loyalty to me."

"Nor you to me. You were so willing to let me cross over."

"Alas, that is true. I have freed myself from human attachment. That is the story of how I've survived. For you, however I felt—"

"You have no one to love," she said. "I, on the other hand, am overflowing."

"That is true." Sari grew pensive, a man searching for a lost memory—family, wife, children. He sighed again. "Love is not a necessity in my life, not anymore." He pointed toward the demonic throng. "But this thing approaching, we must both face it."

"I am lucky," Amanda said. "I have two loves, both equal, both important."

"Then serve those loves, but let us fight this one last battle together. For the sake of the village."

Amanda gave him a stern look. "Both these loves demand freedom from you, freedom for the town, freedom for people to make a choice."

Sari fixed his eyes on Amanda. "This word—freedom—as when fish swim about freely and get caught in a net?"

Amanda stared back. "If they make that choice, then yes."

"Freedom . . . to be ensnared and overpowered."

She nodded. "If that is the choice they make."

Sari shook his head. "Yes, I see you were once blessed with choice, and yet you are not free."

She slowed her words and bit on her syllables. "It is not my demand to be free."

"Yet you want freedom for this village?"

"Freedom to choose their own master, yes."

Sari's eyes narrowed. "Will they be free to choose when you are finished?"

"They will, for the moment. Beyond the moment, who knows? Time changes. Choices are made. Nothing lasts forever."

"Except Bill and his handmaiden?"

"That remains to be seen."

In the town center, people had gathered out of curiosity. When the plague approached, some panicked and ran for shelter. Others stood frozen in place, unsure what to do next.

Brent and Rita emerged from the store to investigate. Seeing Amanda and Sari in the center, they hurried over to catch the conversation. Rita gripped Brent's arm in fear. Brent wrapped his arm around her waist and looked around the square.

Sari stood straight and raised his arms. The foul air began to flow circular in the town square, then formed a funnel and reached skyward. The temperature around him dropped. The heat and smell were drawn into the flow.

Amanda spoke forcefully. "You are no match for my skills, Sari. You've known that all along."

"I am no match for those whose sole intention is destruction," said Sari. "I am a man of reason, but a man nonetheless, though not without powers of my own, learned over the years from some very good teachers."

"But not the book."

"No, I would not dare read the book. It was intended for minds more powerful than mine. I'm afraid that it would do to me what it has done to you."

"Then you choose to die in this place?"

Sari's words flowed gently. "Do you choose to kill me, my Dulami?"

Amanda did not flinch. "I choose to remove you as an obstacle, if that's what you remain."

"Then remove me, if you wish."

Amanda turned toward the horde, extended her arms, and beckoned them to attack.

Sari braced for the onslaught.

"Karam di mephisto," she yelled and whirled around to face him.

Sari threw his arms wide in a sacrificial pose. The noise in the distance approached like a speeding train, hissing and moaning toward his body. He uttered a response. "Deekay agonto, mobus freelus."

At that moment, there was a loud explosion in the center of the square, as if missile fire had found its target. Sari disappeared into the heart of
the fireball.

Yet above the fray, ten feet or so in the air, his image appeared in the middle of the fire. His body was like mist, but his face was clear and his arms were extended toward Amanda.

From the image, a ray of light fired down and struck her in the chest. She fell backward and lay still. The image disappeared. Sari was gone.

Onlookers were shocked into silence. Brent rushed over to check on Amanda. He lifted her wrist and took her pulse. "She's still alive," he announced.

Amanda groaned and turned on her side. Her eyes opened and noticed the crowd. She appeared surprised and dazed. "Where am I?"

"Freeland," Brent said. "Where else? Right smack in the middle of town."

Amanda pushed up and sat quietly in the dust. "Freeland?"

"Yep. You've come home."

She tried to regain her focus. "Where's Stan?"

Brent was taken back. "I don't know. Home, I guess. You haven't seen him?"

"Not since I left town."

"Well, my guess is he's at your house, though with all this racket, I would bet he'll be here shortly."

"What's going on here?"

Brent took a step back. "Hell, Amanda, you tell us. You're the one that brought it here." He pointed a finger at the horizon.

Amanda glanced up and saw the screaming mass overshadowing the town. "Me?"

"Well, either you brought them or they're looking for you. Either way, it's bad news for us."

For a moment, Amanda shut her eyes. "Bill, I guess."

"Bill?" said Brent. "Who the hell is Bill?"

She stood and brushed herself off. "Where's Sari?"

"Gone," Brent said with growing irritation. "You just blew him out of the water, thank you very much. Now we've got no one to protect us, except you maybe, if that's what you came back to do."

Amanda looked around at the small circle of townsfolk. "Right."

Brent slid protectively next to Rita. "I don't know if that's what you plan, but we don't stand much chance here without you."

The surrounding crowd became more panic stricken. Several people cried out in fear.

"Well?" said Brent.

"To tell you the truth," Amanda said as she lowered her head, "I'm as confused as you are."

An audible gasp rose from the onlookers. Someone shrieked, "Oh my God, we're all going to die." Some started to run off.

Rita whimpered, "Brent, honey, do something, please."

Brent took her hand. "It's okay, sweetie. Just hang in there, all right?" He turned back to Amanda. "So? Now what?"

"Plan B."

"Which is?"

"I don't know yet. I'm still working on it."

Brent's eyes widened. "Oh my God, Amanda. What have you done?"

The roar of an explosion woke Stan up. The first thought that hit him was a question. *Where's Amanda?*

A quick search. An empty house. Throwing on some clothes and grabbing the book, he sprinted out the door toward the town square. Immediately he smelled the awful odor. A noise like angry insects poured from the hillsides. "Oh, hell, not good," he groaned.

Stan sprinted down the road and noticed a small group of people gathered near the Circle. In the middle of it all, he saw Amanda looking dazed. Brent and Rita stood nearby. Stan ran over and took her by the arm. "Amanda?"

Amanda started and pulled away. "Stan?"

He glanced up at the sky again. "Jesus, Amanda! What's going on here?"

Her face grew cloudy. "My best guess is Bill. I think he's about to unleash hell on us."

"Where's Sari?"

"Gone," Brent said, "thanks to your wife."

From nearby, a loud voice shouted, "Good morning, citizens of Freeland." It was Bill.

The remaining crowd fell back, revealing the one he had assigned to help with all this chaos. Amanda.

"And good morning to you, my good servant," he said to her. "I hope everything is as you expected?"

"Well—." She pressed against Stan. He wrapped his arm around her waist.

374

Bill surveyed the crowd. His eyes came to rest on Stan. "And you?"

"I know what I see," said Stan, "and right now it's not good. What's with all the theatrics, Bill?"

Bill gave Stan an evil grin. "Not entertaining enough for you?"

Stan pulled a hand from behind his back. "I have the book here. If it's still what you want, then we're not finished with our bargain yet."

Bill brushed his chin with a finger and laughed. "Oh, my friend. You misunderstand. You see, it's not me who desires that book. Now isn't that right, Amanda?"

Amanda broke free of Stan.

Touching his chest with his finger, Bill continued, "Of course, you assumed I wanted it?"

"Yeah, that's what I thought. Guess you got me on that count. But whether you do or don't is not my concern. All that matters is that it was part of our agreement."

"Well put. It was what we agreed upon, but in fact, I intended it all along for your lovely wife. Like Walt, she has a passion for this kind of stuff. I thought it would make a nice welcome home gift."

"Whatever. I have it. You asked for it. We agreed to conditions. Are those still in play?"

Bill's eyes narrowed. His usually cheerful voice took on a somber tone. "I could easily unleash my forces here, agreement or not. I have no qualms about blasting you or this shitty dump of a town into the next universe."

Stan felt his knees buckle. "I'm aware of that."

Bill's grin returned and seemed to grow darker. "Well, what's to stop me?"

"You'd lose a very valuable commodity in the process. And I know you hate to lose at anything."

"Really?"

Amanda drew in her breath. "You'd have to go through me, Bill."

Bill pressed his stick to his chest. His face turned stony. "Ah, so you've switched sides again, my servant. My, you are quite susceptible to outside influences, now aren't you?"

"If being human means being susceptible, then yes."

"So you're throwing yourself into the fire for the sake of these poor, ignorant twits?"

"Yes."

"And that book? You think your little husband here will give it away willingly? You know the power of that thing. I'm not sure he's entirely trustworthy."

Amanda glanced hesitantly at Stan, then back at Bill. She closed her eyes and released a long, slow breath. "I trust him more than you at this point."

"Well, I suppose it's true, what they say. We all have to learn from our mistakes."

"And you, Bill," said Stan. "Seems you've made a mistake here. So, what have you learned?"

"Ah, for me, what's to learn when you've found the ultimate vocation?" As he shrugged, his face brightened. "I know what I like. Everything else is just empty rhetoric."

"Which is exactly what you've given me."

Bill raised his stick, aimed it like a rifle at Stan, and leered. "It's what I do best. You know that as well as anyone."

Stan moved toward Amanda and encircled her with both arms. "So what about it, Bill. Do I still have a deal with the devil?"

Bill arched his back to his full height. He looked taller, more ominous. "There you go with that name calling again. What's to gain from such prejudice?"

"Just unmasking hell for what it is."

Bill pointed a hand toward Stan. "Did I not give you what you wanted?"

"That remains to be seen."

Bill spread his arms wide. "What, the town is loosed from Sari. You have your freedom. You have your wife. I think it should be I who has the complaint."

"There's still the book." Stan raised it to his chest. "I owe this to you, don't I?"

Bill's eyes danced merrily. A sneer spread across his face. "Well, then, hand it over."

As Stan tried to extend the book toward Bill, he felt an invisible pull on his arm from a force so strong, the spine left an imprint in his palm.

"See what I mean?" said Bill. "Ah, the lovely power of the book, which I think nullifies our bargain and leaves me empty-handed. Which in turn makes me very unhappy. And you can guess what happens when you jilt the devil."

For Stan, it clicked. The surprise attack that left him in checkmate. The book that chose its own master. Bill simply manipulated that choice for his own purpose.

Bill leered and spoke with a deliberate meter. "You've underestimated your own desire, my friend, the union of the book's mind with your will. The possessor of the book is also its slave. You couldn't give that to me, no matter how hard you try." Flipping the words off the end of his tongue, he said, "Bargain . . . cancelled."

As Stan lowered the book, he realized the truth. It had attached itself to him, and by doing so, had forced him to renege on his contract. Stan gave Amanda an embarrassed glance. "Sorry, my love. Looks like he's got us cornered."

Amanda pulled away from Stan. "There's one point you've missed here, Bill."

Bill half-curtsied. "Ah, my dear, you're back."

Amanda touched Stan's arm. "Stan is not a student of sorcery, but I am, which means I've read the book from cover to cover."

"And a good student you are," he said with a graceful turn of his hand.

"There's a spell buried deep in the back."

"Yes, indeed. I believe we as sorcerers call it the release clause."

"Find a sorcerer willing to bear the book's burden—"

"And, of course, the book will release the holder."

"Yes."

Bill jammed the tip of his stick in the earth and pressed down. "I'm very familiar with it, my darling. I practically wrote this book. And so, of course, that's where you come back into play."

"I do." Amanda gripped Stan's hand. "You can do this, Stan. If we work together, you can give me the book and be free."

Stan's palms grew sweaty. "Then what happens to you?"

"It's the sorcerer's responsibility to leave the holder and be the book's keeper."

"But, then—"

"The holder also has to leave the sorcerer, has to relinquish all contact and communication. Otherwise, the temptation to retrieve the book is too great."

"Ah, I love these complexities," Bill said heartily. "All in pursuit of what you call freedom."

Stan was bewildered. "But, Amanda, we're husband and wife. How the hell do you expect me to give you up?"

Bill's laughter increased. "Yes, Amanda, how indeed?"

Amanda increased her grip on Stan. "You've got a choice, here, Stan. Either we can both live or both die. Bill's not going to spare either of us without this spell."

Bill mocked Amanda's plea. "No indeed, Stan, she's right, you know. Spoil my game and I'll turn you both to soot."

Stan extended his arm far enough to let Amanda touch the book. "I'm not sure I can let it go."

"The spell will take care of that," she said.

"Okay," Bill taunted. "Now let's all have a little farewell pity party. Come on, Stan. What're you waiting for? Clock is ticking. Time to send Amanda into the wilderness."

Amanda gripped the book and chanted, "Deru mishen, eakus diablan, noso diem."

Bill silently mimicked each word. When Amanda finished, Stan released the book into her care.

Bill threw up his arms and did a tiny dance. "Yes, yes, what fun this all is. Nothing like family separation to brighten my day."

Amanda tucked the book under her arm. The crowd parted, allowing her a path of escape.

"Go on now, little servant," Bill teased. "You've done your deed. Time to say bye bye."

As Amanda backed up another few steps, Stan felt his brain explode with fear and panic. He stepped toward her and held out his hand.

Amanda gave Stan a last longing look and turned west on Paradise Road. In a matter of minutes, she vanished. Even Bill fell quiet as they watched her disappear.

For the second time in a year, Stan had lost his wife. His arms went limp. His head drooped. He was speechless. Then, running his hand over his face, he turned to Bill. "Well?"

"Well what?" Bill sneered.

"Have you got what you came for? Is this reason enough for you to leave?"

"Am I now unwelcome?"

"Yes, without a doubt. You are now officially pond scum."

"Ah, I see. Give a gift, get the boot. How typically human."

"And, of course, you expected—"

"A little courtesy, perhaps."

"Right, a band and a banquet, some roses and a glass of champagne."

Bill leaned on his stick and primly crossed his feet. "At least a meal or two in that dumpy little diner over there would have been nice."

Stan pointed a finger at Bill. "Drop by, knock the door down, have a free cup of coffee. Steal a meal from the kitchen. Hell, take the furniture if you want. Sari's gone. No one gives a shit. Just take you and your bony ass stick and fuck off."

Bill pointed toward the sky. "And my friends here?"

"Yeah, you, your smelly buggers, whatever pestilence and disease you've brought. Just . . . go."

Bill folded his arms and looked around. "Your hospitality is lacking, Stan. We came such a long way to be here."

"Come back in a thousand years or so, when none of us are around anymore."

"Ah, now, that would be such a waste." Bill reached his hand skyward, then aimed it at the Circle. The dark spirits congregated over the roof and hurtled down. The café burst into flames.

Screams rose from customers hiding inside. A woman with her dress on fire ran through the door and fell in the square. It was Dahlia Rutan. For thirty seconds, she screamed and pleaded for help. To no avail. The smell of her burnt flesh drifted toward the terrified crowd.

Bill spun around and aimed his finger at Plymouth's Grocery. The demons swerved from the Circle and hit the building from the side. It flew apart in a giant ball of flame.

The remaining onlookers in the square panicked and scattered in all directions. Brent grabbed Rita's hand and ran.

"Stop!" Stan cried. "What about our bargain?"

"Nullified by your failure to give me the book," he shouted. "That was our agreement. She takes the book, which means our bargain is nullified. That means we're back to square one, and I say," shooting a finger at several people fleeing the scene, "Freeland must pay the price!"

Immediately, the hovering spirits attacked. In a matter of seconds, several bodies exploded, sending small bits of flesh and bone high in the air.

As Brent and Rita ran across the square, Bill spotted them and cried, "Well, now, there's a nice young couple. How about this for grins and giggles?" He jerked a hand in their direction. The spirits gathered in full force and sped toward them.

Brent saw them and threw himself on top of Rita. "No!" he shouted just before he was hit and ripped to pieces. Rita, covered in with blood, screamed in agony on the ground.

"One for the money, two for the show," Bill chanted as he aimed a finger at her.

In desperation, Stan leaped and tried to tackle Bill, but he nimbly dodged the charge and yelled in triumph as Stan collapsed in the dirt. "You, I'll save for last," he snarled. "In the meantime, I'll make you watch the whole damn show!"

Stan jumped up and bull-rushed him again. "You lying son of a bitch!"

Bill stood like a rock and gave Stan several powerful blows to the head with his stick. Stan rolled off him like a limp sack. Then the sorcerer thrust his right arm straight up. Stan flew several feet in the air and landed on his back.

"My, oh my," Bill said. "When was the last time I had so much fun?" He bounced on his feet like a boxer.

With a tango move, he spun around and shoved his finger at Rita. Angry spirits buzzed down and pounced on her. Her wailing pleas echoed across the center. In a matter of seconds, she was blown to smithereens.

The square was now empty. The Circle, gone. Plymouth's Grocery, gone. Sari and Amanda, gone. Brent and Rita, gone. The only person left was Stan, dazed and stretched on his back among all the bloody remains strewn across the plaza.

Bill took his dignified time and strode over. Planting his stick, he towered over Stan triumphantly. His face beamed with triumph. "What do you think? Having a good time?"

Stan caught his breath and lay still. He knew it was his turn, the final gruesome act in Bill's treacherous drama.

As he faced his demise, he realized how he'd been waiting for this moment for over a year. How he'd courted and encouraged it. Even dared it to take him. Now, with his wife gone, the town destroyed, his life in tatters, Bill had become Stan's ticket out of Freeland. The end was not pleasant, but the thought gave him hope. "Do it, you dirty bastard," he growled.

Bill leaned over and mocked him. "Do what, Stan?"

"Get it over with. Finish me off."

"Well, thank you for that invitation. Come to think of it, when it comes to you, I believe I do have something quite fun in mind."

"Doesn't matter. Just do it."

"Soon enough. First I finish off this place, then we play."

Bill extended his arms out and waltzed gracefully with an invisible partner. Raising a finger in mid-motion, he gathered his army over head. "Hello, my pretties. We still have work to do. No rest for the wicked I believe is what's said about us."

Spinning his finger rapidly, he sent demons flying in all directions. Multiple explosions reverberated across town. The ground shook and the air filled with the cries and pleas of dying victims. Dust clouds rose and a monstrous roar echoed like the bellow of some gargantuan beast on the loose.

Stan listened for several minutes to the snap, roar, and crackle of buildings on fire and houses collapsing. Finally, no more voices. Stan knew. Everyone in Freeland was gone. The whole town had been reduced to rubble.

Bill seemed satisfied and stopped to catch his breath. He meandered back to Stan and propped himself on his staff. "Well, now. Not a bad party, huh?"

Stan rolled on his stomach like a repentant priest. He lowered his head and dug his fingers deep in the dirt.

"One thing remains, of course. My special guest—you."

Stan waited for the onslaught. Whatever his end, it wouldn't be pretty. Bill's pent up rage was now aimed at him. His only consolation—these black demons weren't patient. The end would come quick.

Suddenly, in the area where the grocery store once stood, a voice rang out. A man with a distinct African accent spoke with authority. "You've had your fun, Bill, but this one, you must leave alone."

Bill and Stan searched for the voice. It came from a large black man wearing a brown Fulani hat and a tattered green and yellow dashiki. And standing next to him, Stan's brother, Dave.

"Dave!" Stan groaned, his voice barely above a whisper.

"Sorry for the tardiness, my brother," Dave said.

Bill grabbed his stick and held it loosely with his knobby hands. He looked amused. "Ah, welcome—Dave—and I see you've brought a guest. Hopefully someone interesting."

The man in the dashiki held his arms wide. "I'm surprised you would not remember me, Bill. We've met many times."

Bill stroked his chin. His eyes widened. "Why, you old pain in the ass, Marah. How could I forget such a scoundrel as you." He eyed him intently. "And how is it you've wandered out of the African desert to this tiny hole in the road? Not enough sin out there to keep you busy?"

"The same reason as always, Bill. I go where I'm invited to clean up your mess. Obviously, with you wreaking havoc here, there is certainly a need for my services."

Bill rubbed his chin again and wheeled his stick toward Marah. "Still spouting mumbo jumbo, playing priest, that sort of pish posh?"

"As you know, my friend, I've chased you many times across the planet. Seems you never get tired of spreading destruction."

"Destruction? Is that what you call it? I prefer to call it art. Yes, indeed, I create a thing of beauty and you come along and spoil the party. Is that it? Seems to be a pattern, here, don't you think?"

"One I intend to keep, so long as you continue to scatter hell everywhere. So, here we are again, I suppose, a similar song and dance?"

Stan gathered himself up and limped toward his brother.

Bill turned his head toward him. "Not so fast, my servant. I have a vested interest in you." He snapped his arm in a half-circle and threw Stan back on the ground. "You're not for sale, you know."

"Indeed, he's not," Marah said, "though I'm not at all surprised you would claim ownership of something that doesn't belong to you."

"Well, as you know," Bill quipped, "truth is a moving target."

"And you keep moving that target."

"As always, yes."

"Seems you've marked a lot of targets today. Time to put away your toys and go home."

Once again, Stan tried to get up.

"Stay down, Stan," Dave begged.

Stan eased to the ground. "What's going on?"

"Can't explain now. Took me a long time to track down this gentleman, even longer to convince him to help me. Bottom line, we've come to get you out of this rat hole."

Bill did a two-step and spread his arms. "Well, now, if that's your intention, all you had to do was ask. I'll gladly give him to you . . . or what's left of him when I finish."

Bill gathered his black force in a cluster over Stan's head. "There's more of them than there are of you," he taunted. With a dramatic spin, he aimed his finger at Stan.

An awful screaming noise headed straight toward him. The smell, the heat, the hate. All of it palpable to his senses. Stan closed his eyes and braced for the impact.

An explosion of energy came within inches of his eyes. He was blinded and pinned to the ground. The heat burned his skin. The air had a stench so putrid he gagged and vomited. He heard the horrifying sounds of hissing, moaning, teeth gnashing. "Goddamn it," he screamed, "leave me alone!"

At that moment, Marah pumped his hands and shouted, "Nesha devorum."

A rumble like thunder burst within inches of Stan's head. The smell, the noise, the heat, the presence of the horrid spirits disappeared. A grey cloud mushroomed in the air and scattered across the town square.

"I won't let you do this to him, Bill," Marah said as the air cleared. "I'm afraid the party's over."

Bill glared at Marah. "Why, you grubby old meddler. Tell me now, have you ever had a day of fun in your whole dithering, nosy life?"

Marah bowed. "Every time I meet you, Bill, I always take great pleasure in spoiling your work."

"Indeed," Bill said, as he threw his hands forward.

A white light flashed from his fingers and struck Marah, but Marah raised his hands and reflected the light back like a mirror. In a matter of seconds, Bill was immersed in the same brightness. Smoke surrounded him. Thunder filled the air and echoed for several seconds.

When the smoke cleared, Bill looked like he'd just emerged from a fire—hair singed, face blackened, soot covering his arms.

Marah, however, remained quite clean. He took a moment to adjust his hat and straighten his robe. "This trick never works, Bill. You should know better."

Bill dusted himself off and posed on his stick. "I will be careful to avoid you from now on. I'll move as far as I can from wherever you think me to be. I'll be as scarce to you as rain in your desert."

"Then, for once in your miserable existence, keep your promise. Go on. Take your putrid soul and vanish."

Bill's eyes ran up and down Marah's body. He gave him a foul look of hatred.

Marah never flinched. His sharp eyes challenged Bill to try another trick.

The anger on Bill's face dissolved. He grew calm and swung his stick methodically like a pendulum. His demeanor took on a casual, relaxed air. "I will now make my exit," he said with an arrogant grin. "I'm sorry you puny pudding heads don't have the good sense to appreciate my handiwork."

Marah extended a hand toward the hills. "Somewhere in the vast desert seems fitting. There's plenty of room out there for you to play around."

"It does have its charm," Bill said. He glanced toward Stan. "It's been a pleasure."

"Fuck you," Stan spit back.

Bill bowed gracefully. "And to you as well."

For the next few minutes, Marah, Dave, and Stan watched Bill walk west down Paradise Road.

He moved his stick back and forth between his right and left hands and strolled with a leisurely pace that extended his moment in the sun. Though he may have appeared simply as a man out for a casual morning walk, it was clear to everyone watching that Bill was enjoying his last departure. As a final mocking gesture before leaving the road, he curtsied.

"Shit, brother," said Stan in a shaky voice, "that was too damn close."

Dave grinned. "Better late than never."

"A day earlier would've been nice." He grabbed Dave and gave him a sturdy hug.

Marah watched and waited. "Your brother has been persistent all these years."

"I can imagine. He used to bug the hell out of me with all his crazy ideas. Guess it's my good fortune he's not a quitter."

"I had to prepare for this conflict," Marah said quietly. "Bill would surely know if I was not ready. Unfortunately, my preparation did not prove timely for your town. My apologies."

"Well," Stan said, "I'm just happy you showed up. As you can see, Bill had something really nasty planned for me."

"Yes, I'm afraid his wrath was aimed right at you."

Stan took in the ruins that used to be Freeland. Empty now. Buildings charred like burnt tombstones. The town itself a lifeless shell. The wreckage around him—the remnants of bodies and bones, the loss of his friends, his wife—hit Stan hard.

Despite his longing to leave, the carnage he witnessed only magnified his sense of loss. He felt shock overwhelm him. His legs gave out and he stumbled to the ground. For a moment, he kneeled on his hands and knees, face almost touching the ground.

His body began to shake. He collapsed and lay sprawled with his head in the ash and dust as he moaned repeatedly. Then he grew still and stopped moving.

Dave tapped his brother's shoulder and gently turned him over.

Stan opened his eyes and stared at the sky. "I just can't believe it," he said in a hoarse voice. "Everything's gone. The sonofabitch really did screw me over."

"But you're alive," said Dave.

Stan glanced at him, then up at the sky. He covered his eyes and remained silent.

The two men waited, their own silence a memoriam to Stan's grief. Then Dave spoke up. "Time to go, brother."

"Go? Go where?" Stan said, his mind a hurricane of confusion.

"Home," Dave said. "Unlike these poor souls, you've actually got somewhere to go."

"San Diego?"

Dave reached out and gripped Stan's shoulder. "That's right, man. Home."

Stan gathered his thoughts. Home. Somehow that word had a strange sound to it. It had been on the tip of his tongue all these years. But now, faced with gaining his cherished freedom, he thought about its meaning. Where was it exactly, his real home?

He stood up, brushed off the dust, straightened his clothes, and took a few deep breaths. Then his eyes circled around the town square. "Goddamn, he really did torch the place, didn't he?"

"Bill leaves only death and destruction," said Marah.

Taking another deep breath, Stan stopped and faced them. "All right. I'm ready."

Dave gave Stan another hug. "It's a fresh start, Stan, and you can come stay with me, or Mom and Dad, your choice, until you get back on your feet."

As Dave released him, Marah took one last look around. "This town you were trapped in, it had a leader?"

Stan nodded. "Sari."

"Ah, yes, I've heard rumors of him in Africa."

"He was a shaman of some sort."

"Yes, quite legendary."

"Gone now."

"Gone, but not dead. Left the village, yes, but someday he will reappear. Perhaps I will meet him."

Stan scraped his foot in the dirt. "Better you than me."

The three of them hiked out of Freeland. Dave had parked his rental car on a shoulder just up the road. As they jumped in and wound their way toward Boise, Stan rolled down the window and let the warm air blow on his face. It felt fresh. It felt like—freedom.

May 21, 1984

Stan stood in the same spot where he had started this journey seven years ago. Directly in front of The Idaho Statesman. Same colonial building. Same antique windows. He marveled that it hadn't changed or fallen down in a heap. It was the newspaper time had forgotten.

As for Stan, he had definitely changed. He was older and more bruised, still trying to wrap his head around a different civilization. He found himself flinching at all the traffic noises and keeping his eyes on the exits when he ate in restaurants.

Knowing that Sari was still out there only made it worse. Something in his head kept warning him to be careful. It was a running faucet he couldn't turn off. Not yet, anyway.

Tonight he and Dave would be flying back to San Diego. Dave would get back to his former life. Stan would be starting over.

At this moment, however, he was wrestling with a more imminent decision. Returning to the paper, meeting up with Amy and Hank. It was something he talked about with Dave. It was something he had to do.

He knew that once Hank heard his story, he would either laugh him out of the building or plaster him on the front page. Stan could take the laughter, but he was not ready to be plastered anywhere. He desperately wanted to remain incognito.

Still, he felt that he owed them an explanation. For reasons yet to be determined, he harbored guilty for abandoning his post and for leaving Amy. He wondered what kind of angry look Hank would give him. What would Amy's reaction be after seeing her long-lost lover?

He stood still for several minutes, eyes detailing the stonework, the rectangle quality of each red brick. He took a deep breath, shook his hands and fingers to loosen up, and pushed through the front door.

The first thing he noticed was that the lobby had been remodeled. New equipment at the front desk, and a different receptionist—older, less flirtatious.

She eyed him as he meandered across the lobby to her desk. "Can I help you?" she said without much enthusiasm.

"Yeah," Stan said as he fidgeted nervously with his hands. "I used to work here some years ago. Just thought I would drop by and see if any of the old-timers are still around."

The receptionist, whose name tag read "Betty," looked skeptical and pursed her lips. "So, you're here for a visit?"

Stan knew that look. She was puzzled. He guessed that over the next few months he would see that look frequently as he tried to explain why he had popped up again after such a long absence. "Yup, that's right. Looking for Hank Aleano, Amy Nigel?"

Betty stopped. There was something in her eyes she didn't want to reveal. She looked anxiously toward the newsroom door, perhaps hoping that someone would run out, interrupt them, and take the responsibility off her shoulders. But the question had been asked and she was stuck answering it. "Hank dropped dead a year ago." She shifted anxiously in her chair. "Heart attack."

Stan paused and rubbed his hands lightly across her countertop. "Oh," he said, the word sticking to his tongue. His throat dry, his breath shallow, he had to brace himself to stay upright. "Sorry to hear that."

Betty let out a deep breath. "Who else did you want?"

"Amy. Amy Nigel."

Betty leafed through her employee listings. "Nope, no one here with that name. When did she work here?"

"1977, October, the last time I saw her."

"Jesus," Betty murmured. She pushed back in her chair and gave Stan a severe look. "Well, I've been at this desk for two years. Never heard of or met anyone here named Amy."

Stan backed away and glanced out one of the antique windows. "Well, I know it's been a while."

Betty picked up a pencil and ran it lazily through her fingers. "Yeah, you know, in news years, that's a long time. Lot of turnover around here. Paper's been losing money. All the old timers are pretty much gone. We're down to the bare bones."

Stan straightened and looked back at Betty. "Okay, then, I guess that's it."

Betty stopped rolling her pencil. "Where've you been?"

Stan ran the statement through his mind several times. How to answer such a simple question. He knew he'd have to give this some serious thought and come up with a reasonable answer.

But was there any such thing as a reasonable answer? Was there any answer at all that a reasonable person could believe? And if he was sitting in Betty's chair, would he believe that answer? He had his doubts.

Stan decided there really was no rational way to respond. For now, all he could do was lie. "I got called to San Diego on a family emergency," he said. "Turns out that my mom was very sick, so I ended up moving back home."

Betty waited for some additional information. None was forthcoming. She shrugged. "Well, not much I can do to help you. Whoever you used to know here is long gone. Sorry."

Stan didn't bother with any of the normal courtesies. Betty didn't appear to need them anyway. He peered around the lobby, took a long look at the entrance into the newsroom, and headed for the front door.

"You want me to tell someone you're here?" she asked.

Stan turned and ran a hand through his hair. "Nope, like you said, everyone I know, they're all gone." He gave her a weak smile and hurried out.

He found his way to a coffee shop down the street. From his cushioned seat in a beat-up booth, he sat peacefully and watched the pedestrians, cars, and commercial trucks hurry past his window.

It was an odd sensation, his body and brain split in two. One still catching sight of Johnny Nelson and Matty Rolf chatting. The other gawking at strangers in a large city who skittered past his perch.

He had just been loosed from Freeland, but not by much. It seemed that the freedom he had ached for was more elusive than he could have imagined.

"What can I get you?" a waitress said, interrupting his train of thought.

Stan jumped and caught his breath. She stood next to him poised and ready.

He took stock of her. Blond, nice figure, very pretty, maybe in her early twenties, perhaps a student working her way through college. Fresh face, fresh dreams.

"What kind of pie you have?" he said.

She raised her pad and pencil. "Apple, banana cream, cherry. That's about it for right now."

"Cherry," he said.

"Anything else?" She wrote furiously, anxious to move on.

"Coffee, black."

"Okay, you got it." In a split second, she was gone.

Stan returned to his musings and his people watching. The whole scene reminded him of swirling confetti. He tried to sort through all the different bits, but for now, most of it was just a blur. The world had sped up since he disappeared, or had he slowed down? He had no idea, but he was sure he had fallen off a train. It would take some time for him to figure out how to get back on board.

When the waitress returned with his pie and coffee, he tried to strike up a conversation. "You a State student?"

"Yeah, senior," she said with a small bit of warmth. "Gotta make the change to keep going, but next year, hopefully, I'll be doing something a lot more cushy."

"Like?"

"Accounting, taxes, telling people how much they owe Uncle Sam."

Stan took a bite of pie and sipped his coffee. "That's a great career."

"It's a living," she said. "All I care about is getting paid a decent salary . . . and never having to bus another table." She gave him a mischievous grin.

Stan grinned back. "Yeah, but think of all the people you make happy in the process."

"Yeah, right," she huffed and disappeared back into the kitchen.

Stan looked down at his half-eaten pie. He had started something and she had abruptly finished it, or rather, half-finished it. He realized this was the way it would be for a while. His old life gone. His wife gone. The last seven years of his life gone. There would be many more unfinished conversations like this one. He was, after all, starting from square one.

Square one. Square one. How had he managed to travel forward and backward at the same time? This was a mystery much bigger than Sari, Amanda, and Bill. Bigger than himself.

He finished his pie and stayed in the booth for a good hour just drinking in the motion. It would take him days, weeks, months, to climb on board the train. For now, he was simply content to watch it speed by.

EPILOGUE

July 6, 1985

It was the Saturday after the 4th of July. Stan was at Dave's house in Spring Valley enjoying some summer sun by his brother's nice outdoor pool.

Stan had brought copies of his new paper, the El Cajon Reporter, to hand out to friends. He was reading one of his articles when Dave strolled up and stretched out in a deck chair. "How's it going, bro?"

Stan lowered the paper. "Great. Couldn't be a nicer day. Great party. Some outstanding women. Hell, man. You're living the life here."

Dave's eyes circled around his patio. "See anyone in particular you like?"

Stan held his brother's gaze for a moment before returning to his paper. "Yeah, just not interested, that's all."

"Gotta get back on the surfboard, brother."

"In my own time, Dave."

"No problem."

Dave yelled across the pool and greeted one of his friends. They sat together quietly for several minutes before Dave asked, "Paper going all right?"

"We're surviving," said Stan. "Got some new ads in. The sales person I hired is great. All in all, treading water at this point, but I don't mind. I like what I'm doing. I like where I live. Really, Dave. Life's good."

"Folks send their love."

The mention of his parents made Stan wince. "Yeah?"

"They love you, you know."

Stan shifted in his chair. "I'm sure. Just kind of awkward, trying to explain what happened."

"No explanation required."

"Well—"

"Face value, brother. They're just glad you're home."

Stan nodded and glanced up at the sky. "Good to hear. I promise. I'll drop by sometime this week."

"There you go. That's progress."

Stan paused and watched the crowd milling around the pool. "You're a good man, Dave. Hope you know how much I appreciate what you've done for me."

"We are brothers, you know." he said with a mischievous grin. "You'd do the same for me."

Stan browsed through the paper, then put it down and picked up his beer from the deck. "You know, I always wondered what happened to the hermit. He just sort of . . . disappeared."

"Marah? Hell, that man's a ghost. Not a word since he slipped out on us in Boise. Probably chasing a bunch of Bills somewhere out in the desert. No way we'll ever see him again."

"So you found him—where?"

"Not in the yellow pages, that's for sure. Years of research and a lot of travel. I probably know more about exorcism than most of your high-ranking priests." He laughed. "I did some wandering in the Kalahari, where he tends to hang out on his off days. Now there's a slice of hell on earth."

"Strange man there, bro," Stan said and shook his head.

"Strange but effective. Former monk, I think, from somewhere in South Africa. Among those in the know, he comes highly recommended. No idea how old he is. Could be hundred or a thousand for all I know, but along the east coast of Africa, he's numero uno."

"And somehow you convinced him to help?"

"Yeah," Dave said. His gaze drifted. "After a little persistent groveling and hand wringing. I wasn't sure if he'd come with or leave me to die."

Stan squinted at Dave. "What a guy."

Dave gave him that brotherly look—cavalier, off the cuff—and nodded. "I could say the same for you. Guess that makes us joined at the hip."

"Thank goodness."

Dave rose from his chair. "I got someone I'd like you to meet."

"Who?"

"A woman," he said.

"Hey," said Stan, "don't play cupid with me. I don't need that kind of help."

"Shut your pie hole and listen to her story. You might actually learn something."

"How many women do you know?" Stan joked. "I remember when you were just a lonely surfer. No women allowed."

"I got over that and I know plenty. When you're ready to hook up, you know who to call. Now, just stay here. Be nice. I'll bring her over."

Stan picked up the paper again. "Whatever."

Dave strolled around the pool and approached a woman sitting in a striped deck chair. She looked to be in her late twenties—tall, dark hair, very attractive—wearing a turquoise summer T-shirt, dark-blue designer jeans, and a tan pair of summer high heels. Her hair was pulled back in a stylish pony tail. At first glance, she reminded Stan of Amanda.

As she circled the deck and approached, he scrutinized her from behind his cheap set of shades. The afternoon sun peeked around her head. He had to admit. She was stunning.

Dave gave the introductions. "Renee, meet my brother Stan. He's the owner and editor of the brand new El Cajon Reporter. Best damn paper in San Diego. Stan, this is Renee Noland. We play pool together sometimes; that is, when we're not sitting around drinking too much."

Stan extended his hand. "Pleasure to meet you, Renee."

Renee reached out and shook it. "I've heard a lot about you, you know, brother about brother, that kind of thing."

"Don't believe everything he's said. True, we're brothers. We've also taught each other how to lie."

Dave left them to tend to his barbeque. "You two chat while I cook," he said over his shoulder.

Renee pulled over a chair and primly sat down. She took a little time to toy with her hair and adjust her legs. "So, Dave says you've traveled a lot."

Stan did his best to play coy. "Hmm, not really. I've spent a lot of time in the east, traveling around New York, New Jersey, Pennsylvania. Some time in Idaho and Oregon. Nothing too exotic."

"That's more than I've seen. I'm a real California girl. Born and raised here in San Diego. I'd love to get out and travel around the country."

"You should. It makes you appreciate what's here."

Renee had a cherub face. Stan noticed, when she smiled, how her eyes lit up.

She recrossed her legs and adjusted a slim turquoise bracelet dangling around her wrist. "Glad to be home, huh?"

"More than I can say. I have no plans to leave, ever."

One of Dave's friends did a cannonball in the pool and splashed water on them. They laughed and brushed themselves off.

"You own a paper?" she said.

"Yeah, it's a brand new venture. I'm a hardcore writer. I love the business."

"What do you like to write about?"

"Well, I'm really interested in politics." Stan bent down and grabbed one of his freshly minted editions. "Here, here's a copy. Front page, I'm dealing with upcoming elections."

She took a paper and casually leafed through it. "Very nice. Doesn't feel like a small town paper."

"Thanks."

"You're welcome."

Stan took a moment to size her up. "So, mysterious Renee, where have you come from and how do you know my brother?"

Renee gave him another sunlight smile. "Well, truthfully, here's why Dave introduced us. I'm a reporter for the San Diego Union Tribune."

"Oh boo, corporate writer."

"Yep," she laughed, "the man owns me."

"That's okay. Some day you'll see the light and be like me. Sole proprietor, flat broke."

"Maybe. I can see myself doing that in a few years."

"So, what's your connection to Dave?"

Renee shifted in her chair. She spotted Dave chatting with friends. Her face became wistful. "Oh, once in a blue moon, long ago, your brother and I had a fling. Didn't last too long, but the good news is, we're still friends. He knew me when I was a student at San Diego State."

"And now you're a big time reportor."

"I think the word is investigative journalist."

"That sounds like fun."

"He thought you might give me some help on a story I'm covering."

"Oh?" Stan pushed back in his chair, crossed his legs, and wrapped his hands around one knee.

"There are rumors I'm pursuing about a small community way out in the desert, maybe Arizona, maybe somewhere near the Colorado River, out in that vicinity."

Stan stretched out and crossed his arms. "Now why would I know anything about that?"

"Your brother seems to think you might." Renee's face grew serious. A gust of wind whipped through her hair. She casually straightened it and waited. She seemed acutely aware that she had thrown him a gauntlet.

Stan picked up the signal. His intuition told him she knew more than she was letting on. "My brother's a wannabe surfer with a vivid imagination."

"I think your brother's a pretty sharp guy," said Renee. "I agree, he's a lot of things, including a wannabe surfer, but he's not a liar."

Stan glanced down, closed his eyes, and gathered his thoughts. "Sorry," he said. "Didn't mean to imply that."

Renee toyed with her bracelet. "People are going missing across San Diego County. Not in bunches, mind you, but individual disappearances. Five or so in the last year. All of them left strange notes on the scene, explaining where they'd gone, why they suddenly moved to cities like Los Angeles, Portland, Denver, even New York. None of them have ever come back or contacted anyone from their family. They just . . . vanished."

Stan remained perfectly still. "So?"

Renee reached into her pocket and pulled out a crumpled piece of paper. "This, too, always left on their bed. Something like parchment paper, with this symbol."

Stan plucked it from her fingers and scoured it. A circle with lines running across the middle and a strange rune in the center. "It looks like some kind of hieroglyphic."

"Yeah, similar to some old Indian paintings in Arizona. I had a professor at San Diego State analyze it for me. It looks like the markings for an old Anasazi community out in Northern Arizona. That's why we think these folks are out in the desert."

"Holy shit."

"The police don't seem to have much of a clue as to what this all means. I've been trying to put two and two together. My best guess. I think someone local may be kidnaping and shanghaiing them into Arizona."

Stan felt himself react and tried to keep his true feelings under raps.

Too late. Renee read him like a book. "You know something about this?"

"Something similar, yeah," Stan drawled, "but whatever I tell you is off the record. I don't want my name to appear in any form or fashion in any story you write. Is that understood?"

"Sure, Stan. I respect my sources."

"It's more than that. We're talking potential life and death here. I need to know. Can I trust you?"

Renee was taken back. "You can trust me, Stan. Ask your brother. I'm good."

"This is no lighthearted mission you're on." He leaned forward, put his elbows on his knees, and folded his hands under his chin. "And I have to warn you. You may be entering dangerous territory, real dangerous."

Renee seemed shaken. "Jesus, Stan. It's just a story."

"Right," he said, pointing a finger at her. "That's your first mistake."

Renee took a breath, thought for a moment, and exhaled. "You think there's more to this?"

"If what you describe is true, then yes, it's possible."

Another moment of silence. "So, will you help me?"

"Well, I can only help if you're willing to admit that what I've experienced, what Dave knows about me, is true."

"What's that?"

"Occult activity."

"You mean witches, ghosts, that sort of thing?"

"Yes. And . . . magic."

"You know this?"

"Yes."

"For a fact?"

Stan hesitated. "Yeah. For a fact."

"Well, then, I promise to keep an open mind. Now, will you help me?"

"You're sure this is what you want?" Stan watched intently and measured her reactions. "You know, people get tangled in this stuff, sometimes they don't make it back—alive."

"But you did."

"I was lucky. Lucky to get out. Lucky to have a brother who spent a hell of a lot of time and money to get me out."

"Then you've got an insider's view."

"Yeah," he said, "but you can't say that in your paper." He bounced a nervous finger on his knee. "I don't want to be identified. Period. You've no idea how dangerous some of these people are."

Renee brushed back her hair and sat up straight. "Really?"

"Really."

"Okay, now you've got me kind of spooked."

"Good, you should be. You should be careful about putting your name out there as well, putting yourself at risk."

Renee caught sight of a bird sailing overhead. She let her eyes wander as the bird jetted overhead and out of sight. Finally, she returned to Stan. "So, will you help me?"

"Will you be careful?" Stan shot back.

Renee raised her hand in a pledge. "Promise."

"Not just with me. With yourself."

"Okay, Stan," she said. "I, Renee Noland, do solemnly swear to be careful."

"Okay, then I promise to help."

Renee eyes searched for Dave. She found him as he cooked a steak at his grill across the pool. She played once more with her bracelet, then returned to Stan. "Jesus Christ! Long road to a short answer."

Stan reached out and gathered her hands in his. "You don't get it, now. Hopefully, sooner rather than later, you will."

She gave him a long glance. "Well, thanks, I think."

He gently laid her hands in her lap. "You're welcome."

Renee stood up and stretched her arms toward the sky, revealing the length and depth of her beautiful figure. "Nice to meet you, Mr. Spooky Stan." She gave him one more smile, less dazzling, more forced, and headed back to Dave.

Stan felt something stir in his head. Those shapely curves and angles. That bright face. He picked up his paper and relaxed in his chair.

After he read a paragraph or two, he glanced over and saw her chatting with Dave. They both gave him a serious look. Stan guessed that she was relaying her doubts about his sanity. He buried his head again in his paper.

For him, it didn't matter what she believed or didn't believe. All he cared about was that it was a warm summer day in San Diego. He was so appreciative to be here, alive by a pool, with his brother. Free to read, walk, and live anywhere he pleased. Free to talk to anyone he chose about crazy things like shamans and demons and Indian symbols.

Sometimes he worried about his state of mind. Maybe he still suffered from years of oppression in Freeland. Maybe Renee would blow his cover. Maybe Sari or Bill would show up at his door seeking retribution. Maybe Amanda would come looking for him. Some days all these questions crashed over him like large surf. Other days, they subsided into gentle waves.

Dear Amanda. He often had the urge to pack up his things and go look for her. So far, he had resisted. Even if he found her, there was no guarantee she'd be the Amanda he loved, and who knows what the book may have done to her soul.

For the time being, he would remain entrenched in San Diego, soaking in the sun, enjoying life. It could all come crashing down tomorrow, but he didn't care. Freeland was behind him and who knows what weird shamans, demonic powers, and exorcists lived out there in the desert? He willingly discarded the past and future and kept his focus on the present.

It was a good day to be alive. Dave's barbeque smelled great. People around him were happy. Best of all, at the end of the day, he could pick up his gear and go home. He returned to one of his stories, eased back in his chair, and relaxed.

The
ESSENCE
of BEING

DOMINICK JULIANO

BALBOA.
PRESS

A DIVISION OF HAY HOUSE

Balboa Press books may be ordered through booksellers or by contacting:

Balboa Press
A Division of Hay House
1663 Liberty Drive
Bloomington, IN 47403
www.balboapress.com
1 (877) 407-4847

Because of the dynamic nature of the Internet, any web addresses or links contained in this book may have changed since publication and may no longer be valid. The views expressed in this work are solely those of the author and do not necessarily reflect the views of the publisher, and the publisher hereby disclaims any responsibility for them.

The author of this book does not dispense medical advice or prescribe the use of any technique as a form of treatment for physical, emotional, or medical problems without the advice of a physician, either directly or indirectly. The intent of the author is only to offer information of a general nature to help you in your quest for emotional and spiritual well-being. In the event you use any of the information in this book for yourself, which is your constitutional right, the author and the publisher assume no responsibility for your actions.

Print information available on the last page.

ISBN: 978-1-5043-3932-2 (sc)
ISBN: 978-1-5043-3934-6 (hc)
ISBN: 978-1-5043-3933-9 (e)

Library of Congress Control Number: 2015913514

Balboa Press rev. date: 11/20/2015

I dedicate this book
To God
Because He gave
It to me

Acknowledgements

I would like to thank Barry Morgenstern for his
invaluable assistance in editing this book.

I would like to thank Jen Howe and Linda Aliotta
for their assistance with taking and processing the
photos, and Linda Peer for editing assistance.

I would like to thank all my friends who helped with the
proofreading and offered continuous encouragement.

And finally, I would like to thank my wife, Carol, without
whom this book would never have become a physical reality.

Contents

The Introduction

During my life I have come to the conclusion that there is no such thing as a coincidence, that everything that happens is meant to be, and you have to be observant, to see the meaning. You have to look at each experience as more than a coincidence.

This material world that we have all had a part in creating is like a big ditch. We're all in the ditch together. Most people seem to be on autopilot, going through life in the ditch without much thought until something unusual happens, some kind of pain or hardship. There are other people who are always questioning everything, wondering what caused the ditch and why are they in it. Then there are the very few individuals, who know that they are in this ditch, but they only want to know one thing. They want to know how to get out of the ditch. They don't care about the ditch itself or how they got there. They simply want to get out of it.

This book is for those people who are trying to get out of the ditch. They want to escape from this ditch in which we exist, the material world. This is the journey that they have begun, and it is the most important journey they can make. It is a beautiful journey, as I see it, but if you only see the obstacles and hardships along the way, it will take a very long time to reach your goal. You can make the journey harder or easier. You can resist leaving the material world behind as you enter the spiritual world, or you can embrace the change. Some go easily and others go kicking and screaming, but the main thing is that they keep progressing.

Have a beautiful journey and know one thing. No one is going to be left behind for eternity. This material world is a school, and eventually everyone will graduate. It is like the prodigal son who finally wants to come home, to realize himself and return to the kingdom of God.

CHAPTER 1

Jnana Yoga

Jnana Yoga is the yoga of the mind. The word yoga means to attach, to become one with, to unite. A yogi is one who uses many techniques to try to unite and become one with something. So jnana yoga is about the mind, and how we come to think the way we do.

I first heard the term jnana yoga from a hatha yoga master at the Self Realization Fellowship, an organization that would often bring in movies, speakers and yoga masters from India. One time, Brother Stanley and I were at the LA Center on Sunset Blvd. We ate dinner there and then entered the meeting room, which held about 150 people. The introductory speaker told the story of that night's speaker, a master — a young man who came from the Himalayas, was about 30 years old and 5'10", lean and good-looking. He had been for many years, training under his master. He had lived in a remote cave up in the mountains with 8 or 9 others. Their teacher was a hatha yoga master, the yoga of body positions. This master then came out and started demonstrating different positions, all of which were quite amazing. I just couldn't believe what he could do. After about a half hour, as he was sitting on the edge of the stage, he looked at me and asked me to join him on the stage. What he wanted me to do was to touch his feet and to repeat that action every 30 seconds or so. I watched his feet, and the first time I touched them, they were just a normal temperature. Then as I watched, his feet started turning red, as if on fire. Heat waves

were coming off them. This time when I touched his feet they were burning hot and actually burned the tips of my fingers. Then, as I continued to watch his feet, they seemed to return to normal color and then became bluish with cold. This time when I touched his feet, they were frozen solid. From that coldness, they then seemed to thaw and returned to normal.

When I spoke with this master later on in the evening, I asked him how this phenomenon was possible. He said that he had been with his teacher for 12 years, and the group of them had lived in the cave up on the mountainside. Even though they only wore loincloths, they were able to raise their body temperature so high that they could heat the whole cave and maintain a comfortable temperature. If his master were to sit down on snow or ice, it would simply melt 3 feet around him. He also told me about some of the techniques they practiced throughout the day.

Then I asked him if, having learned how to control his body so totally, was there something more important to learn. He simply said the word 'jnana'. Later I would learn that jnana yoga is the yoga of the mind, and that it is the highest form of yoga. This hatha yoga master's path was to be a jnana yoga master.

We continued our discussion and talked about the word jnana. The word itself has different spellings and can be interpreted as wisdom or knowledge, which can make for misunderstandings. For my purposes, I would like to define jnana yoga as yoga of the mind, exploring the mind and understanding how it works. When I bought up the subject with Brother Stanley, he didn't seem to know much about it, so I realized that this wasn't necessarily going to be an easy search. But this would be my goal: to understand how the mind works, what it does, how it functions, how it gets programmed.

There are five different steps or procedures in searching out something. First you hear about it. You may hear about something for years before it actually gets your attention. Secondly, you find yourself discussing it, again maybe for years. With the third step you practice what you have been hearing and talking about, learning how to concentrate and how to contemplate, and then getting into the state of meditation.

Concentration seemed to come fairly easily to me. I learned how to concentrate through bodybuilding and came to the realization that the body does not think, it reacts. It reacts to your thinking. So how does one

learn to think, to understand the process of the whole mind? That was my beginning for the search for the yoga of the mind.

Contemplation is taking something that you have heard about and really starting to think about it. You ask a question, for instance, 'How do I get out of this ditch, how do I start?'

Meditation is the state where the answers come, where you hear God's voice speaking to you. He already knows your thoughts and is ready to answer the questions you need to ask. It takes practice to accomplish this process, and once you start, you will get experiences through the practice. At this fourth level you will experience what you have practiced. The fifth level will be reached when you actually realize what you have experienced, when you truly understand it. I have had many experiences in my life in which I would only totally understand years later. It is then that the real awakening happens.

It was a wonderful experience to witness this master. Stanley and I talked about him a lot. It was at this point that I asked Stanley what the word 'yoga' actually meant. He admitted he didn't know, and it was only years later that I would learn that the word means 'uniting, becoming one with'. One could learn from a master, a master who understood the principle of uniting.

CHAPTER 2

The Programming of the Mind

It seems to me that we have three different processes of the mind. The first process is the brain itself: the first computer. This computer is really advanced beyond all imagination. It is so advanced that it needs five senses to compute, looking, smelling, tasting, touching and hearing, all senses working together.

Now, this human computer is the brain. Weighing approximately 3 pounds it is the world's most advanced computer, one that can even create other computers made out of wires and microchips. And both these kinds of computers can be programmed.

Let's take a minute and look at how this internal programming comes about.

Imagine, for instance, that it all starts when two young people get together, fall in love and decide to get married; just an average couple, from a small town or a big city, and of course they are already programmed, also, into this environment. They both have parents, grandparents, ancestors who contributed to their own programming, but what we want to start with is the conception of the child that they are going to have. We are at the beginning of the programming. If the mother likes classical music, that's being programmed into the unborn child; and if she likes sweet foods, that too will enter the child. Whatever the mother likes, this child will be more aware of than other things, and will like it, or perhaps the child will rebel

and dislike that thing. The environment that she provides for the child will influence the baby. If she has fears, the child will have these fears.

The child is being programmed from the first day it decides to enter the womb. The child enters the womb between 6 to 8 weeks after conception, depending on the child and who is trying to get there first, because it's not easy to just get in and say I'm going to be born here, or I'm going to be born there. From my experience it is my belief that I did the choosing, as did other people I have known. You already have a sort of contract made up before you enter the womb, which is with yourself. It's the individual and where he or she is coming in and the advancement that he left in his previous life that are pivotal. Each individual brings past lessons learned into the new life. Whatever you have learned in previous lives, you take with you, as well as those things that you didn't learn.

In terms of this lifetime the programming starts with the mother's likes and dislikes. If the mother likes Italian food, or Mexican food, or hot dogs and hamburgers, that influences the child. The child is going to absorb whatever the mother is giving it, whether it's food, or music, or arguments or fighting. The fears of the mother are going to be programmed into the child as well. If there is no fear, just a loving relationship and environment, the child will accept all this as his programming.

It is like taking a tape recording and unloading data. That is what happens when this child is developing in the womb. It's amazing; remember that this environment includes the mother and the father, their parents, grandparents, friends and acquaintances. No matter what kind of conversation is going on around the mother, the child is getting these feelings and being programmed. And thus we have the beginning where this child is taking in all this data for about 7 ½ months and being programmed through the mother's environment.

Then the child is born. Depending on many factors, the environment could be either harsh or nice. Perhaps the birth is in a hospital, and the doctor comes rushing in and kind of hurries the birthing along, as if to get it over with, and spanks the newborn as it appears. This is obviously a pretty harsh environment that the baby is meeting, and of course it is all being downloaded into the baby's 'computer' which is not thinking, just accepting data at this point. Because of the harshness of the environment, he has a lot of fear in him. Or then, it could be the opposite. He could

be born in a 'LeBoyer' environment with soft lights, warm temperature, soothing music where the baby is born in a gentle manner, without external pain or conflict. This baby has received a different kind of programming. This will have an effect on the child's life in later years.

This newborn child is wrapped up and placed in a basket, and all the relatives arrive to admire the new baby. They might say things like 'What a beautiful baby, what a wonderful baby.' Perhaps the grandfather will observe, 'But he has no hair.' Or someone will say 'That's not a very pretty baby'. All those comments and emotions will be added to the child's programming. And at some point in the future that child will respond to those words that were already programmed into him.

Of course, the mother bonds with the child. Those first few hours are very important, because the child needs this love. If it gets great love, it is better for the child, and he's programmed with love. On the other hand, perhaps the child is not really wanted, is being born out of wedlock. The child will know this and so be affected by it. Everything is working its way into the child's being, creating his program.

If we step back for a second and look at the child's mind we will see that is has two portions. There is this subconscious mind that just takes in data, and then there's the conscious mind. The newborn's conscious mind is not really functioning yet; it's sort of in a sleep mode. Only in later years will the conscious mind develop completely. So all this child is doing in the beginning is downloading data into its subconscious, not just from the parents but from the grandparents. These adults are not aware of the effect they are having on the child, so they just go on with their lives, loving and fighting, enjoying their daily pleasures of music or food or whatever, their religion, their ethnic life styles, etc.

It's amazing how aware this child is, taking in this programming without analyzing it, just downloading. It's downloading sickness, good health and healing, whatever, and making it into its own environment. It's amazing how this really happens. I first came to this realization many years ago, back in the 1960's, going through various mind processes myself and analyzing the programming I myself experienced. (To be discussed in more detail later on)

But the child that we're considering here, if it's a boy, perhaps he'll be more attached to the mother than to the father. He'll learn a great deal

from the father, and the way the father treats the mother will often be the way the son is going to treat his wife and the other women in his life. If the father's a loving person, the son will be loving. If the father speaks and acts harshly towards his wife and the other women around him, the child is going to pick this up. In this way, habits and ideas are being programmed.

Now the child is a year old, and very aware. He's taking in this environment and programming so fast, that it's unbelievable. He watches everything, watches his parents and learns their emotions through their expressions and actions. If the mother is afraid, she shows it and projects it to the child. If she is fearless, this child will be the same way. The same applies to the grandparents and other adults, who may not be with the child all the time but will still create programming that the child will absorb. This is the way the child develops his own personality over time.

The child is always watching and absorbing as it grows. We all know the expression 'the terrible twos', but really the child is taking in data and learning nonstop. Perhaps the mother opens kitchen cabinets or is working at the stove, so the child wants to do the same without understanding, mimicking the whole process. When the mother stops the child, perhaps fearing the child will be hurt, the program of fear and danger is being downloaded. Whether in a bathtub or a swimming pool, the child is taught to be afraid, that there is danger around water. Born with the natural ability to swim, the child now loses that ability and is programmed to stay away from water. Obviously, these lessons will reappear as the child gets older. Perhaps a little child wants to help take out the garbage and is told he is not strong enough. Years later, when that child is well able to carry out the garbage, something inside him may hold him back, make him hesitate and kind of rebel, even if it doesn't make sense.

As I see it we are born to serve, to do things for others. And it's amazing how we get knocked out of this attitude between birth and about 6-7 years old because of how we've been programmed and how advanced we were when we came in — what we learn in our cumulative lifetimes.

So, a child is still being programmed at the age of 3 to 4. A studious, literary mother may read to the child frequently, creating an environment that encourages the child to love reading. If the mother is not well educated and/or dislikes reading, the child will receive that message and not excel at reading. The child will not have its own books to read and will not

be encouraged to create and write its own stories. All this leads to poor performance in school. Why then do we look around and wonder why one kid seems smart and another one not smart. It's all the programming from earlier childhood, before the child actually started thinking for itself, which is usually around 6 or 7 years old. That's when the conscious mind starts functioning, and the child becomes able to use reason. Then the change starts happening.

By the age of 6 or 7 the child has been downloading data from every aspect of life from parents, television, movies, etc. If the child has been raised in a multi-cultural environment, he will effortlessly learn the languages and nuances of those different cultures. Whether he hears only slang, or proper speech, he will have absorbed it much more easily than if he has to learn the language later in school. It will be even harder once the child has become an adult. And so it is with everything else. If a small child gets whatever she wants whenever she visits her grandparents, she will come to expect such behavior. And if she is taught that she has to earn something, that she has to deserve it, even if she is too young to understand the concept, she'll remember the program that she has to be deserving, that she can't have something because she hasn't earned it. Even when explanations are given to that child, it may not mean anything. She can't rationalize what is being said, because the conscious mind isn't functioning yet. This is continuous in a child's development. It depends on the parents' own initial environment and what they bring to the child. If it's violence, they bring in violence. If there's lots of fear, the child will have a lot of fear. If it's a beautiful environment, the child will be programmed the same way. If the child is in a safe environment, and the parents are happy, the child will be happy. A violent neighborhood will cause the parents to fear for the child's safety, and the child will feel that fear.

In fact, fear is one of the worst emotions that we can possible have. We become afraid of everything. On the other hand, a child of parents without fear becomes fearless himself.

So, we pick up the programming that is all around us, starting from the time we enter the womb, adding data intensively until we are about 6 or 7 years old, when the conscious part of the mind starts to be more active.

Your nationality or religion is programmed. We learn about our culture because it is all around us. If your parents are Italian; you love

the food of Italy, its music, the tightness of Italian family life. Perhaps there are similar characteristics in a Mexican family. Their families seem to have the same kind of deep attachment. Then there is the so-called 'WASP' family (white, Anglo-Saxon protestant), which may create a different environment. Remember, it's all an environment. When I was a kid I hung out with Irish friends in their Irish environment, with Jewish friends in their neighborhood, as well as with Italian kids in another neighborhood. The deeper the programming of our parents, the deeper will be our programming; it is the programming of generations. If your parents are Catholic and take you to church and follow all the rituals involved with the religion, that's your programming. That's very deep stuff. It's the same with the Jewish culture, or the Protestant religion, or Jehovah's Witnesses, the Mormon religion, whatever. You are going to be programmed into the culture and take it with you through life.

If you have parents who are deeply religious, especially from the time of your inception, these programs will be deeply ingrained. Agnostic parents will foster an agnostic set of values, which may be a good thing, because then you will learn these life lessons on your own. You will see other religions as you grow older, go to school, make new friends, etc. and can learn about them, good or bad depending on how you grow out of this situation, when you start thinking for yourself. Like I did; I went through all of this, and I was very lucky because I never really had a deeply religious environment except for my maternal grandmother.

So, the mind is a computer. It takes in so much data that it could fill libraries, and additionally you're recording endless film through visual observation. You're directing a movie and you're creating a multi-sensual film, an almost endless amount of data, volumes of unedited film. This all goes into the subconscious. This is the brain taking in all this data. Now, just imagine. This computer that you have is so great that it can bring you to the point of assembling your own mechanical computer, Windows, Macintosh, whatever.

You take home a big box and open it up. You have a screen, a keyboard and mouse, a modem, speakers and cables, perhaps a printer, etc. laid out before you but this is really no different from the mental computer that you have, although they seem to improve by the month, becoming obsolete in no time. Cell phones are the same, improving all the time. So data is

coming in fast all the time, but who's doing this data, who's developing all this data? It's the human computer, putting it out into the spiritual universe to be turned into the material universe of all these devices.

Okay, you have this computer and you start putting it together. You follow the directions carefully, connecting all the wires to the different parts. You have completed all the steps, and now you are ready to begin, so you push the power button. Nothing happens. You wonder what could be the matter, and the ego immediately suggests 'Boy, you got a lemon." The negativity sets in right away, and you get annoyed, so you call the store clerk, who walks you through all the assembly steps once again. That's when you realize that you never plugged in the power line. You end the conversation, embarrassed that you have been so stupid. Of course the computer comes alive once the electricity has been connected.

What you have learned is that the computer has no life force of its own. Think about any electrical unit, and of course you realize that they all need electricity. Without that power nothing functions. No matter what kind of material unit you have, it has to have a source of power to make it run.

Now, think for a second. What is *your* source of power? What makes you function? What is it that gets this body to work? I call it the essence of being. That is how I conceptualize it. But it's more than just those words, the essence of being. What does the essence of being mean? We will find out eventually.

So you finally have this computer hooked up and working. This computer has been programmed at the factory and will direct you to its installed systems. It will guide you through loading CDs and various other supplemental programs. You are adding data to that computer just as you yourself have received data from outside sources. Remember, we are accepting data from an immense number of sources that are all around us all the time, even though our ability to absorb data has lessened as we have gotten older. Modern science acknowledges that most of our programming occurs before the age of 6 or 7, and there is more awareness of spirituality in today's science as well, which is good. I have heard of many books and lectures series that confirm these beliefs.

However, in addition to all the programming that we have talked of so far, as I see it, I have been programmed by a much higher source than

science. I have been programmed by the essence of being, which I will explain in another chapter.

Inside you is an essence that makes us come alive, that makes us function, that created us just like the one in cooking that my mother taught me to find in every dish. Like in food, this essence is our electricity, what makes us function, what makes us special.

So, now we have these two kinds of computers. We have the spiritual essence of being, and we have the mental computer, our brain, which has created the material computer. Then we have a third program, which I call the universal agreement program, or carnal mind. It is invisible, but we all have agreed to it. As human beings, we all agreed to this invisible program, and the more agreement there is, the more solid it becomes. We are agreeing that we are all human beings.

We all agree that we are human beings, we agree with that concept. We agree that we are material and we get old, get sick, and die. But the truth is that we are created in the image and likeness of God, which is pure spirit, and spiritual beings do not get old, get sick, and die. Why we have all agreed to this is not important. What is important is to see that we have all agreed with this invisible computer called the carnal mind, the universal computer.

It is what we agree to when we call ourselves human beings, for instance or when we engage in a war. War is an agreement even though not everyone has to agree, just enough people to influence the others.

While it may be invisible, believe me, the agreement is there.

We have all agreed that we are human beings. Human beings act and behave a certain way. Human beings agree and/or disagree about weather, religions, politics, global warming. The more people in agreement about something, the stronger the agreement becomes. That is the sad part. If we have agreement on wars, we wage wars.

Let's look at another example, the aging process. At one time, the average human life span was 35-40 years. With time that grew to 45-50 years. We all were told that this was the reality, and we all agreed with that. Decades later we agreed that the average life span was 60-65 years. Then it became 70-75, and we all agreed that we should all be living longer. We agreed that science and better life styles were increasing our life span. Now we're looking past 80 and 90, even to 100 years, and everyone is

agreeing that this is the reality. But what is it: mass agreement. Science understands some of the mechanisms, but it can't understand the reason why we die. Our bodies are totally renewed every 9 years, so it is something else that is making us die. That something else is the carnal mind, the invisible computer of agreement. We agree that human beings get sickness, disease and die. It's all just an agreement, a false agreement. If you have enough agreement, it becomes fact. With minimal agreement, it doesn't become solid fact. So, the more positive thought, the stronger the positive reality. The more negative thought, the stronger the negative reality. The agreement that might is right leads to that reality. Most importantly, the reality, the strength of a reality, is vibration. Everything is vibrating.

CHAPTER 3

Vibrations

When I was younger I was more aware of vibrations. I was aware of people's thinking, both positive and negative. But as I grew older, I sort of went to sleep to that awareness and forgot about the vibrations. Most children are very sensitive to vibrations and, like me, they seem to become less aware as they age. At the same time everyone is always talking about vibrations. 'This person has good vibes, but that one doesn't.'

The whole world is vibrating, even the material world. There is nothing that isn't vibrating. The more aware you are, the more you will feel them and even see them. Every single thought we experience has a vibration. Every single word we speak has a vibration. These positive and negative vibrations go into a field, which we walk into and out of as we meet people and go about our lives. As you listen to people speak you become aware that about 80-90 percent of what people say is negative. There are, unfortunately, very few positive vibrations.

I call it being aware of being aware. You must be aware of your thoughts, so that you can stop the negative thinking and make it positive. You can do this very easily, if you are aware of it. Without awareness, it is very difficult to change. You go with the flow and synchronize with the vibration of the people around you. If it is all negative you fall into that negativity, and you find yourself feeling depressed and unhappy. Those negative vibrations pull energy away from you. Although people are always fighting to get energy,

to be stimulated, to be in control what they don't realize is that each person is a dynamo of this energy. They don't have to fight for it but simply think about it and produce it by means of positive thinking. Therefore, it is very important that you are aware of your thinking, so that you can be more positive and create the positive energy that you need.

What does negative energy produce? It produces negative cause and effect. With each cause there is an effect — which is the law of karma that we will be discussing later on. The same thing happens with positive energy: positive thoughts, words and actions produce positive cause and effect. By being mindful of your thinking you can change your vibrations from negative to positive cause and effect. If you stop yourself every time you have a negative thought and change it to a positive one you will be producing positive energy.

Take the example of someone driving a car. If you get caught in traffic and start thinking about all the negative aspects of this situation you may become anxious and miserable. Negativity can even make you feel fearful.

Fear causes all kinds of problems, including sickness, disease, and even death. Fear is the worst emotion that you can feel, because it can affect the body so negatively. We are all anxious and fearful at times, and it seems so hard to get rid of these emotions — especially when the environment around us is equally negative. This is why it is so important to be aware of where you are — to be aware of that negative environment — to be aware of every single one of your words and actions. You must create positive energy, so that the field around you becomes more positive. The more positive it is, the easier it is to dissolve the negativity that you are feeling.

Negativity creates darkness, as opposed to positive light. Because we are dynamos of energy, we are always creating energy. We are born totally positive but forget that energy over time and allow the negativity of the surrounding world to influence us. We lose touch with the feelings that we have and forget that we can create our own energy but the more we can change that negative field around us, the more we can make it a positive field.

It's like going into a room that is completely dark. You are afraid to step forward, fearing the darkness that is all around. But all you need is one lit candle to dispel the darkness, and now you can see. The more candles you light, the greater is your ability to see more clearly and further into the

corners of the room. Light doesn't comprehend darkness. Darkness doesn't exist in light. It is only in the material world that we allow darkness and negativity to surround us. The spiritual universe doesn't acknowledge this transfer of energy or hear your negative thoughts individually. It absorbs them collectively. It has no respect of individuals, of countries or nations, of religions or race. It just is, an absolutely positive energy. It dissolves all darkness because for this universe darkness doesn't exist. The universe hears those collective thoughts that enter the energy field and understands them.

The more you understand this transfer of energy the more you will understand its power. Even though I had known about the power of negative and positive thinking for a long time, it took me many years to understand how it affected me. Even though I always tried to have a positive attitude about everything, I only gradually became aware of the power of negativity. I saw how much negative thinking existed around me, how people had been programmed to think that way, and how difficult it was for them to change. I learned that you have to work to increase the same awareness in your life, and as you become more aware, you will be amazed at the amount of negativity around you. It comes not just from family and friends, but from our schools, government, news media, and even our churches.

We have all experienced it: going to a party and feeling happier and positively stimulated, because the people there are having a good time, laughing and enjoying one another's company. We don't know why, but we feel better at once. We don't realize that it is the vibration in the room that is stimulating us positively. On the other hand, a funeral immediately makes us feel sad and depressed. The environment is dark and solemn, even the clothes and the music are dark. The feeling of loss creates that negative field and that vibration is absorbed by the people present.

One escapes that field of negativity though love and joy, happy thoughts and remembrances. Think of anything that lifts your spirits. Go into that joy, and you will escape the negativity. Love has a very strong vibration, especially universal love. God's love is unconditional, pure — *universal*. Feel that love and you can escape any form of negativity.

I remember the first time I was told that I was 'asleep'. I was walking with the great master Sai Baba in India. He turned to me and told me

that we did not have a disciple/guru relationship. He told me that the only difference between the two of us was that he was awake and I was asleep. He then told me to wake up and understand who I really was, to realize that I was a dynamo of positive energy. Only by thinking positively can one create positive energy. Only be being aware can one escape the negativity surrounding us all. Until you understand this it is impossible to get out of the negative space. If you live your life on autopilot you will never change that environment. You must be aware of being aware. That is what mindfulness means, to be aware of every single thought you have throughout every single second of the day.

Perhaps this sounds impossible to you. But as the axiom has it: practice makes perfect. At first you may only be able to be aware for a few minutes, then a half hour. Give it time and one day you will wake up to the vibrations within and around you. You will inevitably feel happier, more joyous, more positive, once you have cast the negativity aside. You will want to read more positive books and articles, watch more uplifting television programs. If you go to bed at night with the messages from a spiritual story vibrating in your mind you will have sweet dreams and wake happier and more refreshed. Be aware of being aware as you go to sleep and again as soon as you awake. Feel your awakening in the morning. Don't get up on autopilot, but be mindful of each second, each moment, each thought and action of your day. Be aware of your feelings and words. Keep your vibrations positive and by so doing create good health and a good ambiance around you. Don't let anxiety and fear enter into your life. Don't let other people's negative thoughts influence your beingness. And the saddest part is that they don't even know what they are feeling.

So, once more, be aware of being aware. Listen to yourself think. Listen to yourself speak. Be aware of every single action that you do during every minute of the day. The more you contemplate this concept, the more you will come to understand and embrace it. The only answer to this awareness is positive, uplifting energy. Being in this state of positive beingness breaks the chains that bind you, because negativity tightens everything around you and imprisons you.

There is another axiom that is tremendously important. 'If you can't say something nice about a person, don't say anything at all.' When you speak negatively about someone else you are actually only hurting yourself. That

negative or cruel thought becomes part of your being, creating a vibration that boomerangs back to you. To judge or condemn another is only to judge and condemn you yourself. It shows that you don't understand your own being or that of others: that we have been created out of the image and likeness of God. We are not separated but, rather, all one, all brothers and sisters. We're all going to make it. No one will be left behind. You must decide that you will intentionally never hurt another person, whether by thought, word, or deed. Living one's life through positive vibration is one step on the path to reaching this ultimate realization: that we are all one and the same. Strength comes from uniting, not separating. Positive vibration comes with uniting. Realization comes with uniting.

CHAPTER 4

My Reincarnation

This is the story of my reincarnation.

The year was 1933, sometime in May, and I was entering into this new birth. I had made my contract, and now I was back, on my way in. I had to decide where I was going to be born. I decided that the United States would be a good place, because what I was looking for was total freedom, which I hadn't had in many previous lifetimes. So, I was looking for a mother or father who would give me this total freedom. That was the most important thing for me; the rest would follow. I was looking in New York City, in Manhattan between 73rd and 74th Streets on Third Avenue. I had stopped many places; there were many pregnant women. But none of them suited my situation, my needs. Then I saw a woman who was approximately six weeks pregnant. The vibrations were awesome; they felt good. I was very attracted to her, so I followed her around for quite a while. She lived in a five- story tenement building on Second Avenue and 74th St. It was a typical tenement building of that time. There was a grocery store below. She lived there with her mother and already had a little girl, Fernanda, who was just turning one year old. There was also Tony, who would be my brother and was about eleven years old. My mother had two sons by a previous marriage. They had been abducted by their father years before, and only the younger son had been found at this point.

So, I decided that this was going to be it. My grandmother, Josephine,

who was a wonderful woman, had long, gray hair down to her waist, always worn in a bun. She dressed totally in black and wore glasses. She was really sweet and wonderful, with wonderful vibrations.

After about two weeks of kind of hanging around, I realized that the decision had to be made, because there were other souls looking to enter bodies. I could see them all around me as I was coming in, making the same choices as I was. They all were seeking situations that were right for the lessons they had to learn in this lifetime. So, anyway, I chose my mother, whose name was Rose. She was happy at times, but more often she was fearful and full of anxiety, always worrying about money. She was the sole supporter of this little family and worked very hard. She was about twenty-eight years old, a very attractive woman, not very tall and not heavy. With her I felt sure that I would have the freedom I desired.

Up until the time of entering the body, you are in a kind of free realm. You can expand and contract at will. You have many abilities but are unaware of them. You will realize those abilities as you evolve and learn with each lifetime. If you learn nothing in a lifetime, you will take nothing with you into the next. Learn a lot and you will advance by leaps and bounds. Well, apparently I hadn't learned that much, as I had to come back. But now I had chosen this situation and had to get into the womb.

So, at about eight weeks into the pregnancy, I entered the womb. It is really a funny, peculiar feeling. At one moment you are free and expanded, and then you are suddenly confined to a little space, so you have to contract tremendously. Before entering the body you thought you had a great understanding of this individual, but now you can really feel her beingness. Every emotion, every expression she has, you feel it. You feel her joy, her sorrow, her hunger, her every emotion. The level of the vibrations is very intense. It was quite intense for me, because it had been a long time since I had entered a body, to be born. I was also totally aware of all the emotions and activities going on around me. I could hear my sister crying, my grandmother, my brother. I was aware of my mother leaving for work every morning. I could feel all the emotions that she had that day. I was very aware of all the foods she ate. If she liked a food, so did I. If she disliked a food, I didn't like it either. I felt all the sensations that were in her environment. I responded to all her emotions in kind. The programming was continuous in this situation. She was always a very loving woman to

me, so I felt much loved. My grandmother had a lot of loving vibrations as well. But my sister was very confusing to me. She was either laughing or crying, having strong mood swings as a little girl, but I never took on those feelings, as I didn't have those feelings that came in through her.

So, I had a fantastic mother, but I had no feeling about my father. When the pregnancy was in its third month, we went to court and there I later learned that he had been sentenced to prison for a period of no less than seven years for bootlegging. Apparently for years he had maintained a still right behind the police station, which angered the authorities. My mother had worked alongside him for years, and now the still had been destroyed. She would continue to make alcohol in the following years. She would buy the alcohol from suppliers, bring it home and make all kinds of liquors. She was never a drinker except for a rare glass of wine. My grandmother just drank red wine. When the grapes came down from Poughkeepsie in the fall — big Concord grapes — my mother would buy them by the crate and make wine, which she would later sell. Between making liquor and being a seamstress, she worked very hard. Money was always a concern. When she was stressed over the need for more income, I stressed. When she had enough money and was happy, I was happy. Again, I felt every single vibration in and around her. I was being programmed the way she had been programmed. And that's all it is, being programmed. It is very interesting because you aren't really consciously thinking about these experiences going on around you. You are like a tape recorder, recording the vibrations and sensations around you, as if it were dictation. You keep taking it in, and you have no answer for it at all. The program continues throughout the pregnancy, with data coming in all the time.

Then the day comes when you have outgrown the space in which you have been living. The birth happens. I can remember her rushing to the hospital, Metropolitan Hospital on 97th St. I think, near the East River. I remember the rush to get there, and then, once she had arrived at the hospital, she was placed on a table with wheels. Then I suddenly felt this tremendous sensation of losing liquid. I felt as if I was being drained; very peculiar. I heard a lot of commotion and yelling. People were telling my mother not to push, to hold on. She was trying to hold on, but I was ready to come out. Then suddenly I felt this incredible pressure and pop, I was in the air. There were bright lights, it was cold, and everyone was yelling

and moving about. The doctor held me up and slapped my bottom, and the pain was overwhelming. As I took my first breath, I started crying, screaming. I was totally miserable, with no feeling of well being or comfort, of being separated from my mother. I could feel her vibration and knew that she was close, and eventually after they had cleaned and examined me, I was wrapped in a white cloth and placed on my mother's breast. It was only then, with the return of closeness and comfort, that I stopped crying. To remember this experience is an awesome feeling, but at the time it was misery. Later that day I woke up to find myself separated from my mother once again and started screaming. The nurses fussed over me, talking about my looks and size. I took that all in, again not realizing what it was. Once back at my mother's breast, I stopped crying and returned to a kind of bliss. This pattern continued for quite a little while.

Then I can remember being brought home. My grandmother welcomed me with loving hugs, and my sister, Fernanda, wanted to see me. I heard her voice, but she wasn't speaking it. I could hear everything she was saying in my mind. My brother Tony was always around and I was aware of him even if I couldn't really see him. I wasn't seeing through my eyes but could see everything. I wasn't consciously thinking about all this. I was simply taking in all that was happening. Then there were lots of relatives, lots of cousins. My Aunt Lizzie and my Aunt Jenny, my Uncle Pete, my mother's two brothers all came to welcome me. There were the comments around me — 'Oh, he has no hair. Why is he so bald?' 'Look at how round and beautiful his face is.' I took all the comments in, being programmed. These comments were going into the subconscious mind. All this was going on around me, but I was still very sensitive to my mother and her feelings. I was always watching her face, because I knew that if she were happy, I would feel happy. If she was sad, I could feel it and see it in her face.

When I was almost a year old, I was standing in a doorway, trying to walk. There was a metal storage cabinet in the kitchen. I remember wanting to walk to that cabinet. I started across the room, not noticing that Fernanda was standing there. As I reached for the open door of the cabinet, she slammed it on my finger and cut off the tip. I remember the sensation of pain going through my body, and I screamed. My mother and brother both came running, bound my finger and rushed me to the hospital. I remember lying on the hospital bed with my face covered. I

was screaming with fear, but I could hear my mother trying to calm me, and that eventually helped somewhat. That was my second experience of severe pain.

So, you continue growing and absorbing the world around you, not yet consciously thinking. It is still all subconscious programming. It's amazing how much data you take in. You have no judgment about what you are taking it in. It simply is.

The second clear memory I have occurred when I was about one and a half years old. My brother Tony was sitting on a windowsill. He was hanging up a clothesline from the 1st floor to the utility pole, about 50 feet away. I was watching him, turned away for a second, and then when I turned back, he was gone. I heard a terrible scream. My mother came running and started screaming, so I started screaming as well. Tony had fallen out of the window and had broken his arm. They ran off to the hospital, while I sat on my grandmother's lap. She always tried to make me laugh. She would get up and dance for my sister and me. She was a wonderful woman. She took care of me and Fernanda while my mother worked and Tony was in school. Tony would come home in the afternoon, but my mother would arrive later, as she would pick up the daily groceries on the way home from work. We had no refrigerator, just an icebox with limited space for keeping things fresh during the warm months. In winter, we had a box set outside the window to keep things cold. I remember my mother taking us shopping, going from one store to another, separate shops for fruits or vegetables or meats. We had incredible bakeries. I was totally in love with the bakeries. Cannolis were my favorite treat.

Anyway, my grandmother seemed to take care of me more than my sister. Tony helped a lot, but he couldn't handle both of us. I always found myself being dragged to church. I went to church with her almost every day. I didn't understand what it was about. If she sat, I sat, if she stood, I stood, and if she knelt, I knelt. The mass was in Latin, so I understood nothing. I could never understand why we were doing all this, but if my grandmother told me to do this, I did. It certainly wasn't any fun for me. She would hold my hand and shush me if I started to talk. Obviously church meant keeping quiet. Of course, I was obedient and never yelled or screamed or carried on. That was never behavior like that in my family. When my mother said something, we all stood up like soldiers. We knew,

when she was angry, to sit down and be quiet. My mother was very strict that way, but my grandmother wasn't. She just loved us, no matter what we did. All this went on for years. Some things were memorable, but a lot of things were forgotten. Regardless, you continue to take in data. It is being recorded. So, first it was my mother's vibrations, then my grandmother's, and then my sister and brother started to make an impact on my subconscious. The circle grew to include my aunts and uncles and my cousins. I was taking it all in.

Then I was five years old. I just watched everyone and everything. At that time our family was still living in the same apartment, the longest time we ever stayed in any one place. It was called a railroad flat because it was long and narrow. The kitchen had two windows facing the back yard. From there you went into another room, which in our home was the first bedroom. Then there was a second bedroom and a living room in the front with two windows facing the street. The neighbors often gossiped and hung out in the yard, and sometimes the children were allowed to play there.

Anyway, one day I was jumping on the bed up and down, and my mother told me to stop. Suddenly there was a knock on the door, and I stopped jumping. My mother opened the door, and there stood a man. I can remember him so clearly. He had on a flat-topped straw hat with a black band. He was a tall, big man, about 5'10" with a big mustache and a round face, and weighed maybe two hundred and twenty pounds. My mother hugged and kissed him. I was watching and couldn't understand any of it. My mother told me that this was my father. Well, I had never seen him before, and I had actually believed that my brother Tony was my father because he took care of us and was always there. This man who was my father picked me up, hugged and kissed me, and, although I kissed him back, I didn't feel anything. It was an odd situation. I remember them going to the kitchen to have coffee and Italian pastries. She gave me coffee as she always did, lightened with milk, and we ate up the last of the cannolis.

My parents talked together for a few hours, while my sister and I played with our grandmother, and then, the next thing I knew he was gone. My mother promised that he would return, and indeed, he did come back once a week. But he never lived at home with us. He would come on

Saturday and spend a few hours with us and then leave again. I could tell that my mother really loved him, and I know my sister loved him as well. My brother Tony was like me. He respected my father. I remember sitting on his lap, listening to him talk to me, and I felt no emotion, neither love nor hate. He was just there, and that was the way it was. He would tell us stories, and sometimes he would stay and cook dinner in the evening. He was a fantastic cook, maybe even a little better than my mother, which is a big admission from me, because my mother was a great cook. When my mother cooked, she always put me and my sister on chairs beside her at the stove. She made us taste everything as she cooked and would ask us if the dish needed something. I didn't know what she meant at first, but over time learned to taste for salt and pepper, basil and oregano. She always made it a game, so I loved learning how to cook. We learned to wash and dry dishes at the kitchen sink, standing on stools, while our mother played with us, splashed us with water, making it a game. She never scolded us if we accidentally broke a dish. We had so much fun, whether cooking or washing dishes.

Thursday night was laundry night. She would take out a bucket and put it on a bench with a washboard. I would help her scrub the clothes on the washboard, and it was a game to get the clothes really clean. By the time the laundry was done, we would all be soaking wet from playing around. The programming was always perfect. It was never a hardship to do the daily chores, because my mother made it so much fun.

And so, as I continued to grow up, I was always watching my mother and in touch with her emotions. My sister was much harder to understand. Even though we always played together and were very close, she would sometimes carry on, crying and such, which I didn't understand. Also, my grandmother was aging and went to Uncle Pete's house at times for extended visits, so she wasn't living with us as she had when we were little. I can remember that my mother was always worried about money during these years. It was always a hardship. So I knew I had to make money, that I had to go to work.

CHAPTER 5

Starting School and Working

When I was 6 years old it was time for me to start school. I had heard about school and knew a little about it, but at that time I spoke very little English. My grandmother, who spoke only Italian, had taken care of me. So, when I went to school I understood very little. At my Catholic elementary school the nuns spoke and understood Italian, but used only English in the classroom. The exception was when they were angry: then they would scream in Italian. On my first day of school I arrived in a new pea jacket with a plaid hood. The nun told me to hang my jacket in the closet, yelling at me in Italian. So, I got through my first day and when the final bell rang, all the other kids grabbed their coats and ran out of the room. I sat and waited, not knowing what to do. The nun yelled once again in Italian and told me to get my coat, but when I went to the closet, it was gone. Instead of showing sympathy for the loss of my jacket, she accused me of losing it and gave me 10 swats on my hand with a ruler. I ran screaming out of the school and didn't go back until 6 months later. My mother would drop me off, and my brother would pick me up in the afternoon, but in between I would run off and play hooky with other kids in the neighborhood. No one ever came to check on me. It was if I were totally forgotten.

At this point we moved to another neighborhood. It seemed that from this time on we were always moving every six or seven months. It was

always about money, whether or not we could pay the rent. Rents might only be $6-8 per month, maybe $10, but my mother sometimes couldn't pay it, and we would be evicted. Then she would be out looking for money and was often rescued by my father, who would turn up just then. I remember one time we were thrown out of a tenement building with all our possessions, and my mother placed me on top of a bureau on the sidewalk. She left me there to guard our furniture, alone and afraid for hours, sitting on top of that bureau. Then at dusk I saw my father approaching with a bag of groceries. He asked me what was happening. Just then my mother returned with a truck and we moved from this neighborhood, somewhere on the lower east side of Manhattan, all the way to the Bronx. Somehow she had managed to scrape together some money and saved the day. I remember that first night at the new apartment. It was dark before we were moved in, and then my father started cooking dinner. Everyone seemed to be very happy and at peace. We were all together and had enough money to get by for the moment. I can remember that day like it was yesterday.

So now we were living on the top floor, the 6th floor, of this tenement building in the Bronx. My mother registered me at a new school. I remember the first day there. It was easier now, because I had learned a lot of English on the streets. But I just didn't want to be in school, and after that first day I never went again. I would hang around the neighborhood. The janitor of our building was an Irishman with a wife and two children. Patty was seven and a half years old, a little older than me but the same size. He was a natural hustler and would sing Irish ditties, folk songs, with a sweet Irish voice. He knew everything about the neighborhood and became a great friend. Another kid in the neighborhood was Ritchie Dubois, who also became my friend. His mother was Italian, near the same age as my mother and worked in the courthouse. His sister Marcy was about 8 years older than we were. Ritchie tended to hang out with older kids, and I hung out with Patty.

I was always trying to figure out a way to make money. I noticed that Patty would leave the neighborhood every afternoon, carrying a box, and wouldn't return until late at night. He was going up on Broadway and shining shoes. He got 10 cents a shine. I asked him to teach me how to do it. Patty told me I was too young and wouldn't teach me, even though I was already bigger than he, so I let it go and tried to pick up little jobs

around the neighborhood. I made friends with the iceman, who had a kid helping him, a kid who was a skinny runt like me. He told me he made 5 cents a run, carrying ice blocks to the top floors of the apartment buildings. He told me how hard the job was, carrying 15-20 pounds of ice at a time up all those flights of stairs. I tried to get a job as well and lied about my age, as I was only eight at the time and said I was ten, but the iceman told me to come back when I was eleven. It was tough, but I wanted to work, because I knew how much my mother needed the money. I watched her work so hard for so little money, trying to save for the rent and food. My sister and I were often left home alone with our brother, just making do when there was little food in the house.

In all those tough times my mother was always positive towards me, which I liked very much. I didn't know what negative was, really. She always told me that I would make lots of money when I grew up, and I believed her. I didn't really know the value of money and why everyone had to struggle so much to get it, but I could see that it was really important, that everyone wanted it and hustled for it.

I can remember my grandmother dragging me to church, and my mother insisting that I do my first holy communion. She took me to Sunday school, where I did catechism, learning about the basics of the Catholic religion in preparation for receiving The Host on Sunday. I didn't understand anything about any of this. I only knew what I had seen in church. So I went through all the classes and the bible studies and did my first holy communion. Now I could confess my sins to a priest and take the Host on Sunday. My mother came to church occasionally, but usually she sent my sister and me alone or with our brother, Tony. He didn't like going to church either, so we ended up going by ourselves. We would confess our sins on Friday, get the Host on Sunday, and then on Monday we would start the cycle all over again. We would do our little nonsenses: a little cursing or stealing, making mischief with the other kids in the neighborhood. Then we would confess on Friday, take the Host on Sunday and start again. Sometimes we would wait until Saturday to confess, as we didn't have to be good for so long before Sunday service. The whole thing didn't make any sense to me.

I was 9 years old when I made my Confirmation. Again, I remember going to catechism, and I was always confused about this thing called the soul. I was taught various Catholic dogma about the soul, about Jesus, and other things. I was very curious about the soul. I was told there was something within us, but I wanted to know what it was. How do I know I have a soul? I asked a nun about this, and she said I should talk with a priest. I went to a priest and asked him, 'Father, if you have a soul, how do you know it?' The priest replied, 'You have to have faith.' 'What does that mean?' I asked. He replied, 'Faith is having something you believe in.' And I asked, 'Does that mean you believe in it, but you don't know?' The priest looked at me, then slapped my face and told me to sit down and to stop asking questions like that. I realized at that moment that while I might be calling him 'Father', he didn't know for sure. That was really discouraging to me. I made my Confirmation, but I really didn't go to church much after that. I would go and confess my sins. I would be told to say 10 Hail Marys and 10 Our Fathers. I would do as I was told without thinking. The important thing was to show obedience. They had you two ways, obedience and fear. I realized that there was nothing in this Catholic religion for me and stopped going to church for quite a while.

Now I was 9 years old, and I knew I had to make money. I couldn't fool around anymore. I wasn't going to school. I had gone through all this religion stuff. I went to Patty and told him I wanted to go with him to Broadway and shine shoes. He said okay and told me to get a shine box. What is that? We found an old orange crate, took it apart and made a little shoeshine box out of the front and back of the box, shaping it into about half the size of a milk crate. We bought a little iron shoe stand from the local cobbler, which we screwed to the top of the box. That was it. Then you bought your polishes, black and brown, and your brushes. I was already working Fridays and Saturdays for the iceman, doing all the top floors, getting a nickel an ice block. I could make maybe $1.00-1.50. There were also coal trucks that would come in to the city and dump the coal for a building into a pit at the front of the building. Then you would get a wheelbarrow and move the coal to the back of the building, where the furnace was located. The janitor would pay $5.00 to move all that coal, which took about 8 hours. You worked like an animal.

I wasn't a strong kid, but I always wanted to be, so I would do these

jobs. I was always thinking about strength, and everyone always told me that the harder you worked, the stronger you would get. Well, I took the hardest jobs I could find, and I never got stronger. I was a skinny kid. I only weighed about 85 pounds at 4 feet tall. It seemed that no matter how hard I worked, I couldn't gain weight. I used to always eat anything I could get my hands on. I was never picky. I just wanted to get strong. So everyone suggested that I take up boxing. I tried that, after working all day in coal bins. I would move coal two days a week, Thursdays and Saturdays, and there were a lot of kids doing that stuff. I was lucky that some landlords liked me and would give me the work.

Then I learned about the shoe shining and did that with Patty. So, I got my box all set up and went to Broadway. It was amazing. Broadway was a fantastic place in those days. I rode the subways so much that I knew every stop. It cost a nickel, and you could go any place in Manhattan, the Bronx or Brooklyn. The buses were easy as well. With a transfer you could go either uptown, downtown or cross-town. It was so easy to travel through the city. I knew it inside out. The first time I remember being on Broadway with Patty, he said he would sing, and I would pass the hat. He always wore a little cap. That was the first time I really knew he could sing. We would draw a little crowd and collect 20-30 cents. That was our start. Then we would get up on Broadway, and the first thing we would do is go to Horn and Hardart's, a diner right there on Broadway. It was a huge place, and you could get a big piece of coffeecake and a cup of coffee for 10 cents.

About 3:30PM we would start shining shoes. Patty taught me all the tricks of shining shoes. There were a lot of sailors and soldiers on Broadway, and there was Army-Navy canteen right there, that split Broadway in half. On one side was Broadway and on the other side was 7th Ave. The Coca-Cola sign was right above the canteen. It was quite a busy place at that time. The soldiers and sailors, paratroopers and marines, would go into the canteen to get sodas, hamburgers and hotdogs, and to dance. So it was a great place to shine shoes. We would sit there on the corner and beg guys to let us shine their shoes. Most of the time their shoes were already shiny, especially the paratroopers with their spit shines, but we had a few tricks. Patty taught me, tell them you can tell them exactly where they got their shoes. And if you're right, they have to get a shine. In disbelief, the guys would say, yeah, tell me where I got my shoes. I would say, you got them

on your feet, now put them up. Instead of a left hook, I got the shine. Our secret to the perfect shine was to add a little after-shave lotion or Brylcream, both of which gave a glassy shine. I knew a lot about shining shoes and was up on Broadway every afternoon. We could pick up $4-5.00 in an evening. Of course, you had to stay there and hustle, but it was easier than hauling coal or ice, so I quit those two jobs.

So for two years I spent my working hours shining shoes on Broadway. I made a decent living, so we were able to stay in the same Bronx apartment. In the meantime my friend Ritchie and I always had fun. He was a good guy, but after 3:00 PM I would leave for Broadway. His mother gave him an allowance; he always had a little money in his pocket, and so he never had to worry about making a living. We used to call him the spoiled brat. He wanted to shine shoes, but after Ritchie tried something a time or two, he wouldn't want to do it anymore, and that was the end of it.

In the meantime I was always trying to get strong. I would try anything. I went into boxing. I had never been a good fighter, until an old Italian guy grabbed me when I was about 8 years old. Up until then I used to get beat up all the time. I was the punching bag for the neighborhood. So, he took me aside and told me, 'You can't keep getting beat up like this every day. You have to learn how to fight. I'll teach you a few tricks. First, don't just push back if some guy comes up to you and pushes you around. Soon as that guy walks up to you — just looks at you — give him a one-shot in the stomach. When he folds over, you come up with your knee, and that's the end of it. See how easy it is. Don't argue, don't push or shove, just give him the punch.' The first time I tried it, this big kid went down and then ran. I never lost a fight again. Then, twice a week, when we weren't shining shoes, we went to the local Boy's Club. They had a boxing program, so I joined up because they said if I learned how to box, I would grow up and be strong. So, I started boxing, and all I learned was that you get your brains kicked in. They knew how to box and didn't want to give you a chance to get in a punch. I was actually getting skinnier. I couldn't figure out how to gain weight.

Then one day I remembered about the ad in the back of comic books and Popular Mechanics. There was Charles Atlas, getting sand kicked in his face. After working out for 6 weeks, he was the guy kicking sand in the face of the bully. This sounded good to me, so I sent away for the Charles

Atlas course. It was $2.00. That was a lot of money. I used to make $4-5.00 a night, and I would give my mother most of it. I would keep a $1.00 to spend and would save to buy Army Surplus clothes. There I bought my first Eisenhower jacket and paratrooper boots. They were always too big, so I would stuff newspaper in the toes and give them a great shine. Home relief — welfare in those days — used to give us knickers to wear. Only kids on home relief wore those brown knickers and plaid socks, and of course the other kids ridiculed them. I was ashamed to be on home relief when we were little, standing in line every 6 months to get a pair of shoes. The shoes would quickly wear out, and we would stuff them with paper or cardboard because we couldn't afford to get them resoled. I would promise myself that when I grew up I would never be on home relief again. I would buy my own shoes someday.

All these things added up to needing to make money. My mother would tell me to look down, to always look for money. I took her seriously and always looked down when I walked, and I always found money. She really told me to look down so I wouldn't trip in those oversized shoes, but I took her for her word, and to this day, I look down when I am walking down a sidewalk. And it's amazing, but I always find money. And then she would always say, 'Dominick, you can always make money, no matter what you do.' And I never found it hard to make money. My mother also used to say, 'Dominick, you know you aren't that smart, so you always have to hang around with people who are smarter than you. And always ask questions. Never be afraid to ask questions. Ask them what kind of job they have, and how much money they make.' And so I always used to ask questions. I was never embarrassed to ask. To this day I still do the same thing. I was programmed to do this.

Eventually the Charles Atlas course came in the mail. It was a little brochure with a bunch of exercises called dynamic tension. The first exercise was for the neck. You pushed on the side of your head with one hand towards the other hand, resisting the other way in the next movement. You pushed and resisted back and forth. I did about 15 on each side, and the next morning my neck was so stiff that I couldn't move it. I looked at the brochure and said, 'Well, that's not any good.' There went my Charles Atlas course down the drain.

CHAPTER 6

Just Another Job

By the time I was twelve I had gone through all this nonsense of growing up, doing all kinds of crazy things, learning and being programmed, asking a lot of questions in my neighborhood. The local Italians were all in the Mob, hanging around with gangsters and always encouraging me to join them once I was old enough. They always said they would take care of me, make sure I made a living. That was not the way I wanted to do it. I can remember a story from my childhood. I was walking down the street, about 7 years old, and I heard a scream as I passed by a basement grate where I saw a man hanging by his thumbs, crying for help. When I turned to my mother in horror, she told me to mind my own business and keep on walking. She told me he had done something wrong, maybe squealed on someone, and was being punished by the gangsters, the Mafia, whatever. Just keep walking and ignore him. I walked on, but I never forgot that man, and I knew that something was wrong with this gangster stuff. I wanted no part of it. Being hung by one's thumbs left a big impression on a little boy.

As I got older, I met a lot of these guys. I remember one time when two Italians were having an argument. They both had white shirts on and started slashing at each other with straight-edged razors. Their shirts turned red, and I had a terrible feeling in my own body, like *I* was being cut up. All men used straight edged razors in those days for shaving, and

they would be sharpened on a strap to a fine edge. It was if I could feel that blade. When I would get my haircut after that and the barber would shave up the back of my neck, chills would go through me. That feeling lasted for a long time. I could never even pick up a straightedge razor without that feeling of being cut, and I would never run my finger across it, because they were so sharp. That all stuck with me in the subconscious mind. It put a deep groove in my memory bank.

Anyway, so that's the way it was, and that's the way I grew up until about the age of 12. Then, my brother Tony, who was quite a clever guy, became a cook. He went from job to job and ended up running the dining room at Sutton Place. By this time my brother Frank was also in our lives, and although he never lived with us, he would come around and visit with our mother. I think he lived with his father at that time, was in the Army, and then married and had a couple of children. My mother would often tend those kids, Lucy and Teri, and we all lived in the same neighborhood, never far apart. We were a pretty close-knit family. The war was over, and I remember in 1945 being on Broadway, shining shoes, the night the war ended. It was quite a night. Broadway was my beat and I loved it.

I remembered I knew how to get into any theater through the alleyways to the back entrances. We could sneak into any theater on Broadway. So I did a lot of sneaking in. I saw a lot of stars and all the best bands, watching the dime-a-dance venues. I loved shining shoes and had a lot of great experiences there. I remember seeing Sinatra on Broadway. At the end of the war, he was playing the Paramount Theater, I think, and he came outside and was singing in the middle of Broadway. A lot of the stars would do that now and then, trying to draw a crowd. I saw Harry James and Lucille Ball and Desi Arnez. You could see a show and a movie for 75 cents or $1.00 at that time. We could go to Madison Square Garden and see the big shows there. I saw big fights with Joe Lewis and other famous boxers. I remember when Joe Lewis fought Jersey Joe Walcott; I snuck in to see that fight.

I felt like I owned Broadway in those days. I would get home at midnight or 1:00AM each night, and if I hadn't made my $5.00, I would go buy newspapers for 2 cents apiece and go sell them on the subways for a nickel apiece. Sometimes it took two or three more hours, before I decided I had made enough for that night. Then I would go home. I had

to do that quite often, but I didn't like it as much as I did shining shoes. It was easier to shine shoes, but sometimes you had to do the newspaper thing too, to make the money.

Sometimes I would sell roses in various nightclubs — anything to make a dollar. And all this was before I was 12 years old. Sometimes the police would pick us up for 'disturbing the peace', especially on Friday and Saturday nights, when Broadway was jammed with people. They wanted us off the streets, so they would round up a bunch of us and take us down to the station. Our mothers would have to come down to get us out. My mother wouldn't come, but my sister would. She'd come down and be mad. They would release me to her, glad to get me out of their hair once again. As soon as I was freed, I'd go back to work, to make up for the time lost at the station, while my sister would go home. I have to say they were really nice guys, those policemen, and always gave us coffee and donuts.

When I was 12, my brother Frank was working at a construction site. In New York you had to be 14 years old to work. You had to have working papers, especially if you looked young. I needed working papers. So my mother, who knew people all over the city, said that we would go and see Lizzie, who worked in the working paper bureau. We went and talked with her over dinner (she was a great cook too), and she agreed to help me get the papers. She told us where to go, how to wait for her signal, and then how to answer her questions so that everything sounded legal. So, that's what I did. I waited for my turn, answered her questions, lied about my age, and received the card that allowed me to work.

Now I went to Frank and asked him for a job in construction. Maybe I thought it would make me strong. Frank couldn't believe that I had working papers, but he went to his boss and got me a job as a water boy, working for little salary but for additional income from tips. My job was simply to take a water bucket around to the workers on an hourly basis throughout the day. Taking around the water bucket several times per day became boring. There were about 40 guys that I was taking care of, and I asked them if they would prefer lemonade. So, I bought lemons, honey and 5-6 pounds of ice from the ice man, covered with a piece of burlap to make it last longer. I would cut up the lemons, sweeten the drink with honey, and cool it with the ice. I would take around the lemonade once in the mid-morning and again in the afternoon.

At about noon the guys would break for lunch. I figured maybe they didn't want to pack a lunch every day, so I offered to deliver coffee and a sandwich from the local diners. About 10-11 guys took me up on my offer, so I made a deal with one of the diners, that if I brought in a certain amount of business, I would get my lunch for free. I went for coffee and donuts twice a day as well. The guys liked the lemonade and the delivery of food and coffee and gave me extra tips on payday.

Now, my brother Frank was a hard worker, a hod carrier who mixed and carried plaster up a ladder to the plastering crew. A new school was being built, and the plasterers were finishing the walls and putting up crown moldings on the ceilings. They were master craftsmen. My brother was making about $40 per week, which was pretty good for construction work in those days. Most men made about $20-25, but construction was paying more. I was making about $12-13 as a water boy, and then I was averaging about $1.00 from each guy for the extra stuff I did for him. So I was making anywhere from $40 to $60 per week. So when my brother asked me how I was doing, I told him things seemed to be going great. But when I told him how much I had been making, he became furious with me. He couldn't believe what I was making and said he would never tip me again. I couldn't understand why he wouldn't be happy for my success. From then on, for the rest of the summer, he would hardly ever speak to me, so I decided to quit, rather than continue to anger him. The boss was amazed when I gave notice, but I was determined, so he hired a new boy and I trained him before I left the job.

I was out of a job, but I had my working papers, so I decided to go talk with my brother Tony. He was managing the dining room at the Sutton Hotel, so I figured he could find me a job there. I told him how our mother's friend had gotten me false papers, and so, Tony hired me as a kitchen boy. I was to clean around the kitchen, help the dishwasher, clean the steam tables and scrub the floors. This was a big kitchen, and it was quite messy, so I worked hard, doing a little extra here and there to improve things. I would start around 8AM and by mid-afternoon I was done. That's when the salad man would come in, so I started helping him put together salads. After about four or five weeks, I would have the potato salad and the shrimp cocktails ready before the salad guy even arrived.

My brother Tony didn't realize that I was learning all there was to

know about the salad position. But one night the salad man didn't show up, and Tony was in a panic. When I showed him that I had almost everything ready, he was totally surprised and couldn't believe that I had been doing so much. I told him it was a simple job. Tony wasn't sure I could handle the job, but he ended up giving it to me. My salary went from $12 to $20 per week. It never really mattered to me how much money I made. What was important was that I was making money. I knew that my mother needed money to help out with the rent and food, etc., so if I made a lot of money, I could save some. If I didn't, that was okay, too. I always knew that I could make money.

So I worked as the salad man for about 3 months. Then I started looking around again, always asking who was making what kind of money. I got to be friends with one of the busboys. He was a nice guy, only about 17 years old, and he told me that he was making about $35 per week. He told me about his job, how he came in about 4PM to set up the tables. He would be in charge of five waiters' tables and would set up all the linen, the silverware, the water glasses and finger bowls, which were still used in those days. He would service the tables, making sure that dishes were cleared away and that the customers' needs were met. He had to make sure that everything was done correctly and quickly. This was a high-class dining room, and everything had to be done perfectly. You had to wear black pants and a bow tie and a little white jacket.

Having learned this job, one night as I was getting off, I told Tony that I wanted to be a bus boy. He laughed and said, 'You're never satisfied, are you?' I told him I wanted to advance, to learn things and to make more money at the same time. I knew I could do the job and showed him what I had learned. So Tony hired me as a bus boy and I started the next evening. He got a new salad man and I moved to the dining room. I worked for five waiters and learned very quickly that I had to watch them like a hawk. At that time I was entitled to eight percent of their tips and had to hope that they would give me an honest count. Most of the time they were good about it; only a couple of guys would try to cheat me a little bit. I brought their attention to it, and they realized that I was counting them down. They said, 'You don't miss a trick, do you?' and I simply answered that I liked keeping everybody honest.

That was a good job. I met a lot of nice people, and there was always

new stuff to learn. Sometimes it was very busy and sometimes it was slow, but it was a good job and I met a lot of high-class people. I was always treated nicely.

I remember one evening there was a young lady who came in by herself at about 5:30, and I started setting up her place setting. She asked me how old I was, and I foolishly told her I was twelve. She thought I was older, and I said I was just kidding. I told her that I usually worked until 8-9PM, sometimes later depending on business. Then she asked me what I did for entertainment after work and asked me if I liked swimming. She went on to tell me that she had the key to the hotel pool, which was downstairs, and invited me to join her there later that evening around 9PM. When I got off I went to the pool. She was an attractive girl, a little taller than me, and when I got there, she was the only one there. She told me to lock the door behind me, which I did. Then I realized that she was swimming in the nude. I hadn't brought a swimming suit, but that didn't bother her. Soon I was in the water and we started kissing and such. It was a very lovely evening. After about two hours we got dressed, and she said she would see me the next evening. I agreed, and for three nights we met at the pool. To me she seemed absolutely breathtaking. But on the fourth night she never appeared for dinner. I learned that the family had checked out that morning, and I never saw her again.

So, I kept on working at Sutton Place, moving up from bussing tables to working stag parties. They always had at least two or three stag parties upstairs per week with 20-50, even 100 men in attendance. I found out that the tips were better than in the dining room, so I went to Tony again and asked to work the parties. He warned me that a lot went on during those parties, but I said I was only interested in doing my job. It was a little different, waiters bussing their own tables and doing a lot of the cleanup, and there was a standard menu, but I knew I could handle it. So, begrudgingly, he okayed it. You could make $20-25 per night, which was great. I was working 2-3 nights at the stag parties and the rest of the week in the regular dining room. I did very well for about a year and a half.

CHAPTER 7

Cleanliness is Godliness

This is the story of two boys. They were kids together, born in New York on the lower East Side. One was named Pete, and one was named Tom. They first met when they were eight or nine years old, and they became good buddies. They went to grammar school, to high school, and then graduated. They had a normal childhood, having fun together, being good buddies. One was Italian, and the other was French-Italian. Even though they were such good friends, their parents never met. Their mothers were both divorced and working in NYC, which was very difficult in those days. They were usually working two jobs at a time, so the boys were mostly on their own. The boys both had older sisters, but mainly they just hung around and did everything together. Both were good students, especially in math, and always competed with each other to excel.

After high school graduation they planned to go to college. They worked different jobs. Pete always managed to stick with a job over long periods of time while Tom was always trying out new jobs. They worked and studied their way through college, always enjoying life and their friendship.

Pete's mother was very frugal and always told her son, 'When you work, you should always save a quarter of your salary for a rainy day. The second quarter will be needed to pay for your housing. The third quarter of your salary will be needed for food and clothing, necessary incidentals.

The last quarter is for anything you want, whether it's something necessary or not. You'll have a little extra money to fool around with.'

Pete's mother also told him to keep his home and belongings neat and clean, because cleanliness is next to godliness. She also said, 'When you do things, do them for God. Think of God as your foreman, watching over your work. Be conscientious, be aware of what has to be done. Just do it without looking for reward.'

Pete always remembered his mother's advice and tried to follow it.

Tom's upbringing was a little different. His mother never gave him any advice about saving money. Pete tried to advise him, but Tom was always spending what he had, having a good time. Without practical advice and a mother to set the example, he was on his own most of the time. Pete would advise tidiness and other virtues, and would help out his friend at times. As they contemplated the future after graduation from high school, it was Pete who usually had ideas and was making plans. Tom was more uncertain and disorganized and looked to Pete to lead the way.

Realizing that they were both good in math, Pete thought that they should be able to make good living as an accountant or bookkeeper. Tom agreed, so they went to college and took finance courses, graduating in accounting. Both were excited about the future. They got jobs on Wall St. at a good salary. They got an apartment together overlooking the East River. Pete followed the financial rules set out by his mother. He saved a quarter of his salary, used a quarter for the rent, used another quarter for living expenses and had the rest for pleasure and extras. Pete was a rather contemplative type of person and tended to live a quiet life, socializing at times but also happy to settle in at home with a good book and classical music. On the other hand, Tom was out on the town every night and saved very little of his salary. Pete tried to persuade his friend to be more frugal, with little result.

After four years they were doing well, enjoying the city and working hard. Then one day they both got laid off. Tom was in a panic, not knowing what to do. Pete was disappointed, of course, but quickly realized that the change could be good for both of them. Pete had his savings, so he didn't have to stress about money. His mother had always programmed him, saying, 'You can always make money. Money is easy to make. Think about it and then just do it.'

Tom lacked Pete's confidence. He applied for unemployment compensation and lived off that, while Pete spent more time contemplating the future, planning their next move. Tom kept applying for accounting positions, insisting that he deserved the same salary level as before, but he had no success and grew more and more depressed. Pete, on the other hand, was thinking about other options, not worrying about the salary.

One morning Pete was sitting in Central Park when he decided that it was time to take a job, any job, even if just for the experience. It was time to start taking action and not to just be sitting around. Walking home from the park, he happened upon a rather rundown, dingy restaurant/bar that had a 'Help Wanted' sign in the window. He went up to the steps and entered the restaurant. On the left was the bar, about 20 ft. long. There were tables and chairs on both sides of the entryway, and a little booth tucked away in the corner. There was a young man cleaning up behind the bar. Pete asked for the owner or manager, and the guy told him to walk down the corridor past the restrooms to the office at the back. Pete went down the long hall, past the restrooms and what looked to be a storage room with various stacked chairs, tables and such. The whole place was dirty and grungy, dust all over the place.

Arriving at the door marked Office, Pete knocked and walked in. Before him was a little old Italian guy, sitting behind a desk. The room was dark, lighted only by a desk lamp. Pete, who was always nicely dressed in suit and tie and looked like an accountant told the old man he had come about the Help Wanted sign. The old man replied, 'You don't look like a dishwasher to me.'

Pete said that while he was trained as an accountant, he needed work and didn't care if it was washing dishes. The owner was skeptical and offered only $8 per hour for the position, but Pete quickly accepted the job. The owner questioned him some more, trying to make sure that Pete was sincere, because he was not able to believe that someone with Pete's training and education would want to wash dishes. He even noted that the dishwashing machine was broken, and all the dishes would have to be washed by hand. Pete said that he had washed a lot of dishes as a kid and had always enjoyed it. So, the owner decided to accept Pete at his word, and asked him when he could start. Pete said, 'I can start right now.'

With that, the owner, whose name was Frank, took Pete to the dressing

room, where Pete could change into work shirt and pants. Pete then entered the kitchen and looked around. The place was really dirty. There was a stack of dishes in the sink from the evening before. Frank told him to take care of those dishes and then to plan to return at 5:00 in the evening before the dinner business. Frank commented that business had been pretty slow of late, and obviously seemed frustrated and depressed. He went on to say that the Health Department was threatening to close down the place because of the lack of cleanliness. There just didn't seem to be good maintenance workers out there these days.

Pete set about cleaning the dishes and was finished within an hour. He dried them, put them away and then started cleaning up the immediate area around the sink. Looking to the left, he saw an antipasto station where the waiters and waitresses would make the salads for dinner. There was a filthy steam table there as well. So he first cleaned up the antipasto station and then changed out the water at the steam table and made the stainless steel shine once again. Even though he had been hired as a dishwasher, he was able to just look around, see what had to be done, and do it.

Pete worked the entire afternoon, and was there at 5:00 when the other employees arrived. The waiters and waitresses were amazed to see how clean their work area was. They looked over to the cooks' area to see Pete hard at work cleaning the 3 big ovens, the burners and the stainless steel rack above. He had already cleaned the big serving counter area where the orders came in and the meals went out. The place was cleaner than it had been in months. The head cook arrived and started prepping for dinner, while the steam table cook began to ready his pots for dropping down into the openings of the table, pots from one gallon to maybe three gallons contained things like the sauce and the meatballs, the soups, etc. He was a lazy guy and a sloppy worker, so he was amazed to see everything so clean and shiny. The general atmosphere of the restaurant had been depressing and unpleasant in recent months. The Health Dept. had lately issued it a D rating, and all the employees knew that the business would be shut down if the rating didn't improve. Frank kept telling his employees to make more of an effort to be clean, but the mood was dispirited, and no one seemed to care enough to make the difference.

Except Pete. He looked around and started doing what needed to be done. That first evening only about 20 meals were served, as business

had declined as the energy level went down. The food was good but the service was slow, the dining room less than clean. Pete didn't like this environment, so he took a good look around and really started to clean up the place. He washed and scrubbed the floors. He found an old steam cleaner in a storage closet, got it into proper working condition and cleaned all the old rubber floor pallets, used where the cooks stood.

The owner, Frank, paid little attention. He worked in his office most of the day and came out in the evening to seat his guests, but he was tired and depressed and didn't look around much. Pete kept looking around, trying to decide what needed to be done next, and decided that the whole place needed a paint job. So, he went out and bought a few gallons of off-white paint. He started with the kitchen, and it took about three days. He painted the floors a dark, burnt red. The kitchen was really starting to look inviting. As he watched the customer traffic at night, he began to anticipate the waitresses' needs, perhaps to bus a table or to make an antipasto salad. Even the salads he tried to present in an inviting manner, adding little touches that he had learned from his mother as a growing boy. He tended to keep an eye on the cook as well. The cook was very talented but very sloppy, so Pete would make sure that his working area was kept clean and tidy. The cook asked Pete why he was doing all this extra work. Pete replied, 'Well, I like the work, and it has to be done. And remember, cleanliness is next to godliness.'

The cook had to agree with Pete, remembering that his mother, too, had repeated the same expression many times during his childhood. Pete added, 'Yeah, and remember, you are always cleaning for God, not for yourself.'

Pete also told the cook about an old book he had once read, about a sea captain who told his crew, 'A good mate is one who never has to be asked to do a job. He will simply look around and see what has to be done and do it, even if it doesn't happen to be his job. He does it for God, not for himself.' The staff members listened carefully, taking it all in, and as Pete set the example, they started to watch more closely.

Now, Pete expanded his mission, painting and scouring the restrooms, and did the same with the connecting hallway. His cleaning revealed beautiful parquet flooring. Even Frank finally started to take notice and couldn't believe the changes of the past few weeks. He walked into the

kitchen and was amazed by the change. When he questioned Pete and found out what had been happening, he exclaimed, 'But Pete, where did you get the paint?' He was astonished that Pete had bought the paint with his own money. So, finally, Frank took Pete into the office and sat him down. Naturally he wanted to pay Pete's expenses and to thank him for all the work, but Pete didn't need that. He saw what had to be done and he did it, that was all, and he had a good time as well. He was delighted that the next day's Health Department inspection would go better than the last one had. Frank realized how depressed and worried he had been concerning the restaurant's future, and now he was optimistic once again. It only made sense to give Pete a raise, so that Friday Frank raised his pay to $12 per hour, plus he paid him for all the painting supplies. When Pete saw his paycheck, he thought there was a mistake, but Frank thanked him once more and told him that there was no mistake.

Pete went home and talked with his friend and roommate, Tom. Tom only ridiculed Pete, for working as a dishwasher. Pete didn't like Tom's attitude and tried to explain how important it was that he was working at last. Tom wasn't interested, even when he heard about Pete's raise. It still seemed like a waste of time to him, to be working for less pay than his old wages. Although Pete saw how unhappy his friend was and again tried to encourage him to go out and find employment, Tom didn't hear pay attention

Next day at the restaurant, the health inspector was shocked to see how clean and scoured the restaurant was. He checked the refrigerator, the freezer, the work areas and restrooms and could find no fault. He changed the restaurant's inspection rating from D to B, meaning that there was more work to be done, but Pete had accomplished an incredible amount in just a few weeks. The owner knew that Pete had saved his business and realized that the whole atmosphere of the restaurant was changing. Frank realized that he was feeling better, and so were the other employees. He told Pete how happy he was to have him working there, which made Pete equally happy.

Not satisfied with the inside, Pete now took a close look at the building's exterior. The windows obviously hadn't been washed in months. So he got out the bucket and cleaning supplies and washed them all, inside and out. The restaurant signage and the menu that sat in the window became clearly

visible. He cleaned the window sills and the front steps with the steam cleaner. More people became aware of the restaurant, and business started to increase. The waitresses started making more money, and they were happier. With the higher vibration, all the employees started pitching in, to keep everything clean and spruced up. Even the steam table cook and the head cook, not ones to worry about cleanliness, began to keep their work areas clean and tidy. Pete looked for no credit, he was just happy that the restaurant was doing better. The final convert was the bartender, who hadn't paid much attention to the kitchen improvements. But when Pete scrubbed the floor behind the bar, steam cleaned the floor pallets, scoured the shelves and polished up all the glass and the mirror, even he had to admit that his bar business improved and that everyone seemed happier and more energetic.

After about six weeks the Health Dept. inspector gave the restaurant an A rating. Pete got the credit, of course. The owner was accustomed to spending most of his days at the restaurant. He had no family, and the business was his only real pleasure. Now he was willing to give Pete the keys, to allow him to open up the business and to get the day started. He saw that Pete dedicated himself to the restaurant just as Frank himself always had. And as for Pete, he went through his day quietly dedicating his work to God, pretending that God was the foreman, checking on his work. He was totally content.

At their apartment Pete continued to 'work for God'. Except for Tom's bedroom, the flat was clean, tidy and airy. Tom couldn't be bothered to clean and scrub, even with Pete's encouragement. Tom was still trapped by the notion that he had to get a job worthy of his training and experience, and so as the weeks went by, he continued to be unemployed. Times were hard, jobs were scarce, and salaries were going down, but Tom rigidly held on to his demands. He laughed at Pete's advice to take any job and go from there, and he still ridiculed his friend, calling him 'the dishwasher', not knowing that Pete was now making $20 an hour.

Over time Pete totally renovated the restaurant. He even painted his boss's office. With that, Frank started to reflect the change of energy, dressing more carefully and keeping his papers more orderly. Cleanliness vibrated throughout the whole building. Even the customers were aware of the difference. Three months after Pete was hired there was a line of patrons waiting to eat.

Frank started making an effort to spend more time with Pete. They would breakfast together and talk things over while sipping their cappuccinos. The owner realized that Pete had totally changed the place. Even in the restrooms, there were now signs over each doorway, 'Cleanliness is Next to Godliness'. With tears in his eyes, he thanked Pete once more, gave him a kiss on each cheek and made him accept another raise. Pete was simply thrilled that everyone was so much happier.

Back at home Tom's ridicule continued, but it didn't affect Pete. Tom didn't realize what Pete had accomplished and was astonished to see Pete's latest paycheck. He still thought Pete worked at a dingy, dirty restaurant, even though Pete always encouraged Tom to come down for a cup of coffee or a meal. Pete observed, 'You know, Tom, you go to McDonald's every day to eat, to drink coffee. If you like it there so much, why don't you go down there and apply for a job, any job. Who knows what will happen.' As usual, Tom went into his old routine, not willing to take just any job, etc. However, he began to think a bit more flexibly about other possibilities. He was also embarrassed to realize that he had been unemployed for eight months and was no longer able to contribute to the apartment expenses. He and Pete both knew he would make good on his debt, but it still was bothersome.

Thinking things over during the night, Tom was finally ready to make that change, and the next morning he applied for a job at the local McDonald's. The manager there referred him to general headquarters, where the hiring was done. Once there Tom went in for his interview and said he would take any job, regardless of his qualifications, that he liked eating at McDonald's and knew there must be some kind of job for him. Much to his amazement, he was hired as an accountant, starting at $20 per hour but with room for advancement. He was delighted to go home that evening and inform Pete that he was finally back on track. He had gone out looking for any kind of job and had been rewarded with work he loved, with a salary that would increase over time.

On his way to work the following morning, Tom allowed time to stop by Pete's restaurant, the place he had ignored for the past eight months. He was astonished with the building's appearance, the perfect cappuccino, the warmth and Frank's welcoming graciousness. He saw what Pete had accomplished during all those long weeks and months and determined that

his new career would be just as fulfilling and successful. With new energy and determination, he headed out for his new adventure.

Back at the restaurant, Frank made Pete sit down and relax for a minute or two, because he had something important to say. Frank wanted to make Pete the manager of the restaurant, taking him out of the kitchen. With love, gratitude and respect he told Pete to think of the restaurant as his own. Business was better than ever, and the credit had to go to Pete. Pete accepted the job but, at first, insisted that he continue to wash dishes. Pete was thrilled, as he was so gratified with the job and the restaurant itself. He loved the staff, the patrons, even the building. He quickly became so busy that he realized that he had to hire a dishwasher. He decided to hire a woman to balance the staff more and soon found one in her fifties who was raising two children by herself. He started her at $10 per hour and after teaching her the basics of the job, he taught her his principles about working hard, to looking after for the needs of the place, offering her effort to God. She saw the sign in the restroom, 'Cleanliness is Next to Godliness' and with tears in her eyes, promised to do her best. She knew she would be happy working in that restaurant.

At this point, Pete was doing the bookkeeping as well and the place was incredibly successful. Profits were the highest ever, and Frank couldn't believe his good fortune. Pete suggested that the wealth be shared with a bonus for each employee, and Frank willingly agreed. He now realized that the happiness of the employees was just as important as the bottom line. All the staff, even the new dishwasher, received the bonus with their next paychecks, and of course, they were joyous. And under the sign 'Cleanliness is Next to Godliness', they would continue grow to prosper in the years to come.

Obviously this is a story about more than just two guys, a restaurant and the power of cleanliness: It is a story about Godliness and what it means. Godliness vibrates on a very high level and can change anything. Working through Pete in that dingy restaurant, Godliness raised the vibrations not just of the building but also of the other people who worked there, bringing them together with positive spirit. The energy changed from separation to unification, uniting people so that they wanted to be together.

In time those higher vibrations affected everything and everyone in that restaurant.

On the other hand Tom made no effort to change his life for the better until he realized that he had to take hold of his life, project his inner strengths, find a job, and open a door to greater opportunity. He learned that his own vibrations began to rise as he regained his self-respect and began to make a contribution to his community.

So, this story is really about realizing vibration, learning to embrace the positive and discard the negative. We must always strive to unite, to lift up one another, to look to a higher, more joyful vibration. Higher vibrations can change anything, anyone, even a city or country.

CHAPTER 8

My Start in Bodybuilding

It was 1947, I was 13 years old and I still wanted to be strong. One evening after work I went to a movie theater on Broadway. In those days there was the movie, and then a short vaudeville show. I remember getting my ticket and going in, and after a couple of acts, this guy appeared on the stage. His name was Steve Reeves, and a month earlier he had won the Mr. America title. Now he was touring theaters. This guy was incredible. To me he looked like someone from Mars. He had the most beautiful body I had ever seen in my life, was 6'1" and weighed about 220. I was so stunned by the beauty of his body that I didn't hear anything he was saying. I ran backstage to meet him and to ask him how he got so big and strong looking. He told me that I had to work out, and I asked him what he meant. He told me to get a set of weights and barbells and to lift them. He told me to get a Health and Strength Magazine because it would tell me everything I needed to know. Exasperated, he then told me to get out of there.

I didn't even stay to see the movie. I left the theater, found a newsstand and bought myself the magazine, with him on the cover. I read it from cover to cover and was amazed at how strong all those guys looked. And that was the start of my bodybuilding career. On the back cover of the magazine there was an ad for a set of weights, 255 pounds, the Big 12, for $39. I knew I had to get them, so I got the cash from my stash and went

down to Western Union and got a money order. I sent away for my Big 12, and a big box arrived about 2 weeks later on a Railway Express truck. The driver needed help getting the box down off the truck. I couldn't find anyone to help, so we broke open the box with a hammer and a pry bar and unloaded the weights individually. We stacked up the plates, the bars and the barbells on the sidewalk, I signed for it, and he drove away. I carried all this stuff down to the basement, not knowing what to do with any of it. But there was a set of instructions, written, I remember, by Jules Bacon, a Mr. America of 1943. There was a long sheet, like a poster, with about 30 different exercises. I started with only 6- 7 pounds and tried to squat with a 15-lb. bar. I had absolutely no idea what I was doing. I was doing all these exercises every day and was sore all the time, but I was determined. I got myself another book and was even more determined.

After about 6 or 7 months I actually started gaining weight although I really didn't know what I was doing. Looking at a new Health and Strength Magazine one day, I found an ad for John Terlazzo's Gym on 23rd and 3rd Ave. It wasn't too far from where I lived, so I went down there and found the gym up a set of stairs. Before I could go into the gym I had to join. It was $55 for the first 3 months and then $15 per month. I was stunned; it was so expensive. Terlazzo gave me a tour of the gym, a long room about twenty-five by eighty feet with two bay windows in the front, with the 3rd Ave. El going past them. Places along 3rd Ave. were really cheap in those days. You could get an apartment for $5-6 per month; some places were even $2-3, because no one wanted to live so close to the train. It was so noisy and things in your house would rattle when it went by. I remember my cousin Frank had a flat in a nice building at 3rd Ave. and 79th St. One day he came to our mother and said he had a chance to buy the building for $1600. She screamed at him, that 8 apartments making $2 per month would never be worth $1600. Anyway, I knew that this was a cheap area and wondered why the membership fee was so high.

He said, 'Don't get smart, kid. That's what it is. Take it or leave it.'

Of course, I was thrilled to see all the weights and bars; a full set of barbells from 10 to 120 pounds, and couldn't imagine being able to lift them. Then I remembered that John Terlazzo had been in the 165 pound class of weightlifting, and he could lift them. His brother, Tony Terlazzo, competed in the Olympics and won medals, including a gold. John was on

the team one year, but did not compete. Tony's picture was in the office, along with other champions' photos. I asked about training, and he said that was extra. I knew I couldn't pay for a trainer, but he said I could work out as many hours as I wanted between 7AM and 10PM. So, I went home and got my $55 and joined John Terlazzo's Gym.

The first day I went to train he told me to wear sneakers and sweatpants or shorts and a nice t-shirt, nothing dirty. I continued doing the crazy exercises I had been doing at home in the basement, but I was also watching the other guys, most of whom were weight lifters. They worked on a wooden platform with a 135-pound bar. They would pack it with weights, and I would watch these guys. One of those guys eventually came up to me and asked me what I was doing, wasting my time with those stupid exercises. His name was John Lightgab, and he was a good-looking guy with honey-blond hair, about 5'11" and 175-80 pounds. At that time I weighed about 105 pounds. He offered to show me a routine, some exercises, and told me not to waste my time with those worthless exercises. He also told me to forget about the iron boots that I had been using to provide weight resistance, saying that they were a waste of time too.

So John took me under his wing and taught me exercises like military presses, clean-and-jerk, weightlifting and then bodybuilding exercises like bench presses, inclines and chinning. I couldn't do one chin at that point, so I ignored them. I started doing 5 and 6 sets for each body part and worked up to about 20 sets per body part. I was spending 2, 3, sometimes even 4 hours every day in the gym. But John told me not to work out every day. He said that you needed to work out every other day, or you would get weaker. So, I listened to him and started to get stronger.

Still only 13 years old, I started to gain weight and strength. I asked John how to gain weight, and he told me to drink a lot of milk, 6 quarts per day. He also told me to eat a lot of eggs. 'Just eat a lot of food,' he said.

I didn't know how I could eat that much, but I started out slowly and eventually got up to those 6 quarts of milk, and I got up to 135 pounds that year. When I turned 14, I was faithfully working out 3 times per week. My work hours didn't fit with my workouts, so I quit my job at the hotel. Instead, I got a factory job, making screwdriver handles. I worked the graveyard shift, so I could work out all day. I was making $30 per week, too, which was good money at the time. It was a quota system. I

had to make so many handles for my salary and then got extra pay if I made more. It was an easy job, and basically I could work as much or as little as I wanted.

One day Jack LaLanne came up to the gym while I was working out. He yelled out that he wanted a workout partner, and of course I volunteered. I knew who he was, because I had seen his photo in the magazines. I knew every bodybuilder there was and what each one had won and who was working out where. My body was finally starting to look good. I was gaining weight and getting stronger all the time. So Jack started his routine, and immediately he established a fast pace. 'First I go, then you go. I do a set, you come right after me and do a set.' He was doing different presses and military presses, curls and shoulder presses, laterals and pushups, etc. We worked out for about two and a half hours, a kind of mixed up routine. He jumped from body part to body part, which I had never done. Other guys, though, said that it wasn't a good routine. They called him the 'Jumping Jack', and the nickname stuck. But he was a great guy, good-looking with a stream-lined body, a small man at about 5'5" and 140 pounds.

Then another afternoon when I was working out, another young guy came up to the gym. His name was Artie Zeller and he had just had some posing pictures taken and was showing them around. I thought I recognized him and saw that he had a great body, not very big but streamlined and beautifully balanced. Artie asked me why I was working out at Terlazzo's gym, and of course I said because it was a good gym. Artie said, 'Yeah, but it's too expensive. Come on down to the lower East side. We have a great gym there, not as pretty but more weights. And it's $2.00 per month.' I couldn't believe him, but of course I agreed immediately, and off we went. We climbed 6 stories up to the top floor, and I found myself in the East Side Barbell Club. There were a few guys working out, and boy, it did have weights, solid dumbbells and barbells from 20 pounds and up to 150 pounds. I couldn't believe anyone was strong enough for those higher weights, but Artie told me that there was a guy named Marvin who used them all the time. Artie told me that Marvin was the strongest man in the world.

Artie and I started working out. This was a bodybuilding routine, not strictly for weightlifting, and there was quite a difference between the

two. We started with shoulder work and then went to chest. At that point Marvin arrived. Marvin Eder was about 17 years old at that time, as was Artie, and he looked really terrific. Artie introduced me to him, and we became friends almost immediately. The three of us started working out together, doing back work, neck work, more shoulder work, bicep and tricep work. Then we started squatting, and Marvin showed me how to do it right. He told me that squats stimulate the whole body, that they were really important. I followed him just like a puppy. I learned a lot from Marvin and Artie, and they were great guys. There were other guys like the Hermit, Leroy Colby who came in about a year later and would later become famous. But pretty much I worked out with Marvin and Artie from then on.

Marvin was the boss. You did what Marvin said, and that was it. We averaged about 15-20 sets per body part, and we could spend 5, 6, sometimes 7 hours in a workout. We worked out 3 times per week, and I was still just learning. I was mortified that I couldn't do chins, and these guys did them all the time. Marvin could do 20-30 in a set, adding 40-50 pounds to his waist before doing 10 more. Meanwhile I would do other back exercises, rather than admit I couldn't do them. We had a little park near us with chinning and dipping bars, so I used to go down there before starting my graveyard shift at midnight, and I would do chinning. I pulled myself up, and pulled myself up, again and again. And finally I started doing chins, working my way up to 3 sets of 10, up to 10 sets of 10 and 10 sets of 12. After about 3-4 months I was finally able to go into the gym and do chins with the guys. But whatever I did — such as sets of 10 — Marvin would always say, 'You can do more. You can do better than that.' So I gradually added more sets and more weight. Marvin always forced us to do more. I remember starting bench presses at 135 pounds, and within 2-3 months of working out with Marvin I was doing 200 pounds. He was already pressing 300 pounds. I was 100 pounds behind him all the time.

So, obviously I was totally hooked on working out. Finally, I was strong. I knew it was the right thing for me, and I lived to work out. I'd be doing one workout and already looking forward to the next workout. I was meeting all these great bodybuilders who came up to the gym. It turned out that the East Side Barbell Club was famous in the bodybuilding world. It was there that I met Joe Weider. He came from Jersey and had a little

barbell company there, Weider Weights. He had his own magazine and would put ads in it. He would get photos of all these guys and put them in the magazine. He asked me for pictures, but I didn't have any. So, Artie took me over to the photographer, Lon Hannigan, and I had my first body building photos taken at about 14 ½ years old.

At that time the most famous bodybuilding venue was Muscle Beach in California. Every magazine covered it, talking about the beach and who was down there. It was kind of a competition between the west and east coasts. But Santa Monica and Muscle Beach were the Mecca of the bodybuilding world. Every bodybuilder wanted to get there. I remember they would have contests on the beach. There was so much publicity and the most important contests to enter and win. And so, I would always tell Marvin that we had to go to Muscle Beach, to Santa Monica. He would say, 'Yeah, sure'. Artie wasn't interested either. He said it was too far away, and it would be too expensive to get there. I said we could work and save.

But it turned out that none of these guys worked. Artie's father was a Jewish cantor and gave his son a credit line at the grocery store. So Artie would fix his own food in the little apartment that he shared with his father. We used to call it the Dungeon because the apartment had never been cleaned after his parents' divorce. When you walked into the front hallway, you didn't touch the walls; they were so dirty and dusty. There was a footpath through the dirt on the floor. In that hallway was a clothesline where Artie would hang his laundry like his clean socks. There was a pathway through the kitchen between the sink, the table and the fridge. You didn't touch anything else. To the right was the living room where Mr. Zeller would be singing his prayers. We would greet him on our way into Artie's room, and he would nod his head. Artie kept his room clean, but he had no interest in cleaning the rest of the apartment.

At that time I was trying to learn about other religions. I asked Artie about Judaism, what he believed in. He said he didn't believe in any of it. I was shocked that he really didn't believe in his father's faith. He called him a fool, singing and praying all day long. Artie said that he had been educated in the Jewish faith, but that it was all a waste of time. He learned Hebrew and knew Yiddish, but he believed that all the books of faith were just nonsense. He showed me some examples, and I had to agree with him. Marvin was Jewish as well, but he didn't believe in any of it either. Marvin

believed only in working out, and I had to agree with him as well. I also believed in the need to work, to make a living, but Artie didn't have that need because his father supported him.

Both Artie and Marvin were intelligent guys. They were much smarter and more educated than I was. I would listen to them argue about different things: life, politics, everything. I pretty much stayed out of those arguments because I just didn't know that much. I learned more from these two guys than from anyone before.

About this time Joe Weider started to come to the gym and boast that he was going to open up his own place. We would rag him, when are you going to open this gym? Abe Goldberg, who won best legs and arms in Mr. America that year, was working for Weider in his warehouse and had been promised that Weider would build this gym. We cornered Abe one day and told him that he had to pressure Weider to open the gym now, or it would never happen. We all knew that Weider hated to spend money, so Abe would have to pressure him. Abe finally went to Weider and threatened to quit if the gym wasn't opened. Weider gave in, and they found a little place on 80 Clinton St. There were 3 stories to the building with long stairways between them. On the 3rd floor was a boxing gym. The 2nd story area was like a warehouse, about 75 ft. long and 35 ft. wide.

All of us kids from the East Side Barbell Club starting working on fixing up this area to be a gym. Luckily, one guy was a carpenter, and others were mechanics and experts at other trades. They all knew a little bit about building. So we built Abe Goldberg's Health Studio. It had two huge bay windows in the front, overlooking the street. We built a weightlifting platform right in the front, painted everything white and laid linoleum. We got great weight racks with chrome dumbbells, a lot of equipment that Joe bought, begrudgingly. Of course, none of us kids wanted to have to pay to work out at Abe's gym, so Abe agreed that we could work different jobs. One would wash the floor, one would take care of the locker room, one would manage the little juice bar we set up. Artie worked the front desk, because he didn't like to do manual labor. Little Roy, another good friend of ours, took care of the juice bar, and I took care of the locker room. We had about 7 showers, lockers and benches. Everything was bright and cheery and clean. The gym took off right away, and we got lots of members, including lots of policemen and firefighters.

Once the gym was going, Weider would come up to Marvin and me and say that he wanted to work out with us, at least one day a week. We didn't want to work out with him, and told him that we did 'super sets', meaning we kept up a fast pace, one doing a set as soon as the other was done. The pace would be too slow with a third person. But we finally told him that he could work out alongside us. So he would come up on Thursday nights and after the workout, he would take us out for dinner. We thought that was a great idea, but he always wanted us to order the cheapest thing on the menu, like spaghetti and meatballs. We would tell him that we needed steak and would order it, the most expensive thing on the menu. Artie never wanted to come with us. His schedule varied a lot, so he wasn't always around to work out with Marvin and me. We, on the other hand, would work out 6-7 hours at a time and kept a regular routine. After that I would go to work, at midnight.

Marvin didn't know at first that I was working at the screwdriver plant. I was living with my mother on 14th St. and 2nd Ave. and needed to help with the rent. My sister had gotten married by then and was living on the lower east side, near the gym. Marvin suggested that maybe I could go to work with him and his father, making bagels. Marvin and his father would do the rolling, boiling and baking, before stringing up the bagels for delivery. I wanted to work with them, but I worried that I wouldn't be able to do what I wanted to do, that I would be more tied down, but Marvin said it would be okay. So, a few months later, I started working with Marvin. He would do the rolling, and then I would take the bagels on a board and slide them into a big pot full of boiling water. When they came to the top, I would turn them over, then take them out and put them in the oven to bake. His father would string them by the dozen, getting them ready for delivery, and then about 1-2AM we would go out and deliver them. We would be through by about 6AM, go and have breakfast and then we would go to the gym to work out. I was about 14½, going on 15 years old.

CHAPTER 9

Arrival in Santa Monica

I remember telling my mother that I was going to California. She asked me why, and I told her about Muscle Beach, where all the great bodybuilders were. She told me to go ahead, that I could take care of myself. My mother never told me I couldn't do something. She always encouraged me and told me that I could do it. So, I started planning the trip and saving money.

There were a couple of guys in the gym that were interested in going with me. John was a Jehovah's Witness. I would ask him about his religion, and he would preach to me. I had a lot of questions, but the most important one was how do you know you have a soul. He would look at me like I was nuts and obviously had no idea how to answer. I could see that this wasn't for me. A couple of the other guys would talk about their Protestant churches, but they didn't know anything either. I kept searching but was finding no answers.

So, I kept on bodybuilding and planning for my trip to California. I entered my first contest, Junior Mr. Metropolitan and won it. Soon after I entered the more advanced Mr. Metropolitan and won that contest. Marvin would win any contest he entered, and Artie won some as well.

By the time I had saved about $1400, I was ready to head west. Two other guys went with me. We flew on a 2-engine plane, and the flight had 10-12 stops for refueling. Or at least it seemed like that many. We would get off the plane and walk around until it was time to go again. A funny

thing happened while we were waiting in Arizona. I was wearing a great outfit with light gray peg pants, tightened around the cuff (on Broadway the guys would wear zoot suits, with really tightened peg pants and long coats), a nice, new shirt, and I had the latest thing, a black, plastic belt. So, we got off the plane in Arizona, early in the morning, and already the heat was unbearable. I had never felt heat like that before. I took off my shirt and laid down on the lawn to get some sun. Then, when I went to get up, I found that the black, plastic belt had melted all over my pants. It was just black goop. I tried to wipe it up with my handkerchief and just got black stuff everywhere. I couldn't get into my baggage, so I had to stay like that for the rest of the trip. Luckily, it was cooler in the airplane, so the plastic hardened and didn't get any worse, but the first thing I did when we got to Los Angeles was to change out of those clothes and throw them away.

On our arrival in Los Angeles, in the summer of 1948, we took a room for a week, not knowing exactly where we would be going next. We didn't have any idea where Santa Monica was from LA. We took a trolley car, and the trip was almost 2 hours long. We had to make a couple of transfers along the way. Finally, we arrived at the beach. It was the most fantastic place I had ever seen in my life. It was like landing in Paradise. The weather was balmy, the palm trees beautiful, the beach pristine. We walked down to Muscle Beach, and there we found a big platform about 150 ft. long by 25 ft. wide, with a canvas cover and padding on it. On the end was a big box where all the workout equipment like mats and weights was stored at the end of the day. There were guys working out, kids doing acrobatics, people standing on each other's shoulders two or three high, handstands and foot-to-head balancing, girls being flipped and balanced, wrestling, and gymnasts working on high bars and the rings. It was just a Mecca, I couldn't believe it. I had already appeared in some magazine photos, so a couple of the guys recognized and greeted me. One was a guy named George Gregnola, who was about my age and size and turned out to be a really nice guy. We started a little competition going between the two of us from the east and west coasts. He would do something and then I would better it. I was more muscular and had good abs, weighing about 140-145 lbs. and definitely stronger than he was.

So, we all hung out on the beach for the next 7-8 weeks. We moved to a little apartment, and after about a month decided that it was time

to start making some money again. Much to our surprise, the minimum working age was 16 years old in Santa Monica, and even if you were old enough, there wasn't much work to be found. One of my buddies from NY got someone to send him the plane fare back, but John, the Jehovah's Witness, and I couldn't come up with anything and ran out of money, so we set out to hitchhike back to New York. It took us 8 days to get back and eventually we had to split up to get rides. The only food I had that whole trip was a bag of apples one guy gave to me, and a few lunches that a guy at a restaurant packed up for me. I lost 15 lbs. which I found very depressing. I finally was dropped off by a truck driver at the end of one of the Manhattan tunnels. I snuck into the subway and went home. My mother cooked me a big pot of meatball stew, which I ate before going to sleep. When I woke up I ran to the gym and started working out again.

I stayed in New York, then, until I was about 17 years old. I worked out, entered contests, got pictures in magazines, and gradually I became more famous in the bodybuilding world. Marvin was now 19, and he was just incredible. He was doing weightlifting feats of strength that had never been done before. Artie was also still working out and doing his routine, and he was pretty awesome too, but he wasn't as big. I was now almost 200 pounds, gaining weight fast and drinking six quarts of milk per day, eating a dozen eggs at a time, in fact, eating so much food it was unbelievable. But our workouts were incredibly strenuous and lasted at least 6 hours. We would burn 5000-6000 calories at a time, which was hard to replenish. We did routines like 15 sets of squats, alternating them with pullovers, which expanded the chest. (Steve Reeves was the one who told me about doing pullovers.)

About Steve Reeves: I remember walking up to him at Muscle Beach and introducing myself. He said he had heard of me and knew that I was from the lower east side of Manhattan. I asked him if he remembered me, and of course he didn't. I told him about seeing him at the theater that night so many years before, and how he told me to get lost. He laughed and said he couldn't have done that. I told him I wouldn't hold it against him, and we both laughed. From then on we were good friends. I made a lot of friends on that first trip to Muscle Beach, like Armand Tanny, and Vince Gironda. Jack LaLanne also remembered me from back east.

Back at the gym in New York we were working out, but my dream

was to return to Santa Monica. I wanted Marvin to do something with me so that we could make a lot of money. I was tired of making bagels. But Marvin was always adamant that he couldn't leave his father. I thought we could do a great hand-balancing act, and that we would be able to send lots of money to the parents. He was so strong, it would be easy and incredible with me on top, and we would do great in show business. We would get to travel and make money. There were a couple of acts out there doing really well, but I couldn't get Marvin to do it. We had a chance to become wrestlers, but he wouldn't do that either. I knew I wouldn't be able to get him out of New York.

Then there was a Mr. America competition coming up in 1951, and Joe Weider said that he would send me and Marvin to California for it. We all knew Marvin would win it, and I would place behind him somewhere. We had three months to train, and Marvin just kept getting bigger and stronger. When he came up against other guys, I could really see just how incredible he was. We went to York PA, home to Bob Hoffman who made Health and Strength Magazine famous. Another famous bodybuilder, John Grimek, was there. They would have an annual summer picnic, and at the picnic that year, we won everything there was to win in chinning, dipping, military presses, everything. John was impressed with the both of us and very complimentary, which was quite an honor coming from him.

However, when it came to the Mr. America contest, no one seemed to want to leave New York. Even Artie wouldn't come with us. It wasn't easy getting enough money out of Joe, but at the last minute we finally got some extra living expense money from him. So, we flew to Oakland CA, where the competition was being held. Clancy Ross, another Mr. America, had a gym there, where we worked out. When we finally competed in the Mr. America contest, a guy named Roy Hilligenn, out of South Africa, won. Marvin Eder came in third, after Malcolm Brenner. I don't remember where I placed. There was no question that Marvin should have won. Roy had a good body but nothing like Marvin's. It was just one of those things.

From there we took a train the next day to Santa Monica. Marvin, he was so famous by then that everyone wanted to meet him. One Sunday while we were there, they held a strength lifting contest with bench presses, squats and military presses, plus some chinning and parallel dipping. Doug Hepburn, 350 lbs., who was a champion, big heavy weight lifter, and Paul

Anderson, 370 lbs., who was an Olympic gold medalist, and a couple of other lifters were there. Doug and Paul couldn't do any chinning or dipping, so Marvin and I took 1st and 2nd in those. I did 250 lbs. in parallel dipping, but Marvin ended it all by doing a full parallel dip with two of us big guys hanging on to his legs. It was over 400 lbs. The place went nuts; there must have been 5000 people on the beach that day. We went to the platform and started bench pressing. A few of us were left once we got up to 400 lbs. When we all did that we set a new record. We started adding more weight. However, when we would do one repetition, Marvin would do 3 or 4. I was out at 440 lbs., but Marvin said, "Let's finish this," and did 500 lbs. like it was nothing. Nobody could match him. I ragged Doug and Paul, telling them that they weighed too much and weren't as strong as me and Marvin, pound for pound.

From there we went to squats. Paul Anderson thought he could end the competition by squatting with 1500 lbs., which was unheard of. He lifted the bar, came forward and bent his knees a little bit. I said, 'That isn't a squat. You have to go parallel to make a real squat.' which was hard for those big guys to do. Marvin and I tied at 500 lbs. and won. It was an awesome day; we won everything. That contest went into every magazine in the country. The east coast was victorious that day. We had such a great time, working out, meeting people, entering contests, becoming famous.

I stayed on in California about three more weeks after Marvin returned to New York. I was learning so much about different things. There were all kinds of nutrition guys doing different kinds of diets like vegetarian and fruitarian. Guys were into different religions. Groups were doing all kinds of different things. I realized that Santa Monica was the place for me, that this was where I wanted to be.

I told Marvin that I would be moving to Santa Monica and that I would never return to NY again. He couldn't believe what I was saying, but I meant it. I begged him to join me, but he felt that he couldn't leave his parents. So I told him that I would save up my money once again and move to Santa Monica permanently. And that's what I did.

Before that, however, I joined up with Bob Hoffman who was running a series of summer bodybuilding tours for about six or eight weeks, visiting little towns in New England and the Mid-Atlantic states. It was a good learning experience for me. Grimek was there, Stanko was there, and Jules

Bacon was there, a lot of great Olympic weight lifters. David Shepard and Tommy Kono out of Hawaii, another Olympic champion in 1952 and 1956. John Davis, heavy weight Olympic champion. It was a weight lifting exposition but they needed bodybuilding, because it drew a bigger crowd. A few of us would pose. That's when I met Irvin 'Zabo' Koszewski, six bodybuilders and 8-9 champion weightlifters.

I also met George Eiferman, AAU Mr. America of 1948 and Mr. Universe in 1962. What a character George was. I had just gotten off the stage, and I was going out into the audience so that I could watch the great Grimmick pose. On the way I ran right into George and recognized him from his magazine photos. But he said, 'Dominick Juliano, I have been wanting to meet you!' He shook my hand while I stood there in amazement. He was the famous champion, not me. But that was George, he was so humble and gracious. And we became great friends from then on and for many years to come.

After the tour ended, I returned to California and lived on Muscle Beach for a while, only returning to NY for the Mr. America contest. I had trained a bodybuilder named Malcolm Brenner. I knew how to help him get an extra 10-15% that he couldn't get on his own. He was in great shape and I didn't think anyone could beat him. The competition was at the Armory in Manhattan. Again, the guy who should have won, Malcolm, didn't, but we all won in lesser categories. It just seemed like something was wrong, that the competition was rigged. I was glad to win best back, but still, Malcolm should have won the title.

Was it rigged? Maybe. It sure seemed that way and I heard plenty in later years that might point that way, but far be it for me to say anything now because any proof there might have been is long gone.

The strangest thing about this competition, though, was something else that happened. While on stage, I could hear someone yelling out my name. It turned out to be Ritchie Dubois, who I hadn't seen since I was about 11 years old when we had been separated to keep us out of trouble and sent up into the mountains by the juvenile court system. Like me, in that time he had started working out. This is when you know that there is no such thing as a coincidence. He was a great-looking guy, 6 ft. tall with blond hair and blue eyes. And in meeting again, he swore we would never be separated again, that he would follow me to California. We made quite

a scene, and everyone was laughing and cheering us on. So I told Ritchie to meet us at 7AM the next morning, when we would be leaving New York. Zabo had a car, and Shiftie Shaeffer had another, so we all would be leaving in those together. I got Little Roy and a few other guys to join us, so that all together there were about 7 of us and by 10AM we were ready, and took off for California.

CHAPTER 10

Workout Stories and Boat Dreams

Back in Santa Monica, we lived and hung out on Muscle Beach. By that time most of us were doing extra work in the movie industry, which was easy work and paid well. None of us really wanted to work, so we just did enough to get by. I became famous, and I became strong, which had always been my wish, who knows why. Probably it was something from a past life that was left to be fulfilled in this one. It was a wonderful life, lying around on the beach, enjoying the beautiful girls — starlets even! — who came down to hang out; seeing famous people from the sports and the movie industries.

I remember one morning Ritchie Dubois and I were sunning on the beach, when Ritchie spotted a sailing yacht anchoring out in the harbor in front of us. It was about 75 feet long and seemed to be made of highly varnished wood, gleaming to the hilt. It was absolutely breathtaking. Ritchie said, 'Let's swim out to it.' We were both good swimmers then and figured the boat to be less than a mile out, so we did just that. As we were swimming out, we saw three men get into a dinghy and start off towards the pier. Once we got to the boat, we found a boarding ladder and climbed up. The young ladies who had been left aboard agreed to our request to join them. They told us that they were headed up towards San Francisco and then up along the Canadian coastline. They had already been at sea for about three months. We asked them all about the boat, what it cost,

how much it cost to maintain it and how much it cost to live aboard and travel. We were very interested in the whole adventure. After about an hour we said our good-byes and headed back to the beach.

I said to Ritchie, 'What do you think about 8 or 9 of us putting an act, a routine, together. We could learn how to sail and travel all over, putting on a show to pay for the boat. We could give bodybuilding shows, posing shows, lectures, whatever.'

Ritchie agreed that it was a great idea. So, first I went to Armand Tanny about it, and he thought it was a great idea. He asked me if I had any money, and I said that we would all have to work and save to make it happen, but I thought we could do it in a year. I got at least 8 guys sold on the idea, and I figured that if we all saved a couple thousand dollars each, we would have enough to buy a boat and get started. From there we would be able to find agents that would book us for shows and such. I remember talking with the Hermit, Shaeffer, Zabo, and several other guys. All agreed to the plan. George Eifferman was busy with his lecture tour, so he couldn't commit. Steve Reeves was contracted to a studio for a couple of years and also couldn't join us.

At this point, the Hermit said that he was working at Douglas Aircraft, which was hiring and that we could all work there. So at least eight of us went down and all got hired making parts for airplanes. There was Ritchie, Little Roy, Dave Sheppard, a 1956 Olympic silver medalist weightlifter, and Shifty Shaeffer, who had a good body and was always so much fun to be around that we could make a routine just around him. So we all went to work at Douglas Aircraft and started to make money. Little Roy and I seemed to be the only ones who thought and talked about the routine we would put together as soon as we had all saved some money. Whenever I asked the other guys if they were saving their money, they would all say yes.

I spoke with Armand Tanny again, and he said that he had enough money already. Then he added that his brother Vic wanted to talk with me. It turns out that Vic Tanny was planning on opening up a chain of gyms and needed some guys to help put it together. So, one Sunday morning when we were all at the beach platform, I went over to Vic and said hello. He told me about his gym plans and said that he wanted me to be a part of it. I told Vic that I didn't really know anything about opening gyms, that I was working out at the Dungeon, which Vic owned at 4th and Santa

Monica Blvd. It was a great place to work out, a huge place that could hold 50 guys working out. I remember there was a boxing ring stuck in the corner, and it seemed small compared to the rest of the gym. We did little jobs around there to help out, as we weren't paying any money. I told Vic, 'Nobody wants to pay to work out, at least I don't.'

Vic knew that the other guys and I worked to keep the place nice and clean, so he figured we would take good care of other gyms. I said I didn't have much experience in running a gym, but he said he thought I knew enough.

Then Vic said that the rumor on the beach was that I was the best trainer around. Maybe I didn't realize what I was capable of until someone else pointed it out to me. I had never considered myself a great trainer, even though I understood it. I knew that concentration on certain muscles and body parts was a key to a great workout. I knew that with this concentration you could develop faster than anyone else. Not many guys seemed to know this fact. They had become used to jumping from exercise to exercise, body part to body part. I found that it was a big job to train these guys, as most of them didn't seem to know what they were doing.

Ritchie Dubois was one of those guys. I don't know how he got a body. Besides jumping around from one exercise to another he was always joking around, not concentrating. He distracted everyone else as well. I trained differently: I did it by myself most of the time, if only because my workout was too hard for the other guys. Ritchie couldn't keep up with me, and I told him that he couldn't keep up because he knew nothing about training.

And so, although Vic talked to me about helping open up these health clubs, I hesitated, because it seemed like a lot of work. I said I'd think about it and then told him about our dream to buy a boat and cruise the world. He told me that it wasn't easy to get these beach guys to commit to anything, but he wished me well. I agreed that it didn't seem like all the guys were as committed as me and Armand and Little Roy, but I was still hoping it would happen.

I talked with Ritchie about Vic's plans, and he agreed that no one would want to pay to work out. That's how all the guys felt then. We were considered weirdos and narcissists, out of the mainstream, and none of us thought that regular people would pay to do what we were doing. No one yet realized how healthy it was for the body. I had often tried to talk to guys

active in other sports, to explain to them how body building would be good for their particular sport, that it would build strength and endurance. They all replied that it would only make them muscle- bound, and that it would do more harm than good. In my own mind I could never understand what it meant to be muscle-bound. Bodybuilders on the beach in those days did acrobatics, back flips and handstands. They certainly didn't have tightened tendons or lack of movement. But most people in those days just thought we were crazy.

After working at Douglas Aircraft for about 8 months, Little Roy and I had each saved about $2500. I went to the rest of the guys and asked them if they were ready to go forward, and they just looked at me like I was crazy. None of them was still interested in buying a boat. They didn't want to leave the beach. I also always loved the beach, but after a while I would get kind of anxious, antsy, ready to do something else. The bodybuilding world was wonderful, but it was never enough. I wanted to do other things. Even Little Roy admitted that the beach was enough for him and that he didn't want to leave.

And so, disappointed that my dream was gone, I suggested to Little Roy that we make a trip back east to visit our old friends, Marvin and Artie. We felt closer to the guys back east than with the California guys and always had hoped that they would come out and join us. We agreed on the plan and headed back to New York.

Before leaving for New York, I talk with Vic Tanny again and suggested that he recruit Jack LaLanne. He was a hard worker and had money. Vic said Jack was always doing his own thing. It turned out that he was even planning to create a TV program at that time. I asked Little Roy how he would feel about working with Vic, and he said that it sounded like a lot of work. That was always our reaction when it looked like we would have to work hard. So we figured we'd take our trip and decide about Vic's plans when we got back.

Now unemployed and back on the beach for a few weeks before heading east, I was hanging out with Ritchie one day when we started talking about religion and spirituality, as we often did, and he told me that he had been talking with some people about yoga. I asked what they said about the soul, and he said 'What are you talking about?' I always had one basic question: 'If you have a soul, how do you know it?' Ritchie agreed

that he didn't know the answer to that question. He had faith and feeling that he had a soul but no proof. He then suggested that we go to a place up in Malibu canyon where there was going to be a talk by a man named Krishnamurti, who was renowned as a great yogi.

A few weeks later Ritchie and I went up to the canyon along with a few hundred other people to hear the great yogi speak. Right away I felt that he was special, he had beautiful eyes and looked very loving. I no longer remember what exactly he said, but I was quite impressed at the time. After the lecture there was too big a crowd around him for me to get close, but I heard him say that he was breaking away from Theosophy and that he didn't want to be involved with any organized religion. He planned to write and lecture on his own. The head of the Theosophy organization, Annie Passant, was annoyed because she had nurtured him as a young man and brought him to the States to be the future head of the entire organization.

In the next few years I kept track of him and read some of his books, which I always found interesting. In the end, however, I never got the answer I was seeking to my question about the existence of the soul.

After that trip to Malibu Canyon, I invited Ritchie to join me and Little Roy on our trip back east, but he had decided to sign a 'starlet' contract with one of the studios, Warner Brothers or MGM. I joked with him that this week he was going to be a movie star, because he was always changing his mind about what he wanted to do with his life. It would be a contract like the one Steve Reeves had, where you did photo shoots, took acting lessons every week and were obligated to the studio for a few years.

Little Roy and I returned to New York and got back into the old routine with Marvin and Artie and the others. I was still trying to get them to move out to California, but they weren't interested. Artie was in love with a beautiful girl named Phyllis and spent as much time with her as was possible. The Hermit came back for a visit as well, so he worked out with me and Marvin, while Little Roy did his thing. Melvin Sekolsky, who we called Little Red, was there and other new guys as well. This was at Goldberg's gym, which was getting more crowded all the time. Little Roy took up operation of the juice bar again. There was a lot of money to be made with the juice bar, but most of the guys didn't know how to maximize the profits. We started promoting a few things there, and were very successful.

One day Joe Weider came by and asked us to work out with a guy who was coming in from England named Reg Parks. Marvin and I had our own special training routine, which made it very hard to work in another bodybuilder, but we said we would give it a try. Joe Weider felt sure he would be a champion, and I have to admit that Joe could spot potential. Reg was a good- looking guy, big with black hair, around 6 feet tall and definitely had potential. He did need help, so first we told him to watch Marvin and me work out so that he would be able to break into our routine, which was always fast and hard. Marvin never allowed anything other than fast and hard. Reg was insulted that we considered him a beginner, and I guess we did sound egotistical. When I worked out with Marvin I could only use about 60% of the weights that he used; he was that strong. When Reg Parks started to work out with us, he could barely do anything. I told him to go easy with the weights until he got the hang of the exercises. On bench curls Marvin used 75-80 pounds while I used 50 pounds and Reg could hardly manage 20 pounds. When we did parallel dips, we would hop up on to the bar and then start the exercise. When Reg asked for a stool to get up on the bar, we could only laugh.

That first workout took about 6 hours, and Reg was totally wiped out. I reassured him that in time he would be able to keep up with us because concentration was more important than weight. Reg didn't seem to understand what we were talking about. I tried to get him to think about using the weights for an exercise: to concentrate just on the movement — to use the brain to create weight and to mentally resist both lowering and raising that 'weight'. He actually listened and realized that he could get totally pumped with the mind alone.

A pleasant, polite guy, Reg worked out with us that day, and although at the end of the workout Weider came by to take us all out to dinner and we all talked about working out and how things were different for Reg in England as compared to the States, Reg never came back to work out with us again. We knew he was working in Weider's warehouse in Jersey by himself. He was embarrassed to work out with anyone. We forgot about him, but about eight months later, Reg entered his first posing exhibition at one of Weider's shows. Marvin and I were amazed at how much this guy had developed in that time. We went back stage to compliment him, and he gave us the credit for his progress. We taught him how to concentrate,

to really focus on the exercises — the whole theory of working out — and he thanked us for it. Marvin really appreciated this praise, as did I. We all became great friends after that.

At that time you had to have special briefs for posing. I was always thinking that there had to be a good fabric for making those briefs. The traditional cotton briefs never fit well and had to be trimmed and remade. One day Artie came to me and said we had to go to Macy's. There was a new kind of girdle that was elastic, tube-shaped and came in three colors, blue, white and black. I bought 5 of them at $1.00 apiece. At home I made Artie put one on, sketched a basic design on it in 3 sizes, regular, semi-brief and brief. Then I had my mother sew them, and we had incredible posing briefs. Everyone who saw Artie and me pose wanted a pair. We made some briefs for Reg Parks and he wore them in competitions and posing exhibitions. The local demand was so great that Artie and I decided to go into production. We put an ad in Weider's magazine with Reg posing in the briefs. I was buying the fabric for $1.00 a piece and selling them for $5.00. My mother did the sewing. Immediately, we got orders from everywhere. Melvin Sekolsky would keep us supplied with the fabric; we would buy out the girdles at Macy's on a regular basis. Eventually we found the supplier and started buying girdles by the hundreds in each color. We couldn't keep up with the orders and ended up with a locker full of money orders.

At this point Melvin started getting more involved with fashion photography. At the same time Artie was also getting more interested in photography, although he tended to take more photos in the gym of the guys working out. I was getting antsy to return to California and wanted Artie to come with me, but he was still involved with Phyllis. When I asked her about religion, she said that religion wasn't taught in school, that since she was Jewish and not Catholic, she had never been taught the catechism or Catholic doctrine. She said that her parents weren't active in the Jewish religion either, so she hadn't learned a whole lot. They followed the rules but weren't devout.

We all loved Phyllis, which made Artie crazy with jealousy. We would jokingly threaten to steal her away, which would enrage him. In retaliation, Artie would threaten to steal our girlfriends. One evening we were hanging out around the pickle stand on the corner of Clinton and Rivington

after working out. Artie started teasing Marvin about his new girlfriend. Marvin got angry, and the vein in his neck popped out as he grabbed Artie by the head. Holding him up over the gutter, Marvin threatened to 'snuff the life out of him'. I grabbed Marvin's arms as Artie screamed in terror, and they were like a metal vise. The Hermit grabbed the other arm, and we were finally able to free Artie. That's the way we used to carry on and tease each other, but you had to be careful about teasing Marvin.

Another time, after Marvin and I had finished working, we went over to Artie's to wait for him and the Hermit. The key was under the mat, so we went in and were talking while we waited. I asked Marvin about religion, which always annoyed him. I told him I was looking for answers, that they had to be out there somewhere. So I asked him, demanding a simple yes or no without the usual lecture, 'Do you have a soul?' He looked at me and then started talking. I said 'Stop. Just yes or no.' He started talking again and I said, 'Stop. Just yes or no.' This went on for an hour. It was comical, how he would start explaining this and then that, while I only wanted that simple answer. We ended up in belly laughs, trying to remember where the conversation had started. That's how it always was. When Artie got home with Phyllis, I tried to ask the question again, but eventually we all ended up joking and laughing. We never really came to any answers on anything.

CHAPTER 11

The Cheesecake Man

One Friday night a bunch of us guys were working out in the old Dungeon, Vic Tanny's gym in Santa Monica. We had already been there over 5 hours and after another hour or so, we would all be going out to eat. On Friday nights we would eat out and often went to one particular fancy restaurant in Hollywood for dessert, as the cheesecake there was fantastic.

Zebo and I were joking about cheesecake as we worked out, when an older man approached me. His name was Pierre, and he said that he made the best cheesecake in the world. In exchange for a workout program, he said that he would make one for us. We agreed to that readily, and he told us to come to his house the following evening.

The next evening Zebo and I arrived at Pierre's home, as instructed. His wife welcomed us, and as we talked, we learned that Pierre was the head pastry chef for a hotel in Beverley Hills. Pierre presented his cheesecake to us, and his wife served it to us with coffee. With the first mouthful, I knew that this cheesecake was incredible, better than any I had ever had. I immediately asked him for the recipe, and he replied, 'No, no, I can't do that. This recipe came down through generations of my family, from father to son, and only my son will receive it.'

I thought he was kidding at first, but he was serious. So then I tried another approach. I asked him if he would answer yes or no if I listed various ingredients that I thought were in it. He agreed to that, so I started

listing ingredients and he would answer yes or no. I was far from knowing the recipe, but at least I had a start. I gave him his training program as agreed and said that I would work out with him for 2 weeks, to get him started. In return he gave us the rest of the cheesecake and promised to make us another one, which was fine with me and Zebo.

Back home I was determined to replicate that cheesecake and made three or four of them each day. My workout buddies had tasted the original one. So now they tasted each of mine and would say 'no, that's not it.' I must have made 15-20 cheesecakes that week, and it was costing me a lot of time and money, but I was determined. Totally frustrated, on the following Friday I was ready to give up, but Zebo continued to encourage me, saying that I was getting closer all the time. So I decided to try one more time and tweaking the recipe once again, I made a cheesecake on Saturday morning. When Zebo came over to taste it, he announced that this was it, that I got it, and then added that he thought it would be even better after cooling down for a while.

So, I repeated the recipe exactly and then refrigerated the cheesecake overnight. Then we all got together to taste the last cheesecake, and we really knew we had it. I called Pierre and told him that I was ready to present my own cheesecake to him. Zebo and I went to his house and were greeted by his wife once again. She admired our cheesecake, saying that it looked exactly like Pierre's. Then she tried a piece and exclaimed, 'It's better than Pierre's!' At this point Pierre grabbed a fork and tasted the cheesecake, and as he looked up at me, he exclaimed, 'What did you put in this cheesecake?!' And of course, I replied, 'Oh Pierre, I can't tell you. It's a family recipe that has been handed down through generations from father to son. This recipe will only go to my son.' Pierre had to laugh, but he was frustrated as well, because he really did want to know my recipe. We all had a good laugh over the story of Pierre's cheesecake.

CHAPTER 12

The Hypnotist

There was a guy on the beach named Hymie Schwartz. He looked like a slim and muscular version of Woody Allen with a dark tan. He worked at Douglas Aircraft, one of the few guys on the beach who had a steady job. He worked out hard on the beach and was always a lot of fun. He also always had beautiful girls in tow, and they used to bring him presents all the time as well. Of course, I really wanted to know what kind of line he was giving them, how he was getting them for himself.

One Saturday morning I was hanging out on the beach with some of the guys. Hymie joined us, and I asked him how he did it, how he got all these good-looking girls. He replied that he hypnotized them. I was incredulous; how could he do that? He said that he would show me.

Soon afterwards a pretty girl came along and lay down on her towel. We walked over to her and said hello. We introduced ourselves and talked with her for a few minutes. Then Hymie said, 'Please do me a favor and just look into my eyes.' She kind of giggled but agreed. Then Hymie said, 'I'm going to count to five, and you are going to get sleepier as I count.' You could see that, as he started to count, the girl started to look sleepy and drowsy. By the time he got to five, she was sound asleep. I was amazed.

Now Hymie said to the sleeping girl, 'Now, you are going to be feeling great today, and you're going to have a lot of fun. Also, when I wake you up, you are going to feeling irresistibly attracted to me. You're going to want to

touch me, hold my hand and kiss me. You'll think I'm the greatest looking guy you've ever seen.' I started laughing, but by the time Hymie counted to five again, the girl had awakened and was fully aware of her surroundings. She looked at Hymie, took his hand and started to kiss him. I was shocked. She didn't want him to leave, but we promised to return and walked over to his apartment. It was called 'the Den' and had a black ceiling with stars that sparkled in the dark. I asked Hymie how he had hypnotized the girl, and he replied that it was really easy. I wondered what part of the brain he was hypnotizing and asked him to hypnotize me, but no matter how much he tried, it wouldn't work. He said he didn't really know how he did it, but there were only a few people that he couldn't hypnotize. He had read several books on the subject and assumed that somehow he was able to make contact with and influence the subconscious mind. He also said that women seemed easier to influence than men. He had hypnotized some guys who were going to be entering contests, and he would convince them that they would be able to lift heavier weights than ever before and they really would be able to do it.

One day a few weeks later a bunch of us guys was hanging out at 'the Den'. I asked Hymie to hypnotize some of us, to see if indeed we could become stronger by suggestion. Harry, a tall, skinny guy, was there that day and Hymie chose him as his subject. He did the countdown to five, and sure enough, Harry fell sound asleep. Hymie then told him that he would be stiff and unbreakable as a steel rod. We took two chairs, separated them and then placed Harry so that only his head and heels rested on them. After that the other four of us with an estimated total weight of between seven and eight hundred pounds, sat on him. Harry didn't budge an inch. Amazing! And then, when Hymie brought Harry back from his sleeping state, he remembered nothing.

From that point on we all called Hymie the hypnotist, which he really didn't like very much because he didn't want people to know what he could do. Anyway, he was a nice guy and never took advantage of any of the girls. In the following years I would meet other hypnotists and was fascinated by their ability, but for myself, I never wanted to try it. I didn't feel comfortable with the thought of controlling someone else's mind.

I've thought about that for many years and I now realize what happened. He was able to put her conscious mind to sleep and to program

her subconscious — which never goes to sleep — to accept his orders. I found that very interesting, and now I understand it. This is the way the mind operates, that some things can be invisible to it. In these cases the subconscious mind was in control, not the conscious mind. This is the same way in which we are all hypnotized into agreement in the carnal mind, the universal computer. The important question is: how do we reverse the effects of this hypnosis?

CHAPTER 13

More Muscle Beach Stories

Boy, the people who came down to Muscle Beach. There were lots of famous theatrical groups like the Ganjous, an amazing adagio act with three men and a girl named Merian. They used to pick her up and throw her all over the place. In later years they played all over the world, including many years with the Folies Berger at the Tropicana Hotel in Las Vegas.

They weren't alone, though. There was Karl Karsoni, who had perhaps the greatest hand-balancing act in the world at that time. He worked the act with his two younger twin brothers. Later, after his brothers passed away, he did the act with his wife. And more, maybe 15-20 acts that would come down to the beach and hang out. They were all friends. That's where I learned a lot about hand balancing and acrobatic work and in the process, fell in love with show business. While working out on the beach, I would meet all these people, find out about their lives and points of views, how they got started in show business.

There were many other famous people there. There were always those who not only wanted to work out, but also wanted to figure out the best diet for good health. Johnny Walker was a fruitarian and wrote a couple of books on the subject. Bernard McFaddin, who was almost 70 years old when I met him, was a renowned diet author as well. Jack LaLanne was always interested in fasting as well as fruits and vegetables, and made lots of drinks and food products that he promoted for their health advantages.

I would listen to all the various points of view and would try different

diets. I was vegetarian for a while, but didn't find it very interesting. I lost a lot of weight and had lower energy as well, so I stopped that. I ate vegetables but ate meat as well, to provide strength and energy. I tried fasting, as a lot of people were doing. I remember my first fast when I skipped 3-4 meals and thought I was going to die. I went on to learn different techniques for fasting including breathing exercises. I gradually went from 2-3 days to 7 days and ultimately 21 days. Sometimes on these fasts I would eat one particular food at a time. Someone once told me that I should fast on carrot juice, that it would give me a lot of energy. For 14 days I was drinking about 4 quarts of carrot juice daily. Then I happened to catch a glimpse of myself in a mirror and saw that I was turning orange. I was sure I had jaundice and went to the doctor. When he asked me what I had been eating, and I told him about the carrot juice, he said it was no wonder I had turned orange. So I stopped that fast. It was all a lot of fun experimenting, trying new things.

Nutritional supplements — like vitamins and protein powders — were just starting to come out but I thought that a lot of the stuff that was on the market was worthless. I remember Hoffman or Weider made pills that were supposed to have 96% protein, but I thought it was more like 4-5% protein with the rest was all filler. Eventually all that early stuff had to be taken off the market.

Later they would do a better job of creating products that were closer to what was claimed. We bodybuilders tried all those products, but at the end of it all we realized that if you wanted protein, you ate meat, seafood, and poultry. Over time we learned about protein, carbohydrates, calories etc. We had a system. We knew that we could build muscle and lean-down by eating only protein for a few weeks. If you were more interested in gaining weight alone, you ate more carbs, more calories. Writers and doctors would come down and ask us questions all the time.

One day we were working out in the Dungeon, and a young doctor came in. He wanted me to create a workout program for him and to help him gain weight. I told him about drinking six quarts of milk and eating a dozen eggs per day. He was horrified that I had been doing just that for 6-7 years and made me come down to his office to have my cholesterol checked. So I went down, and the doctor ran several blood tests on me only to find that there was absolutely nothing wrong with me. He was sure that my cholesterol would be sky high, and swore that he always saw the results of such eating in autopsies. I went on to tell him that my workouts usually

went 5-6 hours, and I ate about 5000 calories each day. I knew I could lose up to five pounds in a workout and had to eat like crazy to maintain weight. I liked to keep my weight between 190 and 200 pounds, depending on whether I was about to complete. I felt that more than a 10 pound difference was difficult for the body, so I tried to keep within those limits. That doctor changed his mind about diet, cholesterol and hardening of the arteries.

Another doctor came up from San Diego. His area of interest was the thyroid gland. We told him about our diets and exercise programs, and he wanted to test my thyroid. I wasn't really keen on being tested all the time, but finally I agreed. It was just before a contest, so I had been eating mainly protein. He found that my thyroid was working very fast, which surprised him, but I told him that I found that my body seemed to go faster on protein, and that carbs like spaghetti and bread, seemed to slow it down. I would feel a bit sluggish when I was eating more carbs and carrying a little more weight. Over the next few months the doctor came to see that my thyroid's functioning changed with my diet.

Paul Bragg was another one. He came from Hawaii and was a lot older than most of us, maybe around 50. He was a nice guy and wrote several books, as did Bernard McFaddin. Of course, I was still a teenager and thought all these guys were old. I didn't yet realize that the perception of age is all in the head.

One day on the beach a young, good-looking black guy came up to me and said that he had a book for me to read, a book on breathing, and he thought I would find it interesting. It had a blue cover and no more than 60-70 pages. It was called 'Yoga of the Breath'. I started leafing through it, but when I looked up, the kid had totally disappeared. He wasn't anywhere around on the beach, which I found quite strange.

All the same, I tried out those exercises, which were supposed to produce various results. I found them to be interesting and very stimulating. There were breathing exercises to be done while walking, while standing, before going to bed, on awakening. I practiced them for six or seven months, and the results were tremendous. I learned how one should breathe and realized that most people breathe very shallowly. I could tell that these breathing exercises really worked and they were another way that I proved something for myself empirically — by doing it and finding out for myself whether or not it worked.

In the years that followed, I maintained my breathing awareness, especially when working out. I came to realize that oxygen was being depleted when I worked out and needed to be replenished. Each set would deplete the body's oxygen, so I would breathe deeply between sets. I would take about five deep breaths and hold them for about five seconds. After each breath I would exhale in an exaggerated way, making more room for the next breath. It has been terrific for me, providing each of my body's cells with the oxygen it needs as food. I find that the more they get, the longer they live and the stronger they are.

The last chapter of this book on breathing recommended another book to study, one about hatha yoga. I went and bought it, and it too was had a blue cover and about 150 pages. The first chapter floored me. It explained that you are a soul motivating a body. YOU ARE NOT A BODY; YOU ARE A SOUL. It stunned me that this book was addressing my questions about the soul. The book told me exactly how to realize one's soul, and the answer that I had been looking for everywhere my whole life was a simple exercise. You were to lie down on the floor, and, starting with your toes, tighten and then relax every muscle in your body until you reached the top of your head. Then, once all your muscles were relaxed, you were to become aware of the weight of your body on the ground and then let go of it. At that point you could start to feel yourself lifting out of your body, even while you were able to visualize it.

This was **IT.** I was determined to make this technique work for me and get some answers. Morning, noon and night I would lie down and practice this technique at the Seaside Terrace, where I was living. The book explained that you shouldn't practice the technique when tired or sleepy because you might fall asleep in the middle, which happened to me a few times.

One day after about three weeks of practice, as I was relaxing my body and visualizing leaving my body, I suddenly felt myself lifting, going out. However, in my excitement, I tensed and brought myself back into my body and seemed to hit my head on the floor. I had really been up off the floor. It *was* an actual levitation.

Once I got over the initial excitement, I began the process again. I did it for months, and then one afternoon I was doing the exercise after I had had a particularly good workout and was feeling energized. This time I was suddenly fully out of my body, and it was the most incredible experience I had ever had in my life. I was totally aware of my surroundings. I could see from every angle, and whatever I looked at, I became. I remember floating through the kitchen table, floating through the chairs, floating through and becoming part of the walls, the wallpaper, the wallpaper glue, the plaster and the two-by-fours. I was the couch, the floor, the carpet. I even merged with some cockroaches that were in the corner. I was a part of everything in that room. I felt a total unity with my surroundings. I was the fibers of the wood, and knew the exact being-ness of the wood. It was a magnificent feeling, and at that point I really did know that I was a soul.

I was experiencing something whose full significance I wouldn't understand until years later. And when it was over I remember going back down into my body, like a light collapsing back into a bulb, and then it felt as if I was in prison. I couldn't move right away. I had to take several deep breaths and sort of get adjusted to being back in the body.

This experience was transformational for me but I didn't tell anyone about it. I would continue to ask people if they had felt their soul, but I didn't talk about my experience. I wanted to tell everyone that you are a soul motivating a body, that the body doesn't think but only reacts. You tell it to move and it moves. You tell it to sit and it sits. Once it's programmed, it goes on automatic, but it is still reacting. It reacts to everything around it, your thinking, whatever you see and hear.

This was the real beginning of my understanding of spirituality.

CHAPTER 14

A New Way of Working Out, and Mae West

Of course I wanted to tell everyone at the gym about my great out of body experience but I felt that I couldn't. These guys were totally into bodybuilding and wouldn't understand — plus I couldn't verbalize it yet; I didn't have the words and I was still high from the experience. But now I had a whole new attitude about working out. I felt so much more in control of this body, as if I were in charge of sculpting it. I knew that I was doing all the thinking for the body and that I was in control of changing it. I wanted to see how deeply I could concentrate on the body, changing it into what I wanted it to be. With my new understanding I had to relearn my body, and how best to work it out. For one thing I found that I was concentrating much more deeply, and that I could affect my body parts in size, proportion, and strength just by thinking about them. I was in control of my body. I didn't tell anyone about this, even Ritchie. We had often talked about spirituality, but now I knew that I now had a deeper understanding about the soul, something I had not been able to find anywhere else.

I continued to work out and realized more and more how my thinking —using the vehicle of weights and workouts — could change my body. I realized that perhaps I could even change my body by thought alone. Doing an exercise, I would concentrate so completely on a muscle that I felt I could feel it growing, without even working out. Guys noticed the

change in me, that I was becoming more muscular more rapidly, and they wanted to know my secret. And of course, I did have a secret that no one else seemed to be aware of. Bodybuilders tended to work out on an ego basis, always competing with one another to get a better body. I realized that it had nothing to do with anyone else, that I could make my body stronger or weaker — I could even make it healthier — just by my thinking. It was the soul that was doing the work, not the body. The body was taking orders from me.

Guys were always asking to work out with me, but I usually declined, because my whole method of working out had changed so much. I was doing more *mental* exercise than physical. That was a hard principle to explain, a whole different program. Before I could explain it to others I knew I needed more answers, but no one seemed to be able to help. I had experienced an incredible awakening, but I knew I hadn't yet really grasped its totality. I knew it was important, and that as a result I now had much greater control of my body, but I often wondered how far I could go with it and what it could really mean. In other words: I had a lot of questions, but I found no answers in all the conversations we had.

I realized at the beginning of 1953 that I was starting to lose interest in entering contests — even losing the desire to work out. However, there was one contest I still wanted to win that year: Mr. Muscle Beach. I remember getting ready for that contest and how easy it was to do. There was no longer a great struggle to improve the body; it seemed I could do it overnight just by thinking about it and concentrating those thoughts into my body.

I won Mr. Muscle Beach that year. After that, even though I had little desire to enter other contests I did enter the Mr. America contest with Ritchie that year. That was the year that Bill Pearl won, but I thought that Ritchie should have won, or even me. But again, that was only opinion and ego speaking. 1953 was the year that we thought that the contests were fixed, and that dampened our enthusiasm. Ritchie still dreamed of winning Mr. America, however, and wanted me to train him. I kept refusing, as I had other things to do. George Eiferman had opened up a gym in Hollywood, and we were working out there a lot. He had some rooms on the second floor where we could sleep, so we would help run the gym in return.

One day George said he wanted me to meet a fantastic woman. Of course I was curious and asked to hear more about her. George's only reply was, 'She's quite a woman.' A few days later he took me to a pink and light blue twelfth-floor apartment in the Ravenswood Apts. on Vine. The door was opened by a beautiful woman — 5 feet tall and 120 pounds, strong-looking and full-figured. George introduced us and left. 'Come over here, big boy, and sit down,' the woman said. I didn't yet realize that this was the Mae West I had seen in movies when I was just a kid. If I had thought about it I would have assumed that she was dead. She wasn't.

This very interesting woman said in her beautiful, controlled voiced, 'All right, big boy, take off your shirt and let me see what you look like.' So I posed for her. We talked for a while. Soon we would be great friends. For an entire year I spent a lot of time with her, but I never told anyone, not even George. At the end of that year she began to talk about putting a Vegas show together, which I thought was a great idea.

Mae loved working out, never drank or smoked, and was really quite athletic. I would give her tips on working out, and we would work out together in the mornings. We would take long walks, dreaming up ideas for the show. George thought it was a good idea as well, and so as we headed into 1954, the show was becoming more definite.

At the same time, Ritchie kept nagging me to train him, and I finally agreed. That was one of the hardest jobs I ever had. He needed an extra 10-15% of effort, and he had no concept of concentration in working out. It was a tough 3-4 months to get him in shape for that Mr. America contest, but I finally got it done and promised myself that I would never train anyone else again. Ritchie won that contest. I was in great shape myself, but you never know how these things will turn out. I was glad that Ritchie won; he certainly looked fantastic. And then Hoffman came backstage and said, 'Don't worry, Dominick. Next year is yours'. That was just what he had told Ritchie the year before: 'Ritchie, Next year is yours.' I assumed that many of the contests were fixed, but somehow I didn't think that applied to the Mr. America contest. At that point I lost confidence in the whole thing, and I lost interest as well. I was more interested in finding out who I really was.

In any event the Mae West show was starting up. I remember we did

rehearsals and everything, and we were going to open up at the Sahara in 1954. Before this I had never even heard of Las Vegas and had to ask where it was. Someone said it was in northern Nevada, and of course it isn't; it's in southern Nevada. So much for knowing about geography.

There were eight or nine of us bodybuilders in the show with Mae: George, Ritchie, Zabo, Chuck Pendleton, Krauser, Armand Tanny, Joe Gold, Lester Shaffer and me. We rehearsed for six or eight weeks before the show opened.

We had a lot of fun putting the show together, and there was great camaraderie. We had eight male dancers, a male singer and Hattie McDaniels, who played Beulah, Mae West's maid. There was another guy who played a representative for the Olympics and who introduced us as great athletes from around the world. The show was an immediate success and was called 'Something for the Girls'. On stage and off, Mae was in charge of our lives and wanted to control us completely. We couldn't hang out at the swimming pools; we couldn't date any of the showgirls; we couldn't be seen in nightclubs. As all of us guys wanted to meet women and have fun, we would try to sneak out and break the rules whenever possible. I still enjoyed Mae's company, but she was very controlling and demanding. It was difficult, so I eased myself out of the relationship by getting her interested in Ritchie. I started going out more on my own, and Ritchie got involved with Mae for a while, but it didn't last. Soon after that Chuck Pendleton started going with her. Mae was 61 when I first met her, but she looked like she was in her 30's. Other women were obviously jealous of her looks, her smarts, her voice, and her natural talent as an entertainer.

At one point I snuck off to another hotel pool to visit with Sophie Tucker. She was a fabulous comedienne and was playing at the El Rancho. She had asked me to have breakfast with her so she could be seen with a muscle man. I would go, even though Mae had forbidden it. Vegas was very small-town in those days. There was one road in and one road out. That one road went from downtown LA to downtown Vegas. The El Rancho was only about twenty or thirty feet off the highway. We would sit there by the pool and have our breakfast. One day I saw a sign across the road that offered land for sale, $12 per front foot, 260 ft. deep. I looked at Sophie and said I thought she should buy it. She replied, 'Are

you crazy, Dominick? This town can't last. Gambling is illegal; this town will get shut down, folded up. We're lucky we're working here for now.' Well, what did I know? I was only 20 years old. Anyway, later that day it appeared in the local paper, 'Sophie Tucker seen with muscle man at swimming pool'. When Mae West found out about this, she flipped out. Enraged, she got us all in a meeting and demanded that we tell who had been with Sophie. Of course no one admitted anything. I never did admit it, and after a few weeks, Sophie's show ended. She always laughed at Mae, and promised that, if Mae ever fired me, I would always have a job with her.

Being in Vegas and working for Mae really got me hooked on show business. I realized how much I enjoyed being on stage. This was different from posing in a contest. The audience was different, much more diversified.

About this same time I met Franklin D'Amore, a great guy who owned a restaurant in Hollywood and had had an act for years — first in vaudeville and then on stage in nightclubs all over the States. His was a strongman act, kind of a comedy-acrobatic act. One day I asked him if he would train me to take over his act and he tentatively agreed. He told me to find myself a nice partner and that then he would teach me. I already knew acrobatic stunts and adagio from being on the beach. Everyone on the beach was willing to teach, and we were always playing around, creating little acts in a half hour or so. And, since I always seemed to be getting into trouble with Mae in Vegas, it seemed a good time to leave the show. Most of the guys would drop in and out of the show as time went on, but I never regretted the experience, made good money, and had a lot of fun.

CHAPTER 15

Becoming a Crap Dealer

While in Vegas I made friends with Jimmy Lawler, who had won Mr. Muscle Beach in 1949. He would come backstage a lot and visit with us, and one evening, he was talking about being a crap dealer in Vegas. He suggested that when I turned 21, it would be smart for me to learn how to deal the game. It would be like having a trade, a skill that I would always be able to fall back on. I said I would keep that in mind and consider it when I turned 21.

Back on the beach, I kept working out and even trained a few guys. Even George Eiferman came to me and said that he wanted me to train him for the Mr. Universe contest. I thought he was kidding, but George said I was the only one who could make him concentrate properly. I did end up helping George get ready for that contest, which he won.

I was now 21 and broke once again, so I headed back to Vegas with little Roy. I went to Jimmy, who introduced me to his father-in-law, who owned the Old Pioneer Club at that time. There were only two places that were breaking in dealers. There weren't any dealing schools in those days. You went to work in either the Boulder Club or the Old Pioneer Club as a shill. I got a job at the Boulder Club making $8 per day shilling. You work for the casino, and when there is an empty game you go there and play to start the action going. That was in 1955. I learned to deal by watching, and after about 4-5 months of shilling, I was bored. Even as a kid, I knew

a lot about craps. When I was about 13 years old, when my mother was the superintendent of a building, they had craps games going on. The guy who ran the place offered to teach me how to deal for $20 per night, 2 nights per week. So I already knew a lot about the basic game, the bets and the payoffs.

There was only one place in Vegas that would hire inexperienced dealers, we called them break-ins, and that was the Flamingo Hotel. Once owned by Bugsy Siegal, when I arrived it was owned by Albert Parvin. Getting a job there was almost impossible, and I got discouraged, so I went back to the beach.

There I hooked up with an old friend, Murray Ehrenberg, who had come out from New York. He planned to go work at an Arthur Murray Dance Studio. He figured it was easy work, good money and a place to find a lot of women. He wanted me to learn with him, and I wasn't sure at all, as I was a terrible dancer. But he convinced me to train with him. About 6 weeks into the course I realized it wasn't for me. There were lots of older women coming in to dance with the instructors, and it seemed to be the same older women every night. This studio was in Hollywood. I said to Murray, 'I don't know … it seems like you're a glorified pimp here. You're introduced to these women, and then one seems to always want to dance with you. I don't think this is for me. I think I'll go back to Vegas and see if I can get a job in the Flamingo.'

Murray didn't know about dealing craps, but I told him that it paid a lot more than being a dance instructor.

I returned to Las Vegas and returned to work at the old Boulder Club, lucky that they had an opening. I was still shilling, and everything was at a standstill, job wise. The Flamingo was the only shot to move up as a dealer, and they weren't hiring. I called Murray after about three weeks and told him that he could start as a shill at the Boulder Club, to learn how to deal craps, and he agreed to come. He took the Greyhound bus from LA, and I met him at the bus station downtown on Main St., next to the train station, at 3AM. Murray got that job as a shill and roomed with me in a little trailer, which cost about $40 per month.

After about two months back at the Boulder Club, I became desperate to get out. So one evening I went into the Flamingo Hotel. The hiring boss there was an elderly man, quite good-looking, named Bob Barry. I lied

and told him that I had been dealing craps for 6 months, and he agreed to give me an audition. I tapped out the dealer on one of the games and stepped into place. There were about six players on my end of the crap table. I passed that audition, although Mr. Barry wasn't very impressed with my ability. He told me that I had three months to improve. If I didn't, I would be fired.

I started the next day on day shift at 9AM. It was an incredible job, and I was lucky to have it, with such little table experience. But the guys who were more trained than I just didn't go out and try to get a better job. They gave up before they even tried. I would work at the Flamingo from 1955 up to 1957 or 1958, and it was a good job. No one fired me after three months, so I figured I was hired. During that time I never had a day off and often worked double shifts. You never argued or questioned if told you were going to work an extra shift; you just did it. It went on that way for six months, and I was pretty tired. My mind was full of bets and payoffs, and I was always trying to memorize more. You didn't want to have to figure out payments on a live game; you just wanted to know it. I finally went to the scheduler and asked for a day off. He thought I was joking, but when he looked over the past schedules, he saw that I was right. So he gave me a day off.

It was a good time in my life. I loved Vegas. Life was cheap; you could go to a midnight show with free drinks on the Strip for $3. For another 50 cents you could go to a dinner show and see great stars. I loved the heat. I always had a tan. I was always able to work out. I made a lot of money. Our daily salary was about $22 per day, plus a dollar for the midnight buffet. During the day and evening you could get anything you wanted to eat at the coffee shop, but the buffet was incredible. You worked mainly for tokes (that's what we called tips). Whenever I got the chance, I would return to Muscle Beach for a break, but I was pretty much just working and saving money.

I was still asking spiritual questions, but again, I wasn't getting much in the way of answers. There were numerous religious groups in Vegas and a church on almost every corner. It was amazing that there were so many churches in 'Sin City'. I heard about the Mormon Church for the first time then, as they were very strong. I found no answers there. I was still on my own, asking questions.

Once I had become good friends with Bob Barry, I was able to get off two months at a time, and I would return to Santa Monica. Bob was a compulsive gambler, especially after he had been drinking. He liked to gamble downtown at Binion's Horseshoe Casino, where the big gamblers would go to play, because the Horseshoe would book any bet (the other casinos maxed out at $500 per bet). There was also the Golden Nugget across the street, a small place where the gold prospectors would gather, tying up their donkeys on the hitching post outside. The Nugget had a long bar, where the patrons would stand, and there was sawdust on the floor.

One night I saw Bob Barry gambling at the Horseshoe, and he was really drunk. He asked me for money, and I gave him everything in my pocket, which was $500. After that I could do no wrong, and whenever I wanted time off, I got it. He always paid me back, so I never hesitated to loan him money. This was called having good 'juice', to be in with someone who had influence, and I had good 'juice' in Bob Barry. An older guy at the Boulder Club once offered me some advice. First, always buy with cash, so that you never owe anything to anyone. The second piece of advice was, never make enemies in Vegas. You always tried to be friends with everyone, because the guy who is breaking in today could be your boss tomorrow. Sure enough, that was really good advice, because lots of guys I met ended up being my bosses.

As time went by, Vegas kept growing, kept building new hotels and casinos. Everyone said the town could never last, that it was sure to fold up, but every year it grew a little more. When I first got there in 1954 its population was about 25,000, but it felt like a small town. Everyone knew each other, and life was easy. It was a fun place.

CHAPTER 16

The Self-Realization Fellowship

In 1957 I was still going down to the beach in Santa Monica and just basically hanging around when someone told me about this place in Malibu Canyon called Self-Realization Fellowship. I loved the name and repeated it often. So, I went to the beautiful little lake with a chapel there that had been built from an old windmill. On the rough paths around the lake I first met Stanley, who ran the place with his father. He and his father told me a little of the history of this sanctuary. That was the first time I heard of Yogi Yogananda, who had founded the Self-Realization Fellowship.

Stanley told me that the Fellowship gave meditation classes and lectures and held chapel services on Sundays. Because they always seemed to be working on the grounds and buildings I asked if I could help. Of course they welcomed me, and I found myself out there every day helping to build and improve the paths, fortify the banks of the lake and working on other projects. It was very peaceful.

I learned more about meditation and contemplation there, about being quiet and going more into myself. Up until then I had tried to use reason and logic to figure out answers to my questions, but I had never looked inward before. At first it was very difficult to just sit down and be quiet, to not think. I would practice with Brother Stanley and his father, who had been with Self- Realization for many years.

Then one day I went out onto a little pier which we had just rebuilt. I

sat down on the bench there at about four in the afternoon and tried to be quiet. My mind raced; I was thinking about fifty different things. I prayed for peace and quietness, and then I heard a voice that told me to open my eyes. When I did I saw a sign right in front of me. It said, 'Be still and know that I am God.' I closed my eyes and repeated those words. All of a sudden everything became quiet, and I went into a deep, deep state of silence. It was so awesome, my first really contemplative meditation.

It only seemed like a few minutes had gone by, but when I opened my eyes all I could see was darkness: four hours had passed! Feeling so high from this experience, I returned to the chapel and shared my experience. The people there were happy for me and told me that I was finally beginning to understand. In my newfound happiness, I asked Brother Stanley if I could move in with them and stay by the lake. He told me that I would have to go up to Mount Washington in the LA hills where the main center was located. When I said I had never heard of this center, he handed me *The Autobiography of a Yogi* and told me to read it. Yogananda's photo was on the cover, and I really saw him for the first time, especially the beauty of his eyes. I loved the book. For the first time, I understood what it meant to be a yogi and the different techniques that are used to become 'realized.' I was convinced that I wanted to become a 'brother'.

I filled out an application and had my friend Frenchie fill out one as well, because he was also interested in spirituality and was constantly asking questions. About three weeks later Frenchie got a letter of acceptance. I was happy for him and sure that mine would soon follow. A few days letter I received my letter, but it was for an interview only. I went up to the Fellowship and met Sister Daya, who had been the head of Self-Realization since Yogananda's death a few years before. A beautiful and gracious woman, she told me that as much as she would like to have me at the center, she felt that I still had to deal with some future issues. She seemed to be concerned that I was living with my girlfriend, and I told her that the relationship was ending. She said that it wasn't going to be an easy break, that my girlfriend would try to break down the doors of the center before giving me up. But she went on to say that there was a woman in my future who would be very important to me. Therefore, for my own good, it wasn't yet time for me to leave behind the physical world. I was very disappointed, but I accepted her deep, intuitive understanding.

I was also angry at myself for not having found out about Self-Realization and Yogananda earlier. I was sorry that I had missed signals and messages that would have guided me to Yogananda while he was still alive. I now knew that yoga was the path for me — that through a series of techniques and lessons I could learn and grow. This was something that I could experience for *myself,* unlike Bible studies, in which things are explained TO you.

For instance, one evening while I was working on the ground I met a wonderful old man. I was putting away my tools in a little shed, and there he was, looking like Mahiri Masai, one of the first masters of Self-Realization. The old man greeted me, and said that Brother Stanley had told him about me and the work I was doing on the property. I told him how much I liked the Shrine, how peaceful it was and how conducive to good contemplation. The old man invited me to dinner at his little house up on the hill overlooking the lake. I accepted his invitation and we followed a path up and around to his house. There I met his wife, and we enjoyed a delicious dinner of soup, salad and bread.

After dinner we went into the living room, and the old man told me his story. He had been born and raised in New York City and had followed his father into the garment business. He had always promised himself that when he retired, he and his wife would move to California. Once retired, they moved to the Malibu area and rented a little apartment. They found a realtor and told her that they wanted a little house with a view. The realtor said that she had just such a listing off of Sunset Blvd. in Malibu. They went to see it and liked the house as well as the view overlooking the lake and the ocean on the far horizon. So they bought this little house and after a few months, the wife started taking her morning walks around the lake. She met various people who were there and at Christmas they invited her and her husband to their annual holiday party, to be hosted by Yogananda.

The woman came back to the house and told her husband about the invitation, but the old man wasn't interested because, he told her, he belonged to another religion, and that he was perfectly satisfied with Judaism. She argued that the people at the lake were nice people, and that it would do no harm — the two of them should go to the party. The old man finally agreed. So on Christmas Eve, they walked down the hill and joined

the group that had gathered at the Shrine. A small tent with a dinner table had been set up. Yogananda was seated at one end of the table, and the old man sat at the opposite end, next to another, even older man. He felt uncomfortable there, out of his element, and the other gentleman seated beside him was explaining things about Self-Realization and Yogananda. The old man started complaining to the other fellow about this and that, and the other man said, 'Why don't you go tell Yogananda your problems? I feel sure he could help you.'

At that point Yogananda left the table and went outside to the little garden there. The other older gentleman got up out of his seat and went outside towards Yogananda and fell to his knees at the Yogi's feet. The old man was amazed and disturbed by this show of devotion, but just then, Yogananda looked up and over and suddenly it felt as if a magnet was pulling him towards to the master. When he reached Yogananda, his knees just buckled, and he too fell over and touched the master's feet. At that moment he went into the state of samadhi and totally merged with Yogananda. It only lasted a minute or two, but he had no concept of time. When he regained consciousness, he begged Yogananda to accept him as his disciple, which Yogananda did. His service for Yogananda would be as the purchaser of all goods and supplies bought for Self- Realization's various centers. When I met him he had held this position for four or five years.

I was thrilled to hear this story. The two of us closed our eyes and went into a deep meditation. I, too, could feel the calm and peaceful presence of Yogananda. After some time had passed I awoke and went into the kitchen, where the old man and his wife was sitting. I kissed them good night and left the house. I would never see either of them again.

It was here at the Self-Realization Fellowship that I met the hatha yoga master I wrote about at the beginning of this book, the man who could control the temperature of his body. I asked him if, having learned how to control his body so totally, if there was anything more that he needed to learn. He simply said the word 'jnana'. It was here that I would learn that jnana yoga is the yoga of the mind, and that it is the highest form of yoga.

CHAPTER 17

Mexico and After

Disappointed with my rejection from the Self-Realization Center, I found myself back in Santa Monica and on Muscle Beach. There I would get three or four letters a month asking me about working out or requesting photos. One day shortly after leaving the yoga center I received a letter from an American guy named Steve who was living in Guadalajara, Mexico, inviting me to come down to Guadalajara and give some exhibitions and lectures.

Still depressed, I wanted to do something different, something new. The Self-Realization people talked about 'walking the path' and how at times you slipped and fell down. A change could refocus you and help you to get back up again. Going forward was the key, no matter how long it took you. This process would continue over and over again, and you must keep trying to 'walk the path' so that eventually it all comes together. It's like a big puzzle. The big picture is there, but you can only see pieces of it like 'Cleanliness is next to Godliness' and 'As a man thinketh in his heart, so shall it be.' You hold on to them, and with luck someday you will be able to see the whole picture that the puzzle pieces make.

Guadalajara was the piece I was dealing with at that point. I decided to take a motorcycle trip down there and I was able to take Frenchie with me because he had decided not to join the Fellowship Center without me. Even though I tried to convince him to do so he wouldn't change his

mind. So I wrote to this guy Steve, and Frenchie and I started making plans for our trip.

It turned out to be quite an adventure to get to Guadalajara from Santa Monica. First we drove to Tijuana, only to find out that there were no accessible roads from there that went around the Sea of Cortez and then south. We had to cross to Arizona and then head south. There were no hassles with immigration or customs in those days. All you needed was a driver's license. The roads were terrible, sometimes paved or graveled and sometimes just dirt. At some of the little towns, you could tell that they had never seen a motorcycle before. Some roads seemed like cattle trails, and we saw one bus that had been completely demolished in a collision with a cow. Often at a stream there would be a rickety plank bridge and someone collecting a toll, theoretically to raise money for a real bridge. Frenchie had so little trust in those planks that he would walk his bike across. Along the way we would either sleep by the side of the road or knock on a door and ask for food and lodging. Everyone was always accommodating and, for a few pesos, we were well taken care of and everyone was happy.

After about five days we reached Guadalajara and found Steve at the gym he owned, and from there he drove us out to his ranch. His was an interesting story. Originally from a dairy farm in Pennsylvania, he had decided to visit Mexico about eight years before. Once in Guadalajara, he realized that they had no pasteurization of milk and no proper butchers. The poorly cut meat was just laid out and covered with flies. Because he was married to a local girl, the daughter of a rancher with a 28,000-acre cattle spread that produced hides for his shoe factory, Steve was in a perfect position to do something about the meat and dairy issues. He went into business with his father-in-law, returned to the States, bought some cows and shipped them down to Mexico. He opened up a business for pasteurized milk and fresh ice cream, as well as a high quality butcher shop. From the beginning he had been very successful, not just with the local population, but with the several thousand foreigners living in the area.

In the next few days, I gave a few exhibitions and lectures at the gym. Frenchie was enjoying the social life. Then one day Steve, with whom I had become good friends, asked me what was missing from the local diet. I knew it was eggs, as I was a big egg eater in those days and would eat a

dozen eggs for breakfast each morning. He then offered me a proposition — he would bring down chickens from the States, set me up on the ranch and teach me all I needed to know about chickens and eggs. He told me that I could be a millionaire overnight, but I just couldn't see myself as a chicken farmer and declined his generous offer. He kept trying to convince me, and we had a lot of good laughs over it.

At the gym I met another Mexican gentleman who had quite an establishment on a big lake. There was a building there that was used for shows and parties, picnic grounds and a substantial restaurant as well. He asked me to give a posing exhibition there one evening and offered to pay me $300. Of course I accepted, and it was a great success. Bodybuilding was very popular at that time in Mexico, perhaps because the majority of men were either too skinny or too fat.

But Frenchie and I were ready to leave Mexico. However, before our departure I asked my new friend where we should go next — did he know of a nice beach for us to visit. He told us about a place called Puerto Vallarta, an isolated village off the main highway. He gave us the name of a little hotel there and wished us well.

So Frenchie and I took off and spent the next three days on the road. The last seventy miles was called a road, but it was barely a cow trail. At times the road would completely disappear, and we would have to search for it. We had to ford streams, as there were no bridges. We did see a bus one day, traveling along this road, and it must have been about four feet up in the air on huge springs and tires, packed with people and luggage and animals.

Once we got to Puerto Vallarta, however, we had to agree that it was absolutely breathtaking. The beach was pristine, the water incredible. We asked at the little hotel if we could stay on the beach, and they directed us to little palapas down by the water. The local kids were glad to keep us supplied with fruits, vegetables and fresh fish for a few pesos per day. We spent the next few days just enjoying the beach of Puerto Vallarta.

Heading back to the States, it took us about a week and a half to get back to Santa Monica. We needed a rest after being bounced around for so long. Once back, I moved in again with my old girlfriend, Beverley, and Frenchie found another place. A few days later I became terribly sick. For three days I had diarrhea and vomiting, and I wanted to die. When I woke

up on the fourth day I felt much better, but my urine was dark brownish red and my stool was light beige.

So I went to the doctor, who told me that I had infectious hepatitis. He told me to go to bed for three weeks and do nothing. I was to eat like a horse and gain twenty pounds. That was easy for me, so I lay in bed, ate nonstop, meditated and studied my weekly lessons that came by mail from the Self-Realization Fellowship. It was then that I also came across a book called 'The Infinite Way' which I knew it was a book that was 'right' for me. I knew it was true even though I would put it aside for over twenty years before reading it again.

After getting better, I was out of money and decided that it was time to return to Vegas. I had lost my job at the Flamingo, of course. My friend Murray Ehrenberg was working at the Riviera as a craps dealer and he helped me get a job there and I moved in with him. I worked for about six months before getting bored and returning to the beach. As always I stayed in touch with the guys back east, trying to convince them to come west. So I went back to NY for a quick visit and decided that I just had to get Artie out of NYC. I decided to 'kidnap' him. I knew that if I boxed up all of his belongings and shipped them to California he would have to follow. So that's what I did. I found a movie producer/director in Manhattan who was sending his son out to Hollywood to be broken into the 'business.' He would pay me a hundred dollars to help the son drive out to California. So, I packed up all of Artie's belongings, even his typewriter, and left him only one change of clothes. Everything else got taken to Railway Express that afternoon. Our friend Melvin Sekolsky helped me pack the stuff. When Artie came home that evening, he thought he had been burglarized. We were laughed and told him what we had done. Artie was furious, but he really had no choice but to go with me. I knew he would love Santa Monica. We left the next morning for California.

When we got to Santa Monica, Artie moved in with Zebo Kazewski. I needed to leave for Vegas and my job at the Riviera, and wanted Artie to come with me and check it out but he wanted to spend some time in Santa Monica first, and of course he came to love it very quickly, the beach and the life there. So I stayed, but after a few days, when I told him I had to return to Vegas or lose my job, he agreed to come with me. However, he also told me that he had put in his application to work at the post office.

Artie had never had to work a steady job, but he had worked there part-time in the past and thought it would be a good career. He had a few weeks to wait for an interview, so he came along. Meanwhile, Artie's friend, Larry Evans, a master chess player, was living in Santa Monica and also wanted Artie to move to California. Larry had an old Ford that he didn't want to make payments on anymore, so he told us to take it to Vegas and to leave it at a Ford dealer when we were done with it, to just walk away. So, that's what we did. After I returned to work at the Riviera, I was able to buy another car. I got a job for Artie, breaking in as a 21 dealer. He worked for about 2 weeks and didn't like the job very much, even though it was easy work and he had the perfect personality for it. When he met a girl who wanted to go to Santa Monica, Artie agreed to go with her.

Artie returned to Santa Monica and went to work for the post office. He also got involved with photography, which he had always enjoyed. He started taking pictures of bodybuilders, and developed quite a reputation in the bodybuilding world. He had a good body himself, knew all the guys, and so was the one everybody wanted to have take their pictures. I would visit Artie often and wanted to help him set up a photography shop. He had taken photography courses at UCLA, one class more than once because he enjoyed it so much, and it seemed natural that he would make a career out of it. He said he wanted to stay with the post office and to keep the photography on the side, so that's how we left it. He got a little two-bedroom apartment near Wilshire Boulevard and Sixth Street for $90 per month, and he was happy.

CHAPTER 18

Starting the D'Amore Act

I was back in Vegas once again, dealing craps at the Riviera and getting down to Santa Monica whenever possible. When Steve Reeves, who was training for the Mr. Universe contest, wanted me to train with him in York PA, I hesitated, but he talked me into it, and I quit my job at the Riviera. Steve and I worked out together for about six weeks, and in that time I learned a lot. He had a different approach to body building. He had a very precise method and knew his body very well. In those six weeks he went from 175 pounds to 220 pounds of solid muscle. Even the famous John Grimick, the only man ever to win the AAU Mr. America title more than once, was impressed. Using his method and mine together, it was just incredible, what both of us accomplished. One day I posed for Grimick. He took some pictures, and then he told me, 'Dominick, you have the greatest torso in the world.'

I was shocked at that comment, even more so when Steve agreed. Grimick added, 'Just don't get any bigger. Your proportions are perfect now.' I weighed about 200 pounds then. I had a 30-inch waist and Steve had once told me that I would never get it smaller, but he also had told me that I could make my chest bigger. Now I had a 52-inch chest, and I realized that I had achieved the perfect proportions.

Reeves went off to the Mr. Universe contest, and he won it. I went back to Muscle Beach and working out. My friend Ritchie Dubois was really

acting crazy at that time. He had a 'star' contract with one of the studios. They sent you to acting school and gave you a stipend to live on. Ritchie was a carefree guy, kind of impetuous, always jumping from one thing to another. One time a director came from Italy, looking for Ritchie. He wanted him to do the Hercules movies. When this director came down to the beach to find Ritchie, the guys told him to talk to me, that I would know where he was. I told him that I was Ritchie's agent, and when I found out that the contract included over $100,000 for the first movie, with more to follow, I almost fell over. I told the director that I would get Ritchie and that we would meet with him later that evening at his hotel.

I quickly found Ritchie and described this incredible opportunity to him, but he refused to even consider it. He said that he wanted to have nothing to do with the movie industry. He said he was finished with it all. I thought he was crazy, just on another 'kick' that would change again in another few weeks. I tried to point out that after a few movies he would have enough money to do anything he wanted to do, but he announced that he had decided to become an evangelical preacher, and that was that. Shocked, I pointed out that he knew nothing about God, nothing about preaching, and had no answers for any spiritual questions. Ritchie said that he had met a man who promised to train him for the ministry. I begged Ritchie to do this for me, if for no other reason, but he was steadfast. So I phoned the Italian director and told him of Ritchie's refusal. I then suggested that the guy he really wanted was a bodybuilder named Steve Reeves. I let it go at that, not knowing that one day Steve Reeves would become famous as Hercules.

Disgusted with the whole Ritchie business, I returned to Vegas once again and went to work at the Silver Slipper where I had a good friend who was the casino manager. Overall, I was fed up with Muscle Beach and even with Vegas. It seemed like this might be a good time to get more involved with show business. It was time to get the act together, to train a partner, to get going again. So I called Franklin D'Amore and told him that I was ready to do the act. He said fine, that I should get a partner and come back to Santa Monica where he would train us. The act would be called The D'Amores.

I was looking for a partner who had some acrobatic skill, maybe one of the showgirls in Vegas. The first girl I trained was a showgirl named Mary

who was ideal. But after about three weeks of training she announced that she was pregnant. So I had to find another, and it was hard to find the right girl, someone I knew and trusted.

By this time several members of my family had moved out to Vegas from New York. My half-brother Frank had two older daughters, Lucy and Teri. Lucy would have been perfect as a partner, as growing up she had loved to practice acrobatics around the pool, but unfortunately she had gotten married and already had children. Teri was up in St. George, Utah, supposedly going to college, but when I called her, it turned out that her father had just cut her off and she had no place to go. She was alone and afraid. I asked her if she wanted to come with me to California and learn the act, and she jumped at the chance. So I picked up Teri and brought her back to Vegas where I could work swing shift for a few more weeks at the Silver Slipper. During the day I started training Teri, teaching her some acrobatic moves and getting her in shape for the serious work to come in California.

As it turned out, we would be going to Santa Monica with my on-again-off-again girlfriend, Beverley. I had tried to leave her several times, but when I did she became so distraught that I would feel sorry for her and stay. In the end, we packed up the apartment, loaded all our belongings in a trailer and headed for Santa Monica once again.

Back in Santa Monica we got an apartment, and Beverley went to work at Douglas Aircraft. The rest of my life centered on Franklin D'Amore, who was quite a guy. First of all, he had opened California's first pizza restaurant, Casa D'Amore, in 1939. Now in his mid-sixties he had been working in vaudeville all his life as well as running the restaurant. In fact, my mother was then working for him, taking care of his two children. There was room at Franklin's house for my niece Teri to live and space for us to rehearse next door in a retail space that Franklin owned. There had been a fire in that area where we planned to rehearse, but I was able to clean it up and put down some big mats, so that Teri could take falls without injury.

It turned out to be six months of training. Teri was not the easiest of students. Once she got it, she got it, but it took time. She learned a lot of acrobatic work and trained hard for three or four hours a day. She mastered it all except for the part where she had to come over the chair. She just

couldn't get it. Franklin didn't think she would ever get it, which just made me more determined to succeed. I made all her costumes by hand to save money, the music was set, publicity photos were taken, and everything ready except for this one move.

We started out as two hobos, and I drunkenly staggered out onto the stage with her in a sack. I would drop the sack and kick and tumble it all over the floor, laughing and carrying on. Then I would take the sack and shake her out. She kept herself rolled in a ball, and I would do all kinds of tricks with her, back rolls and dropdowns, twisting her around until she was on my shoulders and then standing on my head. At that point we would drop the hobo clothes, and she would emerge as a lovely young lady in a skimpy outfit. I would then sit down and do a full pivot with her on my head. This part of the act was mastered within a few months.

The next part of the act involved the use of a Roman chair, made out of wood, about 60 pounds and painted gold. It was a straight-backed chair with iron supports projecting from the base of the back legs, so that if you put pressure on it, it wouldn't tip over backwards. I would bring this chair out after the applause for the opening. She would join me, face me and step into my hands. I would pitch her into the air, spin her around and then catch her by her feet, one in each hand. Then I would go to the front of the chair, step onto it, hook my feet under a strap on the seat and then slowly go over the back of the chair. I would go all the way down and then lower Teri to the ground with a stiff-arm pullover. At that point the act would stop for more applause.

After a few lines of dialogue I would bring her back over this chair by going back over the chair by myself and straightening my arms out on the floor. Teri would step into my hands, and I would slowly do a pullover and bring her back over the chair. It was quite a feat of strength for me, but all she had to do was stand still. The problem was that during training, every time I tried to bring her back over the chair, she would turn to the left and grab the wall in fear. This went on for months, fifteen to twenty times a day. Every time she would do the same thing. The blackened wall of our rehearsal room was covered with her hand and finger marks. Finally one day I couldn't take it any longer. I moved the chair over by the plate-glass window in the front of the store. Now, if she went to the left, she would go right through the window. I told her once more to stiffen up and look

straight ahead. There was a nail in front of her, and I told her to concentrate on that nail and nothing else. Teri cried and carried on and said that she couldn't do it, but I told her to be like a two-by-four piece of wood. She stepped into my hands, looked forward without moving, and we did it perfectly. We finally had the act ready. We showed Franklin the act, and he congratulated us on finally getting it done.

We were ready to get some experience, so it was lucky for us that at the time it was easy to get booked at benefit shows like the Actors' Guild, where Franklin got us a gig. For free, of course. When we got to the show the room was filled with actresses, actors and other celebrities, maybe three or four hundred people in the audience. We did the act and it was absolutely perfect.

There was a knock on the dressing room door after that first performance and to our surprise it was Cary Grant, coming backstage to congratulate us. He had been in show business with Franklin in the old vaudeville days when he had done a 'blackout act', with white-painted faces and hands in front of a black curtain. He reminisced about the old days and how he had been in shows with Franklin, who he thought was my father. Cary Grant was only one of many stars who came back to congratulate us that evening, showing their appreciation for the quality of our act and for the fact that we were doing it for free.

After that, we did the act for eight or nine other benefits, including the Shriners. Then I felt we were ready to try for a paid booking. We got it with the famous black basketball team, the Harlem Globetrotters, a contract that Teri loved. They were a great bunch of guys. We got a three-month contract traveling throughout the western half of the States. Interestingly, there was another Globetrotter team that traveled throughout the eastern half of the States. We would do our show during the half times of the basketball games. We traveled with the team by bus, accompanied by a competing white team. We performed in auditoriums, schools and basketball arenas all over the West. There were five acts in the half-time show, and we were the finale, the star act.

The guys were a lot of fun, always singing and dancing and playing around. We would stay in a different hotel each night, and for the first time I saw how prejudiced people were in many of the small Western towns. We would have to stay in separate hotels from the team because of their

color, which we found very upsetting. It seemed like this was just a lot of unnecessary trouble and annoyance, but in those days everyone accepted it as the norm.

After the three months' contract was up they wanted to sign us up for another three months, but we decided not to. We were only making about $350 per week, which that had been okay as long as room and board was included. This time it wasn't, we were to pay our own expenses, so we sadly said good-bye to the Globetrotters and returned to Hollywood to talk things over with Franklin. He advised us to go to Europe where he knew a couple of good agents there, like Evaldi in Italy, who would be able to get us work. The problem was that we would have to get to Europe on our own and then try to get bookings. We needed more money before we could consider that, so I decided that we should go back east and do the borscht circuit of Jewish resorts and hotels up in the Catskill Mountains. The summer season was approaching, and you could get work for three months at the resorts there.

Teri and I drove back to New York and I got an agent who booked us for that summer. We had Mondays and Tuesdays off down in the city, and then we drove up and performed for the rest of the week. We played for different stars, like Sammy Davis Jr. and my old friend, Sophie Tucker. She loved having us open the show for her. We played at the Concord and Grossinger's, hotels that were famous in those days.

One of the performers we opened for was Red Skelton. He was a great guy and one day, when I was with him in his dressing room, I shared with him a problem I had: I would get overly nervous before going on stage at each performance. Red laughed and said that he had been in show business for twenty plus years and that he still got nervous before each performance. I thought he was kidding, but he said not to worry about a few butterflies in your stomach. Once you hit the stage, everything would be fine. I felt better about it then: that if a great star could get nervous and keep going, so could I. And actually, from then on, I didn't get nervous anymore. He gave me more confidence somehow, and I remember going on stage that night and not worrying about a thing.

While we were playing in the borscht belt that summer, we spent our days off in New York City and Phyllis contacted me. She was the beautiful girl who had dated my friend Artie many years before. She and

I got together, and I found that I loved her very much. I spent most of the summer with this incredible woman, who was a schoolteacher. She would come up to the Catskills and stay with us. Room and board was free, and it was a great place to be.

About six weeks into the season, things were going along well and I had already made arrangements to go to Europe with the act at the end of the Catskills season. However, on one of our days off in New York, Teri went to Long Island to visit friends and family in the town where she had lived before moving to Vegas. She met up with her old boyfriend John there and found out that he was now dating her once best friend. Teri was terribly jealous, and she decided that she was going to get him back. They started dating again that summer, and I began to realize that they were getting serious. In the meantime I was spending all my spare time with Phyllis, who was free from teaching for the summer.

Then one day I got a phone call from Teri, telling me that she had been in a car accident and was in the hospital. When I arrived at the hospital, there was Teri in bed with a neck brace on. I was concerned for her but also for all the contracts I had lined up for the next five weeks or so. Then Teri totally shocked me when she said she was going to quit the act. She announced that she and John were going to marry. I pointed out how hard we had worked to reach this point, that we were just about ready to go to Europe and have a fantastic time with the act. I asked her if she was really in love with John or whether it was just her ego, beating out her old girlfriend for his love. But Teri was adamant and wouldn't be talked out of the marriage. I wished her well, but I was really disappointed.

It was too late to get another partner, so I had to cancel the rest of our bookings. Our agent suggested trying to find a replacement at one of the dance studios in the area. So Phyllis and I went from one to another, looking for a replacement. One girl was taking acrobatic courses and seemed very good, but she reminded me of my sister, and I just couldn't imagine doing the act with her.

So I spent the rest of the summer in New York with Phyllis. I was in love with her, and we had a wonderful time together. In the fall Phyllis had to return to work and I needed to get another partner. I couldn't find one in the area and knew that it would take a lot of training time after that, so I decided that I had to go back to California. I told Phyllis that I was

leaving. She was heartbroken, and I suggested that we get married. She looked at me and said that there was no one she would rather be with for the rest of her life, but that she couldn't marry me, that she had to marry a professional, a doctor or a lawyer. I couldn't believe that she meant it, but she said that was the way it had to be, no matter how much we loved each other. I told her that she was incredibly programmed, and she just looked at me. She had been taught this from childhood. Where was the place for love? She told me that love would come afterward. She took me to the airport and we said our good-byes. She cried and begged me to stay, but I pointed out that sooner or later she would find a doctor or a lawyer, and it would have to end. I had to leave, and so I flew back to California and returned to Hollywood, Franklin and the restaurant.

Although Phyllis and I parted ways, I will be forever grateful for the very special gift she gave to me. As a child I had received very little schooling and as a result, I read and wrote English with great difficulty. That summer Phyllis spent hours teaching me the basics of reading and writing, which, of course, would change my life.

Now that I was back in California I had gotten back with my old girlfriend Beverley, who was still working at Douglas Aircraft. She had been in regular contact with me through letters and phone calls while I was doing the act back east. Now she hung around the restaurant all the time. I couldn't figure out how to be done with her. I tried to end the relationship many times, and even Franklin was getting a bit annoyed by the situation, but there didn't seem to be anything I could do that worked. At one point I told her she needed therapy, and she agreed to go to a psychiatrist. I took her to a few counselors, but nothing seemed to help. She always made me feel guilty that I had taken her virginity, that I had taken the best years of her life. At one point I talked by phone about this with Phyllis, and she recommended a famous psychiatrist, so I made an appointment. I remember that he charged $50 per hour, and I asked him to give us only half an hour for $25. I brought Beverley, and he interviewed each of us for about 15 minutes each. At the end of the session he took me aside and suggested that I return for a few sessions because I had the biggest guilt complex he had ever seen. The moment he said that, I realized that I had mistaken guilt for love and I was cured on the spot. From then on it was totally finished. I had no desire or reason to see this woman anymore. I

told her that it was time for her to leave Hollywood and return to Santa Monica, that it was time for her to get on with her life, that I wanted nothing more to do with her. I got more and more agitated and with a wave of anger, I pounded on the table with my fist where we sat and cracked it in half. I told Beverley that I was going to find a woman and fall in love with her so deeply that I would never even think of Beverley again. That was the end of it, and I never saw her again.

I was still trying to find a partner for the act, and I found another girl, Karen, who was a fast learner. Franklin had gotten us a booking with the Steve Allen Show, a very popular TV show at the time. It was to be a live show, not taped, so everything had to go perfectly. Not only that, but Steve wanted the show to be spontaneous, so there was no rehearsal time at the TV studio. Karen had learned most of the act quite quickly, but there was still one trick that she would miss, not every time but occasionally. I was worried about her not being dependable. Franklin could see that she wasn't turning completely with the pitch when I threw her up and around, but he couldn't figure out how to fix the problem. Then Franklin suggested that we get her hypnotized. He had a friend that was performing nightly at Ciro's on Sunset Strip as a hypnotist and suggested that we go to the show and have her hypnotized there.

We went to the nightclub, were seated at our table and ordered cocktails. Meanwhile, Franklin met with his friend backstage and pointed Karen out to him. Once the show had started, the hypnotist called for volunteers to come up on the stage, but Karen refused to go. The 10 people on stage were divided into two groups, and at the same time, the performer suggested that people in the audience might be hypnotized as well. He assured them that nothing bad would happen, and that everyone in the room would be totally alert by the end of the evening.

He told the first group of volunteers that at the count of five they would go to sleep. As the hypnotist spoke to these people, telling that they were getting sleepy, sure enough their heads started dropping and they fell sound asleep. Out in the audience, others were asleep, and it appeared that Karen was one of them. The second group of volunteers was also put to sleep with a second count of five. Now Karen was definitely sound asleep. The first group of volunteers was told that they all had little clowns dancing on their noses. The second group was told that they could see those clowns

dancing, as could those who were sleeping in the audience. Then they were all awakened. The first group members were cross-eyed, trying to focus on the clowns on their noses, while the rest of the volunteers all laughed at the 'dancing clowns'.

Then the hypnotist looked at Karen and told her that on the count of three she would be in a deep sleep again. He talked to her about the approaching Steve Allen Show, and how she was having trouble with the pitch-to-hand part of the act. He told her that from now on she would do it perfectly, with complete confidence. He left her there asleep and returned his attention to the ten volunteers on stage. He put them all back into a deep sleep and told them that they would wake up normal, happy and lively, with no more nose clowns. The hypnotist almost forgot to wake up Karen, as well as others in the audience. They were all awakened, but Karen was told that she wouldn't see me when she woke up. Sure enough, she woke up, and the first thing she asked was where I had gone. Even when I spoke to her and touched her face, she didn't see me. It was amazing. Finally, the hypnotist put her to sleep one last time, and when she woke up, I was back, and everything was back to normal.

I was curious to see if her performance would be perfect. We went to the studio at about 10AM for the noon broadcasting of the show. It was live during the day and taped for the evening show. She showed absolutely no hesitation about doing the pitch, and did it as if it was nothing. Even Franklin was amazed. The show was fine, and Karen did everything perfectly. I really didn't understand how it worked, how anyone could so completely surrender her mind to the power of suggestion, but I saw it happen and had to believe that it was possible.

Karen and I took off onto the road again and were booked into the Orange County trade shows, doing a show at a different venue every night. Karen was a pretty girl and did a good job, but she dreamed of being a famous singer. She practiced all the time, and when I asked about her commitment to the act, she admitted that she considered it only temporary work. I wasn't willing to work with someone who wasn't dedicated to the act, so I fired her.

After completing the trade show contracts, I returned to Hollywood once again and started to look for another partner. I found a young girl and worked with her for about six weeks, but it wasn't going to work out.

I already had a booking for Bimbo's in San Francisco. Bimbo was a good friend and would always book me with a new partner when I needed it. There were a few acrobatic girls on the beach. One of them was Marianne, who was married to a friend of mine, Serge. I asked her to do the act with me for two weeks. I knew I could train her quickly, as she was great at acrobatics and adagio. She agreed, we trained in our little rehearsal room and had the act ready in two days. She was magnificent, and the costumes fit her, so we were all set and went up to San Francisco the following Friday and opened up on Saturday night.

CHAPTER 19

Meeting Elaine

The first night with Marianne at Bimbo's in San Francisco was a great success. Bimbo, a great guy and a sharp dresser who always wore spats, didn't think the act was perfect yet, but it definitely was very good. He felt that there was something missing, but he wasn't quite sure what it was. I'd had the same thought, but I didn't have the answer, either. Anyway, it went well.

The second evening I was dressed in my hobo outfit backstage, waiting for the ballet act to go off before we went on. I was tying Marianne into the hobo sack when I saw a stunningly beautiful young lady coming up the stairs. 'Hi,' she said, looking at me, 'my name is Elaine.' I introduced myself as Franklin, the name I used for the act, and she replied, 'No, you're not a Franklin.' I told her my real name and she said 'That's more like it. I like that name.' She said that she had seen the act the night before and liked it. I thanked her and invited her for a drink after the show. She said maybe and went on.

We did an 8:00 and 11:00 pm show at Bimbo's, so between shows that night I met up with Elaine outside our dressing room and we went out to the lobby for a drink before the second show. Talking with her that evening I felt as if I had known her all my life. She was very tall, 5'10" in stocking feet, 6'1" in her spike heels, and she weighed 140 pounds. I felt like a midget next to her, but she didn't seem to mind. For some reason

we started talking about religion. She had been raised a Baptist, but when I asked her what she knew about John the Baptist, she couldn't answer. She said that she was a Baptist because she loved her grandmother who was a Baptist. She said she didn't go to church but believed in the Baptist faith. I started talking about spirituality, yoga, and meditation because I was growing and exploring, even experiencing— and rejecting — other yoga masters who, unlike Yogananda, were fakes and only in it for money.

After the second show that evening I asked Elaine out on a date for the following night, but she declined. When I saw Elaine again the next night I realized that she was as attracted to me as I was to her. So, after I watched the ballet act that she was in, I asked her a second time to go out with me after the show. Again she turned me down. The third night I said, 'Elaine, I'm asking you out for a third time, and I don't ask a fourth time. If you go with me, great, but if you don't, that's it.' She looked at me and then said, 'All right, I'll go out with you.'

I dropped Marianne off at the hotel after the second show that night, and then Elaine and I went out for a drink and a bite to eat. We had a good time and got talking about spirituality again. I talked about meditation and contemplation, and she took it in like a sponge. Everything I said she just soaked up. I told her that yoga techniques work, and I taught her a few breathing exercises, which she seemed excited about learning.

After a passionate evening together, I dropped her off at her hotel and went back to mine. But only a few hours later I heard knocking on the door. It was Elaine. She said that she wasn't letting me go and had arrived with her bag in hand. She announced that she was going to stay with me. Of course I agreed. We both knew that there was something special happening — that we were soul mates. For the rest of the contract at Bimbo's, Elaine and I were together every night.

One day, towards the end of the last week, she told me that she had to tell me something: she had children, three boys, six, four and almost one year old. I was amazed — perhaps shocked is a better word. I had always preached that whatever you do, don't get involved with a married woman or a woman who has children. I had seen fighting and arguing between husbands and wives throughout my childhood, even after they had children, and I swore it would never happen to me. The next day she took me to her babysitter's, and we picked up the three boys: Dana, the

blue eyed baby with curly blond hair; four year old Donald with straight hair; and David, the oldest, who was both bright *and* handsome. I took them all to breakfast and then went to the beach, where we spent the afternoon. Dana kept calling me Daddy. Elaine said he had never before called anyone Daddy. I was kind of in shock; 'I don't know …. Three children …'

She said, 'So, what's three children?' I said that it was a lot, but she pointed out that they were a package deal. I had to laugh, but really, I was so attracted to Elaine that the problem of having children didn't seem very important at the time.

With my show contract completed, I got ready to leave. We said our good-byes and promised to keep in touch. By the time I got back to Los Angeles I was already missing her. We called each other every day and every night; it seemed like we were on the phone all the time. I told Franklin about Elaine. When I told him how tall she was his response was that she was too big to do the act with me. I said that I still wanted to continue with it. The upshot was that I needed Marianne, so I talked it over with her and asked her to come to the Catskills. She was willing, but we had to talk it over with her husband Serge. As it turned out, he wasn't crazy about the idea, but he could see that Marianne really wanted to do it. So he agreed to stay home with their children while Marianne came with me for the season. In hopes of giving him some peace of mind I told him that we would stay at my sister's apartment on Orchard St. on the lower east side of Manhattan when we weren't doing the show.

I called Elaine and told her I was going to New York for the summer. She told me that the ballet show was ending at Bimbo's, and that she wanted to come to New York too. She said that we had to be together. I couldn't see how it would work out but agreed anyway and told her to come. My sister had 7 kids; what could 3 more matter? I pictured all 13 of us in the little apartment, and had to laugh: there was a kitchen and two bedrooms that you walked through to get to the living room in the back. I knew that my sister wouldn't care; she liked having me around and loved kids.

Serge gave us an old Buick, and Marianne and I drove to New York. My agent was only able to book us into the Catskills for about two weeks because we had started planning late and most of the hotels were already

booked. A week later, I picked up Elaine and the kids at the airport and took them to my sister's apartment. It was a total menagerie with ten kids running around. Elaine's kids were very well disciplined, except for Dana, who seemed to run wild all the time. Everyone had to keep an eye on him.

Elaine and I went up to the Catskills during our work week, leaving the kids with my sister, and then returned to the city on the weekend. In the meantime, unfortunately, Serge was going crazy back in California. He was calling Marianne all the time, trying to track down where she was. Marianne didn't know what to do about it, but Serge was really upset, saying he was going to fly to New York. We had just completed the second week of work, and everything seemed to be going well, when Serge arrived. He insisted that Marianne come home with him. I tried to change his mind — that I had a whole summer full of work — but he was adamant. So they took the Buick that he had lent us and drove back west.

Now I needed to break in someone fast. Luckily my sister's friend Elba — a pretty girl about 5'1" and 108 pounds — was available. So I started rehearsing with her on the roof of the apartment building for hours at a time. All the neighborhood kids would be up on the roofs watching us. We got the act together really quickly, but we had one problem. When Elba was up on my head, we would always drift to the left. I couldn't get her to correct a twisting motion that she would do with her left ankle, which caused me to compensate and move in the same direction. We would drift left by 20 feet or so each time she was on my head.

We got a 3-night booking that next week and went up to Grossinger's. We were opening for Sammy Davis Jr. He gave an incredible performance on stage for two hours and then would go to the lounge and entertain for another two hours for free. We talked a lot, and I asked him how he could work so hard for so many hours, believing that his body wouldn't be able to take it. He said he loved it and just couldn't slow down. He had a small body and he needed to take care of it, but he would just laugh at me. Elaine and I loved hanging out with him after work and always had a great time.

Elaine and I were having a ball, totally happy and compatible together. We continued to have frequent spiritual conversations, which amazed me. We agreed that we must have been together in a past life somewhere. Elaine was 25 at this time and I was going on 30; we had been living together for about four weeks now. Nothing seemed to faze us.

Meanwhile, working with Elba was really difficult. I had to start on the right side of the stage, to compensate for the movement towards the left. I couldn't get another partner, but I also couldn't get any more bookings, as the hotels were all set for their summer season.

The end of summer was approaching and there I was with Elaine and the three kids, living in my sister's apartment and not really knowing what to do. Money was going fast, so I was trying to figure out another act that I could do with Elaine. She was a good dancer, so I created a scenario where I was a statue, painted gold, up on a pedestal, and she would dance around it and bring it to life. My old friend, Melvin Sekolsky, was a famous fashion photographer by that time, and had a great studio. I had Melvin take a series of pictures of me and Elaine, with me painted gold and her dressed in a skimpy gown, doing this dance routine. We even did a few advertising jobs with him, to make a little money. I remember his secretary was a young, beautiful woman named Ali MacGraw, who would later become a famous Hollywood actress. She was his girl Friday. She ran the studio, booked the models, coordinated the contracts, everything. She would fit us in between the paying appointments, so that Elaine and I could get our portfolio together. It was a fun environment at the studio. Ali always managed to find us some work, and Melvin loved to cook big feasts for all of us in the evenings. Melvin used 3 floors of the six-story building he owned for photo shoots and would use the others to build sets for various advertisements.

We thought our new act was okay. It ran about seven minutes, which was pretty routine for novelty acts in those days. We worked a couple of nightclubs, and it was all right, but we knew that act wasn't fantastic. I was never really comfortable with it.

At the same time I was still involved in the tramp act with Elba. And that was the one that Joe Weider was interested in. He was putting on the East Coast Mr. America contest and contacted me to enter the contest and to do the act with Elba. I said I would do the act for $500, which made Joe crazy, but he had already started advertising us at the contest, so he had to pay me. I also told him that he could take 25 pictures and no more. It turned out to be a good time for me. I won the contest in my class. Joe got his pictures and then asked me to write five articles, one on each body part. I said he would have to pay for it, and again he argued

with me because he didn't like to pay anyone. He felt that the publicity he gave the bodybuilders in his magazines was good enough, but I told him that I had to make a living. He finally agreed to give me $100 per article, which was a steal for him. I wrote the articles and delivered them over at Joe's warehouse in Jersey. He wanted me to continue writing for his magazines, but I was done and wanted my money. He told me to make up stuff, anything, just keep the articles coming. I declined and he eventually paid me. Occasionally he would take me Elaine and me out for dinner, which was always nice, but Joe was a little too frugal for me.

I was finding it more and more difficult to do the act with Elba, so I had to end it. I wasn't making much, but the apartment was just too crowded, so Elaine and I and the kids moved into a little apartment on 79th St. that we rented for $25 per week. It had one bedroom, a living room and a kitchen. We were there two weeks when the building got condemned, and everyone was forced to move. I kept trying to find work, and even asked Joe Weider to back me in a couple of things, but he wouldn't do it. So I told Elaine that we would have to go back to Vegas where both of us would easily be able to find work.

I tried to get a booking at Latin Quarters where my good friend Karl Karsoni was playing, but they were booked solid for a year ahead. Karl tried to get me in, but the owner, a guy named Lowes, couldn't afford to add us. He was already over budget and losing over $100,000 a year. He was wealthy from other businesses and kept Latin Quarters open kind of as a hobby. However, he was interested in opening up a casino in Monte Carlo, and we talked it over many times. I thought it would be a great idea to bring American craps there and said I would be glad to work for him, if the opportunity ever came up. Anyway, Karl loaned us a few hundred dollars, and we found an ad in the newspaper to drive a car west. It was an old, beat-up taxicab that the owner wanted delivered to Salt Lake City, Utah. It was blue, yellow and red, and the first time I saw it, I really didn't think it would survive the trip. The owner said it would, and jokingly, told us not to pick up any fares along the way. He promised that our gas costs would be paid once we reached Salt Lake. (The gas bill for that trip cross country was $60.)

We loaded the car with the three kids and our belongings, and stocked up on peanut butter and jelly. We ate a lot of PB and J sandwiches on that

trip. The car survived, and by the time we got to Vegas I had maybe $30 left. I went straight away to my bank, where I had kept an account for years. I asked for $1000, and it was given to me on the spot. This was about 1963 and Las Vegas was going through a financial slump. Real estate had really fallen, so I was able to find a nice, two-bedroom apartment for only $90 per month. I even thought that maybe this was the beginning of the end for Las Vegas. But anyway, I got Elaine and the kids settled, and then I had to continue north with the taxicab, to deliver it to SLC.

Once back in Vegas, I was lucky to have a friend named Al Holden who was a boss at the California Club downtown. I went to see him and told him that I needed a job, and he hired me to work on the graveyard shift, starting right away. It turned out to be a good job. In the meantime Elaine got a job with the Bluebell Girls in the Lido show at the Stardust Hotel and Casino. Money started coming in again. It was the old Vegas story. You could arrive in town totally busted, but just a few months later you would have a new car, apartment, even a new house if you were willing to work hard.

My sister, Fernanda, had become fed up trying to make ends meet in New York City and announced that she was coming out to Vegas. I thought it was crazy to travel with seven kids, but she was determined, and I promised to have everything set up for her. She took a train west with the kids and their belongings. At the same time my mother decided to join us, as she was tired of working for Franklin in Hollywood. We got them all settled in the apartment next to ours. There were the ten kids and four adults, including my mother. Then one of the kids broke a window, and we all got evicted. So we found another apartment complex and rented two neighboring apartments. Fernanda got a job working as a maid at a hotel, and my mother helped to take care of all the kids, the oldest of whom was maybe 12 at the time. So there we were in Vegas.

CHAPTER 20

Doing the Act With the Twins

In Vegas I was now working with Al Holden, and his wife had twin sisters, Eileen and Irene. He suggested that it would be an interesting idea if I figured out a way to do my act with the twins, who were five foot one and cute, with blond hair and blue eyes. The twins were both cocktail waitresses at the time and were delighted with the idea of going into show business. We started rehearsing during the day, when we were all off work, and I got the idea of bringing them both over the Roman chair, one sitting on top of the other. I figured that would make the act really incredible. We rehearsed upstairs at the old Silver Slipper Casino in a big banquet room with a good stage. Rehearsals went along fine, and anyway, there was no real hurry, as both Elaine and I were working.

We always had a good time; the girls were a lot of fun. Things were going smoothly, but I was continually trying to get them lined up correctly — on top of one another — so that I could bring them over the chair. I must have tried 500 times, but I just couldn't do it. Then I remembered my friend, Karl Karsoni, and how he had worked with his twin brothers on stage, creating an amazing illusion of impossible stage entrances and exits.

So, we started a routine with the twins, where one would run off the stage in one direction only to suddenly seem to appear from the other side of the stage. It was a funny routine and I would work first with one of the girls and then the other, and then I would get bewildered at who was

where. At the end of the act I would finally 'realize' that there were two girls, not one, and I would introduce them as my twin sisters. Of course, I would get their names mixed up. It always got a big laugh.

We played several clubs in Vegas, plus the Flamingo Hotel, where my act had always been popular. We played Bimbo's in San Francisco a few times, coming and going as needed. It was a cute act, and we all had a lot of fun doing it, but at the end of the day, we just couldn't make enough money splitting the $750 that we got at the Flamingo three ways. We needed double that, especially since the twins were used to making good money as cocktail waitresses. They also liked to spend their money, too, and were always in the beauty parlor or out clothes shopping.

My friend Franklin came to Vegas to see the act, which he was pleased with, and to meet Elaine. We went to see her show that night, and I asked him to pick her out. He picked the one he thought was the most beautiful, and. of course, it was Elaine. She joined us at our table after the show. Franklin looked at her and told us that with my strength there was no reason why I couldn't do the act with Elaine. I said that she was too tall, that I wouldn't be able to do all the tricks with her, but Franklin persisted, and Elaine agreed with him that there had to be some way we could do the act together. The beginning of the act would have to be changed, but the pitch, the foot to head, the wardrobe change and going over the chair wouldn't be a problem for either of us. And so Elaine and I started re-working the act together. We got the end of it down, and it was really very impressive, because Elaine was so tall. She had a beautiful figure and kept her weight at about 140 well-toned pounds, which I helped with by giving her a few exercises — ones she didn't like, but was willing to do.

After about six months of planning and preparation we had everything ready except the beginning of the act. But, as it turned out, Elaine took care of that. We were in the lounge of the Tropicana one night, where she wanted to hear the pianist who was performing. Elaine, in addition to everything else, was an accomplished pianist who had studied with Muriel Adler, a renowned Canadian concert pianist. On this particular night, sitting there at the bar, enjoying the pianist, Elaine suddenly screamed 'That's it! I've got it!' She had come up with the beginning of the act.

She would be on stage performing as a newly arrived concert pianist from Carnegie Hall and I would be a drunk in the audience. I would

ridicule her piano playing, announcing that I was a great rock-and-roll player. She would invite me up on stage to play. I would insult her; she would hit me and then do judo and karate on me. Even though we didn't know anything about judo and karate the basic idea sounded pretty good and made me laugh.

We found a guy who taught judo and karate at the police academy downtown, but also gave private lessons on the side. We met with him one evening and explained what we wanted. We told this big Hawaiian guy, maybe 240-250 pounds and 5'11", about the act and that we needed about ten or eleven different moves and throws that would be showy. He said he could do it and started throwing me around the mat. It was pretty obvious to me that I would need to learn how to fall, and he said he would take care of that too. And so for the next several weeks I got beaten up on a regular basis and was black and blue all over. I learned how to take the falls, and Elaine learned how to throw me around.

When my friend Franklin was next in Vegas we had our new routine completed and he said that this was 'it', 'the best;' that we finally had something exceptional. We took the act to Bimbo's 365 Club in San Francisco for a week as well, where we were the opening act for Tiny Tim. It was a total success and Bimbo said we were a first rate act, which made both Elaine and me happy. However, when I tried to get our act booked into one of the big shows in Vegas — like the Lido at the Stardust or the Folies Bergere at the Tropicana — the booking agents said that they got almost all of their acts from Europe. I asked them, did I have to go work in Europe in order to get a booking in the States, and one producer said he thought so. I asked if we could be hired by the Lido in Europe, but it was obviously a complicated situation.

So, Elaine was still working in the Lido and I was working for Al Sachs at the Stardust, dealing craps. We made more this way than with our act, but we loved working together and being in show business. During this time in our lives we also decided to get married, and I went on to adopt the three boys.

Just as an interesting aside: before I started working with Elaine, I had gotten a booking doing the act with the twins at the Hollywood Palace. Bing Crosby was producing the show and auditioned us; he liked the act very much and signed us. Months later, he called on a Monday and said

that the show would be going on that following Saturday. I told him that I was now doing the act with Elaine, but he wanted the twins, that they had worked the show around them. I agreed, contacted the twins, and we rehearsed for a few days. It was just that one Saturday, starting in the morning and completing with the performance at about 9PM that evening. It was to be a live show, and would be taped as well. It was a great evening, and Bing was very satisfied with the show. It played live that night and would go on to be rebroadcast on television a few other times. But as good as the act was with the twins, that evening was the last time I would do it with them.

CHAPTER 21

Donald's Accident

At this time, we were living in an apartment off of Tropicana Blvd., facing the Tropicana golf course. The road wasn't even paved at that time. And right behind the Trop was a 7-11 store, about a two-block walk from the apartment. The kids could walk there on a little sidewalk, and they like to hang out there. We had 10 kids in those two apartments, and it was hard to keep track of them all. They were all good kids, but you had to keep an eye on them, especially Dana, who was always wandering off. My mother had her hands full, as Fernanda worked days, and Elaine and I would need to sleep until about 10AM after working swing shift.

Elaine's son Donald and my nephew Johnny were pals and were always walking up and down the street. One day when Elaine was at a rehearsal and I was out somewhere else, the two boys were on their back from the 7-11 store when they were hit by a car driven by a young woman who became distracted by her little dog. She looked away and drove off the road and up onto the sidewalk, where she hit Donald and Johnny. Johnny got clipped and was thrown about 20 feet, but Donald got hit dead-on. His thigh bones were fractured, and his liver was totally destroyed. An ambulance took him to the hospital where he was found to be in really bad shape. Both Elaine and I were notified. When we met at the hospital Donald was unconscious and the doctor in charge, Dr. Komack, said they would have to operate to try to find out what abdominal damage there

was. Joining us later after surgery, the doctor told us that he didn't think Donald would survive the night. Elaine and I just sat there with him in the recovery room. They didn't even sew up his abdomen; it was just packed with gauze, holding the liver together. Dr. Komack described the liver as looking like hamburger. The leg fractures weren't set either.

And so we were just sitting there, praying for Donald. Then Elaine suggested that we call Sister Daya at Self-Realization Fellowship. We asked her to pray, and of course, she said they all would. Lo and behold, Donald survived that night, and then the next night, and then the next. After about a week he was still alive and talking with us — with his abdomen still open. The liver was now packed together, so Dr. Komack removed all the gauze and sewed him up. It is a fact and an actual miracle that the liver can actually regenerate itself, and Donald's liver did just that. At this point they also got around to setting Donald's two legs and putting them in casts. For six weeks he would lie in the recovery room like this. His liver began to function, and even Dr. Komack considered it a miracle.

Johnny survived this accident with cuts and bruises. The young girl who was driving never came once to visit Donald in the hospital, but luckily for us she had insurance, so all the expenses were covered. We got a lawyer and had to fight to get compensation. After 90 days we were able to bring Donald home. Once the leg casts were off, he started walking, but he had trouble with one leg, because when it had been set, the toe had been left in a pointing position, so he was walking tiptoe. I had to work on that foot for 6-7 weeks to get that foot properly aligned. Elaine and I were in frequent contact with Self-Realization Fellowship, so grateful for their love and prayers. We were practicing the weekly lessons that they sent and were meditating daily. More and more we were 'tuning in'. We were facing many challenges, but our spiritual growth continued. Donald was bringing us closer to self-realization.

Unfortunately, after about 6 months Donald developed epilepsy. This time we drove down to the medical center at UCLA to find out what was happening because the doctors in Vegas couldn't figure out what the problem was. At UCLA they had the answer in two hours. A small portion of his brain, about the size of a dime, had dried up and was no longer functioning properly. Donald was put on a prescription of dilantin, which helped with the symptoms. Elaine and I were both working at our jobs,

taking care of the kids and rehearsing the new act, so it was a chaotic time for us while we were trying to do the best we could for Donald.

As the weeks and months passed, Donald seemed to be healing well. He gained back the weight he had lost, and at 6 years old, he was just a happy and beautiful boy. Life was getting back to normal.

At about this time, Elaine and I bought a little three-bedroom house with a swimming pool right off the Stardust Golf Course. Even though it was a good buy at only $27,000 I wasn't thrilled because I didn't want to be tied down with a house. I realized, however, that it was a good decision: it was convenient to the Stardust, where we both worked, and we all enjoyed living there. Fernanda got a bigger apartment, which I helped her with. My mother was doing fine, and everything was going well.

Then my sister Fernanda started getting restless. She was always broke, what with seven kids and a low-paying job. Even with me helping financially and my mother babysitting the kids, life wasn't easy for her, so she decided to go back to New York. I said I would always help her, but she said she didn't want to depend on me all the time. She contacted Welfare, and they agreed to help pay the train fares to return the family to New York. So Fernanda left with her children and returned to Manhattan. We got my mother into a little apartment of her own because she didn't want to leave Vegas. She was relieved to be on her own again. She worked as a maid in Vegas, but she loved to travel, and for the summer season she decided to go back and work up in the Catskills at the Browns Hotel, where she made good money.

So, it was just Elaine, the kids and me now. We settled into an easy routine of working nights and then fitting in rehearsals around the kids. We had a young babysitter who would come in when we left for work at about 7:00 pm and then sleep after the boys went to bed. We would book our act whenever possible, improving it with practice. We even got booked as the 'relief act' on the Strip for a while, filling in for acts that were booked for months and years at a time with no break. At the Lido Elaine was a designated 'swing' girl, which meant that she could take over almost any part in the show if one of the other showgirls needed a day off.

Everything was going smoothly, but I was getting jumpy again, wanting to work on the act. I was regularly in contact with Franklin, and we often discussed the merits and problems of taking the act to Europe.

Franklin thought it was a good idea, and called his Italian agent, Evaldi, to see what bookings we could get in advance. Evaldi was unwilling to book the act sight unseen. He wanted to see what he could do before committing to us. Needless to say, I was nervous about packing up the whole family and going to Europe without a job. I asked my friend, Karl Karsoni, about his agents in Europe and he recommended Bernard Hilda in Paris, so I called him and sent photo stills of the act. In those days we didn't have tapes and cassettes — the only way to tape an act was with 16mm film, and it was prohibitively expensive. Bernard said that he would see what he could do, but in the meantime all we could do was wait.

Then one day I received notification from Bernard that he could book us into the Hilton Hotel chain in Europe. I thought this was the time to make the move. This was approaching the end of 1966, and we had been in the house for about a year. Both Elaine and I handed in our notices. Al Sachs wanted me to keep on at the Stardust and said that he had big plans for me, but I didn't want to get involved with any of the mob activity that was going on at the casino — but more than that — I really wanted to give show business a shot.

So, we put the house up for sale and in about eight weeks we sold it for $38,000, giving us a nice profit that we consolidated with the money we got from the sale of most of our belongings. We used some of this money to book us — at $96 an adult — on Icelandic Airways, from Las Vegas to Luxembourg, via New York — where we had a nice visit with my mother, who was staying in a little apartment near my sister in Brooklyn.

It had been 80 degrees when we left Las Vegas, but when we got to Luxembourg, it was 5 degrees below zero. We were freezing, and as soon as we got settled in our little hotel, we bought winter clothes for everyone. We had about $5000 in cash and some savings still in Vegas, so I figured we could survive for at least 3 months without work. If we failed, at least we would have had a nice European vacation.

I called the agent, Bernard Hilda, and asked him when we would start at the Hilton but I heard a slight hesitation in his voice. He said that he couldn't book the act before he saw it. I told him that we would be getting a car and driving to Paris. He could book us somewhere, so that he could see the act. Both Elaine and I tried to be confident, knowing that we had a good act; plus the kids were having a ball. We found a used car dealership,

and picked a four-door Ford Opel with a luggage rack on top. It was about four years old and cost $500. Luckily for us in Luxembourg at that time, the seller was responsible for the vehicle passing all inspections so when we got new tires, a rebuilt suspension system, and more the dealer had to pay. He tried to raise the price after the sale, but a deal was a deal, and we had already paid.

We packed up our 'new' car with our suitcases and clothing, our costumes and the Roman chair and headed for Paris. It was now nearing Christmas, and we wanted to have a nice holiday for the kids. We had a book called 'Europe on $5 per Day', and in it we found inexpensive places to stay and eat. Europe was very inexpensive at that time. We found the Hotel Colisse, just off the Champs-Elysee in Paris and booked two attached rooms for two weeks. We met up with Bernard Hilda, and he booked us into a casino for New Year's Eve. He was really concerned that our act wouldn't be good enough for such an extravagant gala event, but we knew we would be fine.

In the meantime Elaine and I celebrated the Christmas holiday with the kids. We drove around Paris and visited famous places. We were also looking for schools at the same time, but during the winter, Paris is dark and dreary. The schools were enclosed and seemed depressing. It didn't help that no one spoke English. I wasn't too concerned about that, because the boys were already starting to pick up a little French. That first time in Paris, just like the rest of our European adventure, I had them learn how to count in the local language and manage the local currency of each country we visited. Anyway, we decided that we wouldn't leave the boys in school in Paris but instead would take them to England and see if we liked it better as a home base.

It was always easy to find babysitters in Europe. They seemed to just love kids and wanted to be with the boys, to spoil them and play with them. And hotel life itself was wonderful. We would have a late breakfast each morning with the boys. Elaine and I would have coffee with croissants and jam while the boys had cocoa. It was all delicious.

So, on New Year's Eve we drove to the casino, which was a short distance outside of Paris. The casino was packed with people, and as we prepared ourselves, I could see that Elaine was a little nervous. We went through our regular ritual of meditation and breathing exercises together,

which allowed us to settle down. It always amazed and pleased me how easily Elaine slipped into meditation — I think that this was because by this time her spiritual growth was progressing faster than mine was. In addition to our own routines, wherever we went we always made the effort to find someone else who was spiritually evolved who was maybe teaching or giving lectures; we were always looking for the right teacher or master. We didn't find anyone during this time that truly inspired us, but we kept on trying.

On this night the success of our meditation allowed us to open for none other than Maurice Chevalier. The act was a huge success, and Bernard came running backstage to congratulate us and to let us know that he would book us right away.

CHAPTER 22

East Grinstead, England and Scientology

Now that we knew that we would be working, we asked Bernard to give us a week or two off so that we could go to England and get the boys into a boarding school. He already had us booked at the Hilton Istanbul for a one-month contract, to begin in two weeks. We drove to the coast and caught the evening ferry across the English Channel. It was an easy passage of about two and a half hours. The interesting thing was that every other passenger said, 'Don't forget to drive on the left side when you arrive in England.' Of course I thought it would be no problem, and we all made a big joke out of it. Needless to say, when we debarked from the ferry, I automatically went to the right and almost smashed into an oncoming car.

Elaine and I had talked it over and decided that for convenience it would be ideal for us to locate somewhere between London and the ferry landing. As we drove north that evening, it was pitch black, and all the little towns were dark and still. Obviously, folks went to bed early in this part of the world. We finally found an open pub along the highway in a little town called East Grinstead. The bartender recommended a little hotel further down the road, so we went there and got a room for the night.

The next morning we went exploring and found out that this quaint, little town had a Montessori school. Because the boys had been in a Montessori school in Vegas we were interested in learning more about it. We went there and found it to be in a grand, old castle with beautiful

grounds. We spoke with Pamela, the secretary, and learned that they would accept David and Donald. Dana was too young to be enrolled, but there was another school down the lane for young children. Once we got the paperwork done, we inquired about room and board. The two older boys could live at the school. There was a doctor on campus who boarded 8 or 9 kids, and he had space for them. It was fortunate, too, that he was a doctor, as he would be able to keep a close eye on Donald's well-being and medications. So, the boys were moved in, ready to start school the next day.

While we were in the office, Pamela asked us whether or not we had ever heard of Scientology. Elaine and I exchanged glances, because a good friend from Las Vegas, George Vlahos, was very interested in Scientology at that time and had told us quite a bit about it. Another Vegas friend had talked to us about it as well. Now we learned that the main center of Scientology was right there up the hill on about 40 acres that was dominated by a large building called the Castle. Our rule of thumb was that, if we heard about something three times, we would investigate it. As we still had several days before returning to work, we asked Pamela where we could stay. She offered us a room in her home, which worked out perfectly. At this point, both Elaine and I were thinking, 'There's no such thing as a coincidence.' Pamela and her daughter lived only a few minutes away from the school in a lovely little bungalow with three bedrooms upstairs and the living area below.

We had to find a place for Dana to live and were lucky enough to find a wonderful local family that Pamela knew: a couple with a little girl about Dana's age. They had a little house with a little yard in the back, very clean and tidy. The husband was a long distance truck driver, or lorry driver, as they say, and was paid only five pounds per week. A pound at that time was about $2.40. Dana was already playing with the little girl. When I asked how much it would be to board Dana, the wife hesitatingly asked for five pounds per week. When I considered everything she would be doing for Dana, I replied that, if she would really care for him and love him like her own, I would pay her ten pounds per week. Her mouth dropped, and then she said, 'He will be our little Lord Fauntleroy.' We all laughed, and Elaine and I felt good about the agreement.

Once Dana was settled, we went over to the Scientology center. There were several buildings on the grounds, with people coming and going.

We went into the main office, and at the time, they were offering five free introductory courses. We signed up for the courses, toured the grounds, and were given a book to read, 'Dianetics' by L. Ron Hubbard. We were also given a book on ethics, to be studied by all followers of Scientology. It was about 150 pages long and discussed things like how you should treat other people with respect, especially those just starting to investigate Scientology. They were not to be judged or questioned. It said that the book should be carried at all times, so that anyone could be corrected if they strayed from this code of ethics.

The first course was 'A Problem's Release'. Any problems you had would be solved, released. They had another one called the 'Money Release', which guaranteed that you would never again have problems with money.

We started the first course the next morning. You went in individually and sat before an 'auditor'. There was a machine on the table, called an E-meter. It had two cans connected by two wires to a meter with a flow needle that moved between positive and negative charges and a dial to register the strength of the flow. If you were asked a question and had trouble answering it, the needle would stick in one place and stop flowing. If you came to understand the problem underlying your answer and were 'released' from it, the needle would float effortlessly, back and forth once again. If you stayed 'stuck' on a problem, they would keep asking you if you had problems, and as you addressed each one, you would be probing more deeply into the past and even into the subconscious. I found this all very interesting. It could take hours to complete this process. Elaine completed this 'Problem Release' in about 20 minutes and came out feeling very good. I then went through the process and it took about an hour. Theoretically, once you went through this process you actually understood what a problem is.

Another course investigated the power and vibration of words. We were reading 'Dianetics', which explained that spoken words vibrate, and the more you understand a word, the higher it vibrates. If your understanding was low, the vibration would get stuck at that lower level. There were about six or seven of us in this class. If your understanding of a word was cloudy or mistaken, you would have to look it up in the dictionary or go through the process with your 'auditor'. I was amazed at how many words I misunderstood. There were ten words we examined, including 'love',

'God', 'righteousness' and 'principle'. They were all spiritual words. After you said each word you would try to define it.

The word 'God' could vibrate at 200-300, which was pretty high. Some of us hardly registered at all. The word 'love' seemed to stick at about 200-300 as well. I had heard the word 'righteousness' many times, but I couldn't really define it. It was a great lesson to realize that we use words all the time that we really don't know understand. It was also fascinating to see these words vibrating on that meter from 1 to 1000.

Within a week we had completed the first five courses. Now they would no longer be free. The next courses would be: Power Release, Power Plus and then Clear. Beyond that were "Operating Thetan" level courses with 4 or 5 releases at that level. It was a very expensive process. The 'Power Release' cost about 350 British pounds, or about $1000 at that time. We decided to think about it as we were on a tight budget at that time.

We met a lot of nice people there including a big guy named John. He must have weighed 220-230 and was about 6' tall. He was in a wheelchair, paralyzed from the waist down, the result of a minor operation on his back about 6 months previously. He was investigating Scientology as we were and also found it interesting. The three of us talked about Ron Hubbard, his book 'Dianetics' and also about some of the science fiction that Hubbard had written. We also talked with our new friend, Pamela about what we were learning and experiencing. She, too, had taken the introductory courses but could no longer afford to advance. In fact, many people at the center worked there to earn enough money to continue taking courses and also to take advantage of the employee discount.

As far as Elaine and I were concerned, as much as we enjoyed learning at the Scientology center, at the end of the day we believed that anything having to do with God should be free. God never charged us for our very lives; life was given freely, as was knowledge, wisdom and love. Elaine and I would laugh that everyone was trying to get money for the very things that God gave for free. I would close my eyes and remember the words of Yogananda once again, 'If they charge for their teachings, run like crazy.'

I never minded paying for working expenses, like salaries and supplies, but this was a tax- exempt religious organization, and the amount of money they were taking in was huge.

Having made our arrangements, it was time to leave East Grinstead.

We went around to Dana's new home and then to the school to say good-bye to the boys, crossed the Channel, drove to Paris and flew to Istanbul the following day.

The Hilton Istanbul was a beautiful hotel, and we had a suite that was included in our contract. Our balcony overlooked the Bosporus, so we would have our breakfast there every morning, watching boats coming and going; it was magical.

We were scheduled to do two shows, one at 8:00 pm in the showroom and one at midnight in the lounge plus a Sunday matinee. A young Turkish photographer approached us and offered to take photos of the act and to be our guide around Istanbul during our stay; we agreed. We would go to a new place every day and had a fantastic time. He got us into some private museums not normally accessible to tourists. We visited the Topkapi Palace Museum, which is enormous and would take days to see completely. We got to see the water cisterns: big caves down by the waterfront that were developed by the Romans and are still in use today. Sometimes we would take a 'beggar' ship or ferry over to the European side for lunch a two-hour trip each way.

We went into the bazaars, which exist all around the city, selling everything imaginable. One day Elaine said that she would like to buy a samovar as a gift for her sister Beverley. We shopped around, comparing quality and prices. The merchants expected you to deal and would offer tea in an effort to keep you — bargaining — in their shops. You might spend two or three hours wheeling and dealing. We found the set we wanted, ornate brass holders with red, blown-glass glasses, the pot for the coals, upon which the teapot sat, all resting on a beautiful brass tray. Elaine was ready to just pay the asking price, but I assured her that we could do much better than that and also that bartering was expected of us. And so we made our plan. If you were the first customer in the morning, the merchant would do almost anything to get you to buy something. That would ensure good luck for the rest of the day.

So we went to the shop the next morning as it opened and went in. The merchant said he wanted $50 for the samovar. I looked disgusted and started to leave the shop, and the ritual began. He sat us down and ordered tea. Elaine couldn't take it and left, but after about two hours of negotiations, I made my last offer of $25 and started leaving once again.

In desperation he agreed, and I even got him to wrap up the samovar suitable for shipping to the States. With our prize in hand we went to the post office. Behind the counter was a huge mound of packages, and I knew we were in trouble. We spent $50 for postage and then watched the clerk hurl the package up in the air and on to the pile. He said it would go by air, but we knew it would go by slow boat. I told Elaine to just forget about it, and we laughed as we returned to the hotel. (Miraculously, we learned, months later the samovar did arrive in perfect condition.) After that we tried to avoid sending packages and simply bought little items that we could carry with us.

When our six weeks in Istanbul were over, we rushed back to England where Elaine was anxious to visit Dana, sure that he had forgotten her. I pointed out that kids have a very flexible sense of time and space and that Dana probably didn't even know she had been gone. Sure enough, he ran to greet us, yelling out in an English accent that he had picked up from his caregivers. Laughing, Elaine asked if Dana had missed us, and he replied, 'But you were only gone a day.'

Elaine couldn't believe it, but she realized that I had been right. We took Dana with us and went to visit the older boys. We all had dinner together, and then David and Donald went back to their house, while Dana spent the night with us at Pamela's. The next day we walked him to school and met his teachers, who all seemed to love him. They said he was quite a character, always outgoing and asking questions. He was obviously very happy, and we now had a little Cockney boy on our hands while David and Donald were already quite the proper, young English gentlemen.

Since the older boys, David and Donald, were living with a doctor, we decided to ask him what he thought about Donald's condition. He expressed some concerns. It seemed to him that Donald just wasn't quite right. He examined him regularly, watching for signs of relapse and felt that in the near future Donald's prescription strength of Dilantin would have to be increased. As it turned out, East Grinstead had a large, highly respected hospital, renowned for its department of plastic surgery, which had been developed during and after World War II. We all agreed that if there were need for a change in Donald's medication, we would have him thoroughly examined there and then go forward with whatever was necessary.

Through everything, Elaine and I had continued with our Scientology studies as well as asking questions about spirituality and looking for local masters — even including an unsuccessful attempt to find a fellow who would feed people from his big, old cast iron pot that never got empty. This story we could never verify.

As to Scientology, we still weren't ready to commit to spending big money at the Scientology center, but there were a few inexpensive courses that we could take, so we were still spending time there. In addition, our Vegas friend George Vlahos had arrived in England to help open up a casino. He was one of our gambling industry friends who had come to England because they were still interested in Scientology and could take courses at the Center at the same time that they were opening new casinos in London and training dealers and staff for them, as well as introducing slot machines to the English gambling world. George was also interested in going out on one of the study ships that the Scientologists operated.

One day we went looking for our wheelchair-bound friend John and found him in one of the study rooms. The astounding thing was, however, that *he was standing up and walking.* This amazing transformation had happened when he went in for a 'Problem Release' and 'Engram Release' combined. To explain: an engram is a first cause in a chain of actions, the source of the pattern. If a person can get to the engram — the original incident — and understand it, then the entire chain of future problems can be broken. What John finally remembered was being in the hospital, unconscious on the operating table. He had left his body and was hovering above when the doctor entered the operating room and started yelling at the staff, as the patient was lying on his back instead of on his stomach. 'Now we have to turn the SOB over. He is so fat, he doesn't deserve to walk,' he screamed. But when they turned him over, he fell off the gurney, which further enraged the surgeon. He continued, 'This guy is so fat, it's a wonder he can even walk.'

It was total chaos in the operating room, trying to get everything sorted out while the surgeon continued to insult his unconscious patient. John watched all this from above, only returning to his body with a jolt when the anesthesiologist started bringing him back to consciousness. It was later, in the recovery room, that he realized that he couldn't walk. Here, at the Scientology Center, when he became aware of this out-of-body memory

through the 'release', he was able to walk again. He now understood the engram that had been planted in his subconscious: that he was too fat to walk.

Elaine and I were impressed with this first-hand story and discussed it for days, wondering how this could happen and how the mind works. We saw the power of programming, not only from within but by suggestion from outside the body. This was another part of the puzzle, tied with the understanding that the body doesn't think, it reacts. We couldn't really grasp it completely, but we saved the memory, to help solve the puzzle at a later time. Another example of the fact that you may *experience* something profound but don't necessarily immediately *realize* its meaning.

John wasn't the only one who was healed through Scientology. One day I was in a 'release' session, and I had been in there for about eight hours, talking about love and other things. My problem was that the needle on the E-meter stuck every time we talked about my brother Frank. I kept saying that I loved him, and the needle kept sticking. Frank's name kept coming up and I kept saying that I really loved him, and the auditor kept telling me to look at the needle. All of a sudden, I said, 'I hate that SOB more than I hate anybody; I hate being near him or seeing him.'

At that very moment I felt as if something was being pulled out of the back of my neck. It felt as if a load was being taken off of me, and the E-meter needle started floating freely. As soon as the hatred and venom was released I realized that I no longer hated Frank, that I loved him, and the needle continued to float freely. The 'auditor' told me that I had realized the truth of 'admitting a lie', that I had to release the surface hate in order to embrace the underlying love. That was a life-changing lesson.

Elaine and I spent a few weeks in East Grinstead, mostly to spend time with the kids, but our agent Bernard Hilda wanted to get us booked again. He said he could get us a two-week contract in Venice. We got everything in order before our departure, and told Pamela that we would return to her bungalow if the room was available. But not to worry, there were many rooms available in the area, as rich Americans were coming over to study at the Scientology center. They would buy up old mansions with 14-15 rooms and then rent them out to other visitors for about 6 pounds per week.

So we drove down through Italy to Venice and played at a beautiful nightclub there for two weeks. We toured Venice, had a great time and

met a lot of good people. There were pensions for the performers, where you rented a room from a family. The rooms were always inexpensive, sometimes $2-3 per day including meals. It was great that we were saving some money.

After Venice, on our next return to England, we only stayed for five or six days, this time at a place called 'The Digs,' owned by an American, because Pamela's room was occupied. It was an old castle with beautiful grounds. The main dining room had three fireplaces, which were ablaze at night to take the chill out of the air. It was a good place to talk with friends, to discuss spiritual subjects. Elaine and I always had our ethics books on hand at these times, as we found that people were always judging others, criticizing them and offering up their own opinions. When it got out of hand I would point out the page of the book referring to the violation of the ethics code and tell them to read it again.

Around this time Elaine and I found that we were starting to distance ourselves from Scientology because we felt that Spiritual Love — a love beyond human love, a greater love — was missing from this community. This was true even in the Sunday quasi-religious services they had with visiting lecturers. In truth, I found that the courses offered much more than these Sunday services.

In any event, for the next several months we came and went with bookings in Spain and Italy. We loved the travel, met some wonderful people and had many great experiences. Each contract was usually about two weeks long, after which we would return to East Grinstead to be with the kids. We attended lectures and courses as available at the Scientology center. David and Donald joined us and were able to take several entry-level courses for free because of their ages. But these were limited for Donald because he was on medication and Scientologists believe that one can't get true, clear results while using medication, alcohol or any other drug.

During this time Donald seemed to be doing okay, but things were starting to happen. He had an epileptic seizure at one point when we were away, so it was recommended that his Dilantin dosage be increased. Luckily, that seemed to stabilize him once again.

When we were in Switzerland, opening for our good friend Rosemary Clooney at the Tivoli Gardens, we met a young fellow who was selling

his paintings on the sidewalk. There was a small one, about eight inches high and eighteen inches long, a beautiful Chinese scene of a river going between two mountain ranges with an oarsman rowing a boat on the river. Elaine, who was an accomplished artist herself — excelling at portraits — particularly liked this landscape and commented to the artist that it must have taken hours to complete. The young man looked right at her and replied that it had taken him exactly three minutes. That seemed impossible to both of us. We wanted to hear his story, so we first bought the painting for $20 and then had him join us at a nearby coffee shop.

The young man had spent twelve years at a remote Chinese monastery. The first year he lived in total silence, not allowed to speak. The second year he was allowed limited speech and chose what he wanted to learn — in his case painting and also the art of healing. The next few years were spent painting, and he was always asked, 'Do you see what you are painting? Are you one with your painting?' It took months, but one day he realized that he was the painting, and the painting was him. Suddenly he was painting faster and faster, effortlessly. By the end of five years, he could complete a painting in three minutes. When asked what it felt like to move so quickly, he replied that to him it felt like slow motion. I asked him to show us, but he simply said, 'What would be the purpose?' We had to agree that there was no purpose except to actually see that speed.

He had also studied the art of healing and told us about his concepts and shared his experiences, but didn't give us a lesson or a teaching. The techniques he had learned were supposed to be able to heal and he had some success. Although we had to leave to do our 7:00 pm show, we arranged to meet again, and during that two-week period we saw him almost every day. He told us stories about other monasteries that were in the area of China in which he had lived. There was one nearby that was devoted solely to levitation and flying. The first time he witnessed this, he looked outside and saw a monk sitting on top of a tall blade of grass. After a while the monk suddenly took flight and returned to his monastery.

Elaine and I appreciated testimonies like this — coming from the person who had experienced them. Although we preferred to experience these phenomena ourselves, this first hand re-telling was the next best thing. And in this case we kept in touch with the young man and his wife for many years afterwards.

I was able to do some healing of my own. Our lead act in Switzerland, Rosemary Clooney, suffered from frequent migraine headaches and took quantities of aspirin to deal with them. One evening, however, she was out of medication and I offered to give her a shoulder massage. There had been an earlier time in my life when I had done some chiropractic study before deciding that being a chiropractor wasn't for me. I knew a few things about how to manipulate the body. So I gave her a shoulder massage and could feel that several neck vertebrae were out of alignment. As soon as I could get her relaxed, boom, I gave her an adjustment. She opened her eyes in amazement, saying that her headache was gone. She said that she had felt a jolt of energy or something go through her body. I replied that if she did, I had nothing to do with it. I had only given her a neck adjustment. I told her I didn't guarantee anything and didn't want any lawsuits. She laughed and from then on I would often give her massages and adjustments. She joked that she was going to follow me around from one booking to the next, just to have me handy.

After our time in Switzerland, we returned once more to England and were aware that Donald's health was gradually worsening. We were getting concerned about him and thought auditing might help, but officially it wasn't allowed because of the medications he was taking. However, Donald had a friend up at the Scientology center, a woman named Marie, whom he would visit when he went to the center with David. She had agreed to audit Donald a few times, even though he was on so much medication. We no longer wanted to leave him behind, so we discussed it with the doctor at the school, and he agreed that it would be good for all concerned if we had Donald with us.

So we took Donald with us on our next contract, which was in Spain. There, one day while Donald was playing on the beach he had an epileptic seizure. Elaine saw him drop and I ran to him, pulling his face out of the sand. I turned him over, wiped the sand away from his face and then just tried to hold on to him. He was such a precious, beautiful boy, and my heart broke to see him like this. We drove to the nearest hospital, where there was a wonderful doctor who examined him, ran a battery of tests and then asked to keep him under surveillance at the hospital for a few days. They were quite wonderful at the hospital. No one ever asked for payment upfront. They simply gave the care that was needed. A bill might

be sent at a later date, but there was never any pressure about treatments or cost. Usually, it was already paid for by the state, even for tourists. It was that simple. After about five days the doctor changed Donald's entire medication regime, and within two days he seemed back to normal. She recommended that we follow up with his treatment once we were back home.

On our return to East Grinstead it was late at night and pouring rain. We dropped Donald off at his house and put him to bed. We discussed the new medications and treatment with the doctor there, and he agreed to follow Donald closely in the coming days. Because our friend Pamela didn't have her room available for us and the whole town seemed to be full we called a friend who had a room available but that no one wanted to sleep in because, he said, it was haunted. Elaine and I laughed and said we would take it, that we wanted to see a ghost.

It was a nice little room under the eaves with a fireplace on one side and a bed tucked in the corner, underneath a window. We got the coal fire going to take the chill out of the room. Elaine was exhausted and got ready for bed while I sat in front of the fire and meditated for a short while. Totally exhausted I soon got into bed myself. Elaine was on the inside against the wall and I was on the outside. The fire's flames were beautifully dancing colors and the coals glowed red. It was all very cozy. Suddenly, as I turned away from the fireplace and looked towards the doorway, I saw a shape — the vague form of a body that seemed to glow with the colors of the fire. It was like a floating mist that came towards me and then went over me and right out the window. The next thing I knew I was starting to lift out of my body to follow it. At that moment Elaine screamed, 'No, don't go, don't go!' and I was slammed back into my body. 'Are you crazy, following a ghost?' I asked her how she knew I had been following that ghost since she had been sound asleep. She said that she had seen the whole thing. She was adamant that I never do anything like that again. I told her that I had only been curious to know more about the ghost, but she assured me that wasn't a good idea. Needless to say, it was quite an experience.

CHAPTER 23

Our Algerian Contract, and Knee Surgery

One day while we were performing in Paris, in early 1968, Elaine and I went to visit one of our booking agents, Bernard Hilda. While we were there, a young couple came in. They were from Algeria, ran a hotel there and were looking to book entertainers. Elaine and I talked it over and agreed to sign a contract. Three days later we were on our way.

Algeria in the 1968 was a fascinating country but not without its problems. The French had controlled the country for decades and then, after a long war of independence, left without training the Algerians to run the infrastructure, the utilities and such.

When we arrived we noticed immediately that everything looked run down, but, luckily for us, our hotel was magnificent. The show was very good and included a ballet, another act besides ours, and a stripper who performed between that act and ours. Our accommodations were comfortable, and the food was delicious.

As part of our contract, Elaine and I were paid half in English pounds and half in Algerian currency. The Algerian money had no worth outside the country, and we were concerned that once back in England, it would only be good for wallpaper. We had to figure out a way to spend all of it. Even though we enjoyed ourselves, shopping and visiting the local tourist sites, we still had a lot of this currency left over. Then one day I was talking with the ballet master, who was French, and he gave me a great tip. He told

me to go to the British Airways ticket office and spend all our currency on plane tickets, going to France, Italy, England, wherever. Once we got back to England, we would be able to cash them in for English pounds. The plan worked perfectly. Elaine and I took a big bag full of Algerian money to the airline office and proceeded to buy return tickets to Rome, Paris, London, etc. By the time we were through, we had almost $1000 worth of tickets. Sure enough, when we were back in England and went to the airline office in London, they cheerfully refunded all our money in English pounds.

But before we could do that we had to finish our time in Algeria doing the act. One night, when I squatted down with Elaine standing on my head, I felt something pinch in my back. I found that I could hardly catch my breath. I let her down from my head, and as I pitched her up and into my hands, I could hardly move or breathe. I felt her slip down to the floor. Unable to walk, I crawled off the stage. The concierge and Elaine got me back to our room, and once there, the concierge brought me a tube of liniment called Dolpec. He massaged this into my back where the nerve was pinched and the muscles were spasming. The heat of the ointment was quite intense, but eventually it helped the muscles to relax and I was able to breathe deeply once again. They covered my back with a towel, to keep the heat in, and by the next day I was able to move around a little bit. Unfortunately, I was unable to do the show and had to cancel the rest of our contract. A few days later we flew back to England. There I was treated by a chiropractor, who explained which vertebrae were out. After several days and a few more adjustments, I was back to normal. He also suggested that I wear a wrap around my waist for support when performing, which worked out pretty well.

In 1969 Elaine and I were getting ready to head back to Paris, where we had a few bookings. We also had a BBC show that we would be doing about two months later. During rehearsal one day, I suddenly felt a clicking in my right knee when I was squatting with Elaine on my head and also when I took her over the chair. Not long after, when I was going over the chair the knee clicked again and the pain was excruciating. The cartilage in my knee had splintered and was catching on the tendon. There was an elderly chiropractor, a friend of a friend, who lived relatively close to us and agreed to see me. We drove to his home, and I entered with my knee

in a locked position because I couldn't straighten it. The chiropractor was examining it, talking with me, distracting me, when suddenly he twisted and turned my knee, straightening it, while I screamed with pain and literally lifted him up in the air with my leg. Once straightened, the tendon was released, and the pain subsided. He advised heat, keeping it wrapped and not using it for a few days.

I had to call Bernard Hilda and cancel the Paris contracts, but after about four or five days I thought I would be able to exercise my knee a little bit. But during one performance when I was going over the back of the chair, the splintered cartilage caught again. I went back to the chiropractor and got another adjustment, but this time I knew what was coming and he couldn't surprise me again. He adjusted the knee and I was able to control my reaction. He told me that obviously the cartilage wasn't healing and would have to be removed, and he made an appointment for me at the local hospital.

At the hospital I was examined and x-rays were taken, which clearly illustrated the problem: that indeed the cartilage was splintered and was hooking onto the tendon. When I asked when the surgery would be scheduled, the doctor said that it would be at least three weeks before I could be fit in. I explained that I needed to have the surgery done immediately because I was scheduled for that BBC television show. He gave me the name of a surgeon who had his office on Harley Street but, because he was a private physician, he would charge me for the surgery. If I had been able to wait there would have been no charge.

I met with the surgeon, and we scheduled the surgery for the next day even though he was quite sure that I would never be able to do the act again, whether in two months or two years. That next morning I arrived at the hospital at 6:00 am and was ready for surgery by 8:00. It was a very nice Catholic hospital run by nuns who took good care of me. There was even a little place for Elaine to sleep because they encouraged spouses to be together as much as possible.

The surgery took a few hours and once I had gotten out of recovery and was back in my room, a nun arrived with a big iron boot and put it on my foot. Still groggy from the anesthesia, I asked her what she was doing, and she replied that she wanted me to lift up my leg. I wasn't in any shape to do anything, but I promised that I would start with the boot first thing

the next morning. I had a four inch incision and the pain was intense, but by the next morning I was down in the physical therapy room, moving my leg up and down with the iron boot, without bending my knee. It was easy to do, as my thigh wasn't injured, just my knee. The nun increased the weight, and I kept doing repetitions until she decided that I had done enough. I may have been a bit uncooperative that first day, but I thought it was great that the hospital staff believed in getting the patient up and going as quickly as was possible.

My knee was really aching, and I wouldn't be allowed to bend it until the stitches were removed, so I stayed in the hospital for about five or six days, working out with the boot each day. I got up to about 60 lbs., easily doing sets of ten. Even the nuns were surprised by my leg strength and were impressed when I showed them pictures of our act. I was released from the hospital, to return when the stitches were ready to be removed. I was eager to start rehearsing once again, but the doctor only laughed. He really didn't believe that I would ever do our act again. I gave him the date and time that the show would be broadcasted and made him promise that he would be watching.

For my convalescence, Elaine and I went home to the little house we were renting in East Grinstead and I was able to watch the American moon landing on the television — which happened during my convalescence — and accept the congratulations of all our neighbors. The stitches were taken out a few days later and I was told to start trying to bend the knee a little at a time. Of course I wanted to start rehearsing right away, but Elaine convinced me to wait a few more days, to give my knee a chance to heal completely. I was still lifting two iron boots, to keep my thighs in shape, but after two weeks I felt that we could no longer put it off. We only had about six weeks left before we would be doing the television show.

I tried to bend the knee on my own, but I just couldn't do it. It was frozen in place. Elaine didn't want to have anything to do with bending my knee, but finally I convinced her that she had to help me. I was sitting on a low bureau in the bedroom. I loaded up the boot with sixty pounds of weight, with her holding it up. My leg was hanging over the edge of the bureau. She stood there holding the boot, but when I told her to let go she couldn't do it. I screamed at her to let go, and finally she did. At that

moment my leg went down, and I screamed with the agony of the pain, but the knee could finally bend. We left the boot on, so that the leg would hang, and rubbed the knee with the heat liniment.

From then on I was able to bend the leg, even though it was still painful. Each day I exercised with the boot, lifting it and bending my knee. I was walking with a cane, but after three days we started rehearsing in our living room. Elaine was shaking, but I was able to get her up to my head. I was able to squat a little bit at a time until I could do a full squat. Once I was down at the floor, I was able to do the pivot around with her on my head. I got a little shaky myself at this point and took her off my head before I tried to get back up.

Each day we did a little bit more. The knee hurt, but there was nothing wrong with my muscles and tendons. After a few days I was able to do the squat, pivot and getting back up with her on my head. Then I got up on the chair, hooked my feet in the strap and started doing some partial squatting over the back of the chair. All the while I was putting heat on the knee and keeping it wrapped at night. The knee continued to hurt, but the strength was there. After six days I pitched Elaine up and took her part of the way over the chair in a partial squat motion, which felt good. I would also do sets of ten doing squats with her on my head as well.

The doctor wasn't very concerned that my knee was still swollen, although it was only four more weeks before the show. He was, however, skeptical about my doing the act again. Now it was time to take Elaine over the chair with the full motion. Although it was painful, I was able to do it with strength and control. I continued practicing doing squats with her on my head.

In the middle of all this we had to move out of our rental house and in with our friend Pamela because of structural problems with the house.

Once safely at Pamela's house we started rehearsing again. I was now able to bring Elaine back and up over the chair, but I was still limping using a cane when I walked. It didn't make sense that I could come over the chair with Elaine on my head, which put tremendous pressure on my knees, but I was afraid to put weight on my leg when I was walking.

All the same, when it was time to do the show I called the surgeon and reminded him to watch our performance on TV. He was still totally skeptical but promised he would. We went through our warm-up back

stage and took our positions, the cane still in my hand. Then, when it was time for me to join the audience as a drunk, I dropped the cane. From that moment on, everything went perfectly. The pitch, the squat, the chair, it was all great. We were back in action again.

CHAPTER 24

Donald's Death

Once back in East Grinstead, in 1966, Elaine and I decided that, because of Donald's worsening health, we would try to stay in England as much as was possible. I contacted our friend George Ganjou, who was a booking agent in London and had a billiard parlor at Piccadilly Square. George booked us often in the London area and got us our first booking at The Talk of the Town, as well as BBC television shows. We also played at the Savoy Hotel, which was a great booking. In this way we were able to work for several months in London while spending a lot of time with Donald.

We also accepted an Italian booking with Evaldi. We were in Venetian and Milanese nightclubs for about six weeks. We stayed in small pensions in those cities, so we were out of touch and virtually impossible to contact while we were performing. By the end of the six weeks, Elaine was anxious to return to East Grinstead.

We flew to Heathrow Airport and were met there by two policemen who asked us to come with them. When asked why, they simply replied, 'It's Donald. He's in the hospital, and we are going to escort you there now.'

From that moment on we were in another world. We cleared customs quickly, our luggage was picked up, and we were taken to a police car. All the way through London we drove with lights and sirens, and at each major intersection, the traffic was blocked off to allow us through. Our escort

included two police cars and a police motorcycle. We got to the hospital in an incredible 35 minutes.

Once we reached the hospital, we were taken to Donald, who had been in a coma for four days. He had developed pneumonia and, because his lungs had calcified, they hadn't been able to detect it. They told us that he had very little time left. Elaine was crying when Donald opened his eyes and said, 'Oh Mommy, Daddy' as he hugged us and talked for a while. All of this amazed the medical staff because he had been unconscious for so long.

After about a half hour Donald said that, since we must be tired after rushing so much to get to the hospital, we should get some rest; he would see us again in the morning. He reassured us that everything would be fine. Elaine and I did as he said and tried to settle down and get some sleep, but at about 4:00 am we gave up trying and checked out of the hotel. On the way back to the hospital Elaine suddenly asked me to stop and phone the hospital, immediately. I found a phone booth and called. They told me that Donald had passed on. I was shaking, hardly able to stand, and returned to the car. Elaine knew immediately that Donald had died. We hugged each other and sobbed.

We continued on to the hospital and learned that Donald's body was now in the hospital mortuary. Elaine declined to see him, but I went. I broke down.

We found a funeral parlor in East Grinstead and make the necessary decisions. Donald was placed in a little pine box with a yellow satin lining. Elaine couldn't bear to go to the viewing, which would last for three days, but I went every day with David and Dana and sat for a few hours. I told Elaine that I had told the funeral parlor to cremate him, and that night we held each other in sorrow.

Eventually, we decided that it was time for bed. Elaine went to bed first because I wanted to meditate. When I joined her in bed, I suddenly jumped up, because I was sure that there was a spider running along my leg. I turned on the light and saw Elaine laughing with delight. I told her we needed to find the spider, but she said, 'No, it's not a spider. It's Donald.'

She went on to explain that she had been talking with him for the past few days, that it had been wonderful and made it easier for her to go through Donald's death. She said that she had suggested that he get into

bed between her and me, and that's what I had felt along my leg. I was amazed at this whole story. It was so incredible that I couldn't quite absorb it. I asked Elaine to tell me more, and she said that she and Donald had agreed that together they would find a new mommy for him, that he would be reincarnated and come back right away. I was dubious, but Elaine was totally confident that she could be a help to him.

It was difficult to get our lives back to normal. I felt like I didn't sleep for days. We were staying in East Grinstead and spent some of our time up at the Scientology center. Elaine was still in contact with Donald. He would leave for periods of time and then come back. Suddenly one day a young man named Neil approached and greeted us by name. He asked us if we knew a woman named Marie, who was his wife. He said that she was pregnant and that she had been in contact with Donald. We were both in shock at the new turn of events. We were taken to meet Marie who told us her story: she was one month pregnant and Donald had chosen her to be his new mother. She told us that in the past she had audited Donald a few times, and they had become good friends. Elaine was upset that she hadn't been part of the process of finding the new mother. At that moment, though, Donald appeared to both Marie and Elaine to talk things over; I wasn't aware of his presence at all.

Then Neil took me aside, and we started talking about Donald. He asked me about his accident and following medical problems. I told him what a fantastic boy Donald had been. He seemed to hesitate, wondering if this new child would have a lot of the same problems. In protest, I brought out my wallet and showed him a picture of Donald. Suddenly, Neil and I felt Donald completely submerge us, wrapping himself around both of us. It was an incredible feeling, and Neil said, 'Oh, yes, he will be my son.'

For the next two weeks Donald was in constant contact with all of us, me, Elaine, Neil and Marie. It turns out that Dana was also in contact with Donald. One morning when he was staying with us he came down from his bedroom and said, 'Boy, did I have fun with Donald last night.' He told us that they had been playing together on the upper bunk of the bunk bed upstairs and that Donald would float in the air 'like a white feather.' It looked like a lot of fun, so Dana wanted to do it too, but Donald had warned him that he would fall down and hurt himself. It wasn't my place to doubt Dana's experience; why couldn't he be in contact with Donald?

Going into the seventh week of Marie's pregnancy Donald told Elaine that it was time for him to enter Marie's body, that he would no longer be in contact with her. It was actually a happy situation. We were glad that he was going to be returning. And from then on we didn't hear any more from him. Neil and Marie were planning to return to their home in Hawaii and left about two weeks after that. We said our good-byes, and added that maybe someday we would come to Hawaii to visit all of them. We left it at that.

Several days later, I happened to be talking with a fellow who was known to be able to contact spirits. I asked him if he had ever been in contact with Donald, and he said yes, quite a lot during the period immediately after his death. He said that Donald had told him about playing with Dana and asked me if a 'white feather' meant anything to me. Of course I knew immediately that he was repeating Dana's very words. For me this conversation confirmed that all of this was real and interconnected.

Elaine and I decided to spread Donald's ashes up on the hill where the Scientology Center was based under a lovely tree where Donald had liked to play. That ended that cycle.

The two of us continued to spend time at the Scientology Center, and as we had some extra money, we decided to take some courses, including Power and Power Release. David wanted to take these courses as well, so he joined us. They were good courses and we learned a lot. The last course dealt with reaching the stage of 'clear'. No one would tell us about his or her experience because you signed a contract not to discuss any course with another person. Elaine and I often discussed the concept of 'clear' with one another, and one evening we came to the conclusion that 'clear' could only mean one thing. It had to do with cause and effect and the law of karma — 'clear' was probably understanding the state of karma and eliminating it. After becoming 'clear' you would no longer create karma, as long as you lived your life properly.

Because Elaine and I had become auditors along the way we had our own E-meter and audited each other. I asked her, 'Are you clear?' and she replied that she was. The needle floated, indicating that she understood the concept. She wouldn't tell me what she was thinking, wanting me to figure it out for myself. When I tried to be 'clear', the needle would stick. I

worked on that problem for several days, until one day it hit me. This time when she asked me whether I understood the state of 'clear', the needle floated. I finally understood the meaning of karma, as well as the meaning of eliminating it.

However, we saw that other people who were getting 'cleared' would continue to do all the old things again. They didn't change even though they supposedly had this new awareness. Jesus had said, 'Your sins are forgiven, but go and sin no more', yet these people were returning to their old ways. Coincidentally at that time Ron Hubbard issued a memorandum, that in order to remain 'clear', all 'clears' had to audit themselves every day. Elaine and I had to laugh because we realized that Hubbard was trying to deal with this problem: people who were 'clear' going back to their old ways and creating new karma.

Finally, we came to the conclusion that Scientology was not for us. We felt that there were a lot of things going on that we didn't like. We saw individuals learning things without real understanding. We stopped attending lectures and taking courses, but we still liked living in the little town and had many friends with whom we had good discussions.

One experience we had in East Grinstead involved David, who was now about 15 years old. We were walking through town one day when a woman approached David and called him by another name. David looked at her and then hugged and kissed her. They then started talking about his most recent past life. She recognized him as a Belgian pilot during World War II who had been shot down by the Nazis. They talked in detail about all the family members he had known in Belgium. After several minutes of listening to this Elaine and I excused ourselves, letting the two of them spend the entire afternoon reminiscing together. It was quite an experience for all of us.

CHAPTER 25

Israel and Beyond

Eventually after Donald's death Elaine and I reentered the show business world, signing contracts that took us around England and beyond. This whole period of our lives lasted about 5 years. We had a great experiences throughout those years and loved being in Europe. We continued to ask questions and to follow our spiritual path as well, studying and learning more and more over time. At this point we were both advancing very quickly, absorbing all kinds of ideas and concepts and meeting all kinds of interesting people.

Through Evaldi we got a very interesting contract: to go to Israel immediately following the 6 Day War. We go via cruise ship from Venice — a 5-day trip. Elaine thought it sounded wonderful, so we drove to Venice and embarked from there. It was a lovely ship, and we had a beautiful suite. One of the waiters was named Juliano, and he took wonderful care of us. We told him that we were late risers in the morning, so he would bring our breakfast to the room each day. We visited the Greek islands as tourists during the day and enjoyed being audience members at the shows on board each evening.

Once in Israel Elaine and I were scheduled to play at the Khalife nightclub in Haifa, which was an interesting experience because the country was still on a war standing. Everyone in the audience was in uniform with their machine guns slung over the backs of their chairs. We had never witnessed anything like that before.

During our opening night performance, I was, as usual, sitting in the audience, about five tables away from the stage, and, because of the unusual national situation, I was surrounded by soldiers. When Elaine began to play the piano and I started my drunken insults, the Israeli servicemen started telling me to shut up. I started getting a bit nervous and when I saw a soldier stand and start to approach me, I stood up and started running away from him, around the floor of the nightclub. Everyone was trying to grab me while I was trying to get to the stage. Finally Elaine was able to calm the audience, saying that I was only a drunk and easy to handle. Even as I staggered up onto the stage, guys were trying to grab me, but Elaine stopped them, and we were able to go on with the act. The audience went wild when she started throwing me around the stage.

Throughout Israel we would take side trips to engage with anyone we heard might be 'realized' or highly spiritual. When we got a few days off we went to Jerusalem with one of the other acts, Carmine, a female impersonator who was always in costume and full makeup because he was undergoing hormone therapy — transitioning to being a woman. In fact, when I had first met him I thought he *was* a woman. Carmine was feminine and beautiful and we always referred to her as 'she.'

The three of us were enjoying visiting the sites of Jerusalem when we met up with a little Arab boy who became our guide. We told him we wanted to go to the Wailing Wall, and he said that he could take us there, but that he couldn't enter the prayer area because he was a Muslim. When we got there I took him by the hand and together we walked past the armed Israeli guards and down the stairs to the enclosure. He was amazed to see the Wall for the first time. We joined the other devotees and wrote out little prayers, which we stuck into the cracks of the wall. We spent some time sitting there in contemplation — a wonderful experience. Afterward we took our young friend to lunch, paid him, and watched him happily take off.

We continued along the supposed route of the Crucifixion, but I was startled to realize that none of it seemed to be uplifting. The reality was that it was all about money. Even when we entered a little cave-like area, where the Crucifixion itself was supposed to have taken place, it was divided into three sections: one each for Protestant, Catholic and Greek Orthodox pilgrims, and money was strewn all over the floor. It was

unpleasant, and both Elaine and I felt that this had nothing to do with true faith and spirituality. Carmine felt more in tune with this experience, but at each place we visited, there just seemed to be squabbling between the different Christian sects. There never seemed to be any agreement on anything. It was fascinating but not enlightening.

Further along, when we were walking down a tiny little street, Elaine looked up and saw a sign for a gym. It seemed like an unlikely location for a gym, so we decided to investigate and opened the door. There before us was an old wooden counter behind which stood a young man, and behind him the entire room was covered with old bodybuilding magazine covers. I recognized many of the men posing on the walls, including myself. The young man looked first at me and then at the wall and then back again. He screamed to his companions, and suddenly several young Arab kids came running and surrounded me. They escorted me back into the gym and showed me around, begging me to pose for them. I declined, but they were very excited to meet me, and I signed my autograph on one of the pictures before we left. Elaine and I were amused by the whole incident.

That contract in Israel was a wonderful experience. We met lots of interesting people, and it was hard to leave, but it was time. We took the ship back to Venice and from there drove back to the Channel and then home to England.

The time we were based in Europe was also amazing because from there we were able to travel and perform throughout the Middle East — including Egypt, Tunisia and Libya — and the Far East, to Japan, Hong Kong, and Thailand.

While we were performing in Thailand we did a lot of touring and shopping. Clothes were very inexpensive, and our costumes could be made for pennies on the dollar. We bought a lot of 24- carat gold jewelry there, too, as it was sold by weight and was very inexpensive. We went to the beautiful floating market and to every Buddhist temple there was. We would drive 50-60 miles through the gorgeous countryside to see the temples of Buddha with statues in jade and gold, standing, sitting and lying down. The taxi drivers who drove us would sit to the right of the steering wheel, steering at an angle. They wouldn't move over behind the wheel, saying that Buddha was sitting there and was the one who was really driving. However, even with all this beauty and magnificence we never

found anyone who was truly 'realized.' When we spoke with the locals they would try to explain their beliefs and customs, but it wasn't 'realization.'

In Hong Kong we played for a week on a huge houseboat that held three nightclubs. From there we went to Japan where we were booked for several weeks. We had a problem because so few people spoke English. To deal with this issue we had some assistants to act as translators and to help with our luggage. These skinny little guys could hardly carry our bags and equipment. But that was nothing compared to the problems of the blond Englishwoman who was traveling with us. She did a strong-woman act that included tearing up telephone books, but had to carry her own supply with her because she never knew if the local telephone books would be big enough to make an impression. The suitcase in which she kept them must have weighed 60 pounds, which she could carry easily in one hand. At the train stations the local porters would scramble around us, hoping to carry her bags and earn a tip. One time this porter kept bothering her, to carry her bags, and she finally said, okay, do it. He went to pick up the suitcase, and the bag didn't budge off the ground. He couldn't even drag it. She pushed him aside, picked up the bag and walked away, while the porter looked at her in disbelief.

When we first arrived in Japan we would either take trains from one destination to another or fly on Old Nippon Airline which seemed to have a plane crash every week. I told our agent, 'no more planes, only trains from now on.' The trains were wonderful — reliable and comfortable, clocking up to 150 miles an hour. We played at several venues out in the countryside and then came into Tokyo, where we played at several huge nightclubs. Everyone in Tokyo did his or her business in these nightclubs. The geishas in these nightclubs were beautiful, smart and multi-lingual. One club, the New Tokyo Theatre, was seven stories high and had posters of all the geisha girls, about 1500 in all. Businessmen would come in and fill out cards stating favorite sports, religion, language needs, etc. This information would go upstairs, where a girl would be chosen to best compliment the customer's preferences. They would not only make intelligent conversation, but they would serve food and drinks to the clients. The more geishas you had serving your entourage, the more successful you appeared.

When we were done in Japan, we booked a 'round-the-world' trip that took us through Hawaii, Santa Monica and New York to London. It was

great to see all the guys in Santa Monica. I remember talking with Artie, when a big hulk of a guy came up behind me and lifted me up. It turned out to be Arnold Schwartzenagger, who said that I had been his idol when he was young, and that I had the best back in the world. He asked how I got it, and I told him I did a lot of chinning. I showed him how I did chins with my elbows open and how to dislocate the scapula of the back to increase mass. He would become a good friend in the years to come.

In 1969, we were booked for three weeks in a beautiful hotel/casino in Tripoli, Libya and flew in from Rome, not realizing that it was a time of growing turmoil. I remember hearing about a leader named Gaddafi, who was leading rebellion in the desert area outside of Tripoli. The nightclub in which we played was owned by a fellow who had started working there when he was a boy. From menial labor he gradually rose through various jobs — bus boy, waiter, elevator operator — learning every job in the hotel. He saved his money and 20 years later was able to buy it. He expanded it, added the casino and eventually became a very wealthy man. He also started Tripoli's first bus and truck companies and had an interest in Alitalia Airlines. During the days, he took Elaine and me to the beach or out on his yacht.

As our contract drew to a close, the nightclub owner came to us and said that he would have to get us out of the country as soon as we were done because Gaddafi's forces were nearing Tripoli and soon would enter the city victorious. He said that he, too, would eventually have to leave but luckily most of his savings were already safely invested in Milan, Italy. It saddened us to see what was happening to him. He booked us on the last Alitalia flight out of Tripoli, and we read in the newspaper just a few days later that Gaddafi had taken over the city. I wondered what had happened to our friend but 5 months later we were playing at a nightclub in Milan, and there he was, walking down the main boulevard. We were delighted to know that he and his family were now living in Milan.

While in Milan Elaine and I met other interesting and spiritual people. One of them took us to the Leonardo da Vinci Museum there, a fascinating place about an extraordinary man. We saw models of helicopters, canons, elevators, gearing systems, and more. I feel sure that Leonardo was a very advanced soul with the incredibly creative mind of an inventor.

Then, when we were in France we spent some time with our good

friend Steve Kirkland. He had been one of the three original partners in The American Health Club System, a chain of gyms that had been started in the States. Unfortunately, in order to avoid paying taxes, the three original partners registered this organization as a religion, and the FBI caught up with them. To avoid prosecution, the three men left the States. One went to Italy, one to France and one to Spain. Steve went to Paris and owned about three gyms there. His children, two boys and a girl, had grown up in France and knew no other culture. They had no interest in anything having to do with the States. When Elaine saw this, she suddenly started having concerns about David and Dana. She worried that they, too, would never want to return to the States. When she suggested that maybe it was time to return home, I pointed out that we were finally getting established and doing very well in Europe. I also didn't see the problem of the boys being Englishmen, but Elaine was adamant. Since we had to stay out of the States for five years in order to avoid any tax liabilities, we decided to at least finish out the contracts we had already booked.

Back in England we looked at David and Dana anew. They both had English accents and obviously felt at home in England. We discussed it with David, who was against returning to the States. All his friends were now in East Grinstead and he was looking forward to going to university in England. His attitude made Elaine even more determined to bring the boys home to the States before it was too late.

Financially, Elaine and I had pretty much broken even during those years. We had the expenses of boarding and educating the boys, and we had invested a lot of money in Scientology courses. Elaine and I ended up living in London with our friend, Merian Ganjou and her husband, about a half hour drive from East Grinstead, where the boys were still in boarding school. The Ganjous' home was a beautiful building on Hammersmith Rd. There were seven apartments altogether on three floors. As things worked out Elaine and I stayed in one while I renovated it. Then we moved to the next apartment that needed to be renovated. During the year we were there, between 1970 and our return to the States in 1971, we painted, plastered, patched and refloored the entire building.

The apartment house was only part of the Ganjou 'empire.' There were three Ganjou brothers, Serge, George and Bob who had retired from show business. The three brothers were all partners in their different interests.

Serge owned a Polish restaurant, George was a booking agent, and Bob managed the act that Merian was now doing with three younger men. Then, when Bob's health started to fail, Merian stopped doing the act and spent most of her time at home with him until his death. Luckily, owning the apartment building made Merian financially secure.

After we'd been in London a little while, we moved the boys and put them in school there, so they could live at home. When we were away, they stayed with the Ganjous.

We had a great time there, but we wanted to move back to the States. Rather than put it off again we decided that this was the time. We still had some outstanding contracts, so we decided to ship the car ahead of us, take a two-month break from work and get the kids settled in Vegas once again.

CHAPTER 27

Trip to Assisi and Rome

In 1970, Luigi Evaldi, our Italian agent, booked our act in Athens, Greece. We were also contracted to perform in Rome and Bologna, and we decided to take David and Dana with us.

We drove down in the car through Italy and then took the ferry from Brindisi to Greece. The trip took about five days, allowing us to see many beautiful places on the way to the Nerida Nightclub — right on the Mediterranean — where we were booked. It was a beautiful white and blue building, but its large patio was full of broken plates as if there had been a really bad brawl the night before. Elaine suggested that maybe they broke plates if they liked the acts, but I wasn't so sure. It seemed very strange to me.

We met Elena, the elegant woman who ran the nightclub and was in total control of the business. We asked her about the broken dishes and she explained that the patrons would buy the plates and break them if they enjoyed the show. The more plates broken, the more they liked the show. Anyway, she took us to the inside nightclub, where we would be performing two days later. Unfortunately, when I saw the stage, I noticed that the ceiling was only nine feet high, too low for us to perform our act. We needed twelve feet of air space to do the show — to accommodate my height, Elaine's height and the height of the chair. Elena explained that the patio was now closed for the winter season, and that from this point

on all entertainment had to be inside. It was all a big mix up, however unintentional, but we couldn't perform there, and so Elena had to book another act.

Now we had over two weeks without work before our next contract in Rome, and since I always believe that there is no such thing as a coincidence, we relaxed and waited for the next adventure to unfold. That afternoon we had lunch with Elena at her home where I noticed a book, 'St. Francis' by Nikos Kazantzakis. I picked up the book to show it to Elaine and got a wonderful feeling. Elaine felt the same thing, and when we asked if we could borrow the book, Elena insisted that we keep it. We promised Elena that we would return during the summer season, when we could perform outside on the patio, and then went to the artists' pension on the beach, where we had planned to stay during our contract. Now we would only stay a night or two. Once we started reading the book about St. Francis we didn't put it down until we were finished with it. Feeling profoundly moved by this true story of the Saint, we decided to go to Assisi immediately.

The next day we crossed Greece, taking the ferry back to Brendisi and driving to Assisi, stopping to see the sites along the way. We loved Assisi, which, in those days, wasn't too big and was filled with the presence of St. Francis. Using Elena's book as our guide, we kept looking for the church that God had told St. Francis to rebuild. Whenever we asked for directions we would be sent to St. Catherine's Cathedral, but it didn't feel right. Finally a Franciscan monk showed us that the church St. Francis' had rebuilt was actually *inside* the big cathedral, a tiny little building — only about twelve feet square, simple and beautiful — tucked away in a corner of the bigger building.

We meditated there for a few hours, enjoying the wonderful vibrations of the little church. In the days afterward we toured around the city and then went up into the surrounding hills where St. Francis spent most of his days, contemplating and meditating.

After four or five days in Assisi we headed for Rome, an easy day's drive. Because the whole of Rome is a museum we spent our free time seeing one site after another, as well as eating in fantastic restaurants. We also looked up our body-building friends Steve Reeves and Gordon Mitchell, who were making a lot of movies in Italy at that time. We found Steve in his

penthouse with great views in the heart of Rome and Gordon in another, nearby, penthouse of a nearby building. Once we all got together, Gordon and Steve took us to a great restaurant — a breathtaking place. As you walked into the cellar location there were salamis and sausages hanging all over from the ceiling and huge wheels of cheeses stacked up around the room. There was no menu, so you simply ordered what you wanted. First there were slices of salamis and cheeses with bread. The second course was a wonderful minestrone soup. A big platter of spaghetti with sauce came next, followed by the meat dishes. Each course was served with a different wine. After hours of eating and drinking — when we were sure that we couldn't eat another bite — a huge platter of piled up crème puffs covered with melted chocolate arrived. It was magnificent.

After that feast, we went to the nightclub where we were going to be playing and met the manager of the club, ordered drinks and watched the show. The place was packed, the energy level high. Everyone was coming up to us, asking for autographs from Steve and Gordon.

With about four days before our booking began, we spent the days touring around with Steve and Gordon when they were free. We loved the Coliseum and the amazing Fountain of Trevi. In our continual search for enlightenment, Elaine and I visited local churches and — as always — sought out locals who were known for their spirituality.

On opening night, the nightclub was packed to overflowing. There had been advertising in the papers, including the fact that our friends, Steve and Gordon, would be there. We were there for two weeks and played to a full house every night. The act was a huge success, and for us the icing on the cake was that it was great to to spend time with Steve and Gordon again.

CHAPTER 28

In Bologna, Italy

From Rome we drove to Bologna — a beautiful city with a long history as a center for colleges and universities — where we had a two-week contract at the casino. Once we were there the casino manager gave us an address for a beautiful apartment where we could stay. It was located over a market and owned by Mrs. Paginelli who had four rooms and a kitchen, but the only room available was the living room, which she rented to the four of us, as David and Dana were traveling with us this time.

Mrs. Paginelli was quite eccentric — she liked to complain about everything, even when there was nothing wrong. She would yell and scream and carry on about the other tenants, and Dana would laugh at her, which made her even madder. Then Dana would tell her how much he loved her, and she would melt. Among the four of us the place got the nickname "Paginelli and the Casa di Potts", the house of Crazies.

We rarely saw the other renters at Mrs. Paginelli's, because Elaine and I got up late and were out late at night. David was in charge of his little brother when we were working or asleep, which kept him entertained. David also loved to read and would remember everything he learned about a new city or country. Each morning the boys went out on their own for their breakfast of cocoa and scones and then wake us up at about 10:00 am. We spent the days together and then cooked their dinner before heading off to the casino or nightclub. We had the use of the kitchen in

the apartment, but we rarely saw Mrs. Paginelli or her daughter, who also lived there. It was Dana who found out that they were sleeping in a little closet off of the kitchen that was kept locked during the day. They would be gone during the day, fix a little dinner at night and then would disappear into their closet for the night.

Bologna was a center for communist activity, and the city government was controlled by the Communist Party. Early on during our stay we met an entertaining gentleman who turned out to own a factory with about thirty employees, all of whom were members of the Communist Party. He had a good business and made lots of money, so he wasn't interested in joining the party.

After years of debate between him and his employees, he finally came up with a solution to their political disagreement. During their month of vacation, he sent them all to Russia for two weeks. He heard nothing while they were gone, but they didn't even stay for the full two weeks. When they returned, they never again tried to convert him to communism. It turned out that the first hotel they stayed in was rundown and the service terrible. The food was incredibly bad everywhere, with none of the variety or flavor that Italians would expect. They traveled to other cities, but found the environment equally depressing. The markets were empty, the people had only worn clothing, and even wanted to buy the clothes off the Italians' backs. So, they soon concluded that Communism didn't work. They quit the party and never brought it up again, which suited the factory owner just fine.

CHAPTER 28

A Death in the Swiss Alps

One spring when Elaine and I had a contract in Geneva, Switzerland we took a fabulous drive from London over the Alps and had an amazing experience.

It was early in the morning and we were on a part of the road with a lot of curves. Elaine told me to slow down, and I agreed that we didn't want to rush through this part of the trip. Then she said that there was a young man sitting between us in the car. I asked her what she meant, and she explained that the fellow she was talking about had just gotten into an automobile accident further up the road. She said that he was confused and didn't know what to do. I was amazed, of course, and asked her if she could really see him, and she replied that not only could she see him but she could feel him. She repeated that he was really confused and in bad shape.

At that very moment we came around a curve and found a car that had flipped over and been totally flattened and there was the body of a young man slumped over behind the steering wheel— the very same young man who was telling Elaine how he was trying to get back into his body but couldn't. My sweet wife was telling him that he should wait until his 'guides' arrived to help him.

In the meantime some other folks in another car had stopped and called for help. When we joined them on the road, it was obvious that the young man had died. At that point Elaine told me that although she

couldn't see the 'guides' she could hear them telling the young man to be calm and follow them, that soon everything would be just wonderful. She then saw them momentarily before they disappeared into a very bright light.

There was nothing more that we could do, so we got back into our car and drove to Geneva, where we checked into our pension, a very nice apartment located over the nightclub where we would be performing.

Just before our departure from London, our friend Franklin D'Amore had cabled us, letting us know that he would be joining us in Geneva to celebrate his 75th birthday. He arrived about 3 days after us and had a companion with him, a very nice woman about 50 years old. She actually seemed older than Franklin, as he needed little sleep and was always on the go. After a week, even Elaine was quite worn out. Each night after the show we would go out to eat and drink and would talk until about 3 AM. To my amazement by 7 AM Franklin was throwing pebbles at my window. We would have coffee, pass the time, pick up Elaine at about 10 AM and then return once again at about noon to pick up his companion. Franklin departed, and we returned to London. Just another example of how those five years in Europe were filled with so many wonderful experiences and memories.

CHAPTER 29

On Our Return to the States

When we arrived at the airport in New York on our return to the U.S. in 1971 Elaine, the kids and I had to go through customs. The only things I had of worth were seven gold coins, but of course we had all our clothes and personal items, as well the equipment for the act. The customs officer noticed that all our belongings had been bought in Europe and was going to charge us duty on everything, which he calculated at $1500. I said to forget it; I wasn't going to pay for old, used clothing. For that much money I could buy a whole new wardrobe for the family. I didn't mention to the officer that I had those seven gold coins hidden in my suitcase. We started walking away, and only then did the customs officer relent and allow us to leave with our luggage.

We stayed with my mother while we were waiting for the car to arrive by ship in New York. I made the rounds of the NY booking agents while we were there and discovered that show business was dying. Most of the nightclubs were closing up, even the Latin Quarters. Business in the Catskills was failing as well. I went to visit my old agent on Broadway and found only a sign on the door with his home phone number. When I called him, he said that after three burglaries— in one of which he was seriously injured — he had decided to close the office. It was hard to believe how much things had changed in just five years. It seemed that the only acts in demand were singers and comedians. He went on to say

that Vegas was the only place left that might have bookings for 'novelty' acts like ours.

Once the car arrived from Europe by ship, we said good-bye to my mother and to Fernanda, who was living in a house with her children in Brooklyn. We drove cross-country to Las Vegas where I again made the rounds, trying to get some bookings for the act. Nothing was available. All the shows had a star, a singer or two and a comedian, just as my agent in New York had said.

I found a little apartment for the family that would be okay temporarily, but I knew that I had to cash in those gold coins as quickly as possible. They were all gold $10 Indian heads that I had bought at different pawn shops throughout Europe. I went to a gold shop and placed the coins on the counter. The owner looked at each one carefully. Some he put to the left and the others were pushed to the right. He offered to buy the four he had put to the left, and when I asked him why, he handed me a coin book and told me to study it at home. Needless to say the others were counterfeit. He gave me $110 for each of the good coins, which was fine. We were able to generate some income because while we were away, the value of gold had risen dramatically and the jewelry that we had bought by weight in places like Thailand and Iran was now often worth ten times what we had paid.

We had always planned to return to Europe to complete the final eight weeks of our contracts once we got the boys settled in Vegas, so I found a 72-foot trailer that we could buy with no money down, as the young couple who owned it could no longer afford the monthly payment of $90. We took over their mortgage, moved the trailer to a nice RV park, skirted it, added an awning and planted a few trees in our little yard. My mother agreed to come out and stay with the kids so that Elaine and I could return to Europe and off we went.

This time when we were in our beloved Holland we were paid $2,500 for one television performance and we got to be with our friend Karl Karsoni, with whom — over the years — we had played almost all around the world.

After that it was on to Iran, where we were booked by the Grey Agency out of London for a 6- week contract, after which we would have to return to London to be in a BBC broadcast for which we had a contract that required us to pay *them* if we didn't show up!

In Iran we were booked at the Souk Cafe No in Tehran. An odd thing happened when we arrived at the nightclub by taxi for our first rehearsal: a guy working in a trampoline act spotted us and told us to leave and get a room someplace other than at the nightclub. So we found a room in a very pleasant hotel and returned to the nightclub where the manager wanted to show us to our on-premise accommodations, but we said that we never stayed where we were working. He was upset, but I was adamant and the issue was dropped. We still didn't know why the trampoline guy had been so insistent.

There were 19 acts on the bill in Tehran, but as soon as the manager saw our act he put us right before the closing act, usually a local star of renown or a headline from Europe. The 19 acts made for a very long show — nor to mention the drinking and carrying on that the audience did all night — but the manager wanted us in place when it started at 6:00 pm. Since we usually went on at about 1:00 am I refused, informing him that we would be there by midnight and not a minute before.

That wasn't the only strange thing going on at that Tehran nightclub. The manager was holding the passports of the poor fellow who was doing the trampoline act and his partner, who were desperate to leave Iran. They couldn't leave, though, because the manager kept involuntarily renewing their contract. They had been there for 3 months instead of the original 1-month agreement. Even their booking agent didn't seem inclined to help them. So, repaying the favor that he had done us earlier, I said, 'Well, why don't you break your leg? It should be a pretty easy thing to fake an accident on a trampoline, and then you wouldn't be able to work.'

Of course that very night our friend suddenly fell with a scream and had to be carried off the stage. At the hospital he was told that his ankle wasn't broken but that he had a very bad sprain and wouldn't be able to work for 4-5 weeks. He was able to leave the country two days later.

Now the manager came to me and said that he wanted my passport and Elaine's. He said that they had to be stamped and that he would keep them safe until our departure. At that time it was my understanding that you should never give up your passport, so I unwillingly handed them over. Suspicious of this guy, we went to the American consulate one afternoon and told the official what was going on. He said that the Souk Café No was notorious for causing trouble, but not to worry about our passports, that we would get them back eventually.

Our act was well received, but we noticed that if the manager didn't like an act it was canceled immediately and you had to pay your own fare out of the country. If he liked your act he tried to make you stay longer and longer. Needless to say, he was getting a pretty bad reputation around the show business world and we were getting nervous because we were approaching the end of our six-week contract.

Another of his tricks played out one evening when he came to us and said that we would be playing for the Shah of Iran, in celebration of his son's fifth birthday, but that we would all be doing it for free. I informed him that I didn't work for nothing. Once that was worked out, we did do the performance and had a great evening. The little boy came up on stage afterward to stand on the chair and to feel how strong my muscles were. The Shah invited us for lunch at the palace with his family and gave us a tour of the treasures there.

As our contract drew to a close it was obvious that I would have to take care of business myself because we learned that the manager was planning to extend our contract two weeks at a time. That wasn't going to happen. I told him that if he wanted to buy out our contract with the BBC— for $5000 up front — I would stay. Otherwise, we were leaving. Since the manager had no intention of paying out that kind of money he was forced to let us leave, making us promise to return. Obviously we had no intention of doing so. Later I would joke with my friend Karl Karsoni, that he should work there, but Karl only laughed and said, 'No way.'

It was unusual for us to have difficulties with our contracts, but there were a few other experiences like that. The one that stands out in my mind has to do with our contract for Japan, Thailand and Hong Kong. Our Japanese agent wanted to make sure that while we were in Thailand we collected his commission as well as our own pay. In Thailand, we were the star act at the Honey Nightclub — which was more like a very large striptease club with fantastic food. I had some warning about trouble with pay because the girls who worked there were always crying about the very difficult time they had getting paid. So, at the end of the first week I went to the office to collect our pay. The manager refused, saying that we would be paid at the end of the 2-week contract. No, I said, we get paid every Friday night as stated in our contract. I also demanded that the agent's fees be included as well, which had the manager sputtering with anger,

but I looked him right in the eyes and said, 'Pay.' He put all the money he owed in an envelope and handed it to me. The next Friday I demanded that he pay us before our performance, which he did begrudgingly. Our contract was over.

CHAPTER 30

Getting Settled Back in the States

Once all our contracts were completed, it was time to return to the States. We said our good-byes to the Ganjous, flew to New York and then went on to Vegas. My mother was glad to see us, as she had been watching the boys while we were finishing up things in Europe. The boys were both in school and having a good time.

When I asked David about school, he said that it was too easy. They had advanced him to the senior class, but he had already passed all the tests necessary for graduation. He was quite amazed at how far ahead he was from the other kids, and the principle of the high school really didn't know what to do with him.

Elaine and I met with the principle, and before we discussed David, I asked him how the boys could concentrate on schoolwork when all the girls were wearing miniskirts and skimpy outfits. The principle said there was nothing he could do, that their mothers were dressed the same way. One mother had come into the office to complain when the principle had sent home her daughter to change into something a little less revealing. That mother had sat there in her miniskirt and no panties on underneath. That was just the way it was.

Concerning David, he would graduate with his class in a few weeks, and the principle recommended that he go to college, even though he was only 16 years old. There was no point in keeping him in high school, so

he might as well go up to the state university in Reno, Nevada. And so David applied to and was accepted by UNR. I told him that as long as he got passing grades, we would support him. He promised to do well and went off on his way.

As for Elaine and me, it was impossible to find any work doing the act. Across the country nightclubs were going out of business, and Vegas acts were being booked from Europe. We talked it over and agreed that I had to go back to being a crap dealer. She decided to wait awhile before deciding whether or not she would return to show business as a showgirl.

I went to the Frontier Hotel and Casino and met with my old friend, Lou DeGreg, who was the assistant casino manager at the time. I told him that I wanted to be a baccarat dealer, and he promised to keep me in mind but that there were no job openings at that time. I waited around a few weeks and then received a cable from our agent in London. He had a job available for us, a six-month contract to work with Liberace in South Africa. It would pay $1500 per week and all expenses. That very same day Lou DeGreg phoned and said that he had an immediate opening for a crap dealer and that if I took the job, he would get me into the baccarat pit as soon as it was possible.

Before deciding whether or not to take the contract with Liberace, I went to work in the Frontier. We would really have loved to spend 6 months in South Africa, but I was making great money, and Elaine didn't want to leave the kids for that long a time. So, we really did finally decide that we would no longer try to get contracts doing our act. That part of our life was completed.

We were happy in our mobile home. My mother was doing well and wanted to live independently, so we found her a nearby apartment. My sister-in-law, Irene lived nearby as well, and my brother Tony had moved to Vegas and now lived in a condo with his family, so there were lots of family members to keep her from being lonely. Only my sister, Fernanda, refused to return to Vegas, which was probably a good decision for her, as it had been a disaster the first time around.

Coming into 1973, Elaine and I were doing a lot of reading and studying about spirituality. Neither of us was interested in pursuing a path within an organized religion. What we wanted was 'realization', to realize what God and life were all about. There were a few yoga teachers

who had come from India and were now based in the States. We went to visit some of them and always felt that we were wasting our time looking for a real master.

As Elaine continued to read and study, she was also doing a tremendous amount of meditation. I was working and knew that if I focused my energy on making money, I would be able to retire in 10 years, so I was more involved with the material world than she was. I think this is a common trait among men, that they concentrate on working, surviving, gaining financial security. It is a very easy mentality to slip into, to think that this is all that is important. I call it putting the cart before the horse, as men concentrate all their energy on filling that cart, not knowing that the cart is already full. We don't realize that we already have it all. I was totally involved in the material world, but a part of me was still trying to meditate and grow spiritually. I did have some good experiences through study and meditation and discussed them with Elaine, but she would say that I now had to 'realize' those experiences, to really understand what they meant. It would take many years before I understood what she was talking about.

CHAPTER 31

Juliano's Hang It All

As must be obvious by now, Elaine had multiple talents in the arts, music, sports, and life generally. And she was now looking for a project into which she could direct all this talent and energy. She had started painting again, and was honing her musical abilities by taking piano instruction with our friend Muriel Adler — another spiritual searcher (in her case a Jewish one). And she also started giving meditation classes on Thursday nights.

Then, one day we were at the Roseland Nursery we saw a macramé plant hanger that cost $18. I pointed out that it was basically three strings, some shells, a shelf and a ring: not more than $2 worth of materials. I told Elaine that she could make that with her eyes closed — since after all, macramé is the art of making things with knots. She laughed and asked me what I meant. So we went to VonTobel's, a large local hardware/arts and crafts store in Vegas at that time, and bought enough supplies to make two or three hangers.

We went home with our purchases, and Elaine just stood there looking at me, 'Now what do we do?' I knew a few knots, like the square knot, but realized that we needed help, so we went to the library and got a book on seamen's knots. There were about 75-80 different knots in the book, so we took some of the more basic ones, and Elaine proceeded to design a plant hanger which was absolutely beautiful. She started expanding her design ideas and making more of them, getting her supplies at VonTobel's,

until she had about 20 of these plant hangers in the house. At that point I asked her what she was going to do with them, and she said that perhaps we could sell them.

We went back to the nursery with several of Elaine's hangers and were told that they would buy all that Elaine could make. Macramé hangers were becoming very popular and were hard to keep in stock, and it was also obvious that these were a good quality product.

From that point on we were making 50-60 hangers per week. We had jute, beads and other supplies all over the house. Within a few months we were making $600-700 per month selling the hangers wholesale to the Roseland Nursery and to another local nursery. We knew there was a lot more money to be made on the retail side of the business, and the house was just getting too cluttered, so I suggested that we open a little shop — a place where we could keep all the supplies, display her hangers and other creations in the front and make them in the back.

So, we checked out a few locations and found a little corner shop on Charleston Boulevard — 20 feet wide by 70 feet deep, which Elaine immediately started to decorate, making it more inviting. She created a macramé curtain that covered the front window and asked me to make her some kind of bench where she could display items for sale. She realized that we could sell supplies as well as finished products. I finished the front of the shop with wood flooring and beams, and separated the back, so that it could be our office and workroom. It took about six weeks to get it all together, but it ended up looking really cute. It took a little longer to come up with a name, but then we got it: Juliano's Hang It All. Elaine made a big sign for the front of the building, and then we painted and decorated the side wall as well.

We had a grand opening with the mayor of Las Vegas in attendance and served champagne and sandwiches. We got great coverage that day from the press and the next day we opened to the public. Macramé was just coming into fashion and it was hard to find any decent books with patterns and examples, but we got supplies and materials from a few California distributors, including a Mr. Fitzgerald, who worked out of San Francisco and had a huge inventory and a good catalog. We used him a lot. Each week we ordered more and more materials, and we soon realized that this little shop was actually a goldmine. The planters sold, the jute and beads

sold, anything we bought or made sold. Some items made just pennies in profit, but the volume kept increasing. We hired two clerks right away, and even with them working the front of the store, we were having trouble keeping up with our wholesale business, which was also growing.

Elaine had her hands full, keeping up with the demands of the shop, while I was still working swing shift at the Frontier and helping her during the days. We expanded our designs to include items like baby bassinet hangers, macramé drapes and wall decorations and hired more ladies to help with the retail part of the business.

Then one day Fitzgerald appeared out of the blue, introducing himself to us. He looked around and admired our little shop. He picked several items to buy, and when I asked him why he was buying so many, he explained that he wanted to showcase them in a book about macramé. 'No,' I said, 'I'm going to print my own book.' Fitzgerald said that if the book was any good he would immediately start buying and distributing it. After Fitzgerald left, Elaine turned to me and asked what this nonsense was all about, publishing a book. I said that if Fitzgerald was interested in publishing a book, there must be money in it.

We studied one of the books that was already in print, which we didn't think was very creative. Elaine had a great imagination and could take any idea or project and turn it into something special. So we designed our first book. It would have a 26-page book with an 8x10 inch color photo of 12 items and the written pattern for each one. We wrote out the patterns and proofread them, while our friend Artie Zeller came up from Santa Monica and took the photographs. Printing a four-color book was a complicated and expensive process in those days, involving color separation with the production of a four plates for each photo (cyan, magenta, yellow and black —which, when put together make the full rainbow of colors).

Besides the patterns themselves, Elaine wanted to include some spiritual messages in the books, so we added short stories and proverbs onto each page. In future years we were amazed by how many people wrote to us saying how much these stories and proverbs meant to them. To us they seemed to increase the book's vibration and its popularity tremendously.

After about 6 months we had a product ready for publishing. From the public library we learned about publishing and found a printer in Vegas who had the web press that we needed. We spoke with the company's

sales representative who was enthusiastic about the book. We started with a small print estimate, but we realized that to be profitable the only course to take would be a large printing: in our case 100,000 books for $20,000 — this would be added to the $2,000 we had already invested. The sales rep was skeptical at the prospect of our selling that many books because the country was in an economic slump, but I told her that there was no room for negative thinking. I was positive that this would be a great success. We came up with the $5,000 advance and eight weeks later we had our book.

In the meantime Elaine and I decided to call up a few book and macramé wholesale distributors. Even though I had all the figures needed to convince them about our book, they seemed very reluctant to commit themselves to our product. All the same, they all asked that we send them copies of the book once it was completed, at which point they would decide whether or not to distribute it. As it turned out, they all wanted a 60% profit for themselves built into the price of the book. I was not impressed with their attitudes and felt that, using the shop as a base, we could do our own distribution to craft stores across the country. Elaine and I went back to the library and consulted numerous phone books from which we got the names and addresses of about 75 macramé shops. We sent them all a little announcement — much like a baby's birth announcement — about our book. The reaction was immediate, with numerous shops writing that they would buy a dozen here, 2 dozen there, etc. It was obvious to us that we didn't need a distributor, that we could do it ourselves. The book would sell for $1.50 and we would keep 60 cents while the retailers would keep the other 90 cents. A much better deal for us.

But before any of this could actually happen I still had to come up with the remaining printing cost of $20,000. This I got from Marco Angioni, my good friend at the Frontier, who agreed to be my partner and help me raise the money. Right away he gave me $5000. Now that Marco was my partner, I told him that there would be no extravagant spending — like going to his beloved hometown in Sardinia and spending money freely — until I had the full $20,000.

Our book was supposed to be delivered approximately six weeks after I paid the printer. When nothing happened after seven weeks, I became curious and wanted to see the printing process, but I wasn't allowed onto

the printing floor. After eight weeks had passed, I demanded to receive our order within another week 'or else.' Two days later the printer called to say that the books were ready. He had them stacked up in his warehouse in a block of boxes that each contained 120 books. The block itself was 18 inches high by 7 feet wide by 30 feet long. I immediately rented a little storage warehouse on Industrial Road for $100 per month to which Marco and I moved all the boxes of books in a rented truck.

Now it was time to call Fitzgerald, the reluctant California book distributor, and send him a copy of the book. As soon as he saw the book, he ordered 50,000 copies. I charged him $20,000 and shipped them off to him by Railway Express. We went through all the orders we had received from the individual shops and sent them out in the next week or so.

I realized that we would need another printing when, after only about a month, we had gone through 75 percent of our stock, but I decided to further investigate the locations of web presses in the Southwest because I didn't trust the guy who had done our first printing and felt sure that something unethical was going on. We found out that the biggest web presses were located in Salt Lake City, Utah.

One weekend Elaine and I took a trip to Salt Lake City to visit Deseret Press, one of the companies with a web press, and asked to speak with a sales representative. I told him who we were and he greeted Elaine and me like old friends. As it turned out, they had actually been the ones who did the actual printing of our books. While we were being wined and dined by the rep, we told him about our need for a second printing, and he said that they would be delighted to do so, but only after we paid the $5000 still owed from the first printing. I was shocked and showed him the receipts from the Vegas printer marked 'paid in full.' When I also learned that Deseret Press had charged $10,000 — not $20,000 — I got even angrier. After we ordered another 100,000 books *directly* from Deseret Press, the sales rep phoned our Vegas printer and asked about the missing $5000. The Vegas guy said that I hadn't paid him yet. At that point I got on the phone and warned him that the money wasn't sent by bank transfer immediately, I would return to Vegas and strangle him. The money was sent, and from that time on we dealt directly with Deseret Press.

We wrote up the new contract with Deseret Press, and when we called Fitzgerald — who ordered another 50,000 books — I passed the savings on

to him, changing only $10,000 this time and shipping the books directly from SLC.

With one book under our belt and publishing incorporated into our life, it was time to work on a second one. This time we created a wall hanging that was featured on the front of the book, and macramé curtains for the windows of a van featured on the back. The book concentrated solely on making these two projects with different knots because we felt that it would be easier to learn macramé if there was one book devoted entirely to the craft of knot making itself. This second book was even more popular than the first, and we found ourselves getting orders for more than 100,000 books every two or three weeks. In less than a year we had sold over one million books, sending them all over the country and beyond. Because of the volume we now had to deal with more distributors and I gave them differing rates depending on the quantities they ordered. At this point we had seven women working for us, both in the shop and at the warehouse.

It now seemed that all I did was work, whether at the casino, at the shop or at the warehouse. Elaine suggested that I quit the casino business, as we were making enough money with the macramé.

We decided that I would give it a try, so I went to the Frontier and asked for three months off. The scheduler said it would be impossible. I asked for two months, then one month, then two weeks. At that point, when he refused to give me any time off, I quit. He was incredulous, but I was gone.

That probably wasn't a very wise decision, but I had often made stupid decisions before on the spur of the moment. Elaine would tell me to think things through first, to try to plan a little before acting on impulse. We promised each other to discuss things in greater depth before just jumping in and doing things prematurely.

As we ended 1973 and started 1974 life was full and busy. Our only disappointment was that David failed at college and withdrew after only one semester. Now 17 years old, he had to go to work. I got him a few different jobs, but he never lasted very long at any one of them. We worried about him but also sympathized because we knew what it was like to be young and to want to follow your own interests.

In a material sense our lives were successful, but I knew that I was

not growing spiritually. Elaine told me to keep meditating, to keep going within. I would try, but there were times when I would lose heart and ask: 'God, are you listening? Are you really there?' I had no reason to doubt the existence of God, but the doubts were still there, and I would wonder if I was praying to nothing. Elaine was growing and progressing, successfully meditating and finding answers to her problems and I didn't want to tell her about my own doubts.

In the business part of our lives it was now time to publish our third book, and we had several new designs. This time Elaine took the photographs herself and planned the layout of each project in the book. Some of our new patterns took 30 or 40 hours to make, and we worked hard to make sure that each step was perfectly described. It was interesting to find out that the only way to make money from these beautiful projects was through the books. Interior decorators often came and asked us to create items for their clients, but they were rarely willing to pay for the time and effort it took to complete them.

With over two million books now in print, we were known throughout the world for our publications. We were sending boxes of books to Spain, Portugal, England and even India.

Unfortunately, even with this success, I still wasn't really happy. Now I started thinking that maybe what I needed was to build and open a gym because, of course, I had continued to work out during all of the trials and successes of publication.

Juliano's
Hang It All

MACRAMANIA

CHAPTER 32

Meeting Sri Sathya Sai Baba

One of my regular morning meditations came to have particular importance because while I was in a state of acute awareness I heard a phrase repeated many times: Sathya Sai Baba, Sathya Sai Baba. It made no sense to me; there was no explanation, just the phrase, coming with great force and clarity. I thought about it throughout the day, wondering if it was a name because I knew that Baba meant father, that Sai could be interpreted as heavenly.

That same week when Elaine gave her regular 7:00 to 10:00 pm Thursday meditation class I was working at the casino — as I often did — until very late. When I got home at 3:00 am I asked her, as usual, if anything interesting had happened. Indeed it had. At one point a woman with long, black hair and wearing an Indian robe burst into the room. She said that she was a hatha yoga instructor, that she had been in Vegas for several years and wanted to tell them all about her master. His name was Sathya Sai Baba. I was shocked. According to the hatha yoga instructor — whose name Elaine had never heard — Sathya Sai Baba lived in India, worked miracles, healed the sick and had even raised the dead. It was then that I told Elaine about the chanting that had intruded on my morning.

Soon after, while taking a coffee break during a shopping trip, Elaine called out to me in surprise because she had happened upon a book about Sai Baba called 'Man of Miracles.' Of course she bought it. There was a

photo of Sai Baba on the cover of the book, a man who was remarkably beautiful.

I read 'Man of Miracles', and when I had finished it I went to Elaine and told her that I had to go to India. She wasn't surprised and, in fact, encouraged me to go. She would take care of everything in our life, including the shop, while I was gone. Needing to get some extra money together before I left, I went back to the Frontier and looked up my old friend, Lou DeGreg, who was pretty annoyed with me for the way I had quit but agreed to give me some part-time work for the short time before I was to leave for India.

From the day I started to work at the casino again I did nothing but make money and, as a result, I had over $6000 by the time I was ready to leave for India. In other words, everything fell into place; everything was just right. It was just like the old saying that when the student is ready the master will appear. I had been searching for a master for years, and now it seemed as if this man was indeed the one.

My old friend, George Vlahos, who was back in the States and working at the Hilton, decided that he wanted to go with me, and as I was still worried about my son David, who seemed to be drifting aimlessly through his young life, I decided that he would come with us as well. We got our tickets to India via Los Angeles, New York and London.

During our layover in Los Angeles, there was a group of people standing nearby, some of whom were dressed in saris. There was one woman — Andre Devi — a very attractive 65-year old, who seemed to be in charge. They too were going to India to see Sai Baba, her master. She laughed when I told her that we were going to see him as well and asked how we had heard about him. I told her my story. She said that we all had special stories about our first encounters with Baba and our desires to see and meet him. From that point on we traveled with her group.

When we arrived in New York we were joined by another group of about twenty people and enjoyed hearing their experiences about finding Sai Baba. One young man reminded me of myself as a boy. He was from Philadelphia and had not yet found a focus in life. He had done some bodybuilding and recognized me from magazine photos. He said I wouldn't believe him if he told me his story about Baba. The story he told was that he woke up one morning, and standing at the foot of his bed

was a small, beautiful Indian man with an afro haircut and dressed in an orange robe, surrounded by a bright light. The young man had never heard of Baba before, but there he was. Baba talked to him for about 15 minutes and told him that he had to come to India. It was indeed an incredible story, but I had no reason to doubt him. I told him my story and how I needed a lot of convincing before I was ready to believe that I, too, should go to India. It was reassuring to hear one story after another like this as I got acquainted with the other travelers.

From London we flew to India, where, at the airport, George, David and I took a train to Bangalore, meeting up with the other travelers at our hotel. We all wanted to continue on to the ashram in Puttaparti because that evening Baba would be producing a lingam — an egg-shaped object that Baba brought up out of his throat. In this way he was gradually returning lost or stolen Shiva lingams to various temples around India. However, it was already late at night, so Andre Devi decided that we should depart in the morning, allowing us to wait for any late arrivals so that we could all go together to the ashram.

The next morning we all piled into cabs and made the 50-mile trip to Puttaparti. George, David and I were in one of the first cabs to reach the ashram and went directly to the Shed, a large, open-sided building about half the size of a football field covered with a metal roof. There was a stage at one end, and as we walked with our luggage in hand we could see Baba speaking there. The audience at the Shed is divided by sex, and we had walked in on the women's side. Baba immediately waved to us to approach. As I neared him, my knees buckled, and I fell to his feet. The vibrations were so strong, and I felt almost breathless. As I got up on my knees from the floor, Baba tapped me on the head and said, 'Well, you finally got here, didn't you?' He then directed us to a man who would get us settled in our accommodations, after which we could return.

We were taken to a small room that had 3 bunk beds, a sink and a little stove. It was very simple, but clean and comfortable. From there we went to the Canteen for lunch, where we met up with the other members of our group. Every person there had an incredible story about meeting Baba. I had decided that to believe a first-hand story was valid, but that a story that had been repeated several times by different people was not reliable.

In the afternoon we usually lined up for darshan (blessing), kept in

place by selected women called saivadals. Each line received a number, and then the lines were called up at random, to enter the Shed and sit as close to the stage as possible. Because the crowds were not too large at this point, we were able to form a large circle, sitting on the floor, with Baba in the center.

Our group was called the California group, and we all wore a particular bandana as identification. If Baba tapped someone and chose him or her to visit with him in a private interview, the entire group was allowed to go. Darshan usually lasted for about an hour, during which Baba spoke to us, blessed little baskets of candies and materialized from his fingertips a sacred ash called Vibhuti, which he would give out to various devotees. If you were skeptical, he would even roll up his sleeves before creating the ash. Our group was chosen for an interview that first day, and after darshan we all went into a smaller area where he spoke with us as a group. Then, if he tapped you on the head, you knew that you had been chosen for a personal interview and would have a few precious minutes alone with Baba.

When Sai Baba chose me, I went into a little room that was about 6 feet square. I sat on the floor before him and he asked me 'What is it that you want?' Before I could answer, he went on to say, 'The first thing I want you to know is that I always hear your prayers. Never doubt it for one minute that I don't hear you.' I was stunned because that had been on my mind so much during the past several months. The joy I felt was incredible. Then Baba said, 'David is not your son; he's my son. You don't have to worry about him anymore.' It felt as if 100 pounds had been lifted off my back, and I exhaled with relief. He said, 'Yes, let it all go.' He talked further about some intimate issues, and then he ended the interview, saying that we would talk again later.

When we were back with the group, Baba talked with us all for a while longer and materialized objects as well. He would wave his hand, and something would appear in it that was appropriate for a particular person. From beginning to end, my first darshan and personal meeting with Sai Baba was truly an incredible experience.

George, David and I stayed at the ashram for three weeks during which we each had several private interviews with Sai Baba. We were very fortunate to see Baba at this time. It was 1974 and European groups were just starting to come to India to see Baba. Previously, he had been known

only in India, so there had been relatively few foreigners at the ashram, and we all got to spend more time with him that would be possible in later times. He predicted that one day in the future, if we were to return, he would be a distant orange dot on the stage with thousands of devotees in attendance. In the years to come, George would visit Baba annually and he always commented on the growing crowds of devotees.

But not everything in India was wonderful. I was appalled by the dire poverty and the number of beggars we saw every day, so one day in a group interview I asked Baba how I should deal with them, because they crowded around us, begging, every time we went outside the ashram. Baba replied that I would soon have my lesson.

One morning as I was leaving the ashram I noticed a young woman. She had three young children clinging to her sari and another at her breast. She indicated that she was hungry, so I instinctively went to the nearest pushcart and bought two kilo of bananas for her. She pushed them aside and, rubbing her thumb and fingers together, indicated that she wanted money. I walked on.

One afternoon I saw a young man, deformed and crumpled up on the ground with a begging bowl before him. I took all the change I had and gave it to him. Later that same day I was walking through the village and was impulsively drawn to look through a gate into a beautiful courtyard. There on a chaise lounge in the shade reclined the very same young man that I had seen earlier. I realized then that, at least for this one individual, his poverty and begging was his profession. These were the lessons that Sai Baba taught me.

CHAPTER 33

Righteousness

One day Sai Baba was giving a lecture to about thirty of us devotees. A woman raised her hand and asked, 'Baba, why have you come back?' He replied, 'Righteousness. I have come back to bring righteousness to the world.' My whole body vibrated with that word — righteousness — and I realized the value of an experiment I had seen in England while studying Scientology. As I have mentioned previously, we had used an e-meter to measure the meaning of words and their vibrations. I, myself, had learned that I knew very little about many words and was using them daily without really understanding their meaning. Six or seven of us would take words like love, god, goodness and 'see' the vibrations of these words through this machine. One of the words was righteousness, and it was one of those that vibrated the most.

Again, here in India we all saw how the word 'righteousness' vibrated more when it was spoken by someone who truly understood its meaning. We all felt it and talked about it together later.

And so Baba explained what righteousness is and what it can do.

Similarly, Jesus said, "Seek yea first the Kingdom of God and His righteousness, and all things shall be added unto you."

Righteousness is God itself. It means to unite, to become one with, absolutely no separation, because it is within every one of us, and it can lift up those around us.

Several years later the word righteousness came to me again when I was meditating and the Biblical story of Sodom and Gomorrah came into my mind. In fact, I felt as if I was right there in the city of Gomorrah, one of the two neighboring cities with several thousand people who lacked understanding and the ability to think on a righteous plane. Their vibrations were very low, the kind of vibrations that come from evil thinking, corruption, and sexual misconduct.

But even in Sodom there was Lot, a very religious, wise man, whom the Lord loved very much. A good man, he loved God and his fellow mankind. His daughters loved him for his goodness. His wife, although skeptical of much of what he believed, also knew that he was a good man and followed him faithfully. One evening during dinner there was a knock on the door. Two men stood there, surrounded by a white light. Lot knew immediately that they were angels and welcomed them in. Without speaking, they sat and started eating dinner with the family. But at the same time, they were speaking to Lot mind to mind, telling him that he and his family had to leave the city because the Lord was going to destroy it. Horrified, he asked for mercy on all the people who would die. One angel responded, "The Lord has said that, if you can find ten righteous men within the city, it will be spared. We will return in two weeks."With that the angels disappeared into the night.

Lot's family didn't understand his distress. Without explanation he left the house. For the next two weeks, day and night, he searched for ten righteous men, talking, asking, and feeling their vibrations. He searched both cities without pause, going door to door. Then, while he was meditating on the last day, the angels returned to him. He told them that he had been unable to find the ten righteous men. They repeated to him that he must leave the city with his wife and daughters, walk up and past the mountain, and never look back, no matter what they might hear behind them. Lot summoned his family and told them to prepare for departure. The wife was filled with questions, but Lot simply said, "We must leave the city."

Obediently, the wife and daughters made their preparations, and the family left the city. Then far away, up on the mountain, the sky became black and filled with thunder. Without thinking, the wife turned back to see what was happening behind her and, at that moment, she turned into a

pillar of salt. Lot and his daughters didn't even realize what had happened because they were looking only ahead. Finally, the skies cleared, the noise ended, and they realized that their wife and mother wasn't there.

The lesson of this parable is about the power of righteousness — the vibration of righteousness. Imagine: just ten righteous men could have saved Sodom and Gomorrah. The vibration of righteousness can be so strong and so high when righteousness is truly understood. Truly, a wise man is righteous — a master is righteous. We can imagine that if ten righteous men could save two cities then two cities of righteous men would be able to save a whole planet. Righteousness has the power to eliminate negativity from normal thinking. It emanates out and has the power to change the vibrations around it — to counteract corruption and immorality. I call this process the "invisible computing" — the destruction of negative energy by the power of positive energy, the energy of righteousness.

But this is only one part of the parable of Lot; the other part of the parable concerns itself with not looking back. In my meditation on righteousness and the Old Testament parable of Lot I heard Jesus say to me: "He who live in the past is dead. He who lives in the future has no future. The one who lives in the now is truly a wise and righteous man." Here, indeed, was the meaning of the parable of Lot.

What is meant by this truly righteous statement? If you live in the past you are dead, because there is nothing there. If you live in the future you are nowhere, because it doesn't yet exist. The only time to live is NOW. A wise and righteous man actually 'is' the now.

And who are the righteous? When I meditate and ask for guidance these are some of the people who come to me:

Mahatma Gandhi, the great leader of the Indian independence movement, was a truly righteous man. He lifted India out of bondage through the principle of nonviolence. He didn't judge or condemn. He simply acted on his belief in equality and freedom. That man, who was small in stature but so great in spirit, lived a life of righteousness until one day an ignorant non-thinker, who had no understanding of the truth, shot him and put out his physical light. He could not, however, extinguish the message of this righteousness man.

Martin Luther King was another beautiful, righteous man — an American who believed in non-violence and non-judgment. He brought the

light to America and shined it on the separation of the races, the separation of black and white. He tried to lift up his people out of the slavery of prejudice and discrimination, of ignorance. He did it in a beautiful way. Through his righteousness — not judging or condemning — he lifted up the spirit of millions of oppressed Americans. For a short time he was able to bring together people of all colors to achieve change, but again, along came an ignorant non-thinker, who thought he was doing something honorable by putting out that beautiful light. The man was killed, but again, the message endured. And then, as has happened so many times before, the veil dropped and the message seemed to slowly start to fade away.

The great Nelson Mandela, who brought righteousness into a country that had suffered through generations of domination and bondage was another truly righteous man. He led South Africa out of the darkness of the apartheid years and, instead of being vindictive — of wanting revenge on his oppressors — he forgave them and united with them through the love of righteousness. His smile lit up the country, his love for all of mankind flowed around the world, and people understood and came to witness him, to experience his loving presence. His vibrations of righteousness uplifted all who were around him. Today that light of his physical being has been lost, but we still have it in his teachings and the example he set in the way he lived his life. If only we can keep those lessons in our hearts and minds. It is more important to carry on the work that Mandela started than to just worship the memory of the teacher. The message is to unite, unite, unite, not to separate. It is a message about love and being together as one. We mustn't forget, letting the veil drop down again. We mustn't worship the teacher — putting up statues in parks and photographs on walls — while forgetting the path he showed us.

In the cases of all three of these men — whose lives I have been blessed to witness — the message is the same: united we stand, and separated we fall. That is the meaning of righteousness: total uniting, total oneness, total God.

It doesn't seem very easy, but it can be done. It only takes a few truly righteous men and women to raise up thousands — even millions — of people. Imagine how this material world would change if we had one hundred righteous individuals, or even one thousand. Be righteous (or: embody righteousness) and you will see the change around you.

But as human beings we so often do the wrong thing: we end up worshipping the messenger and forgetting about the message. What we should be doing is worshipping the message, understanding the message and realizing the message. The messengers may be great, but they were never meant to be worshipped, because when we do so we forget the message, misinterpret it and don't understand it.

As Jesus said to me directly in one of my meditations, 'Why do you praise me? I myself can do nothing, and if I bear witness of myself, I bear false witness, for the I am within me does the work.'

And so, once more I say to you, 'Seek ye first the kingdom of God and His righteousness and all things shall be added unto you' (Matthew 6:33). We must try to seek and understand that righteousness. We must unite, unite, unite.

CHAPTER 34

Take It Further

The first time I heard the phrase, 'take it further', I was in Las Vegas, sitting on my couch on a beautifully mild day. It was approaching winter and the sun was shining in on the black television screen. At that moment — and for the first time — I *really* saw the blackness of the screen.

Suddenly I felt myself flowing towards it, and as I reached the surface of the screen I heard a voice say, 'Take it further.' Then I realized that I had passed through the screen and was behind it. It looked like a huge city there and I was every part of it. I heard the voice say again, 'Take it further.' I found myself at the back of the set where the power was connected and I followed down through the wires to the plug on the wall. Taking it further once again I was in the wall, in the wires between the two by fours, coming up out of the wall and into the circuit breaker box. I was aware of all the breakers and I could see how some wires were frayed. The voice again said, 'Take it further' and I proceeded through the electrical wire, underground, only to resurface on Flamingo Road, following the wire to the top of the power pole. Then I found myself down the road at the relay station where machinery was sending power throughout the city.

Once again I heard the voice, and the next thing I knew I was going through massive wires towards Boulder and then I was at Boulder Dam. I was at the top of a dynamo, massive currents flowing everywhere, which I could feel — but without pain or discomfort. From there I went down

into the dam, into the dynamos themselves. Taking it further, I was going through huge water pipes into Lake Mead itself. I was the breadth and depth of Lake Mead. I was the water, the surrounding cliffs, one with everything. And then the voice said, 'Take it further.' I was going up the canyon, the water rushing all around me and then beyond, up in the mountains. Going further, I found myself up in the clouds, lightening striking and snow swirling around me. The feeling was incredible. I was everything up there.

The voice stopped, and the next thing I knew I was back on my couch in Las Vegas. I sat there for quite some time, thinking about these words.

The lesson was that you can take anything further. You can take this story further. You can stop and think about what you have read, think about how far you can go with it. What is the real meaning, what was the author's real meaning? Take it as far as you can, in the process you will learn a lot. Don't stop, just continue to always take it further, until you get the realization of whatever you are concentrating on. That was my lesson about 'taking it further', and you will hear me use the phrase a lot as I talk in this book.

I wish you 'shanti', the peace that surpasses all understanding.

Shanti, shanti, shanti.

CHAPTER 35

Building the Gym: Having a Goal and Fulfilling It

I don't remember when I first dreamed of building a gym, but it probably started the first time I walked into a gym as a boy. I must almost always have dreamed of having a gym of my own.

In 1976 Elaine and I had just completed the publication of our third macramé book when, one morning I woke up and told her that I wanted to open up a gym. She told me that I should fulfill that dream, as I obviously had been wanting to do it for a long time and needed to get it out of my system. That way, she said, I wouldn't have to come back to do it in another lifetime.

So, right away Elaine started designing the building layout and I met with the realtor about a perfect property I already knew about — a two-acre piece of land that was for sale on Boulder Highway in Las Vegas that I felt would be an excellent location for our gym. At the same time, however, I was working out in a little gym called the Executive Club, about 5000 sq. ft. in the Maryland Parkway Center, a popular shopping center with a health food store, a good deli, a pool hall and a women's fitness center. The owner of the Executive Club approached me and asked me to take over ownership of the gym. Initially I had no interest in buying it because it was worn down from years of neglect. He offered it to me for $2,000 and I countered with $1,500; he agreed, and the bargain was made.

The gym had some good points: a good sets of weights, walls lined with mirrors, a fair amount of equipment, as well as a stream room, a hot tub and showers. And I knew Fat Tony, a crap dealer with whom I worked at the Frontier, who also did home renovations and repair work as a second job. Two other friends, Vito and Skippy, were both experienced in building and electrician skills. My friend Marco was already my partner in the macramé business and joined the group, even if he wasn't very good at repair or renovation work. We all got together to size up the job of renovating this old property. Fat Tony figured that with $50,000 we could really make it into a nice place.

Elaine drew up the plans for the new gym. We split the front into two parts, with a juice/snack bar and a little office. There would also be a counter where protein powders and vitamins could be sold. The floor would be tiled, and the décor would include wrought iron and macramé. But before we could start renovating, the building had to be gutted, and that job alone took us about a month. Once it was torn apart, I walked in and was appalled at the mess. We would fill six dumpsters removing all that garbage.

At the same time we were starting the gym and I was working at the Frontier, we were also shipping out macramé books from the warehouse, while Elaine was working at the macramé shop. We would start work at the gym at 7:00 am and spend all day there, until about 4:00 in the afternoon. Then I would run over to the warehouse and deal with shipment orders. After about three hours there, I would go home, grab a snack and then go to work at the Frontier. I would get home at about 3:00 am, get a few hours of sleep and then start the cycle all over again. This went on for five months.

Finally, Elaine and I stood inside the newly completed gym, turned to me and asked, 'Are you happy now?

I replied that yes, I was happy. During the renovation I felt that my goal was being accomplished, and I was very satisfied with the work we were all doing. Elaine and I had often talked about the need to complete each dream and desire that one had — that they stall your progress through life if not completed — so when I installed the last bit of mirror framing, and put in the last nail I knew that my goal had been achieved, that I could move beyond this project. It was a great feeling, but there *was* one problem

remaining even beyond running the gym and making it a success. I had promised all these guys that, for their help in renovating the gym, I would pay each one $5,000, a total of $20,000!

Our Grand Opening was a great success, maybe because my friend Arnold Schwarzenager graciously agreed to come out from Santa Monica, fitting us into his busy schedule. Many people came to meet him that day and to share in the celebration. We even started out with lifetime members who we knew from the previous gym and I had found a good equipment supplier in Arizona, so the gym was very well equipped and the interior was handsome, with carpeting and Mexican tile.

With the opening behind us, I told Marco that he would have to work hard to take care of the place because I wouldn't have time to be there continually. The truth was that Marco hadn't done much with either of our joint ventures: running the macramé business or the gym construction. Now he would now have to help with maintaining the gym. Marco, assured me that he would be able to handle it easily. The gym would be open 24 hours per day, and he promised that he would be there 10 or 11 hours each day. I would be able to work a few hours here and there, and we would hire some other guys to handle the rest of the schedule.

By this time I was pretty well worn out, and it was clear that I couldn't continue to run everything that was going on. I talked it over with Elaine, and we agreed that now would be a good time to end the partnership with Marco. We were in process of printing another macramé book, and all our cash was going towards that. Furthermore, because of unexpected expenses it had taken almost $90,000 to complete the gym. As both businesses were basically cashless, I proposed to Marco that he take over ownership of the gym and I would take the macramé business: the value of each being basically equal. Marco agreed with pleasure because he too had always wanted to own a gym. He paid the money owed to Fat Tony and made some kind of deal with Vito and Skippy to have part ownership in the gym.

For me the force of the initial desire was completely gone now because the goal had been fulfilled. It was a cycle of action that had been completed, one of many in my life that would not have to be continued in another life. I learned so much about this from watching Elaine, as she was finishing one cycle after another as well.

As for Marco, I don't think the gym ever did really well. He ended up

doing most of the managing, at least breaking even. I went to the gym to work out, but I had absolutely no more desire to own or run it.

And then, several months later, Marco announced that he was going to sell the gym, saying that he just couldn't manage it and work at the casino as well. He knew that George Eifferman, Mr. America of 1948, was moving to Vegas and wanted to open a gym. George looked at the gym and loved it. I told Marco that he should get the $90,000 original investment out of the deal, but in fact, I had nothing to do with the transaction. Marco got some cash down and then received monthly payments. Vito also made some kind of agreement with George and would stay on in management. And so the gym changed hands and was truly, completely out of my life.

CHAPTER 36

Trip to Hawaii

By the time the construction of the gym was complete I was totally exhausted because I had been getting very little sleep during those five months and so one day Elaine announced that it was time for us to take a vacation and get away for a few weeks. I hesitated, but she had already made the reservations and bought the plane tickets. She *knew* that we really needed a break.

We went to Hawaii and stayed at the Hilton Hotel on Waikiki Beach. It was wonderful to hang out on the beach once again, to eat and sleep as desired, and just to relax together again. One day while we were sunning on the beach Elaine remembered that Marie and Neil — our friends from Scientology who had received Donald into the life of their unborn child — were now living in Hawaii. She thought we should look them up and see how Donald had turned out.

We found their number in the phone book and called. I spoke with Neil who said that they would be delighted to have us come for a visit. Donald was now Kye — a Hawaiian name that he had chosen for himself. We agreed to meet for lunch and assured them that we would say nothing about the past and Donald.

The next day we drove out to their house, greeted Marie and Neil and were introduced to Kye, who was about seven years old now and had a striking resemblance to Donald. As we entered the house, Marie turned to

Kye and asked him if he remembered Elaine. He replied that yes he did; she had been his mommy in his last life. We were all surprised and went on to talk about the experience of Donald's passing and Kye's start in life. In the car on the way to lunch, Kye was sitting in the back with Elaine and Marie on each side. He put his arms around their shoulders and said, 'Well, now I have my two mommies.' It was quite moving for all of us.

Neil later told me that when Kye was six years old, a car hit him, just as a car had hit Donald at that age. When he was in the hospital, unconscious, Neil told him either to die and leave or to come back completely healed because the car accident cycle had to end once and for all. A few days later Kye regained consciousness and went on to make a complete recovery. None of us understood why he needed to repeat this cycle of action, but it was wonderful to know that it was over.

That afternoon Elaine and I were able to let Donald go because he was now a wonderful little boy named Kye. It was incredible to experience the cycle of reincarnation. This experience led us into a profound discussion about our recollections of our previous life together: how in the earlier one I had left Elaine and our children to live in a monastery for 30 years, studying, reading, and extensively involved in translating books written in different languages into Italian. I remembered that when I came across a word or phrase that I didn't understand, I would talk it over with my fellow scribes and we would come up with a meaning that *seemed* to work. It was that '*seemed*' that troubled me when I looked back at my actions in the former life. In retrospect it is clear that I might have made many mistakes that would have been repeated as truth and fact in later editions. I now realize that any book —including spiritual books — must be taken with a grain of salt because you can never be sure of its authenticity.

And so, in this lifetime, I picked up my life with Elaine and her three children, just at the same ages as when I had left her. Elaine had struggled to raise those children after I had deserted her, and now we were going forward again, not necessarily with the same children but with the karma that existed between the two of us.

While we were in Hawaii I had another wonderful parental experience. I have not mentioned this before, but back in the early 1950's I had an extended affair with a woman named Carol that resulted in the birth of our daughter, Gina, born in 1953. During the next few years I would visit

her in Santa Monica, where she lived with her mother, whenever I could get away from Vegas. There I enjoyed being involved in her life, playing with her and her half-siblings on the beach, shopping for clothes, caring for them.

One day, when we returned from clothes shopping, I saw that their suitcases were all packed, set out in the living room. Carol announced that she was putting all three children into foster care because she was unable to take care of them. I said that I would take responsibility for Gina. I would get a nanny for her in Vegas and assured Carol that she could come and visit at any time. Carol was adamant that the children stay in California and said that she already had homes set up for them. Nothing I said would change her mind. For hours I pleaded with her, but eventually I had to give up. I was not Gina's legal father — and there was no DNA testing in those days — so I had no legal rights as her biological father. I couldn't understand Carol's logic, but in the end I had to let Gina go.

During the following years I would occasionally hear news about Gina. I usually had some idea where she was living, whether in California or later in Hawaii when her mother moved to the Islands with her. I even heard about a time once, when she was about 12 years old, and met my friend Armand Tanny. She asked him if he was her father, and he replied, 'No, I'm not, but I know who he is.'

Knowing that she was living in Hawaii at the time of my trip with Elaine, I found her phone number and contacted her. We took her out to dinner that night and it was a wonderful experience. I had very deep feelings for her, feelings that I didn't even mention to Elaine. Years later, after Elaine's passing, Gina and I would come to spend much more time together, and we have been close ever since. I am so happy to have such a wonderful daughter.

CHAPTER 37

Another Goal: Boat Dreams 2

Elaine and I had just completed our fifth macramé book, and, as always, we celebrated with all our employees. We took the six women who worked with us for dinner at the Bacchanal Room in Caesar's Palace. After that Elaine and I would take off for a few days of recuperation.

This time we decided to go to southern California and stay at one of the beach towns. We chose Newport Beach where we would walk along the docks and look at all the sailboats. One afternoon we were window-shopping at a broker's office and noticed that there was a post for a 38-foot sailboat, a Downeaster that was for sale. I thought it looked great. Just then a salesman approached us and asked if we were interested in looking at the boat. He said that she was an ideal cruising boat, and that he would be glad to take us out for a sail. We arranged to meet him the next day and then went off to eat dinner. During our meal, Elaine remarked that this was obviously a goal that I needed to fulfill. She saw that I was really stuck on the idea of having a boat. I agreed that it had always been a dream, tucked away in the back of my mind.

As planned, we met the salesman the next morning and went out on the Downeaster. The cockpit was comfortable with lots of cushions, so we relaxed as the young man threw off the lines and guided the boat by motor out of the harbor. It was a perfect morning and, as we left the harbor, I asked Elaine what she thought about all this. She replied that she hadn't

given it much thought, but she knew that I had and that I needed to get this dream resolved, one way or another. I said that I thought we could have so much fun sailing, but she didn't really respond. Once out in open water we did a little sailing before returning to the dock. Back on land the salesman gave us some literature about the boat and we went to talk it over. Again, Elaine stressed that this was something that I needed to accomplish. If not, I would have to come back again in another lifetime to do it. I felt quite sure that we would be doing it together, and she never really answered with a yes or no. Feeling renewed and refreshed, we returned to Las Vegas and the subject of buying a sailboat was dropped once again.

I had often asked Elaine what goals she had yet to fulfill and when I asked her this time she replied that she no longer had any goals left; she had no more desires on this material plane. Instead, she wanted me to write down my list of desires and goals. My first entry was to own a sailboat, and I noted that I thought we would both enjoy the experience. She replied that this was my goal, not hers, and that I shouldn't expect her participation.

I realized — after some contemplation — that my only other goal was to attain realization: to realize who exactly I was. To this Elaine said that the goal of realization was the *only* important one, that all other goals are meaningless. I had to agree with her. As much as I loved my family and friends, the most important goal in life was to realize God. She would ask me what that meant, and I didn't know what to say. She knew the answer but wasn't going to tell me. I would have to find the answer for myself, hence Yogananda's term, self-realization. I would have to find the inner self on my own. She kept prodding me to do more meditating, to let go of daily issues and concentrate more instead. I always agreed, but I don't know if I really knew what I was saying. Perhaps I was just trying to appease her. I meditated and tried to be quiet and still. Sometimes I would have beautiful meditations, and sometimes there would be nothing. For Elaine, on the other hand, every meditation seemed to produce a wonderfully wise observation or truth.

We would have wonderful conversations about these things, but I didn't realize just how close she was to full realization. I was still totally involved with house and family and work: the usual daily worries. I have no idea why I was so obsessed with these daily concerns; I didn't need to worry about anything but — all the same — I seem to have chosen to do

so. These were more pieces of my 'life puzzle' that were piling up around me; pieces that I didn't know how to use. Elaine often laughed at me and just told me to keep on trying, that practice makes perfect. Even when I asked her things like, 'What about David and Dana?' she would reply, 'What about them? They are living and thriving. What do we have to offer them at this point? We have raised them to the best of our ability, tried to instill them with good concepts and set as good an example as is possible. Now they have to go on by themselves.'

I had to agree with her, but it was hard to let go. I was still trying to get them jobs, to arrange things for them, to keep them from making mistakes, while they lived their lives as they wanted. I knew that David and Dana had their own lessons to learn, but I had to remind myself that I had to give them total freedom, just as my mother had done for me as a young man. Unfortunately, the best I could do was to let them go for a while, and then something would happen that would make me interfere in their lives. Elaine would tell me once again to let them go, to let it all go, and the cycle would begin again. Of course she was right. David and Dana turned out just fine, and I can't criticize either one of them.

CHAPTER 38

The First Samadhi

One day early in the morning Elaine and I had eaten breakfast, and we were talking about making love. I said that I felt that there was something more to making love than just the sexual part of it, and she agreed. The wonderful feeling of climax lasted only a few seconds, and then there was always the desire to repeat that feeling. We couldn't come up with an immediate answer, and so we decided to meditate on it.

We went into the living room and decided that we would ask the same question, 'What is the meaning of sex? Why do people crave it?' In silence we asked our questions. I asked once, then again, but heard no answer. I waited in silence for the answer. After some time I heard a sweet, lovely voice say, 'It's the first samadhi.' I opened my eyes and saw that Elaine was already looking at me. She told me that she heard a voice say the same thing, 'It's the first samadhi.'

Now the two of us focused on the word 'samadhi'. I defined it as a state of blending, of becoming one with — merging with — God. She agreed, but she said that we must have more: the true realization of that samadhi. So we went into the bedroom and we undressed. We sat cross-legged on the bed, facing each other, and she told me to forget all about the past. This was to be the first time we had ever made love, totally in present time with no remembrance of the past. We started with a simple touch, really trying to feel one another. I loved the softness of her cheek, and she

discovered how broad my shoulders were. We went from each body part to another, lovingly touching each other. Then, I realized that I was having a sensation throughout my whole body, the feeling that I was merging with her. She felt the same thing, and then, as we continued to touch one another, suddenly we were one. There was no separation; we were melting into one another. It was an incredible oneness, an unbelievable sensation. In a way it was a total climax, where I felt her in every part of my body, as she was experiencing the same thing within her body.

And so we discovered that first samadhi. We had the experience, *and* we realized the experience. This is why people want to have intercourse — to have orgasms over and over again — because it is the first step in merging with another person. As we talked about the experience, Elaine explained that we are programmed to seek this feeling and to experience it repeatedly, but we are rarely in that moment. Rather, we are just reacting to memory, to the programming that makes us always seek the reaction with different people in different situations. We are not really coming to the final stage of completely merging and becoming one. But once you have experienced that first samadhi you seek it over and over again, because it is so wonderful.

The time had flown by without our realizing it — the feelings that we had experienced lasted much longer than the momentary bliss of orgasm. *This*, we realized is what people are always seeking through sex, but which cannot be attained solely through programming. You must realize what you have and reach out to your beloved as if for the first precious time. Try to be in the total state of now, not returning to the memory of something in the past. Don't let the programming become more important than the actual moment. *Then* you will experience your first samadhi.

Following the basic principle to 'take it further' Elaine and I realized that the feeling we had gone through with this first samadhi was actually everyone's desire to become one with God. We unite as one individual to another, but we are not uniting as totally as we can — as we need to do. It is only a first step towards uniting with total spirit. People experience the desire of having sex, but they don't realized what they are really seeking. The real uniting is with God. We have that split second of experience during orgasm without really understanding what we are seeking, and so we keep doing it over and over again.

Take it further: unite instead of separate. Work to overcome the basic trouble with the human race: that people are in a state of separation instead of union. The step of uniting through sex is only the first step of the ultimate union: the union with God.

CHAPTER 39

Elaine's Passing

At one time I was Elaine's spiritual teacher, but by 1978 I'd been left way behind; now she was my teacher.

One day when we were in the shop with the four girls who were working there at the time a young girl walked into the store. I was behind the counter and Elaine was in the back, blocked from the front by a set of louvered shutters that gave the backroom some privacy. Without even seeing the young girl Elaine screamed, 'My angel has come!' I had no idea what was going on as Elaine ran up from the back room and hugged the girl. She said, 'You want a job, don't you?'

The girl said that her name was Roanna, and that yes, she wanted a job. Elaine hired her on the spot, while I muttered something to myself about not needing any more help in the shop. Elaine took Roanna to the back to do her paperwork, and when I called to her to discuss this latest decision, she came up to me and looked me right in the eye. She said, 'Listen, this girl is going to come in handy for you one day very soon.'

She said it with such power that I immediately backed off and let it go at that.

Roanna was a delightful young lady, very pretty and full of life. She was always bubbly and was a quick study. She soon became part of the shop routine. And so the days and months continued to go by smoothly.

Then, one day as I was sitting at the back of the shop, just watching

Elaine as she worked at the desk, she suddenly looked up at me and said, 'Well, have you figured it out yet?'

I asked her what she meant, and she said that it was about who Roanna really was. I didn't know what she was talking about at first but then I realized that Elaine was talking about our past life together, which she had learned about through her study of astrology. The two of us had been married in this other life, but when I was thirty I had left my Elaine, my wife, and our three children to go live in a monastery. Roanna had been one of those children.

As usual, I was skeptical and needed proof, but once I thought about it, I realized that the way Roanna had slipped into our lives without effort, the way we all felt comfortable together, was the proof of what Elaine had said. She had a much greater understanding than I did about the spiritual world surrounding us; she could examine and experience actions and experiences in ways that led to a much fuller understanding than I was capable of.

It was at the same time that Roanna entered out life that I suffered such intense and chronic back pain working at the Frontier Casino that I had to walk with a cane at times. One day my friend Al mentioned that he was going to visit a spiritual healer in Redwood City, California, and suggested I go with him. I was skeptical, but I had nothing to lose. Elaine and I agreed to go see him. She drove up with Al and a friend's wife who had stomach pain, and I flew up the next morning and met them for the final drive to a half-finished log building. I managed to get up the long flight of stairs to the healer's ante-room where about fifty other people were waiting. I wasn't the only one with body aches and pains. Elaine hadn't been able to play tennis for years because of knee pain and Al's neck was very stiff and painful.

Reverend Plume, a small Englishman, entered the room. He sat on a small, wheeled stool and scooted around. He was always talking with someone, looking up and discussing things. I couldn't believe this guy was for real, but I saw that people were being healed. It seemed that he somehow popped something in Al's neck, and whatever he did, the pain and stiffness were gone. Without asking about your condition, Reverend Plume would simply place his forehead on your back and then treat your ailment, wherever it might be. Elaine sat down before him, and after he placed his head on her back, he came around to the front, and it seemed

that he started stuffing tissues of some kind into her knee. Then he hit the tissues with his hand and pulled them out. From that time on, she never again had knee pain.

I didn't want to give the reverend any clues as to my condition, so I left my cane behind and stiffly went forward to the chair where Reverend Plume was waiting. He spoke briefly to me and then put his head on my back. I heard him say, 'All right, I'll try that.' Then he put two of his fingers at the base of my spine and shoved them into my back. I could feel his fingers in my back. He pulled them back and with that motion the pain was gone. I never again had the back pain. It was a great experience. And for such a gift of healing Reverend Plume wouldn't accept more than ten dollars.

Now that Elaine's knee was healed, she started playing tennis again, as she had been very good at it in the past. She entered a few local tournaments and became an 'A' player in the rankings. I took a few lessons and learned to play the game as well, but I was never as good as she was. However, we did have a good time playing tennis together.

Then one morning Elaine came to me and said, 'Last night I could have left.'

She said that her two guides had come to her — explaining that we all have guides and some can be very high spiritually. As an aside, she said that I should acknowledge my guide, that I should thank and love him for all that he did for me. Returning to her own story, she went on to say that she had the choice to leave this material plane, because she didn't need to be here anymore. She said that she had started leaving with her guides, but just before the point of no return she realized that she had to get me ready for her departure, so she turned back and was now telling me about it.

Incredulous: that's what I was. Elaine was saying that she was done with life on this plane. She said that all her material goals had been realized — in the arts, in music, in material success with the macramé — everything. I asked about her teaching, the meditation classes, and she explained that actually, there were very few people around who had any idea of what was going on. She said that there was no reason to stay if not one person in her group really understood what she was teaching. She said that even I had no idea what she was talking about half the time. You can imagine what a blow to my ego that was. It was very difficult for me to

admit that she was always right, so I didn't say anything. I was just glad that she hadn't left.

I know how hard it is for people to comprehend these teachings, and that it is like that razor's edge, because even if you do get a glimpse of the truth, it is too easy to fall off to the side. The path is narrow and hard to follow. It is hard to get past this material universe — especially for men. Men are bound to money, to jobs, to position, to material things. Greed and envy always seem to play a part as well. Even I often questioned my own life. After all, I was a crap dealer, associating with gamblers and their money. In the casino one night — when I was depressed, brought down by the vibrations of my surroundings — I prayed to God to give me a sign, to show me why I was doing this. Soon afterward, while I was on a coffee break a younger dealer sat down beside me and started asking about India and I realized once again that there is no such thing as a coincidence because even here in the middle of a casino here was this young man earnestly searching for a higher truth. I must admit that this didn't happen very often. Few dealers spoke with me about spiritual matters or asked questions. They were stuck in the material universe, worrying only about new cars, new houses, vacations, toys, etc. even if they devoutly went to church every Sunday.

Elaine would tell me that sometimes she was so lonely that she could hardly bear it. She said that she had no one to talk to. Of course I said that she could talk to me, but she said no, she couldn't even talk with me, that I was too stuck in this material world. She told me that I had to get out of it, and I knew that she was so right, but there I was.

One evening we were sitting before the fireplace, where we had displayed a small lingam that she had brought back from India for me. Looking at the fire before her she said that she and the fire were one, that she *was* the fire. At that moment she placed her hands directly into the fire, much to my horror. The flames were dancing around her fingers and she seemed to be playing with them. She created a ball of fire in her hands and then dropped it down again. I was in total shock. I have no idea how long this lasted, but eventually she turned to me and repeated, 'The fire and I are one.'

Elaine said she had to get me ready for her departure. She would talk to me and look at me and ask, 'Who am I?'

I would say that she was my wife, my best friend, and she would walk away in disgust. A few days later she would ask the same question, and I would call her my lover, my soul mate, and she would turn away. I didn't know what she wanted from me. I was trying to meditate more and more on this question, but the harder I tried the further away the answer seemed.

This went on for about six months, during which time Elaine would meditate every night from about 12 midnight to about 3AM. One evening she went to meditate and I was in the bedroom, watching a movie about John the Baptist. I found myself thinking that John had been spiritually insane . . . In that instant I heard another voice say, 'So am I.'

It was Elaine, and for the first time it occurred to me that she, too, might be spiritually mad. When she came back into the room after her meditation, she was radiant with beauty. She said that she was burning up, on fire, and that she had to take a cold bath. I could feel the heat of her body. The house itself was cool, but she needed that cold water to bring down her body temperature. I helped her towel off, and then, once we were back in the bedroom, she turned to me and said, 'I want you to look at me. Don't talk or think, just look at me.'

From maybe twelve inches away, I looked into her eyes, and she asked once more, 'Who am I?' And at that moment I realized that we had merged, that we had become one. We were out of our bodies, totally united. We were conscious that we were separate, and — at the same time — we were now one. We took this oneness and traveled through the city and the state and out over the planet. We went everywhere. This experience lasted for about an hour. It was bliss beyond bliss. It was total oneness, no separation of any kind.

The next thing I knew, boom, I was back in my body with Elaine in front of me. She looked at me and now asked one last time, 'Who am I?'

I said, 'You're God.'

She replied, 'Now you know, and I have to go.'

At that moment I was still high with the experience of one-ness, and I said that I understood. With that we kissed and lay down on the bed. I dozed off to sleep, still in the euphoria of the bliss, and then I heard a voice say, 'Well, what are you going to do, now that she is gone?'

I woke up with a start and touched her cold body. I arose and

uncovering her, touched every part of her body. She was ice cold all over. I told myself, 'She's gone.'

Elaine had given me instructions about her body after death. She knew that there would be an autopsy, but she didn't want anyone to touch her body for three days. I had — of course — agreed. The paramedics arrived and declared her dead. They took her body to the coroner's office. I followed them there and made the request that they wait for three days before the autopsy, for spiritual reasons. The coroner agreed and placed her body in a refrigerated storage unit.

Back at home I was still wrapped up in this high feeling. I thought I was fine. I made arrangements with the mortuary and started contacting our friends and family. One friend John, who was a very spiritual person, was overwhelmed by what we had just gone through and knew how unique our experience had been. He could remember only one other person who had gone through such a death, and that was Yogananda. He also understood why Elaine had ordered us to wait for three days before the autopsy. Because, he said, Elaine had three choices: to take her body with her, to leave her body as she did, or to materialize or dematerialize her body at any time. It was his opinion that she obviously wanted some time before making the final decision.

Anyway, John agreed to go down to the coroner's office with me after three days. When we saw her there, she was absolutely beautiful. She just looked like she was sound asleep. The coroner now had to do an autopsy, and a few days later he phoned me. What he told me was this: for the first time in his professional career he could not find a cause of death. He would have to get another opinion from the coroner's office in Los Angeles. Even after that was done, both coroners found that there was absolutely no biological or anatomical reason for her death. At that point he released the body, I arranged for a viewing and memorial service to take place, after which she would be cremated.

We went through all the arrangements for the memorial service, dressing Elaine's body and such. Even the fellow at the mortuary said that he had never seen such a beautiful body — that there was no sign of death. He almost expected her to just wake up. We held the viewing for three days, and people came from everywhere. From morning to night there was a crowd of people in attendance, all of whom had stories that they wanted

to share about her kindnesses, her healing power, and her loving spirit. I had no idea she had done these things, even though I had always known that she was incredible.

Elaine's father Leo came from California to the viewing. He was totally consumed with grief and didn't stay long. Her mother arrived, looked at me and said, 'So, how did you do it?'

I didn't know what she meant until she asked me how I had murdered her daughter. She was positive that I had killed Elaine and nothing would dissuade her. She walked away and I was left there standing, stunned, with Roanna by my side as she had been all along — helping to plan everything. She was the help that Elaine had predicted. Our long-time friend Marianne was there as well. She too had been one of Elaine's 'angels', a spiritual friend and a tennis partner as well. With the help of them both everything was taken care of.

After the three days of viewing, Elaine's body was cremated. I was starting to feel terrible, but we still had to attend the memorial service, which was held at a little church on Maryland Parkway. The place was packed with mourners, and to my amazement I knew only about a quarter of them. Even the chaplain remembered her fondly because she had attended the service there on several occasions. I came home with her ashes in a little box. The public mourning was completed.

But not my own mourning. I became more and more depressed. About the third week after the memorial I fell apart. Then one night at about midnight I dozed off while I was meditating and dreamed that I was talking with Elaine, telling her that she never gave me a chance to explain how much I loved her. Everything had gone too fast. Suddenly I heard a voice say, 'So, tell me how much you love me.'

'I don't want to tell you in a dream,' I said and with that she told me to open my eyes. There she was, standing right in front of me. I fell to my knees, crying and hugging her and telling her how much I loved her. I could feel her in my arms. I tried to express my love in any and all words: that we had had everything together, and she told me that she knew that. I told her that I loved her with all my being, with everything I could feel. She said, 'All right then. Now I have to go. You have told me.'

She tapped me on the head and disappeared. It was over.

CHAPTER 40

Tithing

When I went to church as a child, my mother or grandmother would give me a nickel or dime to put in the collection plate so that I wouldn't feel ashamed or embarrassed for having nothing to give. I often had that feeling as a child, because I never had any extra money in my pocket. But sometimes in church I only pretended to put that nickel in the collection plate, so that I could run off and buy a cannoli after church. Of course I felt guilty eating my treat, because the coin was meant for the poor, not for me.

That nickel or dime was as close as we could get to tithing — giving one tenth of your earnings as a self-imposed tax for the support of the church. However, there can also be a spiritual meaning to the word tithing: to give of oneself, to give one's time to God. God doesn't want or need your money and doesn't ask for it. Only man does that. God wants your time. He wants you to sit down and give 10% of your time to Him. At first 2 and ½ hours seems like a lot of time, but if you apply the axiom that practice makes perfect, it becomes nothing. You don't have to give it all at once but as a minute here and a minute there throughout the day. While washing the dishes or driving the car, you can be giving time to God. It doesn't matter how or when, just start giving it, and those minutes will multiply. Especially at night before you go to sleep, that is a wonderful time to give your tithing of time. And in the morning before you jump into your day,

give a minute or two of time to God. After a while you may find yourself waking a bit earlier, to allow more time to give.

And believe me, give it in secret. As Jesus said, "Go into your closet, give your tithing of time to God, and you will be rewarded in the open." (Matthew 6:5-8). If you can learn to give 10% of your time in prayer and contemplation of God, you will receive blessing many times over in return. Public tithing at church was created for man to be seen and judged by man. It is not what God wants. Time is your most precious earthly possession because it is the most finite, and the more you surrender it to God, the more you will see God in everything and everywhere. That 10% will grow and become 24 hours of giving, until it is no longer a conscious decision but rather a total state of bliss and joy. If you are feeling sad, you will be able to end it simply by closing your eyes and talking to God.

So, even as you give in secret, so too will you receive in the open. But in terms of receiving something as a reward, let that go. It doesn't matter. It's the giving that is important — giving your precious time to God. As you practice contemplation and then go into meditation, you will lose all track of time. You may be sitting there 20 minutes or four or five hours. You no longer have an awareness of time. Then one day you will suddenly realize that your mind is on God 24 hours a day, because you are united with Him all the time. That's when you know that His omnipresence is truly complete, that there is no place that He doesn't exist. You can close your eyes and unite with it at any time. Wherever you are, you are standing on holy ground.

Just try it, — just give it a chance — and you will see how it works. Remember, do this in secret. Don't tell anyone what you are doing. Then you will receive the full realization of it, and you'll be able to understand it.

Shanti, shanti, shanti.

CHAPTER 41

The Warehouse and Roanna

After Elaine's death I didn't go into the macramé shop for over a month. During that time the business was taken care of by the women who worked there, including Roanna, who was taking care of the bookkeeping and another woman at the warehouse who was handling all the necessary book orders and shipping. When I finally returned, everyone greeted me warmly, but without Elaine there I felt very uncomfortable and would just sit at the desk in the back for a few hours before leaving.

One day the woman who owned the building came to me and announced that she would be raising the rent by 50% with the next lease signing. She was shocked when I told her that, in that case, we would be moving out. I looked around at the shop and it seemed to me that there was no point in keeping the shop because I was no longer enjoying it; and, in fact, the macramé business was starting to lessen. This was in 1978. I still had about 200,000 books in the warehouse and could see that orders were slowing down. I decided not to order anymore and figured that within a few months they would all be gone.

Then, one day Mr. Fitzgerald — one of our main suppliers — called and told me that he had just sold off his entire business. He advised me to do the same, saying that he believed the macramé boom was ending. He gave me the phone number of the woman who had bought all of his supplies and suggested that she might be interested in buying out our

inventory as well. In the meantime I had given my employees plenty of notice, so that they would be able to find new jobs before the shop closed. They were saddened, of course, as we had been together for five years and had had a great experience. They realized, though, that with Elaine gone, my heart was no longer there.

About two months later I rented a truck and moved everything in the shop to the warehouse. Roanna remained with me and together we ran the business from there. Roanna worked each day, I came in for three or four hours, and together we processed orders and shipped out books. I phoned the woman who had bought out Fitzgerald, and she agreed to buy most of the remaining book supply at a bulk rate. We had a little walk-in business because the warehouse was not easy to find, so sales continued to drop. In the meantime, we made the warehouse comfortable and cozy. We had a Franklin stove in one corner, surrounded with sofas, and I spent a lot of time there by myself, just sitting in front of the fireplace after work at night relaxing.

Perhaps, I decided, I needed to go on a vacation. Luckily, just at that time my friend Marco invited me to go with him to visit his family in Sardinia. However, because I wasn't sure that this was what I wanted to do I talked it over with my dear friend, Marianne, who had also been very close to Elaine. My path had crossed with Marianne's many times, but each time one of us was open to a possible relationship the other one was already involved with someone else, so we always remained loving friends.

Roanna and I also talked things over while we spent time going through Elaine's many spiritual books that were stored in the warehouse, reading her comments and markings of passages she had wanted me to read. I asked Roanna how she felt about running the business by herself while I was gone. She had no problem with that, but when I asked her if she would, perhaps, like to go on the trip with me, she hesitated, saying that her grandfather wouldn't approve of her traveling with me because he was very traditional-minded, not allowing her to do certain things even though she was 21 years old.

So I left for Italy with Marco, and we were gone for about three weeks, visiting Rome, Assisi, Milan and Venice before flying to Sardinia, where I enjoyed meeting his mother and brothers. Marco was paying for his brother Paolo's medical studies and had financed his brother Mario's career as an optometrist. His mother was very active in the Catholic Church and

in the local tradition had been made a contessa in recognition of her faith. I asked Marco if there was anyone he had heard of locally who was on the spiritual path. He replied that Sardinians only cared about eating, sleeping and making love, so with that the conversation ended.

The trip was a good break for me and I came home rested and energized, having decided to close the warehouse once and for all. When I told Roanna of my decision she asked me what I would be doing next. She asked me if I would be remarrying, and when I asked her why, she replied that I was still young and had a long life ahead of me. Then, to my amazement, she suggested that *we* marry. She said that she loved me and knew that I loved her. I replied that I didn't love her in that way. She asked if it was because she had been my daughter in a previous life, but I said that past lives had nothing to do with the present. And we left it at that.

During the final month or so that the warehouse was open, Roanna and I spent a lot of time together. One evening she came to me in tears, saying that she had been talking about me and that her mother had called me a murderer. This was the second time that I had been accused of murdering Elaine, and I felt that it must have some meaning — but once again I could only put that piece of life's puzzle to the side, hoping that its meaning and importance would reveal itself to me at some time in the future. Roanna knew that I hadn't murdered Elaine because Elaine had told her before her death that she was preparing to leave her body. So now I told her what had really happened the night of Elaine's death, and Roanna wept once again.

Roanna's mother was a nice enough woman, but she had made up her mind about me. The more time that Roanna and I spent together, the more critical her mother became.

Speaking of relatives, Elaine's father Leo was staying with me at this time, near death from years of alcohol abuse, and Roanna was helping to take care of him. During the three months he stayed with me, we got him sober and started to build up his body once again with good nutrition and supplements. He would then be able to return to his job as a Rolex watch salesman in San Francisco.

After Leo was gone and with the warehouse closed, I had little work for Roanna, although she was still on salary. She brought up the subject of our marrying once again, and for some unknown reason, I agreed. And so we got married.

CHAPTER 42

Love

Here, when I'm discussing my marriage to Roanna, seems to be an appropriate time to talk about love. Of course we all know that when love takes over, there is nothing else. But I don't want to talk about human love. The most all-consuming love of all is God's love, the glue that holds it all together.

Love is a wonderful word. And love itself takes place in two different ways.

The first is human love. This love has conditions even though it is the love of father and mother, love of our children, love of our grandparents, love of state, of country. In all these instances, we love for certain reasons. We love someone who does this, but not when he does that. And the conditions are always shifting. What was acceptable one day may not be the next.

Perhaps a father seems to concentrate less on loving his children and more on other things, like getting on in life or creating a successful business. He may think he is doing it all for his son, so that the son can inherit the business someday. He gives his son the finest education possible and plans for the day when they will be partners. He is totally shocked when his son declines his generous offer and is filled with despair and then anger and hatred. He now threatens his son that he will be completely cut off if he doesn't cooperate. The son walks away, and they never see one another again.

Perhaps he has loving daughters as well, who have respected him and learned from him, but because they are female, it doesn't occur to him that one or more of them would be capable of handling the business. His love makes certain demands and expectations. Even the mother puts conditions on her love. She uses it to manipulate her children into proper behavior, using praise and criticism to mold them to her liking.

But we also have the other love —spiritual love — which has no conditions whatsoever. It is like the sunshine and the rain, falling on each and every person. There are no limitations of country, race or creed. It just flows as pure vibration. This kind of love is wonderful. We can call it love of principle, or the love of God, but it just is love. It is the essence of being.

This kind of love is absolutely breathtaking. It finds no faults, no criticism, no harsh judging or rewarding. It just is. This love vibrates on a high frequency and goes outward. All you have to do is tune into it, and then you can feel it. It's there vibrating all the time. You can enter a room where the energy is negative, and all you have to do is think about love. You can change your entire experience within that room from depression to a state of love just by thinking about it and receiving that higher vibration. The more you understand this, the greater the force of the vibration. You can lift up a entire city with the frequency of love's vibration.

Bring *this* love into your contemplations and meditations and you will feel how it changes your entire attitude about life, about everything. You will become more aware of the inadequacy of human love and will not rely on it anymore. You will have something much greater to embrace.

CHAPTER 43

Building My Sailboat, Starting Karoo's and Meeting Carol

Soon after our wedding I suggested to Roanna that we go to southern California and look at some sailboats. We spent about a week going along the coast looking at boats for sale, but I began to think more and more about building my own boat. I met a young guy somewhere during that week who told me that I could buy a hull and deck and then complete the boat myself. I told him that I liked the Downeaster, but he said that I could save a lot of money building my own and that he would take me to someone who was in the business.

And so I met Hank whose business in Wilmington, California, was centered on building the fiberglass hull and deck of a Yorktown sailboat — named by the designer for the aircraft carrier USS Yorktown, on which he had been an engineer. The package was priced at $6000, and I was assured that to complete the boat wouldn't cost more than $30,000 total. He told me that he could supply all needed equipment and that I would be able to do the finishing work at my leisure. It looked to be a great bargain because the Downeaster and other similar sailboats were going for at least $50,000 at that time. We made the deal, I gave him $6000, and Hank began to build my hull and deck. He said it would be completed in three weeks.

Well, three weeks came and went, and the hull wasn't completed. I called Hank from Vegas and asked for progress reports, but he always had

an excuse for delay. Finally, after six weeks he called and said that the hull and deck were completed. Roanna and I drove down to see it and were really happy with the result. As I was to learn, this kind of procrastination and delay would be a constant throughout the construction process.

In any event, the next step was installing the bulkheads (the interior walls of the boat), which Hank said with my help could be completed in three or four days. Luckily my job at that time was working at the Dunes Hotel and Casino where I was making good money and could take off as much time as I wanted. I would make four or five thousand dollars at a time and then take off a few days so that I could go down to the yard and work on the boat.

So I arrived in Wilmington with a pocket full of cash, ready to get to work on the bulkheads, which were constructed of plywood and then sealed into place with fiberglass. While down there working on this job, I also started designing the interior, which I wanted finished mostly in teak — not like another boat I saw another boat in progress where the interior was covered with very cheap looking indoor-outdoor carpeting. This carpeted interior, I found out to my dismay, was part of the original $25,000 estimate for a completed boat.

This was the beginning of another learning experience: nothing would be as cheap as Hank had predicted. Once I realized that the basic price he had quoted me wasn't going to give me the boat I wanted, I made it clear that I expected better-quality materials with the result that the estimate went up to $35-40,000. Now, whenever I gave Hank a job to do, I would give him a couple of thousand dollars with the understanding that the work would be done in a few weeks. But it was never done and he always seemed to need more money.

Unfortunately, what Hank was doing was robbing Peter to pay Paul. He would get a new boat order, take the money and use it to work on other boats that were further along in construction. He was always stalling his buyers, using their money to do jobs on other boats and then waiting for fresh money to come in so that he could work on the more recent orders.

All the same, however, my boat was moving forward. The basic construction of bulkheads and the flooring had been completed and I was coating them with layers of fiberglass and gelcoat for strength. Hank kept saying that I was overdoing it, that I was doing more than what was

necessary; but I knew that I wanted a boat that could really go cruising and wasn't going to skimp on anything.

When the deck was lifted and fit onto the hull, I went to the four Mexican guys who were working in the yard and learned how they connected the two parts with eight layers of fiberglass on the outside and another eight layers on the inside. I paid them each an extra $50 to make sure they did their best work, and they were thrilled to accommodate. When they worked on my boat first — neglecting other jobs in the yard — Hank yelled at them, but they managed to complete my job on time. I would always tip them during construction, helping to insure good and timely work.

I hired outside workmen to start the finishing work, but as I was never really satisfied with the final product, I ended up doing a lot of it myself. On average I ended up spending about eight days each month working on the boat from early in the morning until late at night. Roanna would help me as much as she could, and we always managed to have a good time.

In general our life together was lovely for two or three years, but it was starting to become clear that Roanna was getting a bit bored and antsy. Before we married we had agreed that there would be no children in this relationship. However, even though I felt intuitively that Roanna would never have children of her own, after the wedding I saw her look longingly at infants, dreaming of having her own babies. They weren't going to be with me because I had had a vasectomy but I knew that she still wanted to have children. She couldn't let it go. Obviously there was something that just wasn't working. Roanna started investigating possible career choices and decided that she would take the tests for becoming a corrections officer, a career that offered security and a pension. She passed the written and physical tests and entered the training program. I wasn't particularly impressed with her decision, but it wasn't for me to stop her. I wanted her to be happy in whatever she decided to do. And so Roanna became a corrections officer and began working full time for Clark County.

I continued working at the Dunes and was trying to get a little closer to being back on my spiritual path. I had lost focus, having been drawn back into the material world, even though I knew better. It was a struggle in my life, even as I always tried to meditate and search for the truth, but for the time being that higher level of spirituality seemed to be lost.

By this time, 1984, it was becoming more difficult to maintain a close relationship with Roanna. She was involved in her new career, and I became involved in another project. A friend at the Dunes and his brother invented a new kind of dough suitable for use in a microwave oven. Using this dough we created a stuffed calzone-type sandwich called a Karoo. Once frozen, this sandwich could be microwaved for a minute or so and then tasted like it had just come out of a real oven.

By this time I had decided to sell the condo in which I had lived with Elaine and the boys, and where Roanna and I still lived. I tried using a realtor, but after a year with no results I put my own ad in the newspaper and sold the house within a few weeks. We moved into an apartment because I wanted to be free, unburdened by a mortgage payment or the responsibilities of ownership. At the same time I was working on the boat whenever possible and had about 60% of the work completed.

My associates involved with the new dough product wanted to open a little bakery where they would bake and I would be the salesman. I knew we could produce Karoo sandwiches for around 25 cents, sell them to small bars and convenience stores for about 60 cents each, and that they would be able to sell them for $2.00 each. The potential was awesome, and I was able to get a few friends to invest in the project. Meanwhile, we were still working in the casino, so I had little time for anything besides work. Roanna, who wasn't impressed with the amount of time I spent promoting the bakery product, started spending more time out with friends, and I could tell that things weren't going well.

I was determined to make a success of this Karoo sandwich and decided that the only way to make it work was to get it into supermarkets. I researched it and learned that I had to get a broker in order to get a product into the markets. Most of the local stores used brokers located in California. I got the name of one in Santa Barbara and made an appointment to present our product. He reluctantly agreed to give me five minutes of his time, so I packed up a dozen different Karoos, put them on dry ice, and drove to Santa Barbara. Once there I microwaved one of them and served it to the broker. He was skeptical at first, but when he tasted the sausage Karoo that I had made for him, he was amazed and called in his associates. I microwaved the rest of the Karoos and we served them up. Everyone agreed that the product was a guaranteed success.

For the next hour we discussed the Karoo's future. We already had a box designed and advertising plans. He offered an order of 10,000 dozen, to be ready for delivery in six weeks. My mouth dropped open in shock. We were using a bakery oven, making our Karoo's individually by hand. There was no way to get into production like that on our own. He couldn't be bothered to deal with a smaller order, or so he said. I asked him for a written order, so that I could get a loan, locate a bigger facility and hire the necessary staff, but he refused because, he suggested, I might get the loan and then skip with the money.

I went back to Vegas and sat down in our little bakery with my associates to discuss the proposition. There was no way to physically expand our shop, and once we put the numbers down on paper, we figured that it would cost nearly $300,000 to meet the first order, money which none of us had.

So that was the end of the Karoo sandwich future, but we had also started selling bran and blueberry muffins to local venues — including the Marriott — which handled a shop at the airport. Our sales to the airport increased to the point where we were selling as many as 3000 dozen muffins each week. It was this account that was keeping us in business.

Unfortunately, however, the grind of working two jobs took its toll on my two partners. First one brother and then the other stopped helping out in the shop and I ended up doing everything by myself, spending way too much time in the bakery. I even had to leave the Dunes for a while and stop working on the boat in order to bake at midnight, deliver the muffins at dawn and then try to create sales during the day. On top of that while Roanna and I were still great friends and loved each other dearly, by this time our lives were heading in different directions.

But there was one bright spot in 1984: While at the Dunes one night I met another woman named Carol who was working as a box person in the crap pit.

The first time I spoke to Carol, I sat down next to her in the employee coffee shop. She didn't look very happy, and I asked where she would rather be. Much to my surprise, she replied, 'Sailing on a boat.' I asked her where she would go and she replied, 'Anywhere.' I then told her that she could to that. All she needed was a boat and $300,000. At least that made her laugh. Anyway, we started having conversations during our breaks, and Carol

seemed very receptive to the things I spoke about. She was in an unhappy marriage with two young children, with her working in the casino and her husband going to school.

By 1985 Carol was divorced and decided to submit her application for a job opening that became available for crap dealers at the Cable Beach Casino in the Bahamas. I thought that it might be a great change for me as well, so I applied for the job too. To our surprise we both got job offers and were issued work permits, but I was committed to running the bakery and couldn't leave. I was doing everything by myself by then. Even Roanna couldn't help, because she had a full schedule with her job and needed her sleep at night, when I had to be up baking muffins.

So Carol went off to work in the Bahamas for a year but would often call me for advice, as she struggled to manage job and single parenthood in a foreign country.

This was also the time that Roanna told me she wanted a divorce. I was surprised, but I had to admit that she was right in saying that our lives had gone off in different directions, and that we hardly saw each other anymore. We still loved each other, but she wanted to follow her career rather than going sailing, which was important to me. And so we separated, and our divorce was finalized the following summer.

I moved in with my good friend Jan Levi, who was an oral surgeon, and continued working at the bakery. I was barely breaking even financially and decided to return to the Dunes once again, to get a little ahead. Carol returned from the Bahamas after a long year, with no intention of going back. Her ex-husband took their two boys for a month and Carol moved in with me at Jan's. She helped out in the bakery as much as she could, and we enjoyed being together for the first time.

She wanted to go sailing. I had the boat. We would now be able to go down to the boat and share that new adventure. Definitely there was no coincidence in the way this relationship unfolded.

CHAPTER 44

Selling the Bakery

It was a long hard summer that Carol and I spent at the bakery, getting up
at 2:00AM to bake our muffins and then delivering them to the airport
deli and 25 or so smaller customers. I was so tired; I just couldn't continue.
So I asked myself what I should do. Should I sell the business? While I
know that there are always lessons to be learned with every endeavor, I
nevertheless had to admit that after a couple of years of trying to make this
bakery a success, I just couldn't do it on my own. I couldn't afford to pay
anyone besides myself — Carol did it as a favor to me — and I needed a
great salesperson if the business was to grow. It seemed that soon I would
be learning what my lesson was, one way or another.

None of my three partners wanted to be involved with the daily
running of the bakery, so we agreed that I would put it up for sale. I owed
each of them $5,000, and I had invested about $30,000 of my own, so I
couldn't just walk away. I had to find a buyer and clear at least $45,000.

I called my dear friend, Marianne, who was a realtor, and she came
down to the bakery with our mutual friend, Doris. We got a fellow from
the culinary department at the university to come over and give us an
appraisal. He assessed every piece of equipment from front to back, asked
about the business itself and who was buying the sandwiches and muffins.
When he returned with his report, I learned that the equipment alone, even
if bought second- hand, was valued at at least $80,000. The business had

little debt and a moderate income, and it had potential for the future, but in truth it was the equipment that made the bakery valuable.

Meeting with Marianne and Doris, I told them that I was only interested in getting the $45,000 out of the sale. They could set the price to make their commission, and I would be finished with the whole thing. At this point Doris said that she knew someone who might be interested: a young woman named Madonna who had had a serious car accident about five years earlier which had left her paralyzed from the waist down. She had received a substantial settlement with which she had just bought a bridal shop but still wanted to diversify into other businesses related to wedding planning. Perhaps she would be interested in a bakery.

I was skeptical, because the bakery involved a lot of hard, physical work, but Doris convinced me that we should at least meet her. The next day Doris brought Madonna to the shop, and we showed her around and had her sample some of the products we made. She was a lovely girl, slender and rather pale, and seemed to really like our sandwiches and muffins. I told her about my hesitation in selling her the shop, saying that it was a tough job, even for someone as strong as me. She explained that she had a brother who was a chef and was planning on moving to Las Vegas in the near future. She felt it would be a perfect fit.

We met the brother a few days later, and he was impressed with the kitchen equipment. He seemed to feel confident that he could make a success of the business. I warned him, as I had warned Madonna, about the amount of work involved. When he said that he would hire assistants, I warned him that, at least initially, he would have trouble making a profit, unless he had extra income from somewhere. He said that they had two young female cousins who would love to work there. I told him that I thought it was important to have an aggressive salesperson as well. To my surprise, Doris said that she would be that sales rep, that she had been in sales all her life and was good at it.

The price was agreed to, and even though I was still hesitant to close the deal, we shook hands on it and the contract was drawn up. Half the amount was given as a down payment, and the rest would be paid over time. My partners agreed to accept those terms — receiving full compensation for their investments over a period of time. I would also be giving the new owners two weeks of assistance with using the equipment

properly and the correct way to make the sandwiches and muffins. I would teach them about the baking, getting supplies, making deliveries, the billing, etc. I worked with them for the two weeks, during which time the two young girls started and seemed to be enthusiastic.

To my surprise, at the end of that training period, Madonna told me that her brother was no longer interested in managing the business. My response was that as far as I was concerned the deal was cancelled, because the girls couldn't handle the heavy work by themselves. Physically it was just impossible. However, Madonna was adamant that they could do it by themselves. I reminded her that any hired help would cost money that the shop would not be able to generate. I had earned an A rating from the health department, and I could see that it could easily be lost if the kitchen wasn't properly maintained, which would make it difficult for me if I had to find another buyer. Again, Madonna said that they would deal with it. I agreed to spend two more weeks with the cousins to make sure that they were able to run the operation, but I said that the deal would be off if they couldn't do it.

For the next two weeks we all worked hard. Even Doris was coming in during the evenings to help with tasks like cleaning. The girls worked hard and learned the ropes. We all knew that one of the most important things for the success of the business would be keeping the contract with the deli at the airport whose manager loved the muffins so much that he and I often shared one with coffee when I delivered them. He had met the girls and personally warned them that they would have to keep up the high standards that I had set. Luckily by my last week training them, the girls were running the entire kitchen on their own, baking the muffins and making the deliveries. And so, the deal was completed, and I left the bakery for good.

The lesson to be learned from this experience definitely involved ego. This young woman, Madonna, came into a lot of money, and she came to think that she was a business woman, capable of running anything. She was always positive and persistent about her abilities and quite sure that anything she touched would be a success. I knew from years of experience that running a business isn't always that easy. Having a degree in business administration is only a starting point. It is the individual who makes a business a success, a person who has common sense and good intuition.

The ego tends not to be sensible. It just jumps in and does what it wants. I knew this from personal experience; I made many mistakes because I acted without thinking or planning.

Not only did I look at Madonna's situation; I had to look at myself as well and wondered if I was being critical only because I thought I was the only one who could run the business. Doris was doing a great job in generating sales, and new orders started to come in. But I knew how demanding the job would be in the weeks and months to come, and I warned Madonna again that she would have to have physical help if she wanted the bakery to be a success, that the girls would burn out, just as I had. She just said that I was a worrywart, that it was no longer my problem. Theoretically she was right, but my intuition warned me that there would be problems in the future.

Free of the bakery at last, I started concentrating on the boat once again and spent a lot of time that winter working at the marina in Long Beach CA where I was keeping the boat, which I had named *Sai Baba*. Carol and her two sons got a little apartment in Las Vegas, and she returned to work as a crap dealer. We could finally begin to see that we were getting closer to realizing our dream to go cruising.

Finally in June of 1988 I was ready to sail, having sold my share in a 20-acre piece of property in Las Vegas that I had bought with a group of people years before. Carol and I moved onto the boat fulltime. One of her sons, Jake, came to live with us, while the other, Chris, chose to live with his father. We organized all our stuff, emptied out the warehouse that I had maintained for years, gave or threw away all that we no longer wanted or needed and loaded up an old station wagon. It was fun and quite liberating to leave the past behind and start a new adventure.

CHAPTER 45

Life On Board Sai Baba

Once Carol, eight-year-old Jake and I arrived in California and moved on board *Sai Baba* at the Long Beach Marina, we began to get her shipshape and ready to go cruising. We moved onboard in June of 1988 and would leave December first. We worked hard but also had a lot of fun. We took a few short shakedown trips, learning more about the boat with each one and making corrections as needed. We made friends with the other cruisers and learned from them as well.

I was more careful and pragmatic than I had been in the past about planning our departure from Long Beach. Common sense told me that we would have to be well stocked with provisions and spare parts for the boat, because they might not be accessible as we headed south. I didn't let my ego convince me that we could just take off and all would be well. Going through the bakery experience with Madonna had been a good 'zen stick' for me, a good tap on the head to remind me to leave the ego behind.

In fact, before our departure I received word that Madonna had stopped making her monthly payments. She had lost the account at the airport and the bakery was going out of business. I was shocked and unhappy with the turn of events, but we were about to depart. So, with my partners' consent we retained a lawyer whose job it was to put a lien on Madonna's other properties and to collect the rest of the money owed to us. Months later I learned the lawyer had been improperly cashing checks that were made

out to me, and that one of the partners was trying to strike a deal with Madonna on his own. To add insult to injury, Madonna sued me for fraud, and I had to appear in court. It was an exhausting experience, but after three days of testimony, during which I recounted all the warnings I had given Madonna and all the help I had given in helping her get established, the judge ruled in my favor, and Madonna was forced to pay up. It would take several more months to resolve the entire situation, but I was delighted to be done with that chapter in my business career.

With that out of the way we were ready to leave, but since one of the hardest parts of cruising is actually getting yourself to take off, we forced ourselves into it by giving notice on our marina slip so that we would have to leave. When the morning of December first arrived, the next occupant of the slip was waiting nearby to bring his boat in, so we had to leave.

Our last adventure before departure was the installation of a deck box that was built to hold our generator. We had a lot of trouble dealing with the carpenter, because he was often drunk and would disappear for days at a time. On that very last morning we found him and after two hours had the deck box installed. At noon we were on our way at last. Several boats escorted us out of the marina, sending us on our way.

Our first destination was San Diego, which we made in an overnight sail, arriving the next morning. As would become our routine, we would sail when the wind was fair, but if it died down or was against us, we would turn on the motor for an assist. Once in San Diego we anchored with other cruising boats and took our dinghy to shore to do our last shopping before heading for Mexico. We met a few new boats while ashore, and rejoined some boats that we had previously met, so that by that evening we had quite a little flotilla ready to depart. One boat was *Blew By You*, sailed by a father and son and accompanied by their dog Bubba, an English bull terrier, we would spend a lot of time with them in the coming months. We learned quickly that we came to know people only by their first names and by the name of their boat.

That first night in San Diego, the party was on *Sai Baba*, and we learned another valuable lesson. Whatever you put out for cruisers to eat or drink will quickly be gone; I kept putting out more food and drink that evening, and they kept right on eating it up. The next day before our departure we had to return to the store and replace what had disappeared so quickly. Of necessity we would use more restraint in the future.

Before leaving Long Beach, we had gotten all the necessary papers for cruising in Mexican waters: boat papers, fishing licenses, documentation for our cat, Lovey, etc. We had copies of all immigration and customs forms, which made the process of entering Mexican harbors relatively painless. We quickly learned that there would always be fees and the numerous stamping of papers, but with good humor and patience it wasn't difficult to deal with. A slight donation placed on the desk of an official also helped to expedite the process, and being from Las Vegas and working in a tip industry, we didn't find it difficult to give a little bit here and there to ease the way.

Our first landing in Mexico was at Turtle Bay. I had seen it in the 1950s when the town was just a little hole in the wall, but now there was a city. Our small flotilla anchored and side-tied together in the bay, and it would have been a pleasant, uneventful stay except for one boat, whose captain was an alcoholic. He was sociable when sober, but we learned that night that he became violent when drunk. In the middle of the night, we woke to a big commotion and found that he was beating up his partner. We untied from the flotilla, moved away to our own anchorage and vowed that we would never make that mistake again. The next day we took off on our own, meeting friends as we went along.

We left Turtle Bay around 6:00 am on a beautifully sunny day with gentle seas, and started down the coast to Cabo San Lucas. It took a few days to get there, because we weren't going very fast, just enjoying the trip. It hadn't quite sunk in yet that we were actually on our way. I think Carol and Jake were more excited than I was, at that point. We arrived in Cabo on December 14th and dropped anchor in the bay there. We were joined by other boats, some new friends and others we had already met along the way. Everyone was excited to be finally living his or her dream, as we headed south.

After a few days in Cabo we took off once again with our friends on *Blew By You*. Crossing the Sea of Cortez was very uncomfortable, because the winds were coming one way, the current was rocking us another way, and the smell of diesel fuel filled the boat. Jake and Carol both got seasick on this stretch of the journey, but overall we rarely got sick in the months and years to come. By Christmas Eve several boats had arrived and anchored in the harbor at San Blas, on the Mexican mainland. We always

called our friends by their boat name, as we were called *Sai Baba* by those who knew us. We, in turn, often heard a familiar boat name on the radio or mentioned by others and knew that friends were nearby.

While crossing the Sea of Cortez, Carol and Jake had kept busy making Christmas decorations for the boat, so we were all decked out for our first Christmas on board. They even painted a little ceramic Christmas tree to bring the spirit of the holiday home. We had a wonderful Christmas dinner and listened to carols as we opened our presents. We had tried to keep it secret, but of course Jake knew that he was getting a fishing rod, which he treasured and enjoyed thoroughly.

We went on one adventure while in San Blas. Another boat, *Odyssey*, had a boy on board who was close in age to Jake, and they had a lot of fun together. One day *Odyssey* rented a ponga, one of the local canoe-like fishing boats, and the captain took us up a narrow river through the jungle to an open area with a fresh-water pond. The whole afternoon was spent in laughter, as we tried to navigate this river and marveled at the banyan trees with their open root system. It was wonderful.

We headed south along the Mexican coast, sometimes stopping in at a harbor and sometimes sailing on through the night. The sailing was breathtaking, especially sailing at night. Each evening we would have a hot, filling meal, thanks to Carol. If it had been up to me, I probably would have been eating peanut butter and jelly sandwiches. After dinner, I took the first watch while Carol got some sleep. At about midnight she came up into the cockpit and took over, while I went below and tried to sleep. I didn't really sleep much, as I was always listening to the sounds of the boat and was aware of any changes in wind or weather, but at least I could rest my body. At about 4:00 am I returned to the cockpit and Carol got some more sleep before waking in the morning and making our coffee and breakfast. At this point we didn't feel that Jake was old enough to handle the responsibility of standing watches, and so he slept through the night. But having said that, as time went on, whatever job we gave Jake, he always did it enthusiastically and thoroughly. We were always proud of him.

All the same, at the beginning, cruising was rather boring for Jake, because there weren't many kids to hang out with. He got along easily with all the adults he met, but it was always more fun for him to be with kids. Carol had brought dozens of books for him, but for the first month

they stayed stowed away under his berth. Finally one day, in desperation he opened a bag of books and pulled one out. From then on, Jake read anything he could get his hands on. Over time, he graduated from kids' books to adult classics like 'Moby Dick'and to the 'Hobbit' trilogy. He seemed to enjoy them all.

Jake also had his feline companion, Lovey. She would dive into the towels of the linen cabinet whenever the motor was started, but if we were under sail, she came up into the cockpit and kept us company. Unfortunately for Jake, Lovey was not a lap cat. She liked to be close but not handled too much, so when Jake held her in a death grip, more often than not he ended up with scratches on his chest. Often, Lovey just sat and looked at us, as if to say, 'What are we doing here?!' and we would imagine writing a book about sailing from her point of view.

Because we didn't want Jake to fall behind academically, Carol had investigated home schooling before we left the States. We found a school based in Baltimore MD — the Calvert School — which many cruising families used to educate their children. Each year we would receive the necessary books, as well as monthly exams to be completed and returned to the school, where a teacher assigned to Jake would review and grade the material. Jake easily fell into a routine where he did his schoolwork each morning and then had the afternoon free to play or read. He excelled at math and science but showed less interest in English, history and social studies. All in all he did very well in all his courses during the three years he was home-schooled.

We arrived in Puerto Vallarta in time for New Year's Eve, where we were in a large marina, surrounded by condos and high-rises. We had several friends in port, and together we navigated the hassle of checking in with immigration, the port captain, the local police, etc. By this time we were already expert at having everything in order and ready to be stamped and signed.

As famed as Puerto Vallarta was as a tourist destination, we quickly realized that basically we were floating in a cesspool. All those beautiful condos and apartments were flushing their sewage directly into the harbor. On top of that, what we initially thought were cats swarming around the garbage cans at the end of the pier turned out to be rats. In jest we ordered Lovey the cat to sit at the bow of the boat and stand guard against

any intruders, but to our amusement, she sat there anyway, just patiently staring at the distant rats. I don't think she would or could have done anything if a rat had actually boarded *Sai Baba*, but luckily we never did have a problem with on-board rodents or cockroaches. We were always very careful to keep it that way.

As we sailed along we kept in contact with our fellow cruisers on the marine radio channel 16, the open channel for marine voice traffic. At some harbors we would have group calls in the morning where friends could pass on advice about the town, give weather forecasts and often offered up 'treasures of the bilge' for sale or exchange. If anyone had a problem on board, there was always someone with the knowledge and/ or a spare part to remedy the situation. If someone lent you a piece of equipment, you might replace it by sending the new part on with another boat headed in his direction. The cruising community was almost always open-handed and generous, as we all knew that we would need each other at some time or other. It gave us a great sense of security knowing that we were never really alone out there.

As our friendships deepened, we often had parties, either beach parties during the day or potluck dinners in the evening. For Jake's ninth birthday celebration we simply announced on the morning radio chat that we would be meeting on the beach that afternoon. Dozens of our fellow cruisers showed up to wish him well and brought him silly little gifts that they had come up with. From beach to beach a dedicated crew always set up a volleyball net and would play the afternoon away. Our tradition on *Sai Baba* was to cook pasta and sauce on Sunday evening, and we always had company to share our food and wine. You never knew who would be anchored or tied up next to you but sooner or later you would meet up with old friends and spend an evening catching up on their latest news and adventures.

We continued south, staying in the places we enjoyed and leaving others more quickly. One memorable stop was at Zihuatenejo, where Jake made friends with a Canadian who was living there. It turned out that they shared a passion for fishing, and Gary offered to get Jake a free ride on a charter fishing boat. They had a wonderful day out on the water, and on their return Jake proudly posed with his catch, a dorado and a huge sword fish. He looked completely happy at that moment.

Our last major stop in Mexico was in Acapulco, where we had a great time. Acapulco was a final Mexican port for boats that were heading out into the Pacific, whether to the Polynesian Islands or west and then north to the Hawaiian Islands. Some boats turned around there and headed back towards the States, while the rest of us were headed south towards the Panama Canal.

One of the boats that was headed for Hawaii included a teenage brother and sister, which seemed like a bad idea to us because they always wanted to be as far from their parents as was possible. In addition, the mother had originally made it clear that she wasn't at all happy to be sailing, but over time she embraced the cruising life and came to love it even more than her husband, announcing in Acapulco that she was going to carry on, even if the rest of the family chose to fly back to the States. In fact, though, they headed out towards Hawaii — being unlucky enough to lose their mast at some point. From the various boats that were in contact with them via radio, we learned that the daughter made her father sign a contract stipulating that she would be able to leave the boat for good the moment they reached dry land.

For us, Acapulco was a fun break from the daily routine. We were allowed to use the facilities of the local yacht club and spent many an afternoon lounging around the patio tables and sipping cocktails. It was a great place to provision and fuel the boat and to make any necessary repairs before we headed into Latin American waters.

239

CHAPTER 46

Separation

The boating community was very uniting, everyone always getting together. We rarely saw separation. People were always willing to help. No matter what problems you had, there was always someone there to help you.

There is an axiom, probably a very old one, that says, 'United we stand, and divided we fall.' Very few people understand the reality of uniting. For some reason it is very easy to have separation. We have been programmed into separation from our birth. The first big separation is when a baby is forced out of the womb, and it is felt very deeply. Following that event, you can see how separation continues — each person is separated from another, taught to be an individual who stands alone.

We call uniting 'love.' When we feel the depth of love we are experiencing uniting. That feeling is rare compared to the amount of our lives we spend in separation. In school we are separated, taught to be independent and have personal control of our possessions. In religion we are taught that ours is right and the other religions are wrong. Where we should be uniting under faith in God, even there we are divided. This separation is taken into war and even unto death — from the beginning of human history to the present.

Great masters have come to the world — and are here today — trying to teach us the principle of uniting: that without uniting we will fall. It seems to be a simple enough concept, and yet we all continue to resist it.

All areas of human society are always in competition with other areas. Even within a so-called unified group we find competition and differing ideas, all because of different programming.

We cannot grasp the concept of unification until we acknowledge that we all have been programmed. Once you realize this, you can start trying to do something about your separation. This is not an easy task, because the programming is so deeply imbedded in our psyche, even from past lives.

These great masters who have taught the concept of uniting belong to every faith. For instance, the very word 'yoga', when used by a yogi, means to become attached to, to become one with. When I meditated on this concept, it was in the form of Jesus that God spoke to me saying, 'My yoke is light. Attach yourself to me while you see the light. Become the light.'

Instead of trying to follow this concept, we separate ourselves from everything that is in existence, through culture, nationalities, and race. It almost seems like a refusal to try to unite.

To have realization you must do away with separation, which takes a great deal of meditation and contemplation. When you realize what God is — that there is only one God, in whose image and likeness we are created — then you are realizing that we must not separate from this essence of being. Unfortunately we do separate ourselves from God because we do not understand what God is. Nor do we understand what the Self is. We look on the outside and see only separation instead of looking inside and uniting with our own godliness.

The only way I know to realize true unification is through contemplation and meditation, by asking for the true meaning of uniting. If you practice meditation you will become united. It can only come from within. As Jesus said to me, 'When the in becomes the out, and the out becomes the in, and they both have merged, you have entered into the kingdom of Heaven.'

Once you realize this concept within, you will be able to see it around you and unite with — rather than separate from — those around you. It will take a great effort to find the truth within because you have been separated from yourself for so long.

Go into your inner sanctuary, your very essence, pray in secret, and be rewarded in the open. We ourselves are the reward; the reward is within us. You are the living temple, the living church, and that is where you will find

the truth. It takes patience and practice and if at first you don't succeed, try and try again. It's a continual process, and you might feel discouraged at times, in the long run you will succeed. Once you see this for yourself you will be able to look outward and feel uniting instead of separation with the world around you. The magnificent truth is that you are already united with the universe; you just have to realize it. Our God is one, the kingdom of Heaven is within and surrounding us.

So, as the puzzle pieces begin to fit together and you begin to find the truth, you will realize that separation is not the answer. You will see the uselessness of war and conflict, that in truth we must all come together and work together to create harmony on earth. Separation doesn't work; it simply creates more chaos and disharmony.

'United we stand, divided we fall.' This is not rocket science. The more you practice it, the easier it becomes. Then you will understand the words of Jesus in Matthew 22:3, 'Thou shall love the Lord thy God with all thy heart, and with all thy soul, and with all thy mind.' Then, taking this realization a step further that, 'Thou shall love thy neighbor as thyself.' Who is this self? This self, we know, was created in the image and likeness of God, and so we are all that image and likeness of God. But since it is obvious that our bodies are not alike what is being said? Perhaps it would be helpful, if, for instance, we look at 12 computers of different colors and shapes that run all kinds of programs: the one thing that makes them all work — that empowers them — is electricity. Without electricity it doesn't matter how they look or how they are programmed; they will not work. The electricity has no preference for one computer over another; it simply is.

Like the electricity that powers the computers, we have the divine spark, the essence of being, that image and likeness of God. This force is exactly alike inside every single one of us. And we need to unite with it instead of separating from it. This simple concept seems to elude us, but we must become conscious of it because without it we do not exist. This consciousness is the realization that we are one with God, one with everything and everyone around us. This consciousness — this divine spark — doesn't move or travel, it simply is. There is no place where it does not exist. Without consciousness we cannot exist. Each of us may use our senses differently to experience our environment, but it is consciousness that makes everything real.

CHAPTER 47

Cruising in Latin America

From Acapulco, we headed south towards Costa Rica, planning to be at sea for a few days. We were traveling with our friends on *Odyssey* and were surprised when they announced via radio that they were turning east and heading up a channel into the port of San Jose, Guatemala. We followed along a few hours behind, because *Sai Baba* wasn't as fast as their boat. This decision turned out to be a mistake. We arrived in the middle of the moonless night and had a hard time seeing anything around or in front of us. Jake was the first to spot *Odyssey*, and so saved us from going aground on the beach. We tied up alongside and went to bed, but much to our amazement, when we awoke the next morning we found ourselves under military guard. It turned out that we had wandered into a naval base, where tourists like ourselves were prohibited. *Odyssey* needed fuel and had to make some necessary repairs, so we were allowed to stay for a few days. The officers in charge of the base, including the Minister of Defense, were gracious towards us and invited Jake and his friend on *Odyssey* to lunch at the officer's club, but they also made it clear that we were not to encourage other boats to make this stop.

On our way once again, we enjoyed some great sailing, wonderful dolphin escorts and abundant fishing for Jake. We were careful to stay 15 miles offshore in international waters as we cruised past Nicaragua, because we had heard reports of a sailboat getting too close to shore and being

confiscated by the Nicaraguan navy. At the end of March we dropped anchor next to several other boats in Playa del Coco, our port of entry in Costa Rica — a beautiful country that we enjoyed for the next month.

In order to clear Costa Rican customs we took a taxi to the capital, San Jose, enjoying both the city and the inland countryside we passed through on the way there. It turned out to be a great country for Americans: we are popular there because our government has invested quite a lot of time and money over the past few decades and has promised the Costa Ricans protection from attack, so they didn't have to support a standing army. Additionally, unlike any other country that we would visit on our voyage, Costa Rica has been wired for telecommunications, making life 'on the road' very much easier.

Once back from the capital, we sailed south to the little town of Puntarenas, a short distance upriver from the coast. There we found a wonderfully decrepit 'yacht club' whose owners tried to meet any and all the needs of the cruising community. They had a broken down couch, a TV and piles of old movie tapes that were free for the viewing. There was a cooler with cold sodas for the taking. All you did was mark off your purchase by your boat's name in a little book and pay at the time of departure. If you needed propane, they would fill your tanks. They recommended a wonderful Chinese restaurant in the nearby village. Run by descendants of Chinese workers who had been brought in to build the railroad, they provided us with menus written in Chinese and Spanish. So, even though the water was dirty and dangerously swift running at times, and the 'yacht club' was full of cockroaches and rats, we were quite content there in Puntarenas.

Further down the coast we stopped in a little bay and found ourselves on the beach of Manuel Antonio National Park, a beautiful nature preserve with silver-faced monkeys swinging about in the trees. We stopped in the port of Golfito, which had once been a major port for the United Fruit Company but was now abandoned. There we gathered up our fuel cans to take to the nearest gas station, only to find ourselves surrounded by several children who insisted on carrying our jerry cans to and from the station. One little boy could barely manage the load, but he was totally determined to earn a tip. I couldn't help but over-tip them all. They reminded me so much of myself as a little boy, willing to hustle and work hard for a living.

Of course, during all this time I was regularly repairing and maintaining the boat. We had some problems with our satellite navigation system, which turned out to be antenna-related. We had to change out the impeller in our water pump on a regular basis, and we were always trying to improve the system for keeping our batteries charged. We polished and varnished regularly, which kept the jobs easy to manage. We checked with other cruisers to see how they dealt with various problems, learning a lot from all of them. And, of course, there were always potluck dinners on the beach or the dock, with wonderful food, music and good company.

At the end of April a friend, Jim Lemos, flew in from Long Beach CA to transit the Panama Canal with us. During the passage we ended up ruining the two water pump shafts we had on board, and although I was able to jury rig the pump well enough to get us to Balboa, I knew we would have to get the shafts replaced there. We called it Mickey Mousing when I had to fix something and didn't really have the necessary equipment or parts. Carol and Jake even bought me a Mickey Mouse hat later on, to wear when I had to get creative.

We arrived in Balboa at night, and it was a nerve-wracking experience. There seemed to be hundreds of ships anchored outside the Canal, waiting to make the transit, and it was very difficult to read the navigation lights. Eventually we found the yacht club and picked up a mooring. While waiting to get processed to transit the Canal, Jim and I went into town and found an ironmonger who could make the new shafts.

We couldn't have picked a worse week to visit Panama. It was just days before an election, and the infamous Noriega was running for reelection. There was violence in the streets and tension in the air, even within the Canal Zone itself. The authorities ended up shutting down the Canal for a few days, but, luckily, *Sai Baba* and another sailboat were the last ones to be allowed through before the shutdown.

When it was time to pick up our new shafts, Jim stayed on board the boat, and I hired a taxi to take Carol, Jake, and me into town. While I was in the shop, Carol and Jake waited outside, just exploring a bit. Suddenly the taxi driver came to me and said that Carol and Jake had been arrested and were being held across the street to this little boxy building — maybe 12 foot square — which turned out to be a police station. I ran over there and found two officers who had confiscated Carol's camera for the capital

offense of taking a photo of a 'military installation'. It turned out that Carol had been taking photos of a nearby impressive sport stadium where the Panama Games had once been hosted, and, in front of the stadium, next to a park sponsored by the Lion's Club, was this little police station that — who knew? — was a 'military installation'. Adding insult to injury, we hadn't bothered to bring along our passports for this little errand. We were in trouble.

It took time and phone calls, but we found out that we were to be driven downtown to headquarters in our hired cab, which terrified our driver who was obviously afraid that he might lose his license now that he was in this mess with us. We ended up going through a high wall where we found ourselves surrounded by soldiers. We were taken inside a building and walked down a long hall. It felt like we were being taken into a dungeon. Once we were placed in a room, an officer entered and, in Spanish, told our driver to go outside and wait with the boy. When Carol realized what was happening, she went from annoyed to berserk, crying hysterically that no one was going to touch her son — that he would stay with us. The officer decided that it would be all right for Jake to stay with us and told the driver to wait outside, and then told another officer to bring Carol some orange juice, because she was obviously beside herself. It would have been amusing if it hadn't been so scary.

At this point the officer turned back to me and in perfect, American English, asked me my name. It took me a moment to realize that I could understand what he was saying, but once I recovered my senses, I told him my name, and we began to learn what was going on. That was when we were told about the 'military installation', and of course, I told him he could keep the photo, the camera, whatever he wanted. At this point the officer apologized, explaining how tense the country was during this election period, and that it would be a good idea if we just returned to the Canal Zone and stayed there. Our driver took us back to the marina and our boat, and it was then that we realized that we were the only boat there. Not only that, but the yacht club was shut down and deserted, so we couldn't even pay our bill.

It is a great adventure to pass through the Panama Canal. It starts with a payment: for *Sai Baba* it was $35, which was calculated on our water displacement — just the same as tankers and freighters are charged — and

a $50 damage deposit (as if our little boat could damage the Panama Canal! And we were actually refunded that deposit).

We were joined on our adventure by another boat called *Dream Chaser*, whose captain, Bill, was a US Navy Seal single-handedly sailing his boat to Bermuda, where he would be second-in- command of the US Naval base there. And there was also Max, our pilot provided by the canal authorities to direct us through the Canal over the next two days. The captain of the boat, me, had to stand with the pilot while four people on the boat (our friend Jim, another guy who we corralled named Larry, Carol and Jake) holding one end of four lines while four other men, two on each side of each lock, guided us through the lock with the lines and controlled our ascent or descent as the water level changed.

It was an incredibly exciting experience as we ascended through the massive locks to Gatun Lake, which was 26 miles long. We spent the night there before being joined by Max once again the next morning and descending through the second set of locks to the Caribbean side of the Isthmus of Panama.

Once we were settled in a marina on the east side of the Canal in Cristobal, we tried to get some cash, as we were totally out of it. Unfortunately for us, the banks were closed and would stay that way until after the elections. Two men in uniform who told us they were narcotics officers, came by that afternoon and kept asking us how much money we had on board. We explained our situation, and finally they left in disgust. Our friend Bill on *Dream Chaser* came over soon after and asked us how much we had given them. It was only then that I realized that they had been trying to get a bribe out of us.

Leaving Cristobal a few days later, we headed to Playa Blanca, a beautiful little harbor a short distance away where we planned on visiting with retired cruiser named Mike Starbuck who lived there in a lovely, airy bungalow near the water and welcomed all cruisers to his place. We took our dinghy to shore the morning after our arrival and Mike came down to the beach to say hello. We were in our bathing suits, as it was hot and sunny, but much to our surprise, Mike wore long pants and a long-sleeved shirt. We soon figured out why. As we were standing there, I realized that something was biting at my feet. We started heading back into the water, trying to ignore whatever was bothering us. It was then that Mike told

us that the sand fleas had just hatched and that they would be a nuisance throughout May. As it turned out, I am sensitive to the bites of these sand fleas and ended up with hundreds of little red bumps that blistered before healing. Luckily, another boat had some Benadryl, which helped to ease the symptoms, but there was no way we were going to stay in that harbor — no matter how beautiful it was — so we thanked Mike for his hospitality and headed on our way.

This is a beautiful part of the Caribbean. The local San Blas Islands are inhabited in large part by the Chichime Indians, who make their living raising and selling coconuts. They live communally on one or two of the main islands and work the other islands together, dividing the profits equally. It seems to be a very simple, pleasant life. Anyway, soon after we anchored at one of these islands, some of the local Indians rowed out to us to say hello. They had craft items to sell, including some beautiful embroidery called mola, for which they are famous, but they also just wanted to visit. Carol and I declined their kind invitation to come ashore, as we had more than enough sand flea bites, but Jake went with them for the afternoon and had a wonderful time.

We had planned to linger in the San Blas Islands for quite a while, but realizing that we were held captive on the boat because of the sand fleas, we decided to head out to sea and turned northeast towards the Cayman Islands. We had an uncomfortable passage with high winds and chaotic seas for three days. The engine quit twice and had to be bled, both the mainsail and genoa sail tore, and we all felt battered and bruised by the time we got to Grand Cayman. As we approached the island, I started noticing that the propeller shaft wasn't moving freely and was heating up. Luckily we got anchored safely, because I found out that two of the engine mounts had broken during that rough passage. I jacked up the engine and removed the mounts. We found an ironmonger who was willing to do the job, but he didn't have the necessary metal and ended up Mickey Mousing the repair job. It took a week, but eventually we had the mounts back onboard and safely installed. We also found a lady who showed us how to properly mend our sails, and we were able to do a competent job.

While waiting on our repairs, we enjoyed touring the island. There really wasn't much of a town, but there were dozens of banks, set up for offshore banking. The waters were quite fantastic and we enjoyed

swimming right off the boat in harbor. There were a few tourist spots, including a pirate cave and a turtle farm, where turtles were raised both for consumption and releasing back into the ocean.

Heading out once again towards the Florida Keys, we sailed along beautifully until we turned north into the wind. We lowered the sails and went to turn on the engine, but nothing happened. I had no idea what the problem was, but we had to do something if we wanted to head north. Carol jokingly suggested that I 'hotwire' the engine. I was skeptical, but we had nothing to lose. I took off the front panel in the cockpit and had to laugh at the jumble of wires I was looking at. Anyway, I found the ones I needed, and sure enough, the engine started right up. We all laughed, glad that we had found a solution to our problem.

The rest of the trip north was uneventful, except when a Coast Guard helicopter flew overhead as we were rounding the west end of Cuba. They circled above us and took photos, and we waved back in greeting. The Coast Guard boarded several other boats in this area, before entering American waters, but we must have looked pretty benign, as they never boarded *Sai Baba*.

Our first landfall in the Florida Keys was a string of islands called the Dry Tortugas, so named because they have no natural water source. All water has to be collected from rain or brought in by ship. We entered a shallow harbor in front of the famous Fort Jefferson and promptly went aground. It turned out that this would be the first of dozens of groundings because *Sai Baba* draws over six feet, and since the waters of the east coast are much shallower than those along the west coast we were often too deep for the passages. Luckily for us, the sand was quite forgiving, and with the tide we were able to get free and move to deeper water to anchor.

Fort Jefferson served as a military prison for decades, the most famous prisoner being the doctor who treated John Wilkes Booth's injuries after the Lincoln assassination. We enjoyed touring the fort and were grateful to be in the knowledgeable hands of the National Park Service Rangers once again. At the visitor center we were surprised to see 2.5 gallon containers full of water, and even more surprised to learn that they were there as a courtesy for us cruisers. It was so nice to have some fresh water after several days at sea, as our boat water had gotten rather stale-tasting over time.

At Fort Jefferson our dinghy engine died. It was a little Seagull engine,

not very powerful but supposedly quite reliable. No one ever told me, though, that the shaft had a little case for transmission oil which needed to be replenished every now and then, so it froze up, and suddenly we were rowing for our lives, trying to make it against the wind and tide out to our anchorage. After learning that lesson, we headed for Key West. It felt great to be back in an American marina once again. We didn't know that each boat coming into the States has to notify the authorities of their arrival immediately, and we later received an official reprimand for waiting until the next day to call in, but we did fly the yellow 'Q' flag — "Q" for quarantine — that next day and waited to be cleared. We completed our paperwork quickly, and the customs official took all our garbage to be burned, as a precaution against foreign contaminants. Carol was worried that our cat's papers wouldn't be complete, but the other officer who came aboard, a young woman, just petted her and welcomed us all home.

Now that we were back on US soil, it was time for Jake to return to Las Vegas for the summer — to visit with his father and brother. Carol and I drove him up to the airport in Miami and got him safely on his way. It was June, and we were ready to start the next leg of our journey, sailing up the eastern US coast.

CHAPTER 48

Cruising the Eastern Seaboard and Crossing the Atlantic Ocean, June 1989-May 1990

After a few days' stopover in Miami and Ft. Lauderdale, we were ready to head north to New York to visit my sister Fernanda. We were told that it would be a really fast trip, but, frankly, I didn't believe it. Much to our delight we caught the Gulf Stream soon after our departure, which gave us a 6-knot push. With great sailing we were doing up to 12 knots per hour, which — since that speed converts to almost 14 miles an hour — was unbelievably fast for *Sai Baba*. We made the trip of about 1200 miles in six days. While Carol made monkey-fist Christmas ornaments out of string and marbles, I tended the sails and was able to really relax and enjoy the beauty of the sea around us.

One night I was on watch and spotted a distant light on the horizon. As it approached, I called out on the radio, saying that we were a little sailboat and asking if anyone saw us. No one answered, and as the light grew closer, I started to be concerned. Finally, after several more calls on the radio, the other ship finally responded and said that it would avoid us. It did, but with a rumbling sound that brought Carol up into the cockpit just in time to see a sheer wall of steel moving past us. It was very unnerving and made us realize just how small we were.

Another night during my watch I saw a red light streak across the water in front of us. Then I saw a green light move across going the other

direction. I was sure that I was seeing some kind of UFOs, and just as Carol came up to go on watch, I turned and exclaimed, 'There's the mother ship!' I went below to the radio and Carol took over the wheel. Just then, someone came on the radio, identified the 'mother ship' as a US aircraft carrier and ordered us to turn to port, which in nautical language means to the left. Confused by the shock of the whole thing, I asked whose port, theirs or ours. Immediately we were told, 'This is the captain of a US Aircraft Carrier. You will turn onto a course of (whatever it was) and hold that course for 15 minutes.' I said 'yes, sir,' and we changed course. It was then that the side of the ship came into view, and we saw several helicopters doing maneuvers across the surface of the water. Those were my UFOs. Another memorable experience.

When we finally arrived at our destination, it was dusk on the Long Island shore and we were unable to find our inlet. So we decided to anchor off the beach and wait until morning. The sea was rolling, but we were perfectly safe. Someone on shore, however, decided that we were in trouble and called the Coast Guard. They came out to us by boat and offered to guide us to calmer waters. We were grateful for their assistance although the first thing they told us to do was to put on our life jackets. Those jackets had been in a deck locker since our departure from California, doing a nice job of padding our propane tanks. We had always felt very safe because *Baba* had a center cockpit which was totally enclosed with canvas, but now we got the jackets out and put them on. Then the Coast Guard crew notified us that their radio wasn't working properly and that we would have to relay information between them and their station. As a result, things were crazy for a while, with me bringing up the anchor, and Carol trying to maneuver the boat and keep radio contact going down below deck at the same time. However, in less than an hour we were led into the Jones Beach Inlet and shown where we could anchor for the night, safe and comfortable.

The next day we headed for Far Rockaway, where my sister lived. We couldn't afford the local marina, so we went along the shore and found a house on nearby Atlantic Beach with an empty dock in front of it. The couple that lived there was pleased to let us rent their dock space.

We split our time between that dock and Fernanda's house until the end of August. Carol's older son, Chris, was able to join us for a few weeks,

and the two of them took a side trip to Washington, DC and Philadelphia. I loved being with all my nieces and nephews and visiting with old NY friends. At this time I actually considered staying on in New York for the winter. I was concerned with Fernanda's health and thought that with my help, she would work out, eat better and improve her quality of life. Carol wasn't comfortable with the idea — especially because of the lack of safety in the neighborhood — so I let that idea pass, and we started planning our trip back to Florida.

On our first day after leaving Atlantic Beach, we had the incredible experience of motoring right in between the Statue of Liberty and Ellis Island and anchoring there for the night. The next day we headed over to lower Manhattan and discovered the South Street Seaport Museum, which had available docking if you joined the museum. It was a fascinating facility, with various ships being renovated and a museum that explored the archeological history of lower Manhattan. We spent three days there and enjoyed being tourists with Jake, who had rejoined us. We even went up to the top of one of the World Trade Center towers and could see *Sai Baba* at the dock, way below us.

While staying at the South Street Port, we recognized a little French boat we'd seen earlier in the week. They needed dockage but had little money and spoke almost no English. By then we had learned that 'antique' boats were allowed to dock for free, so with a little help from us, their boat was declared an antique and they were able to stay.

We left New York and started down along the New Jersey coast, sailing during the day and finding lovely anchorages at night. We made friends with other boats that were heading in the same direction and shared many meals and good times with them. We splurged and spent a night at a marina at Atlantic City in early September, so that we could celebrate Carol's birthday. It was perhaps the only night ever that Jake had a cable TV hookup, so he was happy to stay on board while we went out for dinner. We spent a few days at beautiful Cape May and rented bicycles, so that we could see all the sights.

At this point we decided to make a detour and head up the Delaware River to Philadelphia in order to visit Carol's brother Dane and his family. It was not a particularly beautiful trip, but we got there and found a marina. We called Dane, but at first it seemed that he didn't want to come

down and visit with us. Carol couldn't believe it, and insisted that, if they didn't like the boat or us, they wouldn't have to stay. Of course, we all had a wonderful time together, and the next day we went over to their house and visited with Dane, his wife Diane and their two girls, Morgan and Hillary.

From Philadelphia we motored through the Chesapeake and Delaware Canal, into the Chesapeake Bay — one of the many beautiful areas we visited along the east coast. The summer crowds were gone, and we had lovely days of sailing, peaceful anchorages, and some great meals onshore.

In September there was the threat of a hurricane — Hugo — so we went to Baltimore and got *Sai Baba* safely secured. We loved the newly developed port area and visited the aquarium and science center there. We also made a point to visit the Calvert School, Jake's home schooling center. Luckily for us Hugo skirted the city and we had no problems.

Our next major destination was Annapolis, Maryland, where we arrived in early October for the annual boat show. We anchored on Spa Creek and spent more than a week there. We had a few mishaps there, like the day we punctured the dinghy and another time when our dinghy cable was cut by the officials who were setting up the floating docks for the boat show and didn't like where we had tied up. The boat show itself was fantastic, however, and we spent hours looking at equipment and displays.

Leaving Spa Creek was quite an experience because I couldn't get the anchor up and had to go down into the brown, murky water to release it. I put on my wetsuit and got the oxygen tank set up before going overboard and following the chain down into total darkness. Then, I reached out and grabbed something that felt just like an arm. I shivered, released the anchor and returned to the boat as quickly as I could. It turned out that our anchor had been hooked around a cable on the bottom of the creek. I was glad to be out of there and on our way again.

As we made our way south, we planned to head up the Potomac River and spend some time being tourists in Washington, DC, but we couldn't make any headway against the wind and current and so gave up that idea. We continued on our way.

Toward the end of October, we decided to haul the boat out at Sarah Creek in Virginia. We had hit something hard while sailing in New York Harbor, so hard that the boat stopped completely and Jake almost went overboard, and now we were able to assess the damage and make

the necessary repairs. It was beautiful autumn weather, and we visited Williamsburg while there.

In early November we entered the Intercostal Waterway at Mile 0, a beautiful passage down the eastern seaboard that would in large part protect us from open seas all the way down to Florida. Our only real concern with the Waterway was its depth, because we often found ourselves aground. The regulation depth was 10 feet, but many areas were shallower than that, and we got a lot of practice getting unstuck. The weather was cooling as we made our way through the changing landscape. We celebrated Thanksgiving in Calabash, NC with three other boats and saw the damage caused by Hurricane Hugo in Charleston, SC. We went ashore in Savannah, GA to have a wonderful dinner with friends we had met earlier in the season. We picked pecans at Fort Frederica State Park a few days later. Each day had its problems — going aground, mechanical failure or crummy weather — but that was all a part of it the adventure. The lasting memory is one of happiness, of contentment as we slowly headed south.

We had expected warm weather once we crossed the Florida state line, but it continued to be cool as we headed for Ft. Lauderdale. In fact, Florida had record cold temperatures that winter. We stopped in Titusville for a few days, so that Jake could enjoy Disney World with a cruising buddy. Then we continued until we arrived at the Las Olas anchorage in Ft. Lauderdale a few days before Christmas.

There we were joined by our friends on *Kaleina Lei* who had been traveling south with us. They were cold and tired, and I thought that the wife, Karen, just might leave us for her home in Massachusetts. Christmas morning arrived with frozen ice particles suspended in the air above the warmer water, but we were all ready to celebrate; the boat was cozy and warm, and we had a wonderful day.

The next month or so was spent getting *Sai Baba* ready for extended cruising and waiting for the weather to improve so that we could cross the Gulf Stream and head for the Bahamas. I was looking forward to it so much that one day I looked out to see and thought I saw palm trees in the distance. Unfortunately they turned out to be giant waves created by the clash of wind and current.

We eventually got going and traveled with several other boats, trying

to make our way south/ southeast, but the winds and seas were continually against us and we only got as far as Georgetown in the Exumas. We always managed to have fun, however, even when holed up in some little harbor. There was beautiful snorkeling and diving to be had throughout the islands. There were giant iguanas to admire, and seashells to collect. There were always potlucks on the beach, and recipe exchanges onboard one or another of the boats nearby. Everyone was friendly, and Jake had a great time visiting other boats.

Returning to Ft. Lauderdale, we made our last repairs and did our final provisioning before heading across the Atlantic. On May 17th we started our first ocean passage, leaving from Ft. Lauderdale and heading for Bermuda. We were sometimes in contact with other boats via radio, but for the most part we were on our own. It took eight days, and most of the trip was uneventful. However, just as we were approaching St. George, Bermuda, we developed engine problems, and our jib and mail sails were both causing problems as a squall approached. We called the local coast guard and requested assistance. Two officers came out in their large inflatable boat, which they called *Rubber Ducky*, and proceeded to tow us into the safety of St .George harbor. Those two gentlemen would befriend Jake and take him out on runs during the next several days. Jake had a wonderful time with them, and we were very grateful for all that they did for us.

In order to clear Bermuda customs we took two local officials aboard. One asked me the usual questions about who and what was on board, while the other officer looked around down below. In answer to one question I said quite casually that there were no firearms aboard, which I knew were illegal in Bermuda, but Carol — who was watching the other official almost fainted as he was opening the very locker in which a shotgun was stored, shoved way in the back. Luckily he didn't investigate very thoroughly, because if he had found that rifle, the entire boat would have been confiscated, and we would have been in serious trouble.

Just to be safe for the rest of the trip, before leaving Bermuda I gave the shotgun to our old friend Bill, who had crossed the Panama Canal with us. He was glad to have it, and we never had to worry about that it again.

Our only other near mishap was the firm warning we received that Lovey the cat was not allowed to go on shore. If she did manage to go on

shore, she would have to be quarantined for something like 6 months. Up to now, Lovey had never tried to leave the boat, but this time, with the dock level with the walkway on *Sai Baba*, she came into the cockpit, looked around and simply stepped off onto shore, presumably planning a little walkabout. Luckily Carol was right there, grabbed Lovey and threw her back on the boat before anyone else noticed.

Once we were cleared into Bermuda, we called Bill, who was second in command of the US naval base there. He arranged for us to tie up at the naval yard marina, as we were a documented naval vessel, and we had a wonderful visit with him and his wife. They shopped for us at the PX on base, and even topped off our fuel tanks with the base's inexpensive diesel. We toured the island, made the latest necessary repairs and enjoyed being with our friends. Our experiences in Bermuda just reminded us how generous and helpful people are all over the world.

A week later we headed east once again, towards the Azores Islands. Again, we had radio contact with friends for a few days, but eventually were on our own once again. We had some great sailing days but then a stretch of three days when we had no wind at all. The Atlantic Ocean was like a mirror, and one day, while I was changing the engine oil, Jake went for a swim alongside the boat. We had a life ring floating behind, in case the wind picked up unexpectedly. We did make occasional contact with freighters and other ships which would give us weather reports. We even had one three-day period with a following sea that pushed us and strong winds of about 35-40 knots (46 mph!), which meant fantastic sailing on *Sai Baba*.

Finally, after seventeen days at sea, we spotted the Azores and proceeded to the port of Horta on the island of Faial, where we cleared customs and then found our slip at the marina. There must have been 70 or 80 boats from all over the world there, all with a different story to tell about crossing the Atlantic. It turned out that several boats experienced severe weather during their passage, as they had sailed either south or north of our route. One boat even lost its mast.

At the Horta marina it was the tradition for cruising boats to paint some kind of decoration identifying your boat on the massive concrete barriers that surround the harbor. They were both decorative and imaginative, and we added ours, of course. We made a triangle design and recorded the

boat, the crew and the date for all posterity or at least until the weather wore it away.

We spent three weeks at Horta and had a fantastic time. I had been looking forward to being in a European community once again, and we loved having our first delicious espresso coffee at a nearby cafe. The locals went out of their way to assist us and make us feel welcome. We all participated in a fun regatta, sailing to one of the neighboring islands, whose citizens hosted us for a banquet that evening and gave each boat a sack filled with local cheeses, breads and little souvenir gifts. The grand prize was a beautiful quilt, won by a young man who was single-handedly sailing his little boat. He announced that he would take it home and give it to his mother, and we all cheered. We celebrated the Fourth of July on the marina break wall with a big potluck dinner. We had brought sparklers along for the kids, and a Greek-American fellow entertained us with his accordion playing. It was a magical evening. We never learned much Portuguese, the language of the Azores, but we did manage to figure out the bus system, make our usual repairs and did our provisioning as we got to know the island.

After much discussion with friends on other boats, we decided to sail to the northern end of Spain from the Azores instead of heading directly for Gibraltar and the Mediterranean Sea. We were told that the rias, or rivers, of that area were worth the detour, and so we headed to Galicia. Our passage took ten days and was basically uneventful. We arrived in La Coruna, Spain on July 21st and were ready for our next adventure, sailing in European waters.

CHAPTER 49

The Words I Am

For years I meditated on the words 'I am.' I said them over in my mind thousands of times, until it became rote, automatic. I didn't realize what the phrase meant, until one day I was sitting there, and as I repeated it, I heard the voice say, 'Be still and know that I am God. Stop *saying* I am and *realize* the I am.'

Then the explanation started to become clear. I am all that there is; beside me there is nothing. Whatever I am gives birth to the I; it is one without separation. When I breathe the inhalation is the I, and the exhalation is the 'am'. Whatever 'I' is, 'am' gives birth to it. I am all your senses and give birth to them. Whatever you see around you is the I am.

I am is all that there is. I am that which you gaze upon; I am gives birth to it. Whatever you ask, I am listening and hear and will give birth to it. But it is all one: inhaling the 'I' and exhaling the 'am'. The breath is the same; there is no separation. For I am that I am. Besides me there is no other.

The first time I was told this — sitting at the Lake Shrine on the little pier at the Self-Realization Fellowship in California — I was having a tough time meditating, when the voice of God within told me to open my eyes. There before me was a little sign that read, 'Be still and know I am God.'

I had a glorious meditation, and we were totally one — united. Then

I learned to say those two words, not over and over again as a mantra, but to really say them. 'Be still and know I am God.' The stillness and the darkness will no longer exist, for the 'I am' will give birth to oneness with God. Enter into your sanctuary, be still and listen. Say it once, and you will be heard. God will hear it even before you say it.

So, no matter what you do, know that God is that action. God is everything. There is no place to go that God is not there for you. He is on the highest mountain and in the lowest valley. But remember to go within, for He is there. You may think that you can separate from God, but in reality you can't. For God and you are one. I the Father am the first cause of all; that's what the word father means. God and the cause are one. Without God nothing can exist. Know that He is there also within your brothers and sisters. Look and hear with your spiritual senses, and know that God is the motivator. Your thinking is only an illusion, so brush it away, and you will hear and see and feel God all around and within you.

God *is* your brothers and sisters, so you cannot judge or condemn them. God is that 'I am'. You will feel and see Him in all, once you have cleared away the programming. You will realize true love, true perfection. Sense the perfection with all your senses, because that is God. Beside Him there is nothing else.

'My peace be given unto you, not as the world gives it, but as I Am gives it.' Unite, unite, unite.

When 'united we stand, and divided we fall' is realized, and when the prodigal son and daughter have come home, the I awaits you, to put the ring of wisdom on your finger, and the Divine Mother, the 'am', will put the purple robe of love on your shoulders. You have come home. The visible becomes the invisible, and the invisible becomes the visible, and you have entered into the Kingdom of Heaven.

CHAPTER 50

Cruising in Spanish and Portuguese Waters and then the Mediterranean Sea

Once cleared into Spain, we had the usual repair jobs, including replacing *Sai Baba's* impeller and leaking fuel lines, but this time we also had to make repairs on the rudder, which involved bringing the boat up against a wall, tying her in place, and then waiting until the tide went out, so that the boat's keel rested on the sand. All our friends were making similar repairs, so we learned from one another and helped out when needed.

Our only real disappointment while in Galicia was eating out. I had told Carol and Jake how delicious and inexpensive the restaurants would be, only to find out that the value of the American dollar had dropped tremendously since the years I had been in Europe with Elaine and the kids. Our first meal out in La Coruña, we went to the main plaza and thought we ordered a little sample of cheeses, so that we could pick one and have it with some bread and wine. We got our little sampler and enjoyed it, thinking we would order more, only to discover that those few pieces of cheese cost $25. I was in shock. The second time we ate out I ordered paella and sangria, expecting a delicious, generous feast. Instead, both were terrible, skimpy and of poor quality, so we didn't eat out too many times after that.

We spent the rest of the summer heading down the coast, visiting the three rias of northern Spain which are famous for their mussel beds, but we

were disappointed in the amount of industrialization and pollution we saw. We traveled some of the time with Spanish-speaking friends on *Tunnix*, which helped make our days as tourists much more interesting. Among many memorable sites, we visited the famous cathedral at Santiago de Compostela. In Oporto, Portugal, we visited a wonderful center dedicated to the sampling of various vintages of port, the local fortified wine, and in Lisbon we spent a day at an internationally acclaimed tile museum.

Every time we entered a new harbor the local officials would come aboard, very politely check our credentials and then stamp our book. They these folks were always pleased if we tried to speak a little of the local language — if only to say hello and thank you — we always made the effort. When we entered Portugal and went through the usual formalities, we were also given a little book of transit.

We had decided to spend the early part of winter of 1990 in the port of Vilamoura on the south coast of Portugal. It was relatively modern, and the rates were reasonable. Sailing in the Mediterranean is not recommended during the winter months, because there are frequent, severe storms, so we stayed in Villamoura until the end of December, and then would travel east only as far as Estepona, Spain.

Vilamoura was a perfectly acceptable place to stay, but the marina seemed deserted and lacked ambience. We used to say that the local coast looked like Legoland, because the condominium buildings along the coast were very blocky and unattractive. We would walk to a little town down the beach when we wanted a good chicken dinner out. All the patrons sat at communal tables and received half of a chicken, bread, salad and a pitcher of the local wine. It was delicious, inexpensive, and we always had a good time.

We did some local touring while in Vilamoura and had a few guests onboard. Carol's father joined us for a few days, as did my daughter, Gina, and her son, Dominick, who was stationed with the US Army in Germany. We tried to show them as many sights as was possible and even booked a day's tour by ferry to Tangier, Morocco, which seemed exotic to all of us.

After Christmas we were ready for a change and decided to head for Gibraltar, where several cruising friends were staying. We arrived at dusk on New Year's Eve, and at least six boats welcomed us by radio as we approached. It was party time on *Sai Baba* that night. We supplied

the popcorn and pizza, and everyone brought something to eat or drink. It was so much fun to be with old friends and to bring in the New Year together. The local tradition involved shooting off any expired flares that were onboard, and Jake was in his glory. Carol and I kept watch that no flares set the boat on fire.

Built on a huge rock at the entrance to the Mediterranean and controlled by the British, Gibraltar is separated from the mainland and Spain only by a military air landing strip. Relations were strained between the two governments at that time, as Spain claimed ownership of the Rock, and the Brits had no intention of surrendering it. It was easier to shop at the local Safeway than to go to the markets on the Spanish side of the air field, but because all the fresh vegetables and fruits were flown in from England, everything was ridiculously expensive.

How expensive? Well since there is a legend that says that as long as there are apes on the mountain of Gibraltar, the British will remain in control, we decided to go see them and bring them the grapes that they are reputed to enjoy. We went to the Safeway and bought a bunch, which I calculated cost us 25 cents each. So I ate one to see what such an expensive grape tasted like. Jake told me that I couldn't have any that they were for the apes. I figured that if the grapes cost about 25 cents each and I wanted to have one, I could and would.

While we were in Gibraltar, we had a very interesting visit with a British fellow who claimed to be a psychic medium. We went to his home with several other people and watched him go into a trance. He then started communicating with a doctor and two other men who had lived in the 19th century. They described their environment and life style through the medium. I asked why they hadn't progressed further along the spiritual path, and they never answered that question. They seemed quite content with their lives, wherever they had ended up. The medium himself also seemed content to maintain his friendship with these three souls and not take it any further.

Leaving Gibraltar and heading east along the Costa del Sol - the southern coast of Spain - we ended up in Estepona for the rest of winter. There we hunkered down and waited for better weather. Carol and Jake took some Spanish lessons in the nearby town, I worked on the boat as always, and we enjoyed wonderful days and evenings with our cruising

friends. At the end of January, Carol wanted to surprise me with a grand paella feast for my birthday and went to a local restaurant with a Spanish-speaking friend to place the order. The price was outrageous, but when they turned to leave, the owner of the restaurant talked it over with our friend and agreed on a new price. A few days later two enormous platters of paella were delivered to *Sai Baba*. *This* was the paella that I remembered — so delicious — and that evening we had eight people eating in the cockpit and eight people eating down below. I think that was the record for entertaining friends on *Sai Baba*.

With the weather starting to clear, we made our way from port to port along the coast of Spain. We sailed east as far as Alicante before heading out to sea towards the Balearic Islands, the most famous of which is Mallorca. Ibiza was very high-end and expensive, so we didn't linger there for long. Mallorca was busy and overbuilt, lacking the ambience that I remembered from years before. We most enjoyed staying on Minorca, the furthest east of the islands. It was more rural and slower paced, and we found it very peaceful. It helped that we were traveling with our friends on *True Blue*, as they spoke excellent Spanish.

At this point that we actually had a schedule to keep, something that we usually tried to avoid. Carol's mother wanted to celebrate her 70th birthday with family, and as three of her four children were living in Europe that summer, she and her husband rented a villa in Opio, Provence, in the south of France, and arranged for all of us to gather there. In order to arrive in the nearby port of Cannes by the third week in June, we would have to sail north across the Golfe de Lyon and start making our way along the French Riviera. It was time for a new adventure.

Traveling along the Mediterranean coast that summer was a wonderful experience. We made landfall in France at Saintes-Maries de-la-Mer. Tradition holds that the three Marys — Mary Magdalene, Mary Jacobe, mother of James the Less, and Mary Salome, mother of James and John —landed here, having voyaged from the Holy Land. That area of France, known as the Camargue, was quite beautiful, and the weather was perfect. We had a fun time in St. Tropez, tied up to the dock alongside huge yachts, which we called 'gin palaces'. Making our way east, we arrived at Cannes and were lucky enough to get a slip in the city marina. There we stayed for the next three weeks. It was an easy bus or car ride to Opio, and soon we

joined all of Carol's family for a week's reunion and birthday celebration for her mother. Carol's son Chris was able to join us as well, so her little family felt complete. Our days were filled with swimming and playing tennis, being tourists in the beautiful lavender-growing countryside, and eating great feasts each evening, prepared by a local woman.

We were able to take the family out for an outing on *Sai Baba*, sailing over to Ile St. Marguerite to visit the infamous Fort Royal, a prison that supposedly housed the mysterious Man in the Iron Mask in the 17th century. We found a patio restaurant for lunch and had a great afternoon together. Another day we took Chris out for a sail. Previously, he had been prone to a bit of seasickness, but this day's sailing started out smooth and calm, and so he announced that he wanted a more exciting ride. Unfortunately, we rounded a point of land at that moment, and the seas immediately got rougher. It was one of those times when you should be careful what you wish for.

It was in Cannes that we had to say good-bye to Jake. Bored with life at sea, he now wanted to return to Vegas, to play soccer and be with other kids. We didn't want to see him go, but we knew that life on board had gotten lonely for him, so we put him on the plane with Chris when it was time to fly back to the States. He was very much missed.

However we weren't lonely for long because, to our surprise, we learned that an old friend of Carol's was also staying in Opio at the time of our visit. She came on board and traveled with us for the next few weeks as we left Cannes and continued east along the French coast. While in Antibes we convinced her that she shouldn't be traveling with cash and took her to the nearby American Express office to change her money into traveler's checks. Not half an hour after leaving that office, we were surrounded by a group of Gypsy children, and the travelers' checks disappeared. I grabbed one of the girls, but when she started to scream — as if I were assaulting her — I let go in surprise and all the children escaped. We returned to the AmEx office, but they didn't believe our story, so I had to speak to a higher authority by phone, presenting myself as a traveling yacht owner, before they would replace the checks.

Next was Monaco, which I was really looking forward to. Years before, when I had stayed in Monte Carlo with Elaine and looked down over the harbor, I had dreamed of tying up my own yacht there some day.

Unfortunately my dream didn't come true because the harbor master told us that here were no slips available. Additionally, the outer harbor water was too deep for anchoring, so we had to sail back into France and find a slip there. We did have fun visiting Monte Carlo, though. While Carol and her friend visited the Oceanographic Museum, I went down to the waterfront, ordered a coffee and croissants and just sat there, enjoying life to the fullest.

We had planned to sail along the coast into Italy, but several friends warned us that the cost of cruising Italian waters and doing anything ashore was way too high, so from Monaco we sailed to Corsica and spent several pleasant days there, going from harbor to harbor as we worked our way south. It was a short passage to Sardinia, where Carol's friend departed. We spent the rest of the summer there.

In Sardinia I was also able to visit with Marco, my old friend from Vegas, and his extended family. Perhaps the best meal we ever had while cruising was as the guests of Marco and his brothers. We never saw a menu, just course after course of incredibly delicious pasta, fish, meats and vegetables, each course served with a different local wine, and finishing up with pastries and liqueurs. It was a perfect afternoon.

The waters of Cagliari harbor in Sardinia were really polluted, but we were well protected, at least from the weather and the seas, and made new friends with the cruising couples we found there. Unfortunately, this was the only time we were robbed. While away from the boat, someone broke in and took our new single-sideband radio, the screen to our radar and Jake's fishing rod. A week later, the thief brought back the old pole, keeping the reel for himself. This was a thief with a sense of humor. Luckily, I was able to save a French boat from a similar fate. A local came running one day and motioned that a robbery was in progress. A young man was leaving the little boat, and I started to chase him. After what seemed like forever, I managed to grab him and his bag of loot, but he slipped loose and escaped. I was gasping for air and just glad to have the bag. The French men returned later and of course were delighted that their belongings were safe. We spoke no common language, but they gave me the flag from their yacht club in Marseilles, and made it clear that we would always be welcome there.

It was also in the Cagliari harbor that I worked for pay for the only

time while cruising. The boat next to us was British, and the captain was working on an old Tunisian fishing boat that a local insurance salesman wanted renovated into a luxury yacht. I ended up doing some interior work for him, and he made it quite clear that we could stay and work for him indefinitely, but we were getting antsy and knew that we didn't want to spend the winter tied up to this wall in such dirty waters. As it was, I could hardly get the boat to move forward on the day of our departure because of the heavy pollution in the harbor. Once out into clear waters I went overboard with an air tank and spent several hours scraping more than two inches of coral-like growth off the bottom of the boat.

Next we decided to head to Tunisia for the winter of 1991-92. From discussions with other boating people it sounded like there was a safe marina there and that it wouldn't be expensive, so we left Sardinia and headed south for our next adventure: wintering in African waters.

We had an easy passage to the northern coast of Tunisia where we had a very interesting — but disturbing — experience. As one might expect in a Moslem country alcohol was both very expensive and widely illegal. However, if you were a cruising boat and able to buy duty-free goods, that same alcohol was ridiculously cheap. At one of the ports where we stopped the port captain asked us if we wanted to buy any alcohol, but since we only drank wine, we weren't interested. Undaunted, the official then asked us if we would buy a case of Johnny Walker whiskey for him. Without thinking we said sure, we can do that. We soon received our order and waited for the port captain to come and pick it up, but he was nowhere to be found. We were ready to leave and so took off for our next port, but soon after our departure we started getting radio calls. It was the port captain, trying to find us so he could collect his liquor. By this time we had started getting nervous, wondering if we would be in big trouble for selling liquor to a local, so we never answered his calls and ended up keeping the whiskey for ourselves.

The marina at Monastir, south of Tunis the country's capital, was relatively new and clean. We paid for a year in advance, because it was inexpensive, and stayed for the next six months. Since French is the second language of Tunisia, we were able to communicate a little, which turned out to be helpful. When we went to connect our electric plug to the dock. The workman there used a wooden matchstick to wedge the wires together,

which certainly wasn't up to US code, but he made us comfortable, and — in any event — none of the boats ever caught fire. There were about 60 boats in our little community, and we made great friendships with many of them. We had potluck dinners all the time and helped one another with boat repair and maintenance. Several of us took a bus trip south for a few days and rode camels into the Sahara Desert at dawn. We took over the local pizzeria and all came together for a wonderful Christmas potluck dinner, complete with a gift exchange and Christmas crackers, supplied by a few of the British cruisers. We had adventures visiting the souk and trying to escape the carpet salesmen, who would never take no for an answer.

During the time we were in Monastir, Bosse, our cruising friend from Sweden, told us a wonderful story. Bosse was solo sailing and as he approached the entrance to the Monastir harbor, he knew he was in trouble because it was dark and the seas were rough; he was exhausted and couldn't quite make out the lights of the entrance though the driving rain.

It was, in fact, so frightening that he started to fear for his life. And then a miraculous thing happened. Suddenly he realized that there were other men on the boat with him, helping him to navigate and steer towards the harbor entrance. As soon as the boat was in calm, safe waters, Bosse was alone once again, but he truly believed that those spirits saved his life that night.

For us, one of our biggest challenges was taking care of Lovey the cat. Little did we know, but there was no such thing as cat litter or bagged cat food in Tunisia. Cats lived outside and were expected to fend for themselves. We had to get creative and tried various materials to make some kind of cat litter. Luckily, one day we spotted a carpenter's shop, and he had a huge pile of fresh wood shavings outside his door. For a dollar or two we were able to buy the shavings, stuff them into large garbage bags and haul them home on our bicycles. As for Lovey's food, we stretched our supply of dry cat food as long as we could, giving her boiled sardines and canned tuna as well, which she loved, of course. Then we told every boat we knew that, when they went home for a visit, they had to bring back a bag of cat food for her. Sure enough, bags of cat food were delivered from England, Scotland, Sweden and Germany throughout that winter. Lovey had a lot of good friends.

In the spring before heading out to sea again, we decided to haul out *Sai Baba* and redo the bottom which many other cruisers did in Tunisia because the bottom paint was so cheap and so toxic — being filled with lead that made it long-lasting — that it would have been totally illegal in the States. We hauled out with several other cruising boats and spent about a week sanding down the bottom, repainting her and doing all the other jobs that needed to be done.

It was strange, but throughout all the time we spent in Monastir we had very little contact with the local people. We would hear the calls to prayer each day from the minarets and mingle with them at the souk and the vegetable market, but they were prohibited from entering the marina, and so we were relatively separated. We did, however, make friends with one young family and were invited for dinner at their home. They served a traditional meal of couscous and vegetables and gave us spoons to eat with. They had escargots in the shell and gave us open safety pins to dig out the meat. They were gracious and wanted to show us all their possessions, but it was very hard to communicate, and we came away with the feeling that in the end they were looking for some kind of gift, whether money or clothes or whatever. The hospitality just didn't feel genuine. There *was* another kind of contact that Carol heard from various women in the marina: being grabbed and harassed when in town. She herself was once grabbed up her skirt from behind as we were walking through a souk. It seemed that Western women were fair game for disrespect, and, eventually, it made us eager to head north to a less hostile environment.

CHAPTER 51

The Moneychangers

Dealing with money reminded me of a meditation I once had about the money changers. It came in so clear, it was like I was right there in the temple that day. I just hope I was not the one saying crucify him.

The moneychangers are still with us. Things have not changed. Over 2000 years ago Jesus walked into the temple in Jerusalem. It was an incredible building, with hundreds of people there. As Jesus walked forward, he felt the presence of God, because he realized that God was within him. He saw the moneychangers there before him and became furious. He upturned the tables and sent the money flying. He freed all the doves and sheep; setting all the caged animals free.

But there is more to this story than just turning over the tables; he had a great realization. Unfortunately for us the reality is that the moneychangers are still with us to this day — nothing is different than it was then. They are all around us and easily visible, changing money for this yearning and that impulse, for material desires. In Washington DC the moneychangers are there, even if we call them by names like 'lobbyist' and 'special interest groups'. They are trading money for favors, for influence.

Wherever you go, you can always see the trade-off: favors for money, money for favors. Even in the old city of Jerusalem you can see the moneychangers today. It is impossible to see the beauty of the sites — to

feel your own connection to the old city — because the moneychangers are all around you. At the stations of the cross the moneychangers are there. You visit the site where the cross was placed and find the moneychangers there. You crawl into a little cave no more than six feet wide and four feet deep and the floor is covered with money. Nothing has changed.

Even in communist societies where all were supposed to be equal, the moneychangers were still there. The top members of the party lived in luxury, with cars, spacious apartments and gourmet food, while the sheep and the doves starved. It's the same in socialism and democracy, the same in the Democratic and Republican parties. The moneychangers are there. In Mecca millions come to pray to Allah and, again, there are the moneychangers. There is always money present. It is nothing about God or people desiring to be closer to God. The sheep and the doves are still being sacrificed for the few, the powerful — the moneychangers.

When are we going to wake up to the fact that we must go beyond money, beyond the changing of money, the changing of goods, to meet the yearnings and desires for the few who control us, the sheep and the doves? It's a matter of waking up to the knowledge that God is within you, that we don't need to go anywhere to find him, that without Him we don't exist. We keep searching for God, but He would never leave us; without Him we would collapse, die. There would be no existence. We think our lives are separate and whole without Him. We travel the world looking for God, just as I did for so many years until finally, one day, I realized that He had never left me.

So, we must search within ourselves for God. Never mind the moneychangers. Let them do what they want. Yogananda called this understanding self-realization — a beautiful phrase — when you realize who you really are. With that realization the moneychangers disappear. Seek God within the temple that is your body. You don't have to go to the religious temples of the world to find God, for you are the Living Temple. You are made from His divine essence and only have to recognize this fact and wake up to the truth. Feel His presence within you; bang your knuckles on that door until you realize who you are — always asking until you learn the truth. The door will be opened and the answers will come, but you must take the step yourself and enter into that silent, divine temple. The more you look, the more you will find, until finally realize

the divinity of your physical temple. You will realize that God has not left you for a moment.

So, let the moneychangers go and realize who you are — the essence of your being.

Oh Father, let us just wake up to Thy divine presence, to your presence within us, without which we are nothing. You are omnipresent; there is no place where you don't exist. Help us to realize this miracle and wake up. You are our very own being and our very own essence, and without you we do not exist. Without You we cannot feel, touch or taste. It is this awareness of Your presence that we called Consciousness. We were created in Your image and likeness of this Consciousness. Thank you, Father, for letting me realize Your omnipresence. It is always there, always constant. Without You we have no consciousness, no awareness. Consciousness is all that there is — the omnipresence of You. Father, wake us up to Thy presence, for it is all one — one consciousness — and we are just little bubbles of it. We must expand it into Thy omnipresence, become consciously aware of Consciousness. When we finally merge totally into full Consciousness, we will have merged the one into the other. *Then* we will be able to look around and see our brothers and sisters as a part of that Consciousness. The Divine Light, that Consciousness, is *in* them all, and *for* all of us. We are nothing without it. We will be able to love You with all our being, all our hearts, and love one another as we love ourselves. We will realize that we have all been created out of one thing: Consciousness. There is only one Consciousness, that of God. Oh Father, it is so hard to explain it. When I hear it from You, it is so wonderful, so unbelievably wonderful, but then it is so hard to put it into words. Please help me to explain it, to help me wake up my brothers and my sisters, so that we can realize the Oneness that we are, with no separation but totally uniting in the one God — in the one God that is pure Consciousness — spiritual Consciousness. It is so hard to explain, but so easy to understand once one grasps the concept. You are everywhere; wherever we stand is holy ground, for You are there within us.

So, we need to ignore the moneychangers and realize the omnipresence of God. We can only change the world if we change within ourselves, and we can only make that change if we realize who we are. One man's

realization of this truth can change an entire city, can amplify the vibrations of that city, with just his own realization, his *self*-realization.

How can I explain this feeling of Oneness? I can hardly function anymore. I see Thy presence everywhere in everything I touch and see and smell. Give me the strength to keep functioning while surrounded by this delusion that I have created for myself and the delusions created by those around me. But, more importantly, let these walls of delusion drop away, so that I can only be in Thy presence. For I know that the Kingdom of Heaven is right here at hand, closer than the hands and feet and the breath itself. All the teachings of Jesus come together so beautifully, when the in becomes the out and the out becomes the in. Then you will have entered into the kingdom of Heaven. What a feeling, what an understanding. If only my brothers and sisters could understand this feeling and go within for the answers. With understanding from within comes understanding of all that surrounds us. With that understanding come merging and so one enters the kingdom of Heaven.

Shanti, shanti, shanti.

CHAPTER 52

Malta

In the spring of 1992 we made our departure from Tunisia and sailed north to Malta, where many of our cruising friends were headed. Although we were in awe as we entered the harbor at dusk, sailing past the walls of Valletta — built by the Knights of Malta in the 16th century — we were concerned about entering Malta with Lovey the cat. We had to smuggle her in, because Malta had a strict quarantine policy in the British tradition. However, after that first time, she became a Maltese resident, and we didn't have to worry about her anymore.

Malta was a fascinating country, and we fell in love with her. Its history was so interesting, from the Phoenician sailors and the landing of St Paul, who shipwrecked on the island while being transported to Rome to stand trial, to the Siege of Valletta by the Turks and the bombing of the island by the Germans during World War II. The Maltese had been conquered dozens of times and always managed to survive and thrive. Carol and I spent many days just wandering the streets of the old towns whose buildings were made of a soft yellow stone.

We arrived in Malta just before Easter weekend and our first adventure was to go to the city of Mosta, famous for its immense cathedral and the miracle that took place there during WW II when a bomb fell through the roof of the church, where people had gathered for safety. The bomb never exploded and all their lives were saved.

There was a grand procession that Good Friday, as Malta is overwhelmingly Catholic, and we went to see it. Some men dragged chains, others symbolically whipped themselves, but all of them were hidden under sheets of white, red or purple and wore pointed hats. They all looked like members of the Ku Klux Klan, and at first it was disturbing. But of course, the Maltese had these garments long before the KKK did and wore them as a sign of humility before Jesus and God.

On that Easter Sunday morning we were getting acquainted with our sailing neighbors in the Msida Marina when I saw a man who looked so sad that I asked him what could be wrong on such a beautiful morning, and he told me that that he had just broken his mother's bones. We were shocked and asked him what he meant. It turned out that land is at a premium on Malta and there isn't enough room to bury everyone. Therefore when you die, you are allowed three years under ground in a grave before you are dug up, and your larger bones were broken into smaller pieces so that they can fit into an urn that is placed in a crypt or wall mausoleum.

I had another death-related incident in the same marina when we took our dinghy over to say hello to a nice couple. This time it was the woman who seemed very sad, and when I asked what was the matter was she told me that her father had recently died — but only after an unusual experience in the hospital: he had looked into the corner of the room and saw a white light and asked his wife if she too saw the light. Although the woman I was talking with had been in the hospital room at the time, she hadn't seen the light — but her mother, the man's wife told the dying man had indeed seen it, but when he then told her that she could come with him, that it was time for him to leave and that they could go together towards the light, the wife had been afraid and refused to go, and so the man died and left this world on his own.

Given my own experiences I had no reason to doubt the story, which I think made her feel better — knowing that we didn't think that she or her mother were crazy.

After several months in Malta, we decided to fly home to the States for the holidays. Carol booked the tickets but made the mistake of booking herself as Carol Juliano, because she always used my name now. When we got to the airport, the officials didn't want to let her on the plane since her passport had her previous married name. Somehow we persuaded them

to let us go, but the same thing happened during our transfer in London, where again, we were finally allowed to board the plane. Carol was upset by all this and said that, once we got to the States, she was either going to change her ticket — at great expense — or I would have to marry her. I said, 'Well, I guess we could do that,' and she said, 'I accept!' And so we were married downtown at the city hall in Las Vegas on Christmas Eve of 1992. It was just a formality to me, but I could tell that it made Carol very happy.

During the time we were in Malta, we became good friends with the owner of a little shop who was Maltese but had lived in the States for several years with his wife and two daughters. We had many wonderful dinners with Charlie, his wife Irene, and all their extended family, especially up at the other end of the island in a resort area called Marfa. There the family had managed to get a 99-year lease on a small boat-storage unit near the shore and had transformed it into a little summer getaway. We ate feasts of rabbit stew, pasta and wonderful loaves of fresh Maltese bread. We played cards, swam in the beautiful water and visited with the other families who had leased the neighboring boat sheds. Not only did Charlie and his family become our friends, but when the time came to find a new home for Lovely, they adopted her as one of their own. As a result, she was spoiled rotten and would die of old age in Malta, fat and content.

We made other good friends when, one day a woman walked up to *Sai Baba* and asked if we were Americans. We said yes, how did you know? She said, because our boat was color-coordinated, a comment we had never heard before. And so we met Barbara and Bob on *Snap Decision* and enjoyed some local sailing with them. They had a beautiful home on the other main island of Malta, Gozo, which is a quieter, more rural island, and we fell in love with it.

It was the only time in our travels when we seriously considered buying a house and settling down. The old farmhouses were called 'houses of character'. They could be bought relatively inexpensively and then fixed up into beautiful villas. We never did find the right house at the right time for the right price, but we stayed at Bob and Barbara's house many times during subsequent winters and enjoyed the hospitality of other couples that had also retired there.

We were very comfortable living in Malta. Being able to speak English

made everything easier, and the local cruising community was always friendly and helpful. There was quite an international feeling to the island, which may have been related to this funny tradition. By the front door of many houses there was a sign carved in stone that would say either God Bless America, God Bless Australia, or God Bless Canada. It turned out that so much of the Maltese population had emigrated in the past — especially after WW II — that it was said if all the emigrants returned to Malta, the island would sink under their weight. Anyway, many of those who did return to the Malta put up those plaques in remembrance of their other home countries.

We stayed in the marina during the summer and then brought *Sai Baba* out of the water and onto the hard for the winter at the Manoel Island Yacht Center. For the next two years we used Malta as our home and made trips from there. We made two wonderful short trips to Sicily, first to Siracusa and then to Catania, where we hired a taxi to take us up near the active volcano, Mt. Etna. We spent most of one summer sailing among the Greek Ionian islands to the west of the Greek mainland. We anchored in beautiful harbors, each one with a legendary history, and took side trips to the Parthenon in Athens and to Delphi, home of the famous oracle.

It was on one of these islands, in the summer of 1994, that we decided to take the dingy and motor over to a larger town to get some much-needed cash. Although we had learned by this time that half of southern Europe goes on holiday in August, and the other half goes on strike, we went to the bank, only to find out that the clerks in charge of processing credit card transactions were on strike. The teller was sympathetic to our problem and told us that we could take a bus up the hill to an automated credit card booth, where — maybe — we would be able to get some money. When we told him that we didn't have enough money for the bus, he took 50 drachmas out of his pocket and handed it to us, saying, 'Just consider this an adventure.'

We were very grateful. We found the bus, found the ATM, got our money, and returned the 50 drachmas to the teller with a bottle of brandy in thanks. It was indeed an adventure.

It's hard to stop telling stories about all the wonderful experiences we had, but all the same, the time came — in the fall of 1994 — when we decided that it was time to return to the States. Carol felt that she was

needed by her sons, as they were growing up and nearing the end of high school. She very much wanted them to go to college. Similarly, I had my own concerns, because two of my relatives were gravely ill and I wanted to spend time with them. We hauled *Sai Baba* onto the hard for the last time, covered her with canvas, winterized her as much as was possible, and said our good-byes. I would return to Malta twice in the next few years — to check her over, to clean and wax the hull, to do all the things that needed to be done — but we would never sail her again.

CHAPTER 53

Trip to India to see Sai Baba

Before that final farewell with *Sai Baba* — on a sunny Maltese morning in August of 1993, Carol and I were sitting in the cockpit, drinking our morning coffee. As often happened, I was reminiscing about my visits to Sai Baba in India, and Carol repeated once again that she wanted to go and see him for herself. Suddenly it just seemed like the right time to go, and so we started planning our trip. We had heard that there were inexpensive plane tickets posted in the Sunday edition of the *London Times* newspaper each week, and we found a great round-the-world ticket that was good for a year. It included seven layovers, the only condition being that you had to keep going forward, from west to east. So, we got our visas, put *Sai Baba* on the hard and flew to London, where our odyssey would begin.

We flew directly from London to Bombay, India. From there we took a train for the 600- mile trip to Bangalore. We had assumed that we would take some kind of rail express, meant for tourists, but for some reason they weren't running. Instead we ended up on a local run, which took 24 hours.

It was pouring rain as we left Bombay that evening, and we found ourselves in a leaky car, packed with Indian men. It was not a comfortable situation at all, so I found a conductor and for a few rupees got us moved to a dry, empty car further down the train. Passengers would come and go as we crossed the beautiful countryside, and at each stop little urchins would come in to sweep the car, while others brought in snacks for sale.

We spoke with one older gentleman who recommended a hotel for us to stay in Bangalore. It turned out to be very clean and comfortable, and the next day we hired a little motorized rickshaw to take us to Whitefield, where Baba's summer ashram was located.

I had assumed that there would be a room available for us at the ashram, as there had been the first time I had come, but all the rooms were taken — by Italian devotees who came every August, bringing with them some new kitchen equipment that they would put to good use in their kitchen assignment (this particular year they brought a donut-making machine) — and so we had to find a room outside the compound.

Our first night outside the ashram wasn't pleasant, and Carol was having serious doubts about this adventure, but the next day we found a very nice room attached to the home of an Indian family— a mother and her three daughters living alone while the husband was working as an engineer in Saudi Arabia. The oldest daughter was a college student in Bangalore, and we had a lot of fun going about the city with her. She also took us to a clothing store, where Carol bought some outfits suitable for darshan.

Once settled, we quickly got into the routine of the ashram. We would attend darshan each morning and afternoon, Carol on one side of the open shed with the women, and me on the other side with the men. The ashram was crowded with pilgrims, but we found our niche in the kitchen and started helping to prepare breakfast and lunch for the Western visitors. There was a canteen for the Indians as well, but the food there was much hotter and spicier than we were used to.

We made many friends during our stay at the ashram. One of them was Victoria, the head cook at the Westerners' canteen who welcomed both of us with open arms. Not so the local monkeys who got into anything that wasn't carefully secured. One day Carol caught some of these monkeys in the act of ripping all of Victoria's laundry off the drying line, but instead of chasing them away, Carol first took a few photos. Much as Victoria hated the little creatures, she loved the photo that we later gave to her. Our rickshaw driver, Ravi, was also very friendly and would always be available if we wanted to go somewhere. He even invited us to his home for dinner. Sadly, as happened in Tunisia, it turned out that what he really wanted was something financial: for me to invest in his rickshaw business.

We celebrated Carol's birthday while in Whitefield. Dressed in her finest outfit, she carried a bowl of candies into the shed, hoping that Baba would bless them, as was the local custom. She had also stitched the OM sign onto a handkerchief for him. As usual we were all packed into the shed, where it was hard to get a seat on the outer edge, but this time Carol was seated there. When Sai Baba arrived, he usually walked among us for a while, but this time he walked straight up onto the stage before us, where he sat as we sang hymns. Carol's heart sank, as she believed that he wouldn't bless her candy on this special day. Then - and this was the only time we ever saw him do this - he left the stage, came back down through the crowd and basically walked straight up to Carol. He blessed her candies and picked up the handkerchief. The custom was that he would take something from one person and give it to another - kind of a blessing for both - but this time, after a few moments, he walked back to Carol and returned the handkerchief to her personally. It was a very special day for us both.

In mid-September the community moved to Puttaparti, a few hours away by taxi, where Sai Baba and his followers spent the winter. There, we were able to get a room on the campus, so everything was very convenient. The crowds seemed to grow by the day, and during certain Hindu holidays there would be tens of thousands of people in and about the ashram.

During darshan of that first day in Puttaparti, Carol sat on the women's side, as was customary. She happened to be seated next to Victoria, our friend in the kitchen, who had lived at Baba's ashrams in India for many years. We waited an unusually long time for Sai Baba to appear, and the longer it took, the more people got up and left, probably thinking that he wouldn't be coming. As they left, Victoria would inch closer to the front, nudging Carol along, until they were seated in the front row. And then Sai Baba came out and went right up to Victoria and Carol. Following Victoria's example, Carol placed her hands on one of Baba's feet, as Victoria did the same with the other. And so they stayed for what seemed like several minutes. Baba was talking with other devotees, but Carol was experiencing something quite wonderful. What felt like pulses of electricity surged up her arms and into her body. She was filled with joy. She wasn't aware of anything else, until Baba turned and walked away. Carol often expressed disappointment that she was never chosen to have a personal

interview with Sai Baba, but it was obvious that the experiences she did have were very special, and for that she was very grateful. Carol learned later on that there is a Hindu belief that you will be freed of all past karma if you see a realized master, hear that master and touch that master. She experienced all these things during her stay in Puttaparti.

Carol wanted to see some of the places I had visited during my first visit to the ashram. We went to Hulliguppal's orphanage, which had grown tremendously during the past two decades, and she saw for herself the vibhuti, the sacred ash, forming on the glass covering Sai Baba's pictures. She held in the palm of her hand the amulet that endlessly dripped out amrita, and we filled a little jar with the sacred nectar. We also went to the meditating tree up on the hill outside the ashram, and she quietly waited while I spread Elaine's ashes, which had sailed with us for all those years.

Of course, I was having incredible experiences every day. Just being in Sai Baba's presence was a blessing, but that didn't stop my ego from longing for personal interviews, like the ones I had had years earlier. Then, one day as I sat in darshan, he looked me right in the eye and I heard in my head, "You know you always have a personal darshan with me."

I knew that it was totally true: that Sai Baba was always with me.

But not only with me. There was, for example, an Australian gentleman who arrived in Puttaparti in a wheel chair because he had been in a devastating car accident and could only move one arm. He had no knowledge or faith in Sai Baba, but his friends insisted on bringing him. I saw him at breakfast that first morning, being cared for by his 'mates', and wished him well. It wasn't long after that, in darshan, that Sai Baba walked up to this fellow and told him to stand up. He got up out of the wheel chair and was healed. A few hours later I saw him walk into the canteen for lunch and when I told him that his shoelace was untied, he knelt down and tied it. I asked him, 'So, what do you think about Baba?' and he replied, 'Well, I don't know what he means to you, but he is God to me.'

And Jesus' image was there as well, but it was different from the traditional blue-eyed Jesus that I grew up seeing. This image was displayed in the tourist shops near the ashram and I was told that this was Baba's picture of Jesus. During a private interview with Baba a devotee had asked him what Jesus really looked like. He told her to click her camera three times, and when she got the film developed, there was this photo. I kept a

copy of it in my wallet, and years later, when I was in a new-age bookstore in Sedona, Arizona I looked up, and there was the identical photograph which a store clerk told me was produced by a local woman who claimed to be in contact with Jesus.

As time approached for our departure from the ashram, Carol and I followed tradition and each wrote a letter to Baba, requesting permission to leave. If Baba took your letter, permission was granted. One morning I was seated about three rows back from the front, holding up my letter and watching Sai Baba as he passed. He walked past me and then, without looking, leaned back and took my letter. We knew it was now time to leave. We traveled east for a few weeks as tourists to other ashrams and historical sites near and along the coast of India before returning to Bombay and continuing our voyage around the world.

But before we left, on our return to Bombay for our departure from India, Carol really wanted to see the Bhrigu Samhita, also known as the Book of Bhrigu, an ancient compilation of many volumes, written on palm leaves, that contains predictions on current and future lives as well as information on the past lives. I had told Carol about it and how my fortune had been told in those books — that in my next and last reincarnation on earth, after this one, I would be reborn in Mysore, as would be Sri Sathya Sai Baba in his last reincarnation of Total Love. However, I wasn't interested in pursuing this path. If I am one with God, any karmic prophecies are meaningless. Rebirth is meaningless. But Carol wanted to see the book and perhaps have her own prophecy read. Unfortunately, we could not keep the appointment before our departure. Although Carol was disappointed, I wasn't. I believe that we can make our own destiny and that, if we realize God, we don't need a book of prophecy.

CHAPTER 54

The Lord's Prayer

Before we leave India, let me share one last story.

Carol and I were at Sai Baba's ashram in the town of Whitefield, near Bangalore and one evening we went out for dinner with three divine mothers — three wonderful women — and after dinner, when we were sitting on the patio in the beautiful night, one of the women asked me, 'Dominick, teach us about the Lord's Prayer.'

My first reaction was to laugh. What did I know about the Lord's Prayer? I immediately remembered my First Holy Communion as a child and how I learned the Lord's Prayer and Hail Mary, among other religious formulas, as part of my preparation for taking communion in church. At that time it was just a matter of memorization, and if I didn't say it really quickly, I would forget the words. In confession my punishment was always to repeat the Lord's Prayer and Hail Mary, and I would say them as fast as was possible, with no thought to their meanings. It was total ritual, total programming.

As I got older, I grew away from the rituals of the Catholic Church, and for years had given little or no thought to the Lord's Prayer. Then the question was asked, and I silently asked God to help me understand it. At that moment I started to hear a voice talking to me, and in response, I simply started repeating what I was hearing.

Our Father: These two words hit me like a bolt of lightning. I felt that

284

I was saying it for every sister and brother in the universe. Our Father, the father of all creation. I remembered Jesus saying, 'Call no man on earth your father," (Matthew 23:9) because you have only one father, and He lives in the Kingdom of Heaven.

Which art in Heaven: At that moment I realized the truth that everything is within. In heaven, closer than the hands and feet and the breath itself. The Kingdom of Heaven is within. Everything on the *outside* is a waste of time because you have to go *inside*.

Hallowed be Thy name: I asked God his name and heard his reply: that he has no name and all names, that everything in the universe is his beingness, his name. Whatever is said is His name. I am that I am. I am everything that you can perceive with your senses and beyond.

Thy Kingdom come, Thy will be done, on earth as it is in Heaven: I realized how totally the Kingdom of Heaven is within me. All I have to do is wake up out of this dream and I will realize Thy presence in Thy kingdom. You are always there, never abandoning me, no matter where I am or what I am doing. As it is with me, it is with everyone. The Kingdom of God is within us all. All we have to do is turn within, to feel that presence, and then let the spirit of God guide us in the outer world. The in becomes the out, and the out becomes the in. When the two have merged I have entered into the Kingdom of Heaven. Thy will be done, not my petty, egotistical will, but Thy will. Thy will is the only will I want to obey.

Give us this day our daily bread: The bread is not made of flour but is the word of God. It is that word which nourishes me, that gives me my strength and my joy in life. Speak to me every day. All I want is to hear Thy word. That will fill and sustain me.

Forgive us our trespasses, as we forgive them who trespass against us: When I forgive 70 times 70 I am not only forgiving myself but all my brothers and sisters, because there is no separation at this point. We are all one, so that when we judge and condemn one another, we are judging and condemning our very selves. In fact we are judging God, because we are one with Him.

And lead us not into temptation, but deliver us from evil: Deliver me out of thought, out of the programming of this material universe. Let me think only of You and Your divine presence in every day and every minute for as long as I live.

For Thine is the Kingdom, the power and the glory, for ever and ever: Each time I say this prayer it comes out a little bit differently. Each time I feel a little closer to You and love You all that much more. So, when you say this prayer, let the words flow, for it is God that is saying them, not you. You will hear His voice and know what each word means. That is the Kingdom and the glory of God.

CHAPTER 55

Selling Sai Baba

From India, we went to Singapore, Tokyo, and then on to Hawaii. From there we stopped to visit family in Los Angeles, Las Vegas, and New York before returning to London, where our round- the-world trip had started. From there we flew back to Malta and returned home to our wonderful sailboat, *Sai Baba*.

When we decided to return to the States, our friend Myra, who owned a chandlery near our boat yard in Malta, said that she would keep an eye on *Sai Baba*. Eventually she wrote to tell us that the boat was in bad shape, that all the canvas had been torn and blown away. She had tried to cover the cockpit area with a tarp, but that had blown away as well. So Carol and I decided that I would go back to the boat, assess the damage and spruce her up.

I flew to Malta and took a taxi from the airport, arriving at the boat after dark. I climbed a ladder to get onboard, as she was up on stilts in the yard, and went below. Inside it looked like we had never left. There wasn't even any dust, as she was tight and well-insulated. The next morning I woke up early and was sickened to see what kind of shape she was in on the outside. The canvas was shredded, the varnish had peeled off, and the hull was dull and faded from sun and wind.

I had brought new canvas, plastic sheeting, and zippers with me and found a man who agreed to make the new dodger and bimini to protect

the cockpit. While he did that, I went to work on the boat itself and put in several 16 to 18-hour workdays. On that first day I washed off the dirt and grime and started to sand the hull. On the second day — once the sanding, cleaning and waxing were done — I started the varnishing. I ended up giving the exposed wood five coats of varnish, and she really started to look good. From there I started on the hull, which had to be sanded down before it could be repainted. The canvas man returned with the completed dodger and bimini, as well as a larger canvas cover to protect more of the boat's cockpit and deck area. I then started painting the bottom and continued the next day, managing to put on 3 coats of bottom paint. By the end of that day I was so tired that could hardly stand up.

There I was, standing on the ground, looking up at *Sai Baba*. I was so worn out, so tired, that I said to myself, 'It's time to sell her.' I even said, 'Oh God, I really want to sell this boat. I would take anything, even $20.00, if it was offered to me right now.'

At that very moment, someone came up behind me and said, 'Hey, I hear this boat is for sale.' My heart seemed to stop, my legs almost buckled, and I realized that if this fellow offered me $20.00, I would have to take it. It turned out that he was a very nice guy, a diesel mechanic about 45 years old and retired from the British navy, who had been renovating a 50 ft. boat for 5 years. Now that it was completed, he had run out of money. He and his wife decided that, if they sold their boat and bought a smaller one, they would be able to afford to go cruising. He invited me onto his boat, which was nearby in the boat yard. I was impressed by how pristine and clean it was and how immaculate his engine room was. It was kept the way I had always maintained *Sai Baba*.

I invited the couple onboard *Sai Baba*, and they were totally impressed with her as well. The woman loved the galley area and said, 'Yes, this is the boat for us.' The man reacted the same way when he saw the engine room, which was clean and sparkling. We sat down with some tea and started to discuss the deal. I told them that I hoped to get about $80,000 for her, which worked out to about 60,000 British pounds. He told me that he couldn't afford that and offered me 45,000 pounds, which worked out to about $60,000. Since I had made a deal with God to accept as little as $20.00, I obviously couldn't say no, so I agreed to the price, and we shook hands on it.

Once the deal had been made, the fellow called his lawyer in London and made arrangements to transfer the funds to our bank account in Las Vegas. I would have to bring Carol back to Malta to clean out our personal items from the boat and to say good-bye. The British couple had already sold their boat and would have to be off it in just a few weeks, so the transaction happened quickly. I agreed to leave almost the entire inventory of boat equipment, including the dinghy, the outboard engine for the dinghy, the life raft, my tools, my diving equipment, our nautical electronics and charts, and even all the kitchen and linen supplies.

I flew back to Vegas and, after Carol arranged for a few days off from work, we returned to Malta. Within a few days we had boxed up and shipped off our clothes and mementos. Once we were notified that the money transfer had been made, we signed the final closing papers and said our good-byes to our wonderful home of over six years. We had been so happy on her, but we now sadly realized that our life on *Sai Baba* had come to an end.

CHAPTER 56

The Law of Cause and Effect

Let us now take a moment to talk about karma. I like to call it the planting of the seeds while others call it the law of cause and effect. In any case, it is the same because every effect, every action comes from a cause. It is a law of nature — it exists — and every human comes to realize its immutable nature at some point. Things happen because they were caused, *not* because God is judging or condemning us. And God is perfection. God just IS. There is no right or wrong, no good or evil, no reward or punishment, just God. A god who judged or punished would not be our God of pure love.

All people of faith can name the things that we consider attributes of God — God is the cause, pure love, everything that *is*, total understanding, and in that understanding is just God, the "is"- ness. He holds the entire universe together solely by His existence. There is no judgment of personalities, no respect of nations, of governments, of religions.

So, along the line we realize that God exists just to be. We realize that there was and is no judgment or punishment from Him. We realize that we humans would have to be the ones to do judge or punish. And so we came to create the agreement of cause and effect. We would be the ones to reward and punish ourselves. It doesn't matter when or how we agreed to it; the fact is that we are the ones who have brought these concepts into existence through our mutual agreement.

And so we have to take responsibility for this law, because we agreed

to it. Once you become aware of this law you can see the results all around you. You see people punishing themselves, rewarding themselves, and you can see that it isn't government or society that imposes this law. We do have a system of laws at all levels of government, based on the principle of cause and effect, but these have sprung from our intuitive acceptance of personal responsibility. We know that the world around us is unaware of much that we do in our lives, so we will be our own judges and juries.

Jesus called it the planting of the seeds, (Matthew 13: 3-9) and he tried to teach us about it, but just a handful of people seem to grasp the truth of it. I had to think about it for any years. I sat, closed my eyes, and asked the question, 'What does the law of cause and effect really mean?' and waited for an answer. This time — during these contemplations/meditations — I went through all the stages that I always experience when I'm seeking enlightenment. First, lots of thoughts come in, and I say 'Be still, be still,' and sometimes I have to get angry with my mind, 'Be!' Then it happens, you enter this field, and the questions start being answered, It can be Jesus, or Gautama, or Joe Goldsmith, or Martin Luther King, but they are all God. It is all God. You are there, and it's God, but you know who is saying it. I have learned that since practice makes perfect I must repeat my quest over and over and be patient with myself.

And so it was that I came to my understanding of karma, of cause and effect, of Jesus' parable of the sowing of the seeds We see how crime against society is punished, and how people are imprisoned for breaking the laws. We hear these individuals claiming their innocence, saying that they have been falsely accused and convicted. But we know that in accordance with the law of cause and effect, something brought them to that imprisonment. It may not be what they were accused of, but rather other deeds whether good or bad that they were responsible for in the past.

Take my own case. I have been born several times and have memories of several lives. During the Roman Empire I was a Centurion, and the things I did! I should have punished myself, and I did. In one lifetime I fell madly in love with a Jewish woman and I converted to Judaism. I felt what it feels like to be persecuted, and after I left that lifetime I decided I didn't want to be punished. In other words: I had learned from one lifetime what to do (or not to do) in the next. Each time we come into life with a script — for instance, not to be punished — but at some point we fall back

on our "programming" and we punish — and reward — ourselves all the same, until, eventually we wake up to the realization that we are doing it to ourselves even though what we really are is God. God is consciousness, and we are not separate, we can never be separate from God.

You might ask how we go about punishing ourselves. One of the most obvious is through our bodies. We reward ourselves with good health, and we punish ourselves with sickness, disease and death. Always remember, the body doesn't think; it only reacts. It reacts to our thoughts and beliefs. If we believe in sickness, our body gets sick. If we don't believe in sickness, the body stays healthy. It is part of a belief system that what we believe takes place in the body. I've known people who can eat junk food and stay in good health. And there are those people who try to eat what they consider a healthy diet and become sick. It is the law of cause and effect that makes this happen.

Also, there is no such thing as a coincidence. When you get into a car accident, there is a reason that it occurred. Somehow, in some way, you are reaping the effect of something that was previously put into motion. You may think that it is impossible that you would want to punish yourself, but in fact, you know that there have to be rewards and punishments from somewhere, even if no one is there to judge. Once you have created a cause it belongs to you, and you will be the judge and jury of how it comes out. In fact no one does a better job of judging ourselves than ourselves. God just is. God does not judge or punish.

Do not take my word for this concept; investigate it for yourself through concentration, contemplation and meditation.

This is a hard principle to understand and to accept. Obviously, consciously, we don't know that we agreed to it or why. It has been a part of our beingness for so long that we have no memory of its beginning, or why we chose that path.

The fact is that whatever you do you are going to create an effect, a reaction, and you are going to consider that effect as either a reward or punishment to yourself. When you contemplate or meditate about this relationship you will get answers to your questions. But you will also learn a lot just by observing society around you, watching the way that people around you react.

Knowing and understanding about cause and effect is one thing,

stopping the endless repetition is quite another — knowing how to get off the merry-go-round. That is why a master is someone who has gotten the better of this material world we have created and wants to go beyond it.

The relationship between cause and effect is there to be stopped, and can be done by realization, realizing how and why we have created this system. Knowing that we have agreed to be judged and that we judge ourselves makes a lot of sense. This concept can be extended to a family consciousness — with its internal causes and effects — a city cause and effect, a state one and even national cause and effect. Every level of society is part of this agreement.

Even if you don't accept or understand the concept of the law of cause and effect, you can still stop it. You tell yourself that you don't know what the truth is, but you can see what is happening to people all around you, rewarding and punishing themselves continually as they go through life. You can see this relationship through the endless wars and destruction between nations, even as it is obvious that nothing is accomplished by this great wrong. But we have collectively agreed that war can be justified and go forward.

Killing is strongly condemned by all the great religions, and theoretically we have all agreed to this precept, but yet, we go ahead and justify killing in 'certain circumstances' even though through Moses and the Ten Commandments God said, 'Thou shall not kill', — which should be pretty easy to understand. And Jesus reinforced the concept when he said, 'They that live by the sword shall die by the sword.' (Matthew 26:52) Certainly it is true that if we kill people, we will have to pay the consequence, even if it doesn't take place on the same battlefield. But even so all our young soldiers who go off so patriotically to kill for their country create an immense cause, for which there will be an immense effect. You can see the pain in the faces of these soldiers when they return to society and try to pick up the lives they left behind, because at some level they know inside that what they have done will have consequences.

With raised awareness it will become clear in time that the only people who profit from war and destruction are the moneychangers. They love the profit to be made from war and are unconcerned by its effects created. And so we will have to stop agreeing with the moneychangers if this cycle is to end.

How long will we continue these self-created cycles of destruction? When will we say to ourselves, 'I'm tired of punishing myself?' Once we desire to give it all up, we have taken a great step. We have the answers within us. They cannot be found outside us, in religions or social law. For we are the living temple, not made by man's hands, and we will be the ones to end the cycle of judge and jury.

We can do it, but first we must acknowledge the initial agreement. Secondly, we have to desire to stop it. By contemplating and meditating on it, your understanding will grow, and once you completely understand it, the process will stop instantly. The past will no longer exist, with all its causes and effects, once you have that total realization.

How exactly do we stop this cycle about which many great masters have taught us? They all say one thing; forgiveness. But what is forgiveness? It is the ability to let go. And in letting go, who do we forgive? Ourselves, because we are the ones who do the rewarding and punishing, no one else. As Jesus said: 'We must forgive 70 times 70' (Matthew 18:22) and that's a lot of forgiving. But of course it must be ourselves that we forgive. Because we are all the self, and when we truly forgive, we forgive everybody. As we say every time we recite the Lord's Prayer: forgive us our trespasses, as we forgive those who trespass against us. In other words, forgiveness for one — ourselves — is forgiveness for all. Jesus speaks not only of forgiveness, but also of judgment: 'Judge not, lest you yourself be judged' (Matthew 7:1) because when we do something to someone else, we are doing it to ourselves. When we condemn someone, we are condemning ourselves. Therefore we must forgive, totally and unconditionally. This forgiveness will be a great comfort because as you start contemplating your past, you will see more and more incidents of which you are ashamed. These must all be forgiven and let go.

But how do you forgive yourself for things you can't remember, things that happened in the long ago or even in previous lives? We are still punishing ourselves for things we did in past lives, even if we have no conscious memory of them. That need to punish and reward ourselves came with us into this life. We came here knowing that we would have to be our own judge and jury.

As I said earlier, Jesus taught me a most profound thing, that 'He who lives in the past is dead. He who lives in the future has no future.

He who lives in the now is truly a wise man.' You have to remember that everything takes place in the now — in present time. There is nothing to be done about the past, so you must forgive it and let it go. It is merciful that we can't remember previous lives, because there is nothing we can do to correct those wrongdoings. We could have been despicable murderers and rapists, warmongers and dictators. Anything imaginable is possible in our past. So, instead of continuing to reap the effects of those past lives, it is time to forgive it and let them go. The reward of realization will come, if only you will put in the energy necessary to attain it. It takes a complete realization before you can 'as is' it, — eliminate the agreement of cause and effect.

If you do nothing else in this world just remember not to hurt anyone in thought, word, or deed.

So, you must forgive yourself 70 times 70. There is no future, only this very now. In the realization of the now — in becoming one with the now - the law of karma is totally erased.

Shanti, shanti, shanti.

CHAPTER 57

I Am the Field

Let me end this contemplation of my life and beliefs with some thoughts on three words that I have found in many metaphysical books, words that I have heard teachers discuss but never really explain.

The first word is *omniscience*. When knowledge is total, it is total wisdom. Total wisdom is in the Field that I spoke about in Chapter 3 — the Field of positive vibrations. That means that all wisdom belongs to the I Am. That I Am is the Field.

The second word is *omnipotent*, which means all power. It too belongs to the I Am, which is the Field.

These two words join together and become the third word: *omnipresence*, which means all presence. There is no place where it doesn't exist, where the I Am doesn't exist. It occupies all space. It doesn't move or travel, because it just is. Therefore, wherever I am, the I Am is there. That is the All and the All, and the I Am is the All and the All.

It all takes place within this Field.

What takes place within this Field? All the wisdom and power of existence is present in this Field. Every great master who has lived in the material universe came out of the Field. All the teachings of these great masters exist in the Field. These teachings exist there in the I Am, in the omnipresence of the Field. Nothing exists outside that omnipresence. I Am that I Am, and besides Me there is no other. There is no such thing

as empty space. So, all this wisdom is in the Field and has been drawn upon by the great teachers. It is all a matter of tuning in and receiving this wisdom.

But 'tuning in and receiving' may not be easy and may require an investment of time and space — it simply takes as long as it takes. The more effort you put into the undertaking, the faster will be your ability to understand. It is, in fact, just like learning music. First you have to enter the Field of music to succeed. Then you must practice your instrument; if you don't practice, you'll never become an accomplished musician. Luckily you can tune into the wisdom because you are the Field and the Field is within you — it occupies all space. As Jesus taught me, wherever you stand is holy ground, because wisdom and power occupies all space. There is no place where you can separate from this Field, whatever continent or ocean you are on.

So, all these teachings are within the Field, and the Field occupies all space. As Jesus taught me, when the in becomes the out, the out becomes the in — and when the two have merged — then you will have entered into the kingdom of Heaven which is the same thing as the Field and the I Am. I Am that I Am, and besides me there is nothing else.

You can tune into any one of these wonderful lessons that are in the Field. If you are a Buddhist, you would tune into the words of Gautama. If you are a Christian, you would tune into the words of Jesus. You will tune into the master from whom you want to learn. But it is all the same I Am that is teaching you.

Anything you want to learn is in the Field. All the answers of science already exist in the Field. There is no such thing as you creating an original concept. You are simply receiving information that already exists in the Field. That Field is omnipresent consciousness, and without it nothing exists. You don't exist without it. The I Am is incarnated in you.

Now we understand that the Field occupies all space and is the I Am, and everything comes out of the I Am. The I is all that there is, and the Am gives birth to all that the I is. But they are one. In this Field there is no separation. Everything is one because it is all the I Am.

So, you tune into the Field when you want to learn something. The more you practice, the more perfect it becomes. The question is how do you understand all this, how do you tune into the Field.

First you must learn how to concentrate. From there you go on to contemplation. Once there, meditation gives you all the answers. Learning how to concentrate isn't hard. It just takes patience and practice. When I try to help someone learn to concentrate, I suggest that they find something for which they have an affinity. It might be a candle, a flower, an apple, a master's portrait, anything. Place it before you and gaze at it. The normal mind is usually racing about, so you have to work to slow it down. Once you actually start concentrating on the chosen object, a wonderful thing starts to happen — you become one with that object on which you are concentrating.

That step brings you into the contemplative state. You realize what it all is, and that brings you into the meditative state, where you will find the answers to all your questions. With practice you will no longer have to concentrate on an object, but simply go into the meditation mode. That process takes you into the Field completely.

So, if you want to learn or understand something, you must follow the path of first concentrating on your question and then finding the answer through meditation. It will take you into the Field of omnipresent consciousness, and there you will find your answer.

For years I have been asked, 'So, where do you get all this?' I answer that I got it from God. Initially I was embarrassed to say this, because I would get a certain look from people. I understood the reaction, because I used to do the same thing to Elaine when she tried to teach me. To hear the truth without knowing how to grasp it is frustrating, but I can only say that I got it from God. And of course, that is the reality. The I Am is the I Am and that is God. There is nothing else.

Concentration brings you to meditation, and meditation brings you to the state of experience where realization takes place.

All the great teachers are here, waiting to help you progress. All you have to do is ask - Jesus, Gautama, Lao-tzu, Sai Baba, Yogananda, Joel Goldsmith, any great teacher — and all that teaching will be in the Field. In the I Am of that Field there are no favorites. It has no respect for personality or background. It simply is. That I Am is total truth and omnipresence and is available to anyone who seeks it.

Once you enter this Field of perfect consciousness and realization and hear the words of your teacher, it is the I Am that is teaching you. It

is all there in the Field. For myself, being taught made me want to teach others what I learned. Interestingly other people who are becoming more and more in tune with the I Am have told me the same thing: that as they learn, they want to share this new knowledge and put it back into the Field because everything flows to and from the Field. Anyone who is meditating will enter the Field, learn from it and in turn pass it along. It is all one. It is all the I Am.

This may take some contemplation and meditation, but you can see that once you enter this Field — which is the entire universe — you are one with all. When you remember that Jesus said, 'Don't you know that you yourselves are God's temple and that God's Spirit dwells in your midst?' (1Corinthians 3:16), you can now understand what he meant. We are sons and daughters of the most high. All we have to do is wake up. Jesus also said, 'Ye are the light of the world' (Matthew 5:14). You are the I Am, and the I Am is you. All of us are that One. It is a total uniting with the Field. There is no separation in the Field. We tune into that Oneness through meditation. We become that meditation itself as One.

No negativity exists in the Field. Negativity comes from our programming, our thinking. The negativity that we believe in doesn't really exist. Thinking comes out of nothing, and returns to nothing. It is simply an illusion. The Field is absolute perfection and so cannot have negativity. It is the omnipresence of the Field that is the reality.

As Jesus taught me, Those who live in the past are dead, and those who live in the future have no future, but it is the wise man who lives in the now, in that perfection of the Field. There is no time or space in the now. You become the now and in doing so, receive the answers to all the mysteries of the universe.

Gautama said that you need to free yourself of all concepts, even the very concept of God. You don't know what God is. This was a very hard lesson for me to learn. I had to understand that I didn't really have a true concept of God and would have to go deep into meditation to find the answer which is that God is the total Field, the omnipresent consciousness. We were created out of that image and likeness of that omnipresent I Am.

Once you realize your I Am, all negativity drops away. There is no more judging or condemning. There is only pure love. The love is the glue that holds it all together, this perfect love. It has nothing but perfection in it. It

is total and omnipresent. There are no conditions to this love, only pure, flowing love. Within this perfection there is no up or down, left or right, only being the Now. You must be the Now, and you can attain this level of knowing only through meditation. It takes practice, but there is time. Practice does make perfect. It takes as long as it takes. Have patience with yourself. You have come down through the ages and have now reached this lifetime where you are putting it all together. This is what I call your tithing, the willingness to commit your time to the realization of the I Am. The more you tithe, the more the realization happens.

And then you will truly know the righteous men and women. They have realized the perfection of the Field. They no longer see people as individuals, as they no longer criticize or judge. They see only love. Jesus told Mary Magdalene, I find no fault with you. Your sins are forgiven. He saw no good or bad in her, just God, the omnipresent Now. It was the same when he was on the cross. He saw nothing to judge in the murderer who was beside him. He saw only perfection, the temple of the soul, which is the I Am.

For his part, Gautama wanted to learn only three things. Why does old age exist? Why does sickness and disease exist? And why does death exist? Once he entered Nirvana — the total Field — he realized that these are only illusions that take place in the mind. The reality is the I Am.

This concept is already inside you and you have already arrived — you are one with the Field. The secret to it all is to wake up, to unite into the One. The "Am" gives birth to everything that the "I" is. Don't separate anything. The divine father and the divine mother are one. The breath going in and the breath going out are one. You cannot separate. It's your total consciousness — your total being — that makes you aware of being aware.

You are with all these great souls in the Field — the I Am — and you can tune into any of the wonderful wisdom there. God is all the wisdom, the I Am of you, the consciousness of you. Without that consciousness you do not exist. You have no awareness. That consciousness is the image and likeness of God. We are not human beings. We are spiritual beings. The concept that we are human beings is an illusion and must be discarded. The spiritual being is the I Am. The entire wisdom of the Field is within you, and all you have to do is tune into it. You are the book of life. It is

written within every cell and every atom of your body. It is the I Am. Don't separate but unite, unite, unite. That is the secret of everything.

As Jesus taught me, the crucifixion is the past and dead. The resurrection is the proof that the illusions of the human body do not exist, that you never die but always go forward. He asked us to take his lessons and go forward, to do them more forcefully than he. The crucifixion taken alone only allows for punishment of oneself over and over again. There is no reason to do this. He went through that punishment for us. He asked only that we go forward. The resurrection is eternal life without the illusions of the human body. It is the I Am. You will find out these truths when you go into meditation and ask for understanding. He will speak to you and tell you the truth, for He is the I Am. It is all total uniting. There is no separation between me and you and Jesus. We are all one, the I Am. I Am that I Am. When Moses went up on the mountain, he realized the I Am and brought back the word of God to his people. That is the destination for all of us, to realize the I Am and let go of the old illusions. United we stand, and separated we fall.

The love of the I Am is the glue of it all. This pure love binds us all together, this pure essence of love. Contemplate, meditate, experience it and then realize your experience. Know that it all takes place within the Field. You will become the teacher teaching the next teacher. You will receive and then pass on your new understanding.

Again, remember that practice makes perfect. The more you practice, the easier it will become. Tithe your time. Give your time to God. That is all He wants. Sooner or later you will give your total time to Him; when waking or sleeping you will be in this state of oneness with the I Am. You will realize what oneness means. And then you will look at your brothers and sisters with pure love. There is nothing else there, and that love binds us all together.

This divine consciousness is the Essence of your Being.

So, I bless you as the I Am and ask you to be patient with yourself.